Global Environmental Politics

Global Environmental Politics has provided an accurate, up-to-date, and unbiased understanding of the world's most pressing environmental issues for thirty years. The eighth edition continues this practice by covering critical new developments in global environmental politics and policymaking.

Updated case studies on key issues such as climate change, endangered species, ozone depletion, desertification, whaling, hazardous wastes, toxic chemicals, and biodiversity detail the ongoing development of major environmental treaty regimes, and new case studies on mercury and marine biodiversity showcase the challenges of creating new treaties during a period of significant global change. There is also new material on the implementation of the Sustainable Development Goals, the 2030 Agenda for Sustainable Development, trade and environment, and the impact of the COVID-19 pandemic on environmental diplomacy. Updated information about global environmental trends, paradigms, and actors completes this comprehensive introduction to contemporary international environmental politics.

Global Environmental Politics is vital reading for students of environmental politics and anyone wishing to understand the current state of the field and to make informed decisions about which policies will best safeguard our environment for the future.

Pamela S. Chasek is a professor of political science at Manhattan College. She is the executive editor of the *Earth Negotiations Bulletin*, a reporting service on environment and development negotiations. She is also the author and editor of several books and numerous articles on international environmental policy, including *Transforming Multilateral Diplomacy: The Inside Story of the Sustainable Development Goals*, *The Roads from Rio*, *The Global Environment in the 21st Century*, and *Earth Negotiations*.

David L. Downie is a professor in the environmental studies program and department of politics at Fairfield University. Prior to Fairfield, he taught graduate courses in environmental policy and helped to direct a number of educational programs at Columbia University. He has attended nearly 100 global environmental negotiations since 1990 and is the author of numerous publications on the creation and content of international environmental policy.

Global Environmental Politics

Eighth Edition

Pamela S. Chasek and David L. Downie

Routledge
Taylor & Francis Group

NEW YORK AND LONDON

Eighth edition published 2021
by Routledge
52 Vanderbilt Avenue, New York, NY 10017

and by Routledge
2 Park Square, Milton Park, Abingdon, Oxon OX14 4RN

Routledge is an imprint of the Taylor & Francis Group, an informa business

First edition published by Westview Press 1991
Seventh edition published by Westview Press 2017, reprinted by Routledge 2018

Library of Congress Cataloging-in-Publication Data
Names: Chasek, Pamela S., 1961– author. | Downie, David Leonard, author.
Title: Global environmental politics / Pamela S. Chasek and David L. Downie.
Description: 8th edition. | Abingdon, Oxon ; New York, NY : Routledge, 2021. |
Includes bibliographical references and index.
Identifiers: LCCN 2020032565 (print) | LCCN 2020032566 (ebook) |
ISBN 9780367227586 (hardback) | ISBN 9780367227623 (paperback) |
ISBN 9780429276743 (ebook)
Subjects: LCSH: Environmental policy. | Sustainable development.
Classification: LCC GE170 .C46 2021 (print) |
LCC GE170 (ebook) | DDC 363.7/056–dc23
LC record available at https://lccn.loc.gov/2020032565
LC ebook record available at https://lccn.loc.gov/2020032566

ISBN: 978-0-367-22758-6 (hbk)
ISBN: 978-0-367-22762-3 (pbk)
ISBN: 978-0-429-27674-3 (ebk)

Typeset in Sabon
by Newgen Publishing UK

Contents

Figures

Tables

Boxes

Photos

Preface

Environmental issues affect the welfare of all humankind both directly and through their interaction with other aspects of world politics, including economic development, trade, humanitarian action, social policy, and even security. For more than thirty years, *Global Environmental Politics* has sought to provide an up-to-date, accurate, and unbiased introduction to the key issues in the study and practice of international environmental politics and policy.

This new edition examines key historical developments and trends in global environmental politics, the major national, institutional, and subnational actors, the factors that enhance or hinder prospects for effective policy, insights provided by the scholarly study of global environmental politics, and the development, content, and remaining challenges and potential future paths of global policies that address climate change, sustainable development, biodiversity, chemicals and wastes, desertification, marine biodiversity, mercury, stratospheric ozone depletion, environment and trade, and other issues.

The eighth edition contains entirely new and updated sections and subsections, which examine critical developments that have occurred in global environmental politics since the seventh edition, including achievements and setbacks related to climate change, toxic chemicals, hazardous waste, mercury, endangered species, whales, marine biodiversity, and the 2030 Agenda for Sustainable Development and its seventeen Sustainable Development Goals (SDGs).

Chapter 1 describes the emergence of global environmental politics. First, we examine the trends that shape global environmental politics. Understanding global environmental politics, including environmental treaties and treaty conferences, requires understanding international regimes. Finally, we look at the paradigms that have dominated public understanding of environmental policymaking. Subsequent chapters in this book explore these and other key issues in global environmental politics.

Chapter 2 examines the main actors in global environmental politics. States are the most important actors because they negotiate international legal instruments, create global environmental regimes, and adopt economic, trade, and regulatory policies that directly and indirectly affect the environment. At the same time, nonstate actors also play major roles. International organizations, treaty secretariats, NGOs, scientists, and multinational corporations help set the global environmental agenda, initiate and influence the process of regime formation, and carry out actions that directly affect the global environment.

Chapters 3 and 4 look at the development of ten important global environmental regimes: ozone depletion, climate change, hazardous wastes, toxic chemicals, mercury, biodiversity loss, marine biodiversity in the high seas, trade in endangered species, whaling, and desertification and land degradation. The first two sections of Chapter 5 examine why it has proven so difficult to create and implement effective global environmental policies. The subsequent section outlines methods to improve regime implementation, compliance, and effectiveness.

Chapter 6 examines how environmental issues and global environmental politics fit into the SDGs and how pursuit of these goals, in turn, impacts global environmental politics.

This chapter also discusses trade and the environment and how the evolution of global environmental politics cannot be understood completely outside the context of the historic and current relationship between industrialized and developing countries. Chapter 7 concludes our discussion with some thoughts on the past, present, and future of global environmental politics.

Acknowledgments

Like global environmental politics itself, this book has gone through significant transformations. While its purpose remains the same, the contents of *Global Environmental Politics* have evolved significantly during its three sets of authors. Janet Welsh Brown and Gareth Porter initiated the project and wrote the first two editions. Pamela Chasek wrote the third edition (2000), and David Downie joined the project in 2004. Through the last five editions, including this one, our collaboration has yielded a significantly restructured, larger, more theoretically informed, and essentially new book compared with its first incarnation. The later editions also benefited from reviews of key content by issue experts at the International Institute of Sustainable Development, the *Earth Negotiations Bulletin*, the United Nations, Manhattan College, Columbia University, Fairfield University, and other policy and research institutions—as well as extremely helpful anonymous peer-reviews, including by scholars who use the book in their undergraduate or graduate classes. Special thanks go to Kiara Worth and the other *Earth Negotiations Bulletin* photographers for their amazing images. We also want to thank our editors, and everyone at Routledge, for their support and positive attitude throughout this process.

In addition to all our colleagues who were thanked in earlier editions of this book, we thank Julia Frees and Jackie Graf for their research assistance.

Most importantly, David Downie thanks his family—especially Laura, William, and Lindsey—for their fun, patience, good humor, support, scuba, and making the good things in his life possible. Pamela Chasek thanks Kimo Goree for his understanding as she spent endless hours in front of the computer, especially when quarantined during the COVID-19 pandemic. She also thanks her sons, Sam and Kai, and her parents, Marvin and Arlene, for their patience, support, and love from a distance.

Pamela Chasek
David Downie

Selected Acronyms

AOSIS	Alliance of Small Island States
CBD	Convention on Biological Diversity
CBDR	common but differentiated responsibilities
CFCs	chlorofluorocarbons
CITES	Convention on International Trade in Endangered Species of Wild Fauna and Flora
CO₂	carbon dioxide
COP	Conference of the Parties
CSD	Commission on Sustainable Development
EC	European Community
EEZ	exclusive economic zone
EU	European Union
FAO	Food and Agriculture Organization of the United Nations
FTA	financial and technical assistance
G-77	Group of 77
GDP	gross domestic product
GEF	Global Environment Facility
GHGs	greenhouse gases
GNP	gross national product
HCFCs	hydrochlorofluorocarbons
HLPF	High-level Political Forum on Sustainable Development
HFCs	hydrofluorocarbons
IGOs	intergovernmental organizations
IISD	International Institute for Sustainable Development
IMF	International Monetary Fund
INC	Intergovernmental Negotiating Committee
IPBES	Intergovernmental Science-Policy Platform on Biodiversity and Ecosystem Services
IPCC	Intergovernmental Panel on Climate Change
IUCN	International Union for Conservation of Nature
IWC	International Whaling Commission
LDCs	least developed countries
MARPOL	International Convention for the Prevention of Pollution from Ships
MDGs	Millennium Development Goals
MEAs	multilateral environmental agreements
MOP	Meeting of the Parties
NGOs	nongovernmental organizations
ODA	official development assistance
ODS	ozone-depleting substance(s)
OECD	Organisation for Economic Co-operation and Development
PFOS	perfluorooctane sulfonate
PIC	prior informed consent

POPs	persistent organic pollutants
SDGs	Sustainable Development Goals
TRAFFIC	Trade Records Analysis of Flora and Fauna in Commerce
UN	United Nations
UNCCD	United Nations Convention to Combat Desertification
UNCED	United Nations Conference on Environment and Development
UNCSD	United Nations Conference on Sustainable Development
UNDP	United Nations Development Programme
UNEA	United Nations Environment Assembly
UNEP	United Nations Environment Programme
UNFCCC	United Nations Framework Convention on Climate Change
UNGA	United Nations General Assembly
WHO	World Health Organization
WMO	World Meteorological Organization
WSSD	World Summit on Sustainable Development
WTO	World Trade Organization
WWF	World Wildlife Fund/Worldwide Fund for Nature

Chapter 1

The Emergence of Global Environmental Politics

Abstract

The emergence of environmental problems as major issues in world politics reflects growing awareness of the stresses human activities place on the earth's resources and life support systems. This chapter first highlights global demographic, economic, and environmental macrotrends that drive global environmental politics. Then, in introducing the study of global environmental politics, the chapter outlines how much of global environmental politics focuses on efforts to negotiate and implement multilateral agreements, regimes, or other forms of cooperation to protect the environment and natural resources. The chapter concludes by examining how global environmental policy is shaped not only by political and economic interests, scientific developments, and technological innovation, but also by broad sets of beliefs held by the general population, governments, institutions, and political leaders. Some of these paradigms justify extensive, and sometimes essentially unlimited, exploitation of nature and discount the impact of pollution and deteriorating ecosystems on economic and social well-being. Despite widespread recognition of the need for sustainable development, globalization and the resilience of aspects of the traditional paradigms have complicated attempts to adopt more widespread practices and policies that would support global sustainable development.

Keywords: environmental footprint, globalization, paradigm shift, population growth, precautionary principle, regimes, sustainable development, sustainable consumption

Until the late 1980s, most governments regarded global environmental problems as minor issues, marginal both to their core national interests and to international politics in general. Then the rise of environmental movements in industrialized countries and the emergence of global environmental threats that affect the welfare of all humankind—such as ozone-layer depletion, climate change, and dangerous declines in the world's fisheries—elevated global environmental issues to a higher status in world politics. Today, environmental issues are understood as globally important not only in their own right but also because they affect other aspects of world politics, including economic development, trade, human health, humanitarian action, and even security.[1]

Global concern about the environment evolved in response to expanded scientific understanding of humanity's increasing impact on the biosphere, including the atmosphere, oceans, forests, fresh water, soil cover, and many animal and plant species. Many by-products of economic growth—such as the burning of fossil fuels, air and water pollution, hazardous waste, toxic chemicals, plastics, and increased use of natural resources—put cumulative stresses on the physical environment that threaten human health and economic well-being.

The realization that environmental threats have serious socioeconomic and human costs and that unilateral actions by individual countries cannot solve these problems produced increased calls for international cooperation to halt or reverse environmental degradation.

This chapter, in introducing global environmental politics, highlights important economic and environmental trends, introduces and defines key concepts, and traces some of the major intellectual currents and political developments central to the evolution of global environmental politics.

Global Macrotrends

Global demographic, economic, and environmental macrotrends describe key factors that drive global environmental politics.[2] Humanity's potential stress on the environment is to some extent a function of three key factors: population, resource consumption, and waste production. One way to measure this impact is through an ecological footprint, which measures humanity's demands on the biosphere by comparing humanity's consumption against the earth's regenerative capacity, or biocapacity. The ecological footprint measures the amount of key ecological assets—including cropland, pasture land, forest, and fishing grounds—"that a given population requires to produce the natural resources it consumes (including plant-based food and fiber products, livestock and fish products, timber and other forest products, space for urban infrastructure) and to absorb its waste, especially carbon emissions."[3] Since the 1970s, humanity's annual demand on the natural world has exceeded what the earth can renew in a year. Today, we would need the equivalent of about 1.7 earths to provide the resources we consume annually and absorb the pollution and wastes we emit, and that number is increasing.[4]

Population Growth and Resource Consumption

Population growth affects the environment by increasing the demand for resources (including energy, water, food, and wood), the production of waste, and the emission of pollution. These relationships are not fixed, however, and most of the negative impacts result from how we carry out certain activities. Nevertheless, given the dominant economic and social patterns that have existed since the Industrial Revolution, the rapid growth of human population over the last 100 years has significantly influenced the environment and will continue to do so throughout this century.

Today, the global population is over 7.8 billion. It took fifty years for the global population to increase from 1.6 billion in 1900 to 2.5 billion in 1950. It then took only thirty-seven years to double, reaching 5 billion in 1987. It passed the 6-billion mark only twelve years later, reached 7 billion in late 2011, and is on pace to reach 8.5 billion by 2030, 9.7 billion by 2050, and nearly 11 billion in 2100 (see Figure 1.1).[5]

Projections of future population growth depend on fertility trends, which are affected by economic development, education, disease patterns, population-related policies, and other factors. The world's human population is currently growing at a rate slightly below 1.1 percent annually. Although significantly lower than the peak growth rate of 2.1 percent from 1965 to 1970, this still means a net addition of more than about 80 million people each year.

Historically, population growth has been accompanied by large increases in the consumption of natural resources, including fresh water, forests, topsoil, fish stocks, and fossil fuels. In addition, per capita consumption of natural resources has been rising much faster than population growth.[6] This increase is positive in that it reflects improving living standards for billions of people. At the same time, the aggregate human consumption of natural resources has largely passed sustainable rates.[7]

Nearly all projected increases in human population will occur in developing countries, where per capita consumption is also increasing most rapidly (see Table 1.1). The United

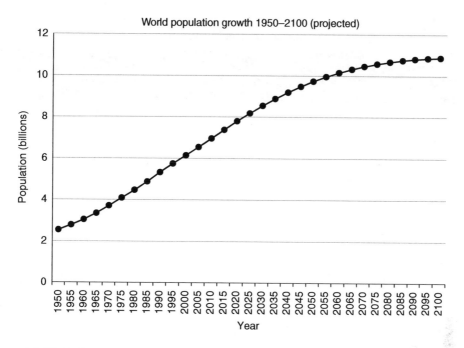

Figure 1.1 World Population Growth 1950–2100 (Projected)

Source: United Nations, Department of Economic and Social Affairs, Population Division (2019). World Population Prospects 2019, custom data acquired via website.

Nations (UN) estimates that Africa will add more than 1 billion people by 2050, about 50 percent of the global population increase. Eastern, central and southern Asia, which includes China, India, and other expanding economies, will add nearly 600 million. The global middle class is expected to grow from 1.8 billion in 2009 to nearly 4.9 billion by 2030.[8] As more developing countries pursue the lifestyles of North America, Japan, and Europe, the future will likely bring higher per capita rates of consumption unless resources are consumed more efficiently and recycled more effectively.

Despite large increases in the consumer class in a number of developing countries, the current gulf in consumption levels within and among countries continues to draw attention, as do the social and environmental consequences that some analysts argue these gaps produce. High-income countries, such as the United States, have far greater ecological footprints per capita than low-income countries.[9] In 2017, high-income countries had the highest footprint per capita (approximately 27 metric tons per person), 60 percent higher than the upper-middle-income countries (17 metric tons per person) and more than thirteen times the level of low-income countries (2 metric tons per person).[10] The United States has more private cars than licensed drivers,[11] and the average size of new, single-family houses in the United States has grown by more than 60 percent since 1973[12] despite a decrease in the average number of people per household.[13] If everyone on the planet consumed resources at the level Americans do, it would take the planet nearly five years to regenerate the renewable resources used and absorb the wastes produced.[14]

At the other end of the spectrum, 9 percent of the world's workers—and their families—live on less than $1.90 per person a day.[15] About 2 billion people lack access to safe, clean drinking water in their homes. More than 780 million lack even a basic drinking water service, including 140 million who drink from untreated surface water (lakes and streams).[16] One out of every three people lacks safely managed sanitation services, the overwhelming majority of

Table 1.1 Population of the World and Selected Regions and Groups of Countries for 2019, 2030, 2050, and 2100, According to the Medium-Variant Projection

	Population (millions)			
	2019	2030	2050	2100
World	7713	8548	9735	10,875
Region				
Sub-Saharan Africa	1066	1400	2118	3775
Northern Africa and western Asia	517	609	754	924
Central and southern Asia	1991	2227	2496	2334
Eastern and southeastern Asia	2335	2427	2411	1967
Latin America and the Caribbean	648	706	762	680
Australia/New Zealand	30	33	38	49
Oceania	12	15	19	26
Europe and North America	1114	1132	1136	1120
Least-developed countries	1033	1314	1877	3047
Landlocked developing countries	521	659	926	1406
Small Island developing states	71	78	87	88

Data source: United Nations, Department of Economic and Social Affairs, Population Division (2019). *World Population Prospects 2019: Highlights* (ST/ESA/SER.A/423), page 6. https://population.un.org/wpp/Publications/Files/WPP2019_Highlights.pdf

whom live in southern Asia and sub-Saharan Africa, including millions of people—mostly in rural areas—who defecate in the open.[17] In the world's poorest, least developed countries, more than 20 percent of health-care facilities have no water, sanitation, or waste management service.[18] Eighty percent of global wastewater goes untreated, containing everything from human waste to toxic industrial discharges, and eventually enters the environment, including watersheds.[19]

Today, the world's industrialized or developed countries (Organisation for Economic Co-operation and Development (OECD) members) comprise only about 15 percent of the world's population but use about 38 percent of the world's energy (see Figure 1.2). The United States, with less than 5 percent of the global population, accounts for about 17 percent of the world's energy consumption, about 80 percent of which is produced by fossil fuels—coal, oil, and natural gas[20]—and spends about ten times more on direct and indirect fossil fuel subsidies than on education.[21] Meanwhile, Africa accounts for about 16 percent of the global population but only 7 percent of global energy use.[22] In fact, the average American consumes about 3.5 times more energy than the average global citizen, three times more than the average person in China, and ten times more than the average person in India.[23] Approximately 600 million people in sub-Saharan Africa and at least 350 million people in Asia live almost entirely without access to any electricity.[24] This includes approximately 167 million people in India, 52 million in Pakistan, 13 million in Indonesia, 76 million in Nigeria, 68 million in the Democratic Republic of Congo, and 57 million in Ethiopia.[25]

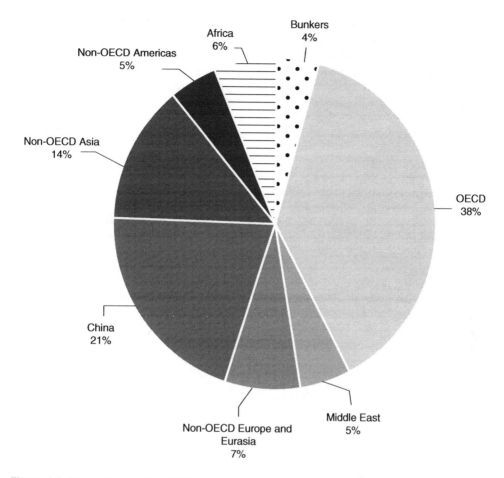

Figure 1.2 Global Energy Use 2017

Note: Bunkers, as defined by the International Energy Agency, are the energy consumption of ships and aircraft.

Source: International Energy Agency, *Key World Energy Statistics*, 2019 (Paris: International Energy Agency, 2019). Data rounded to nearest whole number.

However, energy consumption and carbon dioxide emissions in developing countries are increasing rapidly, driven by industrial expansion, infrastructure improvement, population growth, urbanization, and rising incomes. In 1980, China and India together accounted for less than 8 percent of the world's total energy consumption; by 2018, their combined share had grown to 29 percent.[26]

Natural Resources and Pollution

Perhaps the largest aggregate impact that humans have on the biosphere is their carbon footprint (see Box 1.1), which has grown more than eleven-fold since 1961. The United States and China have the largest national carbon footprints, with China emitting more than 27 percent of global carbon emissions, followed by the United States with about 15 percent.[27] In 2017, the United States emitted almost four times as much carbon dioxide (CO_2) as the entire continent of Africa.[28] China has a much smaller per capita footprint than the United States (7 tons per person in 2017 compared with 16 tons in the United States,[29]

❖ BOX 1.1   WHAT IS A CARBON FOOTPRINT?

A carbon footprint is a measure of the impact our activities have on climate change. Many daily activities cause emissions of greenhouse gases, including burning gasoline when driving, burning oil or gas for home heating, or using electricity generated from coal, natural gas, and oil. These are considered to be the *primary footprint*—the sum of direct emissions of carbon dioxide from the burning of fossil fuels for energy consumption and transportation. More fuel-efficient cars have a smaller primary footprint, as do energy-efficient light bulbs and appliances.

The *secondary footprint* is the sum of indirect emissions of greenhouse gases during the life cycle of products used by an individual or organization. For example, the greenhouse gases emitted during the production of plastic for water bottles, as well as the energy used to transport the water, contribute to a much larger secondary carbon footprint than drinking tap water. Products with more packaging will generally have a larger secondary footprint than products with a minimal amount of packaging.

Source: Maggie L. Walser, "Carbon Footprint," in: *Encyclopedia of Earth*, ed. Cutler J. Cleveland (Washington, DC: Environmental Information Coalition, National Council for Science and the Environment). First published in the Encyclopedia of Earth July 14, 2010; last revised May 15, 2018; https://editors.eol.org/eoearth/wiki/Carbon_footprint/

although China's footprint continues to increase), but its population is more than four times as large. India is the third largest national emitter of CO_2, but its per capita footprint is only about 1.8 tons per person.[30]

However, an energy sector transition is underway in many parts of the world. In 2014, renewable energy became the second largest source of electricity, behind coal. For the first time, in April 2019, renewable energy sources (including solar, wind, hydro, and geothermal) supplied more electricity in the United States than coal,[31] and most existing US coal-fired power plants are now more expensive to operate than new renewable energy production.[32] According to International Energy Agency projections, energy demand is expected to grow at 1 percent per year through 2040, about half the average annual rate since 1990, due to increased energy efficiency in end uses and structural changes to the economy. CO_2 emissions from power generation are expected to grow at only one-fifth of the rate at which power output will increase between now and 2040, breaking the long-standing one-for-one relationship.[33] The International Renewable Energy Agency (IRENA) reports that the renewable energy sector employed 11 million people globally in 2018, 700,000 more than in 2017. This included 855,000 jobs in the United States.[34] Nearly three times as many Americans work in the renewable energy sector as in coal mining or other fossil fuel extraction.[35] Jobs in energy efficiency have also experienced significant growth, and that sector now employs more than 3 million people in the United States alone.[36]

Despite this progress, however, current efforts are not remotely sufficient to move the world onto a pathway consistent with the global goal of limiting global warming to 1.5–2°C (see Chapter 3).[37] 2019 was the warmest year for which observational records exist, following only 2016. 2010–2019 was the warmest decade on record. The world's five warmest years have all occurred since 2015, with nine of the ten warmest years occurring since 2005.[38] If present rates continue, global temperatures will rise by about 3°C (5.4°F) by the end of the century.[39]

The combination of increasing consumption, rising populations, climate change, and current economic, political, and social practices and policies has resulted in many critical natural resources being exploited at unstainable and unprecedented rates.[40] The world's freshwater resources are under serious stress. Increased water consumption, rising population, and climate change mean that about 80 percent of the world's population lives in countries with areas classified as having high levels of threat to water security.[41] For at least one month of the year, more than 4 billion people live with water scarcity. For at least four to six months of the year, 1.8 to 2.9 billion people face severe water scarcity, and half a billion face severe water scarcity year round.[42] A recent MIT study concluded that increasing demand and the impacts of climate change will produce a high risk of very severe freshwater shortages by 2050 in a large portion of Asia, including much of China and India.[43] Thirty-three of the world's major cities, each with over 3 million residents, already face extremely high water stress, and several have recently faced acute and dangerous water shortages, including São Paulo in Brazil, Cape Town in South Africa, and several cities in India.[44]

Agricultural use, mainly crop irrigation, accounts for 69 percent of total global water consumption. Industrial uses account for 19 percent and household use for 12 percent.[45] By 2050, the global demand for water in these sectors is expected to increase 20 to 30 percent above current levels.[46] Forty percent of global grain production could be at risk if the combination of unsustainable pressures on water resources and degradation of the natural environment continues at current levels, with poor and marginalized populations disproportionately affected.[47]

The convergence of population growth, rising demand for lumber and fuelwood, and the conversion of forests to agriculture has also put increasing pressure on the world's forests, especially in developing countries. In 1990, the world contained about 4.13 billion hectares of forested area (1 hectare equals about 2.47 acres). Since then, about 420 million hectares has been lost through deforestation, with about 12 million hectares lost each year in 2010–2015 and about 10 million hectares lost annually in 2015–2020.[48] From 2010 to 2015, about 6.6 million hectares of natural forests were lost annually, but this has accelerated to 10–12 million hectares (29.6 million acres) since then.[49] Satellite imagery showed that rainforest destruction in Brazil accelerated to the equivalent of about one and a half soccer fields every minute in 2019 as a result of policies enacted by President Jair Bolsonaro.[50]

Deforestation contributes to greenhouse gas (GHG) emissions and the loss of biodiversity, including the extinction of species and the loss of genetic diversity within species. Scientists began warning in the 1980s that the destruction of tropical forests, which hold an estimated 50 to 90 percent of all species, could result in the loss of one-fourth to one-half of the world's species within a few decades.

Biodiversity is not confined to the tropical forests, however, and humans are dramatically transforming virtually all of earth's ecosystems. Despite the growing number of nature reserves, national parks, and other protected areas, including the addition of more than 6.1 million square kilometers between 2010 and 2014 (an amount roughly the size of Australia),[51] a recent UN report concluded that 35 percent of the world's richest biodiversity zones remain entirely unprotected.[52]

The International Union for Conservation of Nature (IUCN), an organization that includes governments and environmental organizations among its members (see Chapter 2), lists more than 28,000 specific species as threatened with extinction. This represents 27 percent of all assessed species, including about 40 percent of amphibians, 25 percent of mammals, 34 percent of conifers (cone-bearing trees), 33 percent of reef corals, and 14 percent of bird species.[53] In 2019, the Intergovernmental Science-Policy Platform on Biodiversity and Ecosystem Services (IPBES; see Chapter 2) released the most comprehensive study to date on biodiversity and the ecosystem services it provides. Based on a review of more than 15,000 scientific publications, government reports, and other sources, and involving the work of more than 450 experts, the report concluded that 20 percent of native species in most major land-based habitats have already been lost and nearly 1 million animal and plant species are currently threatened with extinction, more than ever before in human history. The number

Photo 1.1 In 2019, the Intergovernmental Science-Policy Platform on Biodiversity and Ecosystem Services released the most comprehensive study to date on biodiversity and the ecosystem services it provides. Delegates at the meeting pose for photos to celebrate the adoption of the Global Assessment.

Courtesy Diego Noguera, IISD/*Earth Negotiations Bulletin,* http://enb.iisd.org

of birds living in just the United States and Canada has already fallen 29 percent since 1970, a decline of 2.9 billion birds.[54] The principal drivers of population declines and past and possible future extinctions are land-use changes due to human activity, climate change, human harvesting or killing of specific animals and plants, pollution, and invasive species introduced by human activity.[55] A 2020 study concluded that severe disruptions to biodiversity from climate change could occur as soon as 2030.[56] A 2020 report by the UN was even more stark, stating that "Biodiversity is declining at an unprecedented rate, and the pressures driving this decline are intensifying," and as a result, "Humanity stands at a crossroads with regard to the legacy it leaves to future generations."[57]

Many of the world's major fisheries are overfished or on the verge of collapse. The declining marine catch in many areas, the increased percentage of overexploited fish stocks, and the decreased proportion of non-fully exploited species provide strong evidence that the state of world marine fisheries is worsening.[58] The Food and Agriculture Organization of the UN (FAO) estimates that about 90 percent of the world's marine fish stocks are already being fished at or beyond their maximum sustainable rates; with about 33 percent considered overexploited (or currently fished at biologically unsustainable levels) and nearly 60 percent being fished at their maximum sustainable rates.[59] Atlantic salmon in the Gulf of Maine are already on the list of endangered species and could soon be followed by other staples such as tuna, swordfish, and even cod, which could cripple the economies they support (fishing provides some 200 million jobs worldwide).[60] In addition, inefficient fishing practices waste a high percentage of each year's catch and cause severe environmental damage.[61] FAO estimates that at least 20 million metric tons (about 44 billion pounds) of bycatch (unintentionally caught fish, seabirds, sea turtles, marine mammals, and other ocean life) die every year when they are carelessly swept up and discarded by commercial fishing operations, while other analyses put the level at close to 63 billion pounds.[62]

Marine environments are also under siege from land-based sources of pollution, believed to account for nearly 80 percent of the total pollution of the oceans.[63] These include excess sediment and runoff from mining, deforestation, and agriculture; biological contaminants in sewage; toxic chemicals; plastics; excessive nutrients from fertilizers and sewage; radioactive substances; heavy metals; oil; industrial, agricultural, and residential trash; noise; and invasive species.[64]

Large quantities of plastics and other debris can be found in the most remote parts of the world's oceans.[65] Plastic persists almost indefinitely in the environment and has a significant impact on marine and coastal biodiversity.[66] Harmful levels of plastic debris have been found in a variety of sea animals and birds. Microplastics—tiny pieces of plastic ranging from rice-size particles to microscopic bits of plastic polymers and added chemicals, which were originally part of plastic bags, straws, bottles, and other items or from the synthetic fibers used in clothing, carpeting, and other products—can travel in air and water and have been found in remote national parks, the Arctic, deep ocean, and most sea animals, including fish eaten by humans.[67] Eleven billion metric tons of plastic are projected to accumulate in the environment by 2025.[68] A 2016 study concluded that, if present rates continue, by 2050 there will be more plastic in the world's oceans than fish (by weight).[69]

Humans are also having increased negative impacts on wetlands. Different types of wetlands cover about 13 million square kilometers worldwide.[70] Wetlands serve important functions, such as sources of drinking water; water filtration; fish nurseries; rice paddies; flood and erosion control; natural irrigation for agriculture; protection against coastal storms; places for recreational activities; absorption of excess nutrients, sediments, and pollutants; absorption of slow floodwaters; and natural sinks for CO_2.[71] In the United States alone, wetlands provide approximately $23 billion worth of coastal area storm protection.[72]

Wetlands are also some of the most important biologically diverse areas in the world, providing essential habitats for many wildlife and plant species. Despite an international treaty dedicated to their protection, the Ramsar Convention on Wetlands of International Importance especially as Waterfowl Habitat, and their designation as important resources by the European Union (EU) and other regional bodies, wetlands are increasingly being filled in or otherwise destroyed to make way for buildings, farms, and urban and suburban development or damaged by unsustainable water use and pollution. Between 64 and 71 percent of the world's wetlands have been destroyed in the last 100 years, and only 20 percent of what remains is protected.[73] Noting their ecological and economic importance, an influential study concluded: "Given the increasing human population and its dependence on water and wetlands, full recognition of the values and benefits of [these natural resources] is a pressing imperative."[74]

Land degradation, water shortages, increasing demands for food, climate change, changing diets, urbanization, the use of food crops for biofuel, increasing prices, certain agriculture policies, and other factors combine to make it difficult for hundreds of millions to free themselves from the threats of starvation, severe hunger, and malnutrition.[75] Most of the unforested land available to meet current and future food requirements is already in production. Further expansion will involve fragile, marginal, and currently forested lands. As land becomes increasingly scarce, farmers face incentives to turn to intensive agriculture, including the use of dramatically higher levels of irrigation and chemicals. This, in turn, can contribute to soil erosion and salinization, deteriorating water quality, and land degradation.

FAO estimates that 821 million people, including more than 237 million in the least developed countries, live with nearly constant undernourishment—a condition in which an individual's food consumption is not sufficient to maintain a healthy, normal life.[76] Global food production must increase by nearly 50 percent by 2050 just to meet increased demands due to population increases.[77] There is also increasing demand for meat and fish among the growing number of middle-class consumers in China, India, and other developing countries (although per capita meat and fish consumption in these countries remains far below that in Australia, Europe, Japan, and North America). Because it takes many kilograms of feed to produce a kilogram of animal meat or aquaculture fish, grains that feed animals use a significant amount of resources and raise prices.[78] Meat production is also extremely water intensive. The production of 1 kilogram of beef requires an average of 15,000 liters of water compared with 1500 liters of water needed to produce 1 kilogram of potatoes and an average of 2500 kilograms for a kilogram of rice.[79] Food production costs have also increased in many areas, including the cost of seeds (partly because of patents and other intellectual property rights), fuel (for machinery and vehicles), fertilizers, pesticides, water, land, and labor. Weather variability, including from climate change, has also affected international food supply and prices.[80] Prominent examples include the historic heat waves, droughts, and storms in Australia, Brazil, Russia, the United States, and other critical food production areas over the last decade.

Biofuel production is another factor. Biofuels are liquid renewable fuels such as ethanol (fermented from plant materials) and biodiesel (a fuel made from vegetable oils or animal fats) that can substitute for petroleum-based fuels. Although potential biofuels made from algae, seaweed, grasses, saplings, or plant waste would have significant economic and ecological benefits, the production of many current biofuels requires significant amounts of pesticides, fertilizer, water, and energy, and is arguably not environmentally benign. Manufacturing most of the biofuels currently in use, especially those made from corn, sugar cane, and palm oil, also shifts valuable resources (e.g., land, water, labor, and capital) away from the production of food crops into the production of feedstock for biofuels. For example, in 2018, about 38 percent (about 5.6 billion bushels) of US corn was used in the production of ethanol.[81] Diverting land and corn from growing food for people or animals raises corn prices.[82]

Environmental quality in many urban areas continues to be a major problem, and the situation could worsen. It was only in 2008 that the world's urban population surpassed the rural population. By 2050, about 66 percent of the world's population, about 6.7 billion people, is expected to live in urban areas, a large increase from the 4.2 billion in 2018.[83] The number of cities with at least 10 million inhabitants is projected to rise from thirty-three in 2018 to at least forty-three in 2030[84] (see Table 1.2). The largest increases in urban populations are expected in the world's two poorest regions, south Asia and sub-Saharan Africa.[85]

Although cities can provide significant economies of scale for environmentally friendly technology, buildings, and practices, under current conditions, increasing urbanization has produced more water and air pollution and higher rates of natural resource consumption. Air pollution in many major urban areas is already at harmful levels, and it continues to worsen in most cities in Asia and Africa.[86] The World Health Organization estimates that nine out of every ten people on the planet regularly breathe polluted air and that ambient (outdoor) and indoor air pollution causes 7 million deaths a year.[87] Municipal waste systems in many cities cannot keep pace with urban expansion. Although conditions have improved in some cities, an estimated 828 million people live in urban slums, up from 776.7 million in 2000.[88]

The trends described in this section are some of the most important forces that shape global environmental politics. They have resulted from the intense economic development, rapid population growth, inefficient production, and unsustainable resource consumption prevalent in many parts of the world. This is not to say that population growth and economic development are necessarily harmful. Indeed, most would argue that they are not. Rather, it is the manner in which much of this economic development occurred, one characterized by high levels of resource consumption and pollution, that produced these troubling changes in the global environment.

Table 1.2 The World's Twelve Largest Megacities, 2020

Rank	Megacity	Population (in thousands)
1	Tokyo, Japan	37,435
2	Delhi, India	29,400
3	Shanghai, China	26,317
4	São Paulo, Brazil	21,650
5	Mexico City, Mexico	21,846
6	Cairo, Egypt	20,484
7	Dhaka, Bangladesh	20,283
8	Mumbai, India	20,185
9	Beijing, China	20,035
10	Osaka, Japan	19,222
11	Karachi, Bangladesh	16,093
12	Chongqing, China	15,872
	New York (largest city in United States)	8601
	New York-Newark metroplex	~20,000

An Introduction to Global Environmental Politics

Environmental problems do not respect national boundaries. Transboundary air pollution, the degradation of shared rivers, and the pollution of oceans and seas are just a few examples of the international dimensions of environmental problems. The sources, consequences, and actors involved in an environmental issue can be local, national, regional, or global. If the sources or consequences are global, or transcend more than one international region, or the actors involved in creating or addressing the problem transcend more than one region, then we consider the activity and its consequences to be a global environmental issue.[89] The main actors in global environmental politics are states (national governments), international organizations, environmental nongovernmental organizations (NGOs), corporations and industry groups, scientific bodies, and important individuals (see Chapter 2).

Global environmental issues can be analyzed in many ways. From the economist's point of view, environmental problems represent negative externalities—the unintended consequences or side effects of one's actions that are borne by others (and for which no compensation is paid). Externalities have always existed, but when the use of helpful but polluting technologies, such as coal-fired power plants, synthetic fertilizers, pesticides, herbicides, gasoline-powered vehicles, and plastics, expanded rapidly, the externalities they produced became serious global issues.

In this sense, the negative externalities that lead to environmental degradation are similar to the "tragedy of the commons." For many years, the image of open grazing land, or a commons—land that no person or government owned or controlled—has been used as a metaphor for the overexploitation of earth's common land, air, and water resources.[90] In the metaphor, the common land eventually becomes degraded due to overgrazing. The root cause is the lack of awareness among the herders of the long-term impact of their actions and the absence of a method to oblige them to take into account the harmful effects that their own herds' grazing had on the land and, consequently, on the other herders who shared it. In sum, without sufficient knowledge about the impact of their actions, empathy for how these impacts affect others, and structures to moderate the behavior, people (or states in the modern world) tend to pursue their own self-interest in utilizing the earth's common resources until they become degraded or polluted, resulting in the tragedy of the commons. Rapidly declining ocean fish stocks are an oft-cited modern example. How to address externalities and the damage they inflict on environmental resources that, by their very nature, no one can own is a central challenge in global environmental politics.

Oran Young, a pioneer in the scholarly study of global environmental politics, grouped international environmental problems into four broad clusters: commons, shared natural resources, transboundary externalities, and linked issues.[91] The commons are geographic areas, natural resources, and global systems that belong to all humankind rather than to any one country. These include Antarctica, the high seas, deep seabed minerals, the stratospheric ozone layer, the global climate system, and outer space. They may be geographically limited, as in Antarctica, or global in scope, such as the ozone layer and the climate system. Shared natural resources are physical or biological systems that extend into or across the jurisdiction of two or more states. These include non-renewable resources, such as pools of oil beneath the earth's surface; renewable resources, such as migratory animal species; and ecosystems that transcend national boundaries, such as regional seas and river basins.

Transboundary externalities result from activities that occur within the jurisdiction of individual states but produce results affecting the environment or people in other states, such as air and water pollution. Transboundary externalities also include the consequences of environmental accidents, such as the 1986 explosion at the Chernobyl nuclear power plant in the former Soviet Union or the accident at a gold-processing plant in Romania in 2000 that spilled cyanide and heavy metals into a large river system, killing fish and contaminating drinking water in parts of Romania, Bulgaria, Hungary, and Serbia. Linked issues refer to cases where efforts to address environmental concerns have unintended consequences affecting other issues, and vice versa. The most common linked issues occur when efforts to promote certain types of economic development or trade negatively impact the environment.

Different combinations of factors, including internal economic and political forces, foreign policy goals, and the impact of international organizations, NGOs, and corporations, can influence a state's policy preferences on different environmental issues (see Chapter 2). Since the actual costs and risks of environmental problems are never distributed equally, some governments are less motivated than others to participate in international efforts to address them (see Chapter 5). States also possess different views about what constitutes an equitable solution to a particular environmental problem. Yet, despite their often disparate interests, to successfully address most international environmental issues, states must strive for consensus, at least among those that significantly contribute to a specific problem.

Consequently, an important characteristic of global environmental politics is veto power. For every global environmental issue, there exist one or more states whose cooperation is so essential to a successful agreement to cope with the problem that these states have the potential to prevent effective international action. When these states oppose an agreement or try to weaken it significantly, they become veto (or blocking) states.

The role of veto states is central to the dynamics of bargaining and negotiation in global environmental politics. On the issue of a whaling moratorium, for example, four states, led by Japan, accounted for three-fourths of the whaling catch worldwide; they could therefore make or break the effectiveness of a global regime to save whales. Similarly, the major grain exporters (Argentina, Australia, Canada, Chile, the United States, and Uruguay) were in a position to block the initial attempts to reach consensus on a biosafety protocol under the Convention on Biological Diversity (CBD) for fear that the proposed provisions on trade in genetically modified crops would hamper grain exports (see Chapter 4).

Veto power is so important that powerful states are generally not free to impose a global environmental agreement on less powerful states if the latter are both strongly opposed to it and critical to the agreement's success. For example, industrialized countries could not pressure tropical-forest countries such as Brazil, Indonesia, and Malaysia to accept a binding agreement on the world's forests during the 1992 UN Conference on Environment and Development (UNCED). Comparatively weaker states can also use veto power to demand compensation and other forms of favorable treatment. This occurred during the expansion of the ozone-layer regime, when a coalition of developing countries successfully demanded the creation of a financial mechanism to assist them in meeting the higher costs of using new non-ozone-depleting chemicals (see Chapter 3).

Nevertheless, while less powerful states can play veto roles and sometimes prevent or weaken an effective agreement or bargain for special treatment, in general, the major economic powers wield greater leverage because of their larger role in global production and consumption and their ability to provide or deny funding for a particular regime.

A related characteristic of global environmental politics is that the political dynamics within an issue area often reflect national economic interests or the positions of influential interests within a state. Countries sometimes seek to prevent or weaken international action out of concern for its short-term economic impact (e.g., the George W. Bush and Trump administrations' perspective on climate change), although at times the economic costs of the problem or the economic opportunities it creates cause a country to support stronger international action.

Trade relations can also impact negotiation positions and outcomes. For example, a country's ability to give or withhold access to markets can influence states that benefit from such access and cause them to accept a policy proposal if those benefits are more important than the issues at stake in the environmental negotiations. Thus, Japan and the Republic of Korea accepted international agreements on driftnet fishing and whaling because they feared loss of access to US markets. Issues surrounding the international hazardous waste trade have often been shaped by the relationship between some industrialized countries that seek to export both waste and materials for recycling and the related interests of some developing countries to import such materials. Trade relations between tropical timber exporters and consuming nations are critical to the dynamics of tropical deforestation.

Yet, while economic power, interests, and trade dynamics can affect the outcome of bargaining on environmental issues, military power is not particularly useful for influencing such outcomes. Unless a country is willing to use military force to prevent another country from emitting a certain type of pollution or consuming a particular natural resource, military power is largely irrelevant. Indeed, even if a government was willing to take military action and accept the loss of life and international political problems that would accompany it, for most environmental issues it simply would not be effective. For example, how could military action, short of engaging in a massive invasion or bombing campaign, prevent a country from emitting GHGs, cutting more trees, or allowing their plastic trash to reach the ocean?

Many different intergovernmental organizations (IGOs)—including large UN agencies, global and regional financial institutions, scientific organizations, and treaty secretariats—play important roles in global environmental politics. These roles include agenda setting, providing independent and authoritative information, helping to develop norms or codes of conduct (soft law) to guide action on particular environmental issues, convening and managing treaty negotiations, helping to implement global environmental treaties, providing funds, and influencing the environmental and development policies of particular countries (see Chapter 2).

States and IGOs are the most important actors, but another characteristic of global environmental politics is that public opinion and NGOs can affect the creation, content, or implementation of international environmental policy. Public opinion, channeled through electoral politics and NGOs into national negotiating positions in key countries,

---

✦ BOX 1.2 MAJOR UNITED NATIONS SUSTAINABLE DEVELOPMENT CONFERENCES

Earth Summit Series

1972	United Nations Conference on the Human Environment (Stockholm Conference) (Stockholm, Sweden)
1992	United Nations Conference on Environment and Development (Earth Summit) (Rio de Janeiro, Brazil)
2002	World Summit on Sustainable Development (WSSD) (Johannesburg, South Africa)
2012	United Nations Conference on Sustainable Development (Rio de Janeiro, Brazil)

United Nations General Assembly Millennium and Sustainable Development Goals

2000	UN Millennium Summit (UN Headquarters, New York)
2015	UN Sustainable Development Summit (UN Headquarters, New York)

---

has influenced certain aspects of the global bargaining on whaling, endangered species, hazardous wastes, persistent organic pollutants (POPs), and ozone depletion. NGOs have also provided important input to global negotiations and have been integral parts of some implementation strategies (see Chapter 2).

Another characteristic of global environmental politics is that large global conferences convened by the UN (which are different in form and function from the negotiations associated with treaties) have provided critical venues and marked significant milestones in its development (see Box 1.2). The first of these conferences, the historic 1972 Stockholm Conference on the Human Environment, placed global environmental concerns on the international agenda and established the first global, intergovernmental organization focused on the environment—the UN Environment Programme (UNEP; see Chapter 2). The foundation of the conference was the growing realization that "many of the causes and effects of environmental problems are global: this is, beyond the jurisdiction and sovereignty of any nation-state. Global frameworks and other institutions are necessary in order to help organize and coordinate international action."[92] Stockholm also marked the beginning of an explosive increase in government agencies, NGOs, IGOs, and multilateral environmental agreements (MEAs) focused on the environment.[93]

Twenty years later, in 1992, governments gathered in Rio de Janeiro for UNCED, often called the Earth Summit. Countries adopted three important, albeit nonbinding, agreements: the Rio Declaration on Environment and Development, which set out a number of important principles that continue to influence global environmental policy; Agenda 21, a voluntary list of actions and sustainability goals for countries and others to pursue during the twenty-first century; and the Statement of Forest Principles.[94] Governments also officially adopted two major global treaties at the Earth Summit, the climate and biodiversity conventions, which had been negotiated independently of the UNCED process but on parallel tracks with the intention that governments would officially sign them in Rio.

Like the Stockholm Conference twenty years earlier, the Earth Summit launched a significant expansion of international environmental policy and treaty regimes. Over the

✦ BOX 1.3 SELECTED GLOBAL ENVIRONMENTAL TREATIES SINCE 1970

1971	Ramsar Convention on Wetlands of International Importance
1972	Convention on the Prevention of Marine Pollution by Dumping of Wastes and Other Matter (London Convention)
1973	Convention on International Trade in Endangered Species of Wild Fauna and Flora (CITES)
1973	International Convention for the Prevention of Pollution from Ships (MARPOL)
1976	Convention for the Protection of the Mediterranean Sea against Pollution
1979	Convention on the Conservation of Migratory Species of Wild Animals
1980	Convention on the Conservation of Antarctic Marine Living Resources
1985	Vienna Convention for Protection of the Ozone Layer
1987	Montreal Protocol on Substances That Deplete the Ozone Layer
1989	Basel Convention on the Control of Transboundary Movements of Hazardous Wastes and Their Disposal
1992	United Nations Framework Convention on Climate Change
1992	Convention on Biological Diversity
1994	United Nations Convention to Combat Desertification
1997	Kyoto Protocol to the United Nations Framework Convention on Climate Change
1998	Rotterdam Convention on the Prior Informed Consent Procedure for Certain Hazardous Chemicals and Pesticides in International Trade
2000	Cartagena Protocol on Biosafety to the Convention on Biological Diversity
2001	Stockholm Convention on Persistent Organic Pollutants
2001	International Treaty on Plant Genetic Resources for Food and Agriculture
2010	Nagoya Protocol on Access to Genetic Resources and the Fair and Equitable Sharing of Benefits Arising from Their Utilization to the Convention on Biological Diversity
2013	Minamata Convention on Mercury
2015	Paris Agreement to the United Nations Framework Convention on Climate Change

next twenty-five years, new or strengthened conventions, protocols, and policy agreements emerged on climate change, biodiversity, desertification, POPs, biosafety, access to and benefit sharing of genetic resources, mercury, and ozone depletion (see Chapters 3 and 4).

To date, the global community has largely not been able to repeat these breakthroughs at subsequent conferences. The World Summit on Sustainable Development (WSSD), held in Johannesburg in September 2002, was only able to review implementation of the agreements adopted at the Earth Summit. In 2012, the international community returned to Rio for the UN Conference on Sustainable Development, often referred to as Rio+20. This meeting had a larger mandate, received far more attention, and in general enjoyed a more productive atmosphere than the 2002 conference. It also set the stage for future advancement on a number of issues, including the official proposal for developing the Sustainable Development Goals (SDGs), adopted by the UN General Assembly in 2015, in its outcome document, *The Future We Want* (see Chapter 6).

Yet, perhaps the most critical venues for global environmental politics are meetings convened to negotiate the creation, expansion, and implementation of legally binding agreements and other environmental policies in specific issue areas (see Box 1.3). Government representatives gather on a regular basis to examine and sometime strengthen global policy to address biodiversity, climate change, endangered species, fisheries, hazardous waste, mercury, oceans, stratospheric ozone, toxic chemicals, wetlands, whales, and other issues. Preparing for and implementing the results of these conferences can influence not only international and domestic environmental policy but also aspects of economic, trade, and development policy. It is important, however, not to focus solely on the negotiations that create a particular treaty, as doing so can obscure the evolving constellation of binding rules, normative principles, institutions, operating procedures, review mechanisms, and implementation activities that compose environmental policy. Understanding global environmental politics, including environmental treaties and treaty conferences, therefore, requires understanding international regimes.

International Regimes in Global Environmental Politics

International regime is the name given by scholars (and now some practitioners) of international policy to a system of principles, norms, rules, operating procedures, and institutions that actors create to regulate and coordinate action in a particular issue area of international relations. Principles are beliefs of fact, causation, and rectitude. Norms are standards of behavior. Rules are specific prescriptions or proscriptions for action. Operating procedures are prevailing practices for work within the regime, including methods for making and implementing collective choice. Institutions are mechanisms and organizations involved in managing, implementing, evaluating, and expanding the regime and its policies.[95]

Regimes are essentially international policy, regulatory, and administrative systems. A regime usually centers on one or more formal international agreements, but key elements can also include the relevant actions of important international organizations, parts of other interrelated international agreements, and accepted norms of international behavior among actors active in the issue area (including governments, international organizations, NGOs, multinational corporations, and others). These elements together form the entire suite of principles, norms, rules, procedures, and institutions that seek to govern and guide behavior on the issue.

Regimes of varying strength and effectiveness are found in most areas of international relations, including trade, finance, environment, communications, travel, human rights, and security. As a result, regimes have received a good deal of theoretical and empirical attention from scholars of international relations—especially into how, why, and under what circumstances states attempt to cooperate or create international institutions and what factors influence the success of such attempts.[96]

One important line of progenitor theories is marked by concern for the impact and mitigation of structural anarchy, especially the difficulty of establishing international cooperation.[97] (*Anarchy* in this usage does not mean chaos but the absence of hierarchy, specifically the lack of a world government or other formal hierarchical structures to govern international politics.) A second line flows both from constitutionalist scholars who study treaties and the formal structure of international organizations, and from researchers employing the institutional process approach, which concentrates on examining how an organization's day-to-day practices, processes, and methods of operation influence outcomes.[98]

A third line of antecedents starts with the premise that despite structural anarchy, extensive common interests exist among states and their people and that scholars and statesmen must learn how these interests can be realized. Present in eighteenth-century enlightened optimism, nineteenth-century liberalism, and twentieth-century Wilsonian idealism, in the 1970s this view influenced a branch of legal and political scholarship concerned with world order and international law that argued that custom, patterned interaction, and the needs and wants of civilian populations are important sources of international law and require the respect of states.[99]

Functionalism represents a fourth important line of predecessors. Functionalism, often associated with the work of David Mitrany, argues that the scholarly and political focus of international cooperation should concentrate not on traditional interstate politics but, rather, on providing opportunities for technical (non-political) cooperation among specialists and specialized organizations to solve common problems.[100] Functionalists argue that such technical cooperation can begin a process in which increasing interdependence and spill-over (technical management in one area begetting technical management in another) will present opportunities for organizing more and more government functions technically and internationally rather than politically and nationally—a process that will slowly erode or bypass domestic regulators in favor of peaceful global institutions.

Although attractively optimistic, functionalism proved inadequate to explain the totality of actions and outcomes in international relations in which states did not want to relinquish control and technological determinism did not respond automatically to most aspects of increasing interdependence. However, functionalist insights did influence several important theoretical approaches.[101]

Neofunctional integration theory critiqued and extended functionalism, arguing that gradual, regional integration is most important for understanding and creating effective international governance.[102] This approach also lost favor, particularly when Ernst Haas, formerly a leading proponent, argued that focusing exclusively on regional encapsulation had become inadequate for addressing new, turbulent issue areas of international relations characterized by high degrees of complexity, interdependence, and competing national interests, which we now know include environmental issues. Haas argued that the interplay of knowledge, learning, and politics is critical to understanding and managing such issue areas as well as the conduct and adaptability of international organizations created to address them.[103]

Research on transnational relations, which are nongovernmental interconnections and interactions across national boundaries, argued similarly that interdependence can fracture international politics into distinct issue areas and that states are neither the only important actors in international politics nor even totally coherent actors.[104] These insights culminated in complex interdependence, proposed by Robert Keohane and Joseph Nye as an alternative to realism as a paradigm for understanding international relations.[105]

The study of regimes resulted from these lines of inquiry. If international relations are increasingly interdependent, influenced by new types of actors and interactions, and fractured into issue areas across which power and interests vary, then how actors choose to manage these issue areas—the regimes they create to manage them—becomes important to the conduct and study of international politics.

States and other actors create regimes through multilateral negotiations. Negotiations take place when at least some states consider the status quo unacceptable or that negative consequences and high costs will occur if existing trends continue. Although reaching agreement on how to manage the problem is in a state's best interest, so is gaining as much as possible while giving up as little as possible. Nevertheless, the expected value of the outcome to each state, and hence the total value of the outcome, must be positive (or at least neutral), or else there would be no incentive to negotiate or to accept the outcome. In multilateral negotiations, states will not come to an agreement unless they believe they will be better off in some way than they would be with no agreement.[106]

Most regimes center on a binding agreement or legal instrument. For global environmental problems, the most common kind of legal instrument is a convention (treaty). A convention may contain all the obligations expected to be negotiated, or it may be amended at a later date or supplemented by a new, more detailed legal instrument, often called a protocol, which elaborates more specific norms and rules. Because the members of most international regimes are states, regime rules apply to the actions of states. These governments then assume responsibility for ensuring that companies and other actors within their jurisdiction change their behavior to the extent necessary for the country as a whole to comply with the rules of the regime.

If a convention is negotiated in anticipation that parties will negotiate one or more protocols, it is called a framework convention. Framework conventions usually establish a set of general principles, norms, and goals for cooperation on the issue as well as how members of the regimes will meet and make decisions. The latter usually takes the form of a regular Conference of the Parties (COP), an annual, biannual, or otherwise regularly scheduled gathering of all parties to the convention as well as interested observers (observers often include representatives from non-party states, international organizations, NGOs, and industry groups). Framework conventions usually do not impose major binding obligations on the parties but are then followed by the negotiation of protocols, which spell out specific obligations on the overall issue in question or on narrower sub-issues.

A nonbinding agreement can form the centerpiece of a regime to the extent that it establishes norms that clearly influence state behavior. This type of agreement is often referred to as soft law. Nonbinding agreements, codes of conduct, and guidelines for behavior exist for several global environmental problems, including land-based sources of marine pollution and sustainable forest management, with varying degrees of effectiveness. Some consider the SDGs a soft-law regime for worldwide sustainable development because they outline agreed goals and broad norms of behavior. Although nonbinding agreements can influence state behavior to some extent, regimes based on legal instruments are usually more effective.

Global Environmental Regimes

Today, regimes exist on a wide variety of global environmental issues, from whale protection to climate change to hazardous wastes. As demonstrated in Chapters 3 and 4, global environmental regimes can vary significantly in their history, purpose, rules, strength, and effectiveness. Environmental regimes change over time, often expanding and becoming stronger but sometimes weakening or changing in scope. The whaling regime was created in 1946 to perpetuate commercial whaling by establishing international regulation, but it evolved into a ban on commercial whaling in 1985 (see Chapter 4). The regime that seeks to control marine oil pollution began with the 1954 International Convention for the Prevention of Pollution of the Sea by Oil, which established rules only for ships within 50 miles (80 kilometers) of the nearest coast, allowing for significant and deliberate oil spillage outside this area.[107] This led some states in 1973 to create the International Convention for the Prevention of Pollution from Ships, also known as MARPOL or the Maritime Pollution Convention, which limits oil discharges at sea, prohibits them in certain sensitive zones, and sets minimum distances from land for the discharge of other pollutants. However, shipping interests in crucial maritime states opposed MARPOL so strongly that it did not enter into force until

Photo 1.2 For many years, governments have not been able to agree to even negotiate a forests treaty. Instead, governments adopted the non-legally binding UN Forest Instrument, which includes four global objectives on forests to be achieved by 2030.

Courtesy Dan Birchall, IISD/*Earth Negotiations Bulletin*, http://enb.iisd.org

a decade later. States also negotiated the Convention on the Prevention of Marine Pollution by Dumping of Wastes and Other Matter (London Convention, 1972), which prohibited the dumping of specific substances, including high-level radioactive wastes, and required permits for others. This was the first marine-pollution agreement to accept the right of coastal states to enforce prohibitions against pollution and became an important forum for negotiating further controls on ocean dumping.

Many regimes are strengthened as efforts shift from creating an initial framework convention to negotiating and implementing specific protocols. For example, the regional regime controlling cross-border acid rain and air pollution in the northern hemisphere began with the 1979 Convention on Long-Range Transboundary Air Pollution, which did not commit signatories to specific emissions reductions. States later strengthened the regime by adding eight protocols that financed the monitoring and evaluation of long-range air pollutants in Europe (1984) and mandated efforts to reduce sulfur emissions (1985 and 1994), nitrogen oxides (1988), volatile organic compounds (1991), heavy metals (1998), POPs (1998), and acidification and ground-level ozone (1999).[108] The heavy metals and POPs agreements also represented significant expansions of the core mandate established by the original convention.

The ozone regime also began with a framework convention (see Chapter 3). The 1985 Vienna Convention for the Protection of the Ozone Layer did not require countries to control the chemicals that deplete stratospheric ozone; indeed, it did not even mention these substances by name. The 1987 Montreal Protocol then required actual reductions in certain halons and chlorofluorocarbons (CFCs), the most prominent ozone-depleting substances (ODS). Then, beginning in the late 1980s, significant advances in scientific understanding of the threat, the discovery of alternative chemicals, and the use of innovative regime rules allowed governments to reach a series of historic agreements in the 1990s and 2000s that now mandate the near-complete phase-out of all ODS.

Some treaties and regimes, like the 2001 Stockholm Convention on Persistent Organic Pollutants and the Montreal Protocol, have very clear, binding controls (see Chapter 3); others do not. The 1992 Convention on Biological Diversity (see Chapter 4), for example, does not obligate parties to achieve measurable conservation objectives but instead requires the development of national strategies for conserving biodiversity. Similarly, the 1994 UN Convention to Combat Desertification (UNCCD; see Chapter 4), which established a regime to address land degradation in the drylands, calls for countries to draw up integrated national programs in consultation with local communities.

Some regimes, such as the ozone regime, are considered successes, even if they have not completely solved the environmental issues they address. However, many regimes are mixed successes at best. Nevertheless, negotiation of the central agreement and other aspects of the regime (such as the related activities of international organizations) provide greater opportunities for addressing the environmental issue in question than when no regime exists (because either negotiations failed or none were attempted).[109] Thus, even though the bio-diversity and climate regimes have not come close to solving those problems—in fact, each problem continues to accelerate, with potentially disastrous results—the situation would be worse, and the prospects for future improvements more remote, if the regimes did not exist.

Evidence for this conclusion exists in issues that have no extant regimes or for which initial attempts to create a regime failed. For instance, several efforts to create a regime for the protection of coral reefs have failed to gain traction, and coral reefs continue to degrade rapidly around the world. Many countries have laws protecting coastal mangroves, but many of these same countries also sanction their enclosure or even allow their removal for coastal development or to create ponds for shrimp farms. Without an international regime leading all countries to adjust their behavior simultaneously, this situation is likely to continue, and mangroves (and the ecological and economic value they have) will continue to disappear.

Theoretical Approaches to International Regimes

Several major theoretical approaches have been used to explain how international regimes come into existence and why they change.[110] These include structural, game-theoretic, institutional-bargaining, and epistemic-community approaches. Each helps to explain one or more international regimes, but none individually can account for all the regimes described and analyzed in this book.

The structural, or hegemonic power, approach descends from political realism and holds that the primary factor determining regime formation and change is the relative strength of the state actors involved in a particular issue and that "stronger states in the issue system will dominate the weaker ones and determine the rules of the game."[111] This approach suggests that strong international regimes are a function of a hegemonic state that can exercise leadership over weaker states and that the absence of such a hegemonic state is likely to frustrate regime formation.

The structural approach can be viewed in two ways, one stressing coercive power and the other focusing on public goods. In the coercive-power variant, regimes are created and maintained by hegemonic states that use their military and economic leverage over other states to bring them into regimes, as the United States did in setting up trade and monetary regimes immediately after World War II and establishing the dollar as the stable currency for international payments.[112] The second variant views the same post-war regimes as the result of a hegemonic power's adoption of policies that create public goods, that is, benefits open to all states that want to participate.

While useful for explaining the creation of post-World War II economic systems, the structural approach cannot explain the creation and persistence of global environmental regimes. In the 1970s and 1980s, the United States was not a military hegemon but part of a bipolar system with the Soviet Union. Beginning in the mid-1980s, the United States faced the rise of competing economic powers in Japan and Europe. Moreover, the EU, whose member states negotiate on global environmental issues as a single bloc, became a near-economic equal to the United States in the late 1990s. Finally, and perhaps most importantly, the United States did not seek to create many of these environmental regimes. From 1981 to 1993 and from 2001 to 2009, both crucial periods in the creation and expansion of many global environmental regimes, the United States had presidents ideologically hostile toward international environmental regulation; consequently, the United States did not take many lead positions—as the theory argues a hegemonic state must do. The creation and expansion of these regimes depended on wide consensus among several states, not on imposition by the United States.[113] In addition, global environmental regimes did not weaken significantly during the presidency of Donald Trump, as predicted by the theory, even though he was even more opposed to restricting the US economy to protect the environment.

Another approach to understanding regime creation is based on game theory and utilitarian models of bargaining. In game theory, bargaining scenarios are examined under different conditions with regard to the number of parties involved, the nature of the conflict (zero sum or non-zero sum), and the assumptions that the actors are both rational (they will try to pursue outcomes favorable to themselves) and interconnected in some way—that is, they cannot pursue their own interests independently of the choices of other actors. This approach suggests that small groups of states, or coalitions, are more likely to succeed in negotiating an international regime than a large number, because each player can more readily understand the bargaining strategies of the other players. Political scientist Fen Osler Hampson took this approach into account when he analyzed the process of regime creation as an effort by a small coalition of states to form a regime by exercising leadership over a much larger number of national actors.[114]

While providing important insights, this approach also does not capture important realities. Most basically, a successful global environmental regime must include all states that have a large impact on the issue, including potential veto states. Veto states follow their own interests (as all states do), so a veto state in a small group will likely be as prone to opposition as it would be in a large group of states. And if veto states are left outside the small group, they will still be able to frustrate regime formation when the regime is enlarged, or they may simply refuse to join, limiting the regime's success.

Another approach is the epistemic-communities model, which emphasizes the impact of international learning and transnational networks of experts and bureaucrats, primarily on the basis of scientific research into a given problem, as a factor influencing the evolution of regimes.[115] This approach, advanced initially by political scientist Peter Haas to explain the creation of and compliance with the Mediterranean Action Plan, identifies shifts in perspectives about an issue among an international network of individuals with specialized knowledge of the problem and relevant and potentially influential positions in governments, international organizations, scientific agencies, and NGOs as the critical factor in the convergence of state policies in support of creating or strengthening a regime. These elites constitute a transnational epistemic community that shares a common understanding about the causes and impact of a particular problem as well as similar beliefs regarding the need to address it and how to do so, and are in position to help shape policy due to their positions of potential influence within relevant institutions.

The importance of scientific evidence and expertise in the politics of many global environmental issues cannot be ignored. Indeed, a significant degree of scientific understanding and consensus has sometimes been a minimum condition for serious international action. The impetus for agreement in 1990 that the world should phase out CFCs completely came from incontrovertible scientific evidence that damage to the ozone layer was much greater than previously thought and that CFCs were largely responsible. The Kyoto Protocol was made possible, in part, by the Second Assessment Report of the Intergovernmental Panel on Climate Change, which confirmed that the earth's temperature is increasing and that there is a "discernible human influence" on climate.

However, on other issues, such as the whaling ban, the hazardous waste trade, desertification and land degradation, Antarctica, and the ocean dumping of radioactive wastes, scientists have contributed little to consensus building within lead states or to most regime-formation or strengthening activities at the global level. In some of these cases, scientific elites were not particularly influential in policymaking, whereas in others, key actors explicitly rejected scientific findings as the basis for decisions.[116] The lack of significant progress in global climate policy over the last twenty years—despite significant increases in scientific knowledge and consensus and repeated calls by influential scientific elites within key governments and the regime itself for more action—is perhaps the prominent example.

The case studies presented in Chapters 3 and 4 (and many discussions in the study of international relations) also suggest that theoretical approaches based solely on a unitary actor model (one suggesting that state actors can be treated as though they were a single entity encompassing an internally consistent set of values and attitudes), ignoring the roles of domestic sociopolitical structures and processes, are likely to form poor bases for analyzing and predicting the outcomes of global environmental negotiations. Positions usually reflect domestic political balances, and these can change when those balances shift. For example, after Barack Obama was elected president, the United States dramatically shifted its stance from opposing to supporting global negotiations to create a regime to reduce mercury emissions. Although the structure of an issue in terms of economic interests may indicate which states are most likely to join a veto coalition, domestic political pressures and bargaining can tip the balance for or against regime creation or strengthening.

A more complete and nuanced analysis of regime formation and strengthening, therefore, should link international political dynamics with domestic politics and view the whole as a two-level game.[117] While representatives of countries are negotiating at the international level, officials must also negotiate with interest groups within their domestic political systems. Because the two processes often take place simultaneously, the arenas influence each other and become part of the negotiations at each level.

A theoretical explanation for the formation of global environmental regimes must also leave room for the importance of the rules of the negotiating forum and the linkages between the negotiations on regimes and the wider relationships among the negotiating parties. The legal structure of the negotiating forum—the rules of the game regarding who may participate and how authoritative decisions are to be made—becomes particularly important when the negotiations take place within an already established treaty or organization.[118] As the ozone, whaling, and toxic chemicals cases illustrate, such regime structures can be crucial in determining the outcomes of individual negotiations (see Chapters 3 and 4).

Paradigms in Global Environmental Politics

Public policy and regimes are shaped not only by political and economic interests, scientific developments, and technological innovation, but also by broad sets of beliefs held by the general population, governments, institutions, and political leaders. In times of relative stability, public policies and systems of behavior tend to flow in accordance with dominant paradigms, or sets of beliefs, ideas, and values. Not everyone needs to believe in the paradigm for it to impact policy. The paradigm simply needs to be the assumed truth among a significant portion of the population, particularly among decision makers. A dominant paradigm is challenged when contradictions appear between its assumptions and observed reality. If these contradictions are not resolved, eventually it gives way to a new paradigm through a process known as a paradigm shift.[119]

The paradigms that dominated public understanding of environmental management during the period of rapid global economic growth in the 1700s, 1800s, and 1900s, and which still influence decision making today, were based on assumptions that humans exist largely apart from nature, natural resources are essentially limitless, and market forces will correct situations in which they are not. One set of beliefs has been referred to as the *exclusionist paradigm* because it excludes human beings from the laws of nature. Humans stand apart from nature and cannot fundamentally harm it (nor can environmental changes harm humans on a significant scale), either because a deity provided the earth for humans to use or because nature is too vast for humans to affect it in any fundamental way (outside of local impacts related to agriculture, urbanization, etc.). A closely related paradigm has been called *frontier economics*, which shares the core assumption of the exclusionist paradigm but incorporates the sense of unlimited resources characteristic of a society living on an open frontier. There is no need to conserve natural resources, because humans can always go in search of more—either across the sea or by moving further into another frontier. Similarly, there is no need to worry about pollution, as the oceans and atmosphere are so vast that we can put effluents into them forever.[120] For centuries, the traditional international legal principles of state sovereignty (including control over resources within a state's borders) and unrestricted access to the planet's common resources, such as the oceans and their living resources, buttressed these paradigms.

In capitalist economies, these paradigms both reflect and are incorporated into two related assumptions (and indeed paradigms) of neoclassical economics: the free market will tend to maximize social welfare, and there exists an infinite supply of both natural resources and sinks for disposing of the wastes that accrue from exploiting those resources—provided that the free market is operating efficiently. Humans will not deplete a resource, according to this worldview, as long as technology is given free rein and prices are allowed to fluctuate enough to stimulate the search for substitutes; in this way, absolute scarcity can be postponed indefinitely into the future.[121] Waste disposal is viewed as a problem to be cleaned up after the fact, and will be eventually encouraged by market forces, but should not be pursued at the cost of interference with market decisions.[122] Since conventional economic theory is concerned with the allocation of scarce resources, and nature is not considered a constraining factor, these paradigms consider the environment largely irrelevant to economics. Despite a different economic and political ideology, the former Soviet Union and other communist states also shared this assumption.

Sustainable Development: Rise of an Alternative Paradigm

In the 1960s, assumptions central to the exclusionist paradigm, frontier economics, and traditional economic perspectives on environmental issues came under attack. The 1962 publication of Rachel Carson's *Silent Spring*, which documented the dangers posed by synthetic pesticides, marked the beginning of an explosion of popular literature about new threats to the environment and human health, including radiation, lead, toxic wastes, and air and water pollution. The first mass movement for environmental protection, which focused on domestic issues including air and water pollution, developed in the United States in the late 1960s, culminating with the first Earth Day on April 22, 1970. Throughout this period, research and writing on environmental issues raised awareness that economic activity without concern for the environment carried high costs to society. Parallel changes in public attitudes to pollution also occurred in other industrialized countries. The burst of environmental concern in the United States contributed to the passage of a series of landmark pieces of legislation, including the National Environmental Policy Act in 1969, the Clean Air Act and establishment of the US Environmental Protection Agency in 1970, and new rules to combat water pollution in 1972. These laws and those that built on them dramatically decreased air, water, and soil pollution in the United States. The National Environmental

Policy Act also directed federal agencies to support international cooperation in "antici-pating and preventing a decline in the quality of mankind's world environment."[123]

But the United States was not alone. As noted earlier, the first global environmental con-ference in history, the UN Conference on the Human Environment, convened in Stockholm in 1972. The motto of the Stockholm Conference, "Only One Earth," was a revolutionary concept for its time. The conference approved a landmark declaration and a 109-point action plan for advancing international environmental cooperation, including creating a new inter-national organization, UNEP, to provide a focal point for environmental action and coord-ination of environmentally related activities within the UN system. In preparation for, or as a result of, Stockholm, environmental ministries and agencies were established in more than 100 countries (most governments did not have such ministries before 1972). Stockholm also marked the beginning of the explosive increase in environmentally focused NGOs.

This rise of environmental consciousness attacked the central assumptions of fron-tier economics and the exclusionist paradigm but did not produce a widely accepted set of alternative assumptions about physical and economic realities that could become a com-peting worldview. The essential assumptions of classical economics remained largely intact. Confronted with evidence that existing patterns of resource exploitation could cause irre-versible damage, proponents of classical economics continued to maintain that such exploit-ation was still economically rational.[124]

Over time, however, an alternative paradigm began to take shape. Two of the intellec-tual forerunners of this paradigm were the *Limits to Growth* study, published by the Club of Rome in 1972, and *Global 2000: The Report to the President*, released by the White House in 1980.[125] Each study applied global-systems computer modeling to projected interactions among population growth, economic output and growth, natural resource consumption, and pollution patterns, and concluded that if current trends continued, many ecosystems and natural resources would become seriously and irreversibly degraded and that these environ-mental developments would then have serious and negative economic consequences. Because each study suggested that economic development and population growth were on a path that would eventually strain the earth's carrying capacity (the total amount of resource consump-tion that the earth's natural systems can support without undergoing degradation), and that this in turn would then limit subsequent opportunities for economic growth, the viewpoints underlying their conclusions were often referred to as the *limits-to-growth* perspective.

Defenders of the traditional paradigms criticized these studies for projecting the deple-tion of non-renewable resources without considering technological changes and market responses. They argued that overpopulation would not become a problem because people are the world's "ultimate resource," and they characterized the authors of studies as "no-growth elitists" who would freeze developing countries out of the benefits of economic growth. They argued that human ingenuity would enable humanity to leap over the alleged limits to growth through new and better technologies.[126] These arguments found a following among those concerned about economic growth. The development of an alternative paradigm was set back in the early 1980s, when the Reagan administration in the United States and the Thatcher government in the United Kingdom embraced policies consistent with the exclu-sionist paradigm, frontier economics, and neoclassical economic views of the relationship between market forces and the natural world.

Despite these political developments, knowledge about ecological principles and their relationship to economic development continued to spread. A global community of practitioners and scholars began to emerge, allied in the belief that ecologically sound eco-nomic policies should replace policies based on the traditional paradigms.

By the mid-1980s, *sustainable development* had emerged as the catchphrase of the search for an alternative paradigm, and the term was heard with increasing frequency around the world. An important milestone was the 1987 publication by the World Commission on Environment and Development of *Our Common Future* (often called the Brundtland Report, after the commission's chair, former Norwegian prime minister Gro Harlem Brundtland). The UN established the commission to examine the impact of environmental degradation and natural resource depletion on future economic and social development. The commission's report is considered a landmark in part because it helped to define, legitimize, and popularize the concept of sustainable development. Drawing on and synthesizing the views and research of hundreds of people worldwide, it also codified some of the central beliefs of the emerging sustainable development paradigm.

The Brundtland Commission defined sustainable development as "development that meets the need of the present without compromising the ability of future generations to meet their own needs."[127] The central themes of its report criticized existing economic and social systems for failing to reconcile those needs. It asserted that the earth's natural systems have finite capabilities and resources and that continuing current policies carried the risk of causing irreversible damage to critical natural systems.

The sustainable development paradigm emphasizes the need to redefine the term *development*. It posits that economic growth cannot continue at the expense of the planet's natural capital (its stock of renewable and non-renewable resources) and vital natural support systems such as the ozone layer, biodiversity, and a stable climate. That means reducing the amount of resources used per unit of gross domestic product (GDP), shifting from fossil fuels to renewable energy, and reusing and recycling rather than consuming and discarding. It implies a transition to sustainable systems of natural resource management, efforts to stabilize world population, and a more measured approach to consumption.

The sustainable development paradigm also holds that future generations have an equal right to use our planet's natural resources—a concept known as *intergenerational*

Photo 1.3 Youth activists participating in a Fridays for Future climate strike outside the UN Framework Convention on Climate Change negotiations in Bonn, Germany, in 2019 call for intergenerational equity.

Courtesy Kiara Worth, IISD/*Earth Negotiations Bulletin*, http://enb.iisd.org

equity[128]—and the need for greater equity among and within nations. Highly industrialized countries such as the United States, which use a disproportionate share of the world's natural resources, are seen as pursuing an unsustainable type of economic growth, as are societies in which grossly unequal distribution of land and other resources produce negative impacts. To meet current and future needs, developing countries must meet the basic needs of the poor in ways that do not deplete the countries' natural resources, and industrialized countries must examine attitudes and actions regarding unnecessary and wasteful aspects of their material abundance.[129]

Advocates of sustainable development note that although the central measure of macro-economic growth in traditional economic paradigms, GDP, is an effective measure of broad economic activity, it fails to reflect the natural resource-related capability of an economy to provide material wealth in the future or to take into account the relative well-being of the society in general. Thus, a country could systematically deplete its natural resources, erode its soils, and pollute its waters without that loss of wealth and its long-term negative economic impact showing up in calculations of GDP. Moreover, the economic expense of trying to fix these problems would actually add to GDP, with no consideration given to the significant opportunity costs of spending money on rectifying environmental damage rather than using it for investments in education or infrastructure.

In the second half of the 1980s, some economists began to study how to correct this anomaly in conventional accounting and how governments and international organizations could use alternatives to GDP, such as real net national product, sustainable social net national product, or index of sustainable economic welfare, which incorporate changes in environmental resources as well as other indicators that measure human welfare.[130] One example is the annual UN Development Programme's (UNDP) *Human Development Report*, which began using human indicators to rate the quality of life in all countries in addition to economic ones, including literacy, life expectancy, and respect for women's rights. The World Bank's work on national capital accounting and the UN's System of Environmental-Economic Accounts also pioneered the inclusion of social and environmental aspects when assessing the wealth of nations. The OECD's Global Project on Measuring the Progress of Societies began employing broader indicators than traditional GDP or similarly based analyses. The Environmental Performance Index started ranking countries on twenty-one elements of sustainability covering natural resource endowments, past and present pollution levels, environmental management efforts, and contributions to protecting the global commons.[131] The EU now uses a broad range of social and environmental indicators, often regrouped in sets of sustainable development indicators, and supports the use of similar, internationally recognized indicators in neighboring countries and developing countries.[132] The Himalayan kingdom of Bhutan famously measures well-being not through GDP but through a Gross National Happiness Index that provides an overview of performance across nine domains: psychological well-being, time use, community vitality, cultural diversity, ecological resilience, living standard, health, education, and good governance.[133]

The use of these and related approaches reflected an increasing awareness that free markets alone often fail to ensure human health or the sustainable use of natural resources. Market mechanisms can provide incentives to substitute for dwindling resources and pursue less polluting technologies, but they can also actually increase incentives to deplete certain resources, such as when more poachers pursue particular animals because their increasing scarcity has raised prices on the black market or when fishing boats or miners use more destructive technologies to increase their yields.

Because market mechanisms on their own also usually do not prevent or remedy negative externalities, one deduction from the sustainable development approach was that prices should reflect the real costs to society of producing and consuming a given resource or emitting pollution that harms people or the environment. Conventional economic policies, however, systematically underprice or ignore natural resources as well as the costs of pollution and related externalities.

Public policies that do not correct for these market failures tend to encourage pollution, more rapid depletion of renewable resources, wasteful consumption, and the degradation of environmental services (i.e., the conserving or restorative functions of nature; for example, the conversion of CO_2 to oxygen by plants and the cleansing of water by wetlands). Adjusting the markets to send different price signals, removing government subsidies for environmentally harmful activities, and exchanging income taxes for green taxes are means to address this problem.

The sustainable development paradigm gained significant credibility through the 1992 Earth Summit. The Earth Summit presented the first post-Cold War opportunity for industrialized countries (sometimes referred to in those discussions as "the North") and developing countries ("the South") to hold formal discussions on how they might combine economic and social development concerns with those of environmental protection to put the concept of sustainable development into action.[134] The priorities endorsed and the agreements reached in Rio included the principle of common but differentiated responsibilities—the concept that all countries have a common responsibility to protect the global environment, but also different levels of responsibility that reflect how much they contributed to the problem and the resources they have to contribute to a solution. In practice, this means that industrialized countries should address international environmental problems first, as they were primarily responsible for them, and developing countries would try to put into practice more environmentally sound development policies if the industrialized countries agreed to provide support, that is, new and additional financial resources, technology transfer, and assistance with capacity building, education, and training. Yet, while UNCED saw agreement on many important principles and goals, including the need for sustainable development, nearly thirty years later, few countries have lived up to their Rio commitments or completely embraced the sustainable development paradigm.

Globalization and Sustainable Development

Within many governments, including China, India, and the United States, ideas that appear to be descended from the exclusionist paradigm and frontier economics still dominate many policies. Many corporations, government ministries, and leaders of particular countries or political parties embrace the language of sustainable development but support actual policies that contradict it. Interest groups dominated by certain industries locked into old paradigms continue to determine many national political agendas. Additionally, while some treaties have proven successful, studies show that most of the explicit goals set out in international environmental agreements have not been met.[135] Some argue that while progress has been made in reducing negative environmental impacts, the prospects for a clear paradigm transition have stalled because of *globalization*.[136]

One can view globalization as a description and/or an organizing principle, goal, or paradigm. As a description, globalization is the name given to the measurable, increasing interconnectedness of global economic, social, transportation, and communications systems. It is the increasing international movement of commodities, money, information, popular culture, and people, as well as the development of economic and legal systems, infrastructures, organizations, and technology to allow this movement. The interrelationships of markets, finance, goods, and services, and the networks created by transnational corporations are particularly important manifestations.

At the same time, the prevalence of policy choices that favor increased economic interconnectedness and other aspects of globalization, and the arguments of those who support or oppose these policies, make it clear that some consider globalization a goal or paradigm for organizing international economic activity. Supporters of the globalization paradigm advocate for the liberalization of international markets, including reducing trade and other national economic barriers, minimizing regulations on the market (especially in highly regulated developing countries), and granting rights to corporations to invest in any country with few restraints or conditions. Governments should not interfere with the free play of the market. Efforts to prioritize social, development, or environmental concerns will actually slow the economic growth required for such goals to be achieved.

Actions by powerful countries and corporations in the 1990s and 2000s supported not only the physical manifestations of globalization (e.g., the increased international movement of goods, investments, services, people, entertainment, and ideas) but also the ascendancy of the globalization paradigm. Some argue that many senior US policymakers saw globalization as supplanting the need for international assistance and even the sustainable development paradigm. "Trade not aid" became a Washington mantra during the George W. Bush administration. Even among US policymakers favorable to environmental and development objectives, the trade and globalization agenda tended to occupy the available political space and crowd out sustainable development concerns.[137] The same argument could be made about key policies in China, India, and Russia, among other large countries.

As governments prepared for the 2012 Rio+20 conference, support for the sustainable development paradigm remained strong, but efforts to actually alter significant aspects of national and international economics to put the concept into practice on a broad scale remained a challenge, and in most capitals not a priority in an era of increasing globalization. In response, the Rio+20 agenda included examining prospects for countries to pursue a *green economy* in the context of sustainable development and poverty eradication. A green economy, according to one prominent definition, is one focused on explicitly linking economic growth to improving human well-being and social equity while also reducing environmental risks, ecological scarcities, and social disparities. In a green economy, growth in income, employment, and social development is driven by public and private investments in economically productive activities that also reduce carbon emissions and pollution, enhance energy and resource efficiency, and prevent the loss of biodiversity and ecosystem services.[138] Traction for the concept was aided by technological developments in key industries, continued disillusionment with the traditional paradigms that seemed to ignore the increasing threats posed by resource depletion and environmental degradation, interest in developing specific guidance for how to pursue sustainable development, and unease produced by the 2008 financial crisis.

Some of the research and policy work on the green economy emphasizes the importance of internalizing environmental externalities in prices to send the right signals to producers and consumers—that is, to get the prices right. Other discussions focus on the importance of government actions that assist research, development, and deployment of new technologies in key sectors; finance infrastructure investments; provide supportive policy environments for green investments by the private sector; and ensure that green economy policies support employment and income generation for the poor.[139] Other discussions point toward the need for greater awareness within the private sector regarding the business opportunities represented by the green economy and the importance of altering their financing and investment patterns.[140]

Supporters of the green economy, as a paradigm or set of policy principles, believe it offers a way to pursue the economic aspirations of both rich and poor countries in a world of increasing globalization and interdependence that also faces climate change, pollution, and ecological scarcity. A green economy can meet this challenge, they argue, by offering a development path that reduces carbon dependency, promotes resource and energy efficiency, and lessens environmental degradation. As economic growth and investments become less dependent on liquidating environmental assets and sacrificing environmental quality, both rich and poor countries can attain true sustainable development.[141]

During the Rio+20 process, however, a number of developing countries argued that the green economy paradigm did not adequately consider the real development needs in many countries, global equity issues, the negative impacts of globalization, or that the concept could be used by rich countries to justify unilateral trade measures against developing countries or as a new conditional standard (in support of the globalization paradigm) that developing countries would have to meet to access aid, loans, and debt rescheduling and forgiveness.[142] They emphasized the importance of upholding the sovereign rights of individual countries to pursue their own development models and enact policies that reflect their own needs, resources, and history. While the green economy paradigm has received less attention since 2012, the SDGs, the 2015 Paris Agreement on climate change, proposals for a "Green New Deal" that have emerged in American politics, and calls in many countries for emphasizing environmental investments as part of COVID-19 economic recovery efforts all provide important platforms for integrating the paradigm into national and international economic, environmental, and sustainable development agendas.[143]

So, what are the prospects for sustainable development and more effective global environmental policy in a world of increasing globalization? There are two primary arguments in this debate. Supporters of globalization, as a paradigm or as a fact of international life, argue that it goes hand in hand with sustainable development and is beneficial for the environment because it is an engine of wealth creation. As societies become richer, the initial process of industrialization results in greater pollution. This happened in Europe and the United States and is happening now in many developing countries. As economic development continues, a point is eventually reached at which most material needs have been met for a significant majority of a country's citizens. At this point, societies develop greater concern for pollution reduction and environmental protection, as western Europe and the United States did. In addition, because of wealth creation, society has the economic and technical ability to implement the necessary measures to achieve environmental goals. Globalization, by delivering the development side of the sustainable development equation, can solve the economic and social problems that contribute to environmental degradation. Along these lines, poverty is seen as a critical component of environmental degradation, and environmentalists who oppose globalization as a policy are sometimes condemned as eco-imperialists for trying to deny poor countries the right to develop.[144]

The opposing argument sees both the globalization paradigm and most aspects of globalization in practice as almost inherently contrary to sustainable development. In this view, globalization extends the exclusionist paradigm into all aspects of international economic relations, promoting and accelerating the overconsumption of natural resources and overproduction of waste on a global scale. It encourages the movement of capital, technology, goods, and labor to areas with high short-term returns on investment without regard for their impact on the communities who live there, the environment, or even long-term economic well-being. Globalization stretches the chains of production and consumption over great distances and across many locations, which increases the separation between sources of environmental problems and their impact. The division of labor associated with globalization increases the transport of raw materials, commodities, semi-processed materials, parts, finished goods, and waste; requires greater energy consumption, resulting in more pollution, including higher carbon emissions; and increases the risk of localized pollution problems and major environmental accidents.[145] Critics also argue that globalization reinforces the sharp inequalities between developing and developed countries, or at least the inequalities between rich and poor, both nationally and internationally.

For example, the ready availability of so many different types of vegetables and fruits throughout the year is partly the result of a shift from subsistence farming in parts of many developing countries to intensive cash cropping and international trade, the wages and profits of which do not translate into sufficient food and social development in many local societies. Agribusinesses, not farmers, often reap the benefits and own the best-quality land. Chemical fertilizers and pesticides are relied on to produce uniform, export-quality produce, whereas fewer chemicals are needed to grow local or subsistence crops. Poor farmers of

❖ BOX 1.4   COMMODITY CHAINS

The reorganization of production under globalization has led to the creation of extended "commodity chains" that spread environmental impacts over many countries. For example, the production of cotton T-shirts can involve as many as six different countries, creating different types of pollution and environmental impacts in each one.[147]

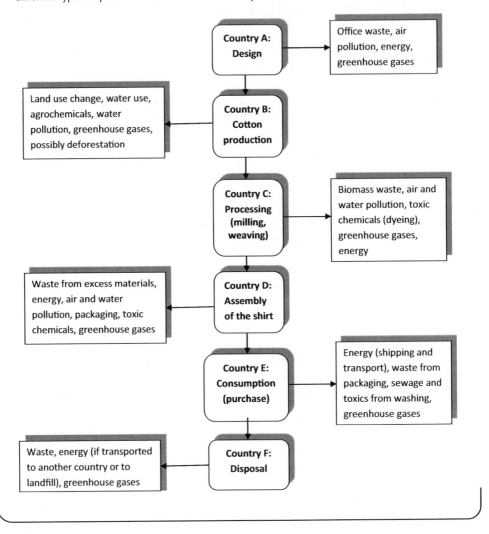

export crops also have perverse incentives, or are even forced by economic circumstances, to cultivate low-quality, marginal land, contributing to soil erosion, habitat destruction, and land degradation.[146] The produce must then be transported to international markets, creating additional environmental externalities. This is an example of how globalization has created extended commodity chains in many economic sectors in ways that impact the environment (see Box 1.4).

The exact relationship between globalization, sustainable development, and the environment is, of course, more complex than either of these two archetypal arguments. Each perspective contains elements of truth, and the specific impact of one aspect of globalization on a particular environmental issue depends on national and international economic and policy choices. The same is true regarding the impact of two other paradigms that impact global environmental politics: the environment-security nexus and the precautionary principle.

Environmental Change as a Security Issue

The environment-security paradigm holds that environmental degradation and resource depletion can affect national security. The central idea is that climate change, resource depletion, and environmental degradation act as threat multipliers that augment other conditions known to cause violence among opposing groups within a state or even among states. As argued by Thomas Homer-Dixon, who helped to pioneer our understanding of this issue, resource scarcity, ecosystem collapse, and other environmental problems can act as tectonic stresses, exacerbating existing political, social, or economic instability to the point where armed conflict occurs.[148] Environmental degradation can help cause or increase the impact of other problems known to contribute to violence within or among states, such as resource disputes, refugee movements, poverty, hunger, and weak governments.

For example, changing climate conditions contributed to the devastating ethnic conflict in Darfur, Sudan.[149] Environmental factors did not cause the violence, but they helped to push other factors, including the political and territorial ambitions of certain individuals and groups, poverty, hunger, population movements, and increasing ethnic and political divisions, past the tipping point into widespread, systematic violence. The government and several rebel groups opposed each other for years, reflecting the political and territorial interests of particular actors as well as long-standing animosity between some elements of the Afro-Arab ethnic groups that dominate in the north and the non-Arab farming ethnic groups in the south. Over time, severe changes in rainfall patterns, increasing drought, and deteriorating soils caused many farmers to block access to the remaining fertile land. Many herders were angry that they were not receiving their share of the land, leading to violent clashes, which were then used by some political leaders as excuses to widen the conflict.

In North America, the collapse of fisheries in northwestern Mexico contributed to the decision by some fishermen to become involved in drug smuggling.[150] Similarly, overfishing and illegal fishing off the coast of Somalia contributed to the increase in piracy.[151] Criminal enterprises, many of which pose threats to local security, are involved in illegal fishing and logging around the world.[152] In Haiti, massive deforestation (less than 2 percent of the nation remains forested) led to severely eroded hillsides, massive soil erosion and runoff, and declining water quality. This exacerbated the already difficult situation for rural farmers trying to work the country's mountainous terrain, and soil runoff from the mountains polluted many of the nation's already overfished coastal areas, eliminating fishing as a source of income for many. With no means to make a living in rural areas, the majority of Haitians moved to city slums, most living without clean water or proper sanitation, producing conditions that worsened the impact of the massive earthquake in 2010, which killed perhaps 300,000 and left at least 1 million Haitians homeless.[153]

US and European military and intelligence communities accept that environmental change and degradation can impact issues related to national security.[154] Of particular concern is climate change, which could produce huge numbers of refugees from flooded coastal areas, increase water and food scarcity, spread disease, and weaken economies in parts of the world that are already vulnerable, unstable, prone to extremism, or suffering significant cultural, ethnic, or economic divisions. Indeed, recent studies indicate that as many as 150 million people currently live on land that will be well below the high tide mark as soon as 2050, and more in the decades that follow, due to climate change and associated sea-level rise.[155]

Africa, for example, although "least responsible for greenhouse gas emissions, is almost universally seen as the continent most at risk of climate-induced conflict—a function of the continent's reliance on climate-dependent sectors (such as rain-fed agriculture) and its history of resource, ethnic and political conflict."[156] Similarly, with conditions in the Middle East already volatile, "climate change threatens to reduce the availability of scarce water resources, increase food insecurity, hinder economic growth and lead to large-scale population movements."[157]

While environmental degradation and the mismanagement of natural resources can fuel conflict among and within states, on the flip side, war and other security issues can affect the environment. Military spending absorbs government finances and policy attention that might otherwise be dedicated to environmental protection. Military operations, even in peacetime, consume large quantities of natural resources. Armed conflict itself produces habitat destruction, overexploitation of natural resources, and pollution. Civil wars in Africa, Asia, and Latin America have destroyed many hectares of forests and wetlands.

Armed conflict also impacts a state's and region's ability to guard protected areas and enforce conservation regulations.[158] This is particularly true during civil war or in very weak states, where the breakdown of the rule of law, increased availability of weapons, and disrupted economic and agricultural production all affect environmental protection. In the Democratic Republic of Congo, for example, armed conflict since 1994 has severely impacted many nature reserves, including some designated as World Heritage sites.[159] Governments, international organizations, and NGOs have faced huge obstacles as a result of the "proliferation of arms and ammunition; displaced people, military, and dissidents; a general breakdown of law and order; uncontrolled exploitation of natural, mineral and land resources by various interest groups; and the increased use of wild areas as refuges and for subsistence."[160] Anti-poaching patrols ceased in many areas for different periods, and increased poaching, harvesting game for food, and habitat destruction seriously affected wildlife populations in some parks. In parts of Bolivia, Colombia, Mexico, Peru, and other countries, rebel groups and drug traffickers, either on their own or in alliance, have sometimes prevented the enforcement of wildlife conservation, habitat protection, or deforestation laws by essentially controlling access to certain areas or bribing or intimidating inspectors and other officials.[161] Illegal gold mining in many parts of the world, including nature preserves, causes severe local environmental and human health impacts and contributes to cycles of lawlessness and violence.[162] The lack of effective security and policing measures at the national and local levels contributes to the illegal deforestation in Brazil undertaken to clear land to create cattle and soybean fields.[163]

The environment and security paradigm augments traditional analyses that assume that environmental degradation is irrelevant to a state's national security interests. This does not imply that the environment is more important than traditional security calculations, but it does argue that an analysis of factors that can negatively affect a state's security must include environmental degradation and resource mismanagement (much as the sustainable development paradigm argues that serious environmental degradation can negatively affect a state's economy). It is not clear, however, that increased awareness of this relationship will lead to new action to ward off resource collapse in vulnerable countries. Nor is it clear that recognition of the serious security problems posed by climate change will lead to meaningfully increased efforts to reduce GHG emissions.

The Precautionary Principle

The neoclassical economic assumptions that underlie elements of the exclusionist paradigm and frontier economics imply that economic policy calculations need not factor in resource scarcity and environmental degradation. If resource scarcity begins to occur, the market will respond by raising prices, which will reduce demand and spur the search for substitutes, thereby averting a crisis. Similarly, there is no need to consider or take steps to avoid environmental problems before they occur, as these can be remedied after the fact if the market demands it. The globalization paradigm argues that priorities should be placed on policies that accelerate global economic growth, as this will provide the resources for environmental protection.

Unfortunately, these deductions fail to account accurately for the physical limitations of the earth's biological and physical systems. It is true that prices will rise and incentives will exist to develop substitutes when scarcity becomes an issue, but for some environmental problems, these market forces will occur too late. Certain environmental impacts cannot be remedied once they occur, at least not on timescales relevant to human economic and political systems. If the ozone layer thins significantly, a rainforest is destroyed, a coral reef dies, the climate system shifts to a different equilibrium, a species becomes extinct, or a human life is shortened by air, water, or toxic pollution, these changes will last, if not forever, then at least for a very, very long time.

Moreover, in some cases, environmental degradation actually increases the incentive to exploit a resource. Declines in rhino, elephant, tiger, and tuna populations increase their price and thus the interest of poachers. Water scarcity due to changes in weather patterns increases pressure on aquifers. Lower crop yields due to climate change can cause farmers to cultivate marginal land, clear forests to increase capacity, or increase the use of fertilizers or pesticides that have a net negative impact on the environment.

In other cases, operating under the exclusionist paradigm simply represents a poor economic decision. Sometimes, the impacts of pollution or environmental degradation cost more than the economic benefits accrued from production. Deforestation in Haiti and some other areas is an example. For the country as a whole, the economic benefits of using the wood or cleared land are short term and smaller than the larger and long-term economic costs associated with the harm caused to fisheries, farming, and freshwater resources created by the severe erosion and runoff from hills and mountains that no longer have trees to hold the soil in place. In other cases, such as climate change or ozone depletion, the economic costs associated with significant consequences of the problem far outweigh the cost of taking steps to prevent them from occurring.

Those holding this position argue that in many situations, the best policy—from an environmental, human health, and economic point of view (and perhaps an ethical one as well)—is to avoid producing certain serious environmental problems in the first place. The difficulty, of course, is that the complexity of many environmental issues prevents clear calculations of a polluting activity's environmental and human health costs, while its short-term economic benefits are usually quite clear. Thus, the lack of scientific certainty about the range, extent, and cost of environmental impacts from particular activities or products can prevent effective policy in the face of strong lobbying by economic interests.

The *precautionary principle* attempts to resolve this dilemma and provide a paradigm and guidance for the development of national and international environmental, economic, and sustainable development policy. The most widely used definition of the precautionary principle was set forth by governments at the 1992 Earth Summit in Principle 15 of the Rio Declaration: "Where there are threats of serious or irreversible damage, lack of full scientific certainty shall not be used as a reason for postponing cost-effective measures to prevent environmental degradation."[164]

Those supporting the use of the precautionary principle argue that it leads to several policy-relevant ideas that augment sustainable development, including:[165]

- The importance and efficacy of taking preventative action, when the lack of action might produce essentially irreversible, unwanted impacts on the environment or human health.
- The need to shift the burden of proof from those seeking to protect human health and the environment to those supporting an activity or product. Rather than forcing others to prove something is definitely harmful, which has traditionally been the case, proponents of, for example, using a chemical would need to show it is not harmful.

- The need to keep science and rational arguments central to decision making involving health and environmental issues, with the understanding that complete scientific certainty or unanimity regarding future harm is not required to make policy designed to protect the environment or human health.
- The importance of asking why we should risk irreversible or very serious harm for a particular product or activity.

Several important global environmental statements and treaty regimes contain elements of the precautionary principle either explicitly or implicitly. For example, the Ministerial Declaration from the Second International Conference on the Protection of the North Sea (1987) states: "In order to protect the North Sea from possibly damaging effects of the most dangerous substances, a precautionary approach is necessary which may require action to control inputs of such substances even before a causal link has been established by absolutely clear scientific evidence."[166] The Montreal Protocol on Substances That Deplete the Ozone Layer (1987) states that parties are "determined to protect the ozone layer by taking precautionary measures to control equitably total global emissions of substances that deplete it."[167] The climate regime includes the concept of precaution as one of its central principles. Article 3 of the UN Framework Convention on Climate Change (1992) states:

> In their actions to achieve the objective of the Convention and to implement its provisions, the Parties shall be guided, *inter alia*, by the following: ...
>
> The Parties should take precautionary measures to anticipate, prevent, or minimize the causes of climate change and mitigate its adverse effects. Where there are threats of serious or irreversible damage, lack of full scientific certainty should not be used as a reason for postponing such measures.[168]

The 2000 Cartagena Protocol on Biosafety expressly allows parties to ban imports of living modified organisms, even where there is a "lack of scientific certainty due to insufficient relevant scientific information and knowledge" concerning health or environmental impacts.[169] The 2001 Stockholm Convention on Persistent Organic Pollutants defines the objective of the regime: "Mindful of the precautionary approach as set forth in Principle 15 of the Rio Declaration on Environment and Development, the objective of this Convention is to protect human health and the environment from persistent organic pollutants."[170] In addition, the treaty states that precaution should be used when considering additional substances to add to the control measures and that the lack of scientific certainty regarding the precise levels of a substance's toxicity or propensity for long-range transport and bioaccumulation shall not be grounds for failing to consider controlling it under the regime.

Local and national laws in a number of countries have also incorporated the principle. Most important is the EU announcement in 2000 stating that the precautionary principle will guide EU policy decisions on environmental and human health issues and is also "a full-fledged and general principle of international law."[171]

Despite the many references to the precautionary principle, arguments exist that it is bad policy or should not be accepted as a principle of international law (on a par with universally accepted principles such as sovereignty). These include that shifting the burden of proof means that decisions will be based on emotion, will cost too much, harm companies, and hinder economic development, or will require proving that something is totally safe, which is essentially impossible to prove in all situations. Others note that its use in treaties or acceptance by international legal bodies as a guiding point of international law is not definitive. For example, the United States and others have blocked inclusion of the full phrase "precautionary principle" in various MEAs or official decisions made by their COPs, arguing that while taking precautions is prudent, the precautionary principle should not be seen as, nor do they accept it as, a general principle of international law that binds states to certain norms or actions.[172] Under this interpretation, references to precaution in treaties that the United States signed or ratified relate only to the specific issue under discussion—not a general international legal principle applicable across all countries and issues.

A number of analysts, legal scholars, and policymakers reject this argument. They believe that inclusion of the precautionary principle (or its key elements under another name) in so many international treaties, its status within the EU, and its emergence in local and national laws prove that "the precautionary principle has evolved from being a 'soft-law' 'aspirational' goal to its present status as an authoritative norm recognized by governments and international organizations as a firm guide to activities affecting the environment."[173]

Clearly, sustainable development and the precautionary principle have become a part of many international environmental policies, having found their way into a number of global regimes, influenced international decision making, and become more and more accepted in debates on national policies in multiple countries. At the same time, the lack of progress made by the global community in addressing climate change, biodiversity, fisheries, and other issues makes clear that neither is yet a truly dominant paradigm. Elements of the exclusionist, frontier economic, and globalization paradigms as inherently positive still influence some global, national, local, and corporate policies, but so, too, do elements of the sustainable development paradigm, the precautionary principle, and calls for a green (or greener) economy.

Will the exclusionist, globalization, sustainable development, precautionary, or green economy paradigm dominate future political and economic perspectives? Will policy continue to reflect elements of all these approaches? Will some future paradigm shift require, as some have argued, a "revolution of social consciousness and values," perhaps led by the younger generations?[174] As economies, populations, cities, energy production, resource depletion, pollution, and climate change continue to grow, the paradigms that influence national and international policy debates could go a long way toward determining what our future world will look like.

Conclusion

Global environmental politics involves actions by, and interactions among, states, IGOs, and other actors that transcend a given region and that affect the environment and natural resources of multiple regions or the entire planet. The emergence of environmental issues in world politics reflects growing awareness of the cumulative stresses that human activities place on the earth's resources and life support systems.

Much of global environmental politics focuses on efforts to negotiate and implement multilateral agreements or other mechanisms for cooperation to protect the environment and natural resources. Some of these agreements stand at the center of global environmental regimes of varying effectiveness that seek to govern or guide state behavior.

Legitimate differences in economic, political, and environmental interests make achieving unanimity among states responsible for, or directly affected by, an environmental problem a political and diplomatic challenge. One or more states often have the ability to block or weaken a multilateral agreement, and finding ways to overcome such blockage is a major concern. For a regime to form and be effective, veto states must be persuaded to abandon their opposition or at least to accept a compromise.

Other obstacles stem from policies and paradigms that justify extensive, and sometimes essentially unlimited, exploitation of nature and discount the impact of pollution and deteriorating ecosystems on economic and social well-being. Despite widespread recognition of the need for sustainable development, globalization and the resilience of aspects of the traditional paradigms have complicated the shift to potential new models centered on a green economy, incorporation of the precautionary principle, and global sustainable development.

Notes

1 e.g., Larry Eliot, "Climate Crisis Fills Top Five Places of World Economic Forum's Risks Report," *The Guardian*, January 15, 2020.
2 United Nations Environment Programme (UNEP), *GEO 5: Global Environmental Outlook—Environment for the Future We Want* (Nairobi: UNEP, 2012); UNEP, *GEO 6: Global Environment Outlook—Healthy Planet, Healthy People* (Nairobi: UNEP, 2019).
3 Global Footprint Network, Ecological Footprint, www.footprintnetwork.org/our-work/ecological-footprint/.
4 Ibid.
5 Population data in this chapter are from United Nations, Department of Economic and Social Affairs, Population Division (2019), *World Population Prospects 2019: Highlights* (ST/ESA/SER.A/423).
6 Peter Dauvergne, *Shadows of Consumption* (Cambridge, MA: MIT Press, 2008), 4.
7 UNEP, *GEO 5*, 4–30; Global Footprint Network, Ecological Footprint.
8 Mario Perzzini, OECD, "An Emerging Middle Class," *OECD Observer*, http://oecdobserver.org/news/fullstory.php/aid/3681/An_emerging_middle_class.html.
9 Global Footprint Network, "Ecological Footprint of Countries 2016," http://data.footprintnetwork.org/#/compareCountries?type=earth&cn=all&yr=2016.
10 United Nations, *Sustainable Development Goals Report 2019* (New York: UN, 2019), 46.
11 e.g., I. Wagner, "Car Drivers—Statistics & Facts," www.statista.com/topics/1197/car-drivers/.
12 Mark Perry, "Today's New Homes Are 1,000 Square Feet Larger Than in 1973," AEIdeas Blog, February 26, 2014, www.aei.org/publication/todays-new-homes-are-1000-square-feet-larger-than-in-1973-and-the-living-space-per-person-has-doubled-over-last-40-years/.
13 United States Census Bureau, "Historical Households Tables: Table HH-4; Households by Size, 1960–Present," November 14, 2018, www.census.gov/data/tables/time-series/demo/families/households.html.
14 Global Footprint Network, "Ecological Footprint of Countries 2016," http://data.footprintnetwork.org/#/compareCountries?type=earth&cn=all&yr=2016.
15 UN, *The Sustainable Development Goals Report 2018* (New York: UN, 2018), 4–7.
16 WHO, "Drinking Water: Key Facts," June 14, 2019, www.who.int/news-room/fact-sheets/detail/drinking-water.
17 UN, *The United Nations World Water Development Report 2019: Leaving No One Behind* (Paris: UNESCO, 2019), 19.
18 WHO, "Drinking Water: Key Facts."
19 UN, "Tackling Global Water Pollution," www.unenvironment.org/explore-topics/water/what-we-do/tackling-global-water-pollution.
20 US Energy Information Administration (EIA), "What is the United States' Share of World Energy Consumption?" December 26, 2018, www.eia.gov/tools/faqs/faq.php?id=87&t=1, and "Petroleum, Natural Gas, and Coal Continue to Dominate U.S. Energy Consumption," July 1, 2019, www.eia.gov/todayinenergy/detail.php?id=40013.
21 David Coady, et al., "Global Fossil Fuel Subsidies Remain Large: An Update Based on Country-Level Estimates." IMF (International Monetary Fund) Working Paper, WP/19/89, May 2019.
22 Calculation based on International Energy Agency (IEA) data, www.iea.org//statistics/?country=WORLD&year=2016&category=Energy%20consumption&indicator=TFCbySource&mode=chart&dataTable=BALANCES.
23 "Energy Use (kg of Oil Equivalent Per Capita)," World Bank, http://data.worldbank.org/indicator/EG.USE.PCAP.KG.OE/countries/1W-US-CN-IN?display=graph.
24 Laura Cozzi, et al., International Energy Agency (IEA), "Commentary: Population Without Access to Electricity Falls Below 1 billion," October 30, 2018, citing IEA data, www.iea.org/newsroom/news/2018/october/population-without-access-to-electricity-falls-below-1-billion.html.

25 International Energy Agency, "Access to Energy: Population Without Access to Electricity, 2017," www.iea.org/sdg/electricity/.

26 Enerdata, "Global Energy Statistical Yearbook 2019," https://yearbook.enerdata.net/total-energy/world-consumption-statistics.html.

27 Global Footprint Network, "Climate Change," www.footprintnetwork.org/our-work/climate-change/.

28 Approximately 5250 $MtCO_2$ versus 1332 $MtCO_2$. Global Carbon Project, "CO_2 Emissions (2018)," www.globalcarbonatlas.org/en/CO2-emissions.

29 Ibid.

30 Ibid.; Global Footprint Network, "Climate Change."

31 Chris Martin, "For First Time, Renewables Surpass Coal in U.S. Power Mix," citing Energy Information Administration data, Bloomberg, June 25, 2019, www.bloomberg.com/news/articles/2019-06-25/for-first-time-ever-renewables-surpass-coal-in-u-s-power-mix.

32 Eric Gimon, et al., "The Coal Cost Crossover: Economic Viability of Existing Coal Compared to New Local Wind and Solar Resources," Energy Innovation, March 2019, https://energyinnovation.org/wp-content/uploads/2019/04/Coal-Cost-Crossover_Energy-Innovation_VCE_FINAL2.pdf.

33 IEA, World Energy Outlook 2019 (Paris: IEA, 2019), www.iea.org/reports/world-energy-outlook-2019.

34 Environmental and Energy Study Institute (ESSI), "Jobs in Renewable Energy, Energy Efficiency, and Resilience (2019)," www.eesi.org/papers/view/fact-sheet-jobs-in-renewable-energy-energy-efficiency-and-resilience-2019.

35 Silvio Marcacci, "Renewable Energy Job Boom Creates Economic Opportunity as Coal Industry Slumps," Forbes, April 22, 2019, www.forbes.com/sites/energyinnovation/2019/04/22/renewable-energy-job-boom-creating-economic-opportunity-as-coal-industry-slumps/#451bc03a3665.

36 EESI, "Jobs in Renewable Energy, Energy Efficiency, and Resilience (2019)."

37 UNEP, Emissions Gap Report 2018 (Nairobi, UNEP, 2018).

38 NOAA, "2019 Was 2nd Hottest Year on Record for Earth Say NOAA, NASA," January 15, 2020, www.noaa.gov/news/2019-was-2nd-hottest-year-on-record-for-earth-say-noaa-nasa.

39 UNEP, Emissions Gap Report 2018, Executive Summary, 4.

40 See, for example, IPCC, Climate Change and Land: An IPCC Special Report on Climate Change, Desertification, Land Degradation, Sustainable Land Management, Food Security, and Greenhouse Gas Fluxes in Terrestrial Ecosystems (Geneva: IPCC, 2019), www.ipcc.ch/report/srccl/.

41 UNEP, GEO 5.

42 Mesfin Mekonnen and Arjen Hoekstra, "Four Billion People Facing Severe Water Scarcity," AAAS Science Advances vol. 2, no. 2 (February 2016), doi: 10.1126/sciadv.1500323.

43 Charles Fant, et al., "Projections of Water Stress Based on an Ensemble of Socioeconomic Growth and Climate Change Scenarios: A Case Study in Asia," PLoS ONE vol. 11, no. 3 (2016): e0150633, https://doi.org/10.1371/journal.pone.0150633.

44 Somini Sengupta and Weiyi Cai, "Water Crisis May Grip a Quarter of Humanity," New York Times, August 7, 2019, citing data from a new study by the World Resources Institute. See www.wri.org/aqueduct.

45 UN-Water, The United Nations World Water Development Report 2019 (Paris: UNESCO, 2019), 13.

46 Ibid., 1.

47 Ibid., 14.

48 FAO, Global Forest Resources Assessment 2020 – Key Findings (Rome: FAO, 2020), 4.

49 UNEP, Annual Report 2018 (Nairobi: UNEP, 2018), 4.

50 See, for example, Ernesto Londono and Leticia Casado, "In Brazil, Amazon Deforest Has Risen Sharply on Bolsonaro's Watch," New York Times, November 19, 2019.

51 UNEP, Annual Report 2014 (Nairobi: UNEP, 2015), 4.

52 UNEP, Protected Planet Report 2018 (Nairobi: UNEP, 2018), 11.

53 As of January 2020. For updated information, see www.iucnredlist.org/.

54 Kenneth Rosenberg, et al., "Decline of the North American Avifauna," Science vol. 366, www.iucnredlist.org/.

55 Intergovernmental Science-Policy Platform on Biodiversity and Ecosystem Services (IPBES), Summary for Policymakers of the Global Assessment Report on Biodiversity and Ecosystem Services of the Intergovernmental Science-Policy Platform on Biodiversity and Ecosystem Services, S. Díaz, et al., eds. (Bonn: IPBES, 2019). See also www.ipbes.net/.

56 Christopher Trisos, et al., "The Projected Timing of Abrupt Ecological Disruption from Climate Change," *Nature* vol. 580 (2020): 496–501.

57 Secretariat of the Convention on Biological Diversity (2020) *Global Biodiversity Outlook 5 – Summary for Policy Makers* (Montréal: CBD Secretariat, 2020).

58 FAO, *State of the World Fisheries and Aquaculture: 2018—Meeting the Sustainable Development Goals* (Rome: FAO, 2018), 4, 8, 39–40.

59 Ibid., 6, 39–41.

60 Ibid., 30–31; U.S. Fish & Wildlife Service. 2018. ECOS Environmental Conservation Online System, Listed Animals, https://ecos.fws.gov/ecp/.

61 J. Samuel Barkin and Elizabeth R. DeSombre, *Saving Global Fisheries: Reducing Fishing Capacity to Promote Sustainability* (Cambridge, MA: MIT Press, 2013).

62 FAO, *Review of the State of World Marine Fishery Resources* (Rome: FAO, 2014), 13–14; Amanda Keledjian, et al., *Wasted Catch: Unsolved Problems in U.S. Fisheries* (Washington, DC: Oceana, 2014), 3.

63 UNEP, Global Programme of Action for the Protection of the Marine Environment from Land-Based Activities (GPA). "Addressing Land-Based Pollution," www.unenvironment.org/explore-topics/oceans-seas/what-we-do/addressing-land-based-pollution.

64 UNEP, GPA, "Why Does Addressing Land-Based Pollution Matter?" www.unenvironment.org/explore-topics/oceans-seas/what-we-do/addressing-land-based-pollution/why-does-addressing-land.

65 e.g., Kara Law, "Plastics in the Marine Environment," *Annual Review of Marine Science* vol. 9 (2017): 205–229.

66 UNEP, *Marine Plastic Debris and Microplastics—Global Lessons and Research to Inspire Action and Guide Policy Change* (Nairobi: UNEP, 2016), 189–190, 195–198, 207–228.

67 e.g., Janice Brahney, et al., "Plastic Rain in Protected Areas of the United States," *Science* vol. 368, no. 6496 (June 12, 2020): 1257–1260; C. Anela Choy, et al., "The Vertical Distribution and Biological Transport of Marine Microplastics Across the Epipelagic and Mesopelagic Water Column," *Scientific Reports* vol. 9 (2019), doi.org/10.1038/s41598-019-44117-2; Rachel Obbard, et al., "Global Warming Releases Microplastic Legacy Frozen in Arctic Sea Ice," *Earth's Future* vol. 2, no. 6 (June 2014).

68 Brahney, et al., "Plastic Rain in Protected Areas of the United States."

69 World Economic Forum and Ellen MacArthur Foundation, *The New Plastics Economy: Rethinking the Future of Plastics* (Cologne and Geneva: World Economic Forum, 2016), www3.weforum.org/docs/WEF_The_New_Plastics_Economy.pdf.

70 Daniela Russi, et al., *The Economics of Ecosystems and Biodiversity for Water and Wetlands* (London and Brussels: IEEP; Gland: Ramsar Secretariat, 2013), 7, 15.

71 Ibid.; National Ocean and Atmospheric Administration, "What Is a Wetland?" https://oceanservice.noaa.gov/facts/wetland.html.

72 Russi, et al., *The Economics of Ecosystems*, 16.

73 UNEP, IUCN, and NGS, *Protected Planet Report 2018* (Cambridge, Gland, and Washington, DC: UNEP, IUCN and NGS, 2018), 8, 20. See also US EPA, "Coastal Wetland Loss Analysis. Summary Findings of Pilot Studies Conducted by the Interagency Coastal Wetlands Workgroup," 2.

74 Russi, et al., *The Economics of Ecosystems*.

75 IPCC, *Climate Change and Land*.

76 FAO, et al., *The State of Food Security and Nutrition in the World 2018* (Rome, FAO, 2018), 2–12, 128, 161.

77 FAO, *The Future of Food and Agriculture—Trends and Challenges* (Rome: FAO, 2017), 46.

78 Asbjørn Eide, *The Right to Food and the Impact of Liquid Biofuels (Agrofuels)* (Rome: FAO, 2008), 14.

79 Water Footprint Network, "Product Gallery," https://waterfootprint.org/en/resources/interactive-tools/product-gallery/.

80 e.g., Eide, *The Right to Food*, 44.

81 U.S. Department of Energy, 2019, "Maps and Data—U.S. Corn for Fuel Ethanol, Feed and Other Use," https://afdc.energy.gov/data/10339, accessed June 21, 2019.

82 Nicole Condon, Heather Klemick, and Ann Wolverton, "Impacts of Ethanol Policy on Corn Prices," *Food Policy* vol. 51 (February 2015): 63–73.

83 UN, World Urbanization Prospects: The 2018 Revision. Annual Urban Population at Mid-Year (thousands), World, 1950–2050, https://population.un.org/wup/DataQuery/.

84 UN, *The World's Cities in 2018: Data Booklet* (New York: UN, 2018), 2.

85 UNHSP, *World Habitat Day Voices from Slums: Background Paper*, 2.

86 Health Effects Institute, *State of Global Air 2018* (Boston: Health Effects Institute, 2018). See also UNEP, *GEO 6*, 78, 486.

87 WHO Press Release, "9 out of 10 People Worldwide Breathe Polluted Air, But More Countries Are Taking Action," May 2, 2018.

88 These are widely used UN figures. See, for example, *UN News*, "Over 200 Million Escape Slums but Overall Number Still Rising, UN Report Finds," *UN News*, March 18, 2010, https://news.un.org/en/story/2010/03/332882-over-200-million-escape-slums-overall-number-still-rising-un-report-finds; and UNDP, "[Sustainable Development] Goal 11: Sustainable Cities and Communities," www.undp.org/content/undp/en/home/sustainable-development-goals/goal-11-sustainable-cities-and-communities.html.

89 For an early effort to categorize environmental problems, see Clifford Russell and Hans Landsberg, "International Environmental Problems: A Taxonomy," *Science* vol. 172 (June 25, 1972): 1307–1314.

90 This metaphor was popularized in Garrett Hardin, "The Tragedy of the Commons," *Science* vol. 162, no. 3859 (December 13, 1968): 1243–1248. The metaphor is useful, but Hardin got facts wrong regarding Medieval commons (generally, there were rules), and he has been criticized for his conclusions of how to respond to such situations and his views on race. See Susan Buck, "No Tragedy of the Commons," *Environmental Ethics* vol. 7, no. 1 (Spring 1985): 49–61; Southern Poverty Law Center, "Garrett Hardin," www.splcenter.org/fighting-hate/extremist-files/individual/garrett-hardin.

91 Oran Young, *International Governance: Protecting the Environment in a Stateless Society* (Ithaca, NY: Cornell University Press, 1994), 19–26.

92 Diane Bui, "The Instance of Environmental Regimes," in *Delegating State Powers: The Effect of Treaty Regimes on Democracy and Sovereignty*, ed. Thomas Franck (Ardsley, NY: Transnational Publishers, 2000), 33.

93 Lars-Göran Engfeldt, "The Road from Stockholm to Johannesburg," *UN Chronicle* vol. 39, no. 3 (September–November 2002): 14–17.

94 UN Conference on Environment and Development, *Agenda 21, Rio Declaration, Forest Principles* (New York: UN, 1992).

95 This definition builds explicitly on the definition developed in Stephen Krasner, ed., *International Regimes* (Ithaca, NY: Cornell University Press, 1983). Compare the definition and use of the term *regime* in John Gerard Ruggie, "International Responses to Technology: Concepts and Trends," *International Organization* vol. 29 (1975): 557–583; Ernst Haas, "On Systems and International Regimes," *World Politics* vol. 27 (1975): 147–174; Robert Keohane and Joseph Nye Jr., *Power and Interdependence: World Politics in Transition* (Boston: Little, Brown, 1977); Oran Young, "International Regimes: Problems of Concept Formation," *International Organization* vol. 32 (1980): 331–356; Robert Keohane, *After Hegemony: Cooperation and Discord in the World Political Economy* (Princeton, NJ: Princeton University Press, 1984); and Stephan Haggard and Beth Simmons, "Theories of International Regimes," *International Organization* vol. 41 (1987): 491–517.

96 For influential discussions of the study of international cooperation, see and compare Friedrich Kratochwil and John Gerard Ruggie, "International Organization: A State of the Art on an Art of the State," *International Organization* vol. 40 (1986): 753–776; James Dougherty and Robert Pfaltzgraff Jr., *Contending Theories of International Relations: A Comprehensive Survey*, 5th ed. (New York: Pearson, 2001), ch. 10; and Joseph Grieco, "Anarchy and the Limits of Cooperation: A Realist Critique of the Newest Liberal Institutionalism," *International Organization* vol. 42 (1988): 485–507.

97 Classic examples include Thucydides, Machiavelli, and Hobbes. Influential modern examples include Hans J. Morgenthau, *Politics Among Nations: The Struggle for Power and Peace*, 5th ed. (New York: Knopf, 1973); Robert Jervis, "Cooperation Under the Security Dilemma," *World Politics* vol. 30 (1978): 167–186; and Kenneth Waltz, *Theory of International Politics* (Reading, MA: Addison-Wesley, 1979).

98 Constitutionalists believe that "international governance is whatever international organizations do; and formal attributes of international organizations, such as their charters, voting procedures, committee structures and the like, account for what they do" (Kratochwil and Ruggie, "International Organization," 755). The institutional process approach examines

influence, how information is produced and digested, who speaks to whom, how decisions are made, and so on. It argues that the outputs of international organizations do not always reflect their charters or official procedures. A classic example is Robert Cox and Harold Jacobson, eds., *The Anatomy of Influence: Decision Making in International Organization* (New Haven, CT: Yale University Press, 1973).

99 For example, Richard Falk, *A Study of Future Worlds* (Princeton, NJ: Princeton University Press, 1975).

100 Important examples and discussions of functionalism include David Mitrany, *A Working Peace System: An Argument for the Functional Development of International Organization* (1943; repr., Chicago: Quadrangle Books, 1966); David Mitrany, *The Functional Theory of Politics* (London: M. Robertson, 1975); and A. J. R. Groom and Paul Taylor, eds., *Functionalism: Theory and Practice in International Relations* (New York: Crane, Russak, 1975).

101 See and compare discussions in Kratochwil and Ruggie, "International Organization," 756–763; Dougherty and Pfaltzgraff, *Contending Theories of International Relations*, ch. 10; and Groom and Taylor, *Functionalism*, ch. 1.

102 Leading examples and discussion include Ernst Haas, *Beyond the Nation State: Functionalism and International Organization* (Stanford, CA: Stanford University Press, 1964); Ernst Haas, "The Uniting of Europe and the Uniting of Latin America," *Journal of Common Market Studies* vol. 5 (1967): 315–343; Philippe Schmitter, "Three Neo-Functional Hypotheses About International Integration," *International Organization* vol. 23 (1969): 161–166; Ernst Haas, "The Study of Regional Integration: Reflections on the Joy and Anguish of Pretheorizing," *International Organization* vol. 24 (1970): 607–646; Kratochwil and Ruggie, "International Organization," 757–759; and Groom and Taylor, *Functionalism*, chs. 11–12.

103 Examples are Ernst Haas, "On Systems and International Regimes," *World Politics* vol. 27 (1975): 147–174; and Ernst Haas, *When Knowledge Is Power: Three Models of Change in International Organizations* (Berkeley: University of California Press, 1990).

104 Robert Keohane and Joseph Nye Jr., eds., *Transnational Relations and World Politics* (Cambridge, MA: Harvard University Press, 1972).

105 Keohane and Nye, *Power and Interdependence: World Politics in Transition* (Little, Brown, 1977). Complex interdependence and turbulent fields share important concerns and insights.

106 This paragraph is adapted from I. William Zartman, ed., *The 50% Solution: How to Bargain Successfully with Hijackers, Strikers, Bosses, Oil Magnates, Arabs, Russians, and Other Worthy Opponents* (1976; repr., New Haven, CT: Yale University Press, 1983), 9–10.

107 R. Michael M'Gonigle and Mark Zacher, *Pollution, Politics, and International Law: Tankers at Sea* (Berkeley: University of California Press, 1979), 58–59, 84–85, 93–96.

108 Not all countries in the northern hemisphere are parties to the Convention or all its Protocols. For example, the United States is a party to the Convention but only four of the Protocols. For details, see www.unece.org/env/lrtap/status/lrtap_s.html.

109 Keohane, *After Hegemony*, provides an influential discussion of why it is easier to make international regimes more effective than it is to create new ones.

110 For an early summary, see Haggard and Simmons, "Theories of International Regimes."

111 Keohane and Nye, *Power and Interdependence*, 50–51.

112 For the former approach, see Robert Gilpin, *The Political Economy of International Relations* (Princeton, NJ: Princeton University Press, 1987); Grieco, "Anarchy and the Limits of Cooperation"; and Susan Strange, "Cave! Hic Dragones: A Critique of Regime Analysis," *International Organization* vol. 36 (Spring 1982): 479–496. Susan Strange, "The Persistent Myth of Lost Hegemony," *International Organization* vol. 41 (Summer 1987): 570, argues that inconsistency in US policy rather than loss of US global hegemony caused erosion of international regimes.

113 Oran Young, "The Politics of International Regime Formation: Managing Natural Resources and the Environment," *International Organization* vol. 43 (Summer 1989): 355.

114 Fen Osler Hampson, "Climate Change: Building International Coalitions of the Like-Minded," *International Journal* vol. 45 (Winter 1989–1990): 36–74.

115 See Peter Haas, "Do Regimes Matter? Epistemic Communities and Mediterranean Pollution Control," *International Organization* vol. 43 (Summer 1989): 378–403.

116 The issue of ocean dumping of radioactive wastes, in which scientific evidence was explicitly rejected as the primary basis for decision making by antidumping states, is analyzed in Judith

Spiller and Cynthia Hayden, "Radwaste at Sea: A New Era of Polarization or a New Basis for Consensus?" *Ocean Development and International Law* vol. 19 (1988): 345–366.

117 Robert Putnam, "Diplomacy and Domestic Politics: The Logic of Two-Level Games," *International Organization* vol. 42, no. 3 (Summer 1988): 427–460.

118 For example, David Downie, "Understanding International Environmental Regimes: Lessons of the Ozone" (PhD diss., University of North Carolina, Chapel Hill, 1996).

119 For an influential and accessible discussion of paradigm shifts, see Thomas Kuhn, *The Structure of Scientific Revolutions* (Chicago: University of Chicago Press, 1962).

120 Harold and Margaret Sprout, *The Ecological Perspective on Human Affairs, with Special Reference to International Politics* (Princeton, NJ: Princeton University Press, 1965); Kenneth Boulding, "The Economics of the Coming Spaceship Earth," in *Environmental Quality in a Growing Economy: Essays from the Sixth RFF Forum*, ed. Henry Jarrett (Baltimore: Johns Hopkins University Press, 1966).

121 For an analysis of neoclassical economic assumptions as they bear on environmental management, see Daniel Underwood and Paul King, "On the Ideological Foundations of Environmental Policy," *Ecological Economics* vol. 1 (1989): 317–322.

122 See Michael Colby, *Environmental Management in Development: The Evolution of Paradigms* (Washington, DC: World Bank, 1990).

123 John McCormick, *Reclaiming Paradise: The Global Environmental Movement* (Bloomington: Indiana University Press, 1989), 67.

124 See Clem Tisdell, "Sustainable Development: Differing Perspectives of Ecologists and Economists, and Relevance to LDCs," *World Development* vol. 16 (1988): 377–378.

125 Donella Meadows, et al., *The Limits to Growth: A Report for the Club of Rome's Project on the Predicament of Mankind* (New York: Universe Books, 1972); Council on Environmental Quality and Gerald Barney, *Global 2000: The Report to the President Entering the Twenty-First Century* (New York: Pergamon, 1980).

126 e.g., Julian Simon and Herman Kahn, eds., *The Resourceful Earth: A Response to Global 2000* (Oxford: Basil Blackwell, 1984).

127 World Commission on Environment and Development, *Our Common Future* (Oxford: Oxford University Press, 1987).

128 e.g., Edith Brown Weiss, "In Fairness to Future Generations," *Environment* vol. 32 (April 1990): 7–11, 30–31.

129 e.g., Dauvergne, *Shadows of Consumption.*

130 For discussion and early examples, see Yusuf Ahmad, Salah El Serafy, and Ernst Lutz, eds., *Environmental Accounting for Sustainable Development* (Washington, DC: World Bank, 1989); Herman Daly and John Cobb Jr., *For the Common Good: Redirecting the Economy Toward Community, the Environment and a Sustainable Future* (Boston: Beacon, 1989); and Robert Repetto, et al., *Accounts Overdue: Natural Resources Depreciation in Costa Rica* (Washington, DC: WRI, 1991).

131 For information, see https://epi.yale.edu.

132 Commission of the European Communities, *GDP and Beyond: Measuring Progress in a Changing World*, http://eur-lex.europa.eu/LexUriServ/LexUriServ.do?uri=COM:2009:0433:FIN:EN:PDF. See also European Commission, "Indicators," https://ec.europa.eu/eurostat/web/sdi/indicators.

133 Centre for Bhutan Studies, *A Short Guide to Gross National Happiness Index* (Thimphu, Bhutan: Centre for Bhutan Studies, 2012).

134 Pamela Chasek and Lynn Wagner, "An Insider's Guide to Multilateral Environmental Negotiations Since the Earth Summit," in *The Roads from Rio: Lessons Learned from Twenty Years of Multilateral Environmental Negotiations*, eds. Pamela Chasek and Lynn Wagner (New York: Routledge, 2012), 1–2.

135 UNEP, *GEO 5.* See also Chapters 3 and 4.

136 e.g., Martin Khor, "Globalisation and Sustainable Development: Challenges for Johannesburg," *Third World Resurgence* vol. 139/140 (March–April 2002).

137 For discussion, see James Gustave Speth, "Two Perspectives on Globalization and the Environment," in *Worlds Apart: Globalization and the Environment*, ed. James Gustave Speth (Washington, DC: Island, 2003).

138 UNEP, *Towards a Green Economy: Pathways to Sustainable Development and Poverty Eradication* (Nairobi: UNEP, 2011).

139 UN, *Secretary-General's Report on Objectives and Themes of the United Nations Conference on Sustainable Development*, December 22, 2010, 5, www.un.org/ga/search/view_doc.asp?symbol=A/CONF.216/PC/7&Lang=E.

140 UNEP, *Towards a Green Economy*, 14.

141 Ibid., 16–17.

142 "Summary of the United Nations Conference on Sustainable Development: 13–22 June 2012," *Earth Negotiations Bulletin* vol. 27, no. 51 (June 25, 2012); Martin Khor, "Global Debate on 'Green Economy,'" *Star* (Malaysia), January 24, 2011.

143 Lucien Georgeson, Mark Maslin, and Martyn Poessinouw, "The Global Green Economy: A Review of Concepts, Definitions, Measurement Methodologies and Their Interactions," *Geo: Geography and Environment* vol. 4, no.1 (2017), doi: 10.1002/geo2.36.

144 Neil Carter, *Politics of the Environment: Ideas, Activism, Policy*, 2nd ed. (Cambridge: Cambridge University Press, 2007), 272–273. For additional views on this argument, see Jagdish Bhagwati, *In Defense of Globalization* (Oxford: Oxford University Press, 2004) and Jennifer Clapp and Peter Dauvergne, *Paths to a Green World: The Political Economy of the Global Environment* (Cambridge, MA: MIT Press, 2005).

145 Carter, *Politics of the Environment*, 273; Ronnie Lipschutz, *Global Environmental Politics: Power, Perspectives, and Practice* (Washington, DC: Congressional Quarterly Press, 2004), 121.

146 Carter, *Politics of the Environment*, 273; Arthur Mol, *Globalization and Environmental Reform* (Cambridge, MA: MIT Press, 2003), 71–72, 126.

147 Source of information on commodity chains and waste chains: Ronnie D. Lipschutz, *Global Environmental Politics: Power, Perspectives and Practice* (Washington, DC: CQ Press, 2004), 124.

148 See, for example, Thomas Homer-Dixon, "On the Threshold: Environmental Changes as Causes of Acute Conflict," *International Security* vol. 16, no. 2 (1991): 76–116; Thomas F. Homer-Dixon, "Environmental Scarcities and Violent Conflict: Evidence from Cases," *International Security* vol. 19, no. 1 (1994): 5–40; and Thomas Homer-Dixon, *Environment, Scarcity, and Violence* (Princeton, NJ: Princeton University Press, 1999). For current news and reports, see the Environmental Change and Security Program website: www.wilsoncenter.org/program/environmental-change-and-security-program.

149 UNEP, *Sudan: Post Conflict Environmental Assessment* (Nairobi: UN, 2007); Clionadh Raleigh, "Political Marginalization, Climate Change, and Conflict in African Sahel States," *International Studies Review* vol. 12, no. 1 (2010): 69–86.

150 See Doug Hawley, "Drug Smugglers Curtail Scientists' Work," *USA Today*, December 27, 2007.

151 Rashid Sumaila, "Fisheries, Ecosystem Justice and Piracy: A Case Study of Somalia," *Fisheries Research* vol. 157 (September 2014): 154–163; Samantha Farquhar, "When Overfishing Leads to Terrorism: The Case of Somalia," *World Affairs: The Journal of International Issues* vol. 21, no. 2 (2017): 68–77.

152 Dan Liddick, "The Dimensions of a Transnational Crime Problem: The Case of IUU Fishing," *Trends in Organized Crime* vol. 17, no. 4 (December 2014): 290–312; Christian Nelleman, UNEP, and INTERPOL, *Green Carbon, Black Trade: Illegal Logging, Tax Fraud and Laundering in the World's Tropical Forests* (Nairobi: UNEP, 2012).

153 Maura O'Connor, "Two Years Later, Haitian Earthquake Death Toll in Dispute," *Columbia Journalism Review*, January 12, 2012.

154 See, for example, Geoffrey Dabelko and P. J. Simmons, "Environment and Security: Core Ideas and U.S. Government Initiatives," *SAIS Review* (Winter/Spring 1997): 127–146; German Advisory Council on Global Change, *Climate Change as a Security Risk* (Oxford: Earthscan, 2007); The White House, *Findings from Select Federal Reports: The National Security Implications of a Changing Climate* (Washington: The White House, May 2015); Office of the Under Secretary of Defense for Acquisition and Sustainment, *Report on Effects of a Changing Climate to the Department of Defense*, January 2019.

155 Scott Kulp and Benjamin Strauss, "New Elevation Data Triple Estimates of Global Vulnerability to Sea-Level Rise and Coastal Flooding," *Climate Communications* vol. 10, no. 4844 (2019), https://doi.org/10.1038/s41467-019-12808-z.

156 Oli Brown and Alec Crawford, *Climate Change and Security in Africa* (Winnipeg, Canada: International Institute for Sustainable Development, 2009), 2.

157 Oli Brown and Alec Crawford, *Rising Temperatures, Rising Tensions: Climate Change and the Risk of Violent Conflict in the Middle East* (Winnipeg, Canada: International Institute for Sustainable Development, 2009), 2.

158 For discussion, see J. Oglethorpe, et al., "Parks in the Cross-fire: Strategies for Effective Conservation in Areas of Armed Conflict," *IUCN Protected Areas Programme: Parks* vol. 14, no. 1 (2004): 2–8.

159 For a recent example, see Abdi Latif Dahir, "12 Rangers Among 17 Killed in Congo Park Ambush," *New York Times*, April 25, 2020.

160 G. Debonnet and K. Hillman-Smith, "Supporting Protected Areas in a Time of Political Turmoil: The Case of World Heritage Sites in the Democratic Republic of Congo," *IUCN Protected Areas Programme: Parks* vol. 14, no. 1 (2004): 11.

161 See, for example, Talli Nauman, "Illegal Drugs Root of Evil for Conservation Community," *Herald Mexico*, August 1, 2006; Hawley, "Drug Smugglers Curtail Scientists' Work."

162 Recent, first-hand reporting includes Richard Paddock and Adam Dean, "In Indonesia, Outlaw Gold Miners Poison Themselves to Make a Living," *New York Times*, December 31, 2019.

163 e.g., Helen Regan, "Brazil's Beef and Soy Exports to the EU Linked to Illegal Deforestation, Study Finds," CNN, July 16, 2020, www.cnn.com/2020/07/16/americas/brazil-deforestation-soy-beef-eu-intl-hnk/index.html.

164 "Rio Declaration on Environment and Development," in *Report of the United Nations Conference on the Human Environment*, Stockholm, June 5–16, 1972, ch. 1, www.un-documents.net/rio-dec.htm.

165 For a representative discussion, see David Kriebel, et al., "The Precautionary Principle in Environmental Science," *Environmental Health Perspective* vol. 109, no. 9 (September 2001): 871–876; Carolyn Raffensperger and Katherine Barrett, "In Defense of the Precautionary Principle," *Nature Biotechnology* vol. 19 (September 2001): 811–812.

166 Ministerial Declaration, Second International Conference on the Protection of the North Sea, London, November 24–25, 1987.

167 Preamble, Montreal Protocol, 26 ILM 1541, September 16, 1987.

168 UN Framework Convention on Climate Change, UN, May 9, 1992.

169 See Article 10 and Article 11 of the Biosafety Protocol.

170 Article 1 of the Stockholm Convention on Persistent Organic Pollutants, May 22, 2001.

171 Communication from the Commission on the Precautionary Principle COM 1.1 Final, Commission of the European Communities, February 2, 2000.

172 Personal observations by David Downie during negotiations related to the Montreal Protocol and the Rotterdam and Stockholm Conventions.

173 Jon Van Dyke, "The Evolution and International Acceptance of the Precautionary Principle," in *Bringing New Law to Ocean Waters*, eds. David Caron and Harry Scheiber (Leiden, Netherlands: Martinus Nijhoff, 2004), 357.

174 Paul Raskin, et al., *Great Transition: The Promise and Lure of the Times Ahead* (Boston: Stockholm Environment Institute, 2002). Compare with Kuhn's analysis of paradigm shifts in science in *The Structure of Scientific Revolutions*.

Chapter 2

Actors in the Environmental Arena

Abstract

This chapter examines the roles that different actors play in global environmental politics. States are the most important actors, since they adopt the broad economic, regulatory, trade, and development policies that affect the environment. But nonstate actors also influence global environmental politics. Intergovernmental organizations (IGOs) help to set the global environmental agenda, initiate and mediate the process of regime formation, and cooperate with countries on projects and programs directly affecting the environment. Treaty secretariats influence operational, implementation, and financing issues within global environmental regimes. Nongovernmental organizations (NGOs) and civil society organizations participate in agenda setting and influence regime negotiations and the environmental policies of states and IGOs. Scientists, indigenous peoples, and local knowledge holders contribute to the understanding of environmental issues and what needs to be done to prevent lasting harm. Multinational corporations influence state positions in regime negotiations and carry out actions that directly affect the global environment.

Keywords: civil society, indigenous peoples, intergovernmental organizations, governments, multinational corporations, nongovernmental organizations, scientists, states, treaty secretariats, UNDP, UNEP, World Bank

States are the most important actors in global environmental politics. States adopt the broad economic, regulatory, trade, and development policies that affect the environment. They decide which issues receive formal consideration by the international community through the decision-making processes within international organizations. States negotiate the international legal instruments that create and implement global environmental regimes. Donor states influence the effectiveness of regimes and other environmental policies through donations to implementation programs, the Global Environment Facility, multilateral banks, bilateral technical and financial assistance, and other programs.

But nonstate actors also influence global environmental politics. Intergovernmental organizations (IGOs) help to set the global environmental agenda, initiate and mediate the process of regime formation, and cooperate with countries on projects and programs directly affecting the environment. Treaty secretariats influence agenda setting and operational, implementation, and financing issues within global environmental regimes. Nongovernmental organizations (NGOs) and civil society organizations (CSOs) participate in agenda setting and influence regime negotiations and the environmental policies of states and IGOs. Scientists, indigenous peoples, and local knowledge holders contribute to the understanding of environmental issues and what needs to be done to prevent lasting harm. Multinational corporations influence state positions in regime negotiations and carry out actions that directly affect the global environment. This chapter examines the roles that these actors play in global environmental politics.

Nation-State Actors: Roles and Interests

Perhaps the most important actions by state actors in global environmental politics concern the creation, content, implementation, and expansion of international environmental regimes. In regime negotiations, a state plays one of four roles: lead state, supporting state, swing state, or veto (or blocking) state. A lead state has a strong commitment to effective international action on the issue, supports ambitious targets, moves the negotiation process forward by proposing constructive options, and attempts to win the support of other states. A supporting state speaks in favor of the lead states' proposals in negotiations.

A swing state has mixed incentives and, in exchange for its acceptance of an agreement, seeks a side-payment or concession to its interests, but typically not one that significantly weakens the regime. However, a swing state sometimes switches to supporting veto states in response to a side-payment, as when some small nonwhaling nations began to support Japan's pro-whaling veto position in exchange for Japanese financial assistance (see Chapter 4). A veto state seeks to block a proposed environmental regime outright, tries to weaken it to the point that it cannot be effective, or refuses to join, thereby severely reducing the global or long-term effectiveness of the regime.

States sometimes shift roles due to changes in government or strategic interests. The United States switched from a veto state that helped to block global negotiations on a mercury treaty for many years, to a lead state that strongly supported efforts to start negotiations following the election of President Barack Obama, to a swing state during the later stages of negotiations. Canada shifted from a swing state in the climate negotiations under the liberal government of Paul Martin, to a veto state under the conservative government of Stephen Harper, to a swing state under Prime Minister Justin Trudeau. The United States changed from a veto state under George W. Bush, to a lead or supporting state under President Obama, to a veto state under Donald Trump. China and India switched from swing states during the first stages of the ozone negotiations to leaders of a veto coalition of developing countries to enhance their bargaining leverage, successfully refusing to join the agreement to phase out chlorofluorocarbons (CFCs) until the industrialized countries agreed in 1990 to provide significant financial assistance to assist developing countries' transition to less harmful chemicals and more advanced technology (see Chapter 3).

There may be more than one lead state on a given issue. For example, Canada and Sweden both played lead roles in initiating actions that led to negotiations on persistent organic pollutants (POPs). Sometimes, a state steps forward to advance a policy that puts it clearly in the lead for a particular period, as Germany did with climate change in 1990 and the African countries did with desertification in 1992. As issues develop over time, the role of lead state may shift from one state or combination of states to another. During some of the early ozone negotiations, Finland and Sweden played important lead roles, heavily influencing early treaty drafts put before the conference. In 1986, the United States stepped into the lead role by proposing a gradual 95 percent reduction in CFCs. In the early 1990s, the European Union (EU) emerged as the lead state in negotiations to phase out other ozone-depleting substances such as methyl bromide and hydrochlorofluorocarbons (HCFCs).

Lead states use a wide range of methods to influence other state actors, including (but not limited to):

- Funding, producing, and/or calling attention to research that defines the problem and demonstrates its urgency, as when Canadian research revealed long-range dangers posed by POPs and when US-based research revealed a threat to the earth's protective ozone layer

- Using their diplomatic clout to encourage an international organization to identify the issue as a priority, as when the United States and Canada persuaded the Organisation for Economic Co-operation and Development to take up the issue of protecting the ozone layer, African countries persuaded the United Nations (UN) to begin negotiations on a treaty to combat desertification, and Sweden and Canada led efforts to get various organizations to address POPs
- Pledging to commit financial or technical resources to addressing the problem or supporting negotiations, such as the incentives that industrialized countries provided in the Montreal Protocol and Stockholm Convention to gain critical developing-country participation, or Japan did in volunteering to help fund the mercury negotiations
- Making a diplomatic démarche to a state that is threatening a veto role, as the United States did with Japan on African elephant ivory
- Working with NGOs that can support their position in other countries and at international conferences, as the Alliance of Small Island States (AOSIS) did when it proposed quantitative limits on greenhouse gas (GHG) emissions in the Kyoto Protocol negotiations
- Seeking to influence public opinion in target states, as Canada did when it supplied US tourists with pamphlets on the acidification of its forests and waters and instructed its Washington, DC embassy to cooperate with US environmental organizations concerned about acid rain

Although economic, scientific, technological, and diplomatic resources cannot ensure that lead states will prevail on an environmental issue, they constitute valuable assets for the creation of a regime. When a big power like the United States plays a lead role through scientific research, unilateral action, and diplomatic initiative, as it did on the issue of ozone protection, it can help to sway states that do not otherwise have clearly defined interests.

States play different roles on different issues. A lead state on one issue may be a veto state on another. Whether a state plays a lead, supporting, swing, or veto role on a particular global environmental issue depends primarily on domestic political factors and the relative costs and benefits of the proposed regime. A second-tier variable, which has been important in some cases, is potential international political consequences, including increased prestige or damage to a country's global image.

Domestic Political Factors

A state's definition of its interests with regard to a particular global environmental issue and its consequent choice of role depend largely on domestic economic and political interests and ideological currents. Whether a government opposes, supports, or leads on an issue often reflects the relative strength and influence of powerful political, economic, and bureaucratic forces and domestic environmental constituencies. Ideological factors related to broader domestic political themes can also play prominent roles in the definition of interests.

Domestic economic interests and their influence on political actors are particularly prominent in promoting veto roles. When the Liberal Democratic Party dominated Japanese politics, for example, whaling companies generally received government support because of close ties to the party.[1] Norway's fishing industry, which claimed that it suffered declining fish catches because of the international protection of whales, prevailed on its government to defend Norwegian whaling before the international community. The United States has played swing or veto roles on certain climate change and chemicals-related issues because of pressure from domestic oil, gas, automobile, and chemicals manufacturers and their supporters in

Congress. In Indonesia, a 2011 study found that seven influential conglomerates controlled more than 9 million hectares of land, including large forest concessions that could remain exempt from any moratorium on forest clearing established under the country's Reducing Emissions from Deforestation and Degradation (REDD) program.[2] The extent of these holdings complicated Indonesia's efforts to reduce carbon dioxide (CO_2) emissions and biodiversity declines caused by logging and plantation development.

Government bureaucracies with institutional interests threatened by potential global action on a particular environmental issue often attempt to influence the adoption of swing or blocking roles. During the negotiation of the Montreal Protocol in the mid-1980s, officials in the US Departments of Commerce, Interior, and Agriculture, together with some members of the White House staff, sought to reopen basic questions about the scientific evidence and the possible damage to the US economy from imposing additional CFC controls to protect the ozone layer but were overruled.[3]

Taking a lead role on a global environmental issue is far more likely if there is little or no domestic opposition. The United States easily took a lead role on whaling, for example, because the US whaling industry had already been eliminated. Similarly, the absence of significant bureaucratic or business interest in opposing a ban on importing African elephant ivory made it easy for Washington to assume a lead role on that issue.

The existence of a strong environmental movement can be an important factor for a state when determining its position, especially if environmental interests compose a potential swing vote in parliamentary or congressional elections. West German and French bids for leadership roles on certain environmental issues in the late 1980s reflected in part the upsurge of public support for strong environmental protection policies. In 1984, the Green Party won 8.2 percent of the vote for West German representatives to the European Parliament. In 1987, a Green Party coalition held nearly 10 percent of the seats in the Bundestag, the German parliament.[4] Polls taken in advance of the 1989 European Parliament election indicated a surge in environmentalist sentiment in Germany and France. These electoral developments contributed to the choice by both countries to become part of the lead coalition proposing negotiations on what became the UN Framework Convention on Climate Change.

But a strong environmental movement does not guarantee that a country will play a lead or supporting role on a particular issue, particularly when it faces concerted opposition from well-connected economic and political interests. US environmental organizations are among the largest and best organized in the world, but they were unable to sway US policy on climate change during the George W. Bush or Donald Trump administrations or successfully lobby the Senate to ratify the Kyoto Protocol or the Biodiversity, Basel, Rotterdam, or Stockholm Conventions.

Conversely, the absence of a strong environmental movement makes it more likely that a state will play a swing or veto role on an international environmental issue. For example, Japanese environmental NGOs are not as strong as those in North America and Europe, and the Japanese political system makes it difficult for interest groups without high-level political links to influence policy. The Japanese government therefore felt little domestic pressure to support environmental regimes on African elephants, whaling, and driftnet fishing. In contrast, US wildlife NGOs placed a great deal of domestic pressure on the US government to take strong positions on these issues.

The ideology or belief system of top policymakers can also shape a country's definition of its interest in an environmental regime. Although the United States had exported very little of its hazardous waste, the George H. W. Bush administration, while supporting elements of the proposed Basel Convention, led the veto coalition against a complete ban on hazardous waste exports to developing countries because of its general opposition to regulatory intervention in national and international markets. The first Bush administration also helped to veto a proposal for industrialized states to set targets for per capita energy use because officials saw this as unwarranted state interference in consumer preferences.

Comparative Costs and Benefits of Environmental Regimes

A second group of variables involve the perceived costs of an environmental threat and the costs and benefits associated with the proposed regime.[5] Exceptional vulnerability to the consequences of environmental problems can drive countries to support, or even take the lead on, strong global action. Thirty-two small island states especially vulnerable to sea-level rise because of global warming formed AOSIS in November 1990 to speak with a single, more influential voice in the climate negotiations and became among the strongest proponents of international action to reduce GHG emissions. Sweden and Norway, which led the fight for the Convention on Long-Range Transboundary Air Pollution, were the major recipients of sulfur dioxide air pollution from other European countries, and their lakes and soils are also acid sensitive, causing the damage from acid rain to appear earlier and more seriously in those Nordic countries than in the United Kingdom or Germany. Canada pushed for strong action on POPs after the discovery that the chemicals tend to bioaccumulate in Arctic food chains and disproportionately affect Inuit communities in northern Canada.

The potential costs of implementing a given global environmental regime, which can differ dramatically from one country to another, also shape negotiation positions. The ozone negotiations provide several examples (see Chapter 3). Because the United States had enacted an early and unilateral ban on aerosols using CFCs, chemicals that deplete stratospheric ozone, it was ahead of Europe and Japan in finding substitutes for CFCs in aerosol cans; it therefore joined Canada and the Nordic states in supporting such a ban, while the European Community (EC) and Japan rejected it. The Soviet Union, fearful that it would be unable to develop new technologies to replace CFCs, opposed any globally mandated CFC cuts until 1987. China and India, which were minor producers at the time but already gearing up for major production increases (including a plan by India's chemical industry to export half its projected CFC production to the Middle East and Asia), feared that the transition to ozone-safe chemicals would be too costly without access to new, alternative technologies and refused to accept controls until after industrialized countries agreed in 1990 to provide significant financial and technical assistance. Moreover, the perceived cost of eliminating the use of methyl bromide in agricultural applications, especially in California, caused the United

Photo 2.1 Saudi Arabia and other countries that rely on oil exports have generally played swing or veto roles in climate negotiations.

Courtesy Kiara Worth, IISD/*Earth Negotiations Bulletin*, http://enb.iisd.org

States in 1995 to push for a large exemption for such use as part of the agreement to phase out nearly all other uses of the chemical.[6]

Since achieving reductions in GHG emissions is easier and/or cheaper for some countries than others, perceived economic impacts have also significantly affected the climate negotiations. For example, EU states are generally net importers of fossil fuels, and most have learned how to continue reducing their use without compromising economic growth. The EU's view that its cost of compliance is manageable, particularly given the huge environmental and economic costs associated with significant climate change, partly explains why it has played a lead role in the negotiations. Meanwhile, other countries that rely on oil, gas, or coal exports (e.g., Australia, Iran, Russia, and Saudi Arabia) or utilize large domestic coal reserves (e.g., Australia, China, India, and the United States) have generally played swing or veto roles.

International Political and Diplomatic Considerations

States also consider potential benefits or costs to broader international interests when considering their position on a particular global environmental issue. A state may hope to gain international prestige by assuming a lead role, or it may decide against a veto role to avoid international opprobrium or damage to its relations with countries for which the issue is of significantly greater concern.

Concern for national reputation or status in the international community was once confined largely to the area of international security. Beginning in the early 1990s, a few states began to see leadership on the global environment as a means of enhancing their international status. In 1994, the EU environment commissioner hailed the prospect of a region-wide carbon tax, which would give the EU a lead role in climate change and result in "the resumption of world environmental and fiscal leadership by the European Union," suggesting that the EU would gain a new kind of international prestige.[7]

At the 1992 Earth Summit, some observers believed that the United States tarnished its image when it stood nearly alone in not signing the Convention on Biological Diversity (CBD). Germany and Japan, among other countries, shared US unhappiness concerning some provisions in the CBD but avoided a veto role for fear of damaging their prestige. A George H. W. Bush administration official stated that Germany and Japan had departed from the US position in part to demonstrate their new status as emerging, independent world powers.[8]

A country's concern about how a veto role might affect its image sometimes focuses on a particular country or group of countries. In negotiations on controlling international trade in hazardous wastes, for example, the decision by France and the United Kingdom in 1989 to alter their position and not play a veto role stemmed in part from a broader national interest in maintaining ties with former colonies in Africa. Japan chose not to block efforts to ban trade in African elephant ivory in 1989 in part because it feared damage to its relations with its most important trading partners, the United States and Europe. Canada ratified the Kyoto Protocol in 2002 in part to protect its "environmentally progressive international image,"[9] although it withdrew from Kyoto in 2011, when the government of Stephen Harper, no longer concerned with this aspect of its international image, objected to its impact on the domestic oil and gas industry.[10] In 2017, President Trump exhibited a similar lack of concern regarding the United States' environmental reputation when he announced that his administration intended to withdraw from the Paris Climate Agreement.

Subnational Actors

National governments, despite their assertion of exclusive rights to act in international relations, are not the only governmental actors in global environmental politics. In recent years, many cities, states, and provinces have enacted their own environmental and energy policies, and these could have a major impact on global environmental problems, especially climate change. Although municipal and state governments are unlikely to usurp national government functions in regime creation and strengthening, they can supplement national efforts, especially when national governments fail to act.

Cities are critical when it comes to climate action.[11] More than 4.2 billion people, or roughly 55 percent of the earth's human population, live in urban areas.[12] Cities already account for more than 70 percent of global energy use[13] and, directly and indirectly, some 75–80 percent of all GHG emissions.[14] A detailed 2018 study of the carbon footprints of 13,000 cities concluded that "concerted action by ... local governments can have a dispro-portionate impact on global emissions."[15]

One of the largest attempts to initiate organized climate action across a large number of cities began in 2005 when a bipartisan group of 132 US mayors, frustrated by the Bush administration's rejection of the Kyoto Protocol, pledged that their cities would try to meet Kyoto's US target: a 7 percent reduction in GHG emissions from 1990 levels by 2012. By November 2019, 1066 mayors, representing large and small cities in all fifty states, had signed the Mayors Climate Protection Agreement.[16] In 2016, Michael Bloomberg created one of the largest coalitions in the world—the Global Covenant of Mayors for Climate and Energy—which now includes over 10,000 cities in 138 countries taking action and supporting further measures to address climate.[17]

The Carbon Neutral Cities Alliance brings together large cities in eleven different countries committed to achieving carbon neutrality or reducing their GHG emissions by 80–100 per-cent by 2050 or sooner—the most ambitious GHG emission reduction targets undertaken by a group of cities—while simultaneously committing to grow their local economies and improve the quality of life of their residents. The cities include Amsterdam, Copenhagen, Hamburg, Helsinki, London, Melbourne, Minneapolis, New York, Oslo, Portland, Rio de Janeiro, San Francisco, Seattle, Stockholm, Sydney, Vancouver, Washington, DC, and Yokohama.[18]

C40 is a network of ninety-six of the largest cities in the world, collectively home to more than 700 million people and representing about 25 percent of the global economy, that have committed to implement climate action plans in line with achieving the ambition of the Paris Agreement to limit global temperature rise to 1.5 degrees Celsius.[19] More than thirty cities in the United Kingdom and fifty in the United States have committed to get 100 percent of their electricity from renewable sources by 2050.[20]

There has also been significant action to reduce GHG emissions at the US state level. By mid-2020, twenty-five states had joined the United States Climate Alliance and committed to reduce GHG emissions by at least 26–28 percent below 2005 levels by 2025 and imple-ment policies that advance the goals of the Paris Climate Agreement.[21] At least twenty-nine states, Washington, DC, and three US territories have adopted renewable energy portfolio standards that set deadlines for utilities to produce a certain percentage of their energy from renewable energy, such as wind, solar, hydro, and geothermal.[22] In 2015, Hawaii became the first state to mandate that all of its electricity be produced from renewable energy sources, setting a 2045 deadline. California, Maine, Nevada, New Mexico, New York, Virginia, and Washington have passed analogous legislation. In 2016, Oregon became the first state to commit to eliminating the use of electricity from coal-fired power plants, setting a 2035 deadline.[23]

Ten northeast and mid-Atlantic states limit GHG emissions through a cooperative effort called the Regional Greenhouse Gas Initiative (RGGI), the first mandatory, multi-state, market-based CO_2 emissions-reduction program in the United States. Within RGGI, Connecticut, Delaware, Maine, Maryland, Massachusetts, New Hampshire, New Jersey, New York, Rhode Island, and Vermont require annual reductions in GHG emissions from power plants. New Jersey returned to RGGI in 2020 after former Governor Chris Christie had pulled New Jersey out of the initiative in 2011, and Pennsylvania and Virginia announced their intention to join.[24] Since the first auction of CO_2 allowances in September 2008, carbon emissions covered by RGGI have dropped by about 40 percent; the auctions have provided more than $91 million for states to reinvest in strategic programs, including energy efficiency, renewable energy, bill assistance, and GHG abatement; more than 14,000 new jobs have been created in the green energy and energy efficiency sectors; consumers have saved hundreds of millions of dollars in lower electric bills; and the states have netted nearly $6 billion in health savings (due to less pollution) and other benefits.[25]

Action at the state and provincial levels is occurring outside the US as well. Australia's most populous state, New South Wales, announced a goal to cut GHG emissions by 35 percent by 2030 compared with 2005 levels and achieve carbon neutrality by 2050.[26] In 2008, the Canadian province of British Columbia introduced North America's first carbon tax, which applies to the purchase and use of fossil fuels and covers about 70 percent of the province's GHG emissions. British Columbia's carbon tax is revenue neutral in that every dollar generated is returned in rebates to citizens, tax credits, reductions in income tax rates, or other measures. Since its introduction, the provincial economy has grown, while GHG emissions have declined.[27] The Canadian province of Quebec started operating a cap-and-trade system in 2013 and a year later linked its system with California's, creating the world's first carbon market operated by subnational governments in different countries.[28] In 2019, the Canadian government initiated a policy that seeks to establish carbon pricing across the country via levies or cap trade systems in different provinces.

Intergovernmental Organizations

IGO influence on global environmental politics has increased significantly since 1972 (see Box 2.1). National governments create IGOs for broad, multisector purposes—for instance, the UN and various regional associations such as the Organization of American States—or for more specific purposes—for instance, the Food and Agriculture Organization of the UN (FAO), World Health Organization (WHO), and International Civil Aviation Organization. IGOs range widely in size and resources, from the World Bank—which in fiscal year 2019 committed more than $60 billion in loans, financing, investments, and guarantees and had a staff of more than 12,000 and an operating budget of about $2.6 billion[29] to the UN Environment Programme (UNEP), which has a staff of less than 900 and a budget of less than $800 million (which includes project implementation).[30]

Most IGOs receive direction from governing bodies comprised of representatives from all governments that are members of the IGO and meet every one to three years to approve budgets and provide formal guidance on priority activities. Although accountable to these governing bodies, and dependent on them for most of their budgets, IGOs have varying degrees of independence, ability, and ambition, differing levels of which can affect regime negotiations and implementation.

An IGO can seek to influence global environmental policy in several ways, including:[31]

- Helping to determine which issues the international community will address through its influence on the agenda for global action
- Providing independent and authoritative information on a global environmental issue
- Seeking to convene international conferences and negotiations
- Seeking to influence negotiations on a global environmental regime
- Helping to develop norms or codes of conduct (soft law) to guide action in particular environmental issue areas
- Influencing national environmental and development policies on issues not under international negotiation but relevant to global environmental politics

- Affecting the implementation of global environmental policies through the provision of funds and technical assistance

No IGO influences global environmental politics by performing all of these functions. IGOs tend to specialize in one or more political functions, although one may indirectly influence another.

❖ BOX 2.1 PROMINENT INTERGOVERNMENTAL ORGANIZATIONS IN GLOBAL ENVIRONMENTAL POLITICS

Many intergovernmental organizations (IGOs) play important roles in different aspects of global environmental politics. These include but are not limited to:

African Development Bank (AfDB)

Asian Development Bank (ADB)

UN Food and Agriculture Organization (FAO)

Global Environment Facility (GEF)

Inter-American Development Bank (IDB)

International Monetary Fund (IMF)

International Maritime Organization (IMO)

Intergovernmental Panel on Climate Change (IPCC)

Intergovernmental Science-Policy Platform on Biodiversity and Ecosystem Services (IPBES)

International Renewable Energy Agency (IRENA)

International Tropical Timber Organization (ITTO)

Organisation for Economic Co-operation and Development (OECD)

United Nations Development Programme (UNDP)

United Nations Environment Programme (UNEP)

United Nations Population Fund (UNFPA)

United Nations Human Settlements Programme (UN-HABITAT)

World Bank

World Health Organization (WHO)

World Meteorological Organization (WMO)

World Trade Organization (WTO)

Setting Agendas and Influencing Regime Development

UNEP is the principal locus for agenda-setting activities in global environmental politics because of its mandate to catalyze and coordinate environmental activities and to serve as a focal point for such activities within the UN system (see Box 2.2). UNEP identifies global environmental issues requiring international cooperation. In 1976, for example, the UNEP Governing Council chose ozone depletion as one of five priority problems, and consequently UNEP convened a meeting of experts in Washington, DC, which resulted in adoption of the World Plan of Action on the Ozone Layer in 1977—five years before negotiations on a global agreement began. UNEP played a similar role in initiating negotiations on climate change.

UNEP has convened and managed the international negotiations that created most of the global environmental conventions of the past three decades, including the Convention on Migratory Species of Wild Animals (1979), the Vienna Convention for the Protection of the Ozone Layer (1985), the Montreal Protocol on Substances That Deplete the Ozone Layer (1987), the Basel Convention on the Control of Transboundary Movements of Hazardous Wastes and Their Disposal (1989), the CBD (1992), the Stockholm Convention on Persistent Organic Pollutants (2001), and the Minamata Convention on Mercury (2013). With FAO, UNEP convened the negotiations that resulted in the 1998 Rotterdam Convention on the

---

✧ BOX 2.2   WHAT IS UNEP?

UNEP The United Nations Environment Programme (UNEP) is the lead United Nations organization on environmental issues. Founded as a result of the United Nations Conference on the Human Environment in June 1972, UNEP's original mandate was to promote, catalyze, and coordinate the development of environmental policy within the UN system and internationally. UNEP's current mission is "To provide leadership and encourage partnership in caring for the environment by inspiring, informing, and enabling nations and peoples to improve their quality of life without compromising that of future generations."

UNEP assists the development and implementation of international environmental policy, helps to monitor and raise awareness of environmental issues, assists developing countries to implement environmentally sound policies, promotes environmental science and information sharing and how they can work in conjunction with policy, seeks to coordinate United Nations environmental activities, and encourages sustainable development at the local, national, regional, and global level.

UNEP's headquarters is in Nairobi, Kenya, and it maintains offices and units in several other countries (such as the office in Geneva that houses the secretariats for the Basel, Rotterdam, Stockholm, and Minamata Conventions). UNEP has a relatively small staff and budget compared with many UN organizations. This reflects its original mandate to acts as a catalyst and coordinator rather than an on-the-ground manager of large programs like UNDP, UNICEF, or WHO.

Source: UNEP website, www.unep.org

Prior Informed Consent Procedure for Certain Hazardous Chemicals and Pesticides in International Trade. UNEP and other IGOs also influence the global environmental agenda and specific issue areas by monitoring and assessing the state of the environment and disseminating that information to governments and NGOs. (See the following sub-section on providing independent and authoritative information.)

Some IGO leaders, such as former UNEP Executive Director Mostafa Tolba, seek to influence environmental diplomacy through direct participation in negotiations. In informal talks with the chiefs of EC delegations during the negotiations on the Montreal Protocol, Tolba lobbied hard for strong controls on CFCs.[32] At a critical Vienna Convention Conference of the Parties (COP) in 1990, he convened informal meetings with twenty-five environment ministers to push for a compromise on the contentious issue of establishing a formal mechanism for providing financial assistance (see Chapter 3). At the final session of the negotiations on the CBD, Tolba took over when talks gridlocked on key issues regarding the financing mechanism and virtually forced acceptance of a compromise text (see Chapter 4).

During the tenure of Klaus Töpfer, UNEP's fourth executive director, UNEP developed the Global Earth Observation System of Systems; initiated the Strategic Approach for International Chemicals Management; improved the scientific base of UNEP; and created the Global Ministerial Environment Forum so that high-level discussions could examine existing environmental challenges, identify new and emerging issues, and set assessment priorities on a regular basis.[33]

Achim Steiner became UNEP's fifth executive director in 2006. During his tenure, UNEP adopted medium-term strategies that streamlined its operations to focus on climate change, disasters and conflicts, ecosystem management, environmental governance, chemicals and

Photo 2.2 The fourth session of the United Nations Environment Assembly convened under the theme Solve Different: Innovative Solutions for Environmental Challenges and Sustainable Consumption and Production.

Courtesy Mike Muzurakis, IISD/*Earth Negotiations Bulletin*, http://enb.iisd.org

waste, resource efficiency (sustainable consumption and production), and environmental monitoring.[34] Following the 2012 UN Conference on Sustainable Development (UNCSD), the UN General Assembly adopted a resolution that allowed UNEP to receive secure, stable, and increased financial resources from the regular UN budget and opened UNEP's Governing Council to full participation by all UN member states, renaming it the UN Environment Assembly of UNEP.[35] In February 2019, Inger Andersen, a Danish economist and environmentalists, was appointed as UNEP's seventh executive director and the second woman to hold that post.[36]

The High-level Political Forum on Sustainable Development (HLPF) is the main United Nations platform on sustainable development and has a central role in the review of progress toward the 2030 Agenda for Sustainable Development and the Sustainable Development Goals (SDGs). The Forum, which replaced the Commission on Sustainable Development (1993–2013), meets annually under the auspices of the Economic and Social Council. Every four years, it meets at the level of heads of state and government under the auspices of the UN General Assembly.

Providing Independent and Authoritative Information

IGOs can also influence global environmental politics by providing independent and authoritative scientific and other information to states, other IGOs, public, corporations, NGOs, and the press. This can take the form of broad environmental monitoring, specific scientific reports produced as part of environmental treaty regimes (e.g., the Ozone Assessment reports), reports by stand-alone scientific bodies, and gathering and disseminating information submitted by treaty parties.

Along these lines, UNEP established the Global Environmental Monitoring System/ Water Programme, which provides information on inland water quality; the Global Resource Information Database, a global network of environmental data centers facilitating the generation and dissemination of key environmental information; and the UNEP World Conservation Monitoring Centre, which acts as a global biodiversity information and assessment center. UNEP is also part of the Global Earth Observation System of Systems, which works on comprehensive, coordinated, and sustained earth observations.

UNEP has also undertaken or participated in many global assessments. A small sample includes: six UNEP Global Environmental Outlook reports (since 1995); nine ozone assessments (1985–2018); four global mercury assessments (most recently in 2018); the Global Marine Assessment (2001 and 2007); the Global Biodiversity Assessment (1995); two global chemicals assessments; the Cultural and Spiritual Values of Biodiversity Assessment (1999); the Millennium Ecosystem Assessment (2005); the Global International Waters Assessment (2006); and the International Assessment of Agricultural Knowledge, Science and Technology for Development (2008).

Many other IGOs also conduct such assessments, as does the UN system as a whole. A few examples include the Global Marine Integrated Assessment, FAO's Global Forest Resources Assessment, FAO's State of the World's Fisheries and Aquaculture, and the Global Assessment Report on Disaster Risk Reduction.

Developing Nonbinding Norms and Codes of Conduct

International organizations also influence global environmental politics by facilitating the development of common norms or standards for government behavior. Nontreaty measures, often called soft law, have been developed to help guide state actions on environmental issues, including codes of conduct, declarations of principle, global action plans, and other international agreements that seek to create norms and expectations without the binding legal status of treaties.[37]

✤ **BOX 2.3 WHAT IS THE FAO?**

The Food and Agriculture Organization of the United Nations (FAO) leads international efforts to defeat hunger, advance agricultural productivity, and ensure food safety. It serves both developed and developing countries, acting as a neutral forum where nations meet to discuss issues, negotiate agreements, and create programs. FAO also serves as a source of knowledge and information, helping developing countries modernize and improve agriculture, forestry, and fisheries practices and ensure good nutrition for all. FAO work currently focuses on food security, natural resource management, forestry and fisheries, early warning of food emergencies, disaster recovery, food safety, and bioenergy, among other issues.

Headquartered in Rome, Italy, FAO maintains an extensive set of regional, subregional, and country offices and works in partnership with institutions of all kinds—United Nations agencies, national governments, private foundations, large NGOs, grassroots organizations, companies, professional associations, and others. Some partnerships operate at national level or in the field; others are regional or global in nature. The total FAO budget for 2018–2019 was $2.6 billion. Of this amount, 39 percent came from assessed contributions paid by member countries, while 61 percent came from voluntary contributions from countries and other partners.

Source: FAO website, www.fao.org.

These nonbinding agreements are usually developed or negotiated by groups of experts representing their governments, usually through processes convened by IGOs. Many UN agencies contribute to these processes, although UNEP and FAO have been the most active on environmental issues. For example, UNEP played an instrumental role in successful efforts to get countries to voluntarily adopt standards limiting or prohibiting lead in gasoline. In 1984, a UNEP-organized working group of experts helped draft guidelines for the management of hazardous waste. In 1987, the same process produced guidelines and principles aimed at making the worldwide pesticide trade more responsive to the threats these substances pose to the environment and human health (see Chapter 3). Since 1963, the Joint FAO/WHO Food Standards Programme (via the Codex Alimentarius Commission) has developed food standards, guidelines, and codes of practice aimed at protecting the health of consumers and ensuring fair trade. The FAO also drafted guidelines on the environmental criteria for the registration of pesticides (1985).

The FAO Committee on Fisheries (COFI) has been the primary global forum for considering major issues related to fisheries and aquaculture policy since its creation in 1965. Until the late 1980s, COFI focused on coastal states' fisheries development, but as overfishing became increasingly difficult to ignore, COFI and the FAO Secretariat began pushing more aggressively for new international norms for sustainable fisheries. The FAO Secretariat collected and analyzed data on global fish catch, issued annual reviews on the state of the world's fisheries, and organized technical workshops. These efforts helped to focus government and NGO attention on such issues as excess fishing capacity and fisheries subsidies. In 1991, COFI recommended that the FAO develop the concept of responsible fisheries in the form of a code of conduct, and the FAO Secretariat convened global negotiations. The resulting 1995 Code of Conduct for Responsible Fisheries is the most comprehensive set of principles and international standards and norms for sustainable fisheries management that currently exists and, despite not being legally binding, has had some influence on state and producer practices.

Soft-law agreements are sometimes chosen as a consensus path to avoid the lengthy process of negotiating, signing, and ratifying a binding agreement while also seeking to change international behavior. However, sometimes, soft-law regimes are adopted because key parties were unwilling to consider or accept mandatory provisions. In Codex Alimentarius cases, the agreed-upon norms are usually not particularly stringent, and state compliance is likely to be uneven at best. The 1985 Code of Conduct on the Distribution and Use of Pesticides and the 1985 Cairo guidelines on international hazardous waste trade are also examples of this pattern.

However, soft law sometimes gets turned into binding international law. For example, over time, the principles included in a soft-law agreement may become widely regarded as the appropriate norms for a problem, and thus they are ultimately absorbed into treaty law. Alternatively, sometimes political pressures may arise from those dissatisfied with spotty adherence to soft-law norms, and thus these parties successfully advocate for international negotiations to turn a nonbinding agreement into a binding one.

Influencing National Development Policies

IGOs also affect global environmental politics by influencing the environmental and development policies of individual states outside the context of regime negotiations. National policy decisions on how to manage forests, generate and use energy, increase agricultural production, allocate government resources, regulate pollution and waste, and manage other economic, development, and environment issues determine how sustainable a country will be and the impact it will have on global environmental issues. IGOs can influence such policies in several ways:

- Providing financing for particular development projects, as well as advice and technical assistance that help shape the country's development strategy
- Providing financing for environmental-protection projects
- Providing financing, technical assistance, training, and capacity building to create or improve government agencies
- Conducting research aimed at persuading state officials to adopt certain policies
- Providing targeted information to government officials, NGOs, the private sector, and the public
- Focusing normative pressure on states regarding sustainable development policy issues

FAO, for example, works with countries to help farmers diversify food production, protect plant and animal health, market their products, conserve natural resources, and engage in integrated pest management to reduce reliance on chemical pesticides. In forestry, FAO provides advice and technical assistance to help countries develop and improve national forest programs and implement management and preservation activities. As noted, FAO is also the world's principal repository of global fishery statistics. It compiles, collates, analyzes, and integrates fishery and aquaculture data, creating a range of relevant, timely, and readily available information products.

The United Nations Development Programme (UNDP), with a budget of about $5 billion annually ($600 million for core operations and the bulk of the rest for implementing projects) and a staff of 8000 working in 170 countries, is a large source of multilateral

✤ BOX 2.4   WHAT IS UNDP?

The United Nations Development Programme (UNDP) is the UN global development organization. Headquartered in New York, UNDP works in more than 170 countries and territories in cooperation with national governments, IGOs, NGOs, and others to implement programs that seek to eradicate poverty and build developing-country capacity to address local, national, and global development challenges. UNDP has 126 Resident Representatives, half of whom are women, who work in country offices and formulate and articulate the vision and strategies for UNDP's engagement and development activities at the country level.

UNDP's strategic plan for 2018–2021 focuses on eradicating poverty in all its forms and dimensions; accelerating structural transformations; building resilience to shocks and crises; and working with partners to achieve the Sustainable Development Goals (SDGs). UNDP's annual *Human Development Report* contains updated global and national statistics while also focusing attention on key development issues. UNDP is among the largest UN agencies, and the UNDP administrator is the third highest-ranking member of the United Nations after the United Nations secretary-general and deputy secretary-general. Its budget for 2020 was approximately $4.9 billion and included funds drawn from assessed contributions from member states and donations from countries, corporations, and foundations.

Source: UNDP website, www.undp.org.

grant-development assistance (see Box 2.4). UNDP's current strategic plan focuses on helping countries achieve the 2030 Agenda for Sustainable Development by focusing on three main areas: eradicating poverty in all its forms and dimensions; accelerating structural transformations for sustainable development; and building resilience to crises and shocks (including those related to environmental change). To do so, UNDP identified a set of "signature solutions" in six key areas: reduce *poverty*; enhance *governance* for peaceful, just, and inclusive societies; increase *resilience* and crisis prevention; support nature-based solutions for *environment* and development; expand *clean energy*; and augment women's empowerment and *gender* equality.[38] UNDP has gone further than any other UN agency in calling for donor countries and developing-country governments to allocate particular levels of resources for human development (health, population, and education) as a norm in the context of what it calls "sustainable human development."

Scientific Bodies

The scientific community has always played a role in global environmental negotiations, going back to some of the earliest negotiations on oceans. Many environmental problems are so complex scientifically, with many different parameters, interrelations, and correlations that cannot easily be stated as precise causal relationships, that the substance of what is being negotiated, what is an appropriate trade-off, what is a reasonable fallback position, and what are effective outcomes can be difficult to define for many years.[39] Thus, policymakers rely on scientists to present facts and projections about specific issues. This information does not determine outcomes, but it can shape them and is often very important to the fact-finding and agenda-setting stages of environmental policymaking (see Chapters 3 and 4).

As a result, stand-alone organizations and international networks of cooperating scientists and scientific institutions have become actors in global environmental policy. Huge teams of scientists can review each other's work, perform integrated assessments, provide evidence of global scientific consensus (consensus does not mean unanimity), and generate ideas that far exceed the aggregation of each individual's particular knowledge.[40] While one could consider some of these scientific bodies as IGOs and others as subsidiary bodies to particular treaty regimes, their potential to impact the agenda, development, and content of global environmental policy warrants their consideration as a sub-category of actors.

One of the first international bodies of scientists to provide independent and authoritative information to international negotiators was the Ozone Trends Panel. Organized by the National Aeronautics and Space Administration (NASA), and thus not an official IGO, the panel worked for sixteen months on a comprehensive scientific assessment of knowledge about the ozone layer that involved more than 100 scientists from ten countries. The panel's March 1988 report made headlines around the world: ozone-layer depletion was no longer a theory. The report increased support for strengthening the Montreal Protocol to mandate a phase-out of CFCs and add additional chemicals to the control regime. Scientific information in subsequent reports provided arguments to phase out other ozone-depleting substances and address a serious class of global-warming chemicals (see Chapter 3).

The best-known example of a scientific body in global environmental politics is the Intergovernmental Panel on Climate Change (IPCC). Established in 1988 by UNEP and the World Meteorological Organization (WMO) at the request of the world's governments, the IPCC is charged with providing detailed reports based on available, peer-reviewed scientific information on key issues relevant to understanding climate change, its impacts, and potential response strategies. The first assessment report of the IPCC, released in 1990, served as the impetus for negotiating the UN Framework Convention on Climate Change (UNFCCC). Since then, the IPCC has released four additional comprehensive assessment reports (1995, 2001, 2007, and 2014) with the next one scheduled for 2022, as well as special reports on specific topics.[41] Each involves the work of thousands of scientists from around the world. In 2007, the IPCC and former US vice president Al Gore were jointly awarded the Nobel Peace Prize for their efforts to augment and disseminate knowledge about human-made climate change and help provide the foundation for measures to address it.

The Millennium Ecosystem Assessment, called for by former UN Secretary-General Kofi Annan, examined the consequences of ecosystem change for human well-being and the scientific basis for action needed to enhance the conservation and sustainable use of those systems. The assessment was coordinated by UNEP and overseen by representatives of different treaties (the CBD, UN Convention to Combat Desertification (UNCCD), Ramsar Convention on Wetlands, and Convention on Migratory Species) as well as national governments, UN agencies, civil society representatives, and the private sector. More than 1300 scientists and other experts from ninety-five countries were involved in its work between 2001 and 2005, evaluating an immense array of scientific literature and ultimately publishing five technical volumes.

To build on the Millennium Ecosystem Assessment and institutionalize such processes, in 2012 governments established the Intergovernmental Science-Policy Platform on Biodiversity and Ecosystem Services (IPBES). IPBES assesses the planet's biodiversity and ecosystem services and provides scientifically sound information to support more informed policy decisions. The first IPBES comprehensive assessment, released in 2019, involved about 150 lead authors from all regions of the world, assisted by 350 contributing authors and many more expert reviewers. Scientists analyzed more than 15,000 scientific publications as well as indigenous and local knowledge. The *Global Assessment Report on Biodiversity and Ecosystem Services* detailed how ecosystems across most of the globe have been significantly altered by multiple human drivers, with the great majority of indicators of ecosystems and biodiversity showing rapid decline. Around 25 percent of assessed species of animals and plants—or about 1 million species—face extinction, many within decades, unless action is taken to reduce the drivers of biodiversity loss.[42]

Treaty Secretariats

Treaty secretariats are a specific type of IGO established by an international treaty to manage the day-to-day operation of the treaty regime.[43] Although most secretariats perform similar core functions, they vary considerably in their additional responsibilities, size, funding, autonomy, degree of activism, and relationships with other IGOs, secretariats, and treaties. Some of the larger secretariats, like the Climate Secretariat, have more than 450 staff members, whereas the Secretariat of the Convention on Migratory Species of Wild Animals has fewer than forty and the Ozone Secretariat fewer than twenty. Several secretariats, such as those for the ozone, biodiversity, and chemicals regimes, are part of UNEP. Some, like the Climate and UNCCD secretariats, are administered by the UN Secretariat. The International Treaty on Plant Genetic Resources for Food and Agriculture Secretariat is administered by the FAO.

Staffed by international civil servants, secretariats are located in different parts of the world, although several clusters exist due to host country willingness to provide financial support and the advantages of locating new secretariats near existing UN offices or other secretariats. The secretariats for the Convention on International Trade in Endangered Species of Wild Fauna and Flora (CITES), the Basel, Rotterdam, Stockholm and Minamata Conventions, and IPCC are located in Geneva, Switzerland. The climate, desertification, migratory species, and IPBES secretariats are in Bonn, Germany. The Ramsar Convention on Wetlands Secretariat is located in Gland, Switzerland; the CBD Secretariat is in Montreal, Canada; and the Ozone Secretariat in Nairobi, Kenya.

Each secretariat is headed by an executive secretary or secretary-general (the choice of titles does not connote relative authority within the regime). It is notable that as of 2020, six of the nine secretariats discussed in Chapters 3 and 4 are headed by women: ozone, mercury, climate change, biodiversity, CITES, and whaling.

The core tasks for nearly all treaty secretariats include the following:

- Arranging and servicing meetings of the COP and all subsidiary bodies
- Preparing and transmitting reports based on information received from parties, the COP, and subsidiary bodies
- Preparing reports on secretariat implementation activities for the COP
- Ensuring coordination with relevant international bodies and NGOs
- Liaising and communicating with relevant authorities, non-parties, and international organizations
- Compiling and analyzing scientific, economic, and social data and information
- Monitoring adherence to treaty obligations
- Giving guidance and advice to parties
- Providing guidance and advice to parties
- Helping to provide awareness-raising activities, training, capacity building, and technical assistance to developing countries
- Raising funds for these and other treaty implementation and awareness-raising activities

Secretariats can also create synergies by coordinating and cooperating with other secretariats. The need for such activity stems from the fragmented system of international policy that addresses integrated environmental systems and issues. For example, the goals, operation, and impact of the CBD intersect with dozens of international wildlife, habitat, and pollution conventions and initiatives. Realization of links within the chemicals and waste sector led countries to integrate the Basel, Rotterdam, and Stockholm Conventions' secretariats (see Chapter 3).

Treaty secretariats may influence the treatment of global environmental issues in ways that are similar to international organizations. A secretariat's level of influence depends largely on its mandate (as set out in the treaty that created it), the extent and nature of additional tasks assigned to it by the treaty parties, its funding, and the professional and personal ability and commitment of its staff. Essentially, however, treaty secretariats have two broad areas of impact in addition to the core roles listed here:

1. Treaty secretariats can influence the behavior of actors by helping to change their knowledge and belief systems.
2. Treaty secretariats can influence political processes through the creation, support, and shaping of norm-building processes for issue-specific international cooperation.[44]

Treaty Secretariats as Knowledge Brokers

Environmental treaty secretariats embody the institutional memory of the regime they serve. A secretariat provides continuity for negotiations that stretch through numerous sessions over a period of years (including both the negotiation and the implementation of the treaty), during which there may be considerable turnover among government negotiators.[45] More specifically, secretariat staff possess expert technical and scientific knowledge about the problem; administrative and procedural knowledge of regime rules, norms, and operations; and diplomatic knowledge of state preferences. All of this is useful when dealing with the complex interlinkages characteristic of international environmental regimes.[46]

As knowledge brokers, secretariats are in a position to manage the horizontal flow of information among national governments and the vertical flow of information among international organizations, national governments, and local stakeholders. While most secretariats do not have the means or mandate for actual scientific research, they have the ability to collect and disseminate knowledge. This information can take the form of syntheses of scientific findings, such as the Ozone Secretariat circulating reports on the impact that HCFCs also have on climate change. More broadly, the CBD Secretariat maintains close links with the scientific community through international scientific cooperative programs and the participation of secretariat staff in relevant scientific symposia. The secretariat gathers scientific information on different issues relevant to biodiversity conservation as well as on administrative, social, legal, and economic aspects of the related issues, such as access and benefit sharing. This knowledge is processed and made available through preparatory documents, the secretariat's website, periodic reports, a newsletter, and a comprehensive handbook.[47]

Knowledge and information management is another key role. The COP, its subsidiary bodies, national policymakers, NGOs and other stakeholders, and other interested actors, such as the media, scientists, and members of civil society, draw on and interpret the information and documentation compiled and disseminated by the secretariat in their analytical, political, and scientific assessments and the related discourses.[48] Secretariat websites contain information about the environmental issue, the treaty regime, past and current negotiations, progress in implementing the relevant agreements, official documents, and press and educational materials.

Secretariats can also act as knowledge brokers by gathering, synthesizing, processing, and disseminating information to states and other actors.[49] They can convene expert panels and academic assessments, which can help to raise concern among external actors to the level needed to have an impact on political activity. For example, the Basel, Climate, Rotterdam,

Photo 2.3 The UN Convention to Combat Desertification Secretariat acts as a knowledge broker by gathering, synthesizing, processing, and disseminating information in various reports to states and other actors.

Courtesy UNCCD Secretariat.

and Stockholm secretariats, among others, hold online webinars and workshops on scientific, technical, and treaty implementation topics. Many secretariats promote the use of side events during meetings of the COP or the subsidiary bodies, in which scientists and other nongovernmental experts share information with policymakers and with each other.

Marketing, a subset of knowledge brokering, moves beyond provision of technical information to the strategic use of information to shape opinions about the environmental issue, the regime, and related political processes, norms, and institutions. It involves the deliberate selection of specific pieces of information and transforms that information in pursuit of specific objectives. This information is often repeated across multiple political fora.[50] Many secretariats use their websites, press releases, and various social media accounts, including Facebook and Twitter, to market their knowledge to various communities.

Treaty Secretariats and the Political Process

Treaty secretariats can influence political processes through the creation, support, and shaping of norm-building processes for issue-specific cooperation, such as the advance informed-agreement provisions in the Cartagena Protocol on Biosafety and the prior informed consent (PIC) procedure under the Rotterdam Convention. They can initiate conferences to follow up on treaties or to introduce relevant new topics to the parties. They administer negotiations on the implementation and expansion of the regime through which secretariat staff can exercise considerable influence "even when they are not key players during the negotiation stage."[51] For example, the Biodiversity Secretariat demonstrated a balanced and continuous effort to facilitate dialogues and negotiations on both the issues of biosafety and access to genetic resources and the fair and equitable sharing of benefits arising from their use, which contributed to the adoption of the Cartagena and Nagoya Protocols.

Secretariats can also influence the political process through capacity building, including assisting countries with implementation activities and influencing domestic policies through, for example, workshops, or providing formal or informal technical advice.[52] Secretariats provide basic informational materials on relevant conventions and their sociopolitical implications, such as those developed by the UNCCD Secretariat. The CITES Secretariat provides training materials for wildlife enforcement officers. The Rotterdam Convention Secretariat provides a training manual to explain the convention and its obligations to those responsible for the export of chemicals. The Ozone Secretariat conducts public outreach activities around World Ozone Day and notable anniversaries of the Vienna Convention and Montreal Protocol. Some secretariats provide booklets and games that explain the issues to children.

Some secretariats and their senior staff stick closely to their administrative and facilitative roles, performing only those tasks specifically assigned to them by the treaty or COP decisions. Others, while also performing the normal administrative and facilitative roles, are more proactive. They seek to push the agenda, looking for new initiatives and trying to get governments to support and implement them.[53] Secretariats in the latter category benefit from skillful and charismatic leadership. More often than not, however, the secretariat's role in regime negotiations is less overt and more facilitative—the important, often unrecognized, and sometimes pivotal role of organizing a smooth process, which can be crucial in steering negotiations toward a successful outcome. For example, inexperience by new members of the Minamata Secretariat led to a number of organizational problems during the first COP for the mercury treaty.[54] In contrast, the Basel, Rotterdam and Stockholm (BRS) Secretariat has improved the organization and operation of the complex and difficult simultaneous meetings of the BRS Conventions, with consequential improvements in some outcomes (see Chapter 3).[55]

Nevertheless, it is important to note that treaty secretariats sometimes become more active players in global environmental politics than some governments and other actors may prefer. When secretariats move beyond fulfilling their basic functions and begin influencing global discourse through knowledge management, advancing the institutionalization or expansion of a convention, supporting particular proposals during negotiations, or proactively assisting in capacity building, they become stakeholders in their own right. Government officials occasionally upbraid secretariat officials for moving beyond a purely facilitative role, arguing that secretariats should not influence policy development. At other times, however, officials praise them for acting effectively in pursuit of the stated goals of the regime.[56]

International Financial Institutions

In terms of direct impact on the development and environmental policies of developing states, some of the most powerful IGOs are international financial institutions because of the amount of financial resources they transfer or loan to developing countries every year in support of particular projects and economic policies.

The Global Environment Facility (GEF) provides the most funding for specific environmental protection projects (see Box 2.5). Established on the eve of the 1992 Rio Earth Summit, the GEF provides grants and concessional funding to developing countries and countries with economies in transition for projects with global environmental benefits in six broad focal areas: climate change, biodiversity, forestry, polluted international waters, land degradation and desertification, and toxic chemicals and wastes. The GEF also provides funding to assist developing countries in meeting the objectives of relevant international regimes in these areas and serves as a "financial mechanism" to the CBD, UNFCCC, UNCCD, and Stockholm and Minamata Conventions. The COP for each convention provides broad strategic guidance to the two governing bodies of the GEF, the GEF Council and the GEF Assembly, and the GEF Council converts this broad guidance into operational criteria (guidelines) for GEF projects. The GEF has provided about $20 billion in grants and mobilized more than $100 billion in co-financing for nearly 4700 projects in 170 countries.[57]

❖ BOX 2.5   WHAT IS THE GLOBAL ENVIRONMENT FACILITY?

GEF   The Global Environment Facility (GEF) was established on the eve of the 1992 Rio Earth Summit to help tackle the planet's most pressing environmental problems. It provides grants to developing countries and countries with economies in transition for projects in six focal areas: biodiversity, climate change, chemicals and waste, land degradation, international waters, and sustainable forest management. The GEF is also a designated financial mechanism for the Convention on Biological Diversity (CBD); the Convention to Combat Desertification (UNCCD); the United Nations Framework Convention on Climate Change (UNFCCC); the Stockholm Convention on Persistent Organic Pollutants (POPs); and the Minamata Convention on Mercury. For each of these Conventions, the GEF assists eligible countries to meet their regime obligations under rules and guidance provided by the Conventions and their Conferences of Parties. The GEF is also associated with other regimes, including several global and regional agreements that address transboundary water systems and the Montreal Protocol on Substances That Deplete the Ozone Layer.

The GEF Secretariat handles the organization's day-to-day operations. It is based in Washington, DC, and reports directly to the GEF Council and GEF Assembly. The GEF Council is the main governing body. It functions as an independent board of directors, with primary responsibility for developing, adopting, and evaluating GEF programs. Composed of representatives from sixteen developing countries, fourteen from developed countries, and two from countries with transitional economies, the Council meets twice each year. The GEF Assembly includes representatives from all 183 member countries. It meets every three to four years and is responsible for reviewing and evaluating the GEF's general policies, operation, and membership. The GEF has seventeen implementing partners, including the World Bank, UNDP, UNEP, FAO, other UN agencies, regional development banks, and NGOs, who work with national governments to implement GEF funded projects.

Source: GEF website, www.thegef.org/

Through its Small Grants Programme, which provides grants of up to $50,000, the GEF has invested nearly $600 million and leveraged other funds to support nearly 22,000 small grants directly to civil society and community-based organizations in more than 125 countries.[58]

As part of the negotiation of the seventh replenishment of the GEF, in which donor countries pledged $4.1 billion to support GEF grants and operations, governments agreed that in combination with its traditional investments under the Conventions, the GEF would start: (1) strategically focusing its investments to catalyze transformational change in key systems that are driving major environmental loss, in particular energy, cities, and food; (2) prioritizing integrated projects and programs that address more than one global environmental problem at a time, building on the GEF's unique position and mandate to act on a wide range of global environmental issues; and (3) implementing new strategies and policies to enhance results, including stronger engagement with the private sector, indigenous peoples, and civil society, and an increased focus on gender equality.

Of the international financial institutions, the World Bank (see Box 2.6) has had the biggest impact on development policies, many of which in turn have affected the

❖ BOX 2.6   WHAT IS THE WORLD BANK?

The World Bank is the largest source of international financial and development assistance to developing countries. It is not a bank in the conventional sense, but a group of development institutions owned by 189 member countries. Together they provide low-interest loans, interest-free credits, and grants to developing countries for a wide array of activities, including investments in education, health, public administration, infrastructure, financial and private-sector development, agriculture, and environmental and natural resource management. Headquartered in Washington, DC, the World Bank has more than 10,000 employees in more than 130 offices worldwide. Since 1947 it has funded over 12,000 development projects.

The World Bank consists of a number of different institutions. The first, the International Bank for Reconstruction and Development (IBRD), was created by the United States and its allies in 1944 to facilitate post-World War II reconstruction. Over the years it was joined by four other institutions: the International Development Association (IDA), International Finance Corporation (IFC), Multilateral Guarantee Agency (MGA), and International Center for the Settlement of Investment Disputes (ICSID). The IBRD and IDA provide financing, policy advice, and technical assistance to governments of developing countries, with IDA focusing on the world's poorest countries, and IBRD assisting middle-income and creditworthy poorer countries. The IFC, MGA, and ICSID work to strengthen the private sector in developing countries by providing financing, technical assistance, political risk insurance, and dispute settlement services.

Source: The World Bank website, www.worldbank.org

environment. Historically, the Bank was driven by a bias toward large-scale, capital-intensive, and centralized projects; by a need to lend large amounts of money each year; and by its practice of assessing projects according to a quantifiable rate of return, such as how the loan contributed to conventional gross national product calculations, while discounting longer-term, less quantifiable social and environmental costs and benefits. In the 1970s and 1980s, the World Bank supported agricultural and development projects in the rain forests of Brazil, Indonesia, and other countries, cattle-ranching in Central and South America, and many other projects that accelerated deforestation, fossil fuel use, and other environmental problems.[59]

In response to persistent, well-orchestrated pressure from NGOs, criticism by some prominent members of the US Congress, and calls for it to become part of the solution to global environmental problems rather than a contributor, in the late 1980s the World Bank began a series of policy, structural, and investment-strategy changes to reduce the negative impacts of its lending. These reforms included mandatory environmental assessments, and public disclosure of these assessments, in advance of project approval and sector-specific policies to guide World Bank investment in such areas as forestry and energy, including a ban on financing logging in primary tropical forests.[60] A separate environmental unit created in the 1980s evolved into a vice presidency for environmentally and socially sustainable development in the 1990s. By the mid-1990s, the Bank had developed a portfolio of environment-sector projects, ranging from support for national environmental agencies to investments in national parks.[61]

Many continued to criticize the Bank, however, saying that its environmental reforms were merely efforts to deflect outside criticism, no major changes had occurred in the Bank's overall performance, and lending imperatives tied to traditional models of economic growth continued to outweigh environmental considerations.[62] In response to continued criticism, in 2001 the Bank adopted a new strategy, "Making Sustainable Commitments: An Environment Strategy for the World Bank," which called for mainstreaming "the environment into investments, programs, sector strategies, and policy dialogue."[63] The strategy placed environmental considerations within the institution's central poverty-reduction mission and highlighted three objectives: improving the quality of life, enhancing the quality of growth, and protecting the regional and global commons.[64]

Yet, three years later, experts maintained that the World Bank still had not succeeded in mainstreaming sustainability into its operations and that Bank staff did not see environmental issues as integral to their operations.[65] Echoing these concerns, in 2008 the Independent Evaluation Group of the World Bank recommended that the Bank remedy internal constraints, including poor knowledge, inadequate capacity, and insufficient coordination concerning environmental challenges.[66]

In June 2012 the World Bank released a new policy framework for 2012 to 2022, aimed at enabling countries to pursue more sustainable development.[67] The strategy identifies seven priority areas for the World Bank's engagement in environment projects: wealth accounting and ecosystem valuation, protection of oceans, pollution management, low-emission development, adaptation, disaster risk management, and small island states' resilience. Among other things, the strategy recognizes the growing role of the private sector in addressing sustainability concerns and the need to ensure that global markets promote sustainable development.

Many environmental NGOs, such as Friends of the Earth, Greenpeace, and the Sierra Club, expressed skepticism, warning that the strategy might rely too much on private-sector interventions and market mechanisms. They argued that the initiative lacked specifics and that greater private-sector involvement in a project could lead to decreased capacity to monitor social and environmental impact.[68] Others praised the strategy, noting that the current economic model, driven by unsustainable patterns of growth and consumption, was putting too much pressure on an already threatened environment.[69]

On October 1, 2018, the World Bank launched a new set of environment and social policies called the Environmental and Social Framework, which applies to all new World Bank project financing. The Framework has three central components: (1) a "Vision for Sustainable Development," which sets out the Bank's aspirations regarding environmental and social sustainability; (2) the World Bank Environmental and Social Policy for Investment Project Financing, which sets out the requirements that the Bank must follow regarding projects it supports; and (3) ten Environmental and Social Standards, which set out the mandatory requirements that apply to borrowers. The World Bank believes that articulating sustainable development as central to its mission and applying the new standards will enhance the commitment and ability of both the Bank and its borrowers to identify and manage environmental and social risks associated with projects and thus enhance national abilities to increase prosperity and reduce poverty in a sustainable manner.[70]

The International Monetary Fund (IMF; see Box 2.7) was even slower than the World Bank and regional banks to acknowledge the need to take environmental considerations explicitly into account in its lending operations. It defined its role as limited to helping countries achieve a balance of payments and pay off their international debts. Only in 1991 did the IMF executive board first consider the extent to which the IMF should "address

❖ BOX 2.7 WHAT IS THE INTERNATIONAL MONETARY FUND?

The International Monetary Fund's primary mission is to ensure the stability of the international monetary system. It provides policy advice and financing to countries in economic difficulties to help them achieve macroeconomic stability and reduce poverty. Founded in 1944, and headquartered in Washington, DC, the IMF is a specialized agency of the United Nations but has its own charter, governing structure, and finances. The highest decision-making body of the IMF, the Board of Governors, consists of one governor and one alternate governor for each of its 189 member countries. However, voting power among the governors is distributed based on the size of each country's share of the global economy. Thus, the US, Japan, China, and EU countries wield primary influence.

The work of the IMF focuses on three main areas: economic surveillance, lending, and technical assistance. Surveillance refers to the monitoring of economic and financial developments and the provision of policy advice, aimed especially at crisis prevention. The IMF lends money to countries with balance of payments difficulties, providing temporary financing and supporting policies aimed at correcting underlying problems. It also provides loans to low-income countries aimed especially at poverty reduction. In recent years, the IMF has also employed elements of its surveillance and technical assistance work to help develop standards and codes of good practice as part of international efforts to strengthen the global financial system. Financing for IMF activities comes mainly from the money that countries pay as their capital subscription when they become members. The size of these payments also varies by the size of their economy.

Source: The IMF website, www.imf.org

environmental issues." It decided that the IMF should avoid policies that might harm the environment but that it should not conduct research or build up its own expertise on the possible environmental consequences of its policies.[71]

Since the World Bank and GEF address environmental issues and support extensive work programs, the executive board decided early on that the IMF should not duplicate the Bank's work and that its mandate and expertise should constrain its ability to address environmental issues. The IMF's involvement in environmental policy is thus limited to areas that have a serious and perceptible impact on a country's macroeconomic outlook. The IMF sees fiscal instruments (emissions and other pollution taxes, trading systems, fuel taxes, and reduced subsidies) as central to promoting greener growth. The IMF argues that when applied effectively, such policies reduce environmental harm, are cost-effective, and strike the right balance between environmental benefits and economic costs. For example, many countries subsidize the production and consumption of fossil fuels rather than charging fees to discourage their use, which in turn would reduce GHG emissions and air pollution and incentivize renewable energy and green jobs. The IMF therefore promotes the use of environmentally oriented fiscal reforms and the sustainable management of renewable resources through its analytical work, technical assistance to member countries, and outreach activities.[72] These efforts can run into domestic obstacles, however, if national authorities are not fully committed to environmental objectives. Thus, the IMF argues, it can integrate environment into its policy dialogue only to the extent that member countries allow it to do so.[73]

Since 2015, the IMF has undertaken a number of initiatives to support the 2030 Sustainable Development Agenda. With regard to the environmental aspects of the Agenda and its SDGs, the IMF supports member countries to address the macroeconomic challenges of climate change. Actions focus on policy advice to contain carbon emissions, including energy price reform and carbon pricing, and on how to support countries vulnerable to natural disasters.[74]

In 2014 a new international financial institution entered the scene, the New Development Bank (NDB). Founded and operated by the BRICS states—Brazil, Russia, India, China, and South Africa—as an alternative to the World Bank and IMF, the NDB seeks to support infrastructure and sustainable development efforts in BRICS and other emerging or underserved economies and to foster greater financial and development cooperation.[75] Together, BRICS states comprise more than 3 billion people, about 40 percent of the world's population, cover more than one-quarter of the world's land area over three continents, and account for more than 25 percent of global gross domestic product (GDP).

Dissatisfaction that their rising economic strength had not yielded commensurate increases in influence at the World Bank and IMF led the BRICS to create a developing country-centered alternative to the existing global development financial institutions.[76] Headquartered in Shanghai, the NDB opened its doors in July 2015 with $50 billion to invest in public infrastructure. Unlike the World Bank, which assigns votes based on capital share, the NDB assigns each participant country one vote, and none has veto power. Although the NDB website lists sustainable development among the initiative's central purposes, as of September 2020, the NDB had neither published specific sector strategies nor released NDB specific indicators and benchmarks related to sustainability, nor has it made any mention of what criteria might be used to assess sustainability.[77] At the same time, its 2019 Annual Report states that since its inception, it had approved $3.5 billion in funding for clean energy projects and that the projects approved in 2019 alone would prevent 2.4 million tons of CO_2 emissions each year that would have occurred if fossil fuel power plants had been built instead.[78]

Regional and Other Multilateral Organizations

Regional and other multilateral organizations also play a role in environmental politics. The most prominent regional organizations have broad political and economic agendas that can also include environmental issues. Others have been specifically established to address environmental concerns, including some, such as the regional fisheries management organizations, that comprise functional groups focused on specific issues.

The EU is the only regional organization whose decisions obligate its members. In the 1950s, six European countries decided to pool their economic resources and set up a system of joint decision making on economic issues. To do so, they formed several organizations, of which the European Economic Community was the most important (the name was eventually shortened to the European Community).[79] The group grew in size, and the 1992 Maastricht Treaty introduced new forms of cooperation among the then twelve members on issues such as defense, justice, and home affairs, including the environment. By adding this intergovernmental cooperation to the existing community system, the Maastricht Treaty created the EU. The EU is unique in that its now twenty-seven member states[80] have established institutions to which they delegate some of their sovereignty so that decisions on specific matters, including agriculture, fisheries, and trade, can be made at the European level. Both individual EU member states and the EU itself, as a "regional economic integration organization," can ratify and join global environmental agreements.[81] During global environmental negotiations, EU states negotiate as a single entity, giving their positions considerable importance.

In 2010, the EU adopted Europe 2020, a ten-year growth strategy that focuses on smart growth (developing an economy based on knowledge and innovation), sustainable growth (promoting a more resource-efficient, greener, and more competitive economy), and inclusive growth (fostering a high-employment economy delivering social and territorial cohesion). The strategy sets goals in the areas of employment, innovation, education, poverty reduction, and climate/energy. The 2020 targets included reducing GHG emissions by 20 percent compared with 1990 levels, increasing the share of renewables in final energy consumption to 20 percent, and increasing energy efficiency by 20 percent.[82]

In 2018, the EU set out a vision for climate neutrality, looking at all the key sectors and exploring pathways for the transition, in line with the Paris Agreement objective to keep the global temperature increase to well below 2°C and pursue efforts to keep it to 1.5°C. The European Parliament endorsed the net-zero GHG objective in its resolution on climate change in March 2019 and its resolution on the European Green Deal in January 2020. The European Green Deal is a road map to boost the efficient use of resources by moving to a clean, circular economy, restore biodiversity, and cut pollution. It outlines the investments needed and the financing tools available and explains how to ensure a just and inclusive transition. As part of the European Green Deal, on March 4, 2020 the Commission proposed the first European Climate Law to enshrine the 2050 climate neutrality target into law.[83]

Other regional organizations have far less of an impact on global environmental policy and politics because their national members are not obligated to implement common policies. At the same time, their permanent secretariats seek to facilitate cooperation and knowledge sharing on many issues, including environmental protection and sustainable development. High-level meetings also provide an opportunity for ministers and heads of governments to meet in person to discuss key issues, sometimes including the environment, and the consensus statements from these meetings can provide insight into regional or national priorities.

The Organization of American States (OAS), one of the oldest regional organizations, was the first to hold a presidential summit specifically focused on the environment when it convened the Summit of the Americas on Sustainable Development in Bolivia in December 1996. The OAS Department of Sustainable Development supports member states' integration of environmental priorities into poverty alleviation and socioeconomic development goals and programs. This includes integrated water management, energy and climate change mitigation, climate change risk management and adaptation, biodiversity protection, sustainable land management, and augmenting environmental laws.

The fifth Summit of the Americas, in Trinidad and Tobago in 2009, focused on environmental sustainability, reaffirming the region's commitment to sustainable development and recognizing the adverse impacts of climate change on the region and the need to reduce GHG emissions.[84] The results of the 2015 Summit of the Americas, held in Panama, included a call to strengthen "progress in the areas of sustainable development and climate change in order to counteract the impacts of climate change, increase the capacity for adaptation of communities and ecosystems vulnerable to climate change, and increase efforts to mitigate GHG emissions."[85] The final communique from the 2018 Summit, held in Lima, Peru, however, regressed significantly from previous OAS summit statements, reflecting the position of the Trump administration. Only one short sentence even made a general reference to sustainable development, and the United States added a footnote containing caveats to implementation of the 2030 Agenda for Sustainable Development.[86]

The African Union includes the promotion of sustainable development as one of its official objectives. At its inaugural summit in 2001, the African Union adopted the New Partnership for Africa's Development (NEPAD) as a blueprint for the continent's future development. NEPAD's primary objectives are eradicating poverty, placing African countries on a path of sustainable growth and development, and halting the continent's marginalization in the globalization process. NEPAD recognizes the need to protect the environment not only for Africa's benefit but also because the continent holds many natural resources of global importance, including a wide range of flora and fauna, paleoanthropological resources, and immense forests that act as carbon sinks. Since these resources could be degraded without support from the international community, implicit in NEPAD's approach are calls for donor countries to support Africa's sustainable development for the sake of both Africans and the international community.

In 2013, African heads of state and government signed Agenda 2063, a vision and action plan to work together to build a prosperous and sustainable Africa over the next 50 years. Agenda 2063 includes calls for Africans to ensure cost-effective, renewable, and sustainable energy for all African households and businesses; to implement sustainable forest management; to act with a sense of urgency on climate change and the environment; and to develop equitable and sustainable use and management of water resources.[87]

Asia-Pacific Economic Cooperation (APEC) was formed in 1989 in response to the growing interdependence among Asia-Pacific economies. Although APEC's primary goal is to champion sustainable economic growth and free trade, its work specifically mentions consideration of three categories of environmental issues: air, atmospheric, and water pollution, especially those related to energy production and use; resource degradation; and demographic shifts, including their impacts on food security and urbanization.

APEC held its first ocean-focused ministerial meeting in 2002 and adopted the Seoul Oceans Declaration.[88] In 2007, APEC leaders adopted a Declaration on Climate Change, Energy Security, and Clean Development, which supported a post-2012 international climate change arrangement that "leads to reduced global emissions of greenhouse gases."[89] In 2011, members committed to reducing energy intensity in the region by 45 percent by 2030. In 2012, APEC leaders agreed to support reducing tariffs on fifty-four environmental products, including solar panels and wind turbines. In 2014, members agreed to work toward doubling the share of renewables in APEC's energy mix by 2030, including in power generation. Priority topics discussed by the government leaders in 2019 included ocean pollution, especially plastics, and illegal fishing.

The Group of 77 (G-77) functions as the "negotiating arm of the developing countries" within the UN system.[90] Established in 1964 by seventy-seven developing countries at the end of the first session of the UN Conference on Trade and Development (UNCTAD), the G-77 now includes more than 130 countries, but the original name remains because of its historical significance. China is an associate member and often plays an influential role. As the largest developing-country coalition in the UN, the G-77 provides developing countries with the means to articulate and promote their collective interests, enhance joint negotiating capacity, and promote economic and technical cooperation.[91] Since the early 1990s, when developing countries became far more involved in the negotiation of multilateral environmental agreements (MEAs), the G-77 has played a key role, particularly on issues related to financial and technical assistance. Although the interests of developing counties are not uniform on many environmental issues, including climate change (see Chapter 3), when they are able to speak with a single voice, they represent a powerful coalition.

The thirty-seven members of the Organisation for Economic Co-operation and Development (OECD) include all of the major industrialized countries, including many EU members, and Chile, Colombia, Israel, Mexico, South Korea, and Turkey. The OECD Secretariat promotes sustainable consumption and production within member states, conducts policy-related research, and provides member-relevant information on climate change, transportation, energy, trade and the environment, subsidies, and other issues.

The Pacific Regional Environment Programme (SPREP) is a regional organization created explicitly to address environmental issues. SPREP promotes cooperation and provides assistance in the Pacific region aimed at protecting and improving the environment and ensuring sustainable development.[92] Its twenty-six members include twenty-one small Pacific Island states and territories and five developed countries (Australia, France, New Zealand, the United Kingdom, and the United States) with direct interests in the region.

SPREP's action program aims to build national capacity and action in four priority areas: climate change resilience, island and ocean ecosystems, improving waste management and pollution control, and effective environmental governance.

Nongovernmental and Civil Society Organizations

The emergence of environmental issues as a major concern in world politics coincided with the emergence of NGOs as important actors in environmental politics.[93] Although business organizations are sometimes included in some definitions of NGOs, we use the term here to denote an independent, nonprofit organization not beholden to a government or a profit-making organization.

NGO influence on global environmental politics stems from three principal factors. First, NGOs often possess expert knowledge and innovative thinking about global environmental issues acquired from years of focused specialization. Second, NGOs are acknowledged to be dedicated to goals that transcend national or sectoral interests, providing them with legitimacy and moral standing. Third, some NGOs represent substantial constituencies within particular countries and thus can command attention from policymakers because of their potential ability to mobilize people to influence policies and even affect the outcome of tight elections.

In industrialized countries, most NGOs active in global environmental politics fall into one of three categories: organizations affiliated with international NGOs—that is, NGOs with branches in more than one country; large national organizations focused primarily on domestic environmental issues; and think tanks, or research institutes, whose influence comes primarily from publishing studies and proposals for action.

Some international NGOs are loose federations of national affiliates; others have more centralized structures. Friends of the Earth International, based in Amsterdam, is a confederation of more than seventy national member groups, half of which are in developing countries, and 2 million members and supporters.[94] At biannual meetings, delegates democratically select priority policies and activities for the federation. Founded in 1971, Greenpeace is one of the largest international NGOs. Its global network of twenty-seven independent national and regional Greenpeace organizations works in more than fifty-five countries and has more than 2.8 million financial supporters and members.[95] Its international activities are tightly organized by a well-staffed headquarters (also in Amsterdam) and guided by issues and strategies determined at an annual meeting.

WWF (formerly known as the World Wildlife Fund and the World Wide Fund for Nature) is one of the world's largest and most experienced independent conservation organizations. Established nearly sixty years ago and headquartered in Switzerland, WWF has 5 million members worldwide and works in 100 countries. WWF's work has evolved from saving species and landscapes to addressing the larger global threats and forces that impact them. WWF organizes its current work around six key areas: climate, food, forests, freshwater, oceans, and wildlife.[96]

The European Environmental Bureau, organized in 1974, is now a confederation of more than 160 environmental organizations based in thirty-five EU and neighboring countries, representing more than 30 million members and supporters. The organization addresses Europe's most pressing environmental problems via agenda setting, monitoring issues and policies, advising, and seeking to influence the way the EU and other states deal with these issues.[97]

The second category of NGOs includes the big US environmental organizations, almost all of which have international programs. Some, such as the Sierra Club, National Audubon Society, Nature Conservancy, and National Wildlife Federation, were formed in the late nineteenth and early twentieth centuries around conservation issues. Others, including the

Environmental Defense Fund and the Natural Resources Defense Council, arose in the early 1970s with the aim of using and changing legal and regulatory processes to protect the environment, with an initial focus on air and water pollution. Other organizations with more specific agendas are also active internationally on their issues, including Defenders of Wildlife and the Humane Society.

Environmental think tanks, normally funded by private donations or contracts, rely primarily on their technical expertise and research programs to influence environmental policy. A prominent example is the World Resources Institute, which publishes highly respected research reports on specific issues. The International Institute for Environment and Development in London drew early attention to the connection between the environment and poverty in developing countries. The International Institute for Sustainable Development (IISD) of Canada focuses on economic law and policy, resilience, energy, water, and sustainable development knowledge and reporting services. In a few countries, government-funded but nevertheless independent institutes seek to influence both the policies of their own governments and international negotiations, such as the Stockholm Environment Institute of Sweden.

Environmentalism in many developing countries grew out of what some of its founders saw as a "lopsided, iniquitous and environmentally destructive process of development" and is often interlinked with questions of human rights, ethnicity, and distributive justice.[98] Southern NGOs traditionally stress land-use issues, forest management, fishing rights, and the redistribution of power over natural resources.[99] They are often more critical of consumerism and uncontrolled economic development than their colleagues in the North. An increasing number of southern NGOs, especially those based in low-lying coastal areas or small islands, are focused on climate change. High levels of urban air and water pollution also draw increasing NGO attention in many countries. Some developing-country NGOs initially became involved in international policy issues through opposition to multilateral bank projects and government policies that displace villages or threaten forests and have tended to regard multinational corporations as enemies of the environment. Critical of their governments on environmental and sometimes other domestic policies, NGO members committed to environmental protection have often been harassed, subjected to political repression, jailed, and even killed.[100] In some countries, however, they have also acquired political legitimacy and a measure of influence on national environmental issues.

India's environmental movement dates back to the Chipko movement, which started in the Garhwal Himalaya in April 1973. Between 1973 and 1980, more than a dozen instances were recorded in which men, women, and children threatened to hug trees rather than allow them to be logged for export. Unlike environmentalists in the North, however, Indian activists were not interested in saving the trees as an end in itself, but in using the forest for agricultural and household requirements.[101] Today, India has a large number of NGOs. Examples include the Center for Science and Environment, which researches, lobbies for, and seeks to communicate the urgency of development that is both sustainable and equitable. The Wildlife Trust of India seeks to protect India's wildlife, especially endangered species and threatened habitats. Established in 1974, the Energy and Resource Institute (TERI) is perhaps the world's largest developing-country nongovernmental institution focused on sustainability, with a staff of more than 1200 scientists, sociologists, economists, engineers, and others working from six offices throughout India.

Some of the most important aspects of Brazil's environmental movement can be traced to the 1980s, when rubber tappers began organizing to resist the destruction of the Amazon forests that support them and that they had tended to for decades. In 1989, after a cattle rancher murdered Chico Mendes, a key leader of the rubber tappers, popular support grew, and the Brazilian government began to take more meaningful action. The country set aside extractive reserves to protect forests where tapping and other sustainable extraction could continue. Today, numerous Brazilian NGOs work with indigenous and local communities to end deforestation, promote forest certification, and protect local livelihoods.

The Green Belt Movement, based in Kenya, is an influential grassroots NGO that empowers communities, particularly women, to conserve the environment and improve livelihoods. Founded in 1977 by the late Wangari Maathai (under the auspices of the National Council of Women of Kenya), it aims to create a society of people who consciously work for the continued improvement of their environment. Programs include tree planting, biodiversity conservation, civic and environmental education and advocacy, food security, and networking and capacity building for women and girls. In 2004, Maathai received the Nobel Peace Prize for her efforts with the Green Belt Movement—the first Nobel Peace Prize given to an environmentalist.[102]

While many environmental and development battles continue to be fought at the community level in developing countries, some NGOs and coalitions in those countries also tackle a broader range of environmental and development issues. Third World Network, for example, is an independent, nonprofit, international network of organizations and individuals that focuses on the needs and rights of peoples in developing countries and promoting a fair distribution of global resources and an ecologically sustainable development that fulfill human needs. To these ends, Third World Network conducts research into economic, social, and environmental issues, publishes books and reports, organizes seminars, and represents southern interests and perspectives at international fora, including UN conferences. Headquartered in Penang, Malaysia, Third World Network also has regional offices in Ghana, Malaysia, Switzerland, and Uruguay and researchers located in Beijing, Delhi, Jakarta, Manila, and New York.[103]

International coalitions of NGOs working on a specific environmental issue, including some with both northern and southern NGO members, have also become a means of increasing NGO influence. Among the most prominent is the Climate Action Network, which is very active during climate change negotiations and has more than 700 member organizations in ninety countries that work to promote government and individual action to limit climate change. The International POPs Elimination Network (IPEN) works to improve chemical policies and raise public awareness with the goal that hazardous substances will no longer be produced, used, or disposed of in ways that harm human health and the environment. Founded by a small number of NGOs, IPEN was formally launched in June 1998 during the first session of formal negotiations on creating a global treaty to control POPs. The network mobilized grassroots support for a global treaty and created a forum for activists from around the world to participate in the negotiations. Since then, IPEN has expanded significantly and broadened its foci, becoming a coalition of more than 700 public health, environmental, consumer, and other NGOs in more than 100 countries, and actively participates in Basel, Rotterdam, Stockholm, and Minamata Convention meetings. IPEN is also active in local efforts to combat toxic pollutants, with more than 100 projects in fifty countries.[104] The Antarctic and Southern Oceans Coalition brings together more than thirty organizations seeking to maintain Antarctica, its surrounding islands, and the Southern Ocean as unspoiled wilderness.

The International Indigenous Forum on Biodiversity (IIFB) was established in 1996 by the indigenous peoples of seven world regions (Africa; Asia; the Arctic; Latin America and the Caribbean; North America; the Pacific; and Eastern Europe, Central Europe, and the Caucasus) to facilitate the full and effective participation of indigenous peoples in the Convention on Biological Diversity. IIFB is an example of increasingly successful efforts by indigenous peoples and their supporters to have their voices heard in international fora and respect paid to the unique and useful knowledge they have regarding particular ecosystems. A number of such groups participate in the work of environmental conventions, including the UNFCCC Local Communities and Indigenous Peoples Platform in the climate talks and the Inuit Circumpolar Conference in the chemicals and mercury regimes.

One of the most important organizations through which NGOs influence environmental politics is the International Union for Conservation of Nature (IUCN). The IUCN is

Photo 2.4 At the 2017 UN Climate Change Conference, Indigenous Peoples underscored their vulnerabilities to climate change and the need to recognize their rights.

Courtesy Kiara Worth, IISD/*Earth Negotiations Bulletin*, http://enb.iisd.org

the world's oldest and largest global environmental organization, with more than 1300 government and NGO member organizations from over 170 countries and more than 15,000 volunteer experts. Its work is supported by almost 1000 staff in forty-five offices and hundreds of partners in public, NGO, and private sectors around the world. Governed by a general assembly of delegates from its member organizations (governments, NGOs, and others) that meets every three years, the IUCN has had a major influence on global agreements on wildlife conservation. The IUCN has been successful in helping to draft environmental treaties and assisting in monitoring their implementation.[105]

Influencing Environmental Regime Formation

NGOs can attempt to influence the development, expansion, and implementation of international regimes in various ways, including:

- Raising public awareness about particular issues and conducting education campaigns
- Influencing the global environmental agenda by defining a new issue or redefining an old one
- Lobbying governments to accept a more advanced position on an issue
- Proposing draft text to be included in conventions in advance of negotiations
- Participating and/or lobbying in international negotiations
- Generating media attention
- Supporting ratification and implementation of an environmental treaty by governments
- Bringing lawsuits to compel national action on an issue
- Organizing consumer boycotts to pressure international corporations

- Providing reporting services
- Assisting implementation of the regime, particularly in developing countries
- Monitoring the implementation of conventions and reporting to the secretariat and/
  or the parties

Examples of NGOs influencing the global environmental agenda include the role played by WWF and Conservation International in building government and public support for banning commerce in African elephant ivory. In particular, the groups published a detailed report on the problem, circulating it to the parties to CITES, and engaged in public education campaigns. Greenpeace's monitoring of and reporting on the toxic waste trade was a key factor in encouraging a coalition of countries to push for a complete ban on North–South waste trade under the Basel Convention. The Inuit Circumpolar Conference, an NGO representing 150,000 Inuit of Alaska, Canada, Greenland, and Chukotka (Russia), participated in negotiations that produced the Stockholm Convention on Persistent Organic Pollutants, and their stories concerning the dangers that toxic chemicals pose for the future of their people put a human face on the need to eliminate POPs.

Pressing for changes in the policy of a major actor is sometimes the best way for NGOs to influence an international regime. In efforts to protect the ozone layer, during the late 1970s a group of US environmental organizations lobbied for a domestic ban on aerosols and the regulation of CFCs. Because they later lobbied for a total phase-out of CFCs before negotiations on the Montreal Protocol even began, they contributed to US international leadership on this issue. Similarly, three US NGOs working with pro-treaty biotechnology firms influenced the Clinton administration's decision to reverse the Bush administration's position and sign the CBD (although the United States Senate has not ratified the treaty).[106]

Although effective consumer boycotts are rare in international environmental politics (they are more common on local and national issues), an NGO-organized boycott of Icelandic products because of Iceland's pro-whaling stand, including protests at fast-food and supermarket chains that sold fish caught by Iceland's fishing fleet, contributed to a temporary two-year halt to that country's whaling.[107] Other notable NGO-led boycotts include Mitsubishi making concessions on forest policy following a campaign spearheaded by the Rainforest Action Network, and Shell agreeing to dispose of its Brent Spar offshore oil platform on land rather than dumping it at sea as originally planned.[108]

NGOs can influence international regimes in a more specialized way by developing ideas or draft text for part of a convention or amendment and circulating and lobbying for them in advance of the negotiations in the hope that a national delegation will include it among their proposals. Although an exceptional case, the Convention Concerning the Protection of the World Cultural and Natural Heritage, signed in 1972 in Paris, was based on a draft produced by IUCN. CITES, adopted in 1973, was also the result of an IUCN initiative that went through three drafts over nearly a decade.[109]

NGOs are especially active and well organized in lobbying at international negotiations. The COPs to most environmental conventions permit NGO observers, enabling NGOs to attend and participate in the proceedings. Certain NGOs specialize in particular conventions and over the years acquire a high level of technical and legal expertise. The Humane Society of the United States has been lobbying at meetings of the International Whaling Commission (IWC) since 1973, and Greenpeace has been active in the COP to the London Convention since the early 1980s. The Climate Action Network is active in climate change negotiations. IPEN is a very active participant during negotiations related to the Stockholm and Rotterdam Conventions.

NGOs also seek to influence international conferences by staging protests and attracting media attention. Greenpeace is noted in this regard, including suspending banners protesting forest destruction and inaction on climate change. Other environmental, youth, indigenous peoples, and women climate activists regularly stage protests at climate change and chemical negotiations. Fridays for Future, for example, has been staging weekly climate strikes since August 2018, when Greta Thunberg began a school strike for climate. Her actions sparked an international awakening, with fellow students and activists uniting around the world to protest outside their local parliaments and city halls. In 2018 and 2019 the students took their climate strike to the UNFCCC. The 2020 COP was postponed due to COVID-19.

NGOs also influence international conferences by providing scientific and technical information and new arguments to delegates. In the process leading up to the whaling moratorium, NGOs supplied factual information on violations of the whaling convention as well as scientific information not otherwise available to the delegations.[110] In some circumstances, governments have included NGOs on their delegations or in discussions prior to negotiations, which give NGOs the opportunity to influence the resulting positions. The Foundation for International Environmental Law and Development (FIELD) has provided advice and legal expertise to AOSIS in climate change negotiations.[111] Greenpeace provided technical support to African countries calling for a ban on the dumping of hazardous wastes in developing countries during negotiation of the Basel Convention.

NGOs can also provide reporting services during global environmental negotiations and related conferences. NGOs at selected UN-sponsored environmental conferences have published *ECO*, which provides a combination of news stories and commentary. The *Earth Negotiations Bulletin*, published by IISD, has provided objective reports from many different environment and development negotiations since 1992.[112] Were a government to attempt to provide such information, the reports would likely be perceived as biased. If the UN or a formal secretariat published daily reports, they would have the status of official documents, and member governments would have difficulty agreeing on their content, style, and tone. However, because the NGO community, including impartial research institutions like IISD, is already providing the information, governments and international organizations have little incentive to step in.[113]

NGOs can sometimes assist governments in treaty implementation. This can include offering assistance in drafting national legislation, providing technical and scientific assistance on relevant issues, and brokering the provision of financial support. NGOs can also influence regimes by monitoring compliance with an agreement once it goes into effect. Investigation and reporting by NGOs can put pressure on parties that are violating provisions of an agreement. They can demonstrate the need for more effective enforcement mechanisms (or for creation of a mechanism where none exists) or help build support for further elaboration or strengthening of the existing regime rules.

The international Trade Records Analysis of Flora and Fauna in Commerce (TRAFFIC), a joint wildlife trade monitoring program of WWF and IUCN, plays a vital role in helping to monitor compliance with CITES bans on trade in endangered species.[114] The World Resources Institute and other NGOs in the United States and the EU produce detailed reviews of national climate action plans. Greenpeace's aggressive reporting of hazardous wastes dumped in violation of the Basel Convention helped build support for a full ban on international shipping of such wastes to non-OECD countries.

Business and Industry

Private business firms, especially multinational corporations, are important and interested actors in global environmental politics. Their core activities, although often essential, consume resources and produce pollution, and environmental regulations can directly affect their economic interests. Corporations also possess significant assets for influencing global environmental politics. They enjoy good access to decision makers in most governments and international organizations, can deploy impressive technical expertise on issues related to their operations, have paid lobbyists and national and international industrial associations that represent their interests, and possess significant financial and technical resources that are important for developing solutions.

Corporations often oppose national and international policies that they believe will impose significant costs on them or otherwise reduce expected profits. At times, corporations have worked to weaken proposed or existing global environmental policies on ozone protection, climate change, whaling, hazardous wastes, chemicals, fisheries, and other issues. Corporations in many countries have provided governments with specific information that can result in those countries successfully pressing for specific exemptions to certain control measures on toxic chemicals in the Stockholm Convention and the use of mercury in particular products and processes under the Minamata Convention.[115] At other times, corporations appear to support international environmental policy but in reality are doing so because it would result in weaker regulations on their activities than the regulations they would otherwise expect to be imposed domestically.

However, corporate interests vary significantly across companies and sectors, and many corporations have supported creating stronger national or international environmental policy. Examples include companies that make products or processes with the potential to replace others that harm the environment, or companies whose operations, locations, markets, or other interests will be harmed by further environmental degradation. Corporations without a direct economic interest in an issue also might support environmental initiatives to enhance their reputation, to attract attention from potential customers, or when senior executives believe such action is simply the right thing to do.

Similarly, corporations in countries with existing strong domestic regulations on an activity with a global environmental dimension tend to support international agreements that will impose similar standards on competitors abroad. For example, on fisheries management issues, the US and Japanese fishing industries are more strictly regulated on aspects of high seas fishing, particularly quotas on bluefin tuna and other highly migratory species, than other Asian fishing states (Republic of Korea, China, Taiwan, and Indonesia); their respective fishing industries therefore pushed the United States and Japan to take strong positions on regulation of high seas fishing capacity in FAO negotiations in 1998.

A particular industry's interests on a proposed global environmental regime are often far from monolithic. On ozone, climate change, biodiversity, and fisheries, companies have often split along national lines or among industry sectors or even subsectors. When companies see a positive stake in a global environmental agreement, they can dilute the influence of other companies that seek to weaken it. In 1992, the Industrial Biotechnology Association opposed the Biodiversity Convention because it feared that the provisions on intellectual property rights would legally condone existing violations of those rights.[116] But the issue was not a high priority for most of the industry, and two of its leading member corporations, Merck and Genentech, believed the convention would benefit them by encouraging developing countries to negotiate agreements with companies for access to genetic resources. After those companies joined environmentalists in calling for the United States to sign the convention in 1993, the Industrial Biotechnology Association came out in favor of signing it.[117]

Similarly, US industries seeking to promote alternatives to fossil fuels began lobbying at UNFCCC meetings in 1994 to reduce the influence of pro-fossil fuel industries, which had previously monopolized industry views on the issue. Similarly, because global insurance companies are concerned about the increased hurricane and storm damage caused by climate change, they support GHG emissions reductions and have tried to raise awareness among corporations regarding the dangers of climate change, including by conducting research projects on its negative economic consequences as well as the future impacts of storms and floods. Companies that made alternatives to ozone-depleting chemicals were very important in supporting the strengthening of the Montreal Protocol,

Influence on Regime Formation

Business and industry affect global environmental regimes by influencing national negotiation positions and by undertaking business activities that either weaken a regime or contribute to its effectiveness. To influence the creation, content, review, or expansion of a regime, corporations often attempt to do the following:

- Shape the definition of the issue under negotiation in a manner favorable to their interests
- Fund and distribute targeted research and other information supportive of their interests
- Initiate advertising campaigns to influence public opinion
- Seek to shape individual governments to adopt particular negotiating or policy positions through lobbying and, in some countries, campaign and other financial or political support
- Hire lobbying firms and work through national and international industry associations to lobby national governments and IGOs
- Provide information and lobby delegations during international negotiations

In a noted example, corporations had great success during the issue-definition phase associated with the creation of the International Convention for the Prevention of Pollution of the Sea by Oil (1954). The major oil companies and global shipping interests (most of which the oil companies owned, directly or indirectly) were the only actors with the technical expertise to make detailed proposals on maritime oil pollution. The technical papers submitted by the International Chamber of Shipping, comprising thirty national associations of ship owners, and the Oil Companies International Marine Forum, representing the interests of major oil companies, defined the terms of the discussion[118] and ensured that the convention would be compatible with oil and shipping interests—and ineffective in preventing oil pollution of the oceans.

In most global environmental issues, corporations seek to employ their domestic political and economic clout in attempts to ensure that governments do not adopt strong policies adversely affecting their interests. The domestic US industry most strongly opposed to a ban on hazardous waste trade, the secondary-metals industry, helped persuade US officials to block such a ban in the negotiation of the Basel Convention. And on ozone depletion, Japan agreed to a phase-out of CFCs only after some of its largest electronics firms indicated that they could eliminate their use.

For many years, industrial lobbies in the United States succeeded in reducing the executive branch's flexibility in climate change negotiations. Some of the most powerful trade associations launched the Global Climate Information Project in 1997. Through a multimillion-dollar print and television advertising campaign, the project cast doubt on the desirability of emissions controls in the Kyoto Protocol, then entering the final stages of negotiation, by arguing that such controls would raise the price of gasoline, heating oil, and consumer goods and reduce the competitiveness of American businesses. An alliance of business and labor interests succeeded in persuading the US Senate to vote 95–0 for a resolution stating that the United States should not participate in a climate treaty that would require GHG reductions without similar commitments from China and other large developing countries or that would result in serious harm to the US economy.[119] The influence of the US oil, gas, and coal industries then influenced the Bush administration's continued rejection of the Kyoto Protocol and the Trump administration's decision to withdraw from the Paris Climate Agreement.

Industry associations have been actively involved in influencing negotiations on several other global environmental regimes. Sometimes, industries with particular technical expertise or relatively unchallenged influence over the issue have been part of a key country's delegation. For example, the Japanese commissioner to the IWC was often the president of the

Japanese Whaling Association.[120] US and Canadian food manufacturers have participated on US delegations to the FAO's Codex Alimentarius Commission, which sets international food standards.[121] The Israeli delegation to several key ozone-layer negotiations included officials from a methyl bromide manufacturer during talks on expanding controls on the chemical.[122] The Global Climate Coalition, an industry group, worked closely with the delegations from the United States and Saudi Arabia during the negotiation of the UNFCCC.

Like NGOs, corporate representatives influence negotiations by providing information and analysis to the delegations most sympathetic to their cause. For example, at different times during the climate change negotiations, coal and oil interests actively advised the US, Russian, and Saudi delegations on how to oppose or weaken proposals that they believed would harm the fossil fuel industry.[123] Industry groups had a particularly strong presence at the negotiating sessions for the Cartagena Protocol on Biosafety, with eight industry groups represented at the first round of negotiations in 1996 and twenty such groups from many different countries present at the final meetings in 1999.[124] Individual corporations, among them Monsanto, DuPont, and Syngenta (formerly Novartis and Zeneca), also sent their own representatives to the meetings. Many industry representatives participate in meetings of the Stockholm and Rotterdam Conventions, submitting information and speaking during the negotiations as well as meeting with particular delegations.[125]

Corporations may facilitate or delay, strengthen or weaken global environmental regimes by actions that directly affect the environment. They may take these actions unilaterally or based on agreements reached with their respective governments. Such actions can be crucial to a government's ability to commit itself to a regime-strengthening policy.

For example, the US chemical industry delayed movement toward an international regime for regulating ozone-depleting CFCs in the early 1980s, in part by reducing its own research efforts on CFC substitutes following the election of President Ronald Reagan, whose administration generally opposed additional environmental regulations.[126] Later, after developing effective substitutes, DuPont gave significant impetus to an accelerated timetable for a CFC phase-out by unilaterally pledging to cease its production of CFCs well ahead of the schedule already agreed on by the Montreal Protocol Parties. In 1989, Nissan and Toyota pledged to eliminate CFCs from their cars and manufacturing processes as early as the mid-1990s. In 1992, Ford Motor Company pledged to eliminate 90 percent of CFC use from its manufacturing processes worldwide by the end of that year and to eliminate all CFCs from its air conditioners and manufacturing by the end of 1994.

Early in the climate change negotiations, the Japanese auto industry, which accounted for 20 percent of Japan's CO_2 emissions, adopted a goal of improving fuel efficiency by 8.5 percent by 2000, encouraging the Japanese government to commit to stabilize national CO_2 emissions at 1990 levels by 2000.[127] More recently, numerous corporations around the world have pledged to reduce their GHG emissions and to improve their environmental accounting.[128]

Industry and Nonregime Issues

Corporations can also have significant influence on a global environmental issues in the absence of a regime or regime negotiations. For example, the agrochemical industry once enjoyed strong influence on the FAO's Plant Protection Service, which was responsible for the organization's pesticide activities. The industry's international trade association even had a joint program with the FAO to promote pesticide use worldwide until the 1970s.[129] This influence was instrumental in carrying out the industry's main strategy for avoiding binding international restrictions on sales of pesticides in developing countries. Instead of binding rules, the FAO drafted a voluntary code of conduct on pesticide distribution and use between 1982 and 1985 in close consultation with the industry.

In a different type of example, in 1991, at the request of UN Conference on Environment and Development (UNCED/Earth Summit) Secretary-General Maurice Strong, Swiss industrialist Stephan Schmidheiny enlisted forty-eight corporate chief executives from all over the world to set up the Business Council for Sustainable Development to support the objectives of the Earth Summit. The group issued a declaration calling for changes in consumption patterns and for the prices of goods to reflect environmental costs of production, use, recycling, and disposal.[130] Four years later, it merged with the World Industry Council for the Environment, an initiative of the International Chamber of Commerce, to become the World Business Council for Sustainable Development (WBCSD), which has become a coalition of more than 200 international companies committed to sustainable development. With members from thirty-five countries and more than twenty major industrial sectors, the WBCSD addresses a range of issues, including corporate social responsibility, access to clean water, capacity building, sustainable livelihoods, harmonization of trade law with MEAs, and development of public–private partnerships in key areas, including energy and climate.[131]

Conclusion

State and nonstate actors play important roles in the creation, content, expansion, review, and implementation of national and international environmental policy. State actors play the primary roles in determining the outcomes of issues at stake in global environmental politics, but nonstate actors—IGOs, treaty secretariats, scientists, NGOs, civil society, and corporations—influence the policies of individual state actors toward global environmental issues as well as the international negotiation process itself. Whether a state adopts the role of lead state, supporting state, swing state, or veto state on a particular issue depends primarily on domestic political and economic factors and the potential positive and negative impacts the proposed regime could have on its political, economic, environmental, human health, diplomatic, and other interests.

IGOs, especially UNEP, have played important roles in regime formation by helping to set the international agenda and by sponsoring and shaping negotiations on global environmental regimes and soft-law norms. The Bretton Woods financial institutions (World Bank and IMF) and various UN agencies, particularly UNDP, influence state development strategies through financial, development, and technical assistance. IGOs also can influence state policy through research and advocacy of specific norms at the global level. Treaty secretariats, a subset of IGOs, can influence the behavior of political actors by acting as knowledge brokers and through the creation, support, and shaping of intergovernmental negotiations and cooperation.

NGOs and scientists influence environmental regimes by defining issues. NGOs and civil society lobby at intergovernmental negotiations, provide information and reporting services, propose convention text, and monitor the implementation of agreements. They have also sought to change the policies and structure of major international institutions, such as the World Bank and the World Trade Organization, with varying degrees of success. They have been more successful when the target institution depends on funding from a key state that the NGOs can influence and less successful when the institution is relatively independent or has no tradition of permitting NGO participation in its processes.

Corporations and industry groups influence regimes by utilizing their technical expertise, privileged access to certain government ministries, and political clout with legislative bodies in attempts to either weaken or strengthen particular aspects of a regime. They can also affect the ability of the international community to meet regime goals by their own actions. They often maximize their political effectiveness in shaping the outcome of a global environmental issue when they can avert negotiations on a binding regime altogether.

Notes

1 David Day, *The Whale War* (Vancouver: Douglas and MacIntyre, 1987), 103–107.

2 Data from the Indonesian Ministry of Forest's *Production Forest Utilization Quarterly Report* in 2011. See "7 Conglomerates Control 9M ha of Land in Indonesia," mongabay.com, May 5, 2011, http://news.mongabay.com/2011/0504-indonesia_conglomerates.html. The REDD program seeks to create economic incentives for developing countries to protect and better manage their forest resources, thereby helping to combat climate change. For information, see www.un-redd.org.

3 Richard Benedick, *Ozone Diplomacy: New Directions in Safeguarding the Planet*, 2nd ed. (Cambridge, MA: Harvard University Press, 1998), 59.

4 The German Green Party was routed in the first all-German elections since 1932 because it opposed reunification. It began to rebound in the mid-1990s and then won thirty-four seats in the German parliament in 1998 and made history by becoming part of a coalition government with the Social Democratic Party.

5 Detlev Sprinz and Tapani Vaahtoranta, "The Interest-Based Explanation of International Environmental Policy," *International Organization* vol. 48, no. 1 (1994): 77–105.

6 Brian Gareau, *From Precaution to Profit: Contemporary Challenges to Environmental Protection in the Montreal Protocol* (New Haven, CT: Yale University Press, 2013) details the development of and strongly criticizes the methyl bromide exemptions.

7 Yannis Paleokrassas, quoted in *Energy, Economics and Climate Change* vol. 4, no. 7 (July 1994): 14. On EU ambitions for global leadership on the environment, see Brian Wynne, "Implementation of Greenhouse Gas Reductions in the European Community: Institutional and Cultural Factors," *Global Environmental Change Report* vol. 3 (March 1993): 101–128.

8 Eugene Robinson and Michael Weisskopf, "Bonn Pushes Tough Stand on Warming; U.S. Puts Pressure on 3 Allies to Drop 2nd Stiff Initiative," *Washington Post*, June 9, 1992, A1.

9 Philippe Le Prestre and Evelyne Dufault, "Canada and the Kyoto Protocol on GHGs," *ISUMA* vol. 2, no. 4 (Winter 2001): 40.

10 Bill Curry and Shawn McCarthy, "Canada Formally Abandons Kyoto Protocol on Climate Change," *Globe and Mail*, December 12, 2011.

11 United Nations Environment Programme (UNEP), *Climate Commitments of Subnational Actors and Business: A Quantitative Assessment of the Emission Reduction Impact* (Nairobi: UNEP, 2015), 11.

12 United Nations, *World Urbanization Prospects: The 2018 Revision – Key Facts*, https://population.un.org/wup/Publications/Files/WUP2018-KeyFacts.pdf, viewed June 22, 2019.

13 IPCC, *Climate Change 2014: Synthesis Report. Contribution of Working Groups I, II and III to the Fifth Assessment Report of the Intergovernmental Panel on Climate Change* (Geneva: Intergovernmental Panel on Climate Change, 2014).

14 World Bank Group, *Cities and Climate Change: An Urgent Agenda—Part III: Cities' Contribution to Climate Change* (Washington, DC: World Bank, 2010), 15.

15 Daniel Moran, et al., "Carbon Footprints of 13,000 Cities," *Environmental Research Letters* vol. 13 (2018): 1–9.

16 For information, see the US Conference of Mayors Climate Protection Center's website: www.usmayors.org/mayors-climate-protection-center/.

17 See www.globalcovenantofmayors.org/.

18 Carbon Neutral Cities Alliance, https://carbonneutralcities.org/.

19 See www.c40.org/about.

20 Rowena Mason, "Most of Britain's Major Cities Pledge to Run on Green Energy by 2050," *Guardian*, November 23, 2015; Sierra Club, "100% Commitments in Cities, Counties and States," www.sierraclub.org/ready-for-100/commitments.

21 See www.usclimatealliance.org/.

22 National Conference of State Legislatures, "State Renewable Portfolio Standards and Goals," www.ncsl.org/research/energy/renewable-portfolio-standards.aspx.

23 Sierra Club, "Oregon Governor Kate Brown Signs Historic Coal Transition Bill into Law," press release, March 11, 2016, http://content.sierraclub.org/press-releases/2016/03/oregon-governor-kate-brown-signs-historic-coal-transition-bill-law.

24 Devashree Saha and Dan Lashof, "Pennsylvania Is Joining RGGI. Here's Why That Matters," World Resources Institute, October 10, 2019, www.wri.org/blog/2019/10/pennsylvania-joining-rggi-heres-why-matters.

25 For details, see www.rggi.org. For analysis of the health impacts, see Abt Associates, *Analysis of the Public Health Impacts of the Regional Greenhouse Gas Initiative* (Cambridge, MA: Abt Associates, 2017).

26 "NSW Government Action on Climate Change," https://climatechange.environment.nsw.gov.au/About-climate-change-in-NSW/NSW-Government-action-on-climate-change.

27 British Columbia, *British Columbia's Carbon Tax*, 2019, https://www2.gov.bc.ca/gov/content/environment/climate-change/planning-and-action/carbon-tax.

28 Province of Quebec, "A Brief Look at the Quebec Cap and Trade System for Emission Allowances," 2014, www.mddelcc.gouv.qc.ca/changements/carbone/documents-spede/in-brief.pdf.

29 The World Bank, *Annual Report 2019* (Washington: The World Bank, 2019).

30 United Nations Environment Assembly of the UNEP, *Proposed Programme of Work and Budget for the Biennium 2018–2019*, UNEP/EA/2/6, April 8, 2016.

31 For a similar discussion that uses different terms, see David Downie, "UNEP and the Montreal Protocol: New Roles for International Organizations in Regime Creation and Change," in *International Organizations and Environmental Policy*, eds. Robert Bartlett, Priya Kurian, and Madhu Malik (Westport, CT: Greenwood, 1995).

32 Richard Benedick, "The Ozone Protocol: A New Global Diplomacy," *Conservation Foundation Letter* vol. 4 (1989): 6–7; and Benedick, *Ozone Diplomacy*, 109–110.

33 UNEP, *State of the Environment and Contribution of the United Nations Environment Programme to Addressing Substantive Environmental Challenges: Report of the Executive Director*, UNEP/GC.23/3, October 21, 2004, https://digitallibrary.un.org/record/541817/files/UNEP_GC_23_3-EN.pdf?version=1.

34 See UNEP, *United Nations Environment Programme Medium-Term Strategy 2010–2013*, UNEP/GCSS.X/8, 2007, www.unep.org/PDF/FinalMTSGCSS-X-8.pdf; and UNEP, *United Nations Environment Programme Medium-Term Strategy 2014–2017*, www.unep.org/pdf/MTS_2014–2017_Final.pdf.

35 See United Nations (UN), *Report of the Governing Council of the United Nations Environment Programme on Its Twelfth Special Session and the Implementation of Section IV.C, Entitled "Environmental Pillar in the Context of Sustainable Development," of the Outcome Document of the United Nations Conference on Sustainable Development*, resolution 67/213 (March 15, 2013), www.un.org/en/ga/search/view_doc.asp?symbol=A/RES/67/213; and UN, *Change of the Designation of the Governing Council of the United Nations Environment Programme*, resolution 67/251 (July 25, 2013).

36 Elizabeth Dowdeswell was UNEP's first female executive director, serving from 1992 to 1998.

37 Andrew Hurrell and Benedict Kingsbury, eds., *The International Politics of the Environment: Actors, Interests, and Institutions* (Oxford: Clarendon, 1992), 2; Pamela Chasek, *Earth Negotiations: Analyzing Thirty Years of Environmental Diplomacy* (Tokyo: United Nations University Press, 2001).

38 United Nations Development Programme, *UNDP Strategic Plan 2018–2021*, DP/2017/38, October 17, 2017, 1, https://undocs.org/DP/2017/38.

39 Gunnar Sjöstedt and Bertram Spector, conclusion to *International Environmental Negotiation*, ed. Gunnar Sjöstedt (Newbury Park, CA: Sage, 1993), 306.

40 Pamela Chasek, "Scientific Uncertainty in Environmental Negotiations," in *Global Environmental Policies*, ed. Ho-Won Jeong (London: Palgrave, 2001).

41 For a list of all of the IPCC Special Reports, see www.ipcc.ch/reports/.

42 IPBES, *Summary for Policymakers of the Global Assessment Report on Biodiversity and Ecosystem Services of the Intergovernmental Science-Policy Platform on Biodiversity and Ecosystem Services* (Bonn, Germany: IPBES Secretariat, 2019).

43 Analytical discussions of secretariats include Frank Biermann and Bernd Siebenhüner, eds., *Managers of Global Change: The Influence of Environmental Bureaucracies* (Cambridge, MA: MIT Press, 2009); and Sikina Jinnah, *Post-Treaty Politics: Secretariat Influence on Global Environmental Governance* (Cambridge, MA: MIT Press, 2014).

44 Our discussion of these two topics builds on the analysis presented in Steffen Bauer, Per-Olof Busch, and Bernd Siebenhüner, "Administering International Governance: What Role for Treaty Secretariats?" Global Governance working paper 29, 2006, Amsterdam et al.: The Global Governance Project, www.researchgate.net/publication/228423716_Administering_International_Governance_What_Role_for_Treaty_Secretariats.

45 Personal observations of the authors during attendance at more than eighty global environmental negotiations since 1990. For discussion, see Richard Benedick, "Perspectives of a Negotiation Practitioner," in *International Environmental Negotiation*, ed. Gunnar Sjöstedt (Newbury Park, CA: Sage, 1993), 224.

46 Bauer, Busch, and Siebenhüner, "Administering International Governance," 5.

47 Ibid., 18–19.

48 Ibid., 10.

49 Jinnah, *Post-Treaty Politics*, 52.

50 Ibid., 53.

51 Oran R. Young, *International Governance: Protecting the Environment in a Stateless Society* (Ithaca, NY: Cornell University Press, 1994), 170.

52 Jinnah, *Post-Treaty Politics*, 52.

53 For an early discussion, see Johan Kaufmann, *Conference Diplomacy: An Introductory Analysis*, 3rd ed. (London: Macmillan, 1996), 93–94.

54 Personal observation by David Downie. See also reports from the meeting by the *Earth Negotiations Bulletin*.

55 Jennifer Allan, David Downie, and Jessica Templeton, "Experimenting with TripleCOPs: Productive Innovation or Counterproductive Complexity?" *International Environmental Agreements: Politics, Law and Economics* vol. 18, no. 4 (August 2018): 557–572, doi: 10.1007/s10784-018-9404-2.

56 Personal observations of the authors and conversations with secretariat and government officials during attendance at global environmental negotiations since 1990.

57 GEF, "About Us," www.thegef.org/about-us.

58 GEF, "GEF Small Grants Programme," www.thegef.org/topics/gefsgp.

59 For a critical analysis of the environmental impacts of projects during this era, see Bruce Rich, *Mortgaging the Earth: The World Bank, Environmental Impoverishment, and the Crisis of Development* (Boston: Beacon, 1994).

60 Navroz Dubash and Frances Seymour, "World Bank's Environmental Reform Agenda," *Foreign Policy in Focus*, March 1, 1999, www.fpif.org/reports/world_banks_environmental_reform_agenda.

61 Ibid.

62 Ibid.

63 World Bank, *Making Sustainable Commitments: An Environment Strategy for the World Bank* (Washington, DC: World Bank, 2001).

64 Independent Evaluation Group–World Bank, *Environmental Sustainability: An Evaluation of World Bank Group Support* (Washington, DC: World Bank, 2008), xvi.

65 e.g., Frances Seymour, "Mainstreaming and Infrastructure," *Environment Matters 2004* (Washington, DC: World Bank, 2004).

66 Ibid., 69.

67 World Bank, *Toward a Green, Clean, and Resilient World for All: A World Bank Group Environment Strategy 2012–2022* (Washington, DC: World Bank, 2012).

68 e.g., Ivy Mungcal, "New World Bank Environment Strategy Draws Mixed Reactions," *Devex*, June 8, 2012, www.devex.com/en/news/78385/print.

69 Ibid.

70 World Bank, "Environmental and Social Framework," www.worldbank.org/en/projects-operations/environmental-and-social-framework.

71 "IMF Reviews Its Approach to Environmental Issues," *IMF Survey*, April 15, 1991, 124.

72 IMF, "Climate, Environment and the IMF," March 2016, www.imf.org/external/np/exr/facts/pdf/enviro.pdf/.

73 Ved Gandhi, *The IMF and the Environment* (Washington, DC: IMF, 1998).

74 IMF, "The IMF and 2030 Development Agenda," www.imf.org/~/media/Files/Topics/SDG/imf-and-2030-development-agenda.ashx.

75 Information on the New Development Bank, including its creation and stated purpose, can be found on its website: https://ndb.int.

76 Raj Desai and James Raymond Vreeland, "What the New Bank of BRICS Is All About," *Washington Post*, July 17, 2014.

77 Chris Humphrey, "From Drawing Board to Reality: The First Four Years of Operations at the Asian Infrastructure Investment Bank and New Development Bank," Working Paper of the G-24 &

Global Development Policy Center of Boston University, April 2020, 15, www.bu.edu/gdp/files/2020/04/Humphrey_AIIB.NDB_.April2020.FINAL_.pdf.

78 Ibid.; New Development Bank, *Annual Report 2019: Investing for Innovation*. Shanghai, China: New Development Bank, 2020, www.ndb.int/annual-report-2019/.

79 Belgium, West Germany, Luxembourg, France, Italy, and the Netherlands formed three organizations: the European Economic Community, the European Coal and Steel Community, and the European Atomic Energy Community.

80 The EU had twenty-eight member states prior to the withdrawal of the United Kingdom on January 31, 2020.

81 The European Community (EC) participates in activities and negotiations within many international institutions, especially the UN, and is a party to more than thirty international environmental conventions and agreements.

82 EU, *EUROPE 2020: A Strategy for Smart, Sustainable and Inclusive Growth*, 3.3.2010 COM(2010) 2020 final, 2010, http://eur-lex.europa.eu/LexUriServ/LexUriServ.do?uri=COM:2010:2020:FIN:EN:PDF.

83 See European Commission, "A European Green Deal," https://ec.europa.eu/info/strategy/priorities-2019-2024/european-green-deal_en; and Deutsche Welle, "EU Unveils Law Committing to Climate Neutrality by 2050," March 4, 2020, www.dw.com/en/eu-unveils-law-committing-to-climate-neutrality-by-2050/a-52632306. For a critique of the 2050 climate neutrality target, see Greta Thunberg, et al., "Climate Strikers: Open Letter to EU Leaders on Why Their New Climate Law Is 'Surrender'," *Carbon Brief,* March 3, 2020, www.carbonbrief.org/climate-strikers-open-letter-to-eu-leaders-on-why-their-new-climate-law-is-surrender.

84 Organization of American States, "Securing Our Citizens' Future by Promoting Human Prosperity, Energy Security and Environmental Sustainability," Declaration of Commitment of Port of Spain, Fifth Summit of the Americas, Port of Spain, Trinidad and Tobago, April 19, 2009, www.summit-americas.org/V_Summit/decl_comm_pos_en.pdf.

85 VIII Summit of the Americas, "Prosperity with Equity: The Challenge of Cooperation in the Americas—Mandates for Action," April 17, 2015, www.summit-americas.org/vii/docs/mandates_en.pdf.

86 VII Summit of the Americas, Lima Commitment, "Democratic Governance Against Corruption," Lima, April 14, 2018, www.summit-americas.org/viii/compromiso_lima_en.pdf.

87 African Union, *Agenda 2063: The Africa We Want* (Addis Ababa, Ethiopia: African Union Commission, 2015).

88 For details of the Summits, and text of consensus statements and other information outlined in this section, see www.apec.org.

89 APEC, "Sydney APEC Leaders' Declaration," APEC Summit, Sydney, Australia, September 9, 2007, www.apec.org/Meeting-Papers/Leaders-Declarations/2007/2007_aelm.aspx.

90 Adil Najam, "The View from the South: Developing Countries in Global Environmental Politics," in *The Global Environment: Institutions, Law and Policy*, 2nd ed., eds. Regina Axelrod, David Downie, and Norman Vig (Washington, DC: Congressional Quarterly Press, 2005).

91 This description is based on "About the Group of 77," Group of 77, www.g77.org/doc; and Najam, "The View from the South."

92 The organization was originally called the South Pacific Regional Environment Programme. For information on SPREP, see its official website at www.sprep.org.

93 See Michele Betsill and Elisabeth Corell, eds., *NGO Diplomacy: The Influence of Nongovernmental Organizations in International Environmental Negotiations* (Cambridge, MA: MIT Press, 2008); Thomas Weiss and Leon Gordenker, eds., *NGOs, the UN, and Global Governance* (Boulder, CO: Lynne Rienner, 1996); Paul Wapner, "Politics Beyond the State: Environmental Actions and World Civic Politics," *World Politics* vol. 47, no. 3 (April 1995): 311–340; and Thomas Princen and Matthias Finger, eds., *Environmental NGOs in World Politics: Linking the Local and the Global* (London: Routledge, 1994).

94 See www.foei.org.

95 See www.greenpeace.org.

96 See www.worldwildlife.org.

97 See https://eeb.org/.

98 Ramachandra Guha, "The Environmentalism of the Poor," in *Varieties of Environmentalism: Essays North and South*, eds. Ramachandra Guha and Juan Martinez-Alier (London: Earthscan, 1997), 15.

99 See Julie Fisher, *The Road from Rio: Sustainable Development and the Nongovernmental Movement in the Third World* (Westport, CT: Praeger, 1993), 123–128; and Monsiapile Kajimbwa, "NGOs and Their Role in the Global South," *International Journal of Not-for-Profit Law* vol. 9, no. 1 (December 2006): 58–64.

100 Global Witness, *Enemies of the State: How Governments and Business Silence Land and Environmental Defenders* (London: Global Witness, 2019).

101 Guha, "The Environmentalism of the Poor," 4.

102 See www.greenbelt.movement.org.

103 See www.twn.my.

104 See www.ipen.org.

105 See www.IUCN.org.

106 Working with Merck and Genentech, the World Resources Institute, the World Wildlife Fund, and the Environmental and Energy Study Institute drafted an interpretive statement and persuaded President Clinton in 1993 to sign the treaty with such a statement attached.

107 For references to the boycott as well as broader discussion, see "Iceland," in *The Europa World Yearbook, 2004* (London: Taylor and Francis, 2004), 2049; Guillermo Herrera and Porter Hoagland, "Commercial Whaling, Tourism and Boycotts: An Economic Perspective," *Marine Policy* vol. 30, no. 3 (May 2006): 261–269; Steinar Andresen, "Science and Politics in the International Management of Whales," *Marine Policy* vol. 13, no. 2 (April 1989), 88–117; and "Burger Chain Targeted," *Los Angeles Times*, June 19, 1988.

108 Scott Couder and Rob Harrison, "The Effectiveness of Ethical Consumer Behavior," in *The Ethical Consumer*, eds. Rob Harrison, Terry Newholm, and Deirdre Shaw (London: Sage, 2005), 89–104.

109 Robert Boardman, *International Organization and the Conservation of Nature* (Bloomington: Indiana University Press, 1981), 88–94.

110 Patricia Birnie, "The Role of International Law in Solving Certain Environmental Conflicts," in *International Environmental Diplomacy: The Management and Resolution of Transfrontier Environmental Problems*, ed. John Carroll (Cambridge: Cambridge University Press, 1988), 107–108.

111 Kal Raustiala, "States, NGOs and International Environmental Institutions," *International Studies Quarterly* vol. 41 (1997): 728.

112 The *Earth Negotiations Bulletin* was initially published as the *Earth Summit Bulletin* and was created by Johannah Bernstein, Pamela Chasek, and Langston James Goree VI. For information, see http://enb.iisd.org.

113 Raustiala, "States, NGOs and International Environmental Institutions," 730. See also Pamela Chasek, "Environmental Organizations and Multilateral Diplomacy: A Case Study of the *Earth Negotiations Bulletin*," in *Multilateral Diplomacy and the United Nations Today*, 3rd ed., eds. James Muldoon Jr., et al. (Boulder, CO: Westview, 2005).

114 See www.traffic.org/.

115 Personal observation and private communications by David Downie during these negotiations.

116 See Gareth Porter, *The United States and the Biodiversity Convention: The Case for Participation* (Washington, DC: Environmental and Energy Study Institute, 1992). The Industrial Biotechnology Association merged with the Association of Biotechnology Companies in 1993 to form the Biotechnology Industry Organization.

117 *International Environment Reporter*, June 2, 1993, 416.

118 Michael M'Gonigle and Mark Zacher, *Pollution, Politics and International Law* (Berkeley: University of California Press, 1979), 58–62.

119 S. Res. 98, "A Resolution Expressing the Sense of the Senate Regarding the Conditions for the United States Becoming a Signatory to Any International Agreement on Greenhouse Gas Emissions Under the United Nations Framework Convention on Climate Change," 105th Congress, 1st Session, www.congress.gov/bill/105th-congress/senate-resolution/98.

120 Day, *The Whale War*, 103–107.

121 Laura Eggerton, "Giant Food Companies Control Standards," *Toronto Star*, April 28, 1999.

122 Personal observation by David Downie. See also Alon Tal, *Pollution in the Promised Land: An Environmental History of Israel* (Berkeley, CA: University of California Press, 2002), 305.

123 Interview with William Nitze, Alliance to Save Energy, June 20, 1994.

124 Jennifer Clapp, "Transnational Corporate Interests and Global Environmental Governance: Negotiating Rules for Agricultural Biotechnology and Chemicals," *Environmental Politics* vol. 12,

no. 4 (2003): 1–23. Prominent industry groups at the negotiations included the Biotechnology Industry Organization (a US-based biotechnology lobby group), BioteCanada, Japan Bio Industry Association, the International Chamber of Commerce, and the International Association of Plant Breeders for the Protection of Plant Varieties.

125 Personal observations by the authors while attending such meetings since 1998.

126 Alan Miller and Durwood Zaelke, "The NGO Perspective," *Climate Alert* vol. 7, no. 3 (May–June 1994): 3.

127 *Daily Environment Reporter*, August 27, 1992, B2.

128 Examples include the Ceres Company Network, Business for Innovative Climate and Energy Policy, Business Environmental Leadership Council, and World Business Council for Sustainable Development.

129 Robert Paarlberg, "Managing Pesticide Use in Developing Countries," in *Institutions for the Earth: Sources of Effective International Environmental Protection*, eds. Peter Haas, Robert Keohane, and Marc Levy (Cambridge, MA: MIT Press, 1993), 319.

130 See Stephen Schmidheiny, with the Business Council for Sustainable Development, *Changing Course: A Global Business Perspective on Development and the Environment* (Cambridge, MA: MIT Press, 1992).

131 See the World Business Council for Sustainable Development website: www.wbcsd.org.

Chapter 3

The Development of Environmental Regimes
Stratospheric Ozone, Climate Change, Hazardous Waste, Toxic Chemicals, and Mercury

Abstract

The development of global environmental regimes generally involves five interrelated processes or stages: agenda setting and issue definition, fact finding, bargaining on regime creation, regime implementation, and regime review and strengthening. This chapter examines the ozone, climate, hazardous waste, toxic chemicals, and mercury regimes. These regimes all seek to prevent the production, use, emission, and/or improper management of specific substances that endanger the environment and human health, and as such, can be considered pollution-control regimes. For each case, we outline the environmental issue, delineate key stages in the regime's development, and discuss the role of lead and veto coalitions in shaping the outcomes. The content, development, and impact of these regimes reveal important similarities and differences in regime politics and help us understand why states may or may not cooperate effectively on global environmental issues.

Keywords: chemicals, climate change, hazardous wastes, mercury, ozone depletion, Basel Convention, Minamata Convention, Montreal Protocol, Paris Agreement, Stockholm Convention, UN Framework Convention on Climate Change

The development of global environmental regimes generally involves five interrelated processes or stages: agenda setting and issue definition, fact finding, bargaining on regime creation, regime implementation, and regime review and strengthening. The length of time each stage takes varies greatly. The stages are not always distinct; the issue-definition stage often overlaps with the fact-finding stage, which may, in turn, overlap with the bargaining stage; the implementation stage continues during the regime-review stage, which often includes fact finding and bargaining. Nevertheless, examining regime development through these stages reduces some of its complexities and provides a useful framework for discussion and analysis.

Agenda setting and issue definition involve bringing the issue to the attention of the international community and identifying the scope and magnitude of the environmental threat, its primary causes, and the type of international action required. An issue may be placed on the global environmental agenda by one or more state actors, by an international organization (usually at the suggestion of one or more member states), or by a nongovernmental organization (NGO). The actors that introduce and seek to define the issue often publicize new scientific evidence or theories, as they did for ozone depletion, climate change, and toxic chemicals. Issue definition may also involve identifying a different approach to international action on a problem, as it did for whaling, hazardous waste, desertification, and trade in endangered species.

Fact finding involves studying the science, economics, policy, and ethics surrounding the issue. This is done both to improve understanding of the issue and to build international consensus on the nature of the problem and the appropriate policies to address it. Fact-finding efforts in different issue areas vary from well-developed to non-existent. Sometimes an intergovernmental organization (IGO) can bring key actors together in an attempt to establish a baseline of facts on which they can agree, as the United Nations Environment Programme (UNEP) did in building support for negotiations on persistent organic pollutants (POPs). Sometimes states create a scientific body to review existing information and develop comprehensive consensus reports, as governments did when they created the Intergovernmental Panel on Climate Change (IPCC). When successful fact finding and consensus building do not occur before negotiations begin, scientific facts are more likely to be challenged by states opposed to international action. This occurred early in international discussions on the ozone layer. However, fact-finding efforts can be agreed on later in the process, even after negotiations begin, potentially resulting in greater consensus on the science and possible policy approaches (something that also occurred in the development of the ozone and climate regimes). At the same time, debates on key scientific and related facts can sometimes continue for years, even after a regime has been created, as we see with the whaling regime.

Regime creation involves bargaining among nation-states (with other actors sometimes playing important roles) on the goals and content of global policy to address the issue. Fact-finding activities often shade into this bargaining stage. Meetings ostensibly devoted to establishing the scope and seriousness of the problem may also include attempts to delineate or discuss policy options.

The nature of global environmental politics means that regime proponents face difficult questions during the bargaining process. To be truly effective, a regime to mitigate a global danger such as ozone depletion or climate change must eventually have the participation of all states that contribute significantly to the problem. However, at some point, negotiators must determine whether to go ahead with a less-than-optimal number of signatories or to accommodate veto state demands to achieve consensus. These can be difficult decisions. Can the regime successfully address the problem without the participation of particular nations? Will the agreement be successful if it has universal support but is weakened by compromises with veto states?

The outcome of the bargaining process depends in part on the bargaining leverage and cohesion of a potential veto coalition. Veto states can prevent the creation of a strong international regime by refusing to participate in it, or they can weaken it severely by insisting on significant concessions. In certain cases, an agreement may form without key members of the veto coalition and thus remain relatively ineffective. In other cases, as happened with forests, a regime cannot be created. In some cases, as with the ozone regime, an effective regime can form or be strengthened through difficult compromises among veto and lead states or when veto states change their position after receiving a particular concession, in response to new scientific information, as a result of changes in their domestic politics, or in response to new technological developments and economic incentives.

Successful regime building does not end with the signing or ratification of a global environmental convention. Once established, a regime must be implemented. Most regimes contain important provisions for parties to review and, if they choose, to augment their effectiveness. In the review and strengthening stage, which takes place in parallel with regime implementation, parties negotiate whether and how to make the central provisions clearer or more stringent, how to improve implementation, and/or how to expand the scope of the regime. Regime strengthening may occur because new scientific evidence becomes available, political shifts take place in one or more major states, new technologies emerge that make addressing the environmental issue less expensive, or the existing regime is ineffective in bringing about meaningful actions to reduce the threat.

Regime review and strengthening takes place within processes established by the regime's central convention. The most important elements usually involve formal agreement by the convention's Conference of the Parties (COP) to strengthen or expand binding rules, normative codes of conduct, or regime procedures. This type of regime strengthening usually takes one of three forms.

First, the COP can adopt a new treaty, usually called a protocol, which establishes new, concrete commitments. Examples of this convention-protocol approach include when parties to the 1985 Vienna Convention for the Protection of the Ozone Layer adopted the 1987 Montreal Protocol and when parties to the 1992 United Nations Framework Convention on Climate Change (UNFCCC) adopted the 1997 Kyoto Protocol and the 2015 Paris Climate Agreement. Parties to the 1979 Convention on Long-Range Transboundary Air Pollution, a regional treaty covering the northern hemisphere, have adopted eight protocols that address particular types and sources of air pollution.

As noted in Chapter 1, a framework convention does not establish detailed, binding commitments, usually because negotiators could not reach agreement on such measures. Rather, framework conventions typically acknowledge the importance of the issue, mandate further study and information sharing, encourage or require the development of national or regional plans to address the threat, and create a COP to further consider the issue. Protocols to a framework convention are entirely new treaties and must be ratified by a certain number of states, as specified in the protocol, to enter into force. Only countries that opt in via formal ratification are bound by the terms of the new protocol. Thus, the United States ratified and is obligated to implement the UNFCCC but did not ratify and was not obligated to abide by the Kyoto Protocol.

The two-stage convention-protocol approach allows the international community to establish the institutional and legal framework for future work even when agreement does not exist on the specific actions to be taken. However, the convention-protocol approach has been criticized for taking too much time. For example, after the UNFCCC was signed, it took five years to negotiate the Kyoto Protocol and then more than seven years for the protocol to enter into force. Eighteen years passed between adoption of the Kyoto Protocol and completion of the Paris Agreement, and national commitments still remain too weak to prevent dangerous climate change.[1] Yet the multi-stage approach is often a necessity. The weaker framework convention is chosen not as a preferred option by lead states but because it represents the limit of what veto states will accept.

In the second type of regime strengthening, a COP formally amends the treaty, changing or adding provisions in the main text or binding annex. Examples include expanding the lists of chemicals controlled in the ozone regime, uplisting species such as the African elephant in the Convention on International Trade in Endangered Species of Wild Fauna and Flora (CITES), and establishing a moratorium on commercial whaling by the International Whaling Commission (IWC). Regime strengthening by formal amendment normally requires reaching decisions by consensus, with all parties agreeing; if that is not possible, some treaties allow approval by vote (usually a two-thirds or three-fourths supermajority of those present and voting). In most cases, states must then formally ratify the amendment, in a process similar to ratification of the original treaty. States that do not ratify the amendment are not bound by it.

In a few regimes, certain amendments do not require formal ratification to become binding commitments; however, in most of these treaties, parties have a period of time during which they can opt out if they do not wish to be bound by the amendment. For example, CITES and the IWC allow amendment by two-thirds and three-fourths majorities, respectively, but both have opt-out provisions for amendments. The Stockholm Convention allows each party to choose (at the time it joins the regime) whether it will be immediately bound when additional toxic chemicals are added to the regime or whether it wants to preserve its right to opt in by formally ratifying the amendment each time controls are placed on a new chemical. These types of opt-out and opt-in arrangements allow changes to take effect, at least for some parties, without long ratification delays, but if they are not designed or managed effectively, they risk creating confusing situations in which different parties are subject to different sets of rules.

In the third type of regime strengthening, some treaties allow the COP to mandate new or stronger actions without a formal amendment or protocol procedure. These mechanisms exist to allow parties to change regime terms or technical details rapidly in response to new information and without the delays produced by ratification requirements. Many regimes allow the COP to make binding decisions on matters related to regime implementation, operation, or other issues, provided that the decisions do not alter the text of the treaty. In most cases, these decisions are reached by consensus (albeit sometimes not all states are perfectly happy), but some regimes allow for supermajority votes if consensus cannot be reached.

Other regimes go even further, allowing COP decisions to alter particular types of binding control measures. For example, the Montreal Protocol allows the Meeting of the Parties (MOP) to adjust the targets and timetables for chemicals already controlled by the regime. (There is no functional difference between a COP and a MOP. Usually a convention has a *COP* but a protocol created under a convention has a *MOP*.) Such decisions should be reached by consensus, but if all efforts at consensus fail, the treaty allows voting approval by a supermajority, although no vote has yet been held on these issues. New ozone-depleting chemicals can be added to the Montreal Protocol only by formal amendments, which require ratification. However, once a chemical is listed in the treaty, this innovative adjustment mechanism allows parties to strengthen the protocol's controls rapidly in response to new scientific information and technological developments. The Basel Convention allows substantive decisions to be made by a two-thirds majority of those present and voting, without any opt-out provision for those who oppose it. The Stockholm Convention provides for the COP to change certain technical annexes and other aspects of the convention without requiring formal ratification by parties (although changes to other aspects of the convention require either formal amendment with ratification or opt-in or opt-out provisions). The Rotterdam Convention allows its COP to add to the list of chemicals covered by its prior informed consent (PIC) procedure, although a consensus of all parties at the meeting is required; there are no provisions for voting.

In this chapter and Chapter 4, we analyze ten different environmental regimes. This chapter discusses the ozone, climate, hazardous waste, toxic chemicals, and mercury regimes. These regimes all seek to prevent the production, use, emission, and/or improper management of specific substances that endanger the environment and human health. As such, they can all be considered pollution-control regimes, which feature specific rules to limit particular substances from entering the environment. Chapter 4 shifts the discussion to regimes that address shared natural resources: physical or biological systems that extend into or across the jurisdictions of two or more states or beyond national jurisdiction. In that chapter, we examine biodiversity, marine biodiversity in areas beyond national jurisdiction, trade in endangered species, whaling, and land degradation and desertification.

These ten regimes span a wide range of issues, actors, interests, political circumstances, and effectiveness. For each case, we outline the environmental issue, delineate key stages in the regime's development, and discuss the role of lead and veto coalitions in shaping the outcomes. The content, development, and impact of these regimes reveal important similarities and differences in regime politics and help us understand why states may or may not cooperate effectively on global environmental issues.

Stratospheric Ozone Depletion

Ozone is a pungent, slightly bluish gas composed of three oxygen atoms (O_3). Ninety percent of naturally occurring ozone resides in the stratosphere, the portion of the atmosphere 10 to

50 kilometers (6 to 30 miles) above the earth. Commonly called the ozone layer, stratospheric ozone helps to shield the earth from ultraviolet radiation (UV). Even though only about 3 of every 10 million molecules in the atmosphere are ozone, the ozone layer absorbs deadly UV-C radiation and most of the harmful UV-B radiation emitted by the sun. (UV-B and UV-C denote electromagnetic radiation of different wavelengths.) Destruction of the ozone layer would be catastrophic, and significant depletion would be very harmful. Increased UV radiation causes more skin cancers and eye cataracts, weakens immune systems, reduces crop yields, harms or kills single-cell organisms, damages aquatic ecosystems, and speeds the deterioration of certain human-made materials, among other serious impacts.[2] The environmental importance of stratospheric ozone contrasts with that of ground-level ozone, a very harmful air pollutant that contributes to respiratory problems and damages plants. Most ground-level ozone is produced by the interaction of chemicals from factory and automobile emissions with sunlight.

In the 1970s, scientists discovered that certain human-made chemicals, called chlorofluorocarbons (CFCs), pose a serious threat to stratospheric ozone.[3] CFCs release chlorine atoms into the stratosphere that act as a catalyst in the destruction of ozone molecules. Created in the 1920s to replace flammable and noxious refrigerants, CFCs are inert, nonflammable, nontoxic, colorless, odorless, and adaptable to a wide variety of profitable uses. By the mid-1970s, CFCs had become the chemicals of choice for coolants in air-conditioning and refrigerating systems, propellants in aerosol sprays, solvents in the cleaning of electronic components, and the blowing agent for the manufacture of flexible and rigid foam. Scientists later discovered that other chemicals were also ozone-depleting substances (ODS), including halons (very effective and otherwise safe fire suppressants), carbon tetrachloride, methyl chloroform, and methyl bromide (see Box 3.2). Each of these substances can release chlorine or bromine atoms into the stratosphere, which then destroy ozone molecules.[4]

The economic importance of these chemicals, especially CFCs, made international controls difficult to establish.[5] The absence of firm scientific consensus on the nature and seriousness of the problem, antiregulatory campaigns by corporations producing or using CFCs, concerns for the cost of unilateral regulation, worries on the part of developing countries that restricting access to CFCs would slow economic development, and opposition by the then European Community (EC) prevented effective action for many years.

The issue-definition and agenda-setting stage began in 1977. The fact-finding process also lasted many years, because scientific estimates of potential depletion fluctuated from the late 1970s to the late 1980s, and no evidence had yet emerged in nature confirming the theory and laboratory findings. Indeed, when the bargaining process formally began in 1982, the exact nature of the threat was unclear even to proponents of international action.[6]

The United States, which at that time accounted for more than 40 percent of global CFC production, took a lead role in the negotiations, in part because it had already banned CFC use in aerosol spray cans, which accounted for a large percentage of total use at that time, and wanted other countries to follow suit, and in part because of concern among key actors in the State Department, Environmental Protection Agency, and Congress.[7] However, for an international ozone-protection agreement to succeed, it was essential that all states producing and consuming CFCs join the regime. Thus, the EC, which opposed controls, constituted a potential veto coalition because its member states also accounted for more than 40 percent of global CFC production (exporting one-third of that to developing countries). West Germany supported CFC controls, but the EC position was effectively controlled by the other large producing countries—France, Italy, and the United Kingdom—which doubted the science, wanted to preserve their industries' overseas markets, and wished to avoid the costs of adopting substitutes. Japan, also a major CFC producer, supported this position.

Large developing countries, including Brazil, China, India, and Indonesia, formed another potential veto coalition. Their bargaining leverage stemmed from their potential to produce large quantities of CFCs in the future—production that, if it occurred, would eviscerate the effectiveness of any regime.[8] Although most developing countries did not play an active role early in the regime's development, they eventually used this leverage to secure a delayed control schedule and precedent-setting provisions on financial and technical assistance (FTA).

Although negotiations began with an explicit understanding that only a framework convention would be discussed, in 1983, the lead states (United States, Canada, and the Nordic states) proposed adding binding restrictions on CFC production to the potential treaty. The veto coalition, led by the EC, steadfastly rejected such regulations. Thus, the ozone regime's first agreement, the 1985 Vienna Convention for the Protection of the Ozone Layer, affirmed the importance of protecting the ozone layer and included provisions on monitoring, research, and data exchanges but imposed no specific obligations to reduce the production or use of CFCs. Indeed, the convention did not even mention CFCs by name. However, because of a late-stage lead-state initiative, the negotiators agreed to resume talks if further evidence emerged supporting the potential threat.[9]

Only weeks later, British scientists published the first publicly available reports about the Antarctic ozone hole.[10] Publication of its existence galvanized proponents of CFC controls, who argued that the discovery justified negotiations to strengthen the nascent regime (despite the lack of published evidence linking the hole to CFCs until 1988–1989).[11] Thus, faced with domestic and international pressure, the veto states returned to the bargaining table in early 1986. These negotiations concluded in September 1987 with agreement on the Montreal Protocol.

During these negotiations, the lead states—a coalition that now included Canada, Finland, Norway, Sweden, Switzerland, and the United States—initially advocated a freeze, followed by a 95 percent reduction, in production of CFCs over a period of ten to fourteen years. The industrialized-country veto coalition—the EC, Japan, and the Soviet Union—eventually proposed placing a cap on production capacity at current levels. However, because many manufacturers outside the United States possessed significant excess production capacity, even if a cap were imposed, European producers likely would still be able to increase their actual output of CFCs. Lead states responded with a series of counterproposals before eventually proposing a 50 percent cut as a final offer. After stating for months that it could not accept more than a 20 percent reduction, the EC relented and accepted the compromise proposal in the final days of the negotiations.

The 1987 Montreal Protocol on Substances That Deplete the Ozone Layer mandated that industrialized countries freeze and then reduce by 50 percent their production and use of the five most widely used CFCs by 2000. Production of three key halons would be frozen on the same terms. Developing countries were given ten extra years to meet each obligation, allowing them to increase their use of CFCs before taking on commitments. Instrumentally, this grace period helped gain agreement from a potential developing-country veto coalition arguing that they deserved access to these important chemicals. Substantively, creating two control schedules was recognition that industrialized countries had emitted almost all of the CFCs in the atmosphere to that point and that developing countries needed access to these chemicals to aid their economic development. As such, the grace period reflects the principle of common but differentiated responsibilities (CBDR), which has become a mainstay of international environmental politics. The principle states that all countries have a common responsibility to address global environmental issues but that some countries have the responsibility to act first or enact more measures because of their contribution to the problem or their access to greater financial and technological resources to address it.

The protocol also included provisions establishing scientific and technological assessment panels to provide parties with independent and authoritative information, requiring parties to report on their ODS production and use, banning trade in CFCs and halons with countries that did not ratify the agreement, creating provisions for reviewing the effectiveness of the regime, and strengthening controls through amendments and adjustments by a decision of the MOP. The MOP meets annually and is the supreme decision-making body of the regime, composed of all countries that have ratified the protocol. Unlike formal amendments, adjustments do not require ratification but instead become binding on all parties immediately after adoption.

The ten-year evolution of the EC position from rejecting all discussion of control measures to proposing a production cap to accepting a compromise 50 percent reduction target reflected several factors: disunity within the EC (Belgium, Denmark, the Netherlands, and West Germany supported CFC regulations), the personal role played by UNEP Executive Director Mostafa Tolba, diplomatic pressure by the United States, pressure from European NGOs, and reluctance of the EC to be seen as the culprit should negotiations fail. The evolution of the lead-state position from seeking a near 95 percent cut to accepting a 50 percent cut reflected the need to include EC countries in the protocol. Understanding that a regime without countries responsible for 40 percent of global production could not succeed, lead states concluded that it was better to compromise at 50 percent cuts (even though these carried higher adjustment costs for the lead states, as they had already taken the lost-cost reduction measures, whereas the EC had done almost nothing) in the hope that these cuts could be strengthened in the future, rather than to create a regime without the EC.

The 1987 Montreal Protocol is widely considered a historic achievement in global environmental politics. Several factors stand out:

- It was the first treaty to address a truly global environmental threat.
- The protocol required large cuts in the production and use of several important chemicals, central to economic activity in significant industries.
- The final agreement was reached in the absence of clear scientific proof concerning the problem, making it perhaps the first prominent example of application of the precautionary principle in a global environmental treaty (even if that precise term does not appear in the treaty).
- The design and effectiveness of key architectural elements of the protocol—including the binding control measures, reporting requirements, assessment panels, differentiated responsibilities for developing countries, and review procedures—have influenced subsequent environmental agreements.
- The protocol contained clear, innovative, and effective mechanisms for expanding and strengthening the treaty in response to new scientific information.
- The protocol has been a significant success, something that cannot be said of nearly all other global environmental agreements.

At the same time, the original Montreal Protocol (before its significant expansion in the 1990s; see Box 3.1) addressed only five CFCs and three halons (ignoring, at least for the time being, other known ODS); required that these chemicals be reduced, not eliminated; neglected to require that CFC alternatives not damage the ozone layer; included no provisions for independent monitoring of ODS production and use; and contained no real provisions for providing FTA to developing countries to help them implement the regime. Thus, while hailing the initial protocol as a great success, some of those most worried about the problem doubted that the new agreement would be sufficient to truly safeguard the ozone layer over the long term.[12]

Regime Strengthening

Within months of the adoption of the Montreal Protocol in late 1987, scientists announced that initial research suggested that CFCs were likely responsible for the creation of the ozone hole, which continued to grow larger every year, although natural processes peculiar to

❖ BOX 3.1 OZONE REGIME MILESTONES

1920: In the late 1920s, Thomas Midgley significantly improves the process of synthesizing CFCs, leading to new formulations and their eventual widespread use as refrigerants, in air-conditioning, and as aerosol propellants.

1974: Scientists F. Sherwood Rowland and Mario Molina publish their discovery that chlorofluorocarbons (CFCs) can deplete stratospheric ozone.

1976: The US National Academy of Sciences releases a report confirming the scientific credibility of the CFC–ozone depletion hypothesis.

1977: The UNEP Governing Council adopts the World Plan of Action on the Ozone Layer, which calls for intensive international research and monitoring.

1978: The United States bans the use of CFCs in aerosol spray cans, about 40 percent of US CFC consumption at that time.

1982: Negotiations begin on a global treaty.

1985: The Vienna Convention for the Protection of the Ozone Layer is adopted.

1985: British scientists publish discovery of the Antarctic ozone hole.

1986: Negotiations begin on a protocol to restrict ozone-depleting chemicals.

1987: The Montreal Protocol on Substances That Deplete the Ozone Layer is adopted.

1989: The Montreal Protocol enters into force on January 1. Later that year, the ozone regime's Scientific Assessment Panel concludes that peer-reviewed scientific research has confirmed that CFCs are depleting stratospheric ozone.

1990: The London Amendment and Adjustment mandates the phase-out of all CFCs and halons, as well as several other ozone-depleting substances, and creates the Multilateral Fund.

1992: The Copenhagen Amendment and Adjustment adds binding controls on hydro-chlorofluorocarbons (HCFCs) and methyl bromide; accelerates the phase-out schedules on CFCs and halons; establishes the Implementation Committee; and creates "essential use exemptions."

1995: Parties phase out methyl bromide with exemptions for critical agricultural uses and quarantine and preshipment applications.

1997: Parties accelerate the methyl bromide phase-out schedule.

1999: Parties accelerate controls on CFC and halons in developing countries.

2007: Parties accelerate the phase-out of HCFCs.

2016: The Kigali Amendment adds hydrofluorocarbons (HFCs) to the chemicals controlled under the Montreal Protocol and mandates 80–85 percent reductions in their production and use over the next thirty years.

2019: The Kigali Amendment enters into force.

Antarctica contributed to its severity. Studies over the next two years confirmed these findings. In March 1988, satellite data revealed that stratospheric ozone above the heavily populated northern hemisphere had also begun to thin. In 1989, the regime's Scientific Assessment Panel concluded that the world's scientific community had reached broad agreement that CFCs were indeed depleting stratospheric ozone.[13]

This period also saw significant changes in the economic interests of key actors. After strenuously objecting to national and international CFC controls for years, in 1988 DuPont announced that it would soon be able to produce CFC substitutes. Other large chemical companies, including several in Europe, soon followed. Now that they could make substitutes, the major CFC manufacturers no longer opposed a CFC phase-out but lobbied instead for an extended transition period and against controls on hydrochlorofluorocarbons (HCFCs), a class of CFC substitutes that deplete ozone but at a significantly reduced rate (see Box 3.2).[14] In response to these scientific and economic changes and to increased pressure from domestic environmental lobbies, the EC abruptly shifted positions.[15]

✤ BOX 3.2 CHEMICALS CONTROLLED BY THE MONTREAL PROTOCOL

- **Chlorofluorocarbons (CFCs):** Inert, long-lived, nontoxic, noncorrosive, nonflammable and extremely versatile chemicals used in refrigeration and air-conditioning systems, in spray cans as aerosol propellants, to make flexible and rigid foams (e.g. seat cushions and Styrofoam), in solvents, and in many other applications. The five most widely used CFCs were controlled under the original 1987 Montreal Protocol. The remaining CFCs were regulated under the 1990 London Amendment.
- **Halons:** Used in sophisticated fire extinguishing systems and first controlled under the 1987 Montreal Protocol.
- **Carbon tetrachloride:** Used primarily as a solvent or cleaning agent but also in fire extinguishers and as an industrial chemical, including in the creation of refrigerants. First controlled under the 1990 London Amendment.
- **Methyl chloroform:** Also used primarily as a solvent. First controlled under the 1990 London Amendment.
- **Hydrochlorofluorocarbons (HCFCs):** Originally developed in the 1950s for air-conditioning but not widely used until reformulations were introduced in 1989 as CFC replacements. While much less destructive than CFCs, HCFCs also contribute to ozone depletion and are stronger greenhouse gases. First controlled under the 1992 Copenhagen Amendment.
- **Methyl bromide:** A powerfully toxic pesticide and insecticide used in agriculture, especially for high-value crops; fumigating structures to kill pests, especially termites; and for quarantine treatment of shipping containers and agricultural commodities awaiting export. First controlled under the 1992 Copenhagen Amendment.
- **Hydrobromofluorocarbons:** Not widely used but added to the Protocol under the 1992 Copenhagen Amendment to prevent new uses.
- **Bromochloromethane:** A new ozone-depleting substance that some companies sought to introduce to the market in 1998. Added to the Protocol in the 1999 Beijing Amendment for immediate phase-out to prevent its use.
- **Hydrofluorocarbons (HFCs):** Developed as replacements for CFCs, HFCs are used primarily in air-conditioning systems. HFCs do not deplete stratospheric ozone but are powerful greenhouse gases. First controlled under the 2016 Kigali Amendment.

By June 1990, when parties to the Montreal Protocol convened in London (MOP2), EC states assumed a lead role in the difficult and ultimately path-breaking negotiations that significantly strengthened the ozone regime. The resulting agreement, the 1990 London Amendment and Adjustment, was historic in its own right, requiring that parties completely phase out the production and use of the original eight CFCs and halons, as well as carbon tetrachloride and all other CFCs and halons by the year 2000 and methyl chloroform by 2005.[16]

Because the long-term success of the ozone regime also depended on getting large developing countries to participate, a second historic achievement in London was the creation of the Multilateral Fund for the Implementation of the Montreal Protocol. The first such fund established under an environmental agreement, the Multilateral Fund assists developing countries and "countries with economies in transition" in implementing the protocol.[17] The fund addressed demands by many developing countries, especially China and India, which had refused to join the regime until it included specific provisions for financial assistance to gain access to CFC alternatives. The Multilateral Fund meets the incremental costs to developing countries of implementing the control measures (the increased cost associated with producing or using ODS alternatives) and also finances the development of national plans, capacity building, technical assistance, training, information sharing, and operation of the fund's secretariat. The Multilateral Fund is replenished every three years. An executive committee made up of seven donor and seven recipient countries is the decision-making body that approves proposals from developing countries, and a free-standing secretariat provides administration. Replenishment levels are negotiated by the MOP. The total budget for the 2018–2020 triennium was $540 million.[18] Since its establishment, the fund has disbursed almost $4 billion to support more than 7000 projects in nearly 150 countries and is widely considered a key ingredient in the success of the ozone regime. The existence and effectiveness of the fund has made it easier, both politically and economically, for many developing countries to agree to accelerate ODS phase-out schedules.[19]

Parties strengthened the regime further in 1992 at MOP4 in Copenhagen. Acting again in response to evidence of accelerating ozone-layer depletion and progress in the deployment of CFC substitutes, parties accelerated the existing phase-out schedules; added controls on methyl bromide, a toxic fumigant used in agriculture and once the second most widely used insecticide in the world; and agreed to phase out HCFCs by 2030.[20] MOP4 also created two other important regime elements. Parties established the Implementation Committee, which examines cases of possible noncompliance and makes recommendations to the MOP to secure compliance.[21] The MOP also created "essential use exemptions" that allow a party to propose continued use of certain ODS for specific purposes beyond the final phase-out date if no viable alternatives exist. The MOP must then formally approve the uses and amounts proposed. While providing a loophole, the inclusion of exemptions was a way to overcome the lowest-common-denominator problem (see Chapter 5) and appease potential veto states that might have blocked the earlier phase-out dates.

By the conclusion of the 1992 negotiations, the European Union (EU) and United States had largely reversed the roles they played during the 1970s and 1980s. This became even clearer in 1993, when the EU led the first in a series of attempts to accelerate HCFC controls. Opposing them was a veto coalition that included the United States (no longer a lead state), Australia, China, and India, which argued that further restrictions on HCFCs would not reduce damage to the ozone layer enough to justify the extra economic costs; would punish firms that had made significant and good-faith investments in HCFC technologies by preventing them from recouping their investment; increase the use of hydrofluorocarbons (HFCs), which, although not ozone depleting, are potent greenhouse gases (GHGs); and detract attention and resources from other measures to protect the ozone layer. Although parties agreed in 1999 to a modest strengthening of the HCFC controls, this stalemate continued until 2007.

A similar division developed with respect to methyl bromide. Since the early 1990s, NGOs had called for a rapid phase-out of methyl bromide because it harms both human health (as a toxic pesticide) and the ozone layer (as an ODS). Many industrialized countries, including the United States and the EU, had taken steps domestically to limit, and in some cases phase out, methyl bromide and supported regulating it under the protocol. However, the United States also helped champion a loophole that allowed parties to continue using methyl bromide for "critical agricultural uses" even after its official phase-out date. This procedure gives the requesting country more latitude in defining what constitutes a critical use than countries have when requesting essential use exemptions for CFCs and halons. The United States pushed for this new loophole in response to domestic lobbying from influential agricultural interests, particularly in California. The EU and other lead states reluctantly accepted this new exemption as the price for securing veto state agreement to phase out most uses of methyl bromide and in the hope that the adjustment procedure would provide opportunities to speed up the control schedule in the future.[22]

This strategy proved correct when parties agreed in 1997 that methyl bromide would be phased out by industrialized countries by 2005 and developing countries by 2015 (see Table 3.1). Potential veto states within the developing-country coalition accepted their new requirements, which far exceeded the previous commitment that only required a freeze

Table 3.1 Montreal Protocol Controls on Ozone-Depleting Chemicals as Amended and Adjusted by the Parties Through 2020

Chemicals	Developed Countries Phase-out Schedule*	Developing Countries Phase-out Schedule*
Chlorofluorocarbons (CFCs)	Phase out by 1996	Phase out by 2010
Halons	Phase out by 1994	Phase out by 2010
Carbon tetrachloride	Phase out by 1996	Phase out by 2010
Methyl chloroform	Phase out by 1996	Phase out by 2015
Hydrobromofluorocarbons (HBFCs)	Phase out by 1996	Phase out by 1996
Hydrochlorofluorocarbons (HCFCs)	Reduce by 35% by 2004, 75% by 2010, 90% by 2015, and phase out by 2020, allowing 0.5% for servicing purposes during the period 2020–2030	Freeze by 2013 at the average 2009 and 2010 levels; reduce by 10% by 2015, 35% by 2020, and 67.5% by 2025, and phase out by 2030, allowing for an annual average of 2.5% for servicing purposes during the period 2030–2040
Methyl bromide	Phase out by 2005	Phase out by 2015
Bromochloromethane (BCM)	Phase out by 2002	Phase out by 2002

* Exemptions exist for continuing production and consumption of small amounts of "essential uses" or for laboratory and analytical uses for some ODS after the phase-out date, and larger exemptions exist for critical agricultural and quarantine and preshipment uses of methyl bromide.

For the controls on HFCs, which are not ozone depleting, see Table 3.2.

by developing countries, in part because the agreement enabled them to receive financial assistance earmarked for methyl bromide projects from the Multilateral Fund and because, like the United States, they knew that if necessary, they could exercise the exemption for critical agricultural uses.

Although control measures and Multilateral Fund replenishments draw the most attention, parties have also strengthened the ozone regime via less glamorous but impactful improvements in reporting, information sharing, and technical details that can sometimes serve to reduce an environmentally harmful act through means other than direct regulations. For example, an unintended consequence of the ozone regime was the creation of a global black market in CFCs. So, in 1997, parties developed a new licensing system and provisions for targeted information exchanges that made it more difficult to sneak CFCs across borders under false pretenses. Similarly, in 1999, parties agreed to report on the amount of methyl bromide used in their country for quarantine and preshipment applications, how it was applied, and measures taken to control its release into the environment. Prior to its control under the protocol, methyl bromide was widely used to clean shipping containers and other items in order to limit the spread of invasive species. These quarantine and preshipment uses are another large, but less controversial, exempted use of methyl bromide. Parties recognized (after a push by lead states) that mandatory reporting on the amounts used for these purposes would provide information useful for discouraging unnecessary or excessive applications and for detecting unapproved diversion of methyl bromide to other uses.

In September 2007, parties marked the twentieth anniversary of the protocol by returning to Montreal for MOP19. In a surprising development, countries agreed to accelerate the

HCFC phase-out by a full decade and augment the interim cuts. This agreement, heralded worldwide in environmental policy circles, represented an important accomplishment for addressing both ozone depletion and climate change (as noted, HCFCs are powerful GHGs). It was also the most significant strengthening of ODS controls in a decade and revealed new attitudes on the part of former veto and swing states, with the United States suddenly switching to a lead position on accelerating the HCFC phase-out, emphasizing the positive climate aspects of the move. In an example of political interlinkages, in addition to protecting the ozone layer, the United States apparently wanted a climate victory in the ozone negotiations to buttress its image and negotiating position in the parallel climate change talks.

China, the biggest producer of HCFCs and leading manufacturer of air conditioners that use HCFC-22 as a refrigerant, shifted from a veto state to a swing state. After initially blocking the agreement, China eventually agreed to the new requirements in exchange for political commitments that the next replenishment of the Multilateral Fund would include substantially more funding for HCFC alternatives, which it did. Australia, India, Russia, and other former veto or swing states also relented and did not block the agreement, following the lead states. The potential veto states also did not want the blame for scuttling a deal on the protocol's twentieth anniversary.[23] As noted by an observer at the talks,

> An agreement on HCFCs was therefore timely and served several interests. Many developing-country delegates saw new policy commitments on HCFCs as a way to ensure continued availability of funding … Industrialized countries saw an agreement on accelerated phase-out of HCFCs as an easy win for climate, [and one that included] action by both developed and developing countries.[24]

The 2007 Montreal Adjustment marked the last major strengthening of ODS regulations. However, in 2016, parties agreed, after years of debate, to use the ozone regime to address HFCs—potent GHGs invented as replacements for CFCs. Because HFCs are not an ODS, they do not naturally fall under the purview of the Montreal Protocol. A coalition of lead states, including many small island developing states, Canada, Mexico, and the United States, repeatedly proposed amending the protocol to control HFCs. Supported by the EU, Norway, Switzerland, and others, they argued that the Montreal Protocol had a responsibility to address HFCs, as these substances might not have existed were it not for the treaty's controls on CFCs and HCFCs, and doing so would allow developing countries to access the Multilateral Fund to assist the transition.

These proposals were blocked for several years by a coalition of veto states, led by India, Iran, Kuwait, Pakistan, and Saudi Arabia, among others. Their primary objection was that, in their view, HFC alternatives were not effective in all air-conditioning applications in very high-temperature countries. They also argued that the HFC alternatives, even if effective for some uses, were more expensive; that implementing controls on HFCs would take resources away from eliminating HCFCs and methyl bromide; that any agreement to control HFCs was impossible without assurances regarding large, future replenishments of the Multilateral Fund and the use of those funds to replace HFCs; that the Montreal Protocol could not legally address chemicals that do not directly affect the ozone layer; and that even if it were legal to do so, addressing non-ODS climate issues under the ozone regime would allow industrialized countries to delay additional binding commitments in the climate regime.[25]

Following years of difficult negotiations, in October 2016, parties finalized an agreement, the Kigali Amendment, to significantly reduce HFCs in exchange for allowing developing countries to access the Multilateral Fund[26] (see Table 3.2). The key to reaching agreement was finding specific approaches acceptable to all that addressed both the funding issue, so that developing countries could continue the HCFC phase-out while also starting to phase out HFCs, and the special situation of developing countries with high ambient temperatures.

Many donor nations, including Australia, the EU, Norway, Switzerland, and at times the United States, underscored that they would continue to support the Multilateral Fund,

Table 3.2 Montreal Protocol Controls on HFCs (Hydrofluorocarbons)*

Most Industrialized Countries	Belarus, the Russian Federation, Kazakhstan, Tajikistan, and Uzbekistan	Most Article 5 Parties**	Bahrain, India, Iran, Iraq, Kuwait, Oman, Pakistan, Qatar, Saudi Arabia, and the United Arab Emirates**
Baseline: Average production/ consumption of HFCs in 2011, 2012, and 2013 plus 15% of HCFC baseline production/ consumption	Baseline: Average production/ consumption of HFCs in 2011, 2012, and 2013 plus 25% of HCFC baseline production/ consumption	Baseline: Average production/consumption of HFCs in 2020, 2021, and 2022 plus 65% of HCFC baseline production/consumption	Baseline: Average production/consumption of HFCs in 2024, 2025, and 2026 plus 65% of HCFC baseline production/ consumption
2019: 10% reduction from baseline	2020: 5% reduction from baseline	2023: Freeze at baseline	2028: Freeze at baseline
2024: 40% reduction	2025: 35% reduction	2029: 10% reduction	2032: 10% reduction
2029: 70% reduction	2029: 70% reduction	2035: 30% reduction	2037: 20% reduction
2034: 80% reduction	2034: 80% reduction	2040: 50% reduction	2042: 30% reduction
2036: 85% reduction	2036: 85% reduction	2045: 80% reduction	2047: 85% reduction

* As amended and adjusted by the parties through 2020.

** An extension of four years will be granted to thirty-four high ambient countries in Africa and the Middle East if suitable alternatives do not exist for certain categories of air-conditioning systems.

including providing the necessary resources to complete the existing requirements to eliminate HCFCs and potential new measures to significantly reduce HFCs.[27] However, negotiating the specific language on financing proved difficult. In the nineteen final paragraphs on financing,[28] developed countries agree to provide "sufficient additional financial resources" to developing countries to offset costs arising out of HFC obligations. Countries receiving funds are expected to replace HCFCs or HFCs with alternatives that are not potent GHGs.

The veto coalition's other demand—special consideration for high-ambient temperature countries—was also not difficult to agree on in principle but had to be met in a way that did not create extensions or exemptions large enough to weaken the amendment or create permanent pollution havens. In the end, all parties agreed to reduce HFC production and use by 80 or 85 percent. In accordance with how the CBDR principle has been implemented in the ozone regime (and reflecting demands by veto states), there are differences in the control schedule for developed and developing countries. As with other phase-down requirements in the ozone regime, all countries would have a calculated baseline from which to reduce. In this case, the baseline includes not only HFC production and consumption but also significant percentages of HCFC production and consumption, because the eventual transition must include the entire air-conditioning sector. Also, to encourage participation, countries that do not ratify the agreement will not be allowed to purchase HFCs from parties beginning in 2033.

However, as shown in Table 3.2, veto state demands also led to differentiation and special exemptions. The veto coalition of high-ambient temperature countries enjoys a later baseline and later and slower interim cuts. The difference in the final cut (80 versus 85 percent) will likely be eliminated in the future. In addition, an extension of four years on all deadlines will be granted to thirty-four high–ambient temperature countries in Africa and the Middle East if suitable alternatives do not exist for certain categories of air-conditioning systems.[29] Finally, Russia and some key allies insisted on a slightly more generous baseline and initial cuts than those required of other industrialized countries.

Lead states among both the developed and the developing countries accepted the differentiation and potential exemption as the price for getting agreement. However, as of late 2020, China and the United States, as well as most of the former veto states, have not ratified the Kigali amendment and thus are not bound by its terms.[30]

While most developing countries will likely ratify in order to be eligible for assistance from the Multilateral Fund and to avoid trade sanctions, large countries that can produce their own HFCs, and have large enough markets to use what they make, do not have the same incentives, and thus their ratification is uncertain. This includes India, China, Russia, and the United States. Saudi Arabia could likely become a producer if it wished and supply all the veto states in the Middle East. Leakage from production in any of these counties could also support a global black market. Thus, the participation of these countries is crucial for the Kigali Amendment to succeed.

The Ozone Regime Today

The ozone regime is widely considered the most successful global environmental regime. The Montreal Protocol was the first environmental treaty ever to be ratified by every member of the United Nations. The amended Montreal Protocol currently mandates the near-elimination of ninety-six ODS and very large reductions in the production and use of most HFCs. The ozone regime has eliminated nearly all production and use of new CFCs, halons, carbon tetrachloride, and methyl chloroform.[31] Despite the exemptions (and perhaps even because of them, as exemptions help keep potential veto states in the regime), methyl bromide production has declined drastically. Although recycling continues, and exemptions exist for using small amounts of CFCs and halons for approved essential uses and larger amounts of methyl bromide for critical agricultural and quarantine and preshipment applications, their use has declined significantly.[32] HCFC production has essentially ceased in industrialized countries, and reductions in developing countries are proceeding. As a result, the atmospheric abundance of all major ODS except HCFCs continues to decline, as do chlorine and bromine levels in the stratosphere.[33] Ozone depletion has stabilized.[34]

Because most countries did not take meaningful action to reduce ODS until they joined the Montreal Protocol, and key alternatives were largely invented or commercialized in response to controls established by the protocol, these environmental improvements must be attributed to the ozone regime. Protecting the ozone layer has, in turn, prevented increased UV radiation from reaching the earth's surface. Studies indicate that the Montreal Protocol and its amendments have prevented tens of millions of cases of fatal skin cancer and many more millions of cases of nonfatal skin cancer and eye cataracts, as well as significant damage to plants and ecosystems, including many food crops, and negative impacts on aquatic organisms.[35] As a result, some estimates expect the residual health and economic benefits of the ozone regime to amount to over $2 trillion by 2060.[36]

In addition, because most ODS are potent GHGs, the ozone regime has also delivered substantial climate benefits. Just the reductions in CFC and halon emissions prior to 2000 prevented the equivalent of approximately 25 billion metric tons of carbon dioxide (CO_2) emissions—or several times as much as the initial targets of the Kyoto Protocol.[37] Overall, ODS reductions from the Montreal Protocol are estimated to have already averted GHG emissions equal to more than 135 billion metric tons of CO_2,[38] and completing the phase-out of HCFCs and implementing the agreement on HFCs will avert even more.

Despite its many successes, stratospheric ozone levels have not recovered completely, and a number of significant challenges must be overcome before they can.[39] There must be a total phase-out of CFCs and HCFCs in all developing countries, including the essential use exemptions for metered-dose inhalers. HCFCs and HFCs cannot be replaced by new ODS

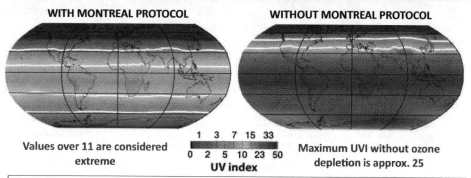

The calculated clear-sky UV index for November <u>2065</u> in the "expected future" (with the Montreal Protocol) compared with that in the "world avoided" (with no Montreal Protocol). From Newman and McKenzie, 2011

Photo 3.1 The Montreal Protocol's Environmental Effects Assessment Panel reported in 2015 that the protocol's success in preventing large increases in UV radiation has now been quantified.

Source: Presentation by Janet Bornman, Min Shao, and Nigel Paul, "Report of the Environmental Effects Assessment Panel" to the 26th Meeting of the Parties to the United Nations Montreal Protocol, 16–21 November 2014, Paris, France. Images on this slide were taken from Paul Newman and Richard Llody McKenzie, "UV Impacts Avoided by the Montreal Protocol," *Photochemical and Photobiological Sciences* 10, no. 7 (April 2011): 1152–1160.

or substances with high global-warming potential or other harmful environmental impacts. Parties must minimize or eliminate methyl bromide, deploy substitutes for the few remaining exempted uses of halons, eliminate illegal trade in ODS, prevent the commercial development of new ODS, and continue to provide funding to developing countries to help them to meet these challenges.

A particularly critical challenge is managing and eventually destroying the many millions of tons of ODS currently contained in wastes and old equipment, collectively known as "ODS banks."[40] Every kilogram of ODS produced since the 1920s but not yet vented to the atmosphere remains in discarded or aging in-use refrigerators, air conditioners, insulating foam, and many other products, and more enters the waste stream every year. Eventually, all of the ODS contained in these banks that are not captured and/or destroyed will reach the stratosphere and slow ozone-layer recovery. Many developing countries lack the regulatory infrastructure, financial resources, expertise, and equipment to manage or destroy ODS banks in an environmentally sound manner, especially given the immense volume of older refrigerators and air conditioners in use or already in the waste stream. Addressing ODS banks will significantly reduce dangerous future emissions but will require FTA for developing countries. However, focusing too many resources on ODS banks might preclude action in other areas, which creates a challenging policy dilemma.

Explaining the Ozone Regime

Four sets of large-scale causal factors shaped the development of global ozone policy: the necessity of accommodating veto states, advancing scientific knowledge and increasing consensus about that knowledge, changing patterns of economic interests among the major actors, and the impact of the extant development and structure of the regime at different points in its history:[41]

1. One major factor affecting the development, timing, and content of the ozone regime is that all countries with significant existing or potential ODS consumption had to be included in the regime for it to succeed. This required lead states to compromise with veto states during key stages of the regime's development. This resulted in the absence of controls measures in the Vienna Convention, the compromise on control measures in the original Montreal Protocol, the broad exemptions for methyl bromide, the long timeline for the HCFC phase-out, and the long timeline, differentiation, and exemptions in the HFC control schedule.

2. Advancing scientific knowledge led to discovery of the threat, galvanized epistemic networks and certain policymakers, changed public opinion, increased concern about the environmental and economic costs of inaction, undercut arguments by control opponents, and, at different times, significantly enhanced prospects for strengthening the regime.[42]

3. Not surprisingly, economic interests tied to CFCs and other ODS—among both prominent companies and certain countries—often prevented stronger controls. Yet, during several crucial periods, the development of effective ODS substitutes altered economic interests, helping parties to strengthen the regime, most significantly in 1990, 1992, and 2007. In addition, the Multilateral Fund significantly affected the calculations of many developing countries, turning veto and swing states into regime supporters in 1990 and enhancing prospects that developing countries would accept stronger control measures.[43]

4. Regime design matters.[44] The framework of the Vienna Convention allowed governments to press forward quickly toward a binding protocol following discovery of the ozone hole. The provisions of the Montreal Protocol allowed governments to strengthen it far more rapidly than would have been possible otherwise. In particular, the requirements to review the effectiveness of the control measures, the mandates for comprehensive scientific and technical assessments, the ability for parties to strengthen existing, binding controls through MOP decisions rather than formal amendments, and the generally effective operation of the Multilateral Fund all created more and faster opportunities for strengthening the regime in response to new developments. More broadly, the prospects for receiving assistance from the Multilateral Fund and provisions that restricted selling CFCs, other ODS, and HFCs to non-parties increased the pace of ratification of the original Convention and subsequent amendments.

The history of global ozone policy illustrates how human activity can upset important global environmental systems, the role that veto coalitions can play in weakening regime rules, how states sometimes shift roles, and the potential impact on global environmental policy of scientific knowledge, technological innovations, changing economic interests, and regime rules. However, if countries fully implement the ozone regime and address ODS banks, then the ozone layer over most of the northern hemisphere and mid-latitudes should fully recover by the 2030s, over the southern hemisphere in the 2050s, and above Antarctica later this century.[45]

Climate Change

Climate change is the prototype of a global commons issue. The earth's climate system affects everyone, and broad international cooperation is required to mitigate global warming. The release of heat-trapping GHGs from human activities, especially the burning of fossil fuels and deforestation, is intensifying the natural greenhouse effect and warming the planet. Global mean temperature in 2019 was 1.1°C above preindustrial levels. 2010–2019 was the warmest decade on record.[46] Without a reduction in emissions that contribute to climate change, the earth's average temperature is projected to increase 1.5°C between 2030 and 2052[47] and another 3.7°C to 4.8°C over the next hundred years.[48]

Developing an effective regime to mitigate climate change is complicated by the multiple sources of GHG emissions, scientific uncertainties regarding the precise scope and timing of future impacts, the need to address the development needs of developing countries, and the lack of political will. Even to stabilize the amount of CO_2 in the atmosphere (which would not reduce the warming caused by existing emissions) requires cutting current emissions by at least one-half. That necessitates major increases in energy efficiency and conservation and a switch from coal, oil, and natural gas to renewable sources of energy, all of which affect powerful economic and political interests.

Emissions from the burning of fossil fuels account for roughly 78 percent of total world GHG emissions.[49] Deforestation and methane emissions contribute most of the rest. Fossil fuel burning has increased atmospheric concentrations of CO_2 by 990 percent since 1916.[50] Since 1990, global emissions have increased by 64 percent, and the atmospheric concentration of CO_2 has increased from 354.35 to 410.27 parts per million (see Figure 3.1). CO_2 levels are now at their highest point in the past 800,000 years.[51]

The top twenty emitters of CO_2, led by China (27 percent) and the United States (14 percent), account for about 76 percent of the world's emissions (see Table 3.3). In 2007, China surpassed the United States as the top CO_2 emitter, and India jumped into third place in the last decade. While emissions from developing countries have increased, and some key industrialized countries have decreased their emissions, developed countries' per capita

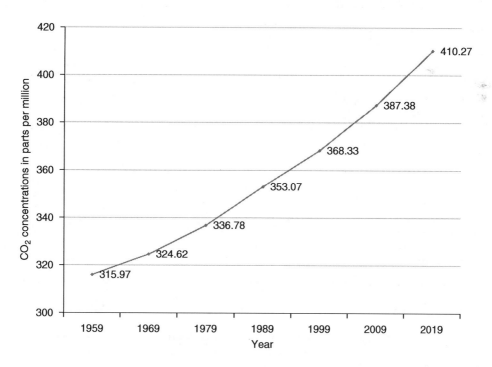

Figure 3.1 Atmospheric Concentration of Carbon Dioxide at Mauna Loa, Hawaii: 1959–2019.

Data source: NOAA Earth System Research Laboratory, ftp://aftp.cmdl.noaa.gov/products/trends/co2/co2_annmean_mlo.txt

Table 3.3 Top Twenty Countries by Total Fossil Fuel Carbon Dioxide Emissions (1000 Metric Tons of Carbon)

Country	1990 emissions	2010 emissions	2016 emissions	% Change 1990–2010	% Change 2010–2016
China	658,554	2,247,534	2,697,856	241%	20%
United States	1,326,725	1,497,865	1,365,231	13%	−9%
India	188,344	564,474	656,578	248%	16%
Russia	565,901	460,551	472,328	−19%	3%
Japan	319,704	310,481	309,759	−3%	−0.2%
Germany	276,425	207,966	198,520	−25%	−5%
Iran	61,954	156,730	180,450	153%	15%
South Korea	65,901	153,580	169,158	133%	10%
Saudi Arabia	58,646	134,653	153,654	130%	14%
Indonesia	41,032	129,970	153,620	217%	18%
Canada	122,739	141,402	148,594	15%	5%
Mexico	104,907	127,127	132,644	21%	4%
South Africa	90,963	123,229	129,982	35%	5%
Brazil	56,966	114,419	126,070	101%	10%
United Kingdom	156,481	134,498	103,361	−14%	−23%
Australia	79,943	99,685	102,511	25%	3%
Turkey	39,776	80,577	101,643	103%	26%
Italy*	115,925	111,252	89,525	−4%	−20%
France**	108,576	98,879	85,022	−9%	−14%
Poland	100,020	84,541	81,548	−15%	−4%
Total Top Twenty	4,539,482	6,979,413	7,458,054	54%	6.9%
Global Total	6,144,000	9,138,791	9,817,000	49%	7.4%

*   including San Marino
** including Monaco

Data sources: D. Gilfillan and G. Marland, "Ranking of the world's countries by 2016 total CO_2 emissions from fossil-fuel burning, cement production, and gas flaring" (Boone, North Carolina: Research Institute for Environment, Energy, and Economics, Appalachian State University, 2019). https://energy.appstate.edu/sites/energy.appstate.edu/files/top2016. totrev.txt.

Research Institute for Environment, Energy, and Economics, "Record High 2010 Global Carbon Dioxide Emissions from Fossil-Fuel Combustion and Cement Manufacture" (Oak Ridge, Tennessee: Carbon Dioxide Information Analysis Center, Oak Ridge National Laboratory, 2012).

T. A. Boden, G. Marland, and R. J. Andres, "National CO_2 Emissions from Fossil-Fuel Burning, Cement Manufacture and Gas Flaring: 1758–2006" (Oak Ridge, Tennessee: Carbon Dioxide Information Analysis Center, Oak Ridge National Laboratory, 2009).

emissions generally remain higher than those of many developing countries,[52] with the notable exception of China, which despite its large population has higher per capita emissions than many industrialized countries.

Scientists have long known that the build-up of CO_2 in the atmosphere can cause climate change. The first scientific article suggesting that atmospheric temperatures will rise as atmospheric CO_2 concentrations increase was published in 1896.[53] A research article in 1938 argued that CO_2 levels were climbing and might be responsible for raising global temperatures.[54] However, the process of issue definition did not really begin until the mid-1980s. The World Meteorological Organization (WMO) and UNEP took the first step by organizing a conference that produced a scientific consensus statement that global warming was a serious possibility.[55] In 1986, WMO, the National Aeronautics and Space Administration (NASA), and several other agencies issued a three-volume report concluding that climate change was already happening at a relatively rapid rate.[56]

The fact-finding process coincided with the issue-definition stage. In 1988, WMO and UNEP, at the request of member states, organized the IPCC in an attempt to establish a common factual basis for negotiations that would focus on policy options. The IPCC's First Assessment Report in 1990 affirmed global warming as a serious threat. The report predicted that if states continued to pursue business as usual, the global average surface temperature would rise at a rate unprecedented in human history. Although the first IPCC report, which like all IPCC reports was based on peer-reviewed publications in scholarly journals, showed increasing scientific consensus on climate change, it failed to establish consensus on the economics of the problem—one of the key points of contention during subsequent negotiations.

This case study illustrates the challenges of climate negotiations, which revolve around perceived economic costs, the CBDR principle, and political will, in five rounds of regime building, review, and strengthening.[57]

Round 1: The United Nations Framework Convention on Climate Change

The first round of intergovernmental climate negotiations began in February 1991 under the auspices of the Intergovernmental Negotiating Committee for a Framework Convention on Climate Change, which had been created by the UN General Assembly. In the beginning, the energy infrastructure of states generally determined whether a state would join a lead-state or veto state coalition with regard to GHG emissions targets and timetables. Initially, three groups of states existed:[58]

- States with few indigenous fossil fuel resources and relatively dependent on imported energy, including Japan and many European states, including Denmark, Finland, France, Italy, the Netherlands, and Sweden.
- States with large supplies of cheap energy resources and a culture of highly inefficient energy use, including Brazil, Canada, China, India, Mexico, Russia, and the United States.
- States highly dependent on fossil fuel exports for income, including the Arab oil states, Australia, Norway, and, initially, the United Kingdom.

The first coalition of lead states (Finland, the Netherlands, Norway, and Sweden) squared off with the United States as leader of the veto coalition. The lead states wanted to negotiate a framework convention in parallel with negotiations on a protocol limiting emissions to be completed no later than a year after the convention. The United States insisted on only a framework convention, with no parallel negotiations on protocols, arguing that regulating carbon emissions would require major changes in fossil fuel consumption and, consequently, lifestyles and industrial structure. In October 1990, Japan broke rank with the United States by committing itself to stabilizing its GHG emissions at 1990 levels by 2000. That left the United States and the Soviet Union alone among industrialized countries in rejecting a target and timetable for controlling GHG emissions.[59]

The EC became the key lead state in the negotiations by virtue of its previous announced commitment to lower its joint CO_2 emissions to 1990 levels by 2000. Australia, Austria, Denmark, Germany, Japan, the Netherlands, and New Zealand also committed themselves to reducing their emissions by 2000 or 2005.

Had binding commitments for controlling GHG emissions been included in the text, developing countries' agreement would have been crucial. The large, rapidly industrializing countries (Brazil, China, and India) already accounted for 21 percent of global emissions in 1989 (about the same as the United States), and as their economies grew, their emissions levels would certainly rise. Since they viewed fossil fuels as a vital component of their success as potential industrial powers, they formed a potential veto coalition.[60]

Negotiations reached a stalemate in early 1992. British, Dutch, German, and other EC members sent officials to Washington, DC, in an unsuccessful effort to persuade the United States to support a binding commitment to stabilize emissions at 1990 levels by 2000. In April 1992, President George H. W. Bush personally called German Prime Minister Helmut Kohl and asked him to drop his government's demand for the stabilization commitment in exchange for Bush's participation in the upcoming Earth Summit. Bush announced his decision to attend the Rio conference only after the final draft text of the convention was completed without reference to binding commitments to reduce GHGs.[61]

In June 1992, 154 countries signed the UNFCCC at the Earth Summit. The convention required Annex I parties (forty industrialized countries) to take steps aimed at reducing their GHG emissions in 2000 to "earlier levels"—a phrase interpreted by the EC to mean 1990 levels—but did not commit governments to hold emissions to a specific level by a certain date. Nor did it address emissions-reduction targets after 2000. But the text did provide for regular review of the adequacy of the commitments.

The UNFCCC entered into force in March 1994, after ratification by the minimum-necessary fifty states.[62] The EC issued a statement upon signing the convention, calling for an early start on negotiation of an agreement with binding targets and timetables. Germany joined with an international network of NGOs and the Alliance of Small Island States (AOSIS) to press for a significant strengthening of the regime (see Box 3.3).

Round 2: The Kyoto Protocol

The first COP to the UNFCCC convened in Berlin in March 1995 and immediately addressed the issue of regime strengthening. In addition to its work on initiating implementation of the UNFCCC, the COP agreed to negotiate, by the end of 1997, quantitative limits on GHG emissions beyond 2000. The COP created a new subsidiary body, the Ad Hoc Group on the Berlin Mandate, to conduct the negotiations (COPs often place large and potentially divisive issues into separate subsidiary bodies that can meet more frequently). However, the COP could not agree on whether the new limits on GHG emissions should represent real reductions from current levels, as opposed to simply reduced levels of future emissions, or which countries would be subject to the new commitments. The EU supported a commitment of substantial reductions, but the JUSCANZ group (Japan, United States, Canada, Australia, and New Zealand), which constituted a new veto coalition, opposed reduced emissions.

AOSIS played a lead role by submitting the first draft of the protocol. The EU maintained its lead-state role by tabling a proposal to reduce emissions of the three main GHGs (CO_2, methane, and nitrous oxide) from 1990 levels by at least 7.5 percent by 2005 and by 15 percent by 2010. The EU proposal allowed some EU member countries, such as Germany, to undertake deeper emissions reductions and poorer EU states to accept lower targets,

✤ BOX 3.3 CLIMATE CHANGE MILESTONES

1988: WMO and UNEP, at the request of member states, organize the Intergovernmental Panel on Climate Change (IPCC).

1990: IPCC's First Assessment Report affirms that global warming is a serious threat.

1991: Formal negotiations for a climate convention begin.

1992: United Nations Framework Convention on Climate Change (UNFCCC) signed in Rio de Janeiro, Brazil.

1994: UNFCCC enters into force.

1995: First meeting of the Conference of the Parties (COP) convenes in Berlin and calls for negotiation of a protocol. IPCC's Second Assessment Report affirms the human influence on climate change.

1997: Kyoto Protocol adopted in Japan, requiring industrialized countries to reduce their greenhouse gas emissions.

2001: IPCC's Third Assessment Report concludes that temperature increases over the twenty-first century could be significantly larger than previously thought, and that the evidence for human influence on climate change is stronger than ever.

2005: Kyoto Protocol enters into force.

2007: IPCC's Fourth Assessment Report says there is strong certainty that most of the observed warming of the past half-century is due to human influences.

2007: Bali Action Plan adopted, including parallel negotiating tracks to determine what will happen after the Kyoto Protocol's first commitment period expires in 2012.

2009: Copenhagen Accord adopted; calls on participating countries to pledge specific actions they will undertake to mitigate greenhouse gas emissions.

2010: UNFCCC COP establishes the Green Climate Fund as a mechanism to assist developing countries in adaptation and mitigation practices to counter climate change.

2011: Ad Hoc Working Group on the Durban Platform for Enhanced Action (ADP) established by the UNFCCC COP to develop a protocol, another legal instrument, or an agreed outcome with legal force under the Convention applicable to all parties.

2012: Doha Amendment to the Kyoto Protocol adopted, setting up a second commitment period from 2013 to 2020.

2013: Parties adopt a decision establishing the Warsaw International Mechanism on Loss and Damage, and the Warsaw REDD+[63] Framework—a series of seven decisions on REDD+ finance, institutional arrangements, and methodological issues.

2014: IPCC's Fifth Assessment Report says that warming of the climate system is unequivocal; human influence on climate system is clear; increasing greenhouse gas emissions and consequential global warming will likely produce severe, pervasive, and irreversible climate change impacts, but these impacts can be reduced by significantly limiting future emissions.

2015: UNFCCC COP 21 adopts the Paris Agreement, the first universal, legally binding climate agreement.

2016: Paris Agreement enters into force.

2018: The IPCC adopts the Special Report on Global Warming of 1.5°C, concluding that limiting global average temperature rise to 1.5°C is still possible but will require "unprecedented" transitions in all aspects of society.

2019: The IPCC adopts the Special Report on Climate Change and Land and the Special Report on Ocean and Cryosphere in a Changing Climate.

2020: Governments submit their revised nationally determined contributions under the Paris Agreement. The COP is postponed for a year due to the COVID-19 pandemic.

provided the overall EU reduction reached 7.5 percent. In sharp contrast, the United States proposed stabilizing emissions of six GHGs at 1990 levels by 2008–2010 for all Annex I (developed) parties.

The United States also proposed allowing countries to meet their targets through emissions trading with other parties. Countries able to exceed their emissions-reduction requirements would be able to sell those excess reductions, or credits, to a country that was having trouble meeting its targets. In theory, this would allow countries with relatively inexpensive options to make more reductions while allowing countries with only very expensive options to do less. If the system worked, it would encourage greater technological innovation (as some countries sought to sell credits for profit) while allowing the world as a whole to achieve the same GHG reductions at a lower cost.

The EU did not oppose the concept of emissions trading but objected to the US proposal because it established few conditions for how the trading would occur. The EU and many developing countries were particularly concerned that the US proposal would assign emissions reductions to Russia and former Soviet bloc states. These emissions were referred to as "hot air" because these countries' emission levels were already down more than 30 percent from 1990 levels as a result of the closure of many obsolete factories and power plants following the collapse of communism. Because emissions-reduction and trading levels would be pegged to 1990 levels, these countries would be able to sell emissions-reduction credits for emissions that no longer existed (hot air). This would allow parties buying the hot air to meet their reduction targets on paper without actually reducing GHG emissions. Other parties argued that the proposed protocol should allow parties to fulfill only a certain percentage of their required reductions through trading.

Australia introduced another important issue: differentiation. Arguing that because its economy depended far more heavily on exports of fossil fuels (coal) than the average Annex I party, Australia said it should not have to reduce its emissions as much as other countries. The demand for differentiation became another way for the veto coalition to seek to reduce its compliance costs by allowing some states to justify lower targets.

As parties gathered for COP3 in Kyoto in 1997, differences between the lead and veto states had grown. The United States agreed to endorse the concept of differentiation to accommodate the greater economic burdens that equal reductions would impose on certain states. The United States also took the position that it could not accept any emissions reductions unless large developing countries also agreed to binding emission reductions—a condition mandated by a unanimous vote in the US Senate.[64] This proposal was unacceptable to developing countries.

Following ten days of intense negotiations, the Kyoto Protocol was adopted.[65] The protocol required industrialized-country parties to reduce their collective emissions of six GHGs (CO_2, methane, nitrous oxide, HFCs, perfluorocarbons, and sulfur hexafluoride) by at least 5.2 percent below their 1990 levels between 2008 and 2012. Countries had different requirements within this collective mandate, ranging from a 10 percent increase for Iceland (which already had very low emissions because of its reliance on geothermal and hydroelectric power) to 8 percent reductions for the EU and most of the countries in Eastern Europe. Switzerland and Canada had 8 and 6 percent reductions, respectively. Russia and New Zealand only had to freeze emissions. Australia could increase emissions by 8 percent. The United States agreed to a 7 percent reduction but won a concession that the three newer GHGs (HFCs, perfluorocarbons, and sulfur hexafluoride) would be calculated from a 1995, rather than a 1990, baseline. The presence of so many different requirements made the overall target less ambitious, and that limited the protocol's impact from the start.

The US proposal for a formal commitment by developing countries to control and eventually reduce their emissions was dropped after China, India, and other developing countries attacked it, making clear that they constituted a broad veto coalition and would not compromise. Arguing for upholding the principle of CBDR, these delegations even rejected an option that would have provided for voluntary adoption of an emissions target by non–Annex I parties.

The Kyoto Protocol could enter into force only after ratification by fifty-five parties, including enough Annex I countries that their collective emissions represented at least 55 percent of their CO_2 emissions in 1990. Designed to ensure that the protocol would have a meaningful impact if it entered into force, the requirement also provided bargaining leverage for industrialized countries willing to withhold ratification in exchange for compromises on particular issues.

President George W. Bush announced in March 2001 that he would not seek US ratification because "I oppose the Kyoto Protocol because it exempts 80 percent of the world, including major population centers such as China and India, from compliance, and would cause serious harm to the US economy," and because of what he called "the incomplete state of scientific knowledge of the causes of, and solutions to, global warming."[66] Although the protocol could enter into force without the United States, it would need the ratification of at least all members of the EU, as well as Canada, Japan, and Russia.

By mid-2004, Russia had become the focus of attention. With more than 120 countries having ratified already—including more than thirty Annex I parties representing 44 percent of 1990 emissions—the 55 percent was now tantalizingly close, even without the United States. If Russia, which represented 17.4 percent of the 1990 emissions of Annex I countries, signed on, the treaty would enter into force. In the end, it was Russia's desire for admission into the World Trade Organization that provided the final incentive. The EU had told Moscow that it would support Russia's admission only after ratifying Kyoto.[67] On November 18, 2004, Russia ratified the protocol, which then entered into force on February 16, 2005.[68]

Round 3: The Copenhagen Accords

Even before the Kyoto Protocol entered into force, attention had already turned to the question of what would happen when the first Kyoto commitment period ended in 2012. Thus, the process of regime review and strengthening began anew. Many believed that negotiations on a successor regime to Kyoto's first commitment period would have to begin in 2008 to avoid a gap between the first and subsequent commitment periods (many believed that a gap between commitment periods would create uncertainty and complications for countries and industry). Negotiations on a successor agreement were expected to take at least two years, and the new agreement's entry into force could take at least another two years. Yet achieving consensus on the nature of such an agreement—including its goals and requirements, burden sharing, inclusion of developing countries, and means to ensure participation by both the United States and China—was not easy.

During four years of negotiations from 2005 to COP15 in Copenhagen in 2009, the internal composition of the lead-state and veto-state coalitions as well as other negotiation dynamics underwent several transitions. The EU was weakened by internal divisions and economic realities, which made it more difficult for it to be a strong lead state. China became an important potential veto state due to its increasing economic strength and new status as the world's largest GHG emitter. This hardened the US position that China must take on binding obligations to reduce emissions. The Group of 77 (G-77) became increasingly fragmented on climate policy, splitting into different groups according to vulnerability to climate change, rates of economic development, levels of GHG emissions, and oil exports. These sub-coalitions played different roles (lead state, swing state, or veto state) depending on which issue was under discussion. These coalitions included:

- BASIC: This coalition of Brazil, South Africa, India, and China played a central role due to their fast-growing economies, increasing geopolitical status, large GHG emissions, and attempts to forge common positions on several key issues.

- Least Developed Countries: These forty-seven countries focused on defending their interests, especially with regard to vulnerability and adaptation to climate change.
- AOSIS: These forty-two island and low-lying states are most vulnerable to sea-level rise and played the role of lead states in pushing for deep cuts in GHG emissions.
- Organization of Petroleum Exporting Countries (OPEC): These twelve countries have economies that rely heavily on fossil fuel extraction and export and opposed measures to reduce GHGs that would significantly impact their economies. They also advocated for financial compensation to offset any adverse impacts.
- Bolivarian Alliance for the Peoples of Our America (ALBA): This coalition, including Venezuela, Cuba, Bolivia, Nicaragua, Ecuador, Dominica, Antigua and Barbuda, St. Vincent and the Grenadines, Saint Lucia, Grenada, and Saint Kitts and Nevis, pushed for developed countries to provide significant financial assistance as part of "their climate debt" and commit to steep emission cuts.[69]
- Central American Integration System (SICA): This coalition pushed for greater recognition as one of the most vulnerable regions to the impacts of climate change.
- Central Asia, Caucasus, Albania, and Moldova (CACAM): This coalition represented these countries' interests as non-Annex I countries with economies in transition.
- Coalition of Rainforest Nations: This coalition strongly favored mechanisms that would pay developing countries to preserve large forests as carbon sinks.
- African Group: This coalition supported large GHG cuts and payments to developing countries to mitigate and adapt to climate change.

In addition to the fragmentation of the G-77, several developed-country subgroups were added into the mix. The Umbrella Group is a loose coalition of non-EU developed countries, usually made up of Australia, Belarus, Canada, Iceland, Israel, Japan, New Zealand, Kazakhstan, Norway, the Russian Federation, Ukraine, and the United States. The Environmental Integrity Group, formed in 2000, comprises Liechtenstein, Mexico, Monaco, the Republic of Korea, Switzerland, and Georgia—countries that do not caucus with either the EU or the Umbrella Group and push for the environmental integrity of the climate change regime.

After two years of deliberations and the release of the IPCC Fourth Assessment Report one month before, delegates attending COP13 in 2007 in Bali, Indonesia agreed on a process for reaching a comprehensive framework agreement for the post-2012 period by 2009. At the heart of the Bali Action Plan were negotiating tracks to be pursued under both the UNFCCC and the Kyoto Protocol. Both processes were necessary because a working group established under the Kyoto Protocol could not consider commitments for developing countries (non-Annex I parties) or include Annex I countries that had not ratified the Kyoto Protocol, namely, the United States. These issues could only be discussed under the UNFCCC.

The two working groups met eight times in 2008 and 2009 as they tried to overcome a host of obstacles. Many of the most difficult issues revolved around broad policy questions concerning the post-2012 period: Should the new commitments be legally binding or voluntary? Which countries would have to reduce their GHG emissions? What targets and timetables should be established? Should these be short-term or long-term targets, or both? Should the controls address GHG emissions in general, like Kyoto, or should they include action on specific sources of emissions, like cement production or deforestation? What types and levels of new technology transfer and financial assistance, if any, should be provided to developing countries? Should developing countries be required to adopt commitments in exchange for such assistance? Should the new agreement take the form of a new protocol, an extension of the Kyoto Protocol, an amendment to the convention, or some other agreement? How should the regime balance action to mitigate climate change and action to help countries adapt to it?

When delegates arrived in Copenhagen in December 2009, they had more than 200 pages of draft text before them—the output of the two working groups. Despite the preparatory work, however, negotiators could not resolve many of the core issues. One critical disagreement concerned the legal form of a Copenhagen outcome. The proposal by the industrialized countries for a single new agreement that combined the outcomes from the Kyoto and convention track negotiations was strongly opposed by developing countries, stating that they would not allow "Kyoto to be killed."

The developing countries' position reflected, in part, their concern that the core principle of CBDR must not be undermined or abandoned.[70] For the first decade of the regime, from 1991 to 2001, the negotiations focused almost exclusively on developed countries' emissions. The basic axis during this period was the EU–US split. Although developing countries engaged in these debates, the negotiations focused primarily on what developed countries would do.[71] However, in their second decade, the negotiations became increasingly about potential developing countries' commitments, dividing the climate change talks over the principle of CBDR.

Several related obstacles involved the world's two biggest GHG emitters and most powerful veto states, the United States and China. The United States insisted that a future agreement contain commitments by both developed and developing countries. China, supported by India, refused to accept any binding commitment to limit its emissions, even if they were differentiated. Meanwhile, most Annex I parties with Kyoto targets were unwilling to accept a second round of targets unless both the United States and the major emerging economies, in particular China, agreed to do their share under a legally binding global agreement.[72]

During the final days in Copenhagen, in an extraordinary process, a small group of heads of state and other high-level representatives from the major economies, including

Photo 3.2 Heads of state from the BASIC countries during informal consultations in Copenhagen in 2009. From left to right in circle: South African President Jacob Zuma (back of head), Chinese Premier Wen Jiabao, Indian Prime Minister Manmohan Singh (in turban), and Brazilian President Luiz Inácio Lula da Silva (front right).

Courtesy Leila Mead, IISD/*Earth Negotiations Bulletin*, http://enb.iisd.org

China and the United States, and main UNFCCC negotiating groups reached consensus on a framework agreement, the Copenhagen Accord.[73] These negotiations were so private that when US President Barack Obama announced the agreement to the media, most delegations had not even seen it. When it was presented to the plenary for adoption, a long and acrimonious debate ensued. A relatively small number of delegations, led by ALBA, blocked formal adoption of the agreement, calling the process that produced it "untransparent and undemocratic" because the text of the Copenhagen Accord appeared "out of nowhere, with expectations that it would then be automatically approved by all Parties."[74] In the end, rather than formally adopt the Copenhagen Accord, the COP agreed to merely take note of it.

In retrospect, the Copenhagen Accord represented a creative compromise that avoided a breakdown of the climate regime. The nonbinding agreement set forth a long-term, aspirational global goal of limiting temperature rise to no more than 2°C, established a process for recording voluntary mitigation targets and actions of both developed and developing countries, and agreed to increase funding for mitigation and adaptation by developing countries, including the goal of mobilizing $100 billion per year by 2020.[75] By 2010, more than 140 countries had endorsed the accord, and more than eighty countries had submitted emissions targets and mitigation actions.

By establishing a process for listing both developed-country targets and developing-country actions, the Copenhagen Accord satisfied US demands for symmetry. By establishing only political commitments for developing countries, it satisfied China's and India's rejection of legally binding obligations. And by focusing on a political rather than a legal outcome, it postponed the decision about whether to continue the Kyoto Protocol.[76]

Round 4: The Paris Agreement

The first challenge after Copenhagen was to restore the diplomatic trust that had been lost as a result of the secretive negotiations; otherwise, there would be little chance of achieving meaningful global action on climate change.[77] Negotiations continued on the two parallel tracks after Copenhagen, with little progress. When COP16 convened in Cancun in December 2010, the Mexican hosts carefully followed a transparent, multipronged process that gave parties the opportunity to bring forward their views and, in the final days, seek compromise on a number of issues, including a second commitment period under the Kyoto Protocol.[78]

The resulting Cancun Agreements included formal affirmation of the IPCC-recommended global target to limit global warming to 2°C above preindustrial levels; agreement to scale up mitigation efforts to substantially reduce global emissions by 2050; establishment of an Adaptation Committee to enable enhanced action on adaptation and promote increased finance, technology, and capacity building; confirmation of the $30 billion fast-start pledges under the Copenhagen Accord and the newly established Green Climate Fund; and establishment of a Technology Mechanism to improve technology transfer and development.[79] Although the substantive outcome was viewed by many as far from perfect, and Bolivia went as far as to oppose the adoption of the Cancun Agreements because they would not reduce emissions sufficiently,[80] most participants left Cancun with restored confidence in the UNFCCC process.[81]

The following year, delegates agreed to the Durban Platform for Enhanced Action, which launched a new negotiating body, the Ad Hoc Working Group on the Durban Platform for Enhanced Action (ADP). This marked the first time that negotiations would take place on a single track.[82] Mere weeks before the end of Kyoto's first commitment period in 2012, governments met in Doha, Qatar. By this time, it was clear that the top-down commitments contained in the Kyoto Protocol might not be the answer. The first commitment period under Kyoto included binding targets for thirty-seven industrialized countries, but while many already accepted that the United States would never ratify the protocol, they did not expect that Japan, Canada, New Zealand, and Russia would refuse to take on a second set of commitments. This, coupled with the fact that major developing countries like China and India did not have Kyoto commitments, meant that by 2012, the Kyoto Protocol only covered about 15 percent of global GHG emissions.[83]

Governments approved the Doha Climate Gateway, which called for adopting a new universal global climate agreement by 2015 to cover the post-2020 period. To address the pre-2020 period, parties adopted an amendment to the Kyoto Protocol establishing a second commitment period from 2013 until 2020, keeping Kyoto operational as a transitional measure.[84]

Meanwhile, the ADP met twelve times, culminating in Paris in 2015. Delegates addressed two work streams: the first focused on a 2015 agreement and the second addressed pre-2020 ambition. The only way that many developing countries, especially India and China, would agree to launch negotiations under the convention on a new agreement would be if developed countries increased their ambition before 2020. Although the ADP negotiations had an underlying North–South dynamic, they also featured a plethora of regional and interest groups. In addition to the groups listed earlier, several new coalitions formed during this round of negotiations. Armenia, Kyrgyzstan, and Tajikistan (later joined by Afghanistan) formed the Group of Mountain Landlocked Developing Countries in 2010 to highlight issues unique to their nations, including significant vulnerability to transportation costs and food insecurity. In 2012, Colombia, Costa Rica, Chile, Peru, Guatemala, and Panama created the Association of Independent Latin American and Caribbean States (AILAC), which calls on developing countries to stop waiting for emissions reductions or financial support from wealthy countries and cooperate among themselves to launch ambitious low-carbon economic development at home and abroad. Also in 2012, the Like-Minded Developing Countries (LMDCs) formed to support maintaining CBDR, meaning that developed countries must act first because they have done the most to create the problem of climate change.[85]

In December 2013, in Warsaw, COP19 asked member states to publicly outline what post-2020 climate actions they intended to take under a new international agreement, known as their intended nationally determined contributions (INDCs). Although some expressed concern that the 2015 agreement was developing into a purely bottom-up arrangement, meaning that states would delineate the extent and nature of their contributions, others saw this as a step forward. What seemed to be lacking, argued some, were top-down commitments and a pledge-and-review mechanism to assess the patchwork of national contributions to determine whether they represented emission reductions substantial enough to stay within the 2°C target.[86]

Perhaps the biggest breakthrough, however, took place outside of the UNFCCC negotiating chambers. In November 2014, US President Barack Obama and Chinese President Xi Jinping made a historic joint announcement. They agreed that climate change is one of the greatest threats facing humanity and that their two countries have a critical role to play. They also expressed determination to move ahead decisively to implement domestic climate policies and to promote sustainable development and the transition to green, low-carbon, and climate-resilient economies.[87] This announcement ended the long-standing game of GHG "chicken" between the United States and China, in which each of them was waiting for, and demanding that, the other take responsibility and develop plans for large, long-term GHG reductions.[88] By taking their public pledge together, they removed a significant hurdle.

At COP20 in Lima, Peru, in December 2014, parties made progress in elaborating the elements of a draft negotiating text under the first work stream. Most developing countries, in particular the LMDCs, however, maintained that there should be differentiation in accordance with parties' obligations under the convention, reflecting the principles of CBDR and equity.[89] The final bargaining phase began in earnest in February 2015 in Geneva, Switzerland, when delegates developed a negotiating text based on the Lima Call for Climate Action.[90] The final eighty-six-page Geneva negotiating text covered all key substantive areas of the ADP's mandate, from adaptation to finance, technology, capacity building, mitigation,

Photo 3.3 Celebrating the adoption of the Paris Agreement: French Ambassador Responsible for Climate Negotiations Laurence Tubiana; UNFCCC Executive Secretary Christiana Figueres; UN Secretary-General Ban Ki-moon; COP21/CMP11 President Laurent Fabius, Foreign Minister, France; and President François Hollande, France.

Courtesy Kiara Worth, IISD/*Earth Negotiations Bulletin*, http://enb.iisd.org

and transparency. Negotiations continued in June and September. But in October, at the final meeting before COP21 in Paris, there was a setback. The co-chairs had issued a revised text as a basis for further negotiations that many found unbalanced and unacceptable. As a result, many of the compromises reached at the June and September sessions disappeared, as parties returned to positions expressed in Geneva eight months earlier.[91] The outcome was a significantly larger negotiating text with multiple options and a wide range of contrasting ideas. Many worried that delegates in Paris would be saddled with an impossible task.[92]

After the debacle in Copenhagen and the six years spent rebuilding trust, the Paris Climate Change Conference in December 2015 could not afford to fail, but there were also concerns that the alternative to a failed conference could be a watered-down or meaningless agreement. Despite the odds, parties adopted the Paris Agreement by consensus during a dramatic session on December 12, 2015, and many agreed that the outcome in Paris met or even exceeded expectations.

The 2015 Paris Climate Agreement represents an evolution in climate governance. The top-down approach of the Kyoto Protocol was replaced by nationally determined contributions (NDCs). A global stocktake will inform collective efforts on mitigation, adaptation, and support every five years beginning in 2023. Through these five-year cycles, parties are to "ratchet up" efforts to limit the increase in global temperature to "well below 2°C above pre-industrial levels and to pursue efforts to limit the temperature increase to 1.5°C above pre-industrial levels."[93] To track progress, parties are bound to a transparency framework, which represents the legally binding portion of the agreement, alongside an obligation to undertake and communicate their NDCs. The Paris Agreement also anchors, strengthens, and creates institutions and mechanisms, particularly for means of implementation.[94] The agreement also represents an evolution in how parties address differentiation. It makes no explicit mention of the annexes of the convention, the historic harbingers of differentiation, but only to developed and developing countries, with subtle realignments in various sections. The NDCs represent, as then US Secretary of State John Kerry called them, a "monument to differentiation": each country determines its "fair contribution" according to its respective capabilities and in light of its "different national circumstances."[95]

Finally, to make the Paris Agreement acceptable to the United States, it had to be written in such a way that President Obama could accept it without seeking congressional approval.[96] In 1997 the US Senate had refused to ratify the Kyoto Protocol, and the political climate in 2015 was no better. As a result, the Paris Agreement is a treaty under international law, but only certain provisions are legally binding. Meeting that test precluded binding emission targets and new binding financial commitments, much to the dismay of many NGOs, AOSIS, and the least developed countries. Poorer countries had pushed for a legally binding provision requiring that rich countries appropriate a minimum of at least $100 billion a year to help them mitigate and adapt to climate change. In the final deal, that $100 billion figure appears only in the preamble, not in the legally binding portion of the agreement. So why did these countries accept it? Perhaps because, as UN Secretary-General Ban Ki-moon said, there was "no Plan B" if the deal fell apart.[97]

Round 5: Beyond Paris

The Paris Agreement gave new hope to the UN climate regime and to environmental multi-lateralism. So many countries rushed to ratify the Paris Agreement that on October 5, 2016, the threshold needed for the agreement to enter into force was met: approval by fifty-five countries accounting for 55 percent of global emissions. After the Kyoto Protocol took more than seven years to enter into force, no one expected the Paris Agreement to take less than a year. Optimism grew as governments at the 39th Assembly to the International Civil Aviation Organization struck the first global climate deal for aviation, a fast-growing source of emissions deemed too difficult to include in the Paris Agreement.[98] Then in October 2016, parties to the Montreal Protocol adopted the Kigali Amendment, which mandates an 80–85 percent reduction in HFCs, a potent greenhouse gas (see Montreal Protocol case). But the excitement surrounding the lead-up to COP22 in Marrakesh in November 2016, marking this rare high point of global cooperation on climate action, was brought to an abrupt halt when Donald Trump was elected president of the United States.[99]

During his campaign, Trump vowed to "cancel" the Paris Agreement and eliminate many of the Obama administration's commitments to cut GHG emissions and provide funding to the Green Climate Fund.[100] While no single country can abolish an international treaty, such a reverse in US policy could easily undercut global efforts to prevent a 2°C temperature increase. In fact, many of the fears expressed in Marrakech on the day after the US presidential elections came to fruition. The Trump administration quickly rolled back regulations on energy suppliers, auctioned off millions of acres of new drilling leases on public land, increased domestic oil production, and took steps to reduce automobile fuel economy standards—all of which reversed three consecutive years of declining US carbon emissions.[101] And, keeping his campaign pledge, on November 4, 2019, the Trump administration formally notified the UNFCCC that it would withdraw the United States from the Paris Agreement on the first day possible under the agreement's rules on withdrawal.[102]

Meanwhile, parties had to finalize important aspects of the Paris Agreement and then effectively implement its provisions. In Paris, countries agreed only on the basic structure of the new climate regime—the cycle of NDCs, reporting, review, stocktaking, and updating. They still needed to elaborate more detailed rules for how the Paris Agreement would work in practice, including rules for reporting and review, international emissions trading, and a host of other issues.[103] Countries spent three years negotiating guidelines for bringing the Paris Agreement to life, and in December 2018 at COP24 in Katowice, Poland, they agreed on most elements of the Paris Agreement rulebook. The rulebook included guidance on how national governments should develop and communicate their climate action plans (NDCs) and how they should review their progress, individually and collectively, with a view to upgrading NDCs every five years until the long-term goals of the Paris Agreement are met.[104]

There were two key issues that countries could not agree on in Katowice. The first was the rules that would delineate exactly how countries can work together across borders to reduce emissions through approaches like international carbon markets. Article 6 of the Paris Agreement allows countries to transfer emissions reductions among themselves. The rulebook needs to specify the rules for how countries will do so.[105] To its proponents, Article 6 offers a path to significantly raising climate ambition or lowering costs while engaging the private sector and spreading finance, technology, and expertise into new areas. To critics, it risks undermining the ambition of the Paris Agreement at a time when there is clear evidence of the need to go further and faster to avoid the worst effects of climate change.[106]

Second, the Paris Agreement asked countries to consider whether they should stand-ardize the time periods covered by countries' NDCs. Before the Paris Agreement was adopted, countries submitted their INDCs in an ad hoc fashion, covering a range of time frames out to 2025 or 2030. In Katowice, countries agreed that all NDCs should use a common time frame from 2031, but they could not agree on a specific number of years.[107]

With COP25 being the final COP before 2020, when parties had to submit new climate action plans under the Paris Agreement, the pressure was on. Many recognized that not enough was being done to meet the three climate goals: reducing emissions 45 percent by 2030; achieving climate neutrality by 2050; and stabilizing global temperature rise at 1.5°C by the end of the century.[108] Throughout 2019, youth took to the streets, inspired by Swedish climate activist Greta Thunberg, to call for climate action. UN Secretary-General António Guterres convened a Climate Summit at UN Headquarters in New York to raise ambition and increase climate action. While sixty-seven countries announced their intention to enhance their NDCs in 2020, these countries only represented 8 percent of total global GHG emissions.[109] The IPCC released two special reports—the Special Report on the Ocean and Cryosphere in a Changing Climate and the Special Report on Climate Change and Land—that presented stark scientific evidence of the impact that climate change is having on land, the oceans, the ice caps, and the world's food supply.

After a last-minute change of venue from Santiago to Madrid (due to anti-government protests and massive unrest in Chile), COP25 opened in December 2019 with high expectations that delegates would finish negotiations on these items in the Paris rulebook.[110] Many also hoped to send a message of intent, signaling to the wider world that the UN climate process remains relevant—and that it recognizes the growing gap between current progress and global goals to limit warming.[111] Ultimately, however, the COP failed to deliver, despite running forty-four hours over time and becoming the longest COP in the UNFCCC's twenty-five-year history. Instead, parties decided to continue consideration of these issues in 2020, never imagining that the COVID-19 pandemic would cause COP 26 to be postponed by at least a year.

The climate regime demonstrates the challenges of negotiating an agreement on an environmental problem that affects everyone on the planet, whether rich or poor. This case also clearly pits the traditional frontier economics and exclusionist paradigms against the sustainable development paradigm. The economic undercurrents loom large over the negotiations and have created numerous veto and lead-state coalitions. The different veto coalitions have hindered progress, making it clear that the UNFCCC and the Paris Agreement will not, on their own, solve climate change. At best, the first round of NDCs, according to scientists, will only cut global GHG emissions by about half of what is necessary to prevent a 2°C temperature increase. At the same time, without the UNFCCC and the Paris Agreement, there would likely have been even less progress. But without the necessary political will—especially among large GHG emitters—it may be up to the youth who take to the streets to remind their leaders that this is a climate emergency and time is running out.

Hazardous Waste

Hazardous wastes are discarded materials that can damage human health or the environment. This includes wastes that consist of or contain heavy metals, toxic chemicals, infectious medical wastes, and corrosive, flammable, explosive, or radioactive substances. Estimates vary, but several billion tons of hazardous wastes are generated each year, although the precise figure is unknown. Industrialized countries generate the majority of this waste, but quantities have increased rapidly in many developing countries. Most hazardous waste remains in the country in which it was produced, but some is shipped across international boundaries for a variety of reasons. Most of this movement is among industrialized countries that belong to the Organisation for Economic Co-operation and Development (OECD), but an increasing amount of waste, especially electronic waste (e-waste), gets exported to developing countries.

In the 1970s and 1980s, laws regulating hazardous waste disposal grew in OECD countries, and many individual firms began to seek cheaper sites for disposal.[112] As a result, North–South hazardous waste shipments began to increase significantly. Developing countries or firms within them, particularly the poorer states in Africa, Central America, South Asia, and the Caribbean, were tempted by offers of substantial revenues for accepting wastes but lacked the technology or administrative capacity to dispose of them safely. Some of this trade was legal, but much was not, with the wastes entering countries covertly as a result of bribes or labeled as something else. In some cases, businesses interested in recycling products containing hazardous materials (such as the ship-breaking industry in South Asia and parts of the e-waste industry) circumvented import rules or ignored or obstructed domestic environmental and human health regulations.

During this period, several notorious cases of illegal dumping occurred. In one, the cargo ship *Khian Sea* went to sea in 1986 in search of a disposal site for 14,000 tons of incinerator ash containing high levels of lead, cadmium, and other heavy metals. The ash came from incinerators in Philadelphia and had previously gone to New Jersey, but New Jersey refused to accept any more after 1984. The ship spent almost two years at sea, during which time its name changed twice. In January 1988, it dumped 4000 tons of ash in Haiti; it dumped the remaining 10,000 tons in November at different spots in the Atlantic and Indian oceans.

The issue-definition stage began in 1984 and 1985, when a UNEP-organized working group of legal and technical experts developed a set of voluntary guidelines on the management, disposal, and trade of hazardous wastes (which became the Cairo Guidelines). Designed to assist governments in developing and implementing policies for managing hazardous wastes, the guidelines also specified notification and consent of the receiving state prior to the export of hazardous waste and verification by the exporting state that the receiving state had disposal requirements at least as stringent as those of the exporting state.

These soft-law guidelines did not satisfy some key actors, most notably African states that received the bulk of illegal hazardous waste exports. Some of these states characterized trade in hazardous waste as a form of exploitation of poor and weak states by rich businesses and countries, and argued that an outright ban was needed, rather than soft-law guidelines or regulations that allow some shipments. This position drew support from NGOs and some officials in industrialized states, particularly in Europe.

The bargaining stage began in 1987, when UNEP, at the request of its Governing Council, organized formal negotiations to control international trade in hazardous wastes (see Box 3.4).[113] During the next eighteen months, major differences emerged between African lead states and industrialized countries that were swing and veto states. African states wanted a total ban on waste exports and export-state liability when illegal traffic did occur, in part

❖ BOX 3.4 BASEL CONVENTION MILESTONES

1987: UNEP adopts the Cairo Guidelines on Waste Trading.

1987: UNEP convenes negotiations aimed at creating a treaty to ban or control the international trade of hazardous waste.

1989: The Basel Convention is adopted.

1991: Twelve African countries adopt the Bamako Convention.

1992: The Basel Convention enters into force.

1994: A Greenpeace publication documents 1000 cases of illegal toxic waste exports.

1995: The Basel Ban Amendment is formally adopted.

1998: COP4 adopts Annexes VIII and IX to the Convention, further clarifying which wastes the Convention regulates.

1999: The Protocol on Liability and Compensation is adopted.

2002: Parties establish the first prioritized plan for implementing the Convention.

2008: COP9 adopts technical guidelines for the environmentally sound management of mobile phones and establishes the Partnership for Action on Computer Equipment.

2011: COP10 adopts an updated strategic plan for implementing the Convention through 2021 that includes specified goals and performance indicators.

2013: The Basel, Rotterdam, and Stockholm Conventions hold their first fully coordinated COPs. The "BRS Triple COP" includes simultaneous and separate COP sessions over a two-week period.

2015: Convening as part of BRS Triple COP, Basel COP12 approves technical guidelines on POP wastes and updated guidelines on mercury wastes.

2017: COP13, meeting as part of the now institutionalized BRS Triple COP, adopts six new or updated technical guidelines, establishes a new partnership on household waste, and agrees to include marine litter and waste containing nanomaterials in the work program of the Open-Ended Working Group.

2019: COP14 agrees on an historic amendment to address certain plastic wastes under the Basel Convention. Parties also create a Partnership on Plastic Waste.

because many developing countries did not possess the administrative, financial, or technical ability to enforce a ban on their own. Waste-exporting states wanted a convention that would permit the trade, providing that importing countries were notified and agreed to accept it—something known as a prior informed consent or PIC regime.

During the final round of negotiations in March 1989, the veto coalition, led by the United States, took advantage of the fact that some poor countries wished to continue accepting wastes and stated that ban supporters had to accept a PIC regime or get no treaty. At the time, the United States exported only about 1 percent of its known hazardous wastes (although this was a large amount by weight), mostly to Canada and Mexico, but it led the veto coalition largely because of the George H. W. Bush administration's ideological position that rejected limitations on its right to export and practical concerns about implementing the proposed treaty. The Organization of African Unity proposed language to ban waste exports to countries that lacked the same level of facilities and technology as the exporting nations and to require inspection of disposal sites by UN inspectors, but key industrialized countries rejected these proposals.[114]

The 1989 Basel Convention on Control of Transboundary Movements of Hazardous Wastes and Their Disposal prohibits the export of hazardous wastes to countries with less advanced storage and disposal facilities unless the importing state has detailed information on the waste shipment and gives prior written consent.[115] Agreements between parties and non-parties were permitted, although they needed to conform to the terms of the convention.

Critics charged that the convention did not go further than existing regulations in most industrialized countries—regulations that had already failed to curb legal or illegal waste traffic. They also noted that the convention lacked precision on key definitions, such as *environmentally sound* and even *hazardous wastes*, and contained no liability provisions to deter illegal dumping or provide clean-up costs.[116]

Regime Strengthening: The Ban Amendment and the Liability Protocol

After three years, in May 1992, the Basel Convention entered into force after receiving the necessary ratifications. It was a weak regime, with limited binding rules and without ratification by major waste-exporting states. In less than two years, however, growing demands for stronger action helped lead states strengthen the regime.

By early 1994, more than 100 countries had passed domestic legislation banning the import of hazardous wastes, although not all of them had the administrative capacity to do so unilaterally.[117] This development shows an important potential consequence of a global environmental regime: the strengthening of relevant domestic law. Some of the credit must also go to Greenpeace, which published a report documenting 1000 cases of illegal toxic waste exports.[118] Even the United States, although not a party to the regime, signaled that it would support a ban on hazardous waste exports if the ban exempted scrap metal, glass, textiles, and paper, which were widely traded for recycling.[119]

Building on these developments, at COP2 a broad coalition, including the G-77, pressed for adopting a complete ban on hazardous waste exports from OECD countries to non-OECD countries, including those exported for recycling.[120] They argued that shipments of recyclables often were not for recycling but for dumping and that the OECD countries would never reduce their creation of wastes as long as they could ship some to developing countries. Australia, Canada, Germany, Japan, the Netherlands, the United Kingdom, and the United States countered that any ban should exempt recyclables. China and a number of Central and Eastern European states supported the G-77 proposal. Greenpeace, demonstrating the impact that NGOs can have within certain regimes at certain times, also made an important contribution by releasing a seven-year study of more than fifty recycling operations in non-OECD countries that provided concrete evidence of widespread dumping of hazardous wastes falsely labeled and shipped as recyclables as well as many other shipments of recyclables that had not been recycled at all but just dumped in developing countries.[121]

Despite intensive lobbying by waste-exporting countries, particularly in support of allowing bilateral agreements on hazardous waste exports for recycling, the G-77 remained firm, agreeing to negotiate only on the timetable for implementing a ban. Confronted with non-OECD unity, the veto coalition began to divide, with some withdrawing their opposition. The veto coalition was also weakened because several of its members, including the United States, had not ratified the Basel Convention and, as non-parties, remained technically outside the decision-making process. They could speak, but their views did not officially count and they could not vote. When debate ended, COP2 approved the ban. Countries opposed to the ban obtained nothing more than a delay in its full implementation.

One year later, at COP3 in 1995, parties significantly strengthened the decision by adopting the ban as a formal amendment to the convention. The Ban Amendment prohibits export of hazardous wastes for final disposal or recycling from countries listed in Annex VII of the convention (industrialized-country parties) to non-Annex VII countries. The Ban Amendment does not prevent a developing country from receiving hazardous wastes from an industrialized country, because they can do so by joining Annex VII.

In 2011, after years of slow progress in ratifying the provision, parties resolved an ambiguity in the text of the Convention regarding amendments (Article 17) by agreeing that to enter into force, the Ban Amendment required ratification only by three-quarters of the parties that were parties at the time of the Amendment's adoption, rather than the total number of current parties.[122] Even with this lower threshold (ninety-seven parties rather than more than 130), however, it took until 2019 for the Ban Amendment to receive sufficient ratifications and enter into force. Nevertheless, Brazil, India, Mexico, Pakistan, and most industrialized countries outside of the EU remain non-parties, including Australia, Canada, Japan, New Zealand, Pakistan, Russia, Ukraine, South Korea, and the United States. One reason inhibiting broader ratification is that some countries have economic interests in maintaining existing, or preserving the potential for, trade in wastes for recycling—including ships, electronics, scrap metal, glass, cardboard, paper, and some chemicals. Although recycling in theory is environmentally benign, this activity in certain industries in many developing countries releases air and water pollutants, toxic chemicals, and heavy metals into local environments and the workers. However, in some counties and sectors, such as ship-breaking in India, Pakistan, and other countries in South Asia, the economic need for jobs and raw materials has proven stronger than the damage to the environment and human health.

Prior to its entry into force, COP began taking decisions designed to support the overall intent of the Ban Amendment. This included creating and updating lists of banned and exempted wastes in the hope that increasing the clarity of what was covered would attract new ratifications, which it did, and assist more effective implementation. The COP also developed new PIC procedures, required parties to use precise custom codes, updated criteria for classifying particular material as hazardous, and assisted developing countries to improve their capacity to monitor and trace shipments of hazardous wastes. These measures enhanced the prospects of key purposes of the Ban Amendment being more widely implemented even if not all Basel parties ratify it.[123]

In December 1999, after six years of discussion, COP5 adopted the Basel Protocol on Liability and Compensation, which addressed developing countries' concerns that they lack sufficient funds and technologies to prevent or cope with the consequences of illegal dumping or accidental spills. The protocol would establish provisions for determining liability and compensation for damage resulting from the legal or illegal transnational movement of hazardous wastes. Twenty-one years later, however, only twelve countries have ratified the liability protocol, and it appears unlikely to enter into force for many years, if ever.

Regime Strengthening: Action Plans, Regional Centers, and Technical Guidelines

Nearly twenty years ago, concerned that the Basel Convention was having little practical effect, in 2002 parties established a prioritized action plan for implementing the convention through 2010 that emphasized the environmentally sound management of specific, priority waste streams such as lead-acid batteries, polychlorinated biphenyls (PCBs), used oil, electronics, and obsolete pesticides. This strategic plan provided guidance to parties, the secretariat, regional centers, IGOs, NGOs, and corporations regarding the regime's priorities, but developing countries could not implement some actions because of inadequate funding.[124]

COP6 in 2002 also created a compliance mechanism to review instances where parties might have failed to operate in accordance with regime provisions and to make recommendations to improve implementation. Modeled somewhat on the Montreal Protocol, the inclusion of a compliance mechanism under the Basel Convention was significant, as similar efforts have not succeeded in other regimes.

Four years later, in 2006, an egregious incident highlighted the original purpose of the convention and the dangers associated with hazardous waste. An old chemical tanker carrying more than 400 metric tons of heavily contaminated wash water (water used to clean its holds) sailed to Nigeria to deliver a different cargo and then docked in Abidjan, a port city of 5 million people and the economic capital of Côte d'Ivoire. Under the cover of night, the contaminated wastewater was transferred to tanker trucks, which then dumped it at sixteen different open-air sites around the city, many near water supplies or farms. At least fifteen people died, thousands were hospitalized, and over 100,000 sought medical treatment, overwhelming local hospitals. Many fishing, vegetable, and small livestock activities were halted, associated businesses closed, and workers laid off. Protests erupted over suspicions of (unproven) government corruption in the scandal.[125] The incident highlighted the absence of effective tracking systems for the transboundary movement of hazardous waste and the concern that these shipments, both legal and illegal, might be producing more environmental damage than recognized.

Seeking to continue strengthening the practical impact of the regime, COP10 adopted an updated action plan and strategic framework for 2012–2021 that, for the first time, included specific goals and performance indicators to measure implementation. Many "said this was long overdue, stressing that without concrete goals and indicators, it is very difficult to measure progress" and that the new system "will increase transparency and accountability around implementation."[126] However, many developing counties expressed concerns that the implementation of the strategic framework, including efforts to reduce the creation of hazardous waste, developing and using guidelines on its environmentally sound management, and stopping illegal traffic, depends to some degree on the provision of sufficient FTA and related efforts, including support for the Basel Convention Regional Centers.[127] The Centers were established to facilitate implementation of the convention in developing countries by building capacity, educating the public, collecting data, reporting, promoting environmentally sound waste management, easing the transfer of cleaner production technologies, and helping to train customs officials. While variations persist in their effectiveness and funding, there are now fourteen regional centers located in different parts of Africa, Asia, the Caribbean, Eastern Europe, and Latin America.

The Basel Convention has also been strengthened through the development of nonbinding technical guidelines designed to assist industry and governments in the environmentally sound management of hazardous waste. More than thirty guidelines have been created or updated for different categories of hazardous wastes, including waste oil, biomedical and health-care wastes, POPs, individual chemicals such as PCBs, obsolete ships, and mobile phones.[128] These important and influential guidelines are an example of effective regime strengthening even when new binding rules are not created.

In a related initiative, parties created the Framework for the Environmentally Sound Management of Hazardous Wastes and Other Wastes. This initiative seeks to develop a common understanding of what environmentally sound management encompasses, tools to support and promote the implementation of environmentally sound management of waste by companies and countries, and strategies to implement environmentally sound management. The COP established an Environmentally Sound Management Expert Working Group, which collects information, develops draft manuals and facts sheets, holds regional meetings, and pursues other practical measures.[129]

Regime Strengthening: E-Waste

Electronic waste, or e-waste, comprises discarded, broken, or obsolete electronic devices, including phones, televisions, computers, printers, monitors, sensors, and CD, DVD, and MP3 players, as well as their parts and components. While the EU has some life-cycle requirements on electronic items, most countries do not. Globally, e-waste generation is growing by more than 40 million tons a year, and experts predict that in the worst-case scenario, it could grow to 120 million tonnes by 2050.[130]

E-waste often contains hazardous materials, including heavy metals such as lead, cadmium, and beryllium and a variety of toxic chemicals, including certain flame retardants. Processing e-waste, particularly in developing countries, can yield very important resources

Photo 3.4 A poster at Basel Convention COP13 asks the question whether electronic waste should be seen as a source of jobs or a danger to human health.

Courtesy Kiara Worth, IISD/*Earth Negotiations Bulletin*, http://enb.iisd.org

but can also cause serious pollution and health problems if proper care is not taken to protect workers and prevent release of the pollutants into the environment via direct dumping, poorly designed and operated landfills, open-pit burning, or incinerator exhaust and ashes. A UNEP report concluded that 90 percent of the world's e-waste is improperly disposed of, dumped, or illegally traded each year.[131]

The immense scope of the e-waste issue was unforeseen when countries negotiated the original convention. Parties initiated serious discussions of the problem in 2006, approving the Nairobi Declaration, which stated that parties will promote awareness of e-waste, clean technology, and green design; encourage information exchange from developed to developing countries; improve relevant domestic waste management; and prevent and combat illegal traffic.[132]

In 2008, parties took more concrete steps, adopting specific technical guidelines for the environmentally sound management of used and end-of-life mobile phones. The guidelines, which are updated as needed, address design considerations relevant to reducing hazardous waste; the collection, refurbishment, and recycling of used mobile phones; the transboundary movement of collected phones; and the management of hazardous waste from end-of-life mobile phones. The guidelines built on the Mobile Phone Partnership Initiative, launched in 2002, in which manufacturers and service providers partnered with the Convention to develop and promote the environmentally sound management of end-of-life mobile phones.

Parties also established the Partnership for Action on Computer Equipment (PACE), patterned after the mobile-phone partnership. The PACE working group provided a forum for dialogue among governments, industry, NGOs, and academic experts; developed technical guidelines for environmentally sound repair, refurbishment, and recycling of computer equipment and components; offered expert advice; and promoted more national action.[133] In 2017, the working group completed its work and COP13 adopted, on an interim basis, guidance on the environmentally sound management of used and end-of-life computing equipment. Recognizing that these were only first steps, in 2019 parties initiated a new partnership and working group process, the details of which should be finalized at COP15 in 2021.

Yet, despite broad agreement on the danger of e-waste and more than a decade of detailed discussion on the draft guidelines, disagreements remained between countries that want the guidelines to allow for domestic markets in, and exports or imports of, electronic equipment for reuse, repair, or recycling and other countries, including many in Africa and Latin America, and environmental NGOs that see aspects of such trade as waste dumping.[134] These differences capture a difficult issue within the waste regime: how to allow countries to pursue legitimate reuse, repair, and recycling strategies for hazardous waste, including e-waste,[135] while also promoting and ensuring environmentally sound management and preventing activities that claim to be reuse or recycling but are actually waste dumping.

Regime Strengthening: Plastic Waste

The most recent large-scale regime strengthening focused on plastic waste. Plastic, particularly marine litter, represents a large and growing global environmental problem. Plastic persists almost indefinitely in the environment and has a significant impact on marine and coastal biodiversity.[136] Large quantities of plastic and other debris can be found in the most remote parts of the world's oceans, and harmful levels of plastic have been found in a variety of sea animals and birds.[137] Some plastics also contain, are made with, or are treated with hazardous substances, including POPs. Microplastics—tiny pieces that range from rice-size particles to microscopic bits that were originally part of plastic bags, bottles, straws, and other items—are present in most sea animals, including fish eaten by humans.[138] UNEP estimates annual global plastic production at more than 320 million tons a year and that only 9 percent of the estimated 6.3 billion tons of plastic waste produced since the 1950s has been recycled and only 12 percent incinerated.[139]

The Basel Convention considered plastic waste for many years and established guidelines for its environmentally sound management and other measures.[140] However, many developed and developing countries and NGOs argued that the accelerating production of plastics and the increasingly serious environmental situation required steps to reduce the amount of plastic waste produced, its discharge into the environment, the amount of toxic materials in certain plastics, and the international transport of plastic waste.[141]

In May 2019, Basel COP14 took historic decisions to address plastic waste.[142] The package included a formal amendment that expanded the scope of plastic waste covered by the Convention. Plastic waste that is difficult or currently impossible to recycle is now listed in Annex II, while plastic waste that is hazardous is listed in Annex VIII. Both types can only be exported if the importing country grants consent and confirms that the waste will be managed in an environmentally sound manner.[143] An expert working group will also examine whether certain plastics should be added to other parts of the Convention.

The COP also acknowledged the urgency of the plastic waste problem; emphasized the need for parties to adopt a life-cycle approach for managing plastics; encouraged parties to set time-bound targets to address plastic waste; urged parties and non-parties, international organizations, companies, and NGOs to enhance public awareness of the plastic problem; strongly encouraged parties and other actors to reduce the use of hazardous chemicals in the production of plastics; and established a working group to update the technical guidelines for the environmentally sound management of plastic waste.[144] Finally, the COP established the Partnership on Plastic Waste, which includes representatives from countries, international organizations, NGOs, and, importantly, the private sector. This new partnership is charged with promoting and improving the prevention, minimization, and environmentally sound management of plastic waste, including microplastics.[145] The agreement to adopt the

Photo 3.5 Members of civil society at COP14 in 2019 implore delegates to support the Norwegian proposal to amend the Annexes to the Basel Convention and establish a Partnership on Plastic Waste to better manage marine plastic litter and microplastics.

Courtesy Kiara Worth, IISD/*Earth Negotiations Bulletin*, http://enb.iisd.org

amendment and establish the Partnership was greeted with extended applause by more than 1000 delegates and observers.[146]

Synergies

The technical guidelines and partnerships are part of a new emphasis on the environmentally sound management of the entire life cycle of hazardous substances—production, use, emissions, waste management, and disposal—and enhancing coordination among actors and initiatives to improve their effectiveness and augment resources. Along these lines, the unprecedented "synergies initiative" seeks more effective global policy on hazardous chemicals and wastes by enabling the Basel, Rotterdam, and Stockholm Conventions to coordinate or even combine certain implementation and administration activities.[147] (See discussion under the toxic chemicals section.)

Moving Forward

The current global regime for managing hazardous waste and controlling its international movement is quite different from the original weak regime created in 1989. The expanded Basel Convention has helped to eliminate some of the worst forms of toxic waste dumping, improved the management of hazardous wastes, and established frameworks, guidelines, and partnerships. The evolution of the Basel Convention shows how veto power can dissipate when faced with a strong coalition that includes developing countries and some developed countries. The information, publicity, and political pressure generated by NGOs, especially Greenpeace and the Basel Action Network, also played an important role. Once the hazardous waste trade became a political symbol uniting developing countries, it overcame the leverage of waste exporters on some (but not all) issues. And once the regime expanded to help reduce the creation of certain wastes and improve the management of all wastes (through technical guidelines, partnerships, promoting environmentally sound management, and other initiatives), its network of supporters and relevance increased.

Yet the hazardous waste regime still faces many challenges. Although promising policy initiatives and economic incentives have emerged to promote more effective management, recycling, and disposal of hazardous waste, several of the central goals of the regime—to reduce the amount of hazardous waste produced, limit its movement, and ensure its environmentally sound management—remain difficult to achieve.

Indeed, illegal transnational shipments and illegal dumping of hazardous waste still occur. In July 2020, Malaysia discovered 1800 tons of toxic electric arc furnace dust at the Port of Tanjung Pelepas. This by-product of steel production contains many hazardous components, including chromium and lead, and is classified as toxic waste under the Basel Convention. It had entered the port illegally, shipped from Romania and falsely declared as zinc, and perhaps would have been dumped illegally somewhere inland if it had not been discovered.[148]

In addition, the United States, one of the largest producers of hazardous waste, still has not ratified the Basel Convention. The Ban Amendment has only recently entered into force, but many countries critical to its overall effectiveness have yet to ratify it. Only twelve countries have ratified the Protocol on Liability and Compensation. Many important issues, such as the increasing production of e-waste and plastics, export of hazardous wastes for recycling, illegal dumping, and the dismantling of ships, continue to require attention.

Finally, parties must grapple with the challenge of securing sufficient funding to support key regime priorities. Efforts spent creating and revising technical guidelines matter little to a developing country that lacks the financial resources or technically trained personnel to administer and enforce them.[149] Addressing these challenges will determine the long-term impact of the hazardous waste regime.

Toxic Chemicals

The development and use of chemicals for commercial purposes accelerated significantly after World War II. Of the millions of chemical substances known in industry and scientific research, tens of thousands have been produced for use in the industrial, agriculture, and service sectors. Since the 1960s, more than 100,000 chemicals have been registered for commercial use in the EU alone,[150] and around the world more than 248,000 different chemical products are commercially available.[151] The global chemicals industry engages in about $3.5 trillion of business annually, and when one includes pharmaceuticals, the total exceeds $5 trillion. These figures are expected to double by 2030.[152] Much of this activity remains in industrialized countries, but the production and use of all types of chemicals are rising rapidly in developing countries.[153] Indeed, China leads the world in combined chemical purchases and sales.[154]

Many chemicals enter the market and become widely used before systematic assessments are made,[155] and detailed analyses of the potential impacts on human health and the environment exist for only a relatively small number of substances that have been sold on the open market.[156] Not all chemicals are hazardous, of course, but toxic substances are produced or used in every country. Toxic chemicals include poisons, carcinogens, teratogens (affecting offspring), mutagens (affecting genes), irritants, narcotics, and chemicals with dermatological effects. Toxins are released into the environment through the normal use of certain products (e.g., pesticides and fertilizers), industrial and manufacturing practices that involve or produce hazardous chemicals, leakage from wastes, mismanagement, accidents, and intentional dumping. Once they have been dispersed into the environment, the complete clean-up of many toxic chemicals is difficult, sometimes impossible, and their harmful effects can continue for many years. The World Health Organization (WHO) estimated that 1.6 million deaths could be attributed to selected chemicals in 2016 alone and that the negative health impacts of toxic chemicals cost economies tens of billions of dollars.[157]

The issue-definition phase began in the 1960s, when concern started to grow about potentially negative impacts from pesticides and other chemicals. Instrumental in this process were both groundbreaking publications, especially Rachel Carson's *Silent Spring*, and high-profile accidents, such as the 1968 tragedy in Kyushu, Japan, in which 1300 people were poisoned after eating rice contaminated with high levels of PCBs.[158] In the late 1960s and early 1970s, new risk assessments led some industrialized countries to adopt domestic regulations on relatively small sets of hazardous chemicals. The United States, for example, banned dichlorodiphenyltrichloroethane, commonly known as DDT, in 1972 and initiated controls on PCBs in 1976.[159]

Stimulated in part by discussion on hazardous chemicals at the 1972 United Nations Conference on the Human Environment in Stockholm,[160] governments adopted several multilateral agreements in the 1970s and early 1980s to help protect oceans, regional seas, and rivers from dumping and pollution.[161] In 1976, UNEP created the International Register of Potentially Toxic Chemicals to gather, process, and distribute information. The Food and Agriculture Organization of the UN (FAO) and UNEP led development of both the 1985 International Code of Conduct for the Distribution and Use of Pesticides and the 1987 London Guidelines for the Exchange of Information on Chemicals in International Trade. Unfortunately, many developing countries lacked the regulatory infrastructure that would enable them to use the information made available through these initiatives.[162]

In 1989, amendments to the FAO Code of Conduct and the UNEP London Guidelines created a voluntary PIC procedure to help countries, especially developing countries, learn about chemicals that had been banned or severely restricted in other countries so that they could make informed decisions before they allowed them as imports. Although the voluntary PIC system was seen as a victory for NGOs, which had long called for its adoption, and for developing countries, because they hoped it would assist them to identify and regulate imports, many supporters also believed that a voluntary system would be insufficient.[163]

The fact-finding stage, in general terms, began during the formal preparations for the 1992 Earth Summit, during which governments agreed to devote an entire chapter in Agenda 21 to chemicals. Among other actions, Agenda 21 called on states to create a mandatory PIC procedure and to improve coordination among the many national agencies and international organizations working on chemicals issues. To this end, governments created the Intergovernmental Forum on Chemical Safety in 1994 to address coordination among governments and the Inter-Organization Programme for the Sound Management of Chemicals in 1995 to address coordination among international organizations (see Box 3.5).[164] The fact-finding process continued in these bodies.

Governments then asked UNEP and the FAO to convene global negotiations with the goal of adopting a binding PIC procedure. The result was the 1998 Rotterdam Convention on the Prior Informed Consent Procedure for Certain Hazardous Chemicals and Pesticides in International Trade, which mandates that parties export certain toxic chemicals only with the informed consent of the importing party.[165] More than 160 countries have ratified the Convention. However, the United States is not a party, and many other countries do not follow, or do not have the capacity to follow, all the required procedures.

During this period, concern began to grow regarding a particular set of toxic chemicals known as persistent organic pollutants, or POPs. Scientists and policymakers usually define POPs as possessing four key characteristics: toxicity, persistence, bioaccumulation, and long-range environmental transport.

POPs are toxic. Although extensive variations occur across substances, species, and exposures, the observed or suspected impacts of POPs on wildlife and humans include

❖ BOX 3.5 ROTTERDAM AND STOCKHOLM CONVENTIONS MILESTONES

1962: Rachel Carson publishes *Silent Spring*.

1976: UNEP creates the International Register of Potentially Toxic Chemicals.

1985: FAO Council adopts the International Code of Conduct for the Distribution and Use of Pesticides.

1987: UNEP Governing Council adopts the London Guidelines for the Exchange of Information on Chemicals in International Trade.

1989: Amendments to the FAO Code of Conduct and the UNEP London Guidelines create a voluntary prior informed consent (PIC) procedure for trade in toxic chemicals.

1992: Agenda 21, adopted by the Rio Earth Summit, calls on governments to create a mandatory PIC procedure by 2000 and improve coordination among both national governments and international organizations working on chemical issues.

1994: The Intergovernmental Forum on Chemical Safety (IFCS) is created to enhance coordination among governments.

1995: The Inter-Organization Programme for the Sound Management of Chemicals (IOMC) is created to coordinate efforts among international organizations.

1995: UNEP's Governing Council calls for international assessment of twelve persistent organic pollutants (POPs) known as the dirty dozen.

1995: The Intergovernmental Conference to Adopt Global Programme of Action for Protection of the Marine Environment from Land-Based Activities calls for a legally binding treaty targeting the dirty dozen.

1996: Formal negotiations begin on a potential global PIC convention.

1996: A UNEP/IFCS working group, established by the IOMC, concludes that scientific evidence supports international action to reduce the risks posed by POPs.

1997: UNEP's Governing Council authorizes formal negotiations aimed at creating a global POPs treaty.

1998: The Rotterdam PIC Convention is adopted.

1998: Formal negotiations begin on a POPs treaty.

2001: The Stockholm Convention on Persistent Organic Pollutants is adopted.

2004: The Stockholm and Rotterdam Conventions enter into force.

2007: The Persistent Organic Pollutants Review Committee (POPRC) concludes its first set of evaluations and formally recommends that parties add nine POPs to the Stockholm Convention.

2008: The working group established by the Basel, Rotterdam, and Stockholm Conventions COPs submit their formal synergies proposal.

2009: Parties to the Stockholm Convention add nine POPs to the control measures.

2011: Endosulfan added to the Stockholm Convention and three chemicals, including endosulfan, added to the Rotterdam Convention.

2013: The Basel, Rotterdam, and Stockholm (BRS) Conventions make history by holding a coordinated, joint COP and identify concrete areas where synergies could be achieved. One chemical added to the Stockholm Convention; four to the Rotterdam Convention.

2015: The BRS Conventions hold their first meeting in the Triple COP format. Three POPs are added to the Stockholm Convention. One chemical (methamidophos) is added to the Rotterdam Convention.

2017: The BRS Conventions meet. DecaBDE and SCCPs added to Annex A of the Stockholm Convention and HCBD added to Annex C (it had already been listed in Annex A). Two pesticides and SCCPs added to the Rotterdam Convention.

2019: The BRS Conventions meet. Parties to the Stockholm Convention add two toxic chemical groups, dicofol and PFOA, which together total about 4000 individual chemical formulations. The Rotterdam Convention establishes a compliance mechanism and adds a pesticide and an industrial chemical to the treaty's PIC procedure.

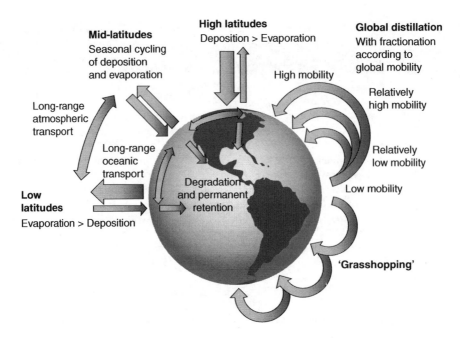

Figure 3.2 Migration of Persistent Organic Pollutants

Source: UNEP, *GEO 3: Global Environmental Outlook* (Nairobi: UNEP, 2002), 236.

reproductive disorders, birth defects, cancers, developmental impairment, damage to central and peripheral nervous systems, immune system impairment, and endocrine disruption.[166]

POPs are stable and persistent compounds that resist photolytic, chemical, and biological degradation. This means that once released into the environment, most POPs remain toxic for years before breaking down.

POPs bioaccumulate. Once ingested, they are readily absorbed by, and remain in, the fatty tissue of living organisms. Over time, POP concentrations can build up in animals and people, potentially reaching 10,000 times the background levels found in the surrounding environment. Fish, birds, mammals, and humans can absorb high concentrations of POPs quickly if they eat multiple organisms in which POPs have already accumulated. Mammals, including humans, can then pass these chemicals to their offspring through breast milk.

Finally, POPs can engage in long-range transport across national borders and have been found in ecosystems, waterways, animals, and people thousands of kilometers from the nearest location of their production, use, or release. POPs travel through air currents, waterways, migrating animals, food chains, and a process known as the grasshopper effect, in which POPs released in one part of the world can, through a repeated process of evaporation and deposit, be transported through the atmosphere to regions far away from the original source (see Figure 3.2).

In the 1980s and 1990s, Canada and Sweden played lead roles in the issue-definition and fact-finding phases by both supporting POPs research and putting POPs on the agenda of several international fora. Much of this work was initiated after scientific studies found very high levels of certain POPs in the Arctic, including in wildlife and even in the breast milk of Inuit women in northern Canada, thousands of miles from the nearest source of emissions.[167] These findings and subsequent studies added a normative component to the issue-definition phase because POPs were now seen as a threat to the food chain, and thus the cultural survival, of the Inuit.[168]

The issue-definition phase reached a turning point in May 1995, when the lead states, NGOs, and representatives of the Inuit and other indigenous peoples used the growing scientific data to successfully lobby the governments on UNEP's Governing Council to call for an international assessment of twelve POPs known as the dirty dozen: the pesticides aldrin, chlordane, DDT, dieldrin, endrin, heptachlor, mirex, and toxaphene; the industrial chemicals PCBs and hexachlorobenzene (which is also a pesticide); and two unintentionally produced substances, dioxins and furans, which are released when certain substances are burned or as a by-product of particular industrial activities.

In response, the Inter-Organization Programme for the Sound Management of Chemicals established a working group to proceed with fact finding. In June 1996, the working group concluded that scientific evidence supported international action to reduce the risks posed by POPs. In February 1997, UNEP's Governing Council endorsed this conclusion and authorized formal negotiations aimed at creating a POPs treaty. Organizations and initiatives with foci outside of chemicals also called for negotiations, revealing the important impact that action in multiple venues can have on initiating or advancing the fact-finding or negotiation stages.

The fact-finding process continued in eight regional workshops on POPs that UNEP and the Intergovernmental Forum on Chemical Safety convened in preparation for the negotiations. More than 138 countries participated in the workshops, which greatly increased awareness of POPs issues, particularly in developing countries and countries with economies in transition. Preparations also included convening preliminary meetings and studying previous negotiating processes on chemicals and specific aspects of the Rotterdam Convention, the regional Aarhus POPs Protocol to the Convention on Long-Range Transboundary Air Pollution, the Montreal Protocol, and other initiatives to see what lessons could be learned.[169]

The bargaining stage officially began in June 1998 and lasted three years. During the negotiations, Canada, the EU, Norway, Switzerland, and NGOs, including those representing northern indigenous peoples, played lead roles. The POPs negotiations were notable for the prominent role given to the Inuit and other northern indigenous peoples to speak to delegates and the press concerning the threats that POPs posed to their health and their cultural heritage of subsistence hunting and fishing.

Countries playing potential veto roles shifted according to the specific issue in question. Interestingly, no governments opposed creating controls on the dirty dozen. The issue-definition and fact-finding phases, combined with UNEP-organized workshops and other efforts that took place before negotiations began, produced a ringing endorsement at the first session of the Intergovernmental Negotiating Committee of the need for global regulations. This reflected not only a general acceptance of the science but also the relatively modest adjustment costs, given that industrialized countries had already established significant controls on the dirty dozen.

Nevertheless, many other contentious issues remained. The EU and NGOs supported creating controls on chemicals beyond the dirty dozen (as was done in the regional Aarhus POPs Protocol). The veto coalition on this issue, which included many developing countries, the United States, and Japan (supported by companies that made or used the chemicals), argued that starting with the twelve on which consensus existed provided the best opportunity for creating a new regime. Even within the dirty dozen, the African Group, Australia, Brazil, China, India, Indonesia, and the United States, among others, stated that they needed individual exemptions for specific uses of certain chemicals, at least for a short period. In addition, while all governments knew prior to the start of the negotiations that they would need to create provisions for providing FTA to developing countries to help them implement the regime,[170] the industrialized and developing countries disagreed strongly on the mechanism for providing financial assistance. Countries also disagreed about possible procedures for adding new chemicals, whether the treaty should include a noncompliance procedure, and what, if any, formal institutional links should be created to other treaties, such as the

Basel and Rotterdam Conventions. Resolving these and other issues required difficult and detailed negotiations, but in the end they succeeded.

The 2001 Stockholm Convention on Persistent Organic Pollutants seeks to protect human health and the environment by eliminating or reducing the production, use, trade, and emission of POPs.[171] The treaty divides POPs into three categories according to their source and the type of control measures placed on them. Substances slated for elimination are addressed in Article 3 and listed in Annex A. Substances whose production and use will be severely limited, like DDT, are addressed in Article 3 and listed in Annex B. POPs produced inadvertently, as unintentional by-products of other activities, are addressed in Article 5 and listed in Annex C. Because the complete elimination of Annex C substances is often technically impossible, parties agree to take specific steps to "minimize and where feasible eliminate" their emission by seeking to apply the relevant "best available techniques" and "best environmental practices," including those spelled out in annexes to the Convention.

The initial treaty mandated that all parties eliminate the production and use of aldrin, chlordane, dieldrin, endrin, heptachlor, hexachlorobenzene, mirex, PCBs, and toxaphene (Annex A); restrict the production and use of DDT to what is needed for disease-vector control and when there are no suitable and affordable alternatives (Annex B); and minimize the release of dioxins and furans into the environment (Annex C).[172]

However, the control measures also include exemptions that address concerns by certain countries that they would have trouble joining the treaty if they could not use one or more of the banned chemicals for specific uses for at least some period of time. As in the development of the ozone regime, these exemptions were accepted by lead states as the price necessary to get all states to agree to the Convention.

Most broadly, African countries and health-related NGOs advocated strongly for a broad exemption for the use of DDT against mosquitoes that spread malaria, a disease that exacts a huge toll on human health and economic well-being in many tropical countries. This position gained near-universal support. As noted, DDT was placed in Annex B, and the treaty allows for an "acceptable use" of DDT for vector-borne disease control. At the same time, the Convention includes mechanisms for reviewing this use so as to reduce it as alternative practices and chemicals are introduced in the affected countries.

The convention also created exemptions that permit specific parties to continue using small amounts of specific POPs for specific purposes for specific amounts of time as well as broader accepted-uses exemptions for uses of certain chemicals. For example, Australia and China called for the continued use of mirex to control termites, including in telephone poles, in remote areas. Botswana and China supported continued use of chlordane to protect wooden dams and certain other structures from insects. Other parties argued that they would need small amounts of aldrin for use as an insecticide during the transition to alternatives. Each party when ratifying the treaty must indicate which exemptions it will claim (e.g., using mirex for termite control). The exemption then lasts for five years. After that, an extension for another five years must be specifically granted by the COP.[173]

In addition, Russia, the United States, and other countries noted that even though new equipment using PCBs was no longer produced, because they were once widely used in electrical transformers and other equipment, hundreds of thousands of tons of PCBs remained in working equipment around the world, and it would be impossible to take them off-line immediately. Thus, an "articles in use" exemption exists for PCBs, but countries must keep the PCBs in this equipment from leaking into the environment while in use or when it is replaced and becomes waste.

To ensure an effective phase-out process, parties must also ban the import or export of all POPs controlled under the convention (except for narrowly defined purposes or environmentally sound disposal), promote the use of the best available technologies and practices for reducing emissions and managing POP wastes, and take steps to prevent the development and commercial introduction of new POPs. Parties must also develop national implementation plans; report on the production, import, and export of controlled POPs; and review the effectiveness of the convention at regular intervals.

As seen in the ozone case, an important factor in the long-term effectiveness of an environmental regime is the process for increasing the scope and strength of its environmental protections in response to new information or technological developments. The Stockholm Convention established specific scientifically based criteria and a step-by-step procedure for identifying, evaluating, and adding chemicals to the treaty (Article 8 and Annexes D, E, and F). This critical feature, which sought to ensure the convention's relevance beyond the dirty dozen, took a long time to develop. During negotiations, the EU advocated a process emphasizing the precautionary principle and allowing the addition of chemicals relatively easily and quickly. The United States, Japan, Australia, and others wanted more sovereign control and a mechanism that relied only on explicit risk analysis of chemicals proven to cause harm.

The agreed-upon process represents a working compromise between these views, incorporating elements of risk analysis that include consideration of specific criteria, use of experts, precaution, flexibility, and sovereign control by the parties (see Figure 3.3).[174] Under the treaty, any party may nominate a chemical for evaluation. A POPs Review Committee (POPRC), made up of thirty-one experts nominated by parties, then examines the nominated chemical in detail. The POPRC first determines whether the substance can be considered a POP under the terms of the treaty by examining its toxicity, persistence, bioaccumulation, and potential for long-range environmental transport according to criteria set out in the convention. If a substance meets the POPs criteria, the committee drafts a risk profile to evaluate whether future emissions would produce significant adverse environmental or human health impacts. If the POPRC determines it would, the committee develops a risk-management evaluation that assesses the relevant costs and benefits of international controls and potential exemptions. Finally, based on these analyses, the POPRC decides whether to recommend that the COP consider controlling the substance under the convention. In carrying out these interrelated tasks, the POPRC is instructed to employ specific scientific criteria for identifying and evaluating candidate POPs (as set out in Annex D of the convention), to follow specific information requirements for developing a risk profile for candidate POPs (Annex E), to consider socioeconomic impacts of controlling a POP in developing the risk-management evaluation (Annex F), and to include a strong perspective of precaution. Each stage (criteria, risk profile, risk-management evaluation) typically takes one year, but some chemicals progress more slowly if the POPRC requires additional time to gather and review relevant information.

As demanded by the EU, precaution informs the process, in that the absence of strict scientific certainty does not prevent the COP from controlling a potentially hazardous substance.[175] At the same time, sovereign control is preserved, as demanded by the United States and others, in that only parties can nominate a POP, and all parties can submit comments and suggest changes to POPRC outputs before they are final. The COP then not only reviews POPRC's recommendation but also considers broader socioeconomic issues and holds final decision-making authority, including on any potential exemptions.[176]

To keep a few countries from preventing global action, the convention allows for voting if all efforts to reach consensus on the listing of a new POP have been exhausted. A three-fourths majority of parties present and voting is required to add a chemical (the EU votes as a unit, so its vote counts for the number of its member states, even if they are not present). This procedure, which has only been used a few times to add chemicals, contrasts with the Rotterdam Convention, which requires consensus. For example, in 2013, opposition by Sudan, and only Sudan, prevented the addition of fenthion to the Rotterdam Convention's PIC procedure, even though fenthion clearly met the technical and procedural criteria. In the Stockholm Convention, opposition by one country would lead to a vote.

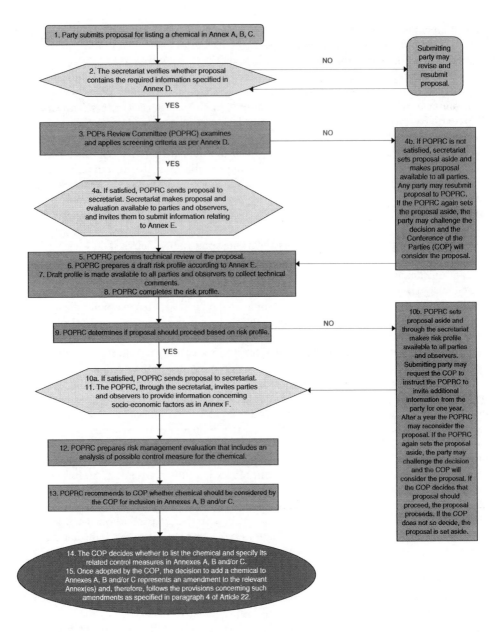

Figure 3.3 Process for Adding New Chemicals to the Stockholm Convention

As noted earlier, to organize the control measures and to make the addition of chemicals more orderly, chemicals slated for elimination go into Annex A, those to be restricted go into Annex B, and unintentionally produced substances go into Annex C. This means that adding chemicals requires amending only the relevant annex, which can be done by a COP decision rather than formally amending the main body of the convention, which would require ratification. However, during the negotiations, states could not agree whether additions to the annexes should be immediately binding on all parties, as preferred by most EU states and many other delegations, or subject to formal ratification, as preferred by Canada, China, India, Japan, Russia, the United States, and others. In a compromise, delegates created opt-in

Photo 3.6 Members of Global Asbestos Action Alliance presented a petition of 7000 signatories from more than 100 countries, calling for action on listing chrysotile asbestos under the Rotterdam Convention.

Courtesy Kiara Worth, IISD/*Earth Negotiations Bulletin*, http://enb.iisd.org

and opt-out provisions. Countries that ratify the treaty can choose to be an opt-in party, which means that they are not required to address a chemical added to an annex unless they formally ratify the change.[177] Otherwise, the addition automatically applies unless they object within one year (the opt-out provision). While potentially confusing, the entire compromise package makes it easier to add chemicals and speeds the implementation of the new controls.[178]

Another critical feature of the convention is the financial mechanism that assists developing countries and countries with economies in transition in meeting their treaty obligations. Although all negotiators acknowledged the importance of providing FTA, different views existed on the proper level and delivery mechanisms. Most developing countries supported a new stand-alone financial institution patterned after the Montreal Protocol's Multilateral Fund. They opposed designating the Global Environment Facility (GEF) as the financial mechanism because of concerns about the GEF's willingness to address POPs as a priority area. The G-77 also insisted that all FTA be new and additional to current programs so that POPs-related activities did not result in less FTA in other areas. Donor countries preferred to use the GEF, arguing that doing so would reduce administrative costs, provide parties with important expertise, and produce synergies with existing programs in other fora, such as the Rotterdam and Basel Conventions.

In the final compromise, industrialized countries agreed to provide FTA to assist countries to implement the convention. Although special obligations are placed on developed countries, all countries with the resources and expertise to do so are called on to provide technical assistance (Article 12). This is one of several examples in the Stockholm Convention in which the CBDR principle is implemented slightly differently than in previous treaties.

The amount of financial and other assistance to be provided by developed countries is unspecified, but it must represent new resources rather than funds redirected from existing development or environmental assistance programs. The GEF was designated as the main financial mechanism, although initially on a provisional basis. It has since been confirmed as the central element. The COP gives instructions to and receives reports from the GEF, reviews the GEF's performance on a regular basis, and has the option to stop using the GEF entirely or as the main conduit for financial assistance. In response to the concerns expressed during the negotiations, the GEF subsequently created a dedicated chemicals focal area, and donor countries have earmarked hundreds of millions of dollars expressly for chemicals.

The Stockholm Convention entered into force in 2004. It currently has 184 parties. The United States remains a non-party. Although the George W. Bush administration supported the treaty and intended to push for its ratification by the Senate, the terrorist attacks on September 11, 2001 put the White House on a war footing, allowing a few opponents in the Senate to block consideration of the treaty out of concern for how the regime might expand.[179] Yet this may have been a tactical error: as a non-party, the United States may speak at the COPs, but its voice does not count in actual decision making, it cannot vote, and it cannot serve as a member of the POPRC.

Regime Strengthening: Adding New Chemicals

Lead-state efforts to strengthen and expand the regime began almost immediately. COP1 in 2005 adopted important decisions on the budget, financial mechanism, operation of the POPRC, and other issues necessary for the regime to operate. Six months later, the POPRC held its first meeting and considered the first set of chemicals proposed by parties for possible inclusion in the Convention. From 2006 through 2008, the POPRC developed and approved risk profiles and risk-management evaluations for nine chemicals and recommended that the COP consider adding these "candidate" POPs to the Convention.

Anticipation was high prior to COP4 in 2009, as participants and observers wondered whether parties would be able to reach agreement to expand the regime by adding the candidate POPs to the Convention. The EU, Norway, Switzerland, and several other countries supported listing all nine substances. Veto states varied depending on the chemical. Veto states were empowered to the extent that they were willing to prevent consensus unless certain exemptions were allowed; if they could credibly claim they would not ratify an amendment (in theory, this only works for countries that produce or use sufficient quantities of a substance to threaten the effectiveness of the controls); or if they were willing to withhold support on an unrelated issue if their position was not adopted. In the end, COP4 added all nine chemicals to the convention, with certain exemptions and acceptable purposes. This significantly strengthened the regime only five years after the treaty entered into force.

By 2020, parties had added eighteen new chemicals to the annexes, and more are under consideration. (See Boxes 3.6 and 3.7.) The country that nominates a POP acts as the lead state on that substance, with support from other concerned parties. In some instances, parties work as a coalition, but one often makes the formal nomination for political reasons. For example, nominations coming from a developing country might carry more influence with other developing countries or countries in a certain region. Lead states push for adopting the recommendations of the POPRC, which usually includes information on potential exemptions. When there are options, lead states push for the inclusion of chemicals in Annex A, which mandates elimination, and for zero or only a limited number of specific, time-limited exemptions. Veto states might oppose the listing entirely, push for inclusion in Annex B, argue for using the broad acceptable purpose exemption category, or push for a large number of specific exemptions. In some cases, listing issues are interrelated. For example, a veto state could offer to relent on listing one chemical in exchange for the creation of more special exemptions for another or a compromise on issues related to FTA.

> ### ✤ BOX 3.6   POPS CONTROLLED UNDER THE STOCKHOLM CONVENTION
>
> Some POPs are subject to more than one type of control measure.
>
> **Annex A: Elimination (with exemptions)**
>
> - Included in the original Convention: aldrin; chlordane; dieldrin; endrin; heptachlor; hexachlorobenzene; mirex; PCBs; toxaphene
> - Added in 2009: chlordecone; hexabromobiphenyl; hexabromodiphenyl ether and hepta-bromodiphenyl ether; alpha hexachlorocyclohexane; beta hexachlorocyclohexane; lindane; pentachlorobenzene; tetrabromodiphenyl ether and pentabromodiphenyl ether
> - Added in 2001: endosulfan
> - Added in 2013: HBCD (hexabromocyclododecane)
> - Added in 2015: hexachlorobutadiene; pentachlorophenol; polychlorinated naphthalenes
> - Added in 2017: DecaBDE; SCCPs (short-chain chlorinated paraffins)
> - Added in 2019: dicofol; PFOA (perfluorooctanoic acid, its salts, and PFOA-related compounds)
>
> **Annex B: Restricted**
>
> - Included in the original Convention: DDT
> - Added in 2009: PFOS (perfluorooctane sulfonic acid, its salts, and perfluorooctane sulfonyl fluoride)
>
> **Annex C: Minimize and Where Feasible Eliminate**
>
> - Included in the original Convention: dioxins; furans; hexachlorobenzene; PCBs
> - Added in 2009: pentachlorobenzene
> - Added in 2015: polychlorinated naphthalenes
> - Added in 2017: HCBD (hexachlorobutadiene)

While the process of adding new substances works well, potential obstacles have been revealed. By creating the POPRC, the Stockholm Convention attempted to separate the scientific and technical consideration of nominated POPs, which are the purview of the POPRC, from the political concerns of parties, which are discussed by the COP. In essence, the POPRC addresses whether the convention can control a substance and how it would do so. Then the COP decides if it should. The lines can blur, however, because the convention asks the POPRC to include certain socioeconomic considerations in the risk-management evaluation phase. This was not an important issue on most of the substances that the POPRC considered at its early meetings, but the shift to evaluating toxic chemicals still in widespread production and use presents a new challenge.[180] Since 2008, a few POPRC members have taken positions that reflect their country's economic and political views as much as the POP's toxicity, persistence, bioaccumulation, long-range environmental transport, and consequential risks to human health and the environment. This has produced some strong exchanges during these POPRC meetings and even some contentious votes.[181]

Ultimately, several "live" chemicals (still in use) have been added to the Stockholm Convention despite strong opposition, including perfluorooctane sulfonate (PFOS) in 2009, endosulfan in 2011, pentachlorophenol in 2015, and dicofol and perfluorooctanoic acid (PFOA) in 2019 (see Box 3.7). India's veto position actually forced a vote in 2015 on the

❖ BOX 3.7   SELECTED POPS ADDED TO THE STOCKHOLM CONVENTION

- **Chlordecone:** Once widely used as an agricultural pesticide (nominated by the EU; added in 2009).
- **Lindane:** A broad-spectrum insecticide; production had decreased in the years before nomination, but it was still produced and used in a few countries (nominated by Mexico; added in 2009).
- **Pentabromodiphenyl ethers:** Used in PCB products, as fungicides, flame retardants, and chemical intermediates, and also produced unintentionally during combustion and as an impurity in certain solvents and pesticides (nominated by Norway; added in 2009).
- **PFOS** (perfluorooctane sulfonic acid, its salts, and perfluorooctane sulfonyl fluoride): Found in firefighting foam, electric and electronic parts, photo imaging, hydraulic fluids, and textiles; widely used in several countries when nominated (nominated by Sweden; added in 2009).
- **Endosulfan:** A broad-spectrum insecticide; widely used in India when nominated (nominated by the EU; added in 2011).
- **Hexabromocyclododecane:** A flame retardant produced in China, Europe, Japan, and the United States and used in building insulation, electronic and electric equipment, automobiles, and upholstered furniture (nominated by Norway; added in 2015).
- **Pentachlorophenol:** Once used as a pesticide and disinfectant and still used as a wood preservative, including for telephone poles in some countries and especially in fiberboard and particle board in India (nominated by the EU in 2011; added in 2015 by a vote).
- **Dicofol:** Pesticide used on a variety of field crops, fruits, vegetables, ornamentals, cotton, and tea (nominated by the EU in 2013; added in 2019).
- **PFOA** (perfluorooctane sulfonic acid, its salts, and perfluorooctane sulfonyl fluoride): Along with PFOA-related compounds, these are widely used in textiles, paper and paints, firefighting foams, electric and electronic parts, surface treatment agents, and in the production of non-stick kitchen and food processing equipment. PFOA has been detected in industrial waste, stain-resistant carpets, carpet cleaning liquids, house dust, microwave popcorn bags, water, food, and Teflon (nominated by the EU in 2015; added in 2019).

addition of pentachlorophenol. Ninety parties voted to add pentachlorophenol, two opposed, and eight abstained.[182]

While lead states and their supporters have the resources to overcome veto states, either by addressing their concerns with exemptions or by resorting to a vote, opt-in countries are not required to ratify the addition of particular chemicals, and several important countries have not. However, there is some evidence that the convention can affect countries that do not ratify a particular chemical by reinforcing or even accelerating global market forces or by affecting national political and regulatory mechanisms. For example, at the time of its listing, endosulfan was still widely used as a pesticide in India. The Indian government tried to prevent its addition to the Stockholm Convention but finally relented when agreement was reached on a broad set of exemptions. However, once endosulfan was listed, India faced pressure from both environmentalists and manufacturers of alternatives to reduce and eventually eliminate its production, showing that the Stockholm Convention can "play an important agenda-setting role that can help influence domestic decision-making even in the presence of particular economic interests."[183]

Regime Strengthening: Financial and Technical Assistance

By COP4 in 2009, the suite of intersecting issues relating to financial resources and technical assistance had become complex.[184] Among other issues, parties needed to review reports on the effectiveness of financial assistance; review needs-assessment reports on the potential costs for developing countries to implement the regime in the future; select regional centers through which capacity building and technical assistance would flow; decide whether the regime should keep the GEF as the financial mechanism; and if so, provide updated guidance on how the COP wanted the GEF to support the convention.

Further complicating matters, the bargaining strategies of many participants led to interlinkages among issues. This is not uncommon during global environmental negotiations, but it forced delegates to search for a complex package deal. For example, many developing countries would not allow a decision on the listing of additional chemicals until a satisfactory resolution was reached on the FTA package. The EU attempted to include noncompliance as part of the overall compromise package. China, India, and others essentially refused to consider a package that included a noncompliance procedure. Some countries dug in their heels on issues relating to certain chemicals in an attempt to get movement on other chemicals or on an unrelated issue.

In the end, these linkages produced a stalemate that almost derailed the meeting, something that would have also prevented adding the first set of new chemicals. Finally, after 4:00 am on Saturday (the negotiations were scheduled to end at 6:00 pm on Friday), a final compromise allowed the COP to add the nine new chemicals, reaffirmed the GEF as the principal entity for the financial mechanism, and requested the GEF to streamline the processes for applying for and receiving financial assistance.[185] Importantly, COP4 also agreed that when donor countries replenish the GEF, they should include funding for the implementation needs of developing countries, as revealed in their Stockholm Convention national implementation plans, and the obligations related to the listing of new chemicals.

One year later, in May 2010, global negotiations for the fifth GEF replenishment concluded, with thirty-five donors agreeing to provide the GEF with $4.34 billion to support GEF activities through June 2014, a 54 percent increase above the 2006–2010 level. Of the total replenishment, $425 million was dedicated to the chemicals focal area.[186] By 2020, the GEF had allocated more than $1.2 billion to projects in more than 135 countries that support Stockholm Convention implementation. The GEF had also leveraged approximately US$4.8 billion in co-financing—from governments, the private sector, international organizations, foundations, and NGOs—to support these POPs projects.[187]

The provision of technical assistance flows through UN agencies, such as UNEP and UNDP, and sixteen autonomous Stockholm Convention regional and subregional centers in Algeria, Brazil, China, Czech Republic, India, Indonesia, Iran, Kenya, Kuwait, Mexico, Panama, Russia, Senegal, South Africa, Spain, and Uruguay. These centers, some of which also act as Basel Convention Regional Centers, serve as official nodes for capacity building, information sharing, training, and technology transfer.

Although significant progress has been made by the COP, the GEF, the parties, and other actors to develop and deploy resources to support implementation of the Stockholm Convention, concerns remain that not enough funds are being earmarked for POPs projects and that too little time, money, and technical assistance are spent on reducing use of POPs, destroying stockpiles, and testing and deploying alternatives. Going forward, the COP will continue to monitor the impact and cost-effectiveness of the GEF, regional centers, and other international organizations. At the same time, political preferences of the donors for the GEF, and of many developing countries for the centers, may leave the current architecture unchanged for many years.

Regime Strengthening: Partnerships and Networks

To help advance the goals of the Convention without harming public health, the regime established the Global Alliance, a DDT initiative modeled somewhat on the partnerships created under the Basel Convention. This network—which includes national health agencies and other government institutions, international organizations including the World Health

Organization (WHO), NGOs, corporations, and scientists and medical experts—works to deploy more effective and cost-efficient products, methods, and strategies to control malaria while reducing the use of DDT.

The COP also created a PCB Elimination Network to strengthen efforts to phase out equipment containing PCBs. Members include experts from multiple treaty secretariats, international organizations, governments, NGOs, research institutions, and industry. The network exchanges information, evaluates PCB use, supports pilot programs in developing countries, promotes improved techniques for managing PCBs, and develops recommendations for further action.

Both alliances seek to identify gaps in existing initiatives, improve coordination among relevant actors, catalyze new action, and take advantage of the global scale of the Stockholm Convention for awareness raising and information sharing. The networks, which likely would not exist without the convention, demonstrate how regimes can enhance the impact of their formal regulations by developing initiatives that coordinate and support action among multiple stakeholders to achieve common goals.[188]

Regime Strengthening: Synergies

Even prior to the Convention's entry into force, Switzerland, the EU, and others began pushing the concept of creating formal coordination among the three main chemicals and waste conventions to achieve synergies and reduce costs. In response, the Basel, Rotterdam, and Stockholm COPs established a joint working group to examine the issue and draft recommendations. By 2007, the joint working group presented recommendations, and at COP3, Stockholm Convention Parties strongly supported pursuing the initiative. This was a distinct break from earlier meetings, where developing countries expressed concern that the process would divert attention and resources away from technical assistance. Formal plans for this groundbreaking initiative had to be approved by all three COPs, which was accomplished by May 2009.

In 2010, parties convened an extraordinary simultaneous meeting of the COPs to the Basel, Rotterdam, and Stockholm Conventions (Ex-COP). The Ex-COP adopted a single omnibus decision on synergies that outlined the intention to offer joint services, organize joint activities, synchronize budget cycles, conduct joint audits, coordinate or combine many secretariat functions, coordinate review arrangements, develop joint clearinghouse and other information and communications activities, and establish a new executive secretary to oversee the secretariats of all three conventions.

In 2013, the three conventions began holding all their COPs together. These "Triple COPs" now meet every two years. Each COP takes turns holding individual plenary sessions on convention-specific issues, while at other times the three COPs meet simultaneously to decide on joint budget, administration, and implementation issues. The joint meetings have had mixed results. Positive results include reduced costs and, more substantively, the ability for parties to consider issues that link two more of the conventions in an integrated fashion at the same time rather than considering one aspect at one COP and another at a different COP several months later. (POPs wastes, financial assistance, and regional centers are three examples.) However, the joint meetings have large and complex agendas and tax the physical and mental stamina of delegates and secretariat staff. This has led to unnecessarily hurried activity at the end of the meetings as well as potential misunderstandings or mistakes. It has also allowed countries to deploy veto and brinkmanship negotiation tactics across treaties by, for example, refusing to allow agreement on a particular issue in one convention unless their positions were reflected in a decision on an unrelated issue in another convention.[189]

Administratively, certain operational elements within the three convention secretariats and regional centers are now merged, especially in the joint secretariat location in Geneva. These include activities relating to information management, public awareness, publishing, meeting planning and operations, budget cycles, and general administrative and support staff functions. This has improved the Secretariat's ability to assist developing countries on issues that overlap conventions; allow it to leverage more co-financing opportunities; and produce financial savings associated with administration, travel, translation, interpretation, facilities, computing, communications, document production, and meetings costs.[190]

Regime Non-Strengthening: Noncompliance Procedures

Creating effective noncompliance procedures has proven a difficult task for most environmental regimes. The Montreal Protocol is one of the very few that have a working procedure for examining potential cases of state noncompliance. Article 17 of the Stockholm Convention states that the COP will develop "mechanisms for determining noncompliance with the provisions of this Convention and for the treatment of Parties found to be in noncompliance." The EU and Switzerland have attached significant importance to developing a robust noncompliance procedure and play a strong lead role. Other industrialized countries and some developing countries attach less importance to the issue, acting as potential swing states. A group of developing countries, often led by China, India, and Iran, constitutes a powerful veto coalition. They link implementation and compliance to the provision of sufficient FTA, arguing that a noncompliance procedure can only be developed after such assistance has been provided and that the lack of such assistance would be noncompliance on the part of donor countries.

Resolving these differences during negotiation of the convention failed, leading to the language in Article 17, which carries no deadline. COP1 created a working group on noncompliance to consider the issue in detail. However, discussions at successive COPs yielded little progress (and sometimes generated heated debate) beyond a preliminary draft text covered with square brackets and alternative formulations supported by different groups. (Square brackets are used to indicate portions of a draft document where parties do not agree.) Progress reached at one COP does not always carry over to the next one. Although parties agree that the noncompliance mechanism for the POPs regime should be facilitative rather than punitive, fundamental differences remain on how to initiate action on potential cases of noncompliance (some countries reject giving either the Secretariat or other parties the authority to initiate the procedure), the information to be examined, whether the provision of specific levels of FTA by donor countries can be evaluated under the noncompliance mechanism, and the composition and decision-making processes for the compliance committee.

The Chemicals Regime Today: Successes and Challenges

The global regime for toxic chemicals has expanded significantly since governments adopted the Stockholm Convention in 2001. Eighteen new chemicals have been added as of 2020. The production, use, and emissions of controlled POPs have declined, as has the use of specific exemptions for the original dirty dozen. The POPRC continues to evaluate candidate POPs nominated by parties. The GEF has created a dedicated chemicals focal area, distributed more than $1.2 billion in support of the Stockholm Convention, and helped to mobilize more than $4.8 billion in additional co-financing. Regional centers serve as nodes for capacity building, technical assistance, and synergistic cooperation with the Basel Convention. Technical guidelines have been developed to help reduce dioxin and furan emissions as well as emissions from POPs waste. Countries and research organizations share data on the presence of POPs in the environment, animals, and humans, and a designated group helps coordinate and expand implementation of the global monitoring plan and develops reports for the COP.[191] Global networks have been created to speed the deployment of alternatives to DDT and the phase-out of PCBs. Awareness regarding the production, use, and impacts of toxic chemicals has increased within many national governments. The synergies initiative has augmented productive coordination within the Basel, Rotterdam, and Stockholm Conventions.

At the same time, and like all of the other regimes discussed in this book, the Stockholm Convention faces significant challenges. Perhaps the most important is addressing live chemicals. The regime has taken the first, difficult steps in this direction, particularly in the POPRC and COP debates on PFOS, endosulfan, and pentachlorophenol. However, many more POPs exist, and concern is rising over a new class of endocrine disruptors that may affect humans at low doses over long periods and might be found in some brands of everyday products, including plastics, pesticides, and detergents.[192] The United States, Israel, and Malaysia, each a producer and consumer of toxic chemicals, are not yet parties to the Stockholm Convention, and a number of important parties—including Argentina, Australia, China, India, and Russia—have not ratified the control measures on some of the chemicals added to the treaty.[193] More voting within the POPRC or the COP could also weaken support for the regime among countries that lose, those concerned with protecting the principle of sovereignty, or those with economic interests likely to suffer. Working to ensure that the opt-in/opt-out structure or the impact of voting does not create situations in which key countries remain outside the regime with regard to individual POPs, and thus weaken the treaty's global impact, remains a key challenge.

Exemptions represent another challenge. Acceptable purpose- and country-specific exemptions might be political necessities to overcome the lowest-common-denominator problem, but they can weaken the impact of listing a particular chemical, especially if the country in question both produces and consumes the substance. Although countries have retired most exemptions for the original dirty dozen, some chemicals added to the convention carry large lists of acceptable purposes and country-specific exemptions. For the regime to be effective over the long term, observers believe that the COP must prevent parties from renewing these exemptions indefinitely and reduce acceptable uses. This could represent a significant challenge, however, if parties "find it difficult to stand in opposition to renewal of another's exemption if they themselves are hoping to find support for continuing an exemption."[194]

Another challenge, common to all environmental regimes, is the need for more financial and technical resources to assist some developing countries in their transition away from the use of toxic chemicals and to improve the management of those that remain. Although donor countries, the GEF, and others have increased assistance, further regime strengthening and effective implementation will require the availability and proper application of sufficient FTA for some states and some substances.

Finally, the synergies initiative, while largely successful, has demonstrated that integrating the regimes allows countries to play veto roles across treaties and introduce time constraints and other complexities to the COPs that can inhibit progress.

Mercury

The 2013 Minamata Convention on Mercury is the first legally binding global treaty designed to protect the environment and human health from anthropogenic emissions of a heavy metal. As such, the Convention represents an historic achievement that could pave the way for future agreements on other dangerous metals. At the same time, its development and provisions show the difficulty of addressing heavy metals when emissions and releases come from multiple sources, some of which are difficult to regulate, and all are linked to important economic interests.

Mercury (Hg) is a is widespread, inorganic, naturally occurring element. In its pure elemental form, mercury exists as a liquid at room temperature and can vaporize quickly.[195] Mercury is released into the air, water, and soil through erosion and weathering of rocks and soil containing mercury ore, volcanic eruptions, and human activities. Once released, mercury can be carried far from its emission source via air, water, and the food chain. Mercury is removed from this global cycle only through burial in deep ocean and lake sediments and subsurface soils.[196]

Of particular concern is methylmercury, a toxin that is produced from mercury, largely in aquatic ecosystems through microbial action, and is biomagnified in aquatic food chains. The human health risks and environmental impacts of exposure to mercury, especially methylmercury, from both acute high-level inhalation and ingestion and long-term accumulation in the body and blood are well documented.[197] They include serious neurological effects, brain and nerve damage, fetal physical and neurological development and birth defects, tremors, lowered fertility, kidney damage, damage to digestive systems, and contribution to cardiovascular disease.

Human use of mercury use dates back at least to 1500 BC, when the Egyptians used it in the paint that adorned ancient tombs.[198] Over time, humans discovered many ways to use mercury, including in large-scale industrial processes, medicine, medical equipment, consumer products, and cosmetics. As use expanded, so did evidence of, and eventually concern for, the impacts of mercury exposure. For example, in the 1500s Spaniards rediscovered the ancient Roman method of using mercury in mining to purify gold, which they brought to the Americas. Miners suffered documented negative health effects in Peru as early as the 1600s, including tremors and hallucinations, from what we now know as extensive mercury exposure.[199] This method is still practiced today, particularly in developing countries. In the eighteenth and nineteenth centuries, industrial workers used mercury nitrate as part of the process of turning fur from small animals, such as rabbits, into felt for hats. The constant inhalation of the vapors caused hatters to experience tremors, hallucinations, and psychosis, giving rise to the expression "mad as a hatter"[200]—which Lewis Carroll turned into a character in *Alice's Adventures in Wonderland*. Although it was clear that extensive exposure to mercury had harmful effects on humans, awareness of the potential for widespread mercury poisoning did not occur until the 1950s, following the tragic contamination of Minamata Bay in Japan.

In 1950, villagers in the small coastal town of Minamata began exhibiting strange and sometimes fatal neurological and other symptoms. It took until 1956 for this strange disease to be officially acknowledged as "Minamata disease," a type of heavy metal poisoning caused by consuming contaminated fish and shellfish. In 1958, research confirmed that chemical waste containing mercury, a by-product of acetaldehyde production, had been dumped into Minamata Bay by Chisso Corporation since 1932. Subsequent research revealed that other companies had also dumped similar waste in the Minamata Bay watershed. It was not until 1968 that the Japanese government officially recognized Minamata disease. Studies indicate that approximately 3000 people fell ill, approximately 1800 died, and many were born with severe birth defects.

Despite widespread attention, Minamata was not the last mass poisoning. Incidences of Minamata disease, eventually traced to dumping of mercury-contaminated waste, were found elsewhere in Japan and in China. In 1971–1972, perhaps 500 people died in Iraq, and more than 6500 were poisoned when they ate or used wheat seed that had been treated with mercury as a fungicide. Panicked farmers then dumped the remaining seed in the Tigris river, polluting the riverbed and marine life and causing additional health impacts.

International Action Begins

The agenda-setting and fact-finding phase launched in the 1970s and 1980s when some countries, especially in western Europe and North America, established individual or regional policies on mercury emissions or mercury used in processes and products, but these were far from comprehensive. (See Box 3.8.) The EU adopted the first international regulations.

✦ BOX 3.8   MERCURY REGIME MILESTONES

1500 BC: Mercury known to the ancient Chinese, Egyptians, and Hindus.

1724: Gabriel Fahrenheit invents the first mercury thermometer.

1932: Chisso Corporation begins producing acetaldehyde in Minamata, Japan.

1956: Minamata disease officially acknowledged.

1960: Researchers in Sweden notice birds dying from mercury-laden fungicides coated onto seeds.

1970: Landmark US Clean Air Act allowed EPA to set limits on many pollutants, including mercury. High concentrations of mercury discovered in fish in the Great Lakes. Researchers confirm coal plants are a significant source of mercury pollution.

1973: OECD urges member states to reduce anthropogenic releases of mercury to the lowest possible levels.

1990: Congress passes an update to the Clean Air Act that adds mercury to the list of toxic pollutants that need to be controlled to the greatest possible extent. Belgium, Denmark, France, Germany, the Netherlands, Norway, Sweden, Switzerland, and the United Kingdom enact the North Sea Directive, which calls for 70 percent reduction, from a 1985 baseline, in the anthropological input of mercury into the North Sea from human activities by 1999.

1997: Canada, Mexico, and the United States agree on the North American Regional Action Plan on Mercury. Objectives include tracking relevant imports and exports of mercury used in manufactured goods and mercury-containing waste.

2002: UNEP's first Global Mercury Assessment is published.

2003: The Convention on Long-Range Transboundary Air Pollution Protocol on Heavy Metals comes into force.

2008: UNEP's second Global Mercury Assessment is published. Minnesota becomes the first US state to ban intentionally added mercury in cosmetics.

2009: UNEP Governing Council authorizes global negotiations on mercury.

2010: Negotiations begin on a mercury treaty.

2013: Minamata Convention is formally adopted in Kumamoto, Japan.

2017: Minamata Convention on Mercury enters into force and COP1 convenes.

2018: Minamata COP2 convenes in Geneva and discusses technical issues to further the implementation of the Convention.

2019: Minamata COP3 reaches agreement on a permanent secretariat and substantive and technical issues aimed at fostering action to address mercury production and use.

These led to calls for international action across the northern hemisphere under the auspices of Convention on Long-Range Transboundary Air Pollution (LRTAP)—not only on mercury but also on lead and cadmium. These were resisted, most prominently by Canada, until a deal was struck in which two LRTAP protocols would be pursued simultaneously, one on heavy metals and the other on POPs. The resulting agreement, the 1998 Aarhus Protocol on Heavy Metals, required parties to reduce their emissions of cadmium, lead, and mercury below their 1990 levels and take other measures to reduce emissions from industrial sources, combustion processes, and waste incineration.[201]

The first global action did not occur until 2001, when UNEP's Governing Council launched a global assessment on mercury and its health effects, sources, transport, and prevention technologies.[202] UNEP's action represented a global political agreement by countries to initiate formal assessment activities—something that had preceded many treaty negotiations.

In 2003, the UNEP Governing Council agreed that the 2001 report and other information provided sufficient evidence on the adverse impacts of mercury to warrant further international action. While some governments supported starting negotiations on a global treaty, a number of veto states prevented consensus, most notably the United States, arguing that a global treaty was not necessary and that greater success could be achieved by supporting national actions, IGO initiatives, and bilateral and regional cooperation. To this end, the Governing Council encouraged states to adopt policies to reduce mercury emissions and instructed UNEP to sponsor technical assistance and capacity-building activities to help countries set and reach mercury reduction goals.

In 2005, the United States again blocked an agreement to start treaty negotiations, causing some environmentalists and other observers to point out that US opposition stemmed from a desire to protect its fossil fuel industry. Other countries using large amounts of coal, including China and India, supported the US position. With no prospects for treaty negotiations, governments compromised by formalizing UNEP's mercury work and creating the Global Mercury Partnership. The Partnership expanded UNEP's mercury activities, eventually establishing dedicated foci in eight areas: artisanal and small-scale gold mining (ASGM); coal combustion; the chlor-alkali industry; mercury in products; mercury air transport and fate research; waste management; mercury supply (including the mining of mercury) and storage of stockpiles; and releases from the cement industry.[203] The Partnership's activities and the efforts of lead states, in particular the EU, helped build support for stronger international action.

As delegates gathered in 2007 for the UNEP Governing Council/Global Ministerial Environmental Forum, "preferences for international cooperation on mercury ranged from starting a negotiating process for a legally binding instrument, to incorporating mercury into existing agreements, [to] concentrating on voluntary actions" via the Partnership.[204] In a compromise between lead states and the United States and other veto states, delegates adopted a "two-track" approach. UNEP would prepare a second inventory on mercury emissions and strengthen the UNEP Mercury Partnership, while, in the second track, an "open-ended working group (OEWG) of government and stakeholder representatives was established to review and assess options for enhanced voluntary measures and new or existing international legal instruments."[205] While this may not have been an optimal outcome for urgent action, it resembled previous compromises on stratospheric ozone and POPs that set the stage for stronger agreements.

The impasse on negotiations dissolved, quite suddenly, at the next Governing Council meeting in February 2009. The major turning point was the election of Barack Obama, which reversed the Bush administration's opposition to negotiations.[206] With the United States now leading the way, other countries did not want to be seen as blocking consensus. The two OEWG meetings held since 2007 also made countries comfortable with starting formal negotiations. Other factors that helped to break the impasse included efforts by lead states in speaking to potential opponents, the positive model of the Aarhus Protocol, consistent information from the WHO on the health threats posed by mercury, UNEP's 2008 Mercury Assessment, and the Global Mercury Partnership. As a result, governments agreed that UNEP should organize an intergovernmental negotiating committee (INC) to complete a legally binding agreement before February 2013.

Mercury Emissions: Why One Treaty Essentially Needed to Be Several Treaties

Following the successful model of the Rotterdam and Stockholm negotiations, UNEP set a schedule of five INCs to complete the treaty, and several very experienced former national delegates and UN officials were hired to assist the process. With the United States as a lead state, and Japan agreeing to provide funding for meetings and host a diplomatic gathering in Minamata to adopt the treaty, the atmosphere at the start of negotiations was extremely positive.[207]

However, despite the road map, widespread concern about the environmental and human health impacts of mercury emissions, and consensus that an international agreement was necessary, significant obstacles soon became apparent. Similarly to other regimes in this chapter, the mercury emissions under discussion were linked to important economic interests. There were also concerns about: uneven adjustment costs to reduce emissions in different sectors; burden sharing that might benefit nations seen as economic competitors; and insufficient capacity in some countries to stop illegal ASGM. The United States also had limits on what it could accept. As with the Paris Climate Agreement, the United States was both a lead state and a veto state. It could use its political and economic leverage (and the goodwill enjoyed by the Obama administration) to push for strong policies and standards already enacted domestically. At the same time, it acted as a veto state on proposals that would require Washington to enact stronger policies, as these would not be approved by the Senate.

Two additional and crucial difficulties stemmed from a key characteristic of the issue area itself. First, the majority of mercury emissions occur in Asia (49 percent), South America (18 percent), and sub-Saharan Africa (16 percent),[208] although amounts and sources vary by country. The fact that most industrialized countries had already reduced mercury emissions and now wanted developing countries to do the same meant that negotiations had to tackle difficult issues related to the CBDR principle, including financial and technological assistance.

Second, reducing mercury emissions on a global scale requires addressing different types of emission sources, of which the majority are in developing countries. Natural sources account for only about 10 percent of global mercury emissions.[209] Major anthropogenic sources include burning fossil fuels, especially coal-fired power plants and industrial boilers, ASGM, industrial processes that use or release mercury or mercury-containing compounds, mining, waste incineration, cremation, deforestation (which exacerbates erosion), and the manufacture, use, and disposal of a wide variety of mercury-containing products. No single or short list of control policies is sufficient to address mercury on a global scale. This complicated the negotiations, because government delegates had to reach agreement on different policies for each major emission source—each with its own set of potential veto states.

Regime Creation

The negotiation process was more difficult than some had expected and resulted in a treaty with far fewer specific emission-reduction requirements than many would have liked. INC-1 convened in Stockholm in July 2010, during which delegates exchanged initial views on key issues and requested the secretariat to prepare documents to support discussions at the next meeting.[210] During INC-2, held in Chiba, Japan in January 2011, the committee focused discussions on some of the more challenging issues that would form the core of the new agreement.

Coal-Fired Power Plants and other Fossil Fuel Burning: Coal combustion for electricity accounts for approximately 21 percent of annual anthropogenic mercury emissions and is by far the largest source of emissions in the United States, Canada, and the EU. Coal combustion and other activities associated with the production of metals account for an additional 12 percent.[211] In addition, because smokestacks release mercury directly into the air, where it travels quickly and far, deposits, and travels again, coal combustion is a significant contributor to mercury in seafood. Most industrialized countries already had the necessary technology to reduce such emissions, but many developing countries did not. Thus, a fixed baseline and significant reductions would create radically different adjustment costs and technical and economic requirements, especially between industrialized and developing countries. Financial and technical assistance could be provided, but the negotiators would then have to solve other difficult questions, such as: What type of facilities would be eligible?

In what industries? Would construction of new coal burning facilities be banned? Which countries could receive the money? How would money be distributed and by whom? Could donor countries avoid essentially subsidizing their economic competitors?

Artisanal and Small-Scale Gold Mining: ASGM differs from the large-scale, industrial mining operations that dig deep into the ground or create vast mining pits on land owned or leased by large, usually multinational mining companies. In ASGM, dry or wet sediment is separated, or rocks and ore are crushed to small pieces or even a sandy mix, and then mixed with liquid mercury for several hours. The mercury separates the gold from the rocks, dirt, and sludge by binding to it, creating a mercury-gold alloy, which is often 40–80 percent mercury. The amalgam is then heated, releasing the mercury into the air and leaving behind pure gold. ASGM is the single largest source of anthropogenic mercury emissions, accounting for about 38 percent of the annual total.[212] Driven by increasing global demand for gold, especially in developing countries with expanding economies, mercury emissions from ASGM increased significantly between 2010 and 2015 to represent an astounding 70 percent of mercury emissions from South America and nearly 80 percent of the emissions from sub-Saharan Africa.[213]

Most ASGM operations are part of the informal economy, and many operate illegally in forests and other remote places without environmental regulations.[214] Operations range in size from a few individuals to hundreds working in a particular location. ASGM produces 12 to 15 percent of the world's gold, employs 10 to 15 million people, including women and children, and is an important part of local and regional economies.[215] In many cases, national laws had already banned some or all activities associated with ASGM, so the act of adopting a global agreement would not change conditions on the ground. Thus, meaningful and politically acceptable incentives and tools needed to be provided so that countries with significant ASGM would have both the motivation and the ability to enforce rules that sections of their population would not like. This created another group of potential veto states.

Cement Production: Cement production accounts for 11 percent of global anthropogenic mercury emissions and is likely to increase, particularly in developing countries.[216] Mercury is released during cement manufacturing because it is present in raw materials used to make cement, especially limestone.[217] Cement production is the principal source of mercury emissions in North Africa and the Middle East, where it accounts for 52 percent and 43 percent of the totals, respectively.[218] This created another potential group of veto states— one with very little leverage on any other issue but that must be brought into the regime for it to be comprehensive and effective over the long term.

Industrial Processes: Several industrial processes use and emit mercury, and, in some cases, mercury is recovered and sold. For example, mercury is used, primarily in China, as a catalyst to make vinyl chloride monomer, which is then used in the production of polyvinyl chloride, or PVC (synthetic plastic). Mercury is not required, but it is a less costly option. In the United States, this is the largest source of stored and in-use mercury.

Products: There is a surprisingly long and diverse list of consumer, medical, industrial, and other products that contain mercury, including appliance and automotive parts, batteries, dental amalgam, electronics, fluorescent lamps and light bulbs, medical equipment including thermometers, barometers, laboratory instruments, antibacterial and antiseptic supplies, pharmaceuticals, and skin-lightening creams and other cosmetics. Mercury can be released during the manufacture, use, disposal, or incineration of these products. While there has been significant success in phasing out mercury in certain products due to domestic regulations or consumer preferences, and the overall emissions are relatively small, each category of products still being manufactured had ardent supporters that opposed its elimination.

Supply (Mining) and Storage: Mercury mining and refining directly emit less than 1 percent of the mercury into the environment. However, most of the mercury used (and released) in ASGM, products, and processes comes from mining or significant stockpiles around the world. This added something else that the treaty had to address, and more potential veto states.

Discussion on all of these issues continued at INC-3 in Nairobi, Kenya, in early November 2011. Working from a new draft text that contained options based on the views expressed by parties at the previous session, delegates negotiated elements of articles related to ASGM, storage, wastes and contaminated sites, awareness raising, research and monitoring, and communication of information. Seven months later, delegates gathered in Punta del Este, Uruguay, for INC-4, and after another week of detailed and difficult talks, agreed on additional draft language. However, since important divisions remained on key issues relating to ASGM, air emissions from coal combustion, releases to water and land from unspecific sources, products, process, and financial and technical assistance, the draft text forwarded to INC-5 included alternative options and square brackets, indicating lack of agreement, around critical passages.

When the final negotiating session convened in January 2013 in Geneva, many expected that delegates would find their way to a new treaty.[219] However, more than once during the week, it appeared that failure might be an option. In the end, however, compromises were reached, largely in favor of veto or swing states, and at nearly 7:00 am on the day after the talks had been scheduled to conclude, delegates adopted a new global environmental treaty. The room erupted in applause.

The Minamata Convention on Mercury was officially introduced at a ceremony in Minamata, Japan, on October 9, 2013 and legally adopted and opened for signature at a diplomatic conference in Kumamoto, Japan, on the following day.[220] Following standard practice, the diplomatic conference authorized continued INC meetings until the treaty entered into force so that delegates could address issues that would speed up its effective implementation. Two additional INC meetings convened in November 2014 in Thailand and in March 2016 in Jordan. On May 18, 2017, the fiftieth country deposited "its instrument of ratification" with the UN, allowing the Minamata Convention to enter into force ninety days later (as specified in Article 31).

The United States became the first official party less than a month after the signing ceremony. Unlike the Basel, Rotterdam, and Stockholm Conventions, the Obama administration did not have to submit the treaty to the Senate, because the Convention does not legally require the United States to do anything more than what was already mandated by US law or Environmental Protection Agency regulations. As discussed earlier, the United States used the same process with the Paris Agreement on climate change.

Key Provisions

The objective of the Minamata Convention is "to protect human health and the environment from anthropogenic emissions and releases of mercury and mercury compounds" (Article 1). Each emissions source is addressed in a different article that underscores its specific dynamics. The strongest binding requirements, albeit with some qualifications, address mercury mining, products, and processes. These provisions, and many others, also show the influence of other environmental regimes, most notably the Stockholm Convention.

Sources. During the negotiations, mercury mining was discussed together with stockpiles and trade. Delegates understood that all supply sources had to be addressed holistically to reduce the availability of mercury on the global market. To this end, Article 3, "Mercury Supply Sources and Trade," requires parties to eliminate existing mining within fifteen years after entry into force. Mercury from existing mines may only be used for use in the manufacture of mercury-added products and manufacturing processes specifically listed in the Convention (Articles 4 and 5, respectively), not ASGM. To limit other sources, parties must identify and report all large stocks of mercury and mercury compounds within their borders as well as other sources of significant mercury supply—such as manufacturing operations that use mercury but can recover it for sale or reuse.

Parties are also prohibited from exporting mercury, from mining or other sources, except to another party or non-party that has provided written consent and only for the purpose of environmentally sound storage or a use permitted under the Convention. A party cannot legally import mercury from a non-party unless that country certifies that the mercury comes from a source allowed under the Convention. Parties must provide information on their implementation of these measures in their required reports (Article 21).

The requirements to identify and report on stockpiles are similar to those in the Stockholm Convention and conform to the adage that one cannot regulate what one cannot measure. The trade measures, including the PIC provisions, are analogous to those in the ozone, POPS, CITES, and other regimes. As with the ozone regime, these rules were aimed to motivate countries to ratify the Convention in order to access mercury on the global market. The reporting requirements increase the odds that a country will take the relevant mandated or suggested action. They also provide information to the COP so that it can examine the efficacy of a treaty over time and make changes if it proves to be ineffective.

Products. Article 4 prohibits manufacturing, importing, or exporting certain mercury-added products, which are listed in Annex A, after a specified phase-out date. These products can still be sold and used but not manufactured. The products include certain types of mercury-containing batteries, electrical switches, fluorescent and other lamps, cosmetics, pesticides, biocides, topical antiseptics, thermometers, and barometers. However, there is a broad exemption for parties that have already taken steps to significantly reduce the manufacture, import, and export of all mercury-containing products as well as individual, time-limited exemptions that parties can utilize on certain products. COPs can add products to Annex A, although certain categories are listed as excluded, including products that are deemed essential for civil protection or military use, when no feasible mercury-free alternative exists, or used to preserve vaccines or in research, traditional, or religious practices. While some lead states and NGOs supported fewer or even no exemptions, the exemptions were added to satisfy veto states and ensure the broadest possible participation, as some countries, like the United States, would have trouble ratifying a treaty with an open-ended future obligation. The Montreal Protocol's essential use exemptions and the Stockholm Convention's country-specific exemptions provided the model.

Processes. Article 5 requires parties to eliminate or reduce the use of mercury or mercury compounds in specific manufacturing processes, as delineated in Annex B. Following the example of the Stockholm Convention, using an annex to list banned products or processes allows COPs to add to this list or adjust the requirements without amending the main text of the Convention, which would require a formal ratification process. Once again, limited country-specific exemptions exist, but these cannot last more than ten years. Parties should not allow new facilities or manufacturing processes that utilize mercury or mercury compounds. As with all the other control provisions, parties must report on implementation and are encouraged to exchange information on relevant technological developments and economically feasible mercury-free alternatives. The COP must review the provisions on products and processes and consider amendments, including to the list of processes in Annex B, within five years of the treaty's entry into force.

ASGM. Despite its immense contribution to global emissions, the provisions for ASGM are far less specific than those for mining, trade, products, or processes. First, ASGM using mercury is already illegal or subject to regulation in most developing countries where it exists. However, countries have struggled to control it or have limited incentives to do so for economic reasons. Thus, accepting specific, binding controls with deadlines for emission reductions would inevitably lead many countries into noncompliance. Second, addressing ASGM requires more resources than many developing countries possess or have been willing to dedicate to this purpose, given other political and economic realities. At the same time, donor countries were not willing to commit to providing such assistance. Thus, the qualified language reflects both the realities on the ground and the availability of financial assistance.

Consequently, Article 7 requires parties "to take steps" to reduce and "where feasible" eliminate the use of mercury in ASGM. Parties must notify the Secretariat if they determine that ASGM in their countries "is more than insignificant"—a term that was intentionally left vague. If so, the party must draft a national action plan to address ASGM, submit it the Secretariat, and update it every three years, outlining the progress made. Parties are encouraged to cooperate and share information on strategies and techniques to reduce mercury emissions, to conduct education and outreach to affected communities, and to provide technical and financial assistance to help countries implement their action plans.

Emissions. Lead states on reducing mercury emissions into the air from burning fossil fuels advocated for establishing binding baseline and reduction targets, such as those applied to ODS emissions in the ozone regime, specific thresholds on emissions levels, or specific rules for specific sectors (power plants, industrial boilers, incinerators, cremation, etc.). However, many of the largest users of coal, including China, India, Indonesia, and Russia, and at times Australia, Canada, and the United States, opposed these suggestions. The United States also could not accept any binding rules that differed from existing domestic laws. Many developing countries refused to accept binding numerical targets without explicitly linked financial assistance, which donor countries would not provide. The resulting compromise language requires different actions to address emissions but does not specify the results.

Article 8 requires parties to inventory and "take measures to control" existing emissions of mercury from specific sources set out in Annex D, which lists coal-fired power plants, coal-fired industrial boilers, waste incinerators, cement production, and smelting processes used for zinc, copper, and gold. Parties have options as to what measures they will use, which should be taken "as soon as practicable" and definitely within ten years, including setting numerical goals for limiting or reducing emissions. However, the obligation to implement any of these measures is subject to a party's "national circumstances, and the economic and technical feasibility and affordability of the measures." This exemption, which is open to broad interpretation, was demanded by veto states, including Brazil, India, Iran, and other developing countries, in order to have flexibility in meeting their energy needs without retrofitting existing plants, as well as the belief that the principle of CBDR required industrialized countries to meet many or all of the costs.

The provisions on emissions from sources not yet built reflect the same concerns but also broader consensus, and adamant arguments by some donor countries, that most countries, including large developing countries, have the resources and responsibility to control emissions from new power plants and other sources, in part because these could and should be built into the business plans for these facilities. Thus, all parties "shall require the use of best available techniques [BAT] and best environmental practices [BEP] to control, and where feasible reduce" emissions from new facilities and "may" establish emissions limits consistent with the BAT employed. The BAT and BEP obligation carries no direct caveat related to the provision of financial assistance (although this could occur), which was the preference of donor states, but the qualified "may" with regard to emissions limits is an example of veto states preventing a mandatory obligation.

Releases. Developing countries, NGOs, and some lead states advocated for specifically addressing mercury released directly into land and water from sources not listed in other articles. They believed that these sources, some of which relate the operations of multinational corporations and others to local conditions, were a particular threat to developing countries but were being ignored at the expense of other issues of greater concern to industrialized countries. Some donor countries objected, arguing that not enough was known about what these sources were, the amount of emissions, and their impact. More privately, they did not want to open another, potentially large, area subject to financial assistance. The conflict on this issue continued until the final hours of negotiations and could have prevented agreement. The final compromise in Article 9 established the potential relevancy of these "Releases" and requires parties to identify, report on, and develop inventories for relevant source categories and, if such releases are present in their country, to develop a plan to address the sources and

Photo 3.7 A delegate poses with a skin cream found to contain mercury after being tested at the first Conference of the Parties to the Minamata Convention.

Courtesy Kiara Worth, IISD/*Earth Negotiations Bulletin*, http://enb.iisd.org

take measures to reduce them. The COP will then use this information to develop additional policies in the future.

Storage, Wastes, and Contaminated Sites. The Convention requires parties to take measures to ensure the environmentally sound management of mercury stockpiles and storage (Article 10), wastes containing mercury, including by adhering to the Basel Convention (Article 11), and sites contaminated with mercury (Article 12). These sources of releases show that the Convention seeks to address the entire anthropogenic mercury life cycle, from mining to disposal.

Effectiveness Evaluation and Compliance. The Convention also sets out a process to evaluate its overall effectiveness six years after its entry into force and periodically thereafter. Similar provisions in the Montreal Protocol and the Stockholm Convention have helped lay the groundwork for regime strengthening. The treaty also sets up a facilitative Implementation and Compliance Committee. As discussed earlier, parties to the Stockholm Convention have had trouble establishing such a committee.

Financial and Technical Assistance. After difficult negotiations, the Convention sets out that all parties, according to their capacity, but especially developed countries, will undertake to provide financial and technical assistance to assist other parties' implementation. In language similar to the Stockholm Convention, the Minamata Convention establishes a financial mechanism, of which the GEF serves as a major component, to help provide financial resources to meet costs associated with implementation. In addition, the treaty establishes a "specific international program" (SIP) to support capacity building and technical assistance. The SIP is seen by many developing countries as a means to provide certain types of assistance faster than utilizing the GEF; a conduit of assistance to countries that the GEF might not fund for political or other reasons; and a means to support certain types of activities that the GEF might fail to prioritize.

Regime Expansion and Evaluation

The Mercury COPs convened annually in 2017, 2018, and 2019 before shifting to biennial meetings. In its first three years, the Minamata Convention did not see the significant strengthening experienced within the ozone regime, the addition of many new substances like the Stockholm Convention, or the expansion into new issues and new types of guidelines and partnerships as seen under the Basel Convention. This largely reflects the issue area and the resistance by some governments to extending the treaty at this point.

Thus far, the COP has addressed implementation issues, which are necessary to the effective operation of the treaty. The COP has worked out details regarding the operation of the SIP, and some donors have made initial pledges. The COP established reporting cycles; agreed on technical issues and guidance related to waste thresholds, contaminated sites, and mercury in wastewater; reached consensus on certain modalities for the review of Annexes A and B; and addressed custom codes related to mercury, an important issue for monitoring and reducing trade. Parties also established a technical expert group to examine possible additional anthropogenic point sources or release categories and develop draft guidance on preparing inventories. A permanent secretariat was established in Geneva and shares some operations with the BRS Secretariat in the spirit of the synergies initiative.

Finally, in a process that reflected the Stockholm Convention's experience, the COP agreed on key elements of GEF's role. From 2014 through 2018, GEF invested $141 million in 110 countries to assist them in conducting Minamata Initial Assessments,[221] developing ASGM National Action Plans, and/or implementing projects aimed at reducing mercury emissions. In February 2019, the $180 million GEF-backed "Global Opportunities for the Long-term Development of the ASGM Sector" (GEF GOLD) launched, with the aim of reducing mercury use in ASGM and facilitating access to mercury-free gold extraction methods. In the current GEF funding period, which covers 2018–2022, the GEF has earmarked an additional $206 million for mercury projects.

While it is too early to evaluate the Convention, its negotiation and creation certainly increased attention to mercury and led more governments and IGOs to make public commitments to address this threat to human health and the environment. Many mercury-containing products will no longer be legally produced in most of the world, and key mercury-based industrial processes will be phased out. The work done by many countries to inventory and reduce or eliminate emissions and the resources mobilized for these efforts would not have occurred without the Convention.

At the same time, the Convention lacks specific targets and timetables for reducing emissions in key sectors, and significant exemptions or caveats exist. New large power plants, industrial boilers, and cement clinkers are still expected to be built in many developing countries, and it is not clear whether these countries will require and enforce BAT and BEP. Also unclear is how the COVID-19 pandemic, and the resulting global economic crisis, will impact the commitment of donor countries to provide funds or developing countries to take firm measures to restrict ASGM. How these and other issues play out in the coming years will determine whether the Minamata Convention can fulfill the regime's motto to "Make Mercury History."

Conclusion

The ozone, climate, hazardous waste, toxic chemicals, and mercury regimes demonstrate how both state and nonstate actors can come together to address transboundary and atmospheric pollution problems. A combination of increasing scientific information, other fact-finding activities, efforts of lead states, action by a facilitating international organization, promises of financial assistance, and domestic policy changes among key states weakened or eliminated opposition from veto states and enabled successful negotiations. Each regime establishes binding controls, including in some cases specific targets and timetables, to limit emissions of specific substances. Each also demonstrates how regimes can strengthen over time, but that such strengthening does not necessarily lead to fundamental success.

Whether a regime can accomplish its objectives depends on the design and strength of its control measures, reporting requirements, review mechanisms, ability to grow in response to new information, and other key elements, and the degree to which parties comply with its core provisions. Negotiating an effective global environmental regime almost always depends on inducing veto states to go along with one or more of the core proposed provisions. In these five cases, numerous issues affected the negotiations. New scientific evidence helped move veto states on some issues (ozone and POPs) but far less on other issues (climate change). International political considerations played a role in the Basel Convention, where French and British desire to maintain close relations with former colonies factored into their views on the hazardous waste trade. Domestic political and ethical concerns played a key role in making Canada a lead state on POPs and Japan a lead state on mercury. Perceptions of economic interests changed significantly in the ozone regime, allowing rapid strengthening, whereas perceptions of economic interests slowed efforts to strengthen the climate regime.

Regime formation usually requires leadership by one or more states committed to defining the issue and proposing policies to address it. In these cases, states motivated by particular vulnerabilities played lead roles: African countries on hazardous waste; Canada and some European countries on POPs; and AOSIS on climate change. However, only in the ozone case did the United States play an early lead role although it was among the lead states in some aspects of the POPs and mercury negotiations.

The ozone and climate regimes both started with framework conventions that established important goals, norms, institutions, and procedures. Governments then negotiated protocols containing binding emissions reductions. Both regimes affect important economic sectors, and their control measures faced significant opposition from powerful interests. Both include references to the importance of the precautionary principle. Both follow the principle of CBDR by mandating that industrialized countries address the issue first, because they were responsible for creating the problem, and include provisions for developing countries to receive FTA to help them meet their regime obligations. Yet, in other ways, the ozone and climate regimes are quite different. The ozone regime is widely considered to be among the most effective examples of global environmental policy. But even with the climate regime, global GHG emissions have increased significantly, and serious impacts of climate change are already being observed.

Each regime also developed at a different speed. Governments concluded negotiations on the Vienna Convention in 1985, eleven years after the discovery that CFCs threaten stratospheric ozone. Scientists discovered the anthropogenic greenhouse effect nearly 100 years before the UNFCCC was adopted. The ozone regime quickly expanded its scope, has strong and effective control mechanisms, and covers all major ODS. The climate regime developed at a far slower pace, and only in 2015 did it include a political commitment to prevent the earth warming more than 2°C—and it still lacks the binding control measures and national commitments necessary to do so.

Although both regimes establish targets, in the ozone regime, all industrialized countries must meet essentially the same mandatory standards, whereas the climate regime is more bottom up, with countries now setting their own nationally determined contributions to emissions reductions, mainly because the top-down Kyoto Protocol approach was largely ineffective in reducing global emissions. Finally, governments significantly expanded and strengthened the ozone regime, primarily because of scientific consensus and the availability of substitutes for ozone-depleting chemicals. In contrast, although the IPCC has demonstrated scientific consensus that climate change is occurring and renewable energy technologies are increasingly available and cost-efficient, most governments have not taken significant action, in part because of domestic politics associated with reducing the use of fossil fuels.

These differences reflect a variety of factors, including characteristics of the issue area; the evolution of scientific consensus; the interests of the major actors, especially the lead and veto states; the design of the respective regimes; the evolution of economic and political interests; and the presence or absence of well-known obstacles to effective cooperation (see Chapter 5). Addressing transboundary and atmospheric pollution problems, however, contrasts with some aspects of the global regimes that address the conservation of natural resources. Chapter 4 examines five regimes for natural resource conservation and management. The conclusion to Chapter 4 reviews and compares all the case studies presented in these two chapters.

Notes

1 UNEP, *Emissions Gap Report 2019* (Nairobi: UNEP, 2019).

2 UNEP, *Environmental Effects and Interactions of Stratospheric Ozone Depletion, UV Radiation, and Climate Change. 2018 Assessment Report* (Nairobi: Environmental Effects Assessment Panel, UNEP, 2018).

3 Mario Molina and F. Sherwood Rowland, "Stratospheric Sink for Chlorofluoromethanes: Chlorine Atom-Catalysed Destruction of Ozone," *Nature* vol. 249 (June 28, 1974): 810–812.

4 WMO (World Meteorological Organization), *Scientific Assessment of Ozone Depletion: 2018* (Geneva: WMO, 2018).

5 The discussion of the ozone regime in this chapter builds on previous writings by David Downie, including "Understanding International Environmental Regimes: The Origin, Creation and Expansion of the Ozone Regime" (PhD diss., University of North Carolina, Chapel Hill, 1996); "Stratospheric Ozone Depletion," in *The Routledge Handbook of Global Environmental Politics*, ed. Paul Harris (New York: Routledge, 2013); and "Still No Time for Complacency: Evaluating the Ongoing Success and Continued Challenge of Global Ozone Policy," *Journal of Environmental Studies and Sciences* vol. 5, no. 2 (2015): 187–194. Other detailed discussions include Karen Litfin, *Ozone Discourses: Science and Politics in Global Environmental Cooperation* (New York: Columbia University Press, 1994); Richard Benedick, *Ozone Diplomacy: New Directions in Safeguarding the Planet*, 2nd ed. (Cambridge, MA: Harvard University Press, 1998); Stephen Anderson and K. Madhavea Sarma, *Protecting the Ozone Layer: The United Nations History* (London: Earthscan, 2002); Edward Parson, *Protecting the Ozone Layer: Science and Strategy* (Oxford: Oxford University Press, 2003); and Ozone Secretariat, *Montreal Protocol on Substances That Deplete the Ozone Layer, 2012: A Success in the Making* (Nairobi: UNEP, 2012).

6 See, in particular, Iwona Rummel-Bulska, "The Protection of the Ozone Layer Under the Global Framework Convention," in *Transboundary Air Pollution*, eds. Cees Flinterman, et al. (Dordrecht, Netherlands: Martinus Nijhoff, 1986), 281–296; and Benedick, *Ozone Diplomacy*.

7 For discussion of the early stages of the negotiations, see Downie, "Understanding International Environmental Regimes"; Benedick, *Ozone Diplomacy*; and Parson, *Protecting the Ozone Layer*.

8 For analysis, see David Downie, "The Power to Destroy: Understanding Stratospheric Ozone Politics as a Common Pool Resource Problem," in *Anarchy and the Environment: The International Relations of Common Pool Resources*, eds. J. Samuel Barkin and George Shambaugh (Albany: State University of New York Press, 1999).

9 Benedick, *Ozone Diplomacy*, stresses US leadership on this point. Benedick led the US delegation to these negotiations.

10 J. Farman, et al., "Large Losses of Total Ozone in Antarctica Reveal Seasonal ClO_x/NO_x Interaction," *Nature* vol. 315 (May 16, 1985): 207–210. While disagreements exist in some accounts regarding the awareness and use of data from US satellites, British scientists using ground-based measurements published the first peer-reviewed reports of the ozone hole.

11 For representative discussion, see Downie, "Understanding International Environmental Regimes," ch. 6; Litfin, *Ozone Discourses*, 96–102; and Benedick, *Ozone Diplomacy*.

12 See, for example, Anderson and Sarma, *Protecting the Ozone Layer*, 93–94, and relevant discussions in Benedick, *Ozone Diplomacy*.

13 WMO, et al., *Scientific Assessment of Stratospheric Ozone: 1989* (Geneva: WMO, 1989).

14 Hydrochlorofluorocarbons (HCFCs) have shorter atmospheric lifetimes, and one HCFC molecule destroys far fewer ozone molecules than one chlorofluorocarbon (CFC) molecule.

15 For example, at the first Meeting of the Parties (MOP), in 1989, European Community members joined eighty nations (including the United States but not Japan or the Soviet Union) to support a nonbinding declaration calling for a complete CFC phase-out by 2000.

16 For the text of the ozone treaties, amendments, and adjustments, as well as official reports from each MOP, visit the Ozone Secretariat's website: http://ozone.unep.org.

17 Countries with economies in transition (CEITs) include the countries in Eastern Europe formerly aligned with the Soviet Union, as well as Russia, Ukraine, and other countries created when the Soviet Union collapsed, which were transitioning from communist to capitalist economies. The Global Environment Facility (GEF) later took over most of the responsibility for assisting CEITs on ozone issues.

18 The fund has been replenished ten times: $240 million (1991–1993), $455 million (1994–1996), $466 million (1997–1999), $440 million (2000–2002), $474 million (2003–2005), $400 million (2006–2008, 2009–2011, and 2012–2014), $437.5 million (2015–2017), and $500 million (2018–2020). It will be replenished again in 2021. The additional $40 million in the 2018–2020 budget is from anticipated payment of arrears and $6 million of interest accruing during the triennium. For information on the history and operation of the fund, see the Multilateral Fund homepage: www.multilateralfund.org.

19 David Downie's observations and conversations with national delegates during the ozone negotiations in 1992–1999 and 2015.

20 A small "servicing tail" is permitted beyond the HCFC phase-out date to allow for the continued use of existing equipment.

21 The Implementation Committee under the Non-compliance Procedure for the Montreal Protocol and the MOP has considered many cases of potential noncompliance, most involving countries with economies in transition and developing countries. Although the regime allows for the application of specified trade sanctions in response to severe cases of intentional noncompliance, the committee and MOP decided that each instance fell below the threshold for sanctions, and opted for consultation and targeted technical and/or financial assistance to remove barriers to implementation and, on occasion, the equivalent of a public rebuke to try harder. For details, see https://ozone.unep.org/institutions.

22 Brian Gareau, *From Precaution to Profit: Contemporary Challenges to Environmental Protection in the Montreal Protocol* (New Haven, CT: Yale University Press, 2012) provides detailed information on the methyl bromide debates. Information about the issue in this and the next paragraph is based on observations by David Downie and his conversations with Australian, EU, NGO, secretariat, US, and other officials during the ozone negotiations from 1992 to 1999. See also the official meetings of these MOPs (which Downie helped to write), available on the Ozone Secretariat website.

23 IISD, "Summary of the Nineteenth Meeting of the Parties to the Montreal Protocol: 17–21 September 2007," *Earth Negotiation Bulletin* vol. 19, no. 60 (September 24, 2007). See also: *Report of the Nineteenth Meeting of the Parties to the Montreal Protocol on Substances That Deplete the Ozone Layer*, UN Document UNEP/OzL.Pro.19/7, September 21, 2007; Keith Bradsher, "Push to Fix Ozone Layer and Slow Global Warming," *New York Times*, March 15, 2007; and David Ljunggren, "Ozone Deal Hailed as Blow Against Climate Change," Reuters Newswire, September 22, 2007.

24 IISD, "Summary of the Nineteenth Meeting."

25 For examples, see UNEP, *Report of the Twenty-Third Meeting of the Parties to the Montreal Protocol on Substances That Deplete the Ozone Layer*, UNEP Document UNEP/OzL.Pro.23/11, December 8, 2011, paragraphs 15–17 and 103–119; UNEP, *Report of the Thirty-Second Meeting of the Open-Ended Working Group of the Parties to the Montreal Protocol on Substances That Deplete the Ozone Layer*, UN Document UNEP/OzL.Pro/WG.1/32/7, August 8, 2012, paragraphs 69–77; UNEP, *Report of the Twenty-Fourth Meeting of the Parties to the Montreal Protocol on Substances That Deplete the Ozone Layer*, UNEP Document UNEP/OzL.Pro.24/10, November 25, 2012; and UNEP, *Report of the Twenty-Seventh Meeting of the Parties to the Montreal Protocol on Substances That Deplete the Ozone Layer*, UNEP Document UNEP/OzL.Pro.27/13, November 30, 2015.

26 UNEP, *Report of the Twenty-Seventh Meeting of the Parties to the Montreal Protocol on Substances That Deplete the Ozone Layer.*

27 See the official negotiation reports from the twenty-fifth, twenty-sixth, and twenty-seventh MOP and OEWG 35, 36, 37, and 38 (https://ozone.unep.org/meetings) and the corresponding reports published by the *Earth Negotiation Bulletin* at https://enb.iisd.org/vol19/.

28 See Decision XXVIII/2 on page 31 of the "Report of the Twenty-Eighth Meeting of the Parties to the Montreal Protocol on Substances That Deplete the Ozone Layer." UN Document UNEP/OzL. Pro.28/12.

29 Algeria, Bahrain, Benin, Burkina Faso, Central African Republic, Chad, Côte d'Ivoire, Djibouti, Egypt, Eritrea, Gambia, Ghana, Guinea, Guinea-Bissau, Iran, Iraq, Jordan, Kuwait, Libya, Mali, Mauritania, Niger, Nigeria, Oman, Pakistan, Qatar, Saudi Arabia, Senegal, Sudan, Syrian Arab Republic, Togo, Tunisia, Turkmenistan, and United Arab Emirates.

30 The United States has not changed its core position. However, a coalition of Democrats and Republicans in the Senate introduced legislation in September 2020 that would cut HFC use by 85 percent by 2035. See Juliet Eilperin and Steven Mufson, "In rare bipartisan climate agreement, senators forge plan to slash use of potent greenhouse gas," *Washington Post*, September 10, 2020, www.washingtonpost.com/climate-environment/2020/09/10/rare-bipartisan-climate-agreement-senators-forge-plan-slash-use-potent-greenhouse-gas/.

31 UNEP, *Information Provided by Parties in Accordance with Article 7 of the Montreal Protocol on Substances That Deplete the Ozone Layer*, UNEP Document UNEP/OzL.Pro.23/7, September 16, 2011. However, evidence of unreported intentional or by-product carbon tetrachloride production exists. See UNEP, *Report of the Twenty-Seventh Meeting of the Parties to the Montreal Protocol on Substances That Deplete the Ozone Layer*, Decision 27/7. See also data compiled by the Ozone Secretariat from national reports: https://ozone.unep.org/countries/data.

32 Compare the information in MOP decisions that approved exemptions from MOPs in the late 1990s and 2000s with those from 2013–2020. See also https://ozone.unep.org/countries/data.

33 WMO, et al., *Scientific Assessment of Ozone Depletion: 2018*.

34 NASA, "2019 Ozone Hole Is the Smallest on Record Since Its Discovery," October 21, 2019, www.nasa.gov/feature/goddard/2019/2019-ozone-hole-is-the-smallest-on-record-since-its-discovery.

35 UNEP, *Environmental Effects of Ozone Depletion and Its Interactions with Climate Change: 2010 Assessment*, 2010; US Environmental Protection Agency (EPA), *Protecting the Ozone Layer Protects Eyesight: A Report on Cataract Incidence in the United States Using the Atmospheric and Health Effects Framework Model* (Washington, DC: EPA, 2010); Arjan van Dijk, et al., "Skin Cancer Risks Avoided by the Montreal Protocol: Worldwide Modeling Integrating Coupled Climate-Chemistry Models with a Risk Model for UV," *Photochemistry and Photobiology* 89, no. 1 (January–February 2013): 234–246.

36 Ozone Secretariat, "#OzoneDay 2019 social media messages," https://ozone.unep.org/sites/default/files/ozone-day/2019/OzoneDay-2019-social-media-pack.pdf.

37 For a representative discussion, see Guus Velders, et al., "The Importance of the Montreal Protocol in Protecting Climate," *Proceedings of the National Academy of Science* vol. 104, no. 12 (March 20, 2007): 4814–4819.

38 Ozone Secretariat, "Montreal Protocol Parties Devise Way Forward to Protect Climate Ahead of Paris COP-21," press release, November 6, 2015.

39 Downie, "Still No Time for Complacency."

40 For a recent analysis, see Megan Lickley, et al., "Quantifying Contributions of Chlorofluorocarbon Banks to Emissions and Impacts on the Ozone Layer and Climate," *Nature Communications* vol. 11, no. 1380 (2020), https://doi.org/10.1038/s41467-020-15162-7.

41 Downie, "Understanding International Environmental Regimes"; Downie, "Stratospheric Ozone Depletion."

42 For detailed and sometimes differing analyses of the complex interrelationships between the development of scientific knowledge and policy developments, see the relevant discussion in, among others, Lydia Dotto and Harold Schiff, *The Ozone War* (Garden City, NY: Doubleday, 1978); Downie, "Understanding International Environmental Regimes"; Downie, "Stratospheric Ozone Depletion"; Peter Haas, "Banning Chlorofluorocarbons: Epistemic Community Efforts to Protect Stratospheric Ozone," *International Organization* vol. 46, no. 1 (winter 1992): 187–224; Litfin, *Ozone Discourses*; Benedick, *Ozone Diplomacy*; Anderson and Sarma, *Protecting the Ozone Layer*; and Gareau, *From Precaution to Profit*.

43 Downie, "Stratospheric Ozone Depletion." For a sometimes differing analysis of different aspects of the impact of changing economic interests on the development of ozone policy, see, among others, the works cited in the previous note and Kenneth Oye and James Maxwell, "Self-Interest and Environmental Management," *Journal of Theoretical Politics* vol. 64 (1994): 599–630.

44 Ronald Mitchell, "Regime Design Matters: International Oil Pollution and Treaty Compliance," *International Organization* vol. 48, no. 3 (summer 1994): 425–458.

45 WMO, *Scientific Assessment of Ozone Depletion: 2018.*

46 WMO, *WMO Provisional Statement on the State of the Global Climate in 2019* (Geneva, Switzerland: WMO, 2019), 2, https://library.wmo.int/doc_num.php?explnum_id=10108.

47 Intergovernmental Panel on Climate Change (IPCC), "Summary for Policymakers." In: *Global Warming of 1.5°C. An IPCC Special Report on the Impacts of Global Warming of 1.5°C Above Pre-Industrial Levels and Related Global Greenhouse Gas Emission Pathways, in the Context of Strengthening the Global Response to the Threat of Climate Change, Sustainable Development, and Efforts to Eradicate Poverty* (Geneva; Switzerland: IPCC, 2018), 4, www.ipcc.ch/site/assets/uploads/sites/2/2019/05/SR15_SPM_version_report_LR.pdf.

48 Intergovernmental Panel on Climate Change (IPCC), *Climate Change 2014: Synthesis Report*, Contribution of Working Groups I, II and III to the Fifth Assessment Report of the Intergovernmental Panel on Climate Change (Geneva, Switzerland: IPCC, 2014), http://ar5-syr.ipcc.ch/ipcc/ipcc/resources/pdf/IPCC_SynthesisReport.pdf.

49 Ibid.

50 D. Gilfillan, G. Marland, T. Boden, and R. Andres, "Global, Regional, and National Fossil-Fuel CO_2 Emissions" (Boone, North Carolina: Carbon Dioxide Information Analysis Center at Appalachian State University, 2019), https://energy.appstate.edu/sites/energy.appstate.edu/files/global.1751_2016.txt.

51 Rebecca Lindsey, "Climate Change: Atmospheric Carbon Dioxide," NOAA Climate.gov, September 19, 2019, www.climate.gov/news-features/understanding-climate/climate-change-atmospheric-carbon-dioxide.

52 D. Gilfillan and G. Marland, "Ranking of the World's Countries by 2016 Total CO_2 Emissions from Fossil-Fuel Burning, Cement Production, and Gas Flaring" (Boone, North Carolina: Research Institute for Environment, Energy, and Economics, Appalachian State University, 2019), https://energy.appstate.edu/sites/energy.appstate.edu/files/top2016.cap_.txt.

53 Svante Arrhenius, "On the Influence of Carbonic Acid in the Air upon the Temperature of the Ground," *Philosophical Magazine* vol. 41 (1896): 237–276.

54 G. S. Callendar, "The Artificial Production of Carbon Dioxide and Its Influence on Climate," *Quarterly Journal of the Royal Meteorological Society* vol. 64 (1938): 223–240.

55 Richard Houghton and George Woodwell, "Global Climatic Change," *Scientific American* vol. 260 (April 1989): 42–43.

56 Daniel Bodansky, "The United Nations Framework Convention on Climate Change: A Commentary," *Yale Journal of International Law* vol. 18, no. 2 (Summer 1993): 461.

57 This case study does not look at the extensive work done by other subsidiary bodies under the convention. For a more holistic look at the work of the UN Framework Convention on Climate Change (UNFCCC) subsidiary bodies, see the UNFCCC website, https://unfccc.int/process-and-meetings.

58 See Matthew Paterson, *Global Warming and Global Politics* (London: Routledge, 1996), 77–82.

59 Japan subsequently backtracked by proposing a process of "pledge and review" in place of binding commitments. Individual countries would set for themselves appropriate targets that would be publicly reviewed. Most EC member states and NGOs opposed the idea. Bodansky, "The United Nations Framework Convention on Climate Change," 486.

60 For country greenhouse gas emissions, contributions to total emissions, and rankings at the time of the negotiations, see World Resources Institute, *World Resources, 1992–1993* (New York: Oxford University Press, 1992), 205–213, 345–355. For an early discussion of different methods of greenhouse gas accounting, see Peter M. Morrisette and Andrew Plantinga, "The Global Warming Issue: Viewpoints of Different Countries," *Resources* vol. 103 (Spring 1991): 2–6.

61 *Earth Summit Update* 9 (May 1992): 1; *Wall Street Journal*, May 22, 1992, 1.

62 "Status of Ratification of the Convention," UN Framework Convention on Climate Change, https://unfccc.int/process-and-meetings/the-convention/status-of-ratification/status-of-ratification-of-the-convention.

63 REDD+ stands for reducing emissions from deforestation and degradation in developing countries, including conservation.

64 US Congress, "S.Res.98 – A resolution expressing the sense of the Senate regarding the conditions for the United States becoming a signatory to any international agreement on greenhouse gas

emissions under the United Nations Framework Convention on Climate Change." 105th Congress (1997–1998), www.congress.gov/bill/105th-congress/senate-resolution/98.

65 See the Climate Secretariat website (http://unfccc.int) for text of the Kyoto Protocol. Also see Herman Ott, "The Kyoto Protocol: Unfinished Business," *Environment* vol. 40, no. 6 (1998), 16 ff.; Clare Breidenrich, et al., "The Kyoto Protocol to the United Nations Framework Convention on Climate Change," *American Journal of International Law* vol. 92, no. 2 (1998): 315.

66 George W. Bush, Text of a Letter from the President to Senators Hagel, Helms, Craig, and Roberts, March 13, 2001, https://georgewbush-whitehouse.archives.gov/news/releases/2001/03/20010314.html. President Bill Clinton did not submit the Kyoto Protocol for ratification after the Senate vowed to reject it. See supra note 64.

67 See, for example, Alex Rodriguez, "Russian Move on Global Warming Treaty Sets Stage for Enactment," *Chicago Tribune*, October 1, 2004.

68 The protocol, like most treaties, specifies a ninety-day delay between the final ratification required and the actual entry into force.

69 Ecuador withdrew in August 2018 and Bolivia withdrew in November 2019.

70 The Climate Group, *The Copenhagen Climate Conference: A Climate Group Assessment*, January 2010, www.theclimategroup.org/_assets/files/TCG-Copenhagen-Assessment-Report-Jan10.pdf.

71 Daniel Bodansky, "The International Climate Change Regime: The Road from Copenhagen," Viewpoints, Harvard Project on International Climate Agreements, October 2010, https://papers.ssrn.com/sol3/papers.cfm?abstract_id=1693889.

72 Ibid.

73 IISD, "Summary of the Copenhagen Climate Change Conference: 7–19 December 2009," *Earth Negotiations Bulletin* vol. 12, no. 459 (December 22, 2009): 1.

74 IISD, "Summary of the Cancun Climate Change Conference: 29 November–11 December 2010," *Earth Negotiations Bulletin* vol. 12, no. 498 (December 13, 2010): 28.

75 UNFCCC, *Report of the Conference of the Parties on Its Fifteenth Session, Held in Copenhagen from 7 to 19 December 2009*, FCCC/CP/2009/11/Add.1, March 30, 2010.

76 Bodansky, "The International Climate Change Regime," 3.

77 IISD, "Summary of the Cancun Climate Change Conference: 29 November–11 December 2010," 28.

78 Ibid.

79 Climate Focus, *CP16/CMP6: Cancun Agreements: Summary and Analysis*, January 10, 2011, http://theredddesk.org/sites/default/files/resources/pdf/2011/Cancun_Briefing_Jan_2011_v.1.0.pdf; UNFCCC, "The Cancun Agreements," http://cancun.unfccc.int.

80 Bolivian Ministry of Foreign Affairs, "Bolivia Decries Adoption of Copenhagen Accord II Without Consensus," press briefing, December 11, 2011, http://pwccc.files.wordpress.com/2010/12/press-release-history-will-be-the-judge.pdf.

81 IISD, "Summary of the Cancun Climate Change Conference: 29 November–11 December 2010," 1.

82 IISD, "Summary of the Durban Climate Change Conference: 28 November–11 December 2011," *Earth Negotiations Bulletin* vol. 12, no. 534 (December 13, 2011): 1.

83 IISD, "Summary of the Doha Climate Change Conference: 26 November–8 December 2012," *Earth Negotiations Bulletin* vol. 12, no. 567 (December 11, 2012): 26.

84 As of October 2, 2020, 145 parties had deposited their instrument of acceptance, enabling the Doha Amendment to enter into force. See UNFCCC, "Status of the Doha Amendment," https://unfccc.int/process/the-kyoto-protocol/the-doha-amendment.

85 Members of the Like-Minded Developing Countries group include Algeria, Argentina, Bolivia, Cuba, China, Democratic Republic of the Congo, Dominica, Ecuador, Egypt, El Salvador, India, Iran, Iraq, Kuwait, Libya, Malaysia, Mali, Nicaragua, Pakistan, Philippines, Qatar, Saudi Arabia, Sri Lanka, Sudan, Syria, and Venezuela.

86 IISD, "Summary of the Warsaw Climate Change Conference: 11–23 November 2013," *Earth Negotiations Bulletin* vol. 12, no. 594 (November 26, 2013): 26.

87 The White House, "U.S.–China Joint Announcement on Climate Change," press release, November 12, 2014, https://obamawhitehouse.archives.gov/the-press-office/2014/11/11/us-china-joint-announcement-climate-change.

88 William Antholis, "The U.S. and China's Great Leap Forward ... For Climate Protection," Brookings Institution Planet Policy Blog, November 12, 2014, www.brookings.edu/blogs/planetpolicy/posts/2014/11/12-us-china-great-leap-forward-climate-protection-antholis.

89 IISD, "Summary of the Lima Climate Change Conference: 1–14 December 2014," *Earth Negotiations Bulletin* vol. 12, no. 619 (December 16, 2014): 43.

90 UNFCCC, "Lima Call for Climate Action," Decision 1/CP.20, February 2, 2015, http://unfccc.int/resource/docs/2014/cop20/eng/10a01.pdf.

91 IISD, "Summary of the Bonn Climate Change Conference: 19–23 October 2015," *Earth Negotiations Bulletin* vol. 12, no. 651 (October 25, 2015): 9.

92 Ibid., 10.

93 UNFCCC, "Paris Agreement" (United Nations: 2015), https://unfccc.int/sites/default/files/english_paris_agreement.pdf.

94 IISD, "Summary of the Paris Climate Change Conference: 29 November–13 December 2015," *Earth Negotiations Bulletin* vol. 12, no. 663 (December 15, 2015): 43.

95 Ibid.

96 For more information on what the Paris Agreement needed to gain US approval, see Daniel Bodansky, *Legal Options for U.S. Acceptance of a New Climate Change Agreement* (Arlington, VA: Center for Climate and Energy Solutions, 2015).

97 Coral Davenport, "Nations Approve Landmark Climate Accord in Paris," *New York Times*, December 12, 2015.

98 International Civil Aviation Organization, "A39-2: Consolidated Statement of Continuing ICAO Policies and Practices Related to Environmental Protection—Climate Change," *Doc 10075 Assembly Resolutions in Force (as of 6 October 2016)* (ICAO 2017), I-72, www.icao.int/Meetings/a39/Documents/Resolutions/10075_en.pdf.

99 Pilita Clark, "Trump Election Casts Shadow over COP 22 Climate Change Talks," *Financial Times*, November 9, 2016, www.ft.com/content/09a302c6-9459-11e6-a1dc-bdf38d484582.

100 Ashley Parker and Coral Davenport, "Donald Trump's Energy Plan: More Fossil Fuels and Fewer Rules," *New York Times*, May 27, 2016, A1, www.nytimes.com/2016/05/27/us/politics/donald-trump-global-warming-energy-policy.html.

101 Stacy Feldman and Marianne Lavelle, "Donald Trump's Record on Climate Change," *Inside Climate News*, December 19, 2019, https://insideclimatenews.org/news/19122019/trump-climate-policy-record-rollback-fossil-energy-history-candidate-profile.

102 See Paris Agreement Article 28, https://unfccc.int/resource/docs/2015/cop21/eng/l09r01.pdf.

103 Daniel Bodansky, "Reflections on the Paris Conference," *Opinio Juris* blog, December 15, 2015, opiniojuris.org/2015/12/15/reflections-on-the-paris-conference/.

104 Nathan Cogswell and Yamide Dagnet, "Why Does the Paris Climate Agreement Need a Rulebook? 7 Questions and Answers," World Resources Institute blog, June 13, 2019, www.wri.org/blog/2019/06/why-does-paris-climate-agreement-need-rulebook-7-questions-and-answers.

105 Ibid.

106 Simon Evans and Josh Gabbatiss, "In-Depth Q&A: How 'Article 6' Carbon Markets Could 'Make or Break' the Paris Agreement," CarbonBrief, November 29, 2019, www.carbonbrief.org/in-depth-q-and-a-how-article-6-carbon-markets-could-make-or-break-the-paris-agreement.

107 Cogswell and Dagnet, "Why Does the Paris Climate Agreement Need a Rulebook? 7 Questions and Answers."

108 UN News, "COP25: UN Climate Change Conference, 5 Things You Need to Know," December 1, 2019, https://news.un.org/en/story/2019/12/1052251.

109 Helen Mountford, et al., "4 Leaders—and Far Too Many Laggards—at the UN Climate Action Summit," World Resources Institute, September 25, 2019, www.wri.org/blog/2019/09/4-leaders-and-far-too-many-laggards-un-climate-action-summit.

110 IISD, "Summary of the Chile/Madrid Climate Change Conference: 2–15 December 2019," *Earth Negotiations Bulletin* vol. 12, no. 775 (December 18, 2019): 1.

111 Simon Evans and Josh Gabbatiss, "COP25: Key Outcomes Agreed at the UN Climate Talks in Madrid," Climate Diplomacy, December 16, 2019, www.climate-diplomacy.org/news/cop25-key-outcomes-agreed-un-climate-talks-madrid.

112 General analyses of the international hazardous waste issue and regime include David Hackett, "An Assessment of the Basel Convention on the Control of Transboundary Movements of Hazardous Wastes and Their Disposal," *American University Journal of International Law and Policy* vol. 5 (Winter 1990): 313–322; Katharine Kummer, *International Management of Hazardous Wastes: The Basel Convention and Related Legal Rules* (New York: Oxford University Press, 2000);

Kate O'Neill, *Waste Trading Among Rich Nations: Building a New Theory of Environmental Regulation* (Cambridge, MA: MIT Press, 2000); Jennifer Clapp, *Toxic Exports: The Transfer of Hazardous Wastes from Rich to Poor Countries* (Ithaca, NY: Cornell University Press, 2001); Henrik Selin, *Global Governance of Hazardous Chemicals: Challenges of Multilevel Management* (Cambridge, MA: MIT Press, 2010). The Basel Convention Secretariat (www.basel.int) and the Basel Action Network (www.ban.org), a prominent NGO, provide extensive information on the regime and the waste issue.

113 An organizational meeting took place in 1987, and five formal negotiation sessions occurred in 1988 and 1989.

114 Carol Annette Petsonk, "The Role of the United Nations Environment Programme (UNEP) in the Development of International Environmental Law," *American University Journal of International Law and Policy* 5 (Winter 1990): 374–377; *International Environment Reporter*, April 1989, 159–161.

115 For the text of the convention, reports from the COPs and other meetings, official documents, updated lists of ratifications, and information on other aspects of the regime, see the Basel Convention website (www.basel.int). For independent summaries and analyses of the COP meetings, see reports by the *Earth Negotiations Bulletin* at https://enb.iisd.org/vol20/.

116 See Hackett, "An Assessment of the Basel Convention"; and Mark Montgomery, "Traveling Toxic Trash: An Analysis of the 1989 Basel Convention," *The Fletcher Forum of World Affairs* vol. 14, no. 2 (Summer 1990): 313–326.

117 During this period, only republics of the former Soviet Union, desperate for foreign exchange and willing to disregard the health and environmental consequences, appeared openly willing to accept significant shipments of hazardous wastes. See Steven Coll, "Free Market Intensifies Waste Problem," *Washington Post*, March 23, 1994.

118 Greenpeace, *The International Trade in Wastes: A Greenpeace Inventory*, 5th ed. (Washington, DC: Greenpeace, 1990).

119 John Cushman Jr., "Clinton Seeks Ban on Export of Most Hazardous Waste," *New York Times*, March 1, 1994; "Basel Convention Partners Consider Ban on Exports of Hazardous Wastes," *International Environment Reporter*, March 22, 1994, A9.

120 Charles Wallace, "Asia Tires of Being the Toxic Waste Dumping Ground for Rest of World," *Los Angeles Times*, March 23, 1994. For a detailed account of the Geneva meeting, see Jim Puckett and Cathy Fogel, "A Victory for Environment and Justice: The Basel Ban and How It Happened," Greenpeace International, September 1994, http://wiki.ban.org/A_Victory_for_Environment_and_Justice:_The_Basel_Ban_and_How_it_Happened.

121 Greenpeace, *The International Trade in Wastes: Database of Known Hazardous Waste Exports from OECD to Non-OECD Countries: 1989–March 1994* (Washington, DC: Greenpeace, 1994). See also Jim Puckett, "The Basel Ban: A Triumph over Business-as-Usual," Basel Action Network, October 1997, http://wiki.ban.org/The_Basel_Ban:_A_Triumph_Over_Business-As-Usual.

122 For analysis, see IISD, "Summary of the Ninth Conference of the Parties to the Basel Convention: 23–27 June 2008," *Earth Negotiations Bulletin* vol. 20, no. 31 (June 30, 2008).

123 See comments by the Basel Action Network as reported in IISD, "Summary of the Meetings of the Conferences of the Parties to the Basel, Rotterdam and Stockholm Convention: 4–15 May 2015," *Earth Negotiations Bulletin* vol. 15, no. 230 (May 19, 2015).

124 See IISD, "Summary of the Ninth Meeting."

125 In February 2007, the company that had leased the tanker, Trafigura, settled with the government for the equivalent of $198 million. As part of the agreement, the Côte d'Ivoire government released three jailed Trafigura executives, dropped criminal charges against the company and its executives, and sealed the investigation results. International Network for Environmental Compliance and Enforcement (INECE), "Côte d'Ivoire Toxic Waste Scandal Triggers Legal Action in 3 Countries," *INECE Newsletter* vol. 14 (April 2007).

126 IISD, "Summary of the Tenth Meeting of the Conference of the Parties to the Basel Convention: 17–21 October 2011," *Earth Negotiations Bulletin* vol. 20, no. 37 (October 24, 2011).

127 Ibid. See also the official meeting reports from the 2015, 2017, and 2019 Basel COPs.

128 See Basel Secretariat, "Adopted Technical Guidelines," www.basel.int/Implementation/TechnicalMatters/DevelopmentofTechnicalGuidelines/TechnicalGuidelines/tabid/8025/Default.aspx.

129 For details, see the ESM section of the Basel Secretariat website: www.basel.int/Implementation/CountryLedInitiative/EnvironmentallySoundManagement/Overview/tabid/3615/Default.aspx.

130 C. P. Balde, et al., *The Global E-Waste Monitor – 2017* (Bonn: United Nations University, ITU, ISWA, 2017).

131 I. Rucevska, et al., *Waste Crime—Waste Risks: Gaps in Meeting the Global Waste Challenge* (Nairobi and Arendal: UNEP and GRID-Arendal, 2015).

132 For information on COP8, see the official report and documents from the meeting, available on the Basel Convention website. See also IISD, "Summary of the Eighth Conference of the Parties to the Basel Convention: 27 November–1 December 2006," *Earth Negotiations Bulletin* vol. 20, no. 25 (December 4, 2006).

133 For details, see the PACE section of the Basel Secretariat website.

134 See the official reports from COP13 and COP14, available on the Basel Convention website. See also IISD, "Summary of the Meetings of the Conferences of the Parties to the Basel, Rotterdam and Stockholm Conventions: 4–15 May 2015."

135 e.g., Josh Lepawsky, *Reassembling Rubbish: Worlding Electronic Waste* (Cambridge, MA: MIT Press, 2018).

136 UNEP, *Marine Plastic Debris and Microplastics—Global Lessons and Research to Inspire Action and Guide Policy Change* (Nairobi: UNEP, 2016), 189–190, 195–198, 207–228.

137 e.g., Kara Law, "Plastics in the Marine Environment." *Annual Review of Marine Science* vol. 9 (2017): 205–229.

138 e.g., C. Anela Choy, et al., "The Vertical Distribution and Biological Transport of Marine Microplastics Across the Epipelagic and Mesopelagic Water Column," *Scientific Reports* vol. 9 (2019), doi.org/10.1038/s41598-019-44117-2; Rachel Obbard, et al., "Global Warming Releases Microplastic Legacy Frozen in Arctic Sea Ice," *Earth's Future* vol. 2, no. 6 (June 2014).

139 BRS Secretariat, "Marine Plastic Litter and Microplastics" (Geneva: BRS Secretariat, 2017). Can be found at www.basel.int/Implementation/Plasticwastes/Overview/tabid/6068/Default.aspx.

140 e.g., "Technical Guidelines for the Identification and Environmentally Sound Management (ESM) of Plastic Wastes and for Their Disposal" (Document UNEP/CHW.6/21); "Framework for the ESM of Hazardous Wastes and Other Wastes" (decision BC-11/1); "Guidance to Assist Parties in Developing Efficient Strategies for Achieving the Prevention and Minimization of the Generation of Hazardous and Other Wastes and Their Disposal" (document UNEP/CHW.13/INF/11); and "Guidance Manual on How to Improve the Sea-Land Interface" (document UNEP/CHW.13/INF/37).

141 See the official reports of COP13 (2017) and COP14 (2019) as well as 2017, 2018, and 2019 meetings of the COP's main subsidiary body, the Open-Ended Working Group.

142 This followed two years of detailed discussion in the COP's main subsidiary body, the Open-Ended Working Group.

143 See Decision BC-14/12. Report of the Fourteenth Meeting of the Conference of the Parties to the Basel Convention, Geneva, 29 April–10 May 2019. UN Document UNEP/CHW.14/28.

144 See Decision BC-14/13.

145 Ibid.

146 Personal observation by David Downie.

147 For official information, see the synergies website: www.brsmeas.org/.

148 See for example, Jessie Yeungm, "Malaysia Finds 1800 Tonnes of Illegal Toxic Waste Dumped at Port," CNN, July 20, 2020, www.cnn.com/2020/07/20/asia/malaysia-waste-dumping-intl-hnk-scli/index.html.

149 David Downie, personal observation and discussions at the Basel and Stockholm COPs in 2013, 2015, 2017, and 2019.

150 Selin, *Global Governance of Hazardous Chemicals*, 40.

151 UNEP, *GEO 5: Global Environmental Outlook—Environment for the Future We Want* (Nairobi: UNEP, 2012), 170.

152 UNEP, *Global Chemicals Outlook II* (Nairobi: UNEP).

153 UNEP, *GEO 5*, 174.

154 Ibid.

155 Lowell Center for Sustainable Production, *Chemicals Policy in Europe Set New Worldwide Standards for Registration, Education and Authorization of Chemicals (REACH)*, 2003, cited in UNEP, *GEO 5*, 223.

156 EPA, *Guidelines for Carcinogen Risk Assessment*, Document EPA/630/P-03/001F (Washington, DC: EPA, 2005), cited in UNEP, *GEO 5*, 223.

157 UNEP, *Global Chemicals Outlook II* (Nairobi: UNEP).

158 Masanori Kuratsune, et al., "Epidemiologic Study on Yusho, a Poisoning Caused by Ingestion of Rice Oil Contaminated with a Commercial Brand of Polychlorinated Biphenyls," *Environmental Health Perspectives* vol. 1 (April 1972): 119–128.

159 Thomas R. Dunlap, *DDT: Scientists, Citizens, and Public Policy* (Princeton, NJ: Princeton University Press, 1981); Janna Koppe and Jane Keys, "PCBs and the Precautionary Principle," in *The Precautionary Principle in the 20th Century: Late Lessons from Early Warnings*, eds. Poul Harremoës, et al. (London: Earthscan, 2002), 64–78.

160 The action plan the conference produced called for improved international efforts to develop and harmonize procedures for assessing and managing hazardous substances and to augment resources available to developing countries for building domestic capacity.

161 Global agreements include the 1972 International Convention on the Prevention of Marine Pollution by Dumping of Wastes and Other Matter (London Convention) and the MARPOL Convention, which includes the 1973 International Convention for the Prevention of Pollution from Ships and its 1978 protocol. Early regional and river agreements include the 1972 Convention for the Prevention of Marine Pollution by Dumping from Ships and Aircraft (Oslo Convention); 1974 Convention for the Prevention of Marine Pollution from Land-Based Sources (Paris Convention); 1974 Convention on the Protection of the Marine Environment of the Baltic Sea Area (Helsinki Convention); 1976 Convention on the Protection of the Rhine Against Chemical Pollution; 1976 Protocol for the Prevention of Pollution of the Mediterranean Sea by Dumping from Ships and Aircraft; and the 1978 Great Lakes Water Quality Agreement.

162 Jonathan Krueger and Henrik Selin, "Governance for Sound Chemicals Management: The Need for a More Comprehensive Global Strategy," *Global Governance* vol. 8 (2002): 323–342.

163 David Victor, "Learning by Doing in the Nonbinding International Regime to Manage Trade in Hazardous Chemicals and Pesticides," in *The Implementation and Effectiveness of International Environmental Commitments: Theory and Practice*, eds. David Victor, et al. (Cambridge, MA: MIT Press, 1998), 228.

164 The participating organizations in the Inter-Organization Programme for the Sound Management of Chemicals are the Food and Agriculture Organization, International Labour Organization, UN Development Programme, UNEP, United Nations Industrial Development Organization, United Nations Institute for Training and Research, World Health Organization, World Bank, and OECD.

165 For the text of the convention, reports, and official documents from the COPs and other meetings, lists of parties, national reports, country contacts, and other information, see the Rotterdam Convention website: www.pic.int. Analyses of the development and content of the convention include Victor, "Learning by Doing"; Richard Emory Jr., "Probing the Protections in the Rotterdam Convention on Prior Informed Consent," *Colorado Journal of International Environmental Law and Policy* vol. 23 (2001): 47–91; and Selin, *Global Governance of Hazardous Chemicals*.

166 For broader discussions of the science of POPs, see Arnold Schecter, *Dioxins and Health Including Other Persistent Organic Pollutants and Endocrine Disruptors* (Hoboken, NJ: Wiley and Sons, 2012); David Downie and Terry Fenge, eds., *Northern Lights Against POPs: Combatting Threats in the Arctic* (Montreal: McGill-Queen's University Press, 2003); Joe Thornton, *Pandora's Poison: Chlorine, Health, and a New Environmental Strategy* (Cambridge, MA: MIT Press, 2000); and Theo Colborn, Dianne Dumanoski, and John Peterson Myers, *Our Stolen Future: Are We Threatening Our Fertility, Intelligence, and Survival?—A Scientific Detective Story* (New York: Dutton, 1996).

167 For examples and discussion of these studies, see Downie and Fenge, *Northern Lights Against POPs*; and Arctic Monitoring and Assessment Programme (AMAP), *AMAP Assessment Report: Arctic Pollution Issues* (Oslo: AMAP, 1998).

168 See Downie and Fenge, *Northern Lights Against POPs*.

169 Personal observations and discussions by David Downie with UNEP chemicals and national government officials during this period and during the negotiating sessions from 1998 to 2001.

170 The decision by the UNEP Governing Council to initiate the talks included specific mandates to address this issue and create a procedure for adding chemicals.

171 For the text of the convention, reports, and other official documents from the COPs and the POPs Review Committee (POPRC), lists of parties, national reports, country contacts, documents from the negotiations that produced the treaty, detailed information on the chemicals controlled under the convention, and other information, see the Stockholm Convention

website: http://pops.int. For detailed secondary-source reports on the COP, see https://enb.iisd. org/vol15/.

172 Very small amounts of DDT can also be used as an intermediate in the production of the chemical dicofol if no DDT is released into the environment.

173 For information on exemptions, including which countries have requested and can use particular exemptions, see http://chm.pops.int/Procedures/Exemptionsandacceptablepurposes/tabid/ 4646/Default.aspx.

174 For a detailed discussion of this process, including the original version of Figure 3.3, see Downie and Fenge, *Northern Lights Against POPs*, 140–142.

175 See, in particular, paragraphs 7(a) and 9 of Article 8 of the Stockholm Convention.

176 Sources of information and analyses of POPRC include Jessica Templeton, "Framing Elite Policy Discourse: Scientists and the Stockholm Convention on Persistent Organic Pollutants" (PhD diss., London School of Economics and Political Science, 2011); David Downie and Jessica Templeton. "Pesticides and Persistent Organic Pollutants," in Paul Harris, ed., *Routledge Handbook of Global Environmental Politics* (New York: Routledge, 2014); and reports on POPRC meetings by the *Earth Negotiations Bulletin*.

177 Opt-in parties include Australia, Canada, China, India, Republic of Korea, and Russia. If it ratifies the convention, the United States would likely be an opt-in party.

178 The opt-in and opt-out options could lead to some parties being bound by controls on new substances while others are not. This could deter countries from listing some chemicals if they believe that doing so will put them at a competitive disadvantage in comparison with opt-in states. Uneven patterns of ratification could also create legal uncertainties with regard to restricting trade in products made with or containing POPs. See Downie and Templeton, "Pesticides and Persistent Organic Pollutants."

179 Because the United States had already controlled the dirty dozen, its costs to implement the original treaty would be low. President Bush participated in a Rose Garden ceremony heralding the convention and stating his intention to push for ratification. In the absence of 9/11, it is logical that he would have done so, if for no other reason than to provide his administration with an environmental victory before the 2004 election.

180 IISD, "Summary of the Fourth Meeting of the Persistent Organic Pollutants Review Committee of the Stockholm Convention: 13–17 October 2008," *Earth Negotiations Bulletin* vol. 15, no. 161 (October 20, 2008).

181 Ibid. Personal observations by David Downie during these meetings and subsequent COPs.

182 For details of the debate and vote, see UNEP, "Report of the Conference of the Parties to the Stockholm Convention on Persistent Organic Pollutants on the Work of Its Seventh Meeting," UN Document UNEP/POPS/COP.7/36; and "Summary of the Meetings of the Conferences of the Parties to the Basel, Rotterdam and Stockholm Conventions: 4–15 May 2015."

183 Downie and Templeton, "Pesticides and Persistent Organic Pollutants."

184 For details of the meeting, see background documents and the official meeting report on the Stockholm Convention's website (http://pops.int) and the daily and summary reports provided by the *Earth Negotiations Bulletin* at www.iisd.ca/chemical/pops/cop4. This section draws heavily on personal observations and notes made by David Downie while attending the meeting; the official report of the meeting; and IISD, "Summary of the Fourth Conference of Parties to the Stockholm Convention on Persistent Organic Pollutants: 4–8 May 2009," *Earth Negotiations Bulletin* vol. 15, no. 174 (May 11, 2009).

185 David Downie, personal observations during the COP.

186 GEF, *Report of the GEF to the Conference of the Parties to the Stockholm Convention on Persistent Organic Pollutants at its Fifth Meeting*, UN Document UNEP/POPS/COP.5/24, March 8, 2011, 4.

187 GEF, "Chemicals and Wastes," www.thegef.org/topics/chemicals-and-waste. See also "Report of the GEF to the Conference of the Parties to the Stockholm Convention on Persistent Organic Pollutants at its Ninth Meeting," UN Document UNEP/POPS/COP.9/INF/30, April 25, 2019.

188 Downie and Templeton, "Pesticides and Persistent Organic Pollutants."

189 Jennifer Allan, David Downie, and Jessica Templeton, "Experimenting with TripleCOPs: Productive Innovation or Counterproductive Complexity?" *International Environmental Agreements: Politics, Law and Economics* vol. 18, no. 4 (August 2018): 557–572; personal observations by David Downie and communications with delegates and observers during the 2013, 2015, 2017, and 2019 COPs.

190 Personal communications.

191 See BRS Secretariat, "Global Monitoring Plan," http://chm.pops.int/Implementation/GlobalMonitoringPlan/Overview/tabid/83/Default.aspx.

192 WHO and UNEP, *State of the Science of Endocrine Disrupting Chemicals* (Geneva: WHO and UNEP, 2013); UNEP, *GEO 5*, 223.

193 The Secretariat maintains an updated list: http://chm.pops.int/Countries/StatusofRatifications/Amendmentstoannexes/tabid/3486/Default.aspx.

194 Downie and Templeton, "Pesticides and Persistent Organic Pollutants."

195 UNEP, *Mercury: Time to Act* (Nairobi: UNEP, 2013), 12. Unless otherwise noted, "common knowledge" facts such as this concerning mercury come from this or similar UN documents.

196 UNEP, *Global Mercury Assessment, 2018* (Geneva: UNEP, 2019), 6.

197 Representative summaries include: WHO, *Exposure to Mercury: A Major Health Concern. Preventing Disease Through Healthy Environments* (Geneva: WHO, 2007); WHO, *Artisanal and Small-Scale Gold Mining and Health. Environmental and Occupational Health Hazards Associated with Artisanal and Small-Scale Gold Mining* (Geneva, WHO, 2016); M. R. Karagas, et al., "Evidence on the Human Health Effects of Low Level Methyl Mercury Exposure," *Environmental Health Perspectives* vol. 120, no. 6 (2012): 799–806; Donna Mergler, et al., "Methylmercury Exposure and Health Effects in Humans: A Worldwide Concern," *Ambio: A Journal of the Human Environment*, vol. 36, no. 1 (2007): 3–11; Phillippe Grandjean, et al., "Health Effects and Risk Assessments," in Nicole Pirrone and Kathryn Mahaffey (eds.) *Dynamics of Mercury Pollution on Regional and Global Scales* (Boston: Springer, 2005).

198 Sources on the historical uses of mercury include: UNEP, *Mercury: Time to Act*; Sharon Zuber and Michael Newman, eds., *Mercury Pollution: A Transdisciplinary Treatment* (Boca Raton: CRC Press, Taylor & Francis Group, 2012); Guido Lombardi, et al., "Five Hundred Years of Mercury Exposure and Adaptation," *Journal of Biomedicine & Biotechnology* vol. 2012 (2012): 472858, doi:10.1155/2012/472858; and Richard Swiderski, *Quicksilver: A History of the Use, Lore and Effects of Mercury* (Jefferson, NC: McFarland, 2008).

199 Lombardi, et al., "Five Hundred Years of Mercury Exposure and Adaptation," 2.

200 Ibid., 5.

201 For details, treaty texts, and lists of parties, see www.unece.org/env/lrtap/hm_h1.html.

202 The outline of historical events in this section is well documented in many UNEP and Minamata Secretariat publications.

203 For details of its operation and history, see UNEP Global Mercury Partnership, "Our Work," https://web.unep.org/globalmercurypartnership/#parentHorizontalTab2.

204 IISD, "Summary of the Fifth Session of the Intergovernmental Negotiating Committee to Prepare a Global Legally Binding Instrument on Mercury," *Earth Negotiation Bulletin* vol. 28, no. 33 (November 10, 2014), 1.

205 Ibid.

206 "Obama Shifts U.S. Policy to Back Global Mercury Control Treaty," ENS Newswire, February 16, 2009. In 2011, the Obama administration also enacted the Mercury and Air Toxics Standards (MATS)—the first federal standard that specifically required power plants to limit emissions of named toxic pollutants, including mercury and arsenic.

207 Personal observation by David Downie, who attended all the mercury negotiations.

208 UNEP, *Global Mercury Assessment*, 10.

209 Ibid., 11.

210 The official reports from each INC meeting, as well as the documents prepared for each meeting, are available on the Minamata Convention Secretariat's website, www.mercuryconvention.org/. See in particular links available via the "History" page: www.mercuryconvention.org/Convention/History/tabid/3798/language/en-US/Default.aspx. See also the daily and summary reports, as well as photos and other material, published by the *Earth Negotiation Bulletin*, at https://enb.iisd.org/vol28/.

211 UNEP, *Global Mercury Assessment*, 15.

212 Ibid., 14–15.

213 Ibid., 12, 16.

214 Recent, first-hand reporting includes Richard Paddock and Adam Dean, "In Indonesia, Outlaw Gold Miners Poison Themselves to Make a Living," *New York Times*, December 31, 2019.

215 UNEP, "Artisanal and Small-scale Gold Mining (ASGM)," 2019, https://web.unep.org/globalmercurypartnership/our-work/artisanal-and-small-scale-gold-mining-asgm.

216 UNEP, *Global Mercury Assessment*, 15–17.
217 For details, see UNEP, "Mercury Releases from the Cement Industry," 2019, https://web.unep.org/globalmercurypartnership/our-work/mercury-releases-cement-industry.
218 UNEP, *Global Mercury Assessment*, 12.
219 Personal observation by David Downie, who attended the meeting.
220 The delay between INC 5 and treaty adoption is standard. After a treaty text is agreed to, it is translated into all six official UN languages and then circulated to countries for several months of review.
221 This includes identifying and quantifying the production and use of mercury and mercury-added products; sources of mercury emissions and releases; contaminated sites; use in ASGM; and what is needed to implement the Convention at the national level.

Chapter 4

The Development of Environmental Regimes

Natural Resources, Species, and Habitats

Abstract

The development of global environmental regimes generally involves five interrelated processes or stages: agenda setting and issue definition, fact finding, bargaining on regime creation, regime implementation, and regime review and strengthening. This chapter examines regimes that address global biodiversity, marine biodiversity in areas beyond national jurisdiction, trade in endangered species, whaling, and land degradation and desertification—issue areas that address shared natural resources: physical or biological systems that extend into or across the jurisdictions of two or more states or beyond national jurisdiction. For each case, we outline the environmental issue, delineate key stages in the regime's development, and discuss the role of lead and veto states in shaping the outcomes. The content, development, and impact of these regimes reveal important similarities and differences in regime politics and help us understand why states may or may not cooperate effectively on global environmental issues.

Keywords: biodiversity, desertification, endangered species, land degradation, marine biodiversity, whales, Convention on Biological Diversity, Convention on Trade in Endangered Species of Wild Fauna and Flora, International Whaling Convention

Like the pollution-control regimes described in Chapter 3, regimes designed to conserve natural resources must overcome conflicts among states' economic and political interests, concerns for protecting state sovereignty, and different opinions on the importance of the precautionary principle and the principle of common but differentiated responsibilities (CBDR). Moreover, natural resources regimes face the additional challenge of trying to protect resources and species that are of international importance but exist within the boundaries of sovereign states or beyond the boundaries of any state.

The regimes described in this chapter focus on shared natural resources: physical or biological systems that extend into, across, or beyond the jurisdictions of two or more states. Shared natural resources include non-renewable resources (for example, underground pools of oil or waterways) subject to the jurisdiction of two or more states, renewable and biological resources (fish stocks, birds, and mammals), and complex ecosystems (forests, regional seas, river basins, coral reefs, and deserts).[1] Many shared natural resources exist in or pass through the commons or the jurisdictional zones of two or more states. Many highly migratory fish and marine mammals, including whales, move through the waters of several coastal states as well as the waters that are part of the high seas, beyond a country's exclusive economic zone (EEZ), the 200-mile territorial waters under the jurisdiction of individual states.[2] Shared resources may also link states far removed from each other geographically, as in the case of migratory birds and fish.

The international management of natural resources must also address transboundary externalities that arise when activities within the jurisdiction of an individual state produce results that negatively affect the welfare of those residing in other states.[3] Such situations involve a very difficult question, one central not only to environmental but also to human rights and humanitarian law: when does the international community have a legitimate interest, right, or obligation to seek significant changes in the domestic affairs of individual states because the activities occurring within their jurisdictions pose severe threats to the well-being of others or to international society as a whole? For example, should states still have unfettered rights to cut huge tracts of their forested land for timber or agriculture when these forests benefit the entire world as biodiversity reserves and as carbon sinks that remove climate change-causing carbon dioxide from the atmosphere? Do countries have a right to try to change how other states manage ecosystems with rich biological diversity because the loss of particular plants and animals could prevent the discovery of new drugs that might cure cancer or other diseases? Do states have the right to tell other states to stop killing, buying, and selling endangered species because extinction is a global concern? Should the ethical perspectives of a large group of countries regarding whales or elephants affect the activities of a smaller set of countries that do not share these views?

In addition to national sovereignty issues, regimes for biodiversity, endangered species, and marine and terrestrial ecosystems may also have consequences for particular economic development strategies or efforts to promote free trade. Are states free to impose import restrictions on products from other countries if their production causes unacceptable environmental harm, such as catching shrimp in a way that endangers sea turtles? (See Chapter 6.) Should a country be prevented from developing a timber industry that would have short-term economic benefits but long-term negative consequences for global biodiversity?

Finally, governments have the option of adopting clear and measurable reduction targets and timetables in regimes that seek to control a particular source of pollution, such as those for ozone and persistent organic pollutants (POPs). However, such approaches are not easily applied, or even possible, when addressing many natural resource issues. Effective protection and management of natural resources often require agreeing on and implementing complex sets of new policies that seek to address a variety of underlying factors that threaten the resource. It is also sometimes more difficult to develop effective indicators to measure implementation or to determine the impact of the regime.

The five cases examined in this chapter highlight different aspects of international natural resource management. The Convention on Biological Diversity (CBD) highlights North–South differences in the distribution of biodiversity resources and how natural resource management can conflict with particular economic, social, and political interests. The need for an agreement on conservation and sustainable use of marine biodiversity in areas beyond national jurisdiction illustrates the difficulties that existing regimes have in protecting resources found beyond national borders.

The Convention on International Trade in Endangered Species of Wild Fauna and Flora (CITES) faces the challenge of combating a globalized black market. The International Convention for the Regulation of Whaling demonstrates how significantly regimes can change and what happens when politics and economics reduce the effectiveness of a regime and throw its purpose into question. The desertification regime illustrates the challenge of finding the right balance between science and policy to reduce land degradation that both harms the environment and impedes economic and social development.

Biodiversity Loss

Biological diversity is most often associated with the earth's vast variety of plants, animals, and microorganisms, but the term encompasses diversity at all levels, from genes to species to ecosystems to landscapes. Scientists estimate that there are approximately 8.7 million species

✦ BOX 4.1 CHARISMATIC MEGAFAUNA

Charismatic megafauna refer to animals that have public appeal, largely due to their phys-ical appearance. Easily recognizable and well-liked, they tend to get more attention than other species. As a result, environmental organizations often use charismatic megafauna such as the giant panda, great ape, male lion, Bengal tiger, humpback whale, and polar bear as advertising icons for their conservation efforts, with consequential advantages for attracting funding for conservation efforts and scientific research.

In an experiment, people were shown different versions of a flyer from a fictional environ-mental organization asking for help protecting an endangered species of great ape or bat. Different flyers had a photo of an attractive example of the ape or bat, an ugly example, or no photo at all. People were willing to give more money to help protect the species when an attractive photo was used. Scientists also note that people like animals that are similar to humans physically and behaviorally, or demonstrate characteristics seen as positive, like empathy, intelligence, strength, or cunning.

The human response to charismatic megafauna has fostered conservation success stories— a positive development, since these species live in biodiverse ecosystems that host a diverse range of plant and animal species, and protecting their habitats will save other species as well. However, concentrating on charismatic megafauna can take public attention and dollars away from protecting many other and equally important species of insects, reptiles, fish, amphibians, and plants. Some endangered species lists might even reflect this bias, because scientists tend to study certain charismatic megafauna at a greater rate than non-charismatic species. For example, well over 100 reports have been published about meerkats, but fewer than twenty papers have been published about the manatee. This aca-demic neglect may work against overall conservation efforts.

Sources: Amber Pariona, "Who are the Charismatic Megafauna of the World?" WorldAtlas, April 25, 2017, worldatlas.com/articles/who-are-the-charismatic-megafauna-of-the-world. html; Rachel Nuwer, "Conservation's Elephant in the Room," Scienceline, March 10, 2011, https://scienceline.org/2011/03/conservation%E2%80%99s-elephant-in-the-room; Jessica C. Walsh, et al., "Trends and Biases in the Listing and Recovery Planning for Threatened Species: an Australian Case Study," *Oryx*, 47(1), 134–143. doi:10.1017/S003060531100161X; Matt Soniak, "Why You Want to Save the Whales, but not the Crickets," *The Week*, March 3, 2014, https://theweek.com/articles/450037/why-want-save-whales-but-not-crickets.

globally, of which approximately 2.2 million are marine. In spite of 250 years of research and over 1.2 million species already identified, it is possible that 86 percent of existing species on earth and 91 percent of species in the ocean still await description.[4] But not all of these species are treated equally. Human perception has led to disparate efforts at conservation. Large, iconic species—elephants, tigers, lions, pandas, and other "charismatic megafauna"— usually receive most of the attention and funding, while the vast majority of species are ignored (see Box 4.1). These forgotten species are often hidden, small, slimy, or "ugly," including many types of insects, snakes, amphibians, and fish. Not only do these species receive less public attention, but they are also less studied and less likely to be protected.

Ecosystems are another aspect of biodiversity. In each ecosystem, including those that occur within or among forests, wetlands, mountains, deserts, and rivers, living creatures interact with each other as well as with the air, water, and soil around them; in this way, they form an interconnected community. Biodiversity also includes genetic differences within species, such as different breeds and varieties, as well as chromosomes, genes, and genetic sequences (DNA).

The *Global Assessment Report on Biodiversity and Ecosystem Services* of the Intergovernmental Science-Policy Platform on Biodiversity and Ecosystem Services (IPBES), which was approved by the world's governments in May 2019, concluded that human actions threaten more species with global extinction now than ever before.[5] The current rate of species extinction is tens to hundreds of times higher than it has averaged over the past 10 million years. An average of around 25 percent of species in assessed animal and plant groups are threatened, suggesting that around 1 million species already face extinction, many within decades, unless action is taken to reduce the intensity of drivers of biodiversity loss—and without such action, the rate of species extinction will accelerate even more.

Governments acknowledge both the intrinsic importance of biodiversity and its value to the well-being of future generations. However, attempts to create an effective global regime for conserving biodiversity have suffered from differences concerning the appropriate definition of the problem and how to balance application of the principle of national sovereignty versus that of the common heritage of humankind;[6] a veto coalition of developing countries whose territories hold most of the world's biodiversity that resist accepting strong legal obligations to enact certain policies within their borders; and inconsistent support from the United States and several other key industrialized states.

In 1987, concern about the rate of species extinction led the United Nations Environment Programme (UNEP) to create a working group of experts to study the potential for an umbrella convention to address biodiversity conservation. As the group began issue definition in 1990, the idea of a biodiversity convention became entangled in North–South struggles concerning the ownership of genetic resources, with developing countries arguing for explicit state sovereignty over the genetic resources within their borders and developed countries arguing the view, previously accepted under international law, that these resources form part of the "common heritage of [hu]mankind." Some developing countries insisted that genetic resources belong to the states in which they are located and that access should be based on a "mutual agreement between countries." They also argued for the inclusion of provisions for non-commercial access to biotechnologies based on plant genetic resources found in the South as a central element in any biodiversity convention. Most industrialized countries initially opposed the inclusion of biotechnology in the convention and attempted to define the scope of the regime to include only the conservation of biodiversity in the wild and mechanisms to finance such efforts.[7]

Formal negotiations on what would become the CBD were completed in five sessions from July 1991 to May 1992 (see Box 4.2). One hundred fifty-three countries signed the convention in June 1992, and the CBD entered into force on December 29, 1993. One hundred ninety-six countries are now parties.[8] Notably, the United States is not a party, although the Clinton administration signed the convention in June 1993. US pharmaceutical and agricultural biotechnology companies had invested heavily in developing genetic material for industrial and commercial use, like multi-resistant plant seeds and various medicines. In general, they opposed the idea of sharing profits with the country of origin of the plant genetic resources they develop and lobbied Congress not to ratify the Convention.[9]

The CBD has three objectives: conservation of biological diversity, sustainable use of its components, and fair and equitable sharing of benefits arising out of the use of genetic resources. Parties are obligated to inventory and monitor biodiversity, incorporate the concepts of conservation and sustainable development into national strategies and economic development, and preserve indigenous conservation practices. The convention takes a comprehensive, rather than sectoral, approach to the conservation of biological diversity and the sustainable use of biological resources, and this has proven to be an implementation challenge. The fact that the treaty encompasses socioeconomic issues, such as the sharing of benefits

❖ BOX 4.2 CONVENTION ON BIOLOGICAL DIVERSITY MILESTONES

1987: UNEP's Governing Council creates a working group of experts to study an "umbrella convention" to rationalize activities in biodiversity conservation.

1991: Negotiations on the Convention on Biological Diversity begin.

1992: 153 countries sign the Convention on Biological Diversity at the Earth Summit in Rio de Janeiro, Brazil.

1993: Convention on Biological Diversity enters into force.

1995: Working Group on Biosafety established to negotiate a protocol on biosafety.

2000: Cartagena Protocol on Biosafety is adopted.

2002: A global target for significantly reducing the rate of biodiversity loss by 2010 is adopted.

2003: Cartagena Protocol enters into force.

2004: The Working Group on Access and Benefit Sharing is established.

2004: Adoption of the Akwé: Kon Guidelines for cultural, environmental, and social impact assessments, and the Addis Ababa Principles and Guidelines for sustainable use.

2005: Ad Hoc Group on Liability and Redress holds first meeting.

2010: Strategic Plan 2011–2020 and the Aichi Biodiversity Targets is adopted.

2010: Nagoya–Kuala Lumpur Supplementary Protocol on Liability and Redress to the Cartagena Protocol on Biosafety is adopted.

2010: Nagoya Protocol Access to Genetic Resources and the Fair and Equitable Sharing of Benefits Arising from Their Utilization is adopted.

2014: Nagoya Protocol enters into force.

2018: Nagoya–Kuala Lumpur Supplementary Protocol on Liability and Redress to the Cartagena Protocol on Biosafety enters into force.

2018: An intersessional working group is established to negotiate the post-2020 global biodiversity framework, which meets in 2019 and early 2020.

2020: Adoption of the post-2020 biodiversity framework postponed due to COVID-19.

from the use of genetic resources and access to technology, including biotechnology, has also complicated implementation. Thus, to strengthen the biodiversity regime, the Conference of the Parties (COP) has negotiated protocols to establish concrete commitments on biosafety and the sharing of benefits from the use of genetic resources and adopted a Strategic Plan for Biodiversity, for the 2011–2020 period, including the Aichi Biodiversity Targets. So how has the Convention done with regard to fulfilling its three objectives?

Conservation of Biological Diversity

Implementation of the CBD has been less focused than in some of the other global environmental regimes. This reflects the more diffuse nature of the regime's rules and norms, the absence of a strong lead-state coalition, the absence of an enforcement mechanism, and a general lack of political will. However, the COP has made progress in both identifying global conservation priority areas and developing work programs on conservation and/or sustainable use in particular sectors.

The COP's first approach to implementation was developing seven work programs in critical areas that sustain biodiversity and provide critical ecosystem services: mountain regions, dry and subhumid lands, marine and coastal areas, islands, inland waters, agricultural systems, and forests.[10] These programs are the main instruments that CBD parties use to achieve the commitments contained in the convention. They include guidelines for national implementation and reforming relevant national laws, policies, or administrative practices. The work programs also identify tasks for furthering implementation at the international level and by the COP as well as opportunities for collaboration between the CBD and other international instruments or processes.[11]

However, the work programs lack overall coherence, and their national implementation has suffered from inadequate policies, funding, and political commitment, as clearly demonstrated in the international community's failure to meet the global target of significantly reducing the rate of biodiversity loss by 2010. The COP adopted this target in 2002, and it was later endorsed by the 2002 World Summit on Sustainable Development (WSSD) and incorporated into the Millennium Development Goals (MDGs).[12] The 2010 *Global Biodiversity Outlook* provided scientific evidence that the global target would not be met and stressed that the five principal pressures directly driving biodiversity loss (habitat change, overexploitation, pollution, invasive alien species, and climate change) remained constant or were increasing.[13] The report concluded that reasons for the global failure to meet the established goals included the insufficient scale of actions taken to implement the convention and meet the challenge of biodiversity loss; insufficient integration of biodiversity issues into broader policies; insufficient attention to the underlying drivers of biodiversity loss; and insufficient inclusion of the benefits of biodiversity (and the costs of its loss) into the operation of economic systems and markets.[14]

In response to this failure, in October 2010 the COP adopted renewed commitments in the Strategic Plan for Biodiversity 2011–2020,[15] which called for more effective and urgent action and included twenty specific Aichi Biodiversity Targets to be met by 2020.[16] The CBD strengthened its review systems to facilitate what governments hoped would be successful achievement of the Aichi Targets.[17] In 2014 the COP established a new Subsidiary Body on Implementation (SBI) to review the ongoing implementation of the Convention, including progress toward meeting the Aichi Targets.[18]

Efforts to achieve these targets, however, were not successful. Both the 2019 IPBES *Global Assessment Report on Biodiversity and Ecosystem Services* and the 2020 *Global Biodiversity Outlook 5* concluded that countries had not made sufficient progress in stemming the direct and indirect drivers of biodiversity loss, and that most of the Aichi Biodiversity Targets for 2020 would be missed.[19] The anthropogenic drivers of biodiversity loss were increasingly global in nature, including habitat loss as a result of land-use change (Aichi target 5), unsustainable agriculture, aquaculture, and forestry (target 7), unsustainable fishing (target 6), pollution (target 8), and invasive alien species (target 9).[20] Countries had made good progress toward only four of the twenty Aichi Targets and moderate progress toward seven. However, there was poor progress on six important targets (reduction in habitat loss; fisheries; sustainable management of agriculture, aquaculture, and forests; pollution reduction; reduction in pressures on vulnerable ecosystems; and extinction prevention), and insufficient information existed to assess progress on the remaining three targets. The lack of significant progress on most of the Aichi Biodiversity Targets was seen as a failure for the Strategic Plan for Biodiversity, an obstacle to achieving the Sustainable Development Goals, and evidence of continued, serious threats to the planet's life support systems.[21]

Cartagena Protocol on Biosafety

Biosafety, under the CBD, refers to precautionary practices that seek to ensure the safe transfer, handling, use, and disposal of living modified organisms (LMOs) derived from modern biotechnology. By the early 1990s, most countries with biotechnology industries had domestic biosafety legislation in place, but there were no binding international agreements regarding genetically modified organisms that cross national borders. Biotechnology, particularly its agricultural applications, was controversial, and national policies varied widely, as exemplified in the contrasting approaches of the United States and the European Union (EU), with the latter installing a far more precautionary approach toward modern biotechnology. In 1999, several European governments joined European environmental nongovernmental organizations (NGOs) in calling for a moratorium on the import of genetically modified foods. Although the moratorium ended in 2004, it provoked a World Trade Organization (WTO) dispute between the United States and the EU, which was decided in favor of the United States in 2006.[22] (See Chapter 6 for discussion of the WTO.)

Parties to the CBD began negotiations on the biosafety protocol in 1996. A powerful veto coalition emerged, called the Miami Group, which comprised the world's major grain exporters outside of the EU, including Argentina, Australia, Canada, Chile, the United States, and Uruguay. The veto coalition argued that proposed trade restrictions in the protocol would harm the multibillion-dollar agricultural export industry, imprecision in several key provisions would create uncertainty and difficulties implementing the treaty, countries would be able to block imports based on their own criteria rather than on sound scientific knowledge, and the increased documentation required under the protocol would create unnecessary and costly bureaucratic procedures.[23] Participation in the regime by at least some veto states was deemed important to the agreement's future success, so crafting acceptable compromises proved difficult.

In January 2000, governments finally reached an agreement and adopted the Cartagena Protocol on Biosafety.[24] The protocol entered into force in September 2003 and requires parties to take precautionary measures to prevent LMOs from causing harm to biodiversity and human health. The protocol has since been supplemented by the 2010 Nagoya–Kuala Lumpur Supplementary Protocol on Liability and Redress to the Cartagena Protocol on Biosafety,[25] which provides international rules and procedures on liability and redress for damage to biodiversity resulting from LMOs. The supplementary protocol entered into force in March 2018.

The successful implementation of the Cartagena Protocol requires additional policy developments that must balance a variety of economic and political interests. One example is the difficulty parties had in reaching agreement on documentation requirements for bulk shipments of LMOs intended for food, feed, and processing (LMO-FFPs). In order to adopt the protocol, negotiators put off an agreement on this issue; according to Article 18.2(a) of the protocol, parties are required to decide on the detailed requirements for such documentation within two years of entry into force. At the second Meeting of the Parties (MOP) in 2005, exporting countries expressed concern that labeling shipments that might include LMOs could interfere with trade. Apart from fears that many commodity producers did not have the capability to account for small amounts of LMOs that a shipment might contain, there was widespread concern that stricter documentation requirements could prove costly, restrict market access, and have a negative impact on countries that rely heavily on agricultural exports. Meanwhile, importing countries wanted to set up documentation requirements that would state which LMOs actually were included in a shipment rather than a longer list of LMOs that might be included. Many developing-country importers, particularly in Africa, stressed that documentation without guidance regarding which LMOs were most likely contained in the shipment posed significant capacity challenges to importing states to detect and monitor the content of incoming shipments.[26] New Zealand and Brazil played the role of veto states, later joined by Mexico, Paraguay, and Peru, and expressed serious objections to establishing any rule that would affect commodity trade in general.[27]

At MOP3 in Curitiba, Brazil, in 2006, Brazil shifted positions and, because of its role as host country, played the role of lead state by preparing drafts and promoting compromise to demonstrate its commitment to a successful outcome of the meeting. Under Brazil's leadership, parties agreed on a compromise package that balanced the interests of importing and exporting states as well as of developed- and developing-country parties. The Curitiba Rules request parties to take measures to ensure that documentation accompanying LMO-FFPs in commercial production clearly states that the shipment contains LMO-FFPs in cases where the identity of the LMO is known. In cases where the identity of the LMO is not known, the Curitiba Rules still allow documentation to state that the shipment may contain one or more LMO-FFPs, and they acknowledge that the expression "may contain" does not require a listing of LMOs of species other than those that constitute the shipment.

The rules were reviewed at MOP7, held in the Republic of Korea in 2014. The African Group wanted to develop a stand-alone document to accompany LMO-FFPs, which importing developing countries have traditionally viewed as a necessity for informed decision making on LMO imports. A number of other countries, including Brazil, Ecuador, the EU, Honduras, Japan, New Zealand, Paraguay, the Philippines, South Africa, and Uruguay, disagreed. Bolivia, Moldova, Norway, Peru, and Qatar suggested keeping the item under review and collecting additional experiences during the third review of the protocol's effectiveness. The EU suggested, and many parties agreed to, compromise text, which states that further review of the need for a stand-alone document is not required, unless a subsequent MOP decides otherwise in light of the experience gained. The compromise was accepted.[28] Although this decision effectively suspended further discussions on the most controversial items relating to LMO-FFPs, several developing-country parties indicated that making decisions on imports of LMO-FFPs would remain a significant challenge in the absence of additional guidance.[29]

Despite these types of implementation issues, the Cartagena Protocol is seen as a historic achievement. It establishes the first international law requiring countries to take precautionary measures to prevent LMOs from causing harm to biodiversity and human health. This precedent is perhaps more impressive considering that many multinational agro-businesses and other related interests, backed in most cases by their governments, did not want an agreement. Furthermore, at MOP5 in 2010 a new phase in the international regulation of biotechnology began: one that focuses on cooperation in managing the risks associated with LMOs rather than on the struggle between those who see biotechnology as a solution for many of the world's pressing problems and those who oppose it because they consider the risks of LMOs greater than the benefits.[30] However, to date only one member of the original veto coalition (Uruguay) has ratified the Cartagena Protocol, leaving many of the world's top grain exporters outside the regime, a situation that hinders the regime's overall effectiveness.

Access and Benefit Sharing

Genetic resources from plants, animals, and microorganisms are used for a variety of purposes, ranging from basic research to consumer products to medicines. Those using genetic resources include research institutes, universities, and private companies operating in many different economic sectors, including pharmaceuticals, agriculture, horticulture, cosmetics, material science, and biotechnology. For example, calanolide A, a compound isolated from the latex of the tree *Calophyllum lanigerum var. austrocoriaceum* found in the Malaysian rain forest, is used as a treatment for HIV-1.[31] An appetite suppressant has been derived from species of Hoodia, succulent plants indigenous to southern Africa and long used by the San people to stave off hunger and thirst.[32]

Since the CBD's entry into force in 1993, developing countries called for an increased focus on the convention's third official objective: fair and equitable sharing of benefits arising from the use of genetic resources.[33] This involves how companies, collectors, researchers, and others gain access to valuable genetic resources in return for sharing the benefits of this access with the countries of origin and local and indigenous communities. In 2004, the COP mandated that the Working Group on Access and Benefit Sharing elaborate an "international regime on access to genetic resources and benefit-sharing."[34]

Sharp divisions between the lead countries (providers of genetic resources) and a veto coalition (user countries) pervaded the negotiations. The Group of Like-Minded Megadiverse

Countries (LMMC), formed in 2002, took the lead on behalf of provider countries. Megadiverse countries are primarily tropical countries that possess rich varieties of animal and plant species, habitats, and ecosystems. Up to 70 percent of the world's biological diversity is located in the megadiverse countries, which include Bolivia, Brazil, China, Colombia, Costa Rica, Democratic Republic of Congo, Ecuador, India, Indonesia, Kenya, Madagascar, Malaysia, Mexico, Peru, Philippines, South Africa, and Venezuela. The LMMC, with the African Group, argued that the current distribution of benefits was unfair. The user countries (i.e., those with industries that commercialize genetic resources) opposed this position, arguing that the current system supports a global biotechnology industry that yields tremendous benefits. These mostly industrialized countries were quite content with the status quo, in which access to genetic resources was arguably free.

After six years of negotiations, parties adopted the Nagoya Protocol on Access to Genetic Resources and the Fair and Equitable Sharing of Benefits Arising from Their Utilization in October 2010 in Nagoya, Japan. The final compromise text was characterized by many as a "masterpiece in creative ambiguity." Instead of resolving outstanding issues by crafting balanced compromise proposals—an endeavor that would have failed—references to the most contentious issues were either deleted from the text or replaced by short and general provisions that allowed for flexible interpretation (but possibly also too wide a berth for implementation).[35]

Particularly challenging issues included the following:

- Whether the scope of the protocol would extend beyond genetic resources to biological resources more generally;
- How the holders of traditional knowledge related to genetic resources would be involved in procedures of access to such knowledge;
- How far countries will cooperate with one another when there are allegations of illegal uses; and
- Whether the scope of the protocol would extend to genetic resources acquired prior to the protocol's entry into force.

On the first point, some developed countries insisted that derivatives of genetic resources be excluded from the protocol and instead be negotiated in bilateral contracts. Developing countries tried to ensure that derivatives, such as naturally occurring biochemicals, were included. The final text states that the protocol shall apply to "genetic resources" and to the "benefits arising from the utilization of such resources,"[36] which includes research and development on the genetic and/or biochemical composition of genetic material. Research on the properties of extracts and molecules from plants, for example, and their development and commercialization as ingredients in pharmaceuticals or cosmetics now have to meet access and benefit-sharing requirements.

With respect to the treatment of traditional knowledge, some developed countries had argued that traditional knowledge relating to genetic resources should be addressed by the World Intellectual Property Organization, the UN's specialized agency responsible for intellectual property services, policy, information, and cooperation. However, others argued that leaving out traditional knowledge made little sense, as it is often used alongside genetic resources, and doing so would significantly reduce the benefits accruing to developing countries and local communities.[37] The protocol states that its rules apply to "traditional knowledge associated with genetic resources within the scope of the Convention and to the benefits arising from the utilization of such knowledge."[38]

It is worth noting that another group that holds traditional knowledge played an important role in the negotiations—women. The Like-Minded-in-Spirit Group of Women, a group of female delegates, including representatives from governments, NGOs, indigenous and local communities, civil society, and industry, was formed in November 2009 to incorporate a gender perspective into the access and benefit-sharing negotiations. This group became the first to ensure that women's voices are heard and their contribution is fully recognized in the CBD. As a result of their efforts, references to the important role that women play in access and benefit sharing and biodiversity conservation, and the need for the full participation of women in all levels of policy making and implementation, appear throughout the agreement.

On international cooperation, developed countries argued that the protocol should focus on compliance with national legislation instead of creating international regulations. However, because only about twenty-five developing countries had access and benefit sharing legislation in place, it was argued that such a requirement would further weaken the effectiveness of the protocol. The final text encourages transboundary cooperation and provides that each party shall take "appropriate, effective and proportionate legislative, administrative or policy measures" to provide that genetic resources and traditional knowledge used within their jurisdiction have been accessed in accordance with "prior informed consent and that mutually agreed terms have been established."[39]

To resolve the question of sharing benefits from new and continuing uses of genetic resources acquired prior to the entry into force of the protocol—one of the key demands of the African Group—delegates also resorted to creative ambiguity. Indeed, there is no direct reference to this issue. Rather, a provision envisages creation of a global multilateral benefit-sharing mechanism to address benefit sharing in transboundary situations or situations where it is not possible to grant or obtain prior informed consent. Such a mechanism, once established, could cover benefits arising from genetic resources acquired outside the framework of the CBD.[40]

The Nagoya Protocol entered into force in October 2014, and by September 2020 had 127 parties. In the end, however, the main strength of the Nagoya Protocol is also its weakness: the creative ambiguities could lead to differing interpretations at the national level, create legal uncertainties, and hinder implementation. National reports submitted to the CBD suggest that parties have made comparatively little progress toward implementing the Protocol.[41] In addition, Australia, Brazil, Canada, Chile, Colombia, Costa Rica, Equatorial Guinea, New Zealand, Russia, Thailand, and the United States are among the provider and user countries that have not ratified the agreement.

Moving Forward

Although parties have made progress on important issues, the biodiversity regime remains weak. The complexity of the biodiversity crisis, the multiple levels at which it must be addressed (ecosystems, species, genes), North–South contrasts in the distribution of biodiversity resources, and the many ways that biodiversity protection can conflict with important, if more short-term, economic, social, and political interests make implementation difficult at best. Yet, at the same time, threats to the planet's biodiversity and ecosystems continue to increase.

As the biodiversity regime moves forward, emerging technologies will continue to be added to the biodiversity, biosafety, and benefit-sharing agendas. Two such issues, synthetic biology and digital sequence information, became the subject of intense debate leading up to COP14 in Egypt in 2018.

Synthetic biology involves the application of engineering principles to biology, including the (re-)design and fabrication of biological components and systems that do not already exist in the natural world.[42] One example is engineered gene drives, which promote the inheritance of a particular gene to increase its prevalence in a population. By practically ensuring that a specific trait will be transmitted to almost all future generations, gene drives may generate serious biosafety concerns.[43] The COP14 decision on synthetic biology[44] called on parties to apply a precautionary approach regarding engineered gene drives, taking into account current uncertainties. It further calls for scientifically sound case-by-case risk assessments and risk-management measures, especially when considering the introduction of organisms containing engineered gene drives into the environment. Genome editing, a group of technologies that allow genetic material to be added, removed, or altered at particular locations in the genome, also attracted a lot of attention, but COP14 only called for further discussions in a working group.[45]

Digital sequence information (DSI) is on the agenda because as biodiversity-based research and development becomes increasingly based on the information content of genetic resources, enabled by genomic technologies, the physical access to biological samples of genetic resources may become unnecessary, and fair and equitable benefit sharing may be harder to achieve. If open access to DSI, necessary to foster scientific research, is not accompanied by benefit-sharing modalities, the CBD's third objective will become increasingly out of reach. While some argue that DSI is outside the scope of the Nagoya Protocol, others stress that failing to address the topic—and therefore not creating a mechanism for fairly and equitably sharing the benefits rising from the use of DSI—would undermine the Nagoya Protocol so fundamentally as to make it worthless.[46]

With the Strategic Plan for Biodiversity 2011–2020 and Aichi Targets[47] expiring in 2020, CBD Parties embarked on the preparation of a new "post-2020" global biodiversity framework in 2019. Parties expected to conclude negotiations and adopt this new framework at COP15 in October 2020, but this meeting was postponed to at least 2021 due to the COVID-19 pandemic. The post-2020 process has engaged a broad range of stakeholders, drawing on evidence from multiple sources, and sought to place biodiversity and ecosystem services in the context of other global agendas relating to development, climate change, land degradation, and disaster risk reduction.[48]

Photo 4.1 Civil society representatives demonstrate outside the negotiations on a post-2020 global biodiversity framework in Nairobi, Kenya.

Courtesy Diego Noguera, IISD/*Earth Negotiations Bulletin*, http://enb.iisd.org

Effective implementation and strengthening of the biodiversity regime also requires greater commitments by states with significant economic, political, or biodiversity resources. Some European states have been active in trying to strengthen the regime, but without increased support from key developing countries and the United States, which remains a non-party to the regime, the convention could remain unfocused and ineffective. In this context, the post-2020 framework has to: honestly assess progress, take into account lessons learned from the failure to achieve the 2010 and 2020 targets, address emerging technologies, and increase implementation and level of ambition. Otherwise, it is possible that the next set of goals will, like those before, come and go without having the needed positive impact on the planet's biodiversity.

Marine Biodiversity in Areas Beyond National Jurisdiction

Oceans represent perhaps the largest biodiversity reservoir on earth. Nearly two-thirds of the world's oceans, which in some areas reach depths of over 10 km (6.2 miles) and represent about 95 percent of the earth's total habitat by volume, is beyond national jurisdiction. No one state has independent governance authority. Areas beyond national jurisdiction (ABNJ) are home to significant biodiversity, including unique species that have evolved to survive extreme heat, cold, salinity, pressure, and darkness.[49] As humanity's technological capacity and demand for resources have grown, so too has the human footprint, and global governance for conservation and sustainable use has not kept pace.[50] Today, ocean biodiversity in ABNJ is under enormous pressure from overfishing, ghost nets,[51] and other debris that entangles marine animals; accumulating plastic, toxic chemicals, and oil released from ships and land-based sources; noise pollution; sewage; fertilizer runoff; and other stressors. All of this is exacerbated by accelerating climate change as the oceans absorb increasing amounts of carbon dioxide, which is increasing ocean acidity, and heat, which contributes to coral bleaching as well as mass movements as species search for more favorable environmental conditions.[52]

The environmental crisis in the ocean directly impacts humans. Billions of people consume some type of seafood at least once a week, and marine fisheries and aquaculture employ over 10 percent of the world's population, many of them women.[53] The vast pool of marine genetic resources provides the basis for innovative medicines. Phytoplankton, kelp, and algal plankton in the ocean produce more than half of the oxygen in the atmosphere as a by-product of photosynthesis.[54] Scientists caution that failure to take swift and effective action to address threats to biodiversity in ABNJ could compromise the ocean's capacity to provide resources and services necessary for human survival.

Countries have created an extensive array of international law and organizations to help govern the oceans, but these have not proven sufficient, and they do not effectively protect, or really regulate, marine biodiversity in ABNJ, commonly abbreviated as BBNJ. The 1982 UN Convention on the Law of the Sea (UNCLOS) sets forth the rights and obligations of states regarding the use of the oceans, their resources, and the protection of the marine and coastal environment. UNCLOS defines EEZs to include the coastal water and seabed extending 200 nautical miles from shore, over which a state has special rights to the use of marine resources, and establishes the limits of the "territorial sea," or the sovereign territory of a state, that extends 12 nautical miles from shore.

UNCLOS' fisheries management provisions (Articles 117 and 118) were strengthened by the 1995 UN Fish Stocks Agreement, which called for a precautionary approach and the use of the best available scientific information toward the conservation and management of fish stocks that move freely in and out of the high seas and through different EEZs. Fisheries are also managed by the UN Food and Agriculture Organization (FAO) 1995 Code of Conduct for Responsible Fisheries, which sets out principles and international standards of behavior to ensure the effective conservation, management, and development of living aquatic resources. There is also a network of seventeen regional fisheries management organizations (RFMOs) in areas that have major deep-sea fisheries. These collect fisheries statistics, assess resources, monitor fishing and other activities, and take important decisions on the management of each fishery.

UNEP, through its Regional Seas Programme, aims to help protect oceans and seas and promote the environmentally sound use of marine resources. The Regional Seas Programme, which includes eighteen Regional Seas Conventions and Action Plans, addresses the accelerating degradation of the world's oceans and coastal areas through a "shared seas" approach—namely, by engaging neighboring countries in specific actions to protect their common marine environment. The International Maritime Organization (IMO), the UN's specialized agency responsible for the safety and security of shipping and the prevention of marine pollution by ships, has adopted several treaties addressing oil pollution, chemicals and other harmful substances, garbage, sewage, and air pollution and emissions from ships.

The Convention on Biological Diversity applies only to activities and processes carried out under a party's jurisdiction or control that may have an adverse impact on biological diversity. Because they have no sovereignty or jurisdiction over the resources located in ABNJ, parties have no direct obligation to the conservation and sustainable use of specific components of biological diversity in those areas. Article 22 of the CBD requires parties to implement the Convention with respect to the marine environment consistently with the rights and obligations of states under UNCLOS.[55] Endangered marine species are also protected under CITES and the 1979 Convention on Migratory Species of Wild Animals and its family of species-specific agreements. In addition, the International Convention for the Regulation of Whaling governs thirteen different great whale species. The 1980 Convention on the Conservation of Antarctic Marine Living Resources and the 1972 Convention for the Conservation of Antarctic Seals under the Antarctic Treaty System apply to species of finfish, mollusks, crustaceans, sea birds, and seals in the waters near Antarctica. Yet even with this complex set of agreements, programs, and organizations, there was still no comprehensive agreement specifically governing marine ecosystems and biodiversity in ABNJ, and evidence indicated that one was needed.

Agenda Setting

The BBNJ agenda-setting phase took place in multiple fora between 1995 and 2004 (see Box 4.3). The second meeting of the Conference of the Parties to the CBD in November 1995 adopted a decision requiring the executive secretary, in consultation with the UN Division for Ocean Affairs and the Law of the Sea, to undertake a study of the relationship between the CBD and UNCLOS with regard to the conservation and sustainable use of genetic resources on the deep seabed.[56] However, little progress was made until 2003, when the UN Open-Ended Informal Consultative Process on Oceans and the Law of the Sea recommended that the General Assembly invite relevant international bodies to urgently consider how to better address threats and risks to vulnerable and threatened marine ecosystems and biodiversity beyond national jurisdiction.[57] The General Assembly then called on the UN Secretary-General to prepare a report on the threats and risks to marine ecosystems and biodiversity in ABNJ as well as details on any existing conservation and management measures.[58] In 2004, member states adopted General Assembly resolution 59/24, which called for establishing an informal working group to study issues relating to the conservation and sustainable use of marine biodiversity beyond areas of national jurisdiction.

Issue Definition in the Working Group

The Working Group, which held nine meetings between 2006 and 2015, was tasked with defining the issues and identifying gaps in the international legal regime concerning the conservation and sustainable use of marine biodiversity in ABNJ. Delegates debated whether mounting pressures on marine biodiversity derived from "implementation gaps"—insufficient and uncoordinated efforts to operationalize existing agreements—or regulatory

✦ BOX 4.3 BBNJ MILESTONES

1995: The Conference of the Parties to the Convention on Biological Diversity (CBD) agrees to study the relationship between the CBD and the United Nations Convention on the Law of the Sea (UNCLOS) with regard to the conservation and sustainable use of genetic resources on the deep seabed.

2002: At the World Summit on Sustainable Development in Johannesburg, governments agree on the need to maintain the productivity and biodiversity of important and vulnerable marine and coastal areas, including in areas beyond national jurisdiction.

2004: "Conservation and sustainable use of marine biological diversity in areas beyond national jurisdiction" is featured as an emerging topic of concern at the fifth meeting of the UN Open-Ended Informal Consultative Process on Oceans and the Law of the Sea (ICP).

2006: The UN General Assembly convenes a Working Group to study issues relating to the conservation and sustainable use of marine biological diversity beyond areas of national jurisdiction (BBNJ Working Group), which meets nine times between 2006 and 2015.

2012: At the UN Conference on Sustainable Development in Rio de Janeiro, states commit to addressing "the issue of the conservation and sustainable use of marine biodiversity in areas beyond national jurisdiction, including by taking a decision on the development of an international agreement under UNCLOS," before September 2015.

2015: The UN General Assembly adopts resolution 69/292, which establishes a preparatory committee (PrepCom) to make "substantive recommendations to the General Assembly on the elements of a draft text" of an international legally binding instrument on the conservation and sustainable use of marine biological diversity of ABNJ.

2016: The first of four sessions of the PrepCom convenes to identify potential areas of convergence of views.

2017: The PrepCom concludes its work and the UN General Assembly, in resolution 72/249 of December 2017, creates an intergovernmental conference (IGC) to negotiate an international legally binding instrument under UNCLOS on the conservation and sustainable use of BBNJ.

2018: The IGC holds its organizational session and first substantive meeting.

2019: The IGC holds its second and third meetings.

2020: The IGC's fourth session is postponed due to COVID-19.

gaps—insufficient international law to engender the necessary level of action by states individually and collectively at regional and global levels.[59]

As the number of delegations pointing to regulatory gaps increased, the Working Group discussed proposals for the development of a new treaty as an additional "implementing" agreement under UNCLOS. This proposal was first put forward by NGOs as early as 2006, and successively tabled by what became a group of key lead states: the EU, later joined by Group of 77 (G-77), Australia, and New Zealand. Yet a potential veto coalition also emerged among countries doubtful of the need for a new agreement: Canada, Japan, South Korea, Russia, and the United States.[60]

A key turning point was reached at the Working Group's fourth meeting in 2011 when participants agreed on a package of issues that could be addressed in a new implementing agreement under UNCLOS:

- the conservation and sustainable use of BBNJ;
- marine genetic resources, including questions on benefit sharing;
- measures such as area-based management tools, including marine protected areas and environmental impact assessments; and
- capacity building and the transfer of marine technology.

This shift may be explained by the momentum generated by the adoption of the Nagoya Protocol on Access and Benefit-sharing under the CBD in October 2010. At previous meetings of the Working Group, it was considered premature to move forward on marine genetic resources (MGRs) before the conclusion of the CBD negotiations. The adoption of the Nagoya Protocol, and the understanding that the Protocol did not apply to MGRs beyond national jurisdiction, removed that procedural barrier and helped generate new ideas. Progress at this meeting also may have been influenced by an informal workshop that enabled government delegates to "break down the issues" and begin identifying a common ground on the way forward outside of the more formal structures of the official Working Group process.[61]

However, when the Working Group reconvened in 2012—after the UN Conference on Sustainable Development formally called on the General Assembly to develop an international instrument under UNCLOS[62]—participants struggled to move forward on the development of a legal framework, with many wondering whether this forum was making any progress or just going in circles.[63] A year later, the UN General Assembly finally set a 2015 deadline for taking a decision. As a result, the Working Group met three times in 2014 and 2015 to discuss the feasibility, scope, and parameters of a new international instrument. At its ninth and final meeting in January 2015, delegates agreed to submit a draft decision to the General Assembly calling for the development of an international legally binding instrument on BBNJ under UNCLOS. The General Assembly subsequently established a preparatory committee (PrepCom) to make substantive recommendations, before official negotiations began, on potential elements of draft text for such an instrument.

Unpacking the Package

When the PrepCom convened in late March 2016, delegates engaged in "unpacking the package" of elements that the Working Group had agreed to in 2011 as the core of a future treaty. This exercise also enabled governments to better understand the elements of the package and the interlinkages necessary for the conservation and sustainable use of marine biodiversity in ABNJ.[64] By the end of the fourth and final meeting of the PrepCom in July 2017, governments had finalized a set of substantive recommendations so that the General Assembly could convene an intergovernmental conference to conclude the text of the agreement. Four of the key areas of discussion, based on the 2011 package, were marine genetic resources, including questions on benefit sharing; measures such as area-based management tools, including marine protected areas; environmental impact assessments; and capacity building and marine technology transfer.[65]

Marine Genetic Resources: Most developing countries called for marine genetic resources found on or under the seabed to be considered the "common heritage of mankind." Applying this principle, which is embedded in UNCLOS, to marine genetic resources could, for example, imply that those who profit from these genes would pay into a global fund that could compensate other nations for the use of shared resources, and this fund could support scientific training or conservation.[66] This is an important issue for developing countries, because thus far they had not received any financial benefits from the use of these MGRs. Entities located or headquartered in three countries have registered more than 74 percent of all patents associated with marine genetic resources: Germany (49 percent), the United States (13 percent), and Japan (12 percent). This figure rises to more than 98 percent if one includes the top ten countries. All international patent claims have been made by entities located in only thirty countries and the EU, while the remaining 165 countries have none.[67]

Some developed countries, including the United States, Canada, Russia, and Japan, opposed extending the "common heritage" language, fearing burdensome and unworkable regulations. They argued that access to high seas genetic resources should be guaranteed to all nations under the "freedom of the high seas," another principle enshrined in UNCLOS. That approach essentially amounts to "finders keepers," although countries traditionally have balanced free access with other principles, such as the value of conservation, in developing rules for shipping, fishing, and research in international waters.[68]

The EU and New Zealand supported a middle-ground position—the development of a new international regime for multilateral benefit sharing that would be part of an integrated approach to the conservation and sustainable use of biodiversity in ABNJ. For example, one proposal would allow nations to prospect for high seas genes but require that they publish the sequences they uncover. Companies could also choose to keep sequences private temporarily, in order to be able to patent them, if they contributed to an international fund that would support marine research by poorer nations.[69] The EU also proposed subjecting access to marine genetic resources to notification or authorization.[70]

The types of benefits to be shared were also discussed, although there was a general understanding that these can be both monetary and nonmonetary. One issue was whether to address questions related to intellectual property rights (IPRs), like patents, which are the usual legal tool employed to derive profit from innovation and thereby provide for monetary benefit sharing. In addition, IPRs may also be useful to monitor the use of marine genetic resources (by screening information on the origin of marine genetic resources in patent applications) and detect possible violations of the benefit-sharing obligations. Predictably Japan, Canada, the EU, Switzerland, Norway, Chile, Singapore, and the United States cautioned against IPR-related provisions in the new agreement, noting that they are addressed in other fora, like the WTO.[71]

Marine Protected Areas: Marine protected areas (MPAs), which can include marine parks, sanctuaries, and reserves, are a regulatory tool for conserving natural or cultural resources. A number of existing agreements already provide for the creation of MPAs; however, those supporting a new treaty argued that these sectoral or regional agreements were not sufficient to create a global network of MPAs. They advocated for a global approach, entailing the creation of a new global decision-making body to coordinate existing regional and sectoral institutions and fill gaps. The veto coalition argued that regional bodies are already well placed, and have significant expertise, to create and manage MPAs, so efforts should focus on enhancing coordination among them.

Those favoring a global model (many developing countries) argued that to make a real difference, the decision-making body of the agreement would have to be mandated to establish, implement, and enforce area-based management tools, including MPAs, while consulting with existing competent bodies. Those favoring a hybrid approach (EU and New Zealand, among others) supported a process whereby existing frameworks, including regional and sectoral bodies, would share responsibilities with the global body in establishing, implementing, and enforcing MPAs and other area-based management tools, with the global body assessing overall effectiveness. Meanwhile, those supporting a regional approach (the United States and Russia, among others) argued that the agreement could strengthen the effectiveness of existing bodies by creating mechanisms for collaboration between and among regional and sectoral bodies, limiting the new agreement to setting standards and principles for consideration by regional and sectoral bodies.[72]

Environmental Impact Assessments: Environmental impact assessments (EIAs) require evaluating the likely environmental impacts of a proposed project or development, with consideration of interrelated socioeconomic, cultural, and human health impacts, to ensure that these factors are known and considered prior to making a final decision. Under UNCLOS, parties have a general obligation to conduct EIAs, but proponents argued that this was largely ineffective due to patchy implementation and because under the Convention they are not required to consider the cumulative impact of multiple stressors on the marine environment.[73] A new treaty could establish common procedures and standards for assessment, monitoring, reporting, and management of EIAs, leading to the development of a central information-sharing mechanism among all the sectoral and regional agreements, and provide greater protection for marine biodiversity.

The Russian Federation expressed skepticism about a centralized body, cautioning against duplication of mandates, bureaucratization, and delays. The United States, Australia, Canada, Japan, China, Norway, and New Zealand preferred that states make decisions on EIAs. The EU proposed that a state party should decide, based on a threshold, whether an EIA is required and ensure monitoring of the effects of activities. IUCN, however, stressed that responsibilities for conducting an EIA and decision making are connected to liability for potential damage and cautioned against allocating such tasks to individual states, given the potential conflicts of interest.[74]

Delegates also debated whether a new agreement that included MPAs and EIAs would also apply to fisheries. The veto coalition argued that the inclusion of fisheries is a "red line" because fisheries are already regulated under the UN Fish Stocks Agreement, which supports a regional, rather than a global, approach, through existing RFMOs. Lead states, however, argued that a new treaty would fill gaps in both the Fish Stocks Agreement and UNCLOS and provide more transparency with regard to RFMOs' work on marine biodiversity in areas beyond national jurisdiction.[75]

Capacity Building and Marine Technology Transfer: Not surprisingly, discussions on capacity building and marine technology transfer mirrored those in all other multilateral environmental negotiations over the past thirty years. Key issues included whether technology transfer should be mandatory, potential inclusion and design of a funding mechanism, potential preferential treatment for certain types of countries, and the relationship to IPRs.

The negotiation positions and alliances on these and related issues reflected development status rather than the lead and veto states' positions that characterized the rest of the negotiations. Developing countries argued that the agreement should define general obligations to promote cooperation for capacity building and technology transfer, recognizing the importance of marine scientific research, and the special cases of small island developing states, least developed countries, and coastal African states, among others. They noted that technology transfer could include voluntary elements but should be mandatory in nature. Donor countries and others, including the EU, Russia, the United States, and South Korea, favored a voluntary funding approach. Australia, China, Canada, and the United States recommended respecting IPRs on the basis of mutually agreed terms. The African Group emphasized that the agreement should balance protection of IPRs and technology dissemination.

Let the Conference Begin

Following more than a decade of discussions, the PrepCom at its fourth and final meeting recommended that the UN General Assembly convene an intergovernmental conference (IGC) to negotiate an international legally binding instrument under UNCLOS on the conservation and sustainable use of BBNJ. In resolution 72/249 of December 2017, the UN General Assembly mandated the IGC to meet for four sessions between 2018 and 2020.

During the first two meetings, in September 2018 and March 2019, governments made some progress in clarifying positions on the package elements. But essentially, the long-standing divisions remained. At the conclusion of IGC-2, IGC President Rena Lee (Singapore) was asked to prepare and circulate a "zero draft" containing treaty text so that in-depth negotiations could begin.

At the third meeting of the IGC in August 2019, delegates discussed the zero draft for two weeks, largely behind closed doors. While progress was made on the inclusion of benefit-sharing modalities in the agreement, key definitions remained unclarified, such as "marine genetic material" or "access to" MGRs. Further discussion was necessary to agree whether access to MGRs would entail collecting the resource in situ (where originally found) or where processed. They also needed to determine whether to include digital sequence data

Photo 4.2 Greenpeace and the High Seas Alliance set up an art installation of marine plastic pollution outside UN Headquarters during the negotiations on marine biodiversity in areas beyond national jurisdiction.

Courtesy Franz Dejon, IISD/*Earth Negotiations Bulletin*, http://enb.iisd.org

and derivatives. Delegations were particularly divided on the question whether fish should be included as a marine genetic resource, due to concerns over impacts on current fisheries management.[76]

On area-based management tools and MPAs, delegates agreed on developing proposals on the basis of best available science, including traditional knowledge of indigenous peoples and local communities, and submitting proposals to establish management tools and MPAs by parties. Divergence of opinions remained on the role of relevant global, regional, and sectoral bodies, and provisions around implementation, monitoring, and review.[77]

Regarding EIAs, disagreement remained on the type of impacts they would address. Developing countries called for a reference to social, economic, and cultural impacts of harmful activities in ABNJ—particularly on coastal states—whereas developed countries preferred a narrow focus on environmental impacts. Similarly, there was no agreement on the role that traditional knowledge might play within the EIA framework. Discussions on capacity building and the transfer of marine technology revealed diverging views on whether it should be mandatory and be complemented by voluntary efforts, or whether it should solely be voluntary.[78]

Delegates agreed that IGC President Lee, assisted by the Secretariat, should prepare a revised draft text, on the basis of the negotiations thus far, for consideration at the final session scheduled for March 2020. The revised draft text[79] was distributed in November 2019, and delegations were asked to submit any textual proposals for consideration at IGC-4 by February 20, 2020. However, due to the COVID-19 pandemic, IGC-4 was postponed. In the meantime, in April 2020 the Secretariat distributed a 423-page compilation of the textual proposals received by the deadline.[80]

While some delegations remained hopeful that negotiations would be concluded at the rescheduled fourth session, others suggested that since divergences existed on a number of issues evidenced by the proposals received, a fifth meeting might be necessary.[81] Governments must still resolve issues that stem from a core disagreement between those who want the regime to be based on the principle that MGRs are the common heritage of humankind and those who place emphasis on the freedom of the high seas. Those who favor the freedom of the high seas approach to MGRs emphasize that access should be unimpeded, while supporters of the common heritage highlight the need for oversight and, more crucially, benefit sharing. The consequences are self-evident. Those subscribing to the freedom of the high seas would support nonmonetary, voluntary benefit sharing based on mutually agreed terms. Those supporting the common heritage are looking into standardized, mandatory benefit sharing, including modalities for monetary benefit sharing. Furthermore, the freedom of the high seas is compatible with a number of regional and sectoral bodies, many that already exist and more that could be established if needed. The common heritage would necessitate a global, international, umbrella structure, envisaged in a rigorous implementing agreement.[82]

Different policy preferences that stem fundamentally from different perspectives on core principles will not be resolved overnight. Any meaningful consensus can only be developed in the space between the two concepts. One suggestion, which was initially tabled at IGC-1, that access-related provisions could be governed under a high seas freedom regime while benefit-sharing modalities would fall under some interpretation of the common heritage principle, signifies the general direction that future trade-offs might take. Yet, most participants agreed that reaching an agreement remains a difficult challenge involving complex trade-offs.[83]

International Trade in Endangered Species

The overexploitation of wildlife resources is a major threat to biodiversity conservation. Together with other factors such as habitat loss, overexploitation can deplete populations and even bring some species close to extinction.[84] International trade in wildlife helps drive demand for hundreds of millions of plant and animal specimens and is estimated to be worth billions of dollars annually. This trade encompasses live animals and plants as well as a vast array of products derived from them, including foods, leather goods, musical instruments, timber, tourist curios, and medicines. Because the trade in wild animals and plants crosses national borders, international cooperation is required to regulate it and prevent certain species from overexploitation and extinction.

CITES was conceived in the spirit of such cooperation. Adopted in 1973, the treaty combats overexploitation of wild animals and plants by delineating threatened species, establishing rules regarding their trade, and imposing trade sanctions against violators.[85] The trade restrictions are designed to limit demand and thus the incentive to harvest the threated species. CITES is an umbrella regime containing a multitude of smaller regimes that address specific species. Under this umbrella, proponent and veto coalitions vary across individual species or groups of species and often cross traditional North–South divisions.[86]

CITES currently covers roughly 5800 species of animals and 30,000 species of plants, divided into three categories, with various levels of controls for each category. Species listed in Appendix I are threatened with extinction and are not to be traded except for scientific or cultural endeavors. Species listed in Appendix II, although not yet endangered, are considered to be affected by international trade that, if left unregulated, would endanger them. Before a country can allow exports of an Appendix II species, a scientific authority must determine that the proposed export will not be detrimental to the survival of the species. The decision to list a particular species in Appendix I or II requires consensus or a two-thirds majority vote by the parties. Species listed in Appendix III are listed voluntarily by range states (states within which the species live) seeking cooperation in the control of international trade, and they do not require a vote. Appendix I lists more than 1000 species; Appendix II lists more than 34,600; and Appendix III lists more than 200.[87]

All 183 member states are required to adopt national legislation that corresponds to the species listings. They have to designate two authorities on a domestic level: a management authority and a scientific authority. The scientific authority advises the management authority, which is in charge of issuing permits and certificates in keeping with the CITES appendices. These authorities work with customs offices, police departments, and other appropriate agencies to record species trading and report to CITES. Thus, the operation and enforcement of CITES can be compromised when national and local officials do not, or cannot, enforce it.

CITES has three main operational bodies: the Standing Committee, Animals Committee, and Plants Committee. Each is a subsidiary body of the COP, which meets every two to three years. The Standing Committee oversees and helps to coordinate the work of the other bodies with policy guidance and budget management. The Animals and Plants Committees work between COPs and report to the COP about their respective mandates. The main implementation tool used by these bodies to monitor CITES' effectiveness is a "review of significant trade," a process whereby the bodies evaluate trade data pertaining to specific species, delving deeper if they notice anything out of place. However, CITES' capacity to actually reduce illegal trade using this process is minimal. The review of significant trade relies on data reported by countries through government agencies; these statistics include information only on legal trading. Because a major causes of species loss is illegal trade, these statistics do not reflect—or have much of an effect on—the illegal movement of species and their derivatives.

The plant species protected under CITES' three appendices compose 85 percent of all of the species covered by the treaty. Legal and illegal collecting of certain rare or commercially desirable plant species poses a major threat to their survival in the wild. Examples include trees that produce high-quality lumber (e.g., big leaf mahogany, Brazilian rosewood), herbs for medicinal use (e.g., American ginseng, goldenseal), and unusual, exotic ornamental species, such as certain orchids, cacti, and cycads. For example, Brazilian rosewood produces a highly prized, red-brown timber that is attractive, heavy, strong, and highly resistant to insects and decay. Its high resonance is ideal for the production of musical instruments, and the tree is harvested for use in high-quality furniture and for its oils and resins. Brazilian rosewood was listed on CITES Appendix I in 1992, making trade in its timber illegal. Nevertheless, deforestation in its native habitat and illegal logging continued, and mature trees with thick trunks are now very rare.[88]

Another example is the African cherry tree (*Prunus africana*), which grows in mountainous tropical forests in central and southern Africa and Madagascar. For centuries it has been harvested for its hard and durable timber as well as for its bark, which has medicinal properties and is used to treat malaria, fever, kidney disease, urinary tract infections, and, more recently, prostate enlargement. As long as all of the bark is not removed, the tree can bear repeated harvests and has been used sustainably for hundreds of years. Indigenous knowledge maintained that, post-harvest, bark grows back more quickly on the side of the tree that faces the sunrise, and it was also believed that medicine made from this east-facing bark would heal a patient faster. Thus, traditionally, only one side of the tree was stripped, yielding about 55 kilograms (121 pounds) of bark. But when completely stripped, a large tree may yield up to 1000 kilograms—worth considerably more on the international market. Harvest limits and protective folklore have given way to market demand, and the African cherry tree appears to be in steep decline, despite its inclusion in CITES Appendix II.[89]

In more recent years, CITES has focused on combating the illegal wildlife trade, which has become one of the largest sources of criminal earnings in the world—ranking alongside trafficking of drugs, people, and weapons. According to UNEP and Interpol (the International

Criminal Police Organization), the global illegal wildlife trade is estimated to be worth $7–23 billion a year. In addition, the illegal fisheries catch is valued at $11–24 billion a year, and illegal logging, including processing, is valued at $51–152 billion.[90]

Illicit wildlife trade ranges in scale from single-item, local bartering to multi-ton, commercialized exports of animals and plants. Wildlife contraband may include live pets, hunting trophies, fashion accessories, cultural artifacts, ingredients for traditional or fanciful medicine, wild protein for human consumption (bushmeat), and other products. The most lucrative include tiger parts, elephant ivory, rhino horn, and exotic birds and reptiles. (See Box 4.4.) Illegal wildlife trade networks encompass a diverse array of actors, including local hunters, regional middlemen, wildlife experts, organized crime syndicates (which sometimes

❖ BOX 4.4 WILDLIFE MARKETS AND ZOONOTIC DISEASE

Almost twenty years ago, a virus appeared in wildlife markets in southern China, and it was unlike any the world had seen. It was winter 2003, and sufferers complained of fever, chills, headache, and dry coughs—all symptoms you might expect during the cold and flu season. This condition progressed into a lethal form of pneumonia that caused severe respiratory failure in a quarter of patients. By the time the epidemic of severe acute respiratory syndrome (SARS) ended seven months later, more than 8000 cases and 800 deaths stretched across thirty-two countries. Fast forward to late 2019, and another virus appeared in wildlife markets in Wuhan, China. Within ten months, this novel coronavirus (COVID-19) spread around the world, over 40 million had been infected, and over 1.2 million had died.

Wildlife markets, which are found around the world, sell wild animals for meat or pets. The markets themselves may be legal, but they sometimes offer illegal species alongside permitted ones. Close interactions with wild animals have caused numerous diseases in addition to COVID-19 and SARS, including Ebola, MERS (Middle East Respiratory Syndrome), and HIV/AIDS. Buying, selling, and slaughtering wild animals for food is one way a zoonotic or animal-borne disease may infect people. When animals are kept in dirty, cramped conditions, such as stacked cages, in wildlife markets, viruses spread more easily, as they intermingle and mutate in ways that make them more transmissible. In fact, two-thirds of emerging infections and diseases now come from wildlife.

Other forms of wildlife trade can be risky as well, including the exotic pet industry and using animals or their parts for traditional medicine or ornamental uses, such as rugs or carvings. In August 2007, for example, a drum maker and his child in Connecticut both became ill with anthrax after his home and workplace became contaminated by goatskin imported from Guinea that carried naturally occurring anthrax spores.

Sources: Patrick Greenfield, "Ban wildlife markets to avert pandemics, says UN biodiversity chief," *The Guardian*, April 6, 2020, www.theguardian.com/world/2020/apr/06/ban-live-animal-markets-pandemics-un-biodiversity-chief-age-of-extinction; Nsikan Akpan, "New coronavirus can spread between humans—but it started in a wildlife market," *National Geographic*, January 21, 2020, www.nationalgeographic.com/science/2020/01/new-coronavirus-spreading-between-humans-how-it-started/; Malavika Vyawahare, "As COVID-19 pandemic deepens, global wildlife treaty faces an identity crisis," Mongabay, May 15, 2020, https://news.mongabay.com/2020/05/as-covid-19-pandemic-deepens-global-wildlife-treaty-faces-an-identity-crisis/.

include terrorists and drug traffickers), global suppliers, front companies, online retailers, corrupt officials, and consumers willing to purchase such contraband.[91]

The internet and social media have contributed to the growth of the illegal wildlife trade, providing an unprecedented technological platform for a burgeoning, undocumented trade in endangered animals, alive and dead (see Box 4.5). The ability to scan the globe for buyers or sellers without leaving one's office, to mask one's identity with increasingly sophisticated software, and to buy and sell online without ever having to meet even a middleman are just three aspects of internet-based endangered species crime that challenge the abilities of national and international law enforcement officials. In addition, many national laws aimed at regulating wildlife trade to ecologically sustainable levels do not yet address aspects of illicit internet sales, and some countries have few laws governing internet commerce at all. Even where laws exist, enforcement is often inadequate because officials do not have the capacity to address internet crime or because they are not focused on online trafficking in wildlife. One such case is the African elephant.

African Elephants

The case of African elephants illustrates CITES' efforts to curb species loss and exemplifies the difficulties inherent in negotiations among numerous parties. The fact-finding stage led to the African elephant's listing under CITES Appendix II in 1977 (see Box 4.6). Beginning in the early 1980s, African elephant populations began to decline precipitously, falling from 1.3 million in 1979 to 625,000 in 1989 to some 400,000 today.[92] In 1985, CITES established a system of ivory export quotas in the countries with elephant herds. Declines continued, however, and a study sponsored by WWF and Conservation International concluded that African elephants were being harvested at a rate far exceeding that considered sustainable. This rate of loss, driven primarily by the international trade in ivory, led to increasing calls to place African elephants in CITES Appendix I and establish a worldwide ban on trade in African elephant ivory.

The bargaining stage began at the seventh meeting of the CITES COP in October 1989, when a unique international coalition consisting of Austria, the Gambia, Hungary, Kenya, Somalia, Tanzania, and the United States initiated an effort to list the African elephant in Appendix I and ban all trade in ivory products. Another unlikely coalition, uniting foes in southern Africa's struggle over apartheid (Botswana, Malawi, Mozambique, South Africa, Zambia, and Zimbabwe), opposed the listing. Underlying their resistance was the fact that several southern African herds had grown in the 1980s as a result of conservation efforts financed through limited hunting of elephants and commercial trade in elephant parts. Despite this resistance, a two-thirds majority of CITES parties voted to place all African elephant herds in Appendix I.[93] The southern African states lodged reservations against the ban and announced plans to sell their ivory through a cartel, with the proceeds to be used to finance conservation.[94]

It was Japan, however, not the lead or veto states, that ultimately determined the viability of the regime. In 1989, the worldwide ivory market was worth an estimated $50–60 million annually. Japan dominated this market at the time, importing more than 80 percent of all African ivory products, making it the potential leader of an effective veto coalition.[95] As the major consumer nation, Japan had been expected to enter a reservation, allowing a significant portion of the ivory market to remain viable and effectively vetoing the ban. However, facing heavy pressure from the United States, the European Community (EC), and national and international NGOs, Japan eventually decided not to oppose the ban. World prices for raw ivory eventually plunged by 90 percent.[96]

In the 1990s, three southern African countries (Botswana, Namibia, and Zimbabwe) called for ending the ivory trade ban, proposing that the African elephant be downlisted from

❖ BOX 4.5 ENDANGERED SPECIES ONLINE

The internet allows criminals, including those involved in wildlife crime, to interact under cover, hide their true identities, and carry out financial transactions in relative privacy. Therefore, website and social media monitoring is vital to understand the level and scope of illegal wildlife trade online. The International Fund for Animal Welfare (IFAW) has researched the vast scale of online trade in protected live animals and their body parts for many years. Its 2018 research report, "Disrupt: Wildlife Cybercrime," focuses on online wildlife trade in four countries—France, Germany, Russia, and the United Kingdom—and on species that are listed on Appendixes I and II of the Convention on International Trade in Endangered Species of Fauna and Flora (CITES). Researchers recorded 11,772 endangered and threatened wildlife specimens offered for sale over a period of six weeks in 2017 via 5381 advertisements and posts on 106 online marketplaces and four social media platforms, worth approximately $3,942,329.

Animals and Products Available for Sale

Category	Ads/Posts	Specimens	% of Specimens
Reptiles	1992	6460	54.88
Birds	1650	2881	24.47
Ivory	996	1288	10.94
Mammals	481	591	5.02
Coral	181	336	2.85
Fish	29	137	1.16
Sharks	21	23	0.20
Mollusks	17	18	0.15
Amphibians	14	38	0.32
Total	**5381**	**11,772**	**100**

In March 2018, twenty-one technology, e-commerce, and social media companies in collaboration with WWF, TRAFFIC, and IFAW joined the first ever Global Coalition to End Wildlife Trafficking Online. As members of this coalition, technology companies pledged to work together to reduce wildlife trafficking across all platforms by 80 percent by 2020. In March 2020, the online technology companies in the Coalition reported removing or blocking over 3 million listings for endangered and threatened species and associated products from their online platforms. These listings included live tigers, reptiles, primates, and birds for the exotic pet trade, as well as products derived from species like elephants, pangolins, and marine turtles.

Source: IFAW, "Disrupt: Wildlife Cybercrime: Uncovering the Scale of Online Wildlife Trade," May 2018, www.ifaw.org/news/disrupt-wildlife-cybercrime-report; IFAW, "Tech Companies Take Down 3 Million Online Listings for Trafficked Wildlife," Press Release, March 2, 2020, www.ifaw.org/eu/press-releases/tech-companies-take-down-3-million-online-listings-for-trafficked-wildlife.

❖ BOX 4.6   CITES MILESTONES ON ELEPHANTS

1963: International Union for Conservation of Nature (IUCN) General Assembly convenes in Nairobi and calls for the creation of an international convention to regulate the export, transit, and import of rare or threatened wild species or the skins and trophies thereof.

1964–1971: IUCN sends out successive drafts of the convention for review by governments.

1972: UN Conference on the Human Environment, meeting in Stockholm, proposes that a conference be convened as soon as possible to prepare and adopt a convention on the export, import, and transit of certain species of wild animals and plants.

1973: The Convention on International Trade in Endangered Species of Wild Fauna and Flora (CITES) is adopted on March 3.

1975: CITES enters into force on July 1.

1977: African elephants are listed under CITES Appendix II.

1985: CITES establishes a system of ivory export quotas in countries with elephant herds.

1989: CITES parties vote to place all African elephant herds in Appendix I.

1997: CITES parties agree to transfer the African elephant populations of Botswana, Namibia, and Zimbabwe from CITES Appendix I to Appendix II and to allow limited commercial trade in raw ivory.

2007: In response to reports of increased illegal trade in ivory, COP bars additional proposals for ivory trade for nine years following one more scheduled for 2008.

2008: The CITES-sanctioned sale of 108 tons of ivory takes place in November and nets nearly $15.5 million for Botswana, Namibia, South Africa, and Zimbabwe.

2010: Tanzania and Zambia propose downlisting their African elephant populations to Appendix II; the proposal fails to get enough votes.

2013: The COP agrees to revise rules for trade in elephants and elephant products, including on employing DNA analysis, monitoring ivory stockpiles, controlling live-elephant trade, and dealing with countries that are persistently involved in illegal trade, but is unable to resolve differences on other key issues to stop illegal trade in ivory and other elephant products.

2016: Proposal to uplist all African elephants to Appendix II fails to get enough votes.

2019: The COP agrees not to have another one-off international ivory sale and calls on governments to close their domestic ivory markets.

CITES Appendix I to Appendix II, since elephant populations in their countries were secure and expanding. These efforts failed at CITES meetings in 1992 and 1994.[97]

At COP10 in June 1997, in Harare, Zimbabwe, the three southern African range states, with support from Japan, again proposed downlisting elephant populations in their countries. The resulting debate was long and acrimonious. The three range states argued that their herds had grown to a combined total of about 150,000 and that their inability to exploit the herds commercially was costing them revenues that could be used to increase their conservation budgets. The United States and other parties feared that even partial easing of the trade ban would result in a new flood of illegal trade in ivory and noted that CITES experts had found deficiencies in enforcement and control measures in Japan and the three African countries. Without adequate controls in place, it would be extremely difficult to track where elephant tusks had originated.

In the final compromise, Botswana, Namibia, and Zimbabwe received permission to sell strictly limited experimental quotas of ivory under a stringent set of conditions.[98] A heavily regulated one-time sale of ivory from these countries was also approved once monitoring deficiencies were adequately addressed. All experimental sales would go to Japan, and all funds obtained by the sale would be invested in elephant-conservation efforts.[99]

At COP12 in 2002, Botswana, Namibia, and South Africa proposed another limited sale of ivory. Parties approved the proposal after agreeing on strict monitoring and verification conditions. In 2004, at COP13, Namibia proposed a 2000-kilogram annual quota of raw ivory, in addition to the trade of worked ivory, leather, and hair products. The proposal involving raw ivory was rejected, but Namibia was allowed to participate in trade in leather and hair products and non-commercial trade in worked ivory amulets known as *ekipas*.[100]

Five years later, at COP14 in 2007, TRAFFIC, a nongovernmental organization working globally on trade in wild animals and plants, reported that illegal trade in ivory had increased since 2005 and implicated Cameroon, China, the Democratic Republic of the Congo, Nigeria, and Thailand as the major players. A compromise was reached to allow Botswana, Namibia, South Africa, and Zimbabwe to have a one-off sale of raw ivory that had been registered in government stocks prior to January 31, 2007, but also bar additional proposals for ivory trade for nine years.[101] Parties also tasked the Standing Committee with developing a decision-making mechanism for ivory trade in time for consideration at COP16 in 2013 and requested the Secretariat to establish a specific fund for African elephants.[102]

In July 2008, at the fifty-seventh meeting of the CITES Standing Committee, delegates gave the go-ahead for the one-off sale of ivory and agreed that China could join Japan as an approved bidder on the ivory. Combined, Botswana, Namibia, South Africa, and Zimbabwe were allowed to sell 108 tons.[103] The Secretariat visited all four African countries to verify the quantity and legality of ivory stocks before allowing the sale to proceed. The sale took place in October and November 2008 with a total profit of nearly $15.5 million to the four southern African states.[104]

Nevertheless, by May 2012, elephant poaching levels were reportedly the worst in a decade.[105] At COP16 in 2013, the member states revised and modernized the rules for the trade in elephants and elephant products, including addressing e-commerce, employing DNA analysis, monitoring ivory stockpiles, controlling live-elephant trade, and dealing with countries that are persistently involved in illegal trade in ivory. However, COP16 did not resolve the debate on one-off ivory sales.

At COP17 in 2016, the debate continued, and Africa remained divided. Noting that elephant populations are not restricted to political borders, Chad, supported by Côte d'Ivoire, opposed having species listings in different appendices. Kenya and others supported the proposal, arguing that an uplisting of all African elephants to Appendix I would signal to the world that elephants deserve the highest protection available under international law. Botswana reversed its position, "unreservedly and voluntarily" relinquished its Appendix II listing of its elephant populations, and supported uplisting to Appendix I. However, China, Brazil, South Africa, Namibia, the EU, and others opposed the proposal, noting that the populations of elephants in Botswana, Namibia, South Africa, and Zimbabwe did not meet the biological criteria for inclusion in Appendix I. In a vote, the proposal to uplist all African elephants to Appendix I was opposed by a two-thirds majority.[106]

Meanwhile, important developments were occurring outside the regime. China shut down its legal ivory market—the largest in the world—at the end of 2017. China's action resulted from a 2015 agreement between Chinese President Xi Jinping and US President Barack Obama in which both countries pledged to end legal ivory sales. The US total ban on sales of African elephant ivory (with an exception for items created long ago) went into effect in July 2016. However, by the end of 2019, Chinese consumers with the means to travel had started purchasing elephant ivory in Japan, Laos, Thailand, and Vietnam.[107]

At COP18 in 2019, Botswana, Namibia, and Zimbabwe tried again to amend the annotation to their Appendix II listing in order to create more opportunities for them to sell ivory. Their proposals failed, and member states agreed not to sanction another one-off international ivory sale. They also called on all governments to close domestic ivory markets. At the same time, an unexpected legal loophole for the illegal ivory trade came up at COP18—prehistoric mammoths. As the permafrost melts on the Siberian tundra, it has revealed preserved woolly mammoths—and perhaps more importantly, their huge ivory tusks. Israel introduced a proposal to include the woolly mammoth in Appendix II, highlighting that trade in mammoth ivory provides a cover for illegal trade in elephant ivory. Russia opposed the proposal, noting that the Convention regulates species threatened with extinction, not extinct species. Canada, the EU, and the US also opposed the proposal, noting that there is no evidence on the scale of the problem. Israel withdrew its original proposal, but CITES parties agreed to commission a study on trade in mammoth ivory and its role in illegal trade in ivory.[108]

Elephant poaching in Africa has declined somewhat since reaching its peak in 2011, but it remains a serious problem, and the continent's elephant population remains threatened. From 2009 to 2014, Tanzania's elephant population fell by 60 percent and Mozambique's by 87 percent.[109] Botswana, home to a third of Africa's remaining elephant population—about 126,000—saw a 600 percent increase in elephant carcasses devoid of their tusks from 2014–2018.[110] The slaughter outstrips the rate at which elephants can reproduce, and some experts warn there could be little time left to save truly wild elephants from extinction.[111]

Controlling International Trade in Endangered Species

The case of African elephant ivory illustrates several distinctive features of the CITES regime. First, CITES is actually an umbrella regime enveloping a multitude of mini regimes across which states' political and economic interests vary from species to species. These mini regimes, while sharing a common organizational structure, are all characterized by an individual set of developmental stages, lead states, and coalitions that often consist of unusual alliances. Veto coalitions can be led by producer nations, consumer nations, or a coalition of both, as is the case with elephant ivory. In addition, not all producer or consumer nations share the same interests. In the elephant case, range states split over listing, largely reflecting differences in the viability of central versus southern African elephant populations.

Second, the role played by science can also vary by species. Although logically associated with the issue-definition and fact-finding stages, scientific knowledge can also play an important role in bargaining and regime strengthening (as seen in the ozone case in Chapter 3). The case of African elephants demonstrates an important scientific role in issue definition and fact finding, via the documentation of the initial population crashes, as well as in the bargaining and regime-strengthening stages, via the documentation of different population trajectories for southern and eastern African elephant populations.

Third, although scientific knowledge can inform debates, economic and political factors often determine specific outcomes. Strong commercial interests on the part of consumer nations or issues such as national sovereignty may lead nations to oppose listings or other conservation measures despite strong evidence of declining populations.

Finally, the impact that a CITES listing has on controlling population declines also varies by species. A CITES listing can be ineffective in stopping overexploitation, particularly if important trading countries file a reservation to the listing, trade is predominantly domestic rather than international (e.g., trade in Chinese tigers and tiger parts), factors other than trade are more important in driving population loss (e.g., habitat loss or climate change), or monitoring is difficult because of the type of product traded (e.g., sawn wood or plant extracts).

Overall, CITES has produced mixed results. Parts of its history illustrate the effectiveness of bans or prohibitions as a mechanism for reducing activities that threaten wildlife or natural resources. However, the history also illustrates how the impact of such measures can be weakened by powerful commercial interests, new technologies, and the ability of parties to opt out by entering reservations on particular species. Meanwhile, threats to endangered

Photo 4.3 NGOs celebrate the adoption of an international trade ban for all eight species of pangolins at CITES COP17. It is estimated that since 2000, more than 1 million pangolins have been traded illegally at the international level, which makes them the most trafficked wild mammal in the world.

Courtesy Kiara Worth, IISD/*Earth Negotiations Bulletin*, http://enb.iisd.org

species continue to multiply and the black market for trade in endangered species grows more sophisticated, driven by both greed and poverty, increasing the danger of extinction for more species even if they are already part of the CITES regime.

Whaling

The history of global whaling policy illustrates how regimes can undergo significant transitions, in this case from a regime designed, albeit ineffectively, to preserve enough whales so that they could be killed indefinitely to a framework for global protection despite resistance from a strong veto coalition. Despite this transformation, however, the international whaling regime has been at a crossroads for over thirty years. The balance of power in the regime's decision-making body, the International Whaling Commission (IWC), rests narrowly with the states favoring a whaling ban.

Emotions and concerns for national sovereignty influence the global debate on whaling far more than scientific analysis or national economic interests (whaling no longer represents a significant economic enterprise on a global or even a national basis). For some governments and many environmental NGOs, whaling is seen as both an act of unnecessary human cruelty to an intelligent species and a powerful symbol of environmental overexploitation. To whaling states, harvesting whales represents the right to preserve cultural traditions, maintain coastal livelihoods, and exercise national sovereignty.

Humans have hunted whales for thousands of years. Advances in technology and larger whaling fleets, particularly in the nineteenth and twentieth centuries, reduced whale populations significantly. In 1946, whaling nations established the International Convention for the Regulation of Whaling, which prohibited killing certain endangered whale species, set quotas and minimum sizes for whales caught commercially, and regulated whaling seasons. The convention, however, was not created as an environmental regime but as a club of whaling nations designed to manage the catch. In fact, the preamble to the Convention states that its purpose is "to provide for the proper conservation of whale stocks and thus make possible the orderly development of the whaling industry."[112] The regime's designated decision-making body, the IWC, met in secret each year to haggle over quotas set so high that far more whales were being killed annually under the new regime than before the regulations had gone into effect. In fact, the total number of whales killed more than doubled between 1951 and 1962. The IWC also had no power to enforce its regulations on the size of catch or even its ban on killing endangered species.

The process of fact finding and consensus building played virtually no role in relations among IWC members. Scientific knowledge was usually subordinated to political and economic interests. The IWC's scientific committee routinely produced data and analyses supporting continued commercial exploitation, and no outside international organization existed that could facilitate a different framework for decisions based on scientific facts. Given this situation, it is not surprising that by the 1960s the survival of the largest species, the blue whale, was in doubt; finback stocks were dwindling; and many other species were experiencing population declines as whalers filled their quotas with younger and smaller whales.

The blue whale, the largest animal on earth—which can be as long as three buses and weigh as much as 200,000–300,000 pounds, with a heart the size of a small car—was too swift and powerful for the nineteenth-century whalers to hunt, but with the arrival of harpoon cannons, it became a sought-after species for its large amounts of blubber. The killing reached a peak in 1931, when 29,649 blue whales were taken. By 1966, blue whales were so scarce that the IWC declared them protected. Today, there are between 8000 and 9000 blue whales in the oceans, and they are considered an endangered species.[113]

Increasing public awareness of the diminishing stocks, including the potential extinction of blue whales, coincided with the emerging environmental movement to turn the tide against commercial whaling. The plight of the whales seized the imagination of many Americans, who were beginning to learn more about the intelligence of cetaceans (marine mammals), and the new awareness led to broad popular support for meaningful protection. Responding to the 1969 Endangered Species Act, the United States declared eight whale species endangered in 1970 and began to take the lead in defining the whaling issue internationally.[114]

The United States first proposed an immediate moratorium on commercial whaling at the 1972 UN Conference on the Human Environment. Adopted by fifty-two of the countries attending the conference, the proposal signaled strong international support for a moratorium. Yet, because it had not been generated through the IWC, it carried no force within the whaling regime itself. In the IWC, the whaling states (Chile, Iceland, Japan, Norway, Peru, and the Soviet Union) not only constituted a powerful veto coalition (they could even choose to leave the regime if they wished) but also held a near majority. A proposal for a whaling moratorium was defeated in the IWC by a vote of six to four, with four abstentions.

Seeing the need to change the regime, the United States, Sweden, and other lead states took advantage of the fact that the IWC does not limit membership to whaling nations and sought to overwhelm the veto coalition by recruiting nonwhaling states to join the commission. Thus, rather than trying to transform the regime by building consensus within the IWC, lead states simply sought to assemble the three-fourths majority required for a whaling ban. To this end, between 1979 and 1982, the anti-whaling coalition recruited a number of developing countries, most of which viewed the whaling issue from the perspective that the oceans and their natural resources are the common heritage of humankind.[115]

The United States also sought to weaken the veto coalition by threatening economic sanctions. It used domestic legislation to ban imports of fish products and to deny fishing permits within the United States' 200-mile EEZ to countries that violated international whale conservation programs. This action put pressure on Chile and Peru, both heavily dependent on US fishing permits and markets, to comply with whale conservation programs.

✤ BOX 4.7 IWC MILESTONES

1946: International Convention for the Regulation of Whaling adopted.

1972: United States proposes an immediate moratorium on commercial whaling at the United Nations Conference on the Human Environment.

1979: Indian Ocean Sanctuary establishes a moratorium on factory ship whaling (except for minke whales).

1982: International Whaling Commission (IWC) approves a five-year moratorium on all commercial whaling.

1987: Japan begins scientific whaling.

1990: IWC extends the moratorium on commercial whaling for another year.

1992: IWC extends the moratorium again. Iceland leaves the IWC.

1994: IWC establishes the Southern Ocean Whale Sanctuary.

2002: Iceland rejoins the IWC.

2010: Australia institutes proceedings before the United Nations International Court of Justice (ICJ) against Japan's scientific whaling program in the Antarctic.

2014: The ICJ rules against Japan, agreeing with Australia that Japan's scientific research program masks a commercial whaling venture in the Antarctic.

2014: IWC passes a New Zealand-sponsored resolution that incorporates more rigorous standards for scientific whaling permits.

2015: Japan resumes scientific whaling in the Southern Ocean.

2018: Japan withdraws from the IWC.

2019: Japan resumes whaling in its coastal waters, harpooning two minke whales on the first day.

2020: Iceland announces that due to changes in public opinion and a decline in the consumption of whale meat, it will not hunt any whales for the second year in a row.

By 1982, enough nonwhaling nations had joined the IWC to tilt the balance. A five-year moratorium on all commercial whaling, to take effect in 1985, passed by a vote of twenty-five to seven, with five abstentions. Four of the veto coalition states (Japan, Norway, Peru, and the Soviet Union), which accounted for 75 percent of whaling and almost all consumption of whale meat and other whale products, filed formal reservations to the moratorium but chose not to defy it openly when it went into effect (see Box 4.7).

Japan, Norway, and the Soviet Union ended their commercial whaling by the 1987–1988 whaling season. Soon thereafter, however, Japan, Iceland, and Norway began to practice what they called "scientific whaling." Article VIII of the convention states that countries can issue special permits to kill whales for scientific research purposes and gives individual governments, not the IWC, the responsibility for setting and regulating these catches. It also states that the scientific information produced by the special permit whaling should be presented, at least annually, to the IWC.

Most IWC members found no scientific merit in the resumed whaling because it killed hundreds of minke whales annually and was conducted by commercial ships. However, other economic and political interests weakened the ability of the United States and other countries to pressure whaling states to end the practice. For example, to avoid a probable Japanese retaliation targeting US fish exports, the United States decided not to ban imports of $1 billion in Japanese seafood annually as retaliation for Japan's whaling, instead choosing the lesser sanction of denying the Japanese permission to fish in US waters.

Although the scientific whaling programs allowed some whaling to continue, veto states also wanted to repeal the whaling moratorium itself. At the 1990 IWC meeting, after the United States had led a majority of IWC members in blocking a proposal to allow limited commercial whaling in the Atlantic and instead extended the moratorium for another year, Iceland, Japan, and Norway threatened to leave the IWC if the moratorium was not overturned at the next meeting. When the IWC voted to retain the moratorium in 1992, Iceland followed through with the threat, leaving the IWC, although it returned in 2002.

In 1993, Japan and Norway again attempted to end the whaling ban. Both governments spent large amounts of money and effort in nonwhaling countries to promote the position that minke whales were no longer endangered and that whaling villages, severely impoverished by the moratorium, were being denied the right to pursue a cultural tradition.[116] In addition, Japan induced six Caribbean IWC members to support its position by providing funds for new fishing vessels and paying their annual IWC membership fees.[117] Despite these efforts, the IWC again voted to extend the whaling moratorium for another year.

Over the objections of the veto states, the IWC strengthened the regime in 1994 by adopting a no-catch area (even for scientific whaling) for all whales inhabiting waters below 40 degrees south latitude. The resulting Southern Ocean Whale Sanctuary created a protected area around Antarctica that could safeguard up to 90 percent of the estimated 3.5 million remaining great whales. The sanctuary is reviewed and open to change every ten years; changes require a 75 percent majority. The whaling nation potentially most affected by the vote was Japan, which was taking 300 minkes from the Antarctic annually, ostensibly for scientific purposes. However, Japan and Norway continued to defy both the whaling moratorium and the provisions for a no-catch area.[118]

Adopting the whaling moratorium and creating a no-catch area suggest a strong regime for the protection for whales. Although certainly reducing the number of whales killed each year, the regime's impact has been severely weakened by outright defiance of the whaling moratorium, incursions into the whale sanctuaries (in both the Southern and the Indian Oceans), and the use of loopholes such as scientific whaling—all by nations that have strong environmental records on many other issues.

Norway registered a formal reservation to the moratorium at the time of its passage, stating that this allowed it to ignore the ban. Despite significant international pressure, Norway has conducted commercial whaling outside the control of the IWC throughout the moratorium, capturing nearly 14,000 whales since 1986.[119] Iceland set its own conservation limits but significantly increased these quotas in 2009 and has caught over 1600 whales since the moratorium.[120] Iceland and Norway, however, whale within their own EEZs. Japan has been the only country whaling in international waters. Japan has conducted its whaling operations mostly under the banner of scientific whaling, with over 16,900 whales captured since 1987.[121] (See Figure 4.1.)

Japan defended its whaling by pointing to the large amount of scientific data it has generated. Some of these data, including stomach contents and reliable estimates of age, cannot be collected without killing the whales. Nevertheless, many scientists contend that, although the data are collected using a high degree of scientific rigor, the resulting information does not provide new and important information relevant to the management of stocks but instead largely supports existing knowledge.[122]

Over the years, the lead states on whale conservation have included Australia, New Zealand, the United States, EU member countries,[123] and the Buenos Aires Group of thirteen countries from Central and South America. This coalition opposes the resumption of any commercial whaling and supports sanctuaries that also prohibit scientific whaling. Their position is that the convention needs modernization that will, among other things, remove language that allows members to unilaterally issue special permits to kill whales for research purposes.[124]

The key veto states have been Iceland, Japan, and Norway, but their coalition has grown steadily since the 1990s. This expansion was engineered largely by Japan, which engaged in what some label as vote buying—that is, building support for its position on whaling through foreign aid and paying IWC membership fees. The head of Japan's Fisheries Agency

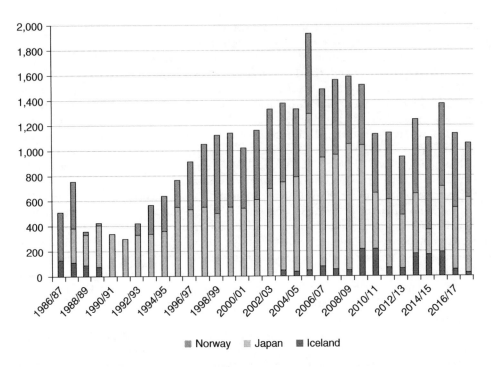

Figure 4.1 Scientific Whaling and Commercial Catches Under Objection: 1986–2017

Note: In 1987–1988, Iceland had a scientific permit and Japan and Norway caught whales in objection to the moratorium. Beginning in 1993–1994, Japan did all of the scientific whaling and Norway continued to catch whales in objection to the moratorium. Iceland did not kill any whales from 1989–2003 but resumed whaling in 2003, after rejoining the IWC in 2002.

Source: International Whaling Commission, "Special Permit Catches since 1985," accessed July 3, 2019, https://iwc.int/total-catches.

confirmed this practice, but government officials subsequently denied it.[125] The veto coalition asserts that whales should be managed just like other marine living resources and that opposition to whaling is contrary to the convention because its purpose is to "provide for the proper conservation of whale stocks and thus make possible the orderly development of the whaling industry."[126] They also argue that parties adopted the moratorium and the establishment of the Southern Ocean Whale Sanctuary without a corresponding recommendation from the IWC's scientific committee that such measures were required for conservation purposes. These positions were set out in a nonbinding resolution, called the St. Kitts and Nevis Declaration, adopted by a vote of thirty-three in favor and thirty-two against, with one abstention, at the IWC annual meeting in 2006.[127]

Regime Strengthening

The fact that certain actors ignore regime rules raises concerns about the IWC's future. The deep and "seemingly irreconcilable philosophical and political divisions" between the veto coalition and the lead states have caused some to refer to the IWC as a dysfunctional regime.[128] As early as 2006, the IWC began exploring how to overcome this central conflict. After a series of intersessional working group meetings from 2008 to 2010, the result, a Proposed Consensus Decision to Improve the Conservation of Whales, was presented at the sixty-second meeting of the IWC, in Morocco in June 2010.[129] Yet delegates were unable to reach consensus on the moratorium, the number of whales that might be taken, special permit whaling, indigenous whaling, sanctuaries, and trade. Japan said that the key stumbling block from its point of view was the demand by the EU and the Buenos Aires Group that Japan end its Antarctic whaling program within a set time frame. Japan believed that reducing its quota from 935 whales in 2010 to 200 in ten years' time represented a significant step forward that should have been acceptable.[130]

As discussions were suspended, the Japanese delegate noted that, although many IWC members emphasized the importance of conservation and management based on science, public opinion against whaling was not based on science. In Japan's view, the two divergent positions on whaling should be mutually acceptable, and IWC members must be willing to accept that different views exist in order to avoid a continued impasse and restore the IWC.[131]

Meanwhile, on May 31, 2010, expressing frustration with the IWC, Australia instituted proceedings before the UN International Court of Justice (ICJ) against Japan, alleging that

> Japan's continued pursuit of a large scale programme of whaling under the Second Phase of its Japanese Whale Research Programme under Special Permit in the Antarctic ("JARPA II") [is] in breach of obligations assumed by Japan under the International Convention for the Regulation of Whaling ("ICRW"), as well as its other international obligations for the preservation of marine mammals and marine environment.[132]

Australia requested the court to order that Japan "(a) cease implementation of JARPA II; (b) revoke any authorisations, permits or licences allowing the activities which are the subject of this application to be undertaken; and (c) provide assurances and guarantees that it will not take any further action under the JARPA II or any similar programme until such programme has been brought into conformity with its obligations under international law."[133]

On March 31, 2014, the ICJ ruled against Japan, agreeing with Australia that Japan's scientific research program masked a commercial whaling venture in the Antarctic. The ICJ ordered a temporary halt to the activities, largely involving fin, humpback, and minke whales, finding that JARPA II was "not in accordance with three provisions of the Schedule to the International Convention for the Regulation of Whaling."[134] The ICJ's ruling, however, only applied to Japan's activities around Antarctica. Not even a month after the ICJ's ruling, Japan announced that it would resume limited scientific whaling in the northwest Pacific.[135]

In September 2014, the IWC passed a New Zealand-sponsored resolution that called for more rigorous standards for scientific permits, as prescribed by the ICJ ruling. Resolution 2014–5, which was passed by a vote of thirty-five votes in favor and twenty against with five abstentions, calls on the IWC Scientific Committee to determine whether the design and implementation of a country's program are reasonable in relation to achieving the stated scientific research objectives, whether the research is likely to lead to improvements in whale conservation and management, whether the research objectives could be achieved by nonlethal means, whether the scale of lethal sampling is reasonable in relation to the program's stated research objectives, and other matters the committee considers relevant.[136]

The existential debate between the whaling moratorium and commercial whaling came to a head at the sixty-seventh IWC meeting in Brazil in September 2018. Japan arrived with a package of proposals called the "Way Forward," aimed at overturning the global ban on commercial whaling once and for all. The Japanese proposal called for setting sustainable use whaling catch limits, enabling the IWC to play a role in both conservation and sustainable use of whales, and establishing a Sustainable Whaling Committee (SWC) for the "orderly management" of whales, including proposing catch limits. The proposal also sought to amend the convention to change the requirements for any "Schedule amendment," which sets out catch limits for commercial and aboriginal subsistence whaling, from a three-fourths vote to a simple majority.[137] Underpinning Japan's position was its oft-repeated position that the 1946 Whaling Convention provides the IWC with a mandate "to provide for the proper

Photo 4.4 Activists protest outside the International Whaling Commission meeting in Florianópolis, Brazil in 2018.

Courtesy Ángeles Estrada, IISD/*Earth Negotiations Bulletin*, http://enb.iisd.org.

conservation of whale stocks and thus make possible the orderly development of the whaling industry."[138]

The lead coalition (EU, Buenos Aires Group, Australia, Brazil, Monaco, Costa Rica, Uruguay, Mexico, Chile, Ecuador, New Zealand, the United States, Panama, Peru, and India) opposed the package proposal. They argued that the proposed modification of catch limits represented a resumption of commercial whaling, the establishment of an SWC would entrench differences, and a simple majority vote ran counter to the text of the 1946 Whaling Convention. Mexico added that conservation had appropriately dominated IWC discussion in recent years and Japan's proposal was exacerbating division.[139]

Support for Japan's proposal came from Togo, Nicaragua, Guinea, Senegal, Norway, Antigua and Barbuda, Iceland, Liberia, Colombia, Solomon Islands, Cambodia, Kenya, St. Kitts and Nevis, Ghana, Grenada, St. Lucia, and St. Vincent and the Grenadines. They argued that the catch quotas were based on the best available scientific information and addressed the convention's purpose to "manage" whales.[140] Twenty-seven member states voted in support of the proposal, forty-one against, and two abstained. Japan responded that it would undertake a fundamental reassessment of its position in the IWC.[141]

In contrast to Japan's commercial whaling proposal, during the meeting, lead states approved the Florianópolis Declaration, which acknowledged that the role of the IWC in the twenty-first century includes the responsibility to ensure the recovery of whale populations, agreed that lethal scientific whaling is unnecessary, and called on the IWC to ensure adequate funding for conservation and nonlethal management issues. In opposition, Japan, the Russian Federation, Antigua and Barbuda, Guinea, Iceland, Liberia, Norway, Senegal, São Tomé and Príncipe, Togo, Ghana, St. Vincent and the Grenadines, St. Lucia, and the Solomon Islands argued that the declaration failed to encompass the concept of sustainable use, including commercial whaling. Delegates adopted the resolution, with forty in favor, twenty-seven opposed, and four abstentions.[142]

Three months later, on December 28, 2018, Japan announced that it would withdraw from the IWC on June 30, 2019, and resume commercial whaling within its own EEZ. Japan sent out its first whaling fleet on July 1, 2019 with permits to catch 227 whales.[143] Japan will no longer carry out "scientific whaling" in the Antarctic Ocean, which some observers argue will benefit more whales than Japan will catch within its EEZ.[144] Even after its withdrawal, Japan said it would participate in the IWC as an observer and conduct whaling within the catch limits calculated by the IWC's method, noting that "the IWC is no longer a respectable body but rather a place for anti-whaling countries to press their views."[145]

Over the years, coalition building on both sides has been characterized more by political maneuvering than by a process that values fact finding and consensus building. Science has played a marginal role in decision making, with its credibility diminished by countries conducting commercial whaling under the banner of scientific whaling, even after the ICJ ruling. Now, with Japan's withdrawal from the IWC, the dynamics are likely to change. Some conservationists believe that Japan will kill fewer whales in a commercial coastal hunt than in its scientific whaling hunts in the Southern Ocean Sanctuary and that without Japan, the IWC can focus more on critical issues facing whales today, including ship strikes, bycatch, climate change, entanglement, habitat degradation, and pollution, including noise, plastics, and chemicals.[146]

The impact of Japan's decision to withdraw from the IWC remains to be seen. Will other pro-whaling nations from the Caribbean and Africa that have been supported financially by Japan also leave the IWC? Is there still a market for whale meat in Japan? Iceland announced in early 2020 that due to changes in public opinion and a decline in the consumption of whale meat, it would not hunt any whales for the second year in a row.[147] Yet at the same time, data show that Norway killed 481 minke whales in 2020, a number that surpasses the toll from the previous three years.[148] As support for whale hunting declines and the income derived from whale watching climbs, it is possible that public opinion and economic realities will prove more important to the future of commercial whaling than the IWC.

Desertification and Land Degradation

Drylands cover over 40 percent of the earth's land surface, providing 44 percent of the world's agriculture and 50 percent of the world's livestock.[149] Over 75 percent of the earth's land area is already degraded, and over 90 percent could become degraded by 2050, affecting the lives of 2 billion people in 169 countries and costing the global economy $23 trillion.[150] Land degradation leads to the reduction or loss of the biological or economic productivity and complexity of land. In the drylands, land degradation is known as desertification. Experts estimate that desertification and land degradation will drive 700 million people out of their homes by 2050 because they will no longer be able to feed themselves or have access to sufficient water.[151]

While many believe that land degradation and desertification require immediate international attention, they have never been priority issues on the global environmental agenda, despite efforts by many African countries since the 1970s. Indeed, desertification was put on the agenda of the 1992 UN Conference on Environment and Development (UNCED or the Earth Summit) only because African countries persisted. When the desertification convention became the first treaty to be negotiated after UNCED, some looked at it as a test of whether desertification and land degradation would finally become an international issue of importance.

Complexity, vagueness, and disagreement on whether desertification was indeed a global problem plagued the issue-definition stage. UNEP and most specialists defined desertification as sustained land degradation in arid, semiarid, and dry subhumid areas resulting mainly from adverse human impact (see Box 4.8).[152] But the term *desertification* evokes images of deserts advancing and destroying productive land, whereas scientists have found no evidence to support claims that the Sahara is expanding at an alarming rate.[153] African countries encountered other problems in defining desertification. A bewildering array of natural and social factors have an impact on land degradation in the drylands, including overpopulation, climatic cycles, social and economic structures, poor pastoral or agricultural practices, bad government and donor policies, and North–South economic relations. It was difficult, therefore, to articulate in a simple and clear way both the nature of the problem and the international actions needed to address it.

In addition, for many African countries, there is a strong link between poverty alleviation and desertification control. Consequently, the African countries' definition of the problem emphasized the need for additional funding but for as-yet unidentified activities. They hoped that a desertification convention would help them gain access to this funding.[154] It was unclear to many developed countries exactly why such assistance should be provided.

Finally, the African countries' attempt to define desertification was hampered because the 1977 UNEP Plan of Action to Combat Desertification was generally acknowledged as a failure. A UNEP evaluation of the plan blamed the failure on African governments and the donor community for not giving the issue priority and for gross mismanagement. UNEP found that only $1 billion of the $9 billion provided by donor agencies from 1978 to 1983 was spent directly on projects in the field.[155]

❖ BOX 4.8   WHY DOES LAND DEGRADATION MATTER?

Land, the ground beneath our feet, is an essential life support system. It is a key building block of our societies and economies. Land provides all species with the means to survive and is a resilient provider of vital ecological services.

- **Food Security:** Twelve million hectares (about 46,332 square miles or the size of Mississippi or Nicaragua) of productive land becomes barren every year due to desertification and drought, which is a lost opportunity to produce 20 million tons of grain.
- **Water Security:** Fully functioning soil reduces the risk of floods and protects underground water supplies by neutralizing or filtering out pollutants and storing as much as 3750 tons of water per hectare.
- **Climate Change:** The world's soils contain 1500 billion tons of carbon in the form of organic matter—two to three times more carbon than is present in the atmosphere. This carbon is released into the atmosphere when land is degraded.
- **Economic Cost:** The annual global cost of reduced cropland and rangeland productivity due to land degradation and land-use change has been estimated at roughly $300 billion.
- **Migration:** In rural areas where people depend on scarce productive land resources, land degradation is a driver of forced migration. Land degradation in tandem with climate change may force 50 to 700 million people to migrate by 2050.
- **National Security:** Forty percent of all intrastate conflicts in the past sixty years have been linked to the control and allocation of natural resources. Where natural assets including land are poorly managed, violence risks becoming the dominant means of resource control, forcing natural resource assets out of the hands of legitimate governments.

Sources: UNCCD, "Land and Human Security," 2019, www.unccd.int/issues/land-and-human-security; UNCCD, *Land in Numbers 2019: Risks and Opportunities* (Bonn, Germany: UNCCD, 2019); IUCN, "Drylands and Land Degradation," Issues Brief, June 2017, www.iucn.org/sites/dev/files/drylands_and_land_degradation_issues_brief_0.pdf.

When the issue of creating a desertification convention was first raised during the UNCED process, most industrialized countries and the World Bank argued that the primary problems were the macroeconomic policies of African governments (such as levying excessive taxes on agriculture and failing to grant enforceable property rights) and that policy reforms, better planning, and more popular participation would achieve better results than a new international program or formal agreement.[156] Unexpectedly, after opposing a desertification convention throughout the negotiations leading up to the Earth Summit, the United States shifted its position in Rio, backing language calling for a convention in the hope of winning African support on forests and on other issues in Agenda 21.[157] Other industrialized countries then followed suit, and the call for a desertification convention became part of Agenda 21.[158]

Negotiations began in May 1993 and were completed over five meetings in fifteen months. A formal fact-finding process was attempted through an information-sharing segment at the first session of the Intergovernmental Negotiating Committee (INC), but the process focused primarily on socioeconomic strategies for slowing and reversing desertification and on reports from individual countries rather than on the scientific understanding of the problem. That process produced general agreement on the importance of such strategies as the integration of arid and semiarid areas into national economies, popular participation in anti-desertification efforts, and land-tenure reform.[159] As a result, the convention would be the first to call for affected countries to provide for effective participation by grassroots organizations, NGOs, and local populations in the preparation of national action programs.[160]

The bargaining stage revolved not around commitments to environmental conservation actions but around financial, trade, institutional, and symbolic issues. The African countries were the lead states and presented detailed draft language for every section of the convention, some of which was accepted as the basis for negotiation.

Differences over financial resources and the financial mechanism nearly caused the negotiations to collapse. As in other global negotiations, some members of the G-77 and China demanded commitments to "new and additional" financial resources and the creation of a special fund for desertification as the centerpiece of the convention. Industrialized countries acted as a united veto coalition in rejecting such provisions. They argued that they bore no responsibility for desertification, unlike ozone depletion, and were therefore unwilling to accept binding obligations to increase their financial assistance to the affected countries.[161] They insisted that existing resources could be used more effectively.

The deadlock on a funding mechanism was broken only after the United States proposed the establishment of a "Global Mechanism" under the authority of the COP, which would improve monitoring and assessment of existing aid flows and increase coordination among donors. Developing countries remained dissatisfied because such a mechanism would not increase development assistance to countries suffering from desertification. They ultimately accepted the Global Mechanism because they could not afford to have the veto coalition walk away and it was the only compromise acceptable to them.[162]

The UNCCD was opened for signature in October 1994 and entered into force on December 26, 1996. Today, there are 197 parties.[163] The convention recognizes the physical, biological, and socioeconomic aspects of desertification, the importance of redirecting technology transfer so that it is demand-driven, and the importance of local populations in efforts to combat desertification. The core of the convention is the development of national, subregional, and regional action programs by national governments in cooperation with donors, local populations, and NGOs.

Implementing and Strengthening the Convention

The UNCCD faced significant challenges during its first six years, including establishing and operationalizing the Global Mechanism and reconciling the convention's emphasis on bottom-up approaches with involvement at all levels by all relevant actors with the logistical

❖ BOX 4.9 UNCCD MILESTONES

1977: UN Conference on Desertification adopts the Plan of Action to Combat Desertification.

1991: Forty African environment ministers meeting in Abidjan, Côte d'Ivoire, call for negotiation of a desertification convention to be included in Agenda 21.

1992: Chapter 12 of Agenda 21 calls on the UN General Assembly to establish a committee to elaborate a convention to combat desertification.

1994: United Nations Convention to Combat Desertification adopted in Paris.

1996: UNCCD enters into force.

1997: First meeting of the Conference of the Parties (COP) and first meeting of the Committee on Science and Technology (CST) meet in Rome.

2002: First meeting of the Committee to Review Implementation of the Convention (CRIC).

2007: COP adopts a strategic plan in response to the Joint Inspection Unit report.

2009: UNCCD convenes first of three Scientific Conferences to consider the theme "Biophysical and socioeconomic monitoring and assessment of desertification and land degradation, to support decision making in land and water management."

2012: Paragraph 206 in the Rio+20 outcome document, *The Future We Want*, recognizes the need for urgent action to reverse land degradation and commits to striving to achieve a land degradation-neutral world in the context of sustainable development.

2013: COP11 establishes a working group to develop a science-based definition of land degradation neutrality in arid, semiarid, and dry subhumid areas.

2015: The 2030 Agenda for Sustainable Development includes Target 15.3 in the Sustainable Development Goals: by 2020, combat desertification and restore degraded land and soil, including land affected by desertification, drought, and floods, and strive to achieve a land degradation-neutral world.

2017: COP 13 adopts the UNCCD 2018–2030 Strategic Framework, which, *inter alia*, strives to achieve a land degradation-neutral world consistent with the 2030 Agenda for Sustainable Development and launches the Land Degradation Neutrality Fund.

2019: COP14 adopts landmark decisions on drought, gender, sand and dust storms, and desertification, land degradation, and drought as a driver for migration. The COP also agrees to include land tenure as a new thematic area under the Convention.

requirements for operating an effective international coordinating body. At the national level, countries affected by desertification had to develop effective action programs in conjunction with donor countries, international organizations, local communities, and NGOs.[164]

Between 1997 and 2003, the COP set up institutional mechanisms intended to enable effective implementation of the convention. The COP established two subsidiary bodies: the Committee on Science and Technology and Committee for the Review of the Implementation of the Convention. After a long-fought battle, the convention designated the Global Environment Facility (GEF) as its financial mechanism once the GEF agreed to establish a program to fund projects to combat desertification. After a decade, it appeared as though the crucial building blocks required for success were in place. Eighty-one affected countries had submitted national action programs, synergies had been developed with the climate change and biodiversity conventions, and there seemed to be a growing understanding in the international community that the root causes of rural poverty are brought on or exacerbated by desertification and drought.[165]

When COP7 convened in Nairobi in 2005, however, delegates resumed the acrimonious debates on many of the same issues that had plagued the convention since its inception. Many of the political problems in this regime, the only multilateral environmental agreement

(MEA) driven by developing countries, stem from the fact that land degradation is not a priority issue for donor governments. As one developing-country official put it, the "scorching breath of the desert is not readily felt by the prosperous public of the rich North."[166]

The tone in Nairobi was also shaped by the critical report from the UN Joint Inspection Unit (an external oversight body). In 2003, parties had requested the Joint Inspection Unit to review the activities of the UNCCD Secretariat. The report confirmed, among other things, that the convention had a major identity crisis: "In the course of the review, it appeared to the inspectors that from the outset there has been a lack of common understanding and recognition of the Convention in its true and proper perspective."[167] The report stated that it seemed unclear whether the convention is environmental, developmental, or both and whether it concerns problems of a purely local or a global nature:

> The very name of the Convention may perhaps be misleading since the fundamental problem is one of land degradation, of which desertification is a key element. The failure and/or unwillingness to recognize the Convention in its proper perspective have inevitably led to undesirable consequences.[168]

The Nairobi meeting ended with agreement that, in response to this report, parties would adopt a long-term strategic plan for implementation of the convention. Although many admitted that this was not a panacea for the UNCCD's problems, they hoped that it would help strengthen the regime.

The strategic plan was adopted in 2007 at COP8 in Madrid. In addition to efforts to create a common vision for the convention and its work programs and mandates, the strategic plan also expanded the UNCCD's mandate by including land degradation:

> To provide a global framework to support the development and implementation of national and regional policies, programmes and measures to prevent, control and reverse desertification/land degradation and mitigate the effects of drought through scientific and technological excellence, raising public awareness, standard setting, advocacy and resource mobilization, thereby contributing to poverty reduction.[169]

The Science-Policy Nexus

Since its inception, the UNCCD had had difficulties finding the right mechanism to channel scientific and technological input into the convention. In its initial institutional architecture, such input was predominantly channeled to the COP through its Committee on Science and Technology and a roster of independent experts nominated by the parties. However, the science and technology committee's large and diverse membership rendered it rather unwieldy, and the discussions rarely included detailed, focused, and meaningful exchanges on specific scientific issues. Government representatives, many of whom lacked scientific training or expertise, typically dominated the meetings. In short, the UNCCD COP was not effectively tapping information available from the scientific community, and the scientific community was not effectively drawing the attention of parties to the scientific aspects of the key issues on the COP's agenda.[170]

The COP tried to address this problem in several ways. First, in 2007, the COP called for scientific-style conferences. Three such conferences were held, but while they enabled more scientists to participate in the work of the UNCCD, it remained difficult to translate the scientific presentations into policy decisions. In 2013, the UNCCD took a different approach and established a new body, the Science-Policy Interface (SPI), to translate science into policy-relevant recommendations. The SPI produces peer-reviewed technical reports as well as science-policy briefs designed to support policy development and also communicates with the larger scientific community. One of the early tests of the SPI was to provide scientific guidance to the operationalization of the land degradation neutrality (LDN) target, and it succeeded.

Land Degradation Neutrality

On the ground, implementation of the convention was also fraught with difficulties. The parties' obligations and the convention's expectations for parties were not quite clear; the robust financial and political capital necessary for its implementation was still not in place; the major tool for on-the-ground implementation, the National Action Plans, were considered irrelevant to mainstream, international development cooperation; and most donors chose to address issues related to land degradation bilaterally rather than under the framework of the convention.[171] There was also little meaningful involvement of local communities in defining, identifying, monitoring, and responding to desertification, even though such participation is a UNCCD centerpiece.[172] These constraints, combined with its dryland-restricted mandate, meant that the UNCCD was hindered from assuming global responsibility for land degradation. As a result, there was no clear indication that any significant amount of dryland degradation had been successfully reversed during the lifetime of the UNCCD.[173]

The need for a shift in focus paved the way for the emergence of the concept of land degradation neutrality, first introduced in a background paper prepared for COP10 in 2011. This led to a proposal at Rio+20 (the 2012 UN Conference on Sustainable Development), which was eventually included in the outcome document, *The Future We Want*, to recognize the need for urgent action to reverse land degradation and to achieve a land degradation–neutral world in the context of sustainable development.[174] Land degradation neutrality also became a part of the Sustainable Development Goals (SDGs) and the 2030 Sustainable Development Agenda adopted by the United Nations General Assembly (UNGA) in 2015. SDG Target 15.3 states: "by 2020, combat desertification, and restore degraded land and soil, including land affected by desertification, drought and floods, and strive to achieve a land-degradation neutral world."[175]

With land degradation neutrality (LDN) center stage, at COP12 in 2015, the UNCCD agreed to a formal scientific definition of LDN put forward by the SPI, and to align the UNCCD's goals and parties' action programs with the SDGs. The UNCCD's "official" definition of land degradation neutrality is a "state whereby the amount and quality of land resources, necessary to support ecosystem functions and services and enhance food security, remains stable or increases within specified temporal and spatial scales and ecosystems."[176] SDG Target 15.3 would be achieved by: (1) managing land more sustainably, which would reduce the rate of degradation; and (2) increasing the rate of restoration of degraded land, so that the two trends converge to give a zero net rate of land degradation.

On the face of it, this is a compelling proposition. Governments commit to ensuring that the rate of restoration at least equals the rate of degradation. Food production and ecosystems are maintained, thus also contributing to political and economic stability. Furthermore, land rehabilitation of up to 12 million hectares of degraded land a year could help close the carbon emissions gap by 25 percent by 2030, thus helping to mitigate climate change.[177]

But not everyone agrees. Some critics argue that the initiative essentially gives governments and powerful interests the right to degrade land as long as they can rehabilitate an equivalent area elsewhere. The assumption appears to be that the area within which neutrality must be achieved is either the nation-state or the natural borders of an ecosystem. However, as some critics say, one banked hectare might not be of the same quality as a hectare that is lost, and the ecosystem services provided by the restored hectare may not be as valuable as those provided by the degraded land. The proposed voluntary reporting could become a meaningless exercise of data manipulation to show zero loss, when in fact productive resources are still diminishing.[178]

Within this context, the next step was implementation. COP13 in Ordos, China, adopted the UNCCD 2018–2030 Strategic Framework with a vision of a future that avoids, minimizes, and reverses desertification/land degradation, mitigates the effects of drought in affected areas at all levels, and strives to achieve a land degradation-neutral world consistent with the 2030 Agenda for Sustainable Development.[179] Meanwhile, the SPI developed a "Conceptual Framework for Land Degradation Neutrality," over 120 countries committed to setting their own LDN targets, and the Secretariat, with governments and the private sector, set up an independent Land Degradation Neutrality Fund.

The "Conceptual Framework for Land Degradation Neutrality" provides a scientifically sound basis for understanding and implementing LDN, and informs the development of practical guidance for pursuing, and monitoring the achievement of, LDN. To achieve the broader development objectives of the UNCCD and the SDGs, the conceptual framework called for LDN interventions to seek to deliver "win-win" outcomes whereby investment in land can also contribute to improved and more sustainable livelihoods. Along those lines, governments are called on to ensure that vulnerable communities are not displaced when lands are targeted for restoration and that the implementation of LDN requires multistakeholder engagement and planning.[180]

The LDN Target Setting Programme supported interested countries in setting voluntary targets to achieve LDN by 2030. The Programme mobilized almost $8 million from multiple bilateral and multilateral donors. To date, over 120 countries have committed to setting voluntary LDN targets, and over eighty of those have already set them.[181]

COP12 also requested the Global Mechanism to increase resources for the full realization of LDN initiatives, including the creation of an independent LDN Fund. The Fund is an impact investment fund blending resources from the public, private, and philanthropic sectors to support achieving LDN through sustainable land management and land restoration projects implemented by the private sector. This is a first-of-its-kind investment vehicle leveraging public money to raise private capital for sustainable land projects. In total, investors have announced commitments of over $100 million out of a target of $300 million.[182]

In January 2019, the LDN Fund made its first investment in Urapi Sustainable Land Use, a program focused on restoring degraded land and promoting sustainable land management involving four coffee cooperatives in Peru. The project aims to reforest nearly 9000 hectares of degraded land into productive agroforestry systems, sequester and reduce carbon dioxide emissions by 1.3 metric tons, and improve the livelihoods of 2400 coffee producers.[183]

The national voluntary targets represent an early step in a much longer process toward the desired long-term impact of LDN. Participating countries now have to implement projects and secure the investment necessary to deliver those responses. While the Global Mechanism and the UNCCD Secretariat have neither the mandate nor the resources to provide intensive support for countries' individual efforts, they can still help maintain the project's initial momentum and support the global effort toward achieving LDN.[184]

Moving Forward

Unlike other regimes, the UNCCD's implementation has not been hindered by issues of national sovereignty or scientific uncertainty. In fact, the knowledge and technical skills exist to halt land degradation in the drylands, but political and economic factors have affected how this expertise is put into practice. Implementation has proven difficult because of the nature of the problem, lack of political commitment, and bureaucratic mistrust, often demonstrated by the developed countries, which have served as a veto coalition exploiting the power of the purse. With the UN's adoption of the SDGs and the UNCCD's embrace of the land degradation neutrality target, the Convention has new focus and direction. COP12 in 2015, situated as it was between the UNGA's adoption of the SDGs and the UNFCCC's adoption of the Paris Agreement, was seen as a watershed event, ensuring that the convention would achieve greater relevance in the global sustainable development agenda, not only through SDG Target 15.3 but also through the convention's relevance beyond arid lands and the relationship between land degradation neutrality and climate change mitigation.[185]

Photo 4.5 Cultural leaders and activists engaged with high-level participants at the interactive dialogue on a values-based approach to land stewardship at UNCCD COP14 in India.

Courtesy Ángeles Estrada, IISD/*Earth Negotiations Bulletin*, http://enb.iisd.org.

At COP14 in 2019, parties continued to improve the relevance of the UNCCD. In response to concerted calls by civil society organizations, parties took a bold, hard-fought step into the politically charged arena of land governance. For the first time, the UNCCD COP formally recognized that equitable land tenure can build an enabling environment for large-scale land restoration and meet one of the Convention's core objectives: improving the lives of people living in drylands. The COP also adopted decisions on how to implement four thematic policy frameworks addressing drought, gender, and sand and dust storms. After lengthy negotiations on drought, delegates agreed, subject to the availability of resources, to establish an intergovernmental working group to explore effective policy and implementation measures for addressing drought under the UNCCD.[186]

Whether the UNCCD continues along this path and receives increased political commitment and financial support from some donor parties and the private sector remains to be seen. The convention also needs to maintain a delicate balance between the global goal of land degradation neutrality and its original focus on the needs at the local level. However, twenty-five years after the convention's entry into force, this new focus and direction may indeed brighten the future of the first sustainable development convention.

Conclusion

The environmental regimes described in Chapters 3 and 4 show that the creation and expansion of strong, effective global environmental regimes almost always depend on inducing one or more key veto states to go along with one or more of the core proposed provisions of the regime. By strong, we mean an agreement that mandates actions that can reasonably be expected to have an impact on the problem if they are implemented, and includes obligations or norms that make it sufficiently clear that parties can be held accountable for implementing them. By effective, we mean one that leads to significant, measurable improvements in the environmental issue. Whether a regime succeeds in effectively addressing an environmental threat depends, of course, on how strong the regime is and on the degree to which parties comply with its core provisions. Success in overcoming the impact of veto states on global environmental negotiations usually results from one or more of the following five developments:

1.   A veto state changes its own understanding of the problem because of new scientific evidence.
2.   A veto state changes its position because its economic interests have changed.
3   A veto state has a change of government, and the new government has a different policy toward the issue.
4   A veto state comes under effective domestic political pressure to change its policy.
5   A veto state fears negative reactions from other governments or adverse international opinion, which it regards as more important than its interest in vetoing a specific provision of the regime.

As Table 4.1 shows, in some of these cases one or more veto states either agreed to the central obligation proposed by the lead-state coalition or accepted the regime in general, often with concessions on the part of the lead states, despite earlier rejection.

New scientific evidence helped move veto states on some issues (ozone depletion and POPs) but has been secondary or irrelevant in others (climate change, whaling, hazardous waste trade, BBNJ, desertification, biodiversity, and African elephants). International considerations were primary in several cases. Japan's concern over economic and diplomatic ties with other major trading nations and its international image helped tilt its stance on the ivory ban. French and British desire to maintain productive relations with former colonies factored into their policy on the hazardous waste trade. Changing economic interests or new political strategies concerning how to pursue those interests can also lead veto states to change position. The United States, the United Kingdom, and France dropped their opposition to phasing out chlorofluorocarbons (CFCs) in part because their chemical industries invented substitutes.

In some cases, domestic political developments played a key role in facilitating agreement. The Obama administration in the United States and the Justin Trudeau administration in Canada pursued significantly different and more productive national and international policies on climate change than their predecessors. The Obama administration also withdrew American opposition to initiating negotiations on mercury. Concern about POPs in the Inuit communities of northern Canada pushed Canada to the forefront of the negotiations to ban certain types of these substances.

Regime formation usually requires leadership by one or more states committed to defining the issue and proposing and supporting strong international policy. Sometimes that role is played by states motivated by particular vulnerability (African countries on the hazardous waste trade and desertification; small island states on climate change) and sometimes by a state that has an advantageous legal or economic situation (the original US call for a phase-out of CFCs). In some cases, such as the BBNJ negotiations, a large lead-state coalition including the EU, the G-77/China, Australia, Mexico, and New Zealand, supported negotiations on a legally binding instrument, although their reasons for support varied, ranging from marine conservation to access and benefit sharing. The absence of lead states seeking to strengthen the regime is a major factor, along with the presence of veto states, that explains why the language in the conservation provisions of the biodiversity treaty remains largely advisory rather than binding.

Lead and veto states are not all equal. Lead states with greater diplomatic clout, economic resources, or negotiating skill outperform those without. In the case of desertification, although African countries formed an active lead-state coalition, their weak political and economic influence contributed to the weaknesses in the regime. The impact of a veto state depends on its ability to keep the regime from being effective. This can vary from issue to issue, and sometimes states that usually have less political or economic influence can have significant veto power if, for example, they are the main home to particular species. In general, however, the states and coalitions with the largest economies, populations, and environmental impacts (such as Brazil, China, India, the EU, and the United States) are the most potent potential veto states.

Table 4.1 Examples of Veto States and Regime Creation or Strengthening*

Issue	Key Veto States	Basis of Veto Power	Veto State Concession
Ozone depletion	European Community	Percentage of CFC production	Agreeing to 50 percent cut
Hazardous waste trade	United States, EU, Japan	Percentage of exports	Agreeing to ban exports
Toxic chemicals	Developing countries that use DDT for malaria control	Percentage of use of DDT; global support for increased malaria control	Acceptance of elimination of DDT but with blanket exception for disease control; acceptance of regular reviews on continued need for DDT
Mercury	Large developing countries, and countries with artisanal and small-scale gold mining	Percentage of mercury emissions	Accepting provisions to reduce emissions without specific guarantees on levels of financial and technical assistance
Climate change	United States, China, India	Percentage of CO_2 emissions	Agreeing to stabilization goal**
Biodiversity loss	United States	Percentage of financing of GEF; biotechnology	Signing the agreement**
Marine Biodiversity in Areas Beyond National Jurisdiction	Canada, Japan, the Republic of Korea, the Russian Federation, and the United States	Ability to access marine genetic resources in the high seas	Meaningful consensus must be developed in the space between two principles: common heritage of humankind and freedom of the high seas***
African elephant ivory	Japan, southern African states	Percentage of imports (Japan); elephant herds (southern African states)	No reservation to CITES uplist
Whaling	Japan and Norway	Percentage of catch	Acceptance of ban on whaling, with an exemption for scientific whaling
Desertification	EC, United States	Percentage of official development assistance	Agreeing to create the Global Mechanism instead of a new source of funds

*   This chart outlines one aspect of the veto coalition situation for each case as a point of comparison.

**   In both of these cases, veto state power has not totally been overcome, because although the United States in each case made certain concessions in the negotiations, the result was a much weaker treaty.

*** To date, there is no such consensus.

Overall, as these cases show, the United States has had greater diplomatic influence on other state actors and intergovernmental organizations than any other state, although the EU as a unit and China are now comparable. When the United States has taken the lead, as it did on ozone depletion, whaling, and the African elephant, the result has been a much stronger regime than otherwise would have been established. In the case of the mercury negotiations, the lead role played by the United States was crucial to agreement on controls of emissions and mining. On the other hand, when the United States has been a veto state, as in the Basel Convention, the Biodiversity Convention, and at different times in the climate negotiations, the result is a significantly weaker regime. It remains to be seen what impact the United States and the other veto states will have on the BBNJ negotiations.

In the case of biodiversity, veto states' efforts combined with several other factors—the complexity of the issue, lack of high levels of media interest, less domestic lobbying by environmental NGOs, and poor design—to prevent the regime from becoming significantly stronger and more effective over time. These issues have also contributed to the Biodiversity Convention receiving far less high-level political attention in major states than do the ozone and climate treaties.

In the case of climate change, the adoption of the Paris Agreement was only possible by avoiding the top-down requirements for emissions reductions, which proved problematic in the Kyoto Protocol, and allowing countries to determine their own greenhouse gas (GHG) emissions reductions. This enabled both China and the United States, as the largest GHG emitters and veto states, to accept the agreement in December 2015.

Many of these regimes examined in these two chapters have grown significantly since their inception. Governments continue to meet and negotiate new pollution controls (as in the ozone and chemicals treaties), list new species (CITES), develop new cooperative programs and helpful guidance (Basel Convention and UNCCD), and even negotiate entirely new protocols within the regime (e.g., the Liability Protocol under the Basel Convention, Cartagena Protocol on Biosafety, the Nagoya Protocol on Access and Benefit Sharing) or new types of agreements that accept political realities while offering a framework for potential success, such as the Paris Climate Agreement.

Global environmental regimes include conventions that enjoy nearly universal participation and have the potential to affect economic development strategies, production technologies, and even domestic political processes in ways supportive of long-term sustainable development. However, as these cases also demonstrate, not all of these agreements have been successful. Serious obstacles exist to negotiating strong, global environmental treaties. Moreover, negotiating a strong treaty on paper does not mean it will be effective in practice. All of the regimes discussed in these chapters face serious implementation challenges, including compliance, financing, technology transfer, and effective translation of regime rules into national policy. The next chapter focuses on these challenges.

Notes

1   Oran Young, *International Environmental Governance: Protecting the Environment in a Stateless Society* (Ithaca, NY: Cornell University Press, 1994), 21.
2   Ibid., 21–22.
3   Ibid., 23.
4   Camilo Mora, et al., "How Many Species Are There on Earth and in the Ocean?" *PLOS Biology* vol. 9, no. 8 (2011), doi: 10.1371/journal.pbio.1001127.
5   IPBES, "Summary for Policy Makers." *Global Assessment Report on Biodiversity and Ecosystem Services of the Intergovernmental Science-Policy Platform on Biodiversity and Ecosystem Services*, eds. E. S. Brondizio, J. Settele, S. Díaz, and H. T. Ngo (Bonn, Germany: IPBES Secretariat, 2019), www.ipbes.net/global-assessment-report-biodiversity-ecosystem-services.

6   National sovereignty over natural resources implies that a government has control over its resources, such as oil, minerals, and timber. Common heritage implies that no one can be excluded from using natural resources, except by lack of economic and technological capacity; conversely, everyone has a right to benefit from the exploitation of the resources. See G. Kristin Rosendal, "The Convention on Biological Diversity: A Viable Instrument for Conservation and Sustainable Use," in *Green Globe Yearbook of International Cooperation on Environment and Development 1995*, eds. Helge Ole Bergesen, et al. (Oxford: Oxford University Press, 1995), 69–81.

7   United Nations Environment Programme (UNEP), *Report of the Ad Hoc Working Group on the Work of Its Second Session in Preparation for a Legal Instrument on Biological Diversity of the Planet*, UNEP/Bio.Div2/3, February 23, 1990, 7.

8   For text of the Convention on Biological Diversity (CBD) and subsequent agreements, official documents from its negotiation and subsequent meetings, and lists of ratifying states, see the official CBD website at www.cbd.int.

9   G. Kristin Rosendal, "Balancing Access and Benefit Sharing and Legal Protection of Innovations from Bioprospecting: Impacts on Conservation of Biodiversity," *Journal of Environment and Development* vol. 15, no. 4 (2006): 428–447. The Senate Foreign Relations Committee approved the ratification of the CBD by a vote of sixteen to three on June 29, 1994. However, in a dramatic move in September 1994, CBD ratification was removed from the Senate's agenda, and since then the ratification issue has never come up for a vote.

10 CBD, "Thematic Programmes and Cross-Cutting Issues," www.cbd.int/programmes/.

11 Elisa Morgera and Elsa Tsioumani, "Yesterday, Today, and Tomorrow: Looking Afresh at the Convention on Biological Diversity," *Yearbook of International Environmental Law* vol. 21, no. 1 (2011), doi:10.2139/ssrn.1914378.

12 See CBD, "COP Decision VI/26 on Strategic Plan for the Convention on Biological Diversity," Doc. CBD UNEP/CBD/COP/6/20 (2002) at para. 11; World Summit on Sustainable Development, "Johannesburg Plan of Implementation," UN Doc. A/CONF.199/20, September 4, 2002, Resolution 2, Annex, para. 44; and UN General Assembly, "2005 World Summit Outcome," Resolution 60/1, October 24, 2005, para. 56.

13 CBD and UNEP–World Conservation Monitoring Centre, *Global Biodiversity Outlook* (Montreal, Canada: Secretariat of the Convention on Biological Diversity, 2010), www.cbd.int/doc/publications/gbo/gbo3-final-en.pdf.

14 Ibid.; and Morgera and Tsioumani, "Yesterday, Today, and Tomorrow."

15 CBD, "COP Decision X/2 2010 on Strategic Plan for Biodiversity 2011–2020," www.cbd.int/decision/cop/?id=12268.

16 The Aichi Targets can be found at www.cbd.int/sp/targets/.

17 See Ana María Ulloaa, Kurt Jax, and Sylvia I. Karlsson-Vinkhuyzend, "Enhancing Implementation of the Convention on Biological Diversity: A Novel Peer-Review Mechanism Aims to Promote Accountability and Mutual Learning," *Biological Conservation* vol. 217 (January 2018): 371–376.

18 CBD, "COP Decision XII/26 2014 on Improving the efficiency of structures and processes of the Convention: Subsidiary Body on Implementation," www.cbd.int/doc/decisions/cop-12/cop-12-dec-26-en.pdf.

19 IPBES, "Summary for Policy Makers," 15; Secretariat of the Convention on Biological Diversity, *Global Biodiversity Outlook 5* (Montreal, Canada: Secretariat of the Convention on Biological Diversity, 2020).

20 IPBES, 33–34.

21 CBD, "COP Decision 14/1 2018 on Updated Assessment of Progress Towards Selected Aichi Biodiversity Targets and Options to Accelerate Progress," www.cbd.int/doc/decisions/cop-14/cop-14-dec-01-en.pdf.

22 For a short analysis of the World Trade Organization ruling, see The European Union Center of the University of North Carolina, "The EU-US Dispute over GMOs," EU Briefings, May 2007, https://europe.unc.edu/files/2016/11/Brief_EU_US_Dispute_Genetically_Modified_Organisms_GMOs_2007.pdf.

23 Nicholas Kalaitzandonakes, "Cartagena Protocol: A New Trade Barrier?" *Regulation* vol. 29, no. 2 (Summer 2006): 18–25, https://object.cato.org/sites/cato.org/files/serials/files/regulation/2006/7/v29n1-4.pdf.

24 For a summary of the negotiations and the protocol, see IISD, "Report of the Resumed Session of the Extraordinary Meeting of the Conference of the Parties for the Adoption of the Protocol on Biodiversity to the Convention on Biological Diversity: 24–28 January 2000," *Earth Negotiations Bulletin* vol. 9, no. 137 (January 31, 2000).

25 *Nagoya–Kuala Lumpur Supplementary Protocol on Liability and Redress to the Cartagena Protocol on Biosafety* (Montreal: Secretariat of the Convention on Biological Diversity, 2011), http://bch.cbd.int/protocol/NKL_text.shtml.

26 IISD, "Summary of the Third Meeting of the Parties to the Cartagena Protocol on Biosafety: 13–17 March 2006," *Earth Negotiations Bulletin* vol. 9, no. 351 (March 20, 2006).

27 Ibid. Exporting parties' pre-existing bilateral trade agreements with large non-parties, such as the United States, were widely acknowledged as one reason why some Latin American parties resisted consensus.

28 IISD, "Summary of the Seventh Meeting of the Parties to the Cartagena Protocol on Biosafety: 29 September–3 October 2014," *Earth Negotiations Bulletin* vol. 9, no. 635 (October 6, 2014).

29 Ibid.

30 IISD, "Summary of the Fifth Meeting of the Parties to the Cartagena Protocol on Biosafety: 11–15 October 2010," *Earth Negotiations Bulletin* vol. 9, no. 533 (October 18, 2010).

31 For more information, see Rhett Butler, "Anti-HIV Drug from Rainforest Almost Lost Before Its Discovery," mongabay.com, September 13, 2005, http://news.mongabay.com/2005/09/anti-hiv-drug-from-rainforest-almost-lost-before-its-discovery/.

32 See Kabir Bavikatte, Harry Jonas, and Johanna von Braun, "Shifting Sands of ABS Best Practice: Hoodia from the Community Perspective," *Traditional Knowledge Bulletin*, United Nations University Institute of Advanced Studies, March 31, 2009.

33 Article 1 of the CBD states:

> The objectives of this Convention, to be pursued in accordance with its relevant provisions, are the conservation of biological diversity, the sustainable use of its components and the fair and equitable sharing of the benefits arising out of the utilization of genetic resources, including by appropriate access to genetic resources and by appropriate transfer of relevant technologies, taking into account all rights over those resources and to technologies, and by appropriate funding.

34 CBD, "Access and Benefit-Sharing: Background," www.cbd.int/abs/background.

35 Ibid., 27.

36 CBD, *Nagoya Protocol Access to Genetic Resources and the Fair and Equitable Sharing of Benefits Arising from Their Utilization, Article 3* (Montreal, Canada: CBD, 2010), www.cbd.int/abs/doc/protocol/nagoya-protocol-en.pdf.

37 Ibid.

38 Ibid.

39 CBD, *Nagoya Protocol Access to Genetic Resources*.

40 IISD, "Summary of the Tenth Conference of the Parties to the Convention on Biological Diversity: 18–29 October 2010," *Earth Negotiations Bulletin* vol. 9, no. 544 (November 1, 2010), 27.

41 CBD, "Analysis of the Contribution of Targets Established by Parties and Progress Towards the Aichi Biodiversity Targets," CBD/COP/14/5/Add.2, October 31, 2018, www.cbd.int/doc/c/7c28/274f/338c8e84ad6f03bf9636dcbf/cop-14-05-add2-en.pdf.

42 Connor McKoy, "Synthetic Biology to Sustain Agriculture and Transform the Food System," Biotechnology Innovation Organization, November 2019, www.bio.org/blogs/synthetic-biology-sustain-agriculture-and-transform-food-system.

43 IISD, "Summary of the UN Biodiversity Conference: 13–29 November 2018," *Earth Negotiations Bulletin* vol. 9, no. 725 (December 2, 2018), 25.

44 CBD, "COP Decision 14/9 on Synthetic Biology," November 30, 2018, www.cbd.int/doc/decisions/cop-14/cop-14-dec-19-en.pdf.

45 Ibid.

46 IISD, "Summary of the UN Biodiversity Conference: 13–29 November 2018," 26.

47 CBD, "COP Decision X/2 2010 on Strategic Plan for Biodiversity 2011–2020."

48 UN Environment World Conservation Monitoring Centre, "Framing the Future for Biodiversity," 2019, www.unep-wcmc.org/featured-projects/framing-the-future-for-biodiversity.

49 IUCN, "Governing Areas Beyond National Jurisdiction," IUCN Issues Brief, March 2019, www.iucn.org/sites/dev/files/issues_brief_governing_areas_beyond_national_jurisdiction.pdf.

50 Pew Charitable Trusts, "Policy Statement: Biological Diversity Beyond Areas of National Jurisdiction (BBNJ)," May 3, 2012, www.pewtrusts.org/en/research-and-analysis/articles/2012/05/03/policy-statement-biological-diversity-beyond-areas-of-national-jurisdiction-bbnj.

51 Ghost nets are fishing nets that have been left or lost in the ocean by fishermen.

52 Pew Charitable Trusts, "Policy Statement: Biological Diversity Beyond Areas of National Jurisdiction (BBNJ)."

53 OECD, "Sustainable Fisheries and Aquaculture Policies for the Future," 2019, www.oecd.org/agriculture/topics/fisheries-and-aquaculture/.

54 IUCN, "Governing Areas Beyond National Jurisdiction."

55 UN General Assembly, "Oceans and the Law of the Sea: Addendum," A/59/62/Add.1, August 18, 2004, 65–66, http://daccess-ods.un.org/access.nsf/Get?Open&DS=A/59/62/Add.1&Lang=E.

56 Convention on Biological Diversity, "Conservation and Sustainable Use of Marine and Coastal Biological Diversity," Decision II/10, November 17, 1995, www.cbd.int/decision/cop/default.shtml?id=7083.

57 UN General Assembly, "Report on the Work of the United Nations Open-Ended Informal Consultative Process on Oceans and the Law of the Sea," A/58/95, June 26, 2003.

58 UN General Assembly, Oceans and the Law of the Sea, Resolution 58/240, December 23, 2003, paragraph 52, https://undocs.org/en/A/RES/58/240.

59 IISD, "Summary of the Working Group on Marine Biodiversity Beyond Areas of National Jurisdiction: 13–17 February 2006," *Earth Negotiations Bulletin* vol. 25, no. 25 (February 20, 2006).

60 Elisa Morgera, "Do We Need a New Treaty to Protect Biodiversity in the Deep Seas?" IISD Reporting Series Policy Update No. 8, January 20, 2015, http://sdg.iisd.org/commentary/policy-briefs/do-we-need-a-new-treaty-to-protect-biodiversity-in-the-deep-seas/.

61 IISD, "Summary of the Fourth Meeting of the Working Group on Marine Biodiversity Beyond Areas of National Jurisdiction: 31 May–3 June 2011," *Earth Negotiations Bulletin* vol. 25, no. 70 (June 6, 2011).

62 UN General Assembly, "The Future We Want," Resolution 66/288, September 11, 2012, paragraph 162.

63 IISD, "Summary of the Fifth Meeting of the Working Group on Marine Biodiversity Beyond Areas of National Jurisdiction: 7–11 May 2012," *Earth Negotiations Bulletin* vol. 25, no. 83 (May 14, 2012).

64 IISD, "Summary of the First Meeting of the Preparatory Committee Working Group on Marine Biodiversity Beyond Areas of National Jurisdiction: 28 March–8 April 2016," *Earth Negotiations Bulletin* vol. 25, no. 106 (April 11, 2016), 18.

65 IISD, "Summary of the Fourth Meeting of the Preparatory Committee Working Group on Marine Biodiversity Beyond Areas of National Jurisdiction: 10–21 July 2017," *Earth Negotiations Bulletin* vol. 25, no. 141 (July 24, 2017), 1.

66 Eli Kintisch, "U.N. Tackles Gene Prospecting on the High Seas," *Science* vol. 361, no. 6406 (September 7, 2018), 956–957, doi: 10.1126/science.361.6406.956.

67 Robert Blasiak, et al., "Corporate Control and Global Governance of Marine Genetic Resources," *Science Advances* vol. 4, no. 6 (June 6, 2018), doi: 10.1126/sciadv.aar5237.

68 Kintisch, "U.N. Tackles Gene Prospecting."

69 Ibid.

70 Morgera, "Do We Need a New Treaty."

71 IISD, "Summary of the Third Meeting of the Preparatory Committee on Marine Biodiversity Beyond Areas of National Jurisdiction: 27 March–7 April 2017," *Earth Negotiations Bulletin* vol. 25, no. 129 (April 10, 2017), 4.

72 IISD, "Summary of the First Session of the Intergovernmental Conference on an International Legally Binding Instrument Under the UN Convention on the Law of the Sea on the Conservation and Sustainable Use of Marine Biodiversity of Areas Beyond National Jurisdiction: 4–17 September 2018," *Earth Negotiations Bulletin* vol. 25, no. 179 (September 20, 2018), 16.

73 Morgera, "Do We Need a New Treaty."

74 IISD, "Summary of the Third Meeting of the Preparatory Committee," 8.

75 Morgera, "Do We Need a New Treaty."

76 IISD, "Summary of the Third Session of the Intergovernmental Conference on an International Legally Binding Instrument Under the UN Convention on the Law of the Sea on the Conservation and Sustainable Use of Marine Biodiversity of Areas Beyond National Jurisdiction: 19–30 August 2019," *Earth Negotiations Bulletin* vol. 25, no. 218 (September 2, 2019), 1; Ina Tessnow-von Wysocki, "Slow Progress in the Third BBNJ Meeting: Negotiations Are Moving—but Sideways," MARIPOLDATA, September 6, 2019, www.maripoldata.eu/slow-progress-in-the-third-bbnj-meeting-negotiations-are-moving-but-sideways/.

77 Ibid.

78 Ibid.

79 United Nations General Assembly, "Revised Draft Text of an Agreement Under the United Nations Convention on the Law of the Sea on the Conservation and Sustainable Use of Marine Biological Diversity of Areas Beyond National Jurisdiction," A/CONF.232/2020/3, November 18, 2019, https://undocs.org/en/a/conf.232/2020/3.

80 "Textual Proposals Submitted by Delegations by 20 February 2020, for Consideration at the Fourth Session of the Intergovernmental Conference on an International Legally Binding Instrument Under the United Nations Convention on the Law of the Sea on the Conservation and Sustainable Use of Marine Biological Diversity of Areas Beyond National Jurisdiction (the Conference), in Response to the Invitation by the President of the Conference in her Note of 18 November 2019 (A/CONF.232/2020/3)," unofficial document, April 15, 2020, www.un.org/bbnj/sites/www.un.org. bbnj/files/textual_proposals_compilation_article-by-article_-_15_april_2020.pdf.

81 For updated information on the negotiations, see the Conference website at www.un.org/bbnj/ and the *Earth Negotiations Bulletin* coverage at https://enb.iisd.org/vol25/.

82 IISD, "Summary of the Second Session of the Intergovernmental Conference on an International Legally Binding Instrument Under the UN Convention on the Law of the Sea on the Conservation and Sustainable Use of Marine Biodiversity of Areas Beyond National Jurisdiction: 25 March–5 April 2019," *Earth Negotiations Bulletin* vol. 25, no. 195 (April 8, 2019), 17–18.

83 Ibid.

84 CITES, "What is CITES?" www.cites.org/eng/disc/what.php.

85 Detailed and updated information on CITES, including its text, history, operation, species covered, current parties, and other issues, can be found on the regime's official website: www.cites.org. For the history of the regime, see also *CITES World*, March 3, 2003, www.cites.org/sites/default/files/eng/news/world/30special.pdf.

86 Ed Stoddard, "CITES Does Not Follow Standard U.N. Divisions," *Environmental News Network*, October 14, 2004, www.enn.com/top_stories/article/169.

87 For updated lists and other information concerning the species listed in each appendix, see www.cites.org.

88 Suzanne Sharrock, *A Guide to the GSPC: All the Targets, Objectives and Facts* (Richmond, UK: Botanic Gardens Conservation International, 2012), 25, www.plants2020.net/files/Plants2020/popular_guide/englishguide.pdf.

89 Ibid., 27.

90 Christian Nellemann, et al., *The Rise of Environmental Crime—A Growing Threat to Natural Resources Peace, Development and Security* (Nairobi: UNEP, 2016), 7.

91 Liana Sun Wyler and Pervaze Sheikh, "International Illegal Trade in Wildlife: Threats and U.S. Policy" (Washington, DC: Congressional Research Service, July 23, 2013), 1, http://fas.org/sgp/crs/misc/RL34395.pdf.

92 See Sarah Fitzgerald, *International Wildlife Trade: Whose Business Is It?* (Washington, DC: WWF, 1989), 3–8, 13–14. See also Adam Cruise, "Why Some Countries Don't Want to Do More to Protect Elephants," *National Geographic*, August 24, 2016, https://news.nationalgeographic.com/2016/08/wildlife-african-elephants-ivory-trade-cites/.

93 David Harland, "Jumping on the 'Ban' Wagon: Efforts to Save the African Elephant," *Fletcher Forum on World Affairs* vol. 14 (Summer 1990): 284–300.

94 "CITES 1989: The African Elephant and More," *TRAFFIC Dispatches* vol. 9 (December 1989): 1–3.

95 World Resources Institute, *World Resources 1990–1991* (New York: Oxford University Press, 1990), 135.

96 "U.S. Ivory Market Collapses After Import Ban," *New York Times*, June 5, 1990, C2; Raymond Bonner, *At the Hand of Man: Peril and Hope for Africa's Wildlife* (New York: Vintage Books, 1994), 157.

97 In each case the proposals were withdrawn prior to a formal vote. WWF, "The Challenge of African Elephant Conservation," *Conservation Issues*, April 1997.

98 "CITES and the African Elephants: The Decisions and the Next Steps Explained," *TRAFFIC Dispatches* (April 1998): 5–6.

99 CITES, "Verification of Compliance with the Precautionary Undertakings for the Sale and Shipment of Raw Ivory," Doc. SC.42.10.2.1, Forty-Second Meeting of the Standing Committee, Lisbon, Portugal, September 28–October 1, 1999.

100 IISD, "Summary of the Thirteenth Conference of the Parties to the Convention on International Trade in Endangered Species of Wild Fauna and Flora: 2–14 October 2004," *Earth Negotiations Bulletin* vol. 21, no. 45 (October 18, 2004): 16.

101 Julie Gray, *TRAFFIC Report of the 14th Meeting of the Conference of the Parties to CITES* (Cambridge: TRAFFIC, 2007), www.traffic.org/site/assets/files/7515/cites-cop14-report.pdf.

102 IISD, "Summary of the Fourteenth Conference of the Parties to the Convention on International Trade in Endangered Species of Wild Fauna and Flora: 3–15 June 2007," *Earth Negotiations Bulletin* vol. 21, no. 61 (June 18, 2007): 21.

103 CITES, "Ivory Sales Get the Go-Ahead," June 2, 2007, www.cites.org/eng/news/pr/2007/070602_ivory.shtml.

104 CITES, "Report on the One-Off Ivory Sale in Southern African Countries," SC58 Doc. 36.3 (Rev. 1), Fifty-Eighth Meeting of the Standing Committee, Geneva, Switzerland, July 6–10, 2009, www.cites.org/sites/default/files/eng/com/sc/58/E58-36-3.pdf.

105 CITES, "Elephant Conservation, Illegal Killing and Ivory Trade," SC62 Doc. 46.1 (Rev. 1), Sixty-Second Meeting of the Standing Committee, Geneva, Switzerland, 23–27 July 2012, www.cites.org/sites/default/files/eng/com/sc/62/E62-46-01.pdf.

106 IISD, "Summary of the Seventeenth Meeting of the Conference of the Parties to the Convention on International Trade in Endangered Species of Wild Fauna and Flora: 24 September–4 October 2016," *Earth Negotiations Bulletin* vol. 21, no. 97 (October 8, 2016): 19.

107 WWF, "Two Years After China Bans Elephant Ivory Trade, Demand for Elephant Ivory is Down," December 31, 2019, www.worldwildlife.org/stories/two-years-after-china-bans-elephant-ivory-trade-demand-for-elephant-ivory-is-down.

108 Ibid.; and IISD, "Summary of the Eighteenth Meeting of the CITES Conference of the Parties: 17–28 August 2019," *Earth Negotiations Bulletin* vol. 21, no. 101 (August 31, 2019): 23.

109 Rachel Nuwer, "Poachers Threaten Elephants in Botswana," *New York Times*, July 2, 2019, D1.

110 Ibid.

111 Brandon Keim and Emma Howard, "African 'Blood Ivory' Destroyed in New York to Signal Crackdown on Illegal Trade," *Guardian*, June 19, 2015.

112 International Convention for the Regulation of Whaling, December 2, 1946, https://iwc.int/convention.

113 Marine Mammal Center, "Blue Whale," www.marinemammalcenter.org/education/marine-mammal-information/cetaceans/blue-whale.html.

114 A revised version of the 1973 Endangered Species Conservation Act banned whaling in US waters or by US citizens, outlawed the import of whale products, and required that the United States initiate bilateral and multilateral negotiations on an agreement to protect and conserve whales.

115 The effort to build an International Whaling Commission (IWC) majority to ban whaling was stymied in the latter half of the 1970s because states such as Canada and Mexico that were otherwise opposed to whaling were primarily concerned about protecting rights to regulate economic activities within their own 200-mile exclusive economic zones and opposed the jurisdiction of an international body over whaling.

116 Teresa Watanabe, "Japan Is Set for a Whale of a Fight," *Los Angeles Times*, April 20, 1993.

117 Paul Brown, "Playing Football with the Whales," *Guardian*, May 1, 1993. The Caribbean states cooperating with Japan were Grenada, St. Lucia, St. Kitts and Nevis, Antigua and Barbuda, Dominica, and St. Vincent and the Grenadines.

118 "During Clinton's Watch Global Whaling Triples," Greenpeace, May 20, 1997.

119 "Catches Under Objection Since 1985," IWC, https://iwc.int/table_objection.

120 Ibid.

121 Ibid.

122 For example, see Dennis Normile, "Japan's Whaling Program Carries Heavy Baggage," *Science* vol. 289, no. 5488 (September 29, 2000): 2264–2265; and Nicholas J. Gales, et al., "Japan's Whaling Ban Under Scrutiny," *Nature* vol. 435 (June 16, 2005): 883–884.

123 Since 2008, EU member countries of the IWC have been bound by a "common position," requiring that they all vote and speak in the same manner at meetings of the IWC (Denmark has an exception related to Greenland). This means that EU countries that formerly expressed some support for sustainable whaling (Sweden, Finland, and Denmark) can no longer do so. See Dan Goodman, "The 'Future of the IWC': Why the Initiative to Save the International Whaling Commission Failed," *Journal of International Wildlife Law & Policy* vol. 14, no. 1 (2011): 66.

124 Ibid.
125 Fisheries Agency head Masayuki Komatsu in an Australian Broadcasting Corporation radio interview. See "Japan 'Buys' Pro-Whaling Votes," CNN.com, July 18, 2001, http://edition.cnn.com/2001/TECH/science/07/18/japan.whale/index.html; and "Japan Denies Aid-for-Whaling Report," CNN.com, July 18, 2001, http://edition.cnn.com/2001/WORLD/asiapcf/east/07/19/japan.whaling. See also Andrew Miller and Nives Dolšak, "Issue Linkages in International Environmental Policy: The International Whaling Commission and Japanese Development Aid," *Global Environmental Politics* vol. 7, no. 1 (February 2007): 69–96.
126 International Convention for the Regulation of Whaling.
127 Goodman, "The 'Future of the IWC,'" 65; IWC, "Resolution 2006–1: St. Kitts and Nevis Declaration," Fifty-Eighth Annual Meeting, St. Kitts and Nevis, June 16–20, 2006, http://archive.iwc.int/?r=2081. The following countries sponsored the declaration: St. Kitts and Nevis, Antigua and Barbuda, Benin, Cambodia, Cameroon, Côte d'Ivoire, Dominica, Gabon, Gambia, Grenada, Republic of Guinea, Iceland, Japan, Kiribati, Mali Marshall Islands, Mauritania, Mongolia, Morocco, Nauru, Nicaragua, Norway, Palau, Russian Federation, St. Lucia, St. Vincent and the Grenadines, Solomon Islands, Suriname, Togo, and Tuvalu.
128 Goodman, "The 'Future of the IWC,'" 64.
129 IWC, *Annual Report of the International Whaling Commission 2010* (Cambridge, UK: IWC, 2011), 6, https://archive.iwc.int/?r=65.
130 Richard Black, "Whaling 'Peace Deal' Falls Apart," *BBC News*, June 23, 2010.
131 IWC, *Annual Report 2010*, 7.
132 International Court of Justice, "Australia Institutes Proceedings Against Japan for Alleged Breach of International Obligations Concerning Whaling," press release no. 2010/16, June 1, 2010, www.icj-cij.org/files/case-related/148/15953.pdf.
133 Ibid.
134 United Nations News Center, "UN Court Rules Against Japan's Whaling Activities in the Antarctic," press release, March 31, 2014, https://news.un.org/en/story/2014/03/465062-un-court-rules-against-japans-whaling-activities-antarctic.
135 Yoko Wakatsuki and Sophie Brown, "Japanese Whaling Fleet Set to Sail Despite Recent Ruling," CNN.com, April 24, 2014, www.cnn.com/2014/04/24/world/asia/japan-whaling/.
136 IWC, "Resolution on Whaling Under Special Permit," Resolution 2014–5, Resolutions adopted at the 65th meeting, 2014, http://archive.iwc.int/?r=3723.
137 IISD, "Summary of the 67th Meeting of the International Whaling Commission: 10–14 September 2018," *Earth Negotiations Bulletin* vol. 34, no. 2 (September 17, 2018): 7.
138 Juliet Phillips, "IWC67: Commercial Whaling Kept at Bay, with all Eyes on Japan's Next Move," Environmental Investigation Agency, October 2, 2018, https://eia-international.org/blog/iwc67-commercial-whaling-kept-bay-eyes-japans-next-move/.
139 IISD, "Summary of the 67th Meeting of the International Whaling Commission: 10–14 September 2018," 7.
140 Ibid.
141 Ibid., 8.
142 Ibid., 10.
143 BBC News, "Japan Whaling: Why Commercial Hunts Have Resumed Despite Outcry," July 2, 2019, www.bbc.com/news/world-asia-48592682.
144 Dennis Normile, "Why Japan's Exit from International Whaling Treaty May Actually Benefit Whales," *Science* (January 10, 2019), doi:10.1126/science.aaw6298.
145 Kyodo News, "Japan Withdraws from IWC to Resume Commercial Whale Hunting," June 30, 2019, https://english.kyodonews.net/news/2019/06/895b5216c64f-japan-withdraws-from-iwc-to-resume-commercial-whale-hunting.html.
146 Dennis Normile, "Why Japan's Exit from International Whaling Treaty May Actually Benefit Whales."
147 Kieran Mulvaney, "Commercial Whaling May Be Over in Iceland," *National Geographic* (May 1, 2020), www.nationalgeographic.com/science/2020/04/commercial-whaling-may-be-over-iceland/.
148 Elizabeth Claire Alberts, "481 and Counting: Norway's Whaling Catch Hits Four-Year High," Mongabay, August 27, 2020, https://news.mongabay.com/2020/08/481-and-counting-norways-whaling-catch-hits-four-year-high/.

149 IUCN, "Drylands and Land Degradation," Issues Brief, June 2017, www.iucn.org/sites/dev/files/drylands_and_land_degradation_issues_brief_0.pdf.

150 UNCCD, "Poor Land Use Costs Countries 9 Percent Equivalent of Their GDP," Press Release, May 15, 2018; and EU Science Hub, "New World Atlas of Desertification Shows Unprecedented Pressure on the Planet's Natural Resources," Press Release, June 21, 2018.

151 EU Science Hub, "New World Atlas of Desertification Shows Unprecedented Pressure on the Planet's Natural Resources."

152 UNEP, *Desertification: The Problem That Won't Go Away* (Nairobi: UNEP, 1992); Ridley Nelson, "Dryland Management: The 'Desertification' Problem," working paper 8, World Bank Policy Planning and Research Staff, Environment Department, September 1988, 2.

153 For a news report on these findings, see William K. Stevens, "Threat of Encroaching Deserts May Be More Myth than Fact," *New York Times*, January 18, 1994, C1, 10.

154 "A Convention for Africans," *Impact* vol. 6 (September 1992): 3.

155 UNEP, *Desertification Control Bulletin (Nairobi)* 20 (1991); Mostafa Tolba, "Desertification and the Economics of Survival," statement to the International Conference on the Economics of Dryland Degradation and Rehabilitation, Canberra, Australia, March 10–11, 1986.

156 *World Bank News,* May 27, 1993, 4; *Crosscurrents* vol. 5 (March 16, 1992): 13.

157 E. U. Curtis Bohlen, deputy chief of the US delegation, recalls that he made the decision personally without consulting with higher US officials. Private communication from Bohlen, August 15, 1994. On the earlier suggestion by African countries of a possible bargain linking African support for a forest convention with US support for a desertification convention, see *Crosscurrents* vol. 5 (March 16, 1992): 13.

158 IISD, "A Summary of the Proceedings of the United Nations Conference on Environment and Development: 3–14 June 1992," *Earth Summit Bulletin* vol. 2, no. 13 (June 16, 1992): 3.

159 IISD, "Summary of the First Session of the INC for the Elaboration of an International Convention to Combat Desertification, 24 May–3 June 1993," *Earth Negotiations Bulletin* vol. 4, no. 11 (June 11, 1993): 2–6.

160 IISD, "Summary of the Fifth Session of the INC for the Elaboration of an International Convention to Combat Desertification, 6–17 June 1994," *Earth Negotiations Bulletin* vol. 4, no. 55 (June 20, 1994), 7–8.

161 IISD, "Summary of the Second Session of the INC for the Elaboration of an International Convention to Combat Desertification, 13–24 September 1993," *Earth Negotiations Bulletin* vol. 4, no. 22 (September 30, 1993): 11.

162 IISD, "Summary of the Fifth Session of the INC," 9–10.

163 Detailed and updated information on the convention, including its text, history, operation, current parties, and other issues, can be found on the regime's official website: www.unccd.int.

164 For more information on the challenges the convention faced, see IISD, "Summary of the Second Conference of the Parties to the Convention to Combat Desertification, 30 November–11 December 1998," *Earth Negotiations Bulletin* vol. 4, no. 127 (December 14, 1998).

165 IISD, "Summary of the Seventh Conference of the Parties to the Convention to Combat Desertification, 17–28 October 2005," *Earth Negotiations Bulletin* vol. 4, no. 186 (October 31, 2005): 16.

166 Ibid.

167 Even Fontaine Ortiz and Guangting Tang, *Review of the Management, Administration and Activities of the Secretariat of the United Nations Convention to Combat Desertification (UNCCD)* (Geneva: UN Joint Inspection Unit, 2005), 7.

168 Ibid.

169 UNCCD, "Ten-Year Strategic Plan and Framework to Enhance the Implementation of the Convention (2008–2018)," document ICCD/COP(8)/16/Add.1, October 23, 2007.

170 Ibid.

171 Charles Bassett and Joana Talafré, "Implementing the UNCCD: Towards a Recipe for Success," *Review of European Community and International Environmental Law* vol. 12, no. 3 (2003): 133–139.

172 Lindsay Stringer, et al., "Implementing the UNCCD: Participatory Challenges," *Natural Resources Forum* vol. 31 (2007): 198–211.

173 Pamela Chasek, et al., "Operationalizing Zero Net Land Degradation: The Next Stage in International Efforts to Combat Desertification?" *Journal of Arid Environments* vol. 112, Part A (January 2015): 5–13, doi: 10.1016/j.jaridenv.2014.05.020.

174 UN General Assembly, "The Future We Want," para. 206.
175 UN, *Transforming Our World: The 2030 Agenda for Sustainable Development*, A.69/L.85, August 15, 2015.
176 UNCCD, "Integration of the Sustainable Development Goals and Targets into the Implementation of the United Nations Convention to Combat Desertification and the Inter-Governmental Working Group Report on Land Degradation Neutrality," Decision 3/COP.12, October 23, 2015, www.unccd. int/Lists/OfficialDocuments/cop12/20add1eng.pdf.
177 UNCCD, "Land Matters for Climate: Reducing the Gap and Approaching the Target," November 2015, www.unccd.int/sites/default/files/documents/2015Nov_Land_matters_For_Climate_ ENG_0.pdf.
178 Noel Oettlé, "Land Degradation Neutrality and a New Fund to Advance the Concept," *Africa Report*, October 2, 2015, www.theafricareport.com/East-Horn-Africa/land-degradation-neutrality-and- a-new-fund-to-advance-the-concept.html.
179 UNCCD, "The UNCCD 2018–2030 Strategic Framework," decision 7/COP.13 (Annex), ICCD/ COP(13)/21/Add.1, October 23, 2017, www.unccd.int/sites/default/files/relevant-links/2018-08/ cop21add1_SF_EN.pdf.
180 Barron J. Orr, et al., *Scientific Conceptual Framework for Land Degradation Neutrality. A Report of the Science-Policy Interface* (Bonn, Germany: UNCCD, 2017).
181 For more information, see UNCCD, "LDN Target Setting Project wins IUCN Impact Award," www. unccd.int/news-events/ldn-target-setting-project-wins-iucn-impact-award.
182 UNCCD, "The LDN Fund," www.unccd.int/actions/impact-investment-fund-land-degradation- neutrality.
183 IDH The Sustainable Trade Initiative, "Land Degradation Neutrality (LDN) Fund Makes First Investment Towards Sustainable Land Management," Press release, January 28, 2019, www. idhsustainabletrade.com/news/land-degradation-neutrality-ldn-fund-makes-first-investment- towards-sustainable-land-management/.
184 Ronnie MacPherson/Greenstate, *Land Degradation Neutrality Target Setting Project: Report of the Terminal Evaluation* (Bonn: UNCCD/IUCN, March 2019), 5, www.unccd.int/sites/default/files/ relevant-links/2019-04/LDNTSP-EvalReport%20final.pdf.
185 IISD, "Summary of the Twelfth Session of the Conference of the Parties to the Convention to Combat Desertification, 12–23 October 2015," *Earth Negotiations Bulletin* vol. 4, no. 267 (October 27, 2015): 22.
186 IISD, "Summary of the Fourteenth Session of the Conference of the Parties to the Convention to Combat Desertification, 2–13 September 2019," *Earth Negotiations Bulletin* vol. 4, no. 290 (September 16, 2019).

Chapter 5

Effective Environmental Regimes

Obstacles and Opportunities

Abstract

Simply negotiating an agreement does not guarantee environmental protection. The most important measure of the effectiveness of an environmental regime—the extent to which it produces measurable improvements in the environment—is a function of three factors. First is regime design, particularly the strength of the key control provisions aimed at addressing the environmental threat, but also the provisions on reporting, monitoring, regime strengthening, noncompliance, and financial and technical assistance. Second is the level of implementation, the extent to which countries adopt appropriate legislation, regulations, and other policies to implement the agreement. Third is compliance, the degree to which countries and other actors actually observe these regulations. This chapter examines some of the factors that inhibit or promote effective international environmental regimes. The first section outlines obstacles that can make it difficult to create and implement effective regimes with strong, binding control measures. The second section looks at variables that inhibit effective implementation and compliance. The third section outlines potential avenues to improve compliance. The final section discusses options for increasing and improving the provision of financial and technical assistance available to help implement global environmental regimes.

Keywords: collective action problems, compliance, finance, implementation, obstacles, regimes, subsidies, system structure, technology transfer, markets

Environmental issues are an important part of international relations. Countries have negotiated more than 280 major multilateral environmental agreements (MEAs)—international agreements focused on environmental protection[1]—and more than 1150 multilateral and 1500 bilateral agreements that contain at least some provisions addressing the environment.[2] However, simply negotiating an agreement, as has been demonstrated in the previous two chapters, does not guarantee environmental protection.

The most important measure of the effectiveness of an environmental regime—the extent to which it produces measurable improvements in the environment—is a function of three factors. First is regime design, particularly the strength of the key control provisions aimed at addressing the environmental threat, but also the provisions on reporting, monitoring, regime strengthening, noncompliance, and financial and technical assistance (FTA). Second is the level of implementation, the extent to which countries and, to a lesser extent, international organizations adopt appropriate legislation, regulations, and other policies to implement the agreement. Third is compliance, the degree to which countries and other actors actually observe these regulations and the extent to which their actions conform to the explicit rules, norms, and procedures contained in the regime.[3]

This chapter examines some of the factors that inhibit or promote effective international environmental regimes. The first section outlines obstacles that can make it difficult to create and implement effective regimes with strong, binding control measures. These obstacles primarily relate to factors at the international level. The second section looks at variables that inhibit effective implementation and compliance. These primarily concern national-level issues. The third section outlines potential avenues to improve compliance. The final section discusses options for increasing and improving the provision of financial and technical assistance available to help implement global environmental regimes.

Obstacles to Creating Effective Environmental Regimes

One can distinguish eight major categories of obstacles that can inhibit creation of strong and effective global environmental regimes: (1) systemic or structural obstacles that stem from the structure of the international system, the structure of international law, and the structure of the global economic system; (2) a lack of necessary and sufficient conditions—in particular, public or official concern, a hospitable contractual environment, and capacity; (3) lowest-common-denominator problems; (4) time-horizon conflicts; (5) obstacles that stem from common characteristics of global environmental issues; (6) obstacles that result from the interconnections of environmental issues; (7) regime design difficulties; and (8) changing views on how to apply the principle of common but differentiated responsibilities (CBDR).[4] Of course, when we think about these categories, it is important to see them as broad, indicative, and heuristic rather than exhaustive and exclusive (see Box 5.1). The categories and individual causal factors are interrelated, and their individual and relative impacts vary significantly across countries and issue areas. They also do not prevent effective policy; they simply make it more difficult to achieve.

Systemic Obstacles

Some impediments to creating strong global environmental regimes result from inherent elements of the global political, ecological, legal, and economic systems. One of the broadest is the anarchical structure of international politics. Anarchy, as used here, means the absence of hierarchy, specifically the absence of a world government with recognized authority to maintain order and make rules. For thousands of years, notable statesmen, philosophers, historians, and political scientists have argued that aspects of this structure have broad consequences for international relations.[5] In particular, states tend to believe they can rely only on self-help to ensure their safety, states usually attempt to balance the power of other states through alliances and armaments, states prefer independence over interdependence, and states often find it difficult to achieve effective international cooperation.[6]

The last consequence is perhaps the most relevant to environmental regimes. Just as in security or economic issues, system structure places pressures on state actors that can make it difficult to create effective environmental regimes (although to a far lesser extent than in security issues). Strong states sometimes attempt to dictate terms to weaker states. States worry that other countries might face fewer costs from an agreement (even if both sides benefit environmentally) or that others might gain more economically or politically.[7] For example, President Trump withdrew the United States from the Paris Climate Agreement, in part, due to concern for its relative economic impacts, arguing that the United States would suffer competitively if it reduced greenhouse gases (GHGs) and gave financial assistance to developing countries but China did not. The administration of George W. Bush refused to join the Kyoto Protocol for the same reason.

❖ BOX 5.1   CATEGORIES OF PROMINENT OBSTACLES TO CREATING EFFECTIVE ENVIRONMENTAL REGIMES

Systemic Obstacles

- Anarchical structure of the international political system
- Incongruence of global political and ecological systems
- Incongruence of fundamental principles of international law and fundamental requirements for effective environmental policy
- Aspects of the structure of international economic systems

Absence of Necessary Conditions

- Inadequate concern
- Inhospitable contractual environments
- Insufficient capacity

Lowest-Common-Denominator Problems

- Strength and effectiveness of an environmental regime depends on securing the agreement, participation, and compliance of veto states

Time-Horizon Conflicts

- Time-consuming process of global policy development and implementation
- Incongruent timescales among environmental systems and most political and corporate systems

Characteristics of Global Environmental Issues

- Links to important economic and social activities and interests
- Unequal adjustment costs
- Scientific complexity and uncertainty
- Time-horizon conflicts
- Different core beliefs
- Large number of actors

Interconnections Between Environmental Issues

- Successfully addressing one problem can require addressing one or more separate but interrelated problems
- Solutions to one issue may exacerbate problems in another issue area

Regime Design Difficulties

- Effective regime design is difficult
- Other political and economic issues influence regime design

Changing Views on the Principle of Common but Differentiated Responsibilities

- Global economic and ecological developments have altered how some countries seek to operationalize this principle

States can fail to agree when some fear that others might "double-cross" them by not fulfilling regime obligations or paying their share of the costs.[8] States sometimes try to free ride and enjoy the benefits produced by others without contributing their fair share, for example, by continuing to emit a certain pollutant when others have agreed to stop, the fear of which can scuttle an agreement or render it ineffective.[9] States sometimes have incentives to pursue policies that appear rational on their own but that result in harming or destroying a common-pool resource, resulting in a "tragedy of the commons."[10] A current example is depletion of ocean fisheries. Many countries allow fishing fleets to catch as much fish as they can in international waters, which is good for them individually in the short run, even though the resource is depleted for everyone in the long run. States sometimes fail to locate mutually advantageous policies because of suspicions, a lack of information, market failure,[11] or misperception of the motives, intentions, or actions of other states.[12] Governments can also compromise environmental negotiations by linking them to unrelated international or domestic political, security, and economic issues.

Another systemic or structural obstacle is the lack of congruence among the global political and ecological systems. The structure of the global political system, which comprises independent sovereign states, is incongruent with ecological systems and not well suited to address complex, interdependent, global environmental problems whose causes, impacts, and solutions transcend political boundaries. Air and water pollution spreads easily to other countries. Persistent organic pollutants (POPs) released in the United States or Mexico affect people, animals, and ecosystems in northern Canada. Some of the mercury released from coal-fired power plants in China, India, Indonesia, and other countries is absorbed and concentrated in fish eaten by people all over the world.

This structural conflict has affected negotiations on global and regional commons issues— such as the atmosphere (ozone depletion and climate change) and the high seas (fisheries and whales)—as well as negotiations on transboundary air and water pollution. For example, upwind and downwind states can hold different views about appropriate rules to control air pollution, as was apparent in efforts to develop specific protocols to the Convention on Long-Range Transboundary Air Pollution and in the US–Canada acid rain negotiations. Similar problems exist in the management of transboundary waterways. Of the more than 260 river basins around the world, one-third of them are shared by more than two countries, and nineteen major river basins are shared by five or more states.[13] This significantly complicates efforts to manage pollution, overfishing, and sustainable use. For example, ten African countries rely on the Nile River and its tributaries. Cooperative management efforts date back to 1902, but pollution, potential overuse, and other disputes threaten the river's health. Egypt at times even threatened the possibility of military action against upstream countries Sudan, Ethiopia, and Uganda for actions or proposals that it perceived as illegal or excessive diversions of water from the Nile.

A similar conflict exists between the foundations of international law and the requirements for effective international environmental policy. Perhaps the most fundamental principle of international law is sovereignty. States have nearly unassailable legal control over activities within their borders, including the use of natural resources. At the same time, however, legitimate actions within one country can create environmental problems for another. Consequently, effective international environmental policy often requires limiting what a state does within its own borders.

This conflict is embodied in Principle 21 of the 1972 Stockholm Declaration, often cited as one of the most important foundations of modern international environmental law. It reads:

> States have, in accordance with the Charter of the United Nations and the principles of international law, the sovereign right to exploit their own resources pursuant to their own environmental policies, and the responsibility to ensure that activities within their jurisdiction or control do not cause damage to the environment of other states or of areas beyond the limits of national jurisdiction.[14]

This principle later became Principle 2 of the 1992 Rio Declaration, but with the words "and developmental" inserted before "policies," making it even more self-contradictory.

Overcoming the inherent tension captured in this principle is one of the most fundamental challenges of global environmental politics. Many states strongly resist regime provisions that, although beneficial to the environment, compromise their national sovereignty. The debate over a forest convention has been strongly affected by states wanting to ensure that they maintain clear sovereignty over their forest resources. Concerns about potential infringements on national sovereignty led to the inclusion of veto clauses that allow each party to block third-party adjudication under the Basel Convention.[15] China, India, and the United States have argued that efforts to curtail GHG emissions should not hamper their right to economic growth or use of domestic coal reserves.

Some argue that elements of the international economic system present an inherent, structural impediment to creating and implementing strong and effective global environmental policy.[16] Different discussions along these lines point to the system's emphasis on resource extraction, globalization, free trade, lowest-cost production, low-cost labor, high levels of consumption and consumerism, and, especially, the failure to include the economic and other costs produced by environmental degradation (externalities) in the cost of activities and products that cause the degradation.

Some aspects of these arguments seem well founded. For example, few of the economic costs associated with the environmental and human health impacts of using toxic chemicals or burning coal or gasoline are included in their price. These costs are passed on to society as a whole rather than paid by the actors actually producing the pollution. Thus, there is little economic incentive for an individual company to reduce pollution when everyone pays its costs. There is an increasing consensus among theorists and politicians from across the political spectrum on the need to include the economic costs of environmental degradation into the larger economic system, although they often reach different conclusions about how to accomplish this.

Many also agree that the emphasis placed by certain international economic forces on developing countries to maximize resource extraction, pay off foreign debts, and industrialize as quickly as possible has produced serious environmental problems. The ultimate impact of free trade and economic integration on certain aspects of the environment also faces scrutiny, particularly when domestic environmental laws, such as the European Union (EU) ban on Canadian fur imports from animals caught in leg-hold traps, are overruled by free-trade rules under the World Trade Organization (WTO).[17] (See Chapter 6.)

Yet it is probably too simplistic to assert that the global economic system only inhibits strong environmental regimes. Indeed, when properly harnessed, these same forces can support effective regimes. For example, in the expansion of the ozone regime, the global economic system accelerated the introduction of more environmentally friendly technology into developing countries much more quickly than many had expected. The financial power amassed by the global insurance industry supports stronger action on climate change. Free-trade rules and economic integration have likely improved overall energy efficiency in Europe. Introducing carbon taxes and similar measures, while lowering other taxes, appears to increase demand for clean energy[18] and to decouple increased economic growth from increased GHG emissions.[19] Thus, the key may be to examine, case by case, how economic interests and systems run counter to, or support, the goals or operation of particular environmental policies rather than reflexively assume that they necessarily inhibit effective environmental regimes.

Absence of Necessary Conditions: Concern, Contractual Environment, and Capacity

As discussed by Peter Haas, Robert Keohane, and Marc Levy, effective environmental regimes require three necessary conditions.[20] First, there must be adequate levels of concern within governments, and perhaps among the public at large, so that states devote resources to examine and address the problem and implement potential solutions. Environmental problems compete with many issues for space on national and international agendas. Concern must exist for the issue-definition, fact-finding, bargaining, and regime-strengthening phases to occur and be successfully completed.

Second, there must be a sufficiently hospitable contractual environment, so that states can gather together, negotiate with reasonable ease and costs, make credible commitments, reach agreement on new policies, and monitor each other's behavior in implementing those policies. In other words, if too many of the negative consequences of system structure, such as fears of cheating or free riding, are present, or if transaction costs (time, money, and effort involved in negotiating a treaty) are too high, then creating strong and effective agreements is difficult.

Third, states must possess the scientific, political, economic, and administrative capacity to understand the threat, participate in creating the global regime, and then implement and ensure compliance with the regime's principles, norms, and rules. Capacity is essentially a measure of the necessary resources a country possesses to address a particular issue, as well as the physical and political ability to deploy those resources effectively.

Concern, contractual environment, and capacity are not obstacles themselves. The presence of each is a necessary but insufficient condition. Thus, their absence significantly inhibits, and sometimes can prevent, the creation and implementation of strong environmental regimes. The concepts are easy to oversimplify, but concern, contractual environment, and capacity encapsulate important, even critical, causal factors and are interconnected with many of the other issues discussed in this chapter.

Lowest-Common-Denominator Problems

Once states begin negotiations to create or strengthen a global environmental regime, an obstacle can emerge: the lowest-common-denominator problem.[21] This problem results from how international environmental negotiations work, the requirements for effective international environmental policy, the structural obstacles outlined previously, the varying levels of concern for particular environmental issues, the need for consensus, and the presence of veto states.

All states are sovereign entities and can choose whether or not to join an environmental agreement. However, because active participation by many countries is required to address global environmental problems, the countries most concerned often need support from countries with far less interest. Thus, an environmental treaty can only be as strong as the least cooperative state allows it to be. The regime's overall effectiveness, thus, is undermined by the compromises made in persuading these states, the veto states, to participate.

For example, during negotiation of the 1991 Protocol on Environmental Protection to the Antarctic Treaty, which protects Antarctica from possible mineral exploitation, opposition from the United States resulted in a fifty-year moratorium rather than the initially proposed permanent protection. As discussed in Chapter 3, from 1977 to 1989, the European Community (EC) acted as a veto state in the ozone-layer negotiations, forcing lead states to accept much weaker rules in the 1985 Vienna Convention and 1987 Montreal Protocol than they had sought. During the Stockholm Convention negotiations, countries critical to its long-term success insisted on specific exemptions so that they could continue using certain POPs, even though the convention calls for eliminating their production and use. This process repeats itself as parties add chemicals to the convention. The lowest-common-denominator problem continues to impede the climate regime. All major emitters of GHGs must cooperate for the regime to succeed. For many years, China, India, and the United States, among others, were reluctant to take actions to curb their domestic emissions. This limited the ability of Europe, the Alliance of Small Island States (AOSIS), and other lead states to move forward with an aggressive emissions-reduction agreement.

Decision-making procedures in many regimes require or strongly encourage consensus on key issues. This also creates lowest-common-denominator problems because it allows one or more states to block agreements that would strengthen a regime, even when the vast majority of countries support the change. For example, in 2015, Sudan was the only country that objected to adding the pesticide fenthion to the prior informed consent (PIC) procedure that operates under the Rotterdam Convention, even after being told by other African countries that listing would provide easy access to more information and not prevent its use. Despite its being inconsequential to the success of the PIC procedure overall, Sudan continued to block adding fenthion in 2017 and 2019 (three other countries joined Sudan in 2019).[22] India was the only country that objected to, and thus prevented, the PIC listing of trichlorfon in 2015. Chile and Indonesia prevented the listing of the severely hazardous pesticide formulation of paraquat dichloride in 2019 despite strong statements of support for listing by other countries. For many years, Kazakhstan, Kyrgyzstan, Russia, and Zimbabwe have led a relatively small number of countries in blocking the addition of chrysotile asbestos to the PIC procedure, despite a large majority of countries supporting the proposal and consistent calls by the World Health Organization (WHO) not only for its listing but also for more countries to ban the substance.

Voting procedures can overcome this type of lowest common denominator. However, in situations in which a regime allows voting (such as the Convention on International Trade in Endangered Species of Wild Fauna and Flora (CITES), whaling, and POPs on some issues), states whose participation is essential to success can create lowest-common-denominator problems by threatening not to participate if the regime is strengthened by a vote. There can also be political costs to forcing a vote. Most treaties have language emphasizing consensus, and once a norm has been established against voting, countries are reluctant to use the voting rules, even in the presence of overwhelming majorities, for fear of harming the contractual environment or creating resentment or mistrust that might harm regime implementation. For example, the Montreal Protocol allows voting, but it has never been used, even when as few as two countries disagreed. Perhaps as a result, however, a norm developed that a single country will not block consensus. In other cases, such as the Convention on Biological Diversity (CBD), the United Nations Framework Convention on Climate Change (UNFCCC), and the UN Convention to Combat Desertification (UNCCD), the voting rules have yet to be adopted and, as a result, all decisions must be taken by consensus, creating even more lowest-common-denominator agreements.

Time-Horizon Conflicts

Another category of obstacles relates to the incongruent timescales of policy development and environmental issues. The process to create and implement effective global environmental policy is neither easy nor speedy. It often operates, as one long-time observer noted, like a slow boat.[23] The international agenda must be set, negotiations convened, appropriate policies identified, agreements reached, implementation strategies agreed to, treaties ratified by enough countries so that they can enter into force and be effective, national and international policies implemented and reported on, environmental problems monitored, and international policies revised in light of new data and lessons learned. The common practice of starting with a framework convention and adopting subsequent protocols takes even longer.

Each step in this process can be time-consuming. As discussed in Chapter 3, the environmental problems posed by hazardous waste shipments were identified in the 1970s, but the 1989 Basel Convention did not come into effect until 1992, and the Ban Amendment, which was adopted in 1995, only entered into force in 2019. The United Nations Convention on the Law of the Sea took nearly ten years to negotiate and another twelve to receive sufficient ratifications to enter into force. The International Convention for the Prevention of

Pollution from Ships (MARPOL) experienced a ten-year time lag from its negotiation to its entry into force, despite the decades of collaborative efforts on oil pollution leading up to it. Scientists discovered the threat to the ozone layer in 1974, but negotiations did not begin until 1982, the first binding controls did not come into force until 1988, developing countries did not have to phase out most uses of chlorofluorocarbons (CFCs) until 2010, and hydrochlorofluorocarbons (HCFCs) will not be phased out until 2030.

Knowledge of the greenhouse effect goes back to 1824, when Joseph Fourier, a French mathematician and physicist, discovered that gases in the atmosphere likely increase the surface temperature of the earth. In 1859, John Tyndall, an Irish physicist, further explained the ability of various gases, including carbon dioxide (CO_2) and water vapor, to absorb radiant heat, proving that the earth's atmosphere has a natural greenhouse effect. In 1896, Svante Arrhenius, a Swedish scientist, published an article suggesting that temperatures would rise 5°C if atmospheric CO_2 doubled. In 1960, Charles Keeling published data clearly showing that CO_2 levels were rising. Nevertheless, formal negotiations on the UNFCCC did not begin until 1991.

Yet environmental issues do not wait for the policy process. As negotiations continue, more species become extinct, forests are cut down, land is degraded, GHGs are emitted into the atmosphere, toxic chemicals are released, and hazardous wastes are not properly managed, making it even more difficult to create and implement effective regimes.

Time-horizon conflicts also stem from an incongruence of environmental systems and political and corporate systems: most political and corporate reward systems operate on much shorter timescales. Addressing environmental problems effectively often requires an informed, long-term perspective. However, because the most serious consequences of many environmental problems may occur in the future, policymakers and other actors sometimes find it difficult to create or implement policies that carry short-term costs even if these actions will prevent much higher costs in the future. In addition, environmental issues often do not develop in linear, predictable patterns, nor do their impacts occur simultaneously in all regions and in all countries. This can mask their global impact or cause some actors to remain less concerned about addressing them immediately.

At the same time, policymakers have shorter time horizons. Major political figures in the United States, for example, face elections every two years (members of the House of Representatives), four years (president and governors), or six years (senators). Many corporations release reports on their revenues, costs, and profits every three months—reports that can significantly affect their stock price and executive compensation. Thus, even if every political figure and corporate leader wanted to address an environmental issue, the time horizons for their most immediate approval processes (elections and quarterly reports) are not in tune with the long-term perspective required.

Biodiversity loss and climate change are obvious examples of issues that are affected by time-horizon conflicts. Efforts to add additional substances to the POPs regime also face this problem. Although thousands of chemical spills occur each year,[24] sometimes resulting in exposure to POPs and other toxic substances, the most widespread threats posed by many chemicals, including potential impacts on reproductive health, may only occur in the future as a result of long-term exposure from their slow accumulation in humans and the environment.[25] Preventing these impacts requires accepting certain current costs for the sake of likely, but future, benefits, something that history indicates is not easy.

Time-horizon conflicts are increasingly important because some environmental issues likely possess critical tipping points beyond which effective policy becomes far more difficult and perhaps impossible. The point at which enough CO_2 enters the atmosphere that significant climate change will be impossible to avoid becomes closer each year, and avoiding it requires global emissions to peak as soon as possible.[26] Fish stocks may decline gradually but then collapse rapidly if too many fish have been harvested. Stocks then take many years to recover, if they recover at all. Once cut, many tropical forests cannot recover into

Photo 5.1 Members of civil society demonstrated in the corridors to remind Convention on Biological Diversity delegates that the decisions made at COP14 will impact future generations.

Courtesy Kiara Worth, IISD/*Earth Negotiations Bulletin*, http://enb.iisd.org

the same ecosystems. Land and water can become so contaminated with radioactivity or toxic chemicals that it is unusable for decades or longer. Coral reefs take centuries to grow. These critical tipping points could enhance the urgency of reaching effective agreements, but they also represent a time-horizon obstacle beyond which truly effective policy may be impossible.

Characteristics of Global Environmental Issues

Another set of obstacles stems from common characteristics inherent in global environmental problems. Although they are certainly not unique to environmental issues, and have impacts that are interconnected and also vary across countries and issue areas, these characteristics are important elements of global environmental politics and have the capacity to exacerbate many of the other obstacles outlined in this chapter. As noted earlier, these categories should be seen as indicative and heuristic rather than exhaustive and exclusive.

One of the most critical characteristics is that environmental issues are inextricably linked to important economic and political interests. Therefore, environmental negotiations are not independent of other economic and political activities and interests. Indeed, environmental issues exist because of these activities and interests. Environmental problems are produced as externalities of individuals, corporations, and nations pursuing other goals and interests. They result from important local, corporate, national, and international economic and political activities, such as energy production, mining, manufacturing, farming, fishing, transportation, resource consumption, livestock husbandry, urbanization, weapons production, and military conflict.

Few, if any, individuals or organizations harm the environment as an end in itself. People do not get up in the morning and announce, "I intend to pollute today." What people do say is, "I intend to manufacture, to produce energy, to farm, to drive my car to work." Environmental degradation is a consequence of these otherwise legitimate pursuits. The fact that many of these activities could be pursued successfully while doing less harm to the environment does not erase the links among the issues.

Creating strong international environmental regimes, therefore, often requires addressing economic, social, and security interests that are important to certain countries or interest groups. Regardless of whether these interests are justified, the links create obstacles to effective action. The presence of important economic interests can lower relative concern, make veto states more determined, and cause powerful domestic economic actors to lobby for their views. They can also enhance fears of free riding, create more opportunities for positional bargaining, and otherwise harm the contractual environment.

There are many examples of the obstacles posed by the links between environmental problems and economic interests. Protecting the earth's remaining biodiversity requires addressing the economic and political pressures that cause habitat destruction, something that has been impossible to achieve in a binding global agreement. In the Nagoya Protocol negotiations and the marine biodiversity negotiations, developing countries called for fair and equitable sharing of benefits arising from the use of genetic resources with the countries of origin and with local and indigenous communities, whereas foreign companies, collectors, researchers, and other users who profit greatly from derivatives of these resources preferred the status quo, whereby they could gain access essentially for free. Addressing climate change requires significant changes in fossil fuel consumption. Complete protection of the ozone layer requires a near total phase-out of methyl bromide emissions, something that major agricultural and shipping interests, including those in the United States, have been hesitant to do.

Economic links even impact scientifically based regime procedures. For example, as discussed in Chapter 3, the Stockholm Convention tasks the thirty-one members of the Persistent Organic Pollutants Review Committee with determining, on the basis of available scientific information, whether a nominated chemical meets the criteria for being considered a POP and then evaluating whether the risks it poses to human health or the environment meet the criteria required for adding the chemical to the treaty's control regime. Information related to economic and social issues is to be considered later in the process and especially by the full Conference of the Parties (COP). However, concerns for national economic and political interests have increasingly affected the work of the committee, complicating and delaying decisions that should have been based entirely on scientific information.[27] Similarly, the analogous technical subsidiary body under the Rotterdam Convention, the Chemical Review Committee, has also seen increasing politicization of what was designed to be a science-based committee.[28]

Sometimes the linkages are particularly difficult to argue against, even for strong proponents of an environmental regime. For example, the total elimination of the POP dichlorodiphenyltrichloroethane (DDT) would prevent its use as an inexpensive tool in the battle against malaria. Even those countries most committed to addressing POPs under the Stockholm Convention agree that this use of DDT should continue (although with methods that reduce its environmental impact) while alternative products and processes are deployed. Similarly, although strongly agreeing in 2009 that the toxic chemical perfluorooctane sulfonate (PFOS) should be eliminated as part of the expansion of the Stockholm Convention, the United States and Switzerland also successfully argued that an exception should be granted so that small amounts of the substance can be used in certain medical devices until replacements are developed. During negotiation of the mercury treaty, governments accepted arguments by African countries, supported by information provided by the WHO, that they should be allowed to continue using a very effective and low-cost preservative for vaccines that contains trace amounts of mercury.[29]

A second characteristic, and one closely linked to the first, is unequal adjustment costs. Addressing an environmental problem means changing the economic, political, and/or cultural activities that ultimately cause the problem. Making these changes, or adjustments, can produce many benefits, but they also carry different economic and political costs in different countries. These variations can reflect differences in a country's contribution to the problem, level of economic development, national enforcement capabilities, existing regulations, resource base, trade profile, method of energy production, and transportation policy; the political and economic influence of an industry within a country; and a host of other factors.

Large variations in adjustment costs in countries essential to a regime act as obstacles to creating a strong regime. Indeed, they are part of the reason why veto coalitions form. In addition to concerns about the costs they will bear, states often also consider potential positional advantages or disadvantages produced by the relative costs to be borne by other states. Thus, states may reject solutions that ask them to bear a larger burden than other states. Alternatively, they may demand special compensation for joining the regime, which in turn can weaken the regime.

Unequal adjustment costs exist in all of the regimes outlined in Chapters 3 and 4, and addressing their impact is a critical and difficult part of global environmental politics. During negotiation of both the 1997 Kyoto Protocol and the 2015 Paris Climate Agreement, many governments argued that their different levels of industrialization, energy profiles, transportation infrastructures, core industries, and even local temperatures made adhering to one set of mandatory reductions in CO_2 emissions inherently unfair. As a result, the Kyoto Protocol contained different, modest targets for developed countries and no mandatory reductions of CO_2 emissions for developing countries, while the Paris Agreement did not include specific mandatory GHG reductions for any country; and the impact of concerns for unequal adjustment costs are vividly reflected in the variation among the nationally determined contributions (NDCs). Although using renewable energy sources to replace fossil fuels will reduce CO_2 emissions, create new jobs, reduce air pollution, and produce far greater long-term benefits for most countries and the planet as a whole, some countries, regions, and companies that rely heavily on fossil fuels will experience higher costs during the transition than those that do not. Controls on carbon emissions also mean enormous adjustment costs for countries and companies whose economies depend on utilizing relatively inexpensive domestic sources of, or exporting, oil, natural gas, or coal, including Australia, Canada, China, India, Iran, Russia, Saudi Arabia, and the United States.

Different governments consistently seek to exclude certain substances from the toxic chemicals regime or press for special exemptions, arguing that a particular industry using the substance would bear higher and unfair burdens if forced to comply with the same standards as companies in other countries that do not use the substance. China, India, Indonesia, and others objected to rules requiring them to install state-of-the-art devices to prevent mercury emissions from existing coal-fired power plants in part because they would face higher costs than the United States and the EU, where such devices were already common.[30] Japan, Norway, and other countries that permit whaling argue that the economic, cultural, or scientific adjustment costs of stopping all whaling would place unfair burdens on particular groups. Some developing countries express concern that efforts to protect biodiversity will include attempts to prevent their use of biodiverse areas for traditional types of economic development—costs that most industrialized countries would not have to bear.

A third obstacle is that environmental issues often involve significant scientific complexity and uncertainty regarding their scope, severity, impact, or time frame. Scientific complexity can challenge the capacity of government bureaucracies to understand the problem and design and implement effective solutions. Scientific uncertainty about the precise time frame or another aspect of an environmental problem can undermine concern and, perhaps most importantly, allow other, more certain economic or political interests to be prioritized. Complexity and uncertainty can lead states to perceive payoffs differently, perhaps reducing incentives to risk cooperation and increasing incentives either to free ride or to ignore the problem altogether, thereby harming the contractual environment.

For example, opponents of strong policies to mitigate climate change emphasize not only the costs of such an agreement (including the links to important economic interests and unequal adjustment costs) but also what they argue are important uncertainties regarding the severity of the problem (the vast majority of scientists and the Intergovernmental Panel on

Climate Change do not share this view). Uncertainty about the precise impacts of long-term, low-level exposure to some toxic chemicals inhibits the chemicals regime from expanding more quickly, despite increasing evidence that concerns many experts. Biodiversity loss, biosafety, and ozone depletion are some of the other issues for which scientific complexity and uncertainty slowed or prevented the creation of strong regimes.

Fourth, states and groups within states sometimes possess different core religious, cultural, or political beliefs and values relevant to environmental issues. Such conflicting beliefs and values can limit the creation of sufficient transnational concern, block potential policies, cause some actors not to participate, and necessitate compromises that weaken the resulting regime. For example, as discussed in Chapter 4, some groups in Iceland, Japan, and Norway have strong cultural links to whaling. They do not view it as a moral issue and thus object to international attempts to curtail their whaling as inappropriate foreign intrusion on their rights and beliefs. Some individuals in Asia believe that products from endangered animal species, such as rhino horn, have important medicinal properties. Even though no corroborating scientific evidence exists, this creates a market for certain endangered species and their products and undercuts international controls designed to protect them. Some political ideologies treat economic development and freedom from government regulations as higher priorities than environmental protection and resist cooperative solutions that they believe would restrict economic or personal freedom.

Fifth, large numbers of actors must cooperate to create and implement effective global environmental policy. This reality increases the impact of other obstacles, including system structure, lowest-common-denominator issues, and time-horizon conflicts. Social science has long acknowledged that reaching cooperative solutions to common problems becomes more

Photo 5.2 Representatives of the Environmental Integrity Group (Georgia, Liechtenstein, Monaco, Mexico, South Korea, and Switzerland) wear shirts saying "science is not negotiable" at the Bonn Climate Change Conference in 2019.

Courtesy Kiara Worth, IISD/*Earth Negotiations Bulletin*, http://enb.iisd.org

difficult as the number of actors increases. More actors mean more heterogeneity of interests. The larger the number of actors, the more likely it is that an agreement, if concluded at all, will be partial in at least one of three ways: (1) covering only some of the agenda topics, (2) leaving some disagreement latent in an ambiguous text, or (3) being signed and accepted only by some states. In addition, the risk of suboptimal outcomes, or lowest-common-denominator agreements, seems to increase as the number of actors increases.[31]

Large numbers can also increase incentives for noncompliance because of reduced fears of detection, particularly if the short-term adjustment costs are high or uneven. This can be particularly dangerous to the success of a regime that seeks to protect the commons, such as the oceans or atmosphere, which all can use but no one controls. If some states fear that others will cheat, they may believe they face a use-it-or-lose-it scenario that compels them to use the resource, leading to its more rapid degradation.[32] The situation is compounded in cases in which many states need to control many private actors in order for the environmental policy to succeed. CITES faces obstacles to compliance because the number of potential violators is so large, especially with the advent of internet sales of endangered species and their products. An immense number of ships can violate ocean pollution and fishing agreements. Thousands of companies in countries around the world work with toxic chemicals or create hazardous waste. The huge number of GHG emissions sources complicates global policy making.

Interconnections Among Environmental Issues

Environmental issues do not exist in isolation. Causes, impacts, consequences, and solutions are often interconnected in surprising ways. Sometimes these connections inhibit successful action. This is the case when one environmental problem exacerbates another, making the problem more difficult to solve because long-term success in one issue also requires effectively addressing the other issue. For example, climate change threatens millions of species with extinction, making the preservation of biodiversity more difficult. Coral reefs face serious threats from warming seas, increased runoff from land degraded by deforestation, and pollution released by industrial facilities. Solving one threat to a reef will not save it unless the others are also solved. Deforestation and land degradation are major contributors to biodiversity loss, through habitat destruction, and to climate change, through the release of CO_2 into the atmosphere and because deforested land can no longer act as a carbon sink by absorbing CO_2 from the air. Thus, effective long-term global policies on biodiversity or climate change will also require action to combat deforestation and land degradation.

Interconnections also create obstacles if addressing one environmental problem exacerbates another. For example, replacing coal-fired power plants with nuclear power plants decreases GHG emissions but creates the potential for immense environmental problems if radiation is released as a result of a natural disaster (as happened in the aftermath of the tsunami that hit Japan in 2011), an accident at the plant (as occurred at the Chernobyl nuclear power plant in Ukraine in 1986), a terrorist attack, or a leak from the storage of nuclear waste. Dams help address climate change by producing electricity without burning fossil fuels, but some also produce harmful environmental impacts such as riparian habitat loss, erosion, loss of river animal and fish populations, and potential declines in water quality. Biofuels can be used to replace gasoline and reduce GHGs, but some biofuels, such as those made from corn or other crops requiring good soil, divert land from food production, often require significant quantities of water and fertilizer, and use large amounts of energy to gather, transport, and refine into fuel.[33]

Several chemicals developed to replace ozone-depleting substances (ODS) exacerbate other environmental problems. As outlined in Chapter 3, companies developed HCFCs and hydrofluorocarbons (HFCs) as substitutes for CFCs. These chemicals proved crucial to protecting the ozone layer while requiring relatively small changes to the huge refrigeration and air-conditioning industries. Unfortunately, most HCFCs and HFCs are stronger GHGs than the CFCs they replaced. Thus, their invention and increased use, which occurred only as part of global attempts to protect the ozone layer, augmented climate change. Similarly, when China replaced halons, the fire suppressants that are also powerful ODS, it did so in part by using firefighting foam mixes that included PFOS. As outlined in Chapter 3, in 2009, parties to the Stockholm Convention added PFOS to the list of chemicals slated for elimination, but China and others argued successfully that an exemption should be granted for use in firefighting foam because it would not be economical to phase out this fire-control substance so soon after eliminating halons. Thus, one solution to the problem of halons as ozone-depleting chemicals exacerbated the problems of toxins in the environment and complicated policy discussions under the Stockholm Convention.

Regime Design Difficulties

Another obstacle to effective global environmental regimes is sometimes the design of the regime itself. As Ron Mitchell puts it, "Regime design matters."[34] Control measures and reporting requirements that are too complex or vague might not be implemented correctly. Treaties without enough flexibility cannot be adjusted in response to new scientific findings. Treaties with too much flexibility may be changed so often that some governments and industries, frustrated with the inability to make long-term plans, may leave or ignore the regime.

Regime design is difficult. All of the issues outlined in the previous sections can inhibit the design of an effective regime. The process requires understanding: the science of the environmental issue, including its causes and consequences, how it interacts with other issues, and how it will evolve over time; the economic and social activities that give rise to the problem and will be affected by it; how to address the issue so that a long-term solution is environmentally, economically, and politically possible; and how to design the solution in the form of an international regime that can be implemented effectively at the national level. This last point is often overlooked. No matter how well-meaning a treaty's intention or how strong its control provisions, it will not yield measurable environmental benefits if states do not, or cannot, implement it.

Equally important is the fact that regimes are negotiated more than they are designed—and negotiated by people and governments with concerns that might run counter to the requirements for a perfectly crafted environmental regime. Environmental treaties are not designed by a small group of experts whose only goal is to eliminate a global environmental problem. In reality, treaties result from negotiations involving hundreds of government representatives from different types of ministries whose collective job is to address the environmental issue but whose individual instructions also reflect concerns for other national and international economic and political goals.

Government negotiators operate within frameworks established by instructions and briefing books given to them by their governments. People from different parts of the government with different perspectives participate in creating these frameworks. In the United States, for example, although Environmental Protection Agency officials might see the negotiations as a means to address the environmental issue, trade officials might want to make sure that a tough stand in the negotiations does not affect relations with a crucial trading partner or upset relationships important to an upcoming trade negotiation. State Department officials might object to a particular regime component, even if it would be very effective, for fear that it will set a precedent that could be demanded in negotiations on other issues. Congressional staff and White House domestic political advisers might not want policies that would upset key political allies or donors to political campaigns. Budget officials might insist on limiting provisions of FTA. None of this is necessarily improper—each person is simply attending to his or her government responsibility—but it does point out how these underlying complexities produce pressures that can influence national negotiating positions away from consensus on optimal regime design.

Similarly, government goals in global environmental negotiations are often broader than just addressing a specific environmental issue. Some developing countries might try to use the negotiations to obtain development assistance masked as environmental investments. Donor countries might try to limit financial obligations in general or to funnel assistance through the Global Environment Facility (GEF) because they think doing so will save money or that they might be able to influence GEF activities more easily than a stand-alone fund. Some governments might push against a particular principle—for example, the precautionary principle—because they do not want it to be accepted as a general principle of international law that could restrain their actions or negotiating positions on other issues. Some might support more monitoring of the issues and building global scientific networks solely as a means to increase scientific training in their countries. Others might push for a strong non-compliance regime because they support strong international adjudication procedures in general. Some countries might have disagreements with particular international organizations, nongovernmental organizations (NGOs), or other governments that affect their negotiating positions.

Thus, environmental regime design should not be seen as the equivalent of blueprints drawn by a small group of brilliant architects who specialize in building hospitals and have been given the time and money to create an outstanding facility that will address one particular disease. They are more like blueprints drawn by a group of several hundred architects who specialize in different types of design and who have been assigned the group task of designing a hospital to address a set of diseases. Plus, many of the architects have other jobs and must make sure that parts of the planned hospital can also be used as a bank, training facility, research center, school, police station, courthouse, travel agency, or construction company. Moreover, they do not agree on which of these other uses is the most important, they do not have enough land or money to construct a building that could do all of these things well, not all of them are particularly good architects, and they do not have a great deal of time before the disease spreads and more people die. Creating and implementing effective global environmental policy is challenging.

Changing Views on the Principle of Common but Differentiated Responsibilities

As discussed in Chapter 1, paradigms influence how environmental issues are viewed and potential policies developed and evaluated, but these paradigms are neither static nor universally shared. Paradigms can be challenged or replaced by alternative paradigms (e.g., the shift from frontier economics and the exclusionist paradigm to limits to growth and sustainable development). The internal definition of a paradigm or conceptions of how it should be put into practice can also change or come into dispute. To some extent, that has happened with the principle of CBDR.

The principle states that all countries have a common responsibility to address global environmental issues but also differentiated responsibilities to act depending on their contribution to the problem or greater financial and technological resources to address it. In many regimes (as shown in Chapters 3 and 4), this principle is reflected by providing developing countries with (1) more time to implement required control measures (e.g., in the ozone and climate regimes) or other provisions that provide them with greater flexibility or exemptions (the POPs regime); and (2) FTA and capacity-building provisions to help them implement regime rules (nearly all global regimes include these, although with varying degrees of specificity and effectiveness). Broad acceptance of CBDR and how to operationalize it within regime operations made some negotiations easier in that it provided a rubric to follow and allowed some discussions to take on elements of bilateral negotiations between industrialized and developing countries, which, although difficult, is theoretically easier than negotiations involving many different groups.

CBDR remains an accepted principle and paradigm in global environmental politics, but a number of developments have caused some countries to change their view regarding how it should be operationalized in specific agreements—from a principle centered on a single division between developing and industrialized countries to one that is more nuanced. These developments include the rapid economic rise of some large developing countries, especially China; the increasing contribution of these countries to many global environmental problems; improved understanding of the environmental vulnerabilities that different countries face; and the vast differences in the economic resources available to different states classified as developing countries—for example, Brazil, Kuwait, and China versus Malawi, Haiti, and Bangladesh. Although observations regarding these developments are empirically correct, their introduction has complicated negotiations on climate change, mercury, chemicals, and other issues.

In climate change, for example, the UNFCCC and the Kyoto Protocol created differentiated obligations for developed and developing countries based on CBDR. The Kyoto Protocol followed CBDR in establishing binding GHG reduction obligations only for industrialized countries. The United States refused to join the Kyoto Protocol in part because it did not establish binding GHG provisions for China and other large developing countries. Since then, China's economy has grown significantly, and its GHG emissions are now by far the largest in the world. This created calls by many countries, including some developing countries, for China and other large developing countries to control their emissions as part of the Paris Climate Agreement, with the understanding that industrialized countries still have to take the lead.

During the negotiation of the Minamata Convention, the United States stated clearly that application of the CBDR principle should not be based simply on whether a county was classified as developed or developing. This sentiment was echoed in different ways by several other developed countries, including the EU and Japan. As a result, no clear division was created for obligations to reduce mercury emissions solely on the basis of development status. During the negotiation of the Stockholm Convention, governments rejected the creation of separate control schedules for developing countries when adding new chemicals, agreeing that an extended timeline, like the one in the ozone regime, would simply shift the production and use of these chemicals to developing countries. As outlined in Chapter 3, the regime instead creates common restrictions with certain exemptions for which all countries can apply. In creating these exemptions, parties assess the situation of developing counties on a case-by-case basis, a more nuanced application of CBDR. In accordance with the traditional paradigm, developing countries in both the mercury and chemicals regimes can access FTA to implement different aspects of the treaties.

Although CBDR remains an important component of global environmental agreements, it is no longer always operationalized purely through a simple division of the world into two groups of countries. Although this likely leads to more effective policy in the long run, it can also pose an obstacle as it creates more coalitions, more options, and more disagreements about when and how the principle of CBDR should be operationalized.

Obstacles to Effective National Implementation of and Compliance with Global Environmental Regimes

Treaties contain many different types of obligations. The most important are sometimes referred to as substantive obligations, particularly obligations to cease or limit a specific activity such as GHG emissions, CFC production, or the release of certain toxic chemicals. Also important are a variety of procedural obligations, such as monitoring and reporting requirements. Compliance refers to whether countries adhere to the mandatory provisions of

---

❖ BOX 5.2   OBSTACLES TO EFFECTIVE NATIONAL IMPLEMENTATION

- Inadequate translation of regime rules into domestic policy
- Insufficient capacity to implement, administer, monitor, or enforce domestic policy
- Misperception of relevant cost and benefits
- Costs of compliance
- Poorly designed regimes
- Many regimes, little coordination

---

an environmental convention and the extent to which they follow through on the steps they have taken to implement these provisions.[35]

Global environmental regimes employ a variety of mechanisms to promote implementation and compliance. These include using binding rules instead of purely voluntary measures; providing eligible countries with FTA to build capacity and help them to fulfill specific regime obligations; requiring regular reporting by the parties; allowing for the public availability and Secretariat, COP, or independent reviews of such reports; reviewing regime implementation and effectiveness; calling noncomplying parties to account publicly; providing incentives; creating formal noncompliance procedures that have the potential to establish penalties or provide assistance; augmenting public education and raising awareness; sharing information; creating focused implementation programs that involve cooperation among the private sector, NGOs, international organizations, and governments; and using NGOs and international organizations to monitor compliance. Of course, not all regimes employ each measure, and their success varies significantly across regimes and among parties.

Most countries that sign and ratify an international convention do so with the intention of complying with its provisions.[36] Nevertheless, complete compliance sometimes turns out to be politically, technically, administratively, or financially impossible, even when a government remains committed to the regime, especially when there are provisions that allow for interpretation. Sometimes compliance becomes sufficiently difficult that a state decides to focus time, effort, and resources in other areas; that is, compliance is still possible, but a state chooses to reduce its effort to comply because of other priorities.

As attention turns from creating new global environmental regimes to implementing and strengthening existing ones, implementation and compliance become important issues. In addition to the general obstacles outlined earlier, the literature and developments within specific regimes suggests that noncompliance can be traced to several different broad categories of factors, including inadequate translation of regime rules into domestic law; insufficient capacity or commitment to implement, administer, monitor, or enforce relevant domestic policy; misperception of the relevant costs and benefits; the costs of compliance; inadequate FTA; poorly designed regimes; and the large number of environmental conventions and the uncoordinated web of requirements they have produced (see Box 5.2).[37] As with the discussion of the obstacles to creating strong and effective regimes, these implementation obstacles overlap significantly and are interrelated. They are also not listed in order of importance, because their impacts vary from country to country and issue to issue. Indeed, scholars and national officials have many different opinions about which obstacles are most important overall or most relevant to particular issue areas.

Inadequate Translation of Regime Rules into Domestic Policy

Some states are unable to or choose not to adopt the domestic legislation necessary to implement and fully comply with an international agreement. This can include failing to adopt some or all of the needed regulations or adopting poorly crafted regulations. For instance, Peter Sand noted that historically, "the main constraint on the implementation of CITES in each Party has been the need to create national legislation. Although this is an obligation under [CITES], several countries have not complied ... Others have only incomplete legislation."[38]

The failure to enact domestic law can stem from a variety of factors. Sometimes, domestic economic or political opposition that did not block a country from negotiating or signing a particular treaty can still prevent the country from ratifying it. If national ratification depends on approval by a legislative branch, as in the United States, then treaty ratification, and consequently, the translation of international regime rules into domestic law, can be prevented by interest groups or lawmakers opposed to its goals or means, by politicians seeking leverage to achieve other political ends, by an overburdened legislative agenda, or by conflicts over resource allocations. For example, since the 1990s, opposition from powerful interest groups and key senators has prevented the US Senate even from holding formal ratification votes on several key treaties, including the Biodiversity, Basel, Rotterdam, and Stockholm Conventions.

Even when a treaty is ratified, interest groups or the political opposition might still manage to prevent or weaken the necessary implementing legislation. Weak legislative and bureaucratic infrastructures or a lack of expertise can also prevent effective regulations from becoming law. The chemicals and wastes treaties, for example, require relatively sophisticated knowledge about toxic substances and their commercial uses, trade, and environmentally sound management to enact all of their provisions effectively into domestic law. Inefficient legislative procedures or political or economic instability also can keep states from fully or accurately enacting necessary domestic legislation. Finally, in democracies with nonintegrated federal structures, the federal government may not always have the jurisdiction to implement international environmental agreements completely at the state or provincial level. For example, in Belgium, each of the autonomous regions must separately adopt environmental legislation. In Canada, the provinces, not the federal government, control some aspects of environmental policy.[39]

Insufficient Capacity or Commitment to Implement, Administer, Monitor, or Enforce Domestic Policy

It is not enough simply to enact laws and regulations. They must also be effectively implemented, administered, monitored, and enforced. Doing so requires sufficient issue-specific skills, knowledge, technical know-how, legal authority, financial resources, enforcement capacity, and commitment at the individual and institutional levels. Insufficient capacity is a particular problem for some developing countries, but it exists in all parts of the world and varies from issue to issue and country to country.

Examples of capacity problems are unfortunately common. Many countries, including industrialized countries, lack the budgets, trained personnel, or commitment needed to enforce or otherwise comply fully and effectively with the rules established by CITES to control trade in endangered species.[40] Compliance with the CBD has been hindered by a lack of national capacity to manage protected areas and to control the impact of development projects. Russia did not comply with its obligations under the ozone regime for several years because its government temporarily lacked the capacity to stop the production and black-market export of CFCs. Full compliance with the Stockholm Convention includes locating, identifying, managing, and destroying stockpiles of obsolete pesticides in an environmentally sound manner, something beyond the technical and financial ability of many countries. African countries continue to express concern that they are sometimes unable to prevent unwanted shipments of obsolete pesticides and products, toxic chemicals, and potentially hazardous wastes from entering their countries, despite relevant provisions in the Basel and Rotterdam Conventions.[41] Several countries in Asia, Africa, and Central and South America express concern for their ability to prevent the use of mercury in illegal, small-scale gold-mining operations.[42] The economic impacts of the 2020 global COVID-19 pandemic seriously affected government budgets around the world, undoubtedly negatively impacting the ability of some countries to monitor and enforce environmental regulations.

Some states that want to comply might not act effectively because they are unaware of what is happening domestically. Two principal sets of factors affect states' abilities to monitor compliance with, and the effectiveness of, domestic environmental laws designed to comply with an international regime: (1) whether states have adequate feedback mechanisms, such as on-site monitoring, reporting requirements, inspections, complaint mechanisms, and close working relationships with relevant NGOs; and (2) the number and size of the potential violators whose conduct the government must monitor.[43] For example, the relatively high level of compliance with the Montreal Protocol results not only from the widely accepted science on ozone depletion and changing economic interests but also the manageable number of facilities that produce the chemicals and require monitoring. Monitoring compliance with CITES, however, remains difficult in part because the number of potential violators is extremely large.

A lack of respect for the rule of law within some countries is an important contributing factor. This problem tends to arise more often in countries where severe economic pressures, political instability, and patterns of corruption lead particular groups, government officials, or the general public to ignore elements of the legal system. For example, sections of the Central African Republic, Democratic Republic of the Congo, and several other African countries are relatively lawless, making it difficult to preserve their significant biodiversity, forest, and ecosystem resources. In some countries, systematic corruption, extreme poverty, and the absence of a meaningful democratic process cause many people to feel alienated from the law-making apparatus, undermining their respect for the law, including regulations on wildlife conservation.[44] Many studies show that illegal deforestation in parts of Africa, Asia, and Latin America reflects, among other factors, lack of government capacity and poverty.[45]

Misperception of Relevant Costs and Benefits

A related obstacle is a lack of understanding of the full set of economic costs and benefits of pursuing environmental goals. Many analyses indicate that even if policymakers wish to ignore nonmonetary concepts relating to environmental and human health protections, purely economic arguments support certain environmental protections. However, such arguments often do not win in domestic policy discussions. Businesses that would need to stop or change operations or incur economic costs make their case clearly in policy debates. Less obvious, however, at least for some, are the significant economic benefits of protecting natural resources; reducing human health impacts from pollution; using energy, water, and material resources more efficiently; and creating green jobs. These are often obscured by the importance placed on short-term adjustment costs (which could be substantial), insufficient analysis of economic changes that will occur if more environmentally benign technology or practices are required, and a failure to include the negative economic impacts of environmental degradation.

For example, arguments in the late 1970s that eliminating CFCs from aerosol spray cans would be extremely costly proved inaccurate when new processes and products actually saved consumers money. Global efforts to remove lead from gasoline have yielded annual economic benefits of approximately $2.4 trillion through the associated improvements in IQ, reductions in cardiovascular diseases, introduction of pollution-control devices (some are not usable on cars and trucks using leaded fuel), and other health and social benefits.[46] Forestry and logging in Kenya actually cost that country roughly $60 million in 2010 because of the economic costs produced by deforestation, especially the impact on the quality and availability of fresh water.[47] The National Academy of Sciences estimated that burning fossil fuels costs the United States about $120 billion a year in health costs, mostly from the health impacts and premature deaths caused by air pollution.[48] The United Nations Environment Programme (UNEP) calculates the negative cost of air pollution to the world's most advanced economies plus India and China to be $3.5 trillion per year due to health impacts and lives lost.[49]

More broadly, experts have long recognized the economic importance of preserving natural systems. For example, a groundbreaking 1997 study estimated the economic value of ecosystem services provided by natural ecosystems in the form of fresh water, cleaner air, pollination, food production, recreation, waste treatment, and other outputs at $16 trillion to $54 trillion per year.[50] A 2014 update to this study estimated that land-use changes that negatively affected ecosystem services cost the global economy $4.3 trillion to $20.2 trillion each year from 1997 to 2011.[51] The Economics of Ecosystems and Biodiversity (TEEB) project is a major international initiative to study and publicize the global economic benefits of preserving biodiversity and healthy ecosystems.[52] A 2012 TEEB report highlighted how short-term economic gains from draining wetlands for farming, building, or water use, and the degradation of wetlands from excessive releases of fertilizers and pollutants in their watersheds, threaten the many billions of dollars' worth of economic and environmental benefits that wetlands provide in preserving water quality, providing habitats and nurseries for fisheries, conserving biodiversity, and mitigating climate change (via carbon storage in peatlands, mangroves, and tidal marshes).[53] A report by UNEP's Finance Initiative in collaboration with a number of asset owners, investment managers, and information providers showed that consideration of the economic impact of environmental degradation and the depletion of natural resources has the potential to lower a country's sovereign debt rating, denoting the purchase of that country's bonds as a greater risk and increasing the interest rate a country might have to offer to attract buyers.[54]

Many large-scale studies conclude that efforts to reduce GHG emissions will prevent significant economic costs associated with sea-level rise, changes in rainfall patterns, droughts, more extreme weather, air pollution, mercury emissions, and an increase in the range of tropical diseases and other health problems.[55] A study by researchers from the European Commission, GEF, McKinsey & Company, Rockefeller Foundation, Standard Chartered Bank, and other organizations estimates that without mitigation and adaptation efforts, climate change will soon carry significant economic costs and could, under certain scenarios, cost some nations up to 19 percent of their gross domestic product (GDP) as early as 2030.[56] This includes Southeast Asia and the Middle East, where, in the absence of effective global action to limit GHG emissions, temperatures could become so high that their negative impacts on human health and labor capacity would significantly decrease economic output.[57]

Also, although many understand that some actors will suffer economic costs from reducing GHG emissions, less widely acknowledged are the larger and broader economic benefits that many studies conclude will result from these efforts, particularly those associated with increased energy efficiency, fewer health problems from air pollution, reduced oil and gas imports, and the creation of new jobs in solar, wind, and geothermal industries.[58] At the national and global levels, the economic benefits of reducing GHG gases appear to outweigh the costs. A report issued in 2016 by the International Energy Agency showed that global GDP grew in both 2014 and 2015 even as GHG emissions levelled off.[59] A World Resources Institute study found that as GDP went up in twenty-one different countries from 2000–2015, their individual and collective emissions of GHGs fell or peaked.[60] A UN-commissioned study estimated that concerted efforts to address climate change and sustainable development would create 20 million additional jobs in the renewable energy sector by 2030 and that a worldwide transition to make all buildings energy efficient would create 2 to 3.5 million more green jobs in Europe and the United States alone, with the potential much higher in developing countries.[61] A 2015 study concluded that investments in low-carbon initiatives to improve public transportation, energy-efficient buildings, and waste disposal in cities could yield \$16.6 trillion in financial savings by 2050 and avoid 3.7 gigatons of CO_2 emissions annually, which is more than India's current emissions.[62]

Costs of Compliance

Even if the long-term benefits are clear, implementation and compliance do require resources. Therefore, compliance with international environmental agreements is affected by the short-term costs of such compliance relative to the country's level of economic development, current economic situation, resource base, and budgetary preferences. Affluent countries experiencing relatively strong economic growth are historically far more willing and able to comply with environmental regulations than poorer states or states with economies that are growing slowly or not at all. States with low per capita incomes are generally reluctant to commit significant funds to comply with commitments to reduce global threats, even if doing so is in the country's long-term interest, because such compliance would likely come at the expense of spending for economic and social development. This underscores the importance of regimes that provide effective, targeted, and sufficient financial and technical assistance to countries that truly need it, and use it, for regime implementation. Even in wealthy countries, competing economic and budgetary preferences or concerns about national economic rivals can inhibit implementation and compliance.

Countries experiencing economic and financial difficulties might refuse or become unable to comply with global environmental agreements. The Russian Federation, for example, did not immediately eliminate CFC production under the amended Montreal Protocol because of its critical economic situation at the time.[63] Budget cuts often impact the ability of countries to combat illegal trade in endangered species under CITES, monitor trade under the Rotterdam Convention, or prevent the trade of hazardous waste or manage it effectively under the Basel Convention. Many developing countries do not have the budgets to effectively combat the use of mercury in illegal gold mining. More broadly, global crises, such as the financial crisis in 2008 and the economic impacts of the COVID-19 pandemic, place financial burdens on countries that can impact their fulfillment of MEA obligations, including those of donor countries to provide particular levels of FTA.

Poorly Designed Regimes

A party's failure to comply with a regime sometimes reflects problems with the regime itself. As discussed earlier, regime design matters. Control measures and reporting requirements that are too complex or too vague allow states to make honest or intentional errors when translating them into domestic law. Regimes that do not pay attention to states' abilities to implement them, the relative costs of compliance, the importance of reporting and monitoring, the interconnections among environmental issues, possible conflicts with rules or practices in other regimes, or the provision of targeted and effective FTA are vulnerable to failure. Implementation and compliance, to some extent, are also a function of regime design.

Vague, weak, or poorly designed regime components can result from simple mistakes, lowest-common-denominator compromises, or intentional negotiating strategies designed to produce imprecise requirements that allow states significant choice regarding which, if any, concrete actions they will take. Regardless of the reason, if a treaty does not contain clear, implementable requirements, parties often have trouble translating the vague language into domestic rules or regulations, or parties can choose to interpret the vague requirements in ways that produce few adjustment costs. The language in the biodiversity and desertification conventions and their related compliance challenges illustrate this point. Although the treaties require countries to develop national plans, there is little guidance on how to enable these plans to actually be effective in conserving biodiversity or combating desertification.

Many Regimes, Little Coordination

Another obstacle to effective implementation and compliance is the sheer number of environmental treaties and other policy initiatives and the uncoordinated web of requirements, norms, and guidelines they include. Because all parties, particularly developing countries, have finite financial, technical, and human resources available, the more complex and confusing the total set of policies needed to implement treaty obligations, the more likely it is that compliance will suffer.

If one counts agreements that expand or alter the provisions of a treaty, countries have created hundreds of multilateral and bilateral environmental accords over the past fifty years. After trade (broadly defined), environment is the most common area of international rule making.[64] It is not uncommon to hear government officials at international meetings note the sheer number of environmental agreements and initiatives as a potential implementation obstacle.[65]

Each environmental regime, as well as many other bilateral and multilateral environmental initiatives, has its own set of control measures, policy guidelines, reporting requirements, monitoring systems, assessment mechanisms, implementation procedures, meeting schedules, financing requirements, and review procedures. In addition, nearly all these regimes and initiatives exist independently of each other. As such, they sometimes place uncoordinated and confusing obligations on states that are difficult to fulfill. One example is reporting requirements that sometimes conflict, or at least remain uncoordinated, in their schedules, procedures, units of analysis, and required methods and formats. This was an issue within the ozone regime for many years and remains an issue within the chemicals and wastes sector, which includes three major treaties and many more international policy initiatives and organizations, although efforts continue to eliminate this problem.

In addition, some regimes establish contrary rules or incentives. For example, HCFCs and HFCs were considered a replacement for CFCs under the ozone regime but are also GHGs subject to controls under the climate regime. Some closely related regimes have uncoordinated membership and regulatory gaps that potentially impede effectiveness. As discussed in Chapter 3, several treaties and other international initiatives exist to address hazardous waste and toxic chemicals, including the Basel, Rotterdam, and Stockholm Conventions, amendments to these conventions, and regional agreements. Although there are increased coordination efforts, some countries have pledged to fulfill obligations under some agreements and amendments but not others. This pattern has become more pronounced as parties add chemicals to the Stockholm Convention and some countries opt out of the new controls, allowing certain chemicals to escape global control.[66]

Opportunities to Improve Effective Implementation and Compliance

Several options exist to improve implementation and strengthen compliance with global environmental agreements. No single option, however, can address all of the obstacles outlined in this chapter. Furthermore, whether these options or incentives can actually lead a government to comply depends on the willingness of states and other actors to take action. However, existing experience with global environmental regimes, academic research, and deductive logic indicate that regime implementation, compliance, and effectiveness can be improved (see Box 5.3). As with other discussions in this chapter, these categories of opportunities are interrelated and are not presented in order of importance.

Raise Awareness and Concern

An obvious factor in improving national implementation and compliance is elevating awareness, concern, and knowledge among government elites and the general public about

> ✦ **BOX 5.3 OPPORTUNITIES TO IMPROVE EFFECTIVE IMPLEMENTATION AND COMPLIANCE**
>
> - Raise awareness and concern
> - Create market incentives
> - Eliminate counterproductive subsidies
> - Augment coordination between regimes and conventions
> - Improve monitoring and reporting
> - Generate publicity
> - Consider sanctions
> - Build domestic capacity
> - Increase and improve financial and technical assistance

environmental issues, including their negative impacts on human health and the economy. For each case in Chapters 3 and 4, there is sufficient expert knowledge to demonstrate the scientific seriousness of the issue; the availability of technological, economic, and policy tools to address it; and the long-term environmental, human health, and economic benefits of doing so.

Significant obstacles remain, however, in part because many government officials and large elements of the public remain unaware of the near-term threats posed by environmental issues, especially to human health, and large gaps exist between the policy goals agreed to at the international level and the actual state of many environmental conditions.[67] There is even less awareness about the significant negative economic costs of environmental degradation, despite an ever increasing number of expert studies, including those outlined earlier. This lack of awareness means that concern for environmental issues often remains relatively low compared with other economic or political interests. The effectiveness of, and compliance with, international environmental regimes cannot improve until officials in more countries acknowledge these facts and raise the priority of environmental issues or until elevated public concern forces them to do so.

Create Market Incentives

As discussed, many economic forces at work today still reward rather than punish unsustainable activity because the local and global costs of pollution and unsustainable resource use have little effect on those responsible. Using market forces to reward environmentally friendly activities would greatly assist the implementation of environmental treaties and the pursuit of the Sustainable Development Goals (SDGs).

Important technologies that are essential to sustainable development become profitable if the environmental and health costs are included in the cost of unsustainable options. Clean energy is the most obvious example. Wind, solar, and geothermal energy sources are all likely economically superior to fossil fuels if one includes the full costs of the health impacts of the air pollution from fossil fuels, the climate impacts of their CO_2 emissions, and the broader environmental and national security impacts of development, extraction, and transportation. Placing a price on CO_2 emissions, therefore, is widely seen as an effective and perhaps critical step toward addressing climate change.[68] The same can be said for addressing most aspects of air and water pollution, rapacious resource use, and some types of deforestation.

Establishing market prices (through taxes, permits, incentives, tradable emission credits, or other measures) for pollution and unsustainable activity can reward efficiency and emission avoidance, encourage innovation, create a level playing field for non-polluting and sustainable technology options, induce the use of low-emission and zero-emission technologies, and reduce the overall cost of sustainable economic growth. Any negative, systemic economic impact of the additional costs could be offset by tax reductions in other areas, such as income taxes or sales taxes on particularly sustainable products or services.

Countries can exploit market forces on their own, through agreements with neighbors or trading partners, or through international agreements. Individual regimes, UNEP, the United Nations Development Programme (UNDP), World Bank, International Monetary Fund (IMF), and other institutions could expand efforts to raise awareness of the broad benefits of employing market mechanisms and perhaps provide incentives. However, efforts by one or a group of countries to use market forces for environmental purposes can run afoul of the WTO if they affect free trade (see Chapter 6). Broad agreement exists that the global trade regime need not stand in the way of more ambitious national and international environmental policy, including market mechanisms, to address climate change or other issues, but the precise frameworks need additional clarification.[69] Similarly, it is not always clear under which circumstances a country can exclude or tax certain imports for environmental reasons or when a country with a particular type of pollution tax relevant to the manufacture of certain products can introduce a tariff on the import of similar products that carry a price advantage because the country of its manufacture has no such tax. This could be particularly relevant to climate change, as some political figures in the EU and the United States have called for consideration of tariffs on goods imported from countries without GHG reduction policies.[70]

Eliminate Counterproductive Subsidies

One method for increasing the use of green energy and the sustainability of agriculture, forestry, and fisheries is eliminating subsidies that support fossil fuel production and consumption, incentivize unsustainable farming practices, and contribute to the degradation of forests, aquifers, and fish stocks. The period from the 1960s through the 1980s saw a rapid, worldwide expansion of subsidies for natural resource production. Although some reductions in subsidies given to agriculture and fisheries occurred in the 1990s and early 2000s, the scale of environmentally harmful subsidies in the energy, road transport, water use, fishing, and agricultural sectors remains staggering.

An IMF Working Paper estimates that globally, the fossil fuel industries received a staggering $5 trillion in direct and indirect government subsidies in 2017 and that reducing these subsidies would lower global carbon emissions by about 28 percent and fossil fuel-related air pollution deaths by 46 percent.[71] The largest subsidizers are China (nearly $1.4 trillion), the United States, (approximately $650 billion—nearly equal to the US defense budget and ten times more than federal spending for education),[72] and Russia (approximately $550 billion). A variety of subsidies, including for boat construction, fuel, and equipment, contribute to overfishing in the world's oceans.[73]

Despite the overall financial and environmental advantages of ending such subsidies, governments keep such policies in place in response to political pressure from key interest groups. It will take a concerted effort to fashion the necessary national and international consensus needed to end, or even severely limit, subsidies impeding conservation. Doing so, however, would make compliance far easier. Actions contrary to many global environmental policies would no longer enjoy artificial economic support, and billions of dollars that currently subsidize environmental degradation would be available to support environmental protection and sustainable economic practices.

Augment Coordination Among Regimes and Conventions

The broadest issue areas in global environment politics involve multiple, overlapping global and regional regimes, international organizations, and soft-law guidelines and procedures. Indicative examples include the atmosphere (ozone, climate, and regional air pollution agreements); chemicals and wastes (the Basel, Rotterdam, Stockholm, and Minamata Conventions; various regional treaties; and the Strategic Approach to International Chemicals Management); biodiversity, wildlife, and habitat protection (CBD, CITES, Ramsar Convention, the Convention on Migratory Species, and a host of wildlife-specific treaties); and oceans and fisheries (the Law of the Sea, the London Convention, MARPOL, the Fish Stocks Agreement, the Food and Agriculture Organization Code of Conduct for Responsible Fisheries, and numerous regional fisheries agreements and third-party certification programs). The UNCCD on its own contains provisions that address biodiversity, climate change, forests, and freshwater resources.

Improved coordination among treaties and organizations would improve regime implementation and compliance by (1) helping to remove obstacles produced by the lack of coordination (outlined earlier); (2) allowing more effective use of limited resources; (3) avoiding unnecessary duplication of tasks; (4) potentially creating opportunities whereby efforts for joint initiatives could improve reporting, monitoring, environmental assessments, financing, and implementation; and (5) potentially strengthening treaty secretariats so that they can manage the coordination and perform other functions more effectively.

The potential for improved coordination is broadly recognized. UNEP has repeatedly addressed the issue, and environmental ministers have discussed it in a variety of fora. As noted in Chapter 3, the Basel, Rotterdam, and Stockholm Conventions have combined their secretariats and coordinate aspects of their implementation. But more could be done. Some countries pushing for enhanced coordination argue that it can reduce duplicated secretariat and other bureaucratic costs, thereby freeing up resources for implementation activities. Opportunities for enhanced coordination that have received particular attention and exhibit promise include examining and eliminating regulatory gaps and conflicts, coordinating reporting schedules and formats, co-locating secretariats and relevant international organizations, coordinating the scheduling of the COPs of related regimes, supporting ratification to remove membership gaps, integrating appropriately related implementation activities, and establishing common regional centers and other programs for capacity building and the provision of FTA.

Improve Monitoring and Reporting

Monitoring and reporting on environmental issues and regime implementation are essential components of regime effectiveness. Without regular and accurate monitoring and reporting by parties, it is difficult to assess the baseline, trends, and current status of an environmental problem; to assess current levels of regime implementation; to identify specific instances or patterns of noncompliance or ineffectiveness; and to develop potential solutions. Studies on institutional effectiveness indicate that regimes employing systems of regular monitoring and reporting have better national domestic implementation and compliance than those that do not.[74]

Most environmental regimes require parties to submit data and reports on issues related to the environmental problem as well as on their implementation activities. Secretariats often compile this information and make it available to other parties and the public. Unfortunately, not all countries submit the required data and reports, and significant variations exist in the quality and timeliness of those that do. In addition, because most countries rely on existing national systems to gather information for regime reporting, the reports sometimes define, estimate, and aggregate the required data in different ways, making comparisons and analyses difficult.

Efforts to improve national reporting and associated monitoring, combined with the ability of secretariats and COPs to review, publicize, and act on the information in a timely fashion, will likely increase regime compliance and effectiveness. In addition to stronger provisions within regimes, another method to achieve these goals is to increase the coordination and integration of the monitoring and reporting requirements among related regimes. For example, observers believe that continuing to improve the quality, submission rates, and harmonization of reporting under the Basel, Rotterdam, and Stockholm Conventions—as well as reporting on mercury wastes and disposal of products containing mercury under the Minamata Convention—would allow far more accurate assessments of global levels and trends in the production, use, generation, transport, management, and disposal of toxic chemicals, hazardous waste, and e-waste. It would also make it easier to monitor progress in implementing these conventions and improve the ability to direct FTA to areas where it would have the most impact.[75] Furthermore, harmonized reporting could help reduce the overall volume of reporting requirements, which could free up human and financial resources to improve implementation on the ground.

Another method is to expand formal and informal relationships with NGOs, intergovernmental organizations, academics, and industry to help monitor environmental issues and regime implementation and compliance. For example, in addition to government reporting, several major private-sector actors and NGOs have monitored aspects of compliance with the Montreal Protocol, including illegal ODS trade.[76] The Carbon Disclosure Project has been instrumental in getting companies to track their CO_2 emissions. International NGOs, such as the Trade Records Analysis of Flora and Fauna in Commerce (TRAFFIC), work closely with the CITES Secretariat to monitor wildlife trade.[77] Since 2007, the International Fund for Animal Welfare has sponsored training programs for law enforcement officers, customs officials, and other authorities in thirty countries around the globe aimed at stopping trade in endangered species and illegal smuggling of other animals.[78]

Generate Publicity

Fear of negative publicity has sometimes proven to be an incentive for treaty compliance. Environmental conventions could create mechanisms through which negative publicity would become a more prominent consequence of refusal to participate in a global regime or failure to implement specific provisions.[79] Social networking, global television networks, and the internet make it easier, cheaper, and faster than ever to collect and distribute information, and evidence exists that such campaigns can have an impact. Countries go to significant lengths to deny or explain implementation lapses during many COPs, which shows that they might be sensitive to more public and systematic exposure. Norway lost money and public support when the EU boycotted Norwegian fish products because of Norway's position on whaling. Negative publicity can also be used to expose and deter corporate noncompliance with national laws. In the EU, the US, and other countries, environmental groups sometimes act as important watchdogs, reporting violations of environmental regime rules to the public, national authorities, and regime secretariats.

Positive publicity might also improve compliance, and some diplomats argue that efforts should be made to publicize regime compliance or special achievements more effectively.[80] Beyond individual regimes, several broader efforts, such as the Environmental Performance Index, rank countries according to various environmental and sustainability criteria.[81] Supporters of such initiatives hope that these types of measures can replace, or at least augment, traditional gross national product rankings and that countries will take steps to attempt to rise in the rankings, or at least avoid being placed near the bottom.

Consider Sanctions

Improving compliance may require additional sticks (sanctions) as well as more carrots, such as capacity building and FTA. Trade restrictions, tariffs, fines, or prohibitions on receiving FTA could be used against parties found to be in willful noncompliance with regime rules. Sanctions could also punish countries that choose to remain outside of a particular regime in an effort to discourage free riders. To be effective, sanctions must be credible and potent. States in conscious violation of a treaty or measures adopted by an MEA must be convinced not only that they will face penalties for the violation but also that the costs of the violation will exceed expected gains.[82]

The ozone regime includes such provisions, prohibiting parties from exporting or importing ozone-depleting chemicals or products that use them to or from non-parties. Trade sanctions can also be invoked on parties for serious, willful noncompliance, although these have never been enacted. CITES allows trade suspensions against countries that do not enact appropriate implementing legislation or have a continuing pattern of violations. The Basel Convention also includes the possibility of sanctions as a potential punishment for non-compliance. However, little support appears to exist among most governments for expanding the use of sanctions as a remedy for treaty violations, and they are seldom used in the regimes in which they do exist. Thus, countries that find themselves in noncompliance with MEA requirements are unlikely to suffer formal adverse legal effects.

Some issues might lend themselves to more robust sanctions, such as illegal, unreported, and unregulated fishing, where sanctions (in this example, curbs on fishing rights, exports, or imports) could be directly related to the failure to comply with a treaty. Other possibilities include adding clear "polluter pays" elements to existing agreements. Many countries, however, oppose the potential use of sanctions, arguing that such sanctions violate national sovereignty and that expanded trade measures could violate international trade agreements or be used as a disguised form of trade protectionism (the latter is of particular concern to many developing countries).

Build Domestic Capacity

Improved compliance sometimes requires programs that strengthen the capacity of developing countries to implement environmental conventions. It also requires commitment by developing countries so that the assistance provided helps to develop permanent infrastructure.

Photo 5.3 As discussions on finance began at the 2019 Climate Change Conference in Madrid, Spain, members of civil society demonstrated in the corridors, calling for stronger financial mechanisms to effectively combat the climate crisis.

Courtesy Kiara Worth, IISD/*Earth Negotiations Bulletin*, http://enb.iisd.org

Governments and international organizations recognize this need. GEF projects on biodiversity, forests, climate change, toxic chemicals, and hazardous waste often integrate capacity-building components into investment projects. Capacity-building activities also exist within many regimes. For example, the CITES capacity-building strategy trains the trainers in a country by holding seminars and providing training materials.[83] The ozone regime supported significant capacity building through its Multilateral Fund. The Basel and Stockholm Conventions regional centers act as nodes for capacity-building programs on issues relating to hazardous wastes and toxic chemicals. The UNCCD's Capacity Building Marketplace helps individuals and organizations share learning, funding, and job opportunities.

Well-targeted capacity building in a variety of areas can augment regime compliance and effectiveness. Areas of particular need include environmental assessment and analysis, monitoring, regulatory infrastructure, enforcement, science education, trade and customs controls and related issues, public awareness, and the use and maintenance of a wide variety of environmentally friendly technologies. Capacity building can also increase government concern for an issue by expanding awareness within the bureaucracy and increasing the number, skills, and visibility of people working on the issue. At the same time, experience shows the importance of ensuring that the funds provided actually go toward relevant capacity building.

Increasing and Improving Financial and Technical Assistance

The line between capacity building and other types of FTA is largely an artificial one. In general, however, capacity building refers to permanent improvements in the ability and self-sufficiency of a country, whereas FTA refers to help with specific implementation and compliance activities. Increasing and effectively targeted FTA remains one of the most important avenues for improving compliance and regime effectiveness (see Box. 5.3). Key areas include obtaining access to new products and processes; technology transfer; developing new or expanded implementation plans, legislation, and regulations; purchasing scientific, monitoring, and communications equipment; financing individual implementation projects; properly disposing of hazardous wastes and toxic chemicals; and introducing substitute technologies.

The mere availability of increased or better-targeted FTA is not a panacea, however. More effective compliance requires assistance targeted toward the most important needs, monitored to avoid waste, provided conditionally in stages to promote real action, continually assessed and reviewed so that procedures can be improved, and coordinated within and across regimes to achieve synergies and avoid duplication and unintended negative consequences.

While not perfect, regimes continue to improve their targeting and monitoring of FTA. A principal challenge, then, is to increase the financial resources available. The successful expansion and implementation of MEAs, including those for climate, biodiversity, desertification, and chemicals, require transitions to environmentally sound technologies and new strategies for natural resource management. As noted earlier, although these technologies and strategies could (and in many cases likely will) yield long-term economic benefits, such transitions require investment in the short run to implement, to deploy more broadly, to ease the transition for those hardest hit, and to overcome resistance from powerful economic and political interests.

Most developing countries consider financial assistance to be an economic or political necessity in order for them to agree to new global environmental commitments and implement many of their existing obligations. Some countries simply do not have the resources to effectively implement MEAs.[84] For others, such as India or South Africa, financial assistance provides valuable economic support so that resources can flow to other social needs. Financial assistance also provides some developing countries, including those with large and growing economies, with important political assistance, easing domestic objections regarding adjustment costs. Such measures also support the CBDR principle and represent a prerequisite to developing-country participation in MEAs, especially those that address problems caused originally or primarily by industrialized countries.

On the other hand, many donor countries are facing their own financial and political challenges, which limit their ability to fund new initiatives or make new commitments to assist developing countries in implementing existing programs. This is particularly true during economic disruptions, such as the one caused by the COVID-19 pandemic. Even in the best of times, donor countries want FTA programs both to target specific actions that will have permanent impacts and to take into account the large economic differences among developing countries.[85]

The Montreal Protocol was the first regime in which the provision of financial assistance was a central issue in the negotiations. It demonstrated that donor and recipient countries participating in a global environmental regime could devise a financial mechanism that equitably distributes power and clearly and effectively links financial assistance with compliance. The biodiversity, climate, desertification, chemicals, and mercury regimes use the GEF as their financial mechanism. As discussed in Chapter 2, the grants and concessional funds disbursed by the GEF complement traditional development assistance by covering the additional costs (also known as agreed-upon incremental costs) incurred when a national, regional, or global development project also targets global environmental objectives. Despite the fact that in 2018 donors pledged $4.1 billion to fund its operations through 2022, the GEF is unlikely to receive sufficient resources from donor countries to fund the entire amount required for developing countries to achieve full compliance with the biodiversity, desertification, chemicals, and mercury conventions, especially since the GEF also must fund projects relating to climate change, forests, and international waters. Although one could argue that a workable coalition of industrialized countries, international organizations, and fast-growing developing countries clearly possesses the resources to address global environmental challenges and achieve truly sustainable development,[86] countries do not always have the short-term interest or ability to make the necessary investments on a systematic basis.

What potential sources exist that could provide the necessary financial resources for implementing global environmental regimes? This section outlines several possibilities proposed by government officials, NGOs, or other experts in different international fora (see Box 5.4). Each is theoretically possible but faces significant obstacles.

❖ BOX 5.4 INCREASING AND IMPROVING FINANCIAL AND TECHNICAL ASSISTANCE

- Focus multilateral and bilateral assistance on the Sustainable Development Goals
- Develop revenue from regime mechanisms
- Pollution taxes
- Exchange debt obligations for sustainable development policy reforms and investments
- Remove trade barriers and subsidies to promote green global trade and investment
- South–South financing and investment
- Triangular cooperation
- Public–private partnerships

Focus Multilateral and Bilateral Assistance on the Sustainable Development Goals

Existing official development assistance (ODA), loan-guarantee programs, and operations of multilateral development banks, each of which dwarfs environmental funding in size, could systematically apply resources to programs that also enhance environmental goals and help achieve the SDGs (see Chapter 6). Overall, ODA flows would not necessarily need to be reduced or enlarged, but governments and international financial institutions such as the World Bank would funnel aid only to proven programs with shared environmental and development goals. Programs focused on energy production or industrialization would support only projects that produce or use green energy rather than oil or coal, employ significant energy-conservation measures, and emit low levels of pollution. Many developing countries have tremendous renewable energy resources, including outstanding conditions for cost-efficient solar power plants in large sections of Africa, the Middle East, and parts of Pakistan and India. Excellent resources for constructing geothermal facilities exist in East Africa and the Pacific Rim, including Indonesia, the Philippines, and the west coasts of Mexico, Central America, and South America. Significant wind-power resources exist in many developing countries.

Similarly, cleaning and redeveloping brownfields—former industrial properties containing hazardous substances, pollutants, or contaminants—would always enjoy priority over clearing land for construction or agriculture. Projects that would clear tropical forests or place roads into or near protected areas would not be funded, nor would products that use or produce toxic chemicals. Reuse and recycling projects would be emphasized over mining projects or production processes that require large amounts of raw materials. Funding would increase to countries following these types of guidelines in their own policies and decrease to countries continuing business as usual. Sustainable agriculture that produces food for local consumption on a regular basis would receive priority over industrial export agriculture that consumes significant quantities of water and fertilizer and can leave countries as net importers of food. Energy efficiency and clean energy initiatives that train people in these increasingly profitable industries, which save money and reduce GHG emissions, would be supported.

Donors or recipients wishing to focus all or part of their ODA programs on health and social issues could effectively pursue these goals while also promoting the social bases of sustainable development, including basic health and nutrition, vaccinations, family planning, land preservation, and education (especially for women and girls). Indeed, better health and education are widely shown to contribute to smaller, healthier families, higher incomes, and less stress on the environment and natural resources.

Develop Revenue from Regime Mechanisms

Environmental regimes have the potential to develop mechanisms to capture certain cost savings that result from environmental protection or to collect fees from services or permits. The climate regime already includes a mechanism for raising revenues, and possibilities exist in other regimes.

One potential source of financing for greater energy efficiency, zero–GHG emission energy sources, technological innovation, and technological diffusion is GHG emissions trading. By making emissions reduction a potential profit source, the competitive nature of market capitalism is employed to combat climate change. In 1990, the United States established one of the first national systems for emissions trading for meeting sulfur dioxide emissions targets in the electric-power sector as a means to reduce acid rain. The EU Greenhouse Gas Emission Trading Scheme commenced operation in January 2005 as the world's largest multi-country, multisector GHG emissions trading scheme. State and regional GHG-trading schemes have been developed in the United States and other countries, including the Regional Greenhouse Gas Initiative, and California and Quebec linked their CO_2 trading systems in 2014 (see

Chapter 2). As national and international systems expand, a small percentage of each auction or transaction could go into a fund for investing in clean energy options in the poorest developing countries.

The central challenge to deploying an effective emissions trading system is designing and then continually improving the system so that it works at both the business and the environmental levels. The success of the emissions trading program in the United States for sulfur emissions argues that this is possible, although maintaining an effective and efficient trading system for CO_2 presents a more difficult challenge. The EU Greenhouse Gas Emission Trading Scheme experienced difficulties for the first few years because an excess of permits drove prices too low. However, some of these problems were fixed, since the system was designed to be adjusted, and governments have expanded the system to cover emissions from more types of sources.[87]

Pollution Taxes

Many ideas exist for state, regional, national, or even coordinated international taxes or user fees to penalize polluters, encourage the use of green technologies and practices, or raise funds for sustainable development. Taxes would be levied on harmful activities or those producing negative externalities. Common proposals include a broad carbon tax, a tax on particular fossil fuels, or fees for particular GHG emissions. A successful example is the excise tax on CFCs enacted by the United States to help implement its obligations under the ozone regime. The tax raised several billion dollars for the US Treasury and acted as a significant incentive for companies to speed their transition to alternatives.[88]

Some taxes could be set quite low but still raise large sums through their aggregate effect. The impact on the poor of larger taxes meant to help change market behavior could be offset by related cuts in income or sales taxes or other programs, such as the tax credit provided as part of the carbon tax program in the Canadian province of British Columbia.[89] Some existing green taxes and proposals seek to be revenue neutral. Others propose that governments use at least some of the revenue to support sustainable development and environmental protection.

In proposals for coordinated action, countries would impose similar pollution taxes and then pool the funds or use them individually to finance sustainable development and environmental regimes.[90] For example, in the early 1990s, the EU called for a tax on air fuel used for international flights to raise funds for environmental projects.[91] In 2009, during the climate change negotiations, the group of least developed countries proposed that developed countries should accept a compulsory levy on international airline tickets and shipping fuel to raise billions of dollars to help the world's poorest countries mitigate and adapt to climate change. The aviation levy, which proponents claim would increase the price of long-haul fares by less than 1 percent, could raise $10 billion a year.[92] An Ecuador-led initiative proposed a 3–5 percent tax on oil exported to industrialized countries that could raise $40 billion to $60 billion annually, which could be used to finance climate mitigation and adaptation activities in developing countries.[93]

Another well-known proposal is to tax large-scale speculative currency trading. A levy of just 0.005 percent could generate $15 billion a year for environmental projects if enacted in countries through which most of such trading takes place. Larger levies, which have been proposed, would raise even more and potentially discourage such speculation, which some argue presents an unnecessary threat to the stability of national currencies.[94] Other possibilities include taxes on certain types of energy production, fossil fuel-powered transportation, the production of certain toxic chemicals or hazardous waste, and the release of heavy metals and air and water pollutants into the environment. In addition to raising funds for implementing globally agreed-upon environmental goals, the taxes would create additional economic deterrents to unnecessary pollution.

Many practical and political issues exist concerning the adoption and administration of such taxes, and the system would be subject to significant concerns about free riders. In addition, some national governments fear that they would lose revenue, that the money raised in their countries would be wasted on inefficient international projects, that the taxes would be used to create slush funds for use by international organizations outside their control, or that the mechanism could contribute to other losses of sovereign control. The US Congress, for example, passed legislation in 1999 making it illegal for the United States to participate in global taxes.[95] Although a national tax, albeit one enacted in concert with other governments and administered domestically with proceeds distributed only by the United States, might pass muster against this legislation and meet at least some of the concern expressed by other countries, it would still face formidable political obstacles.

Exchange Debt Obligations for Sustainable Development Policy Reforms and Investments

Debt obligations create incentives for developing countries to exploit their natural resources at unsustainable rates and use budgetary resources for debt payments at the expense of sustainable development programs. Implementing aggressive debt relief programs in concert with agreements by the debtor country to use a specific amount of the savings for environmental programs offers the potential to tap a source of funds for problems largely neglected by most assistance programs, such as programs needed to combat desertification in Africa.

Several such initiatives have been developed. Under pressure from poor countries and NGOs, the World Bank and the IMF launched the Initiative for Heavily Indebted Poor Countries (HIPCs) in September 1996 to help the poorest and most heavily indebted governments escape from unsustainable debt and focus more energy on building the policy and institutional foundation for sustainable development and poverty reduction.[96] In 2005, the HIPC initiative was supplemented by the Multilateral Debt Relief Initiative, which allows 100 percent relief on eligible debts from three multilateral institutions—the IMF, the World Bank, and the African Development Fund—for countries completing the HIPC initiative process. In 2007, the Inter-American Development Bank also decided to provide additional debt relief to HIPCs in the western hemisphere.

In 2005, leaders of the world's eight leading industrialized countries agreed to cancel the debt of eighteen of the world's poorest nations and to increase aid to, and investment in, Africa.[97] The pledge helped some of the countries that were eligible for the HIPC or Multilateral Debt Relief Initiatives but could not participate because of domestic exigencies or the structural adjustments required. Several broad alliances of religious, charitable, environmental, and labor groups (the best known being the Jubilee Network) continue to advocate for debt cancelation.[98] Although these initiatives represent significant steps, public and private debt levels remain an impediment to successful environmental protection and sustainable development in many developing countries.

Remove Trade Barriers and Subsidies to Promote Green Global Trade and Investment

A variety of options exist for reducing trade barriers and removing subsidies to enhance the global availability of, and investment in, goods and services that benefit sustainable development. As discussed in Chapter 6, the relationship between trade and the environment is complex. However, efforts to remove tariffs and other trade barriers that reduce the flow or increase the price of green energy technologies (such as solar panels) or products that enhance energy or water efficiency increase the cost of sustainable development and take resources away from other efforts. As noted earlier, reducing counterproductive subsidies would have similar benefits. Addressing these issues has been a priority for some countries as part of WTO negotiations and other bilateral and multilateral trade negotiations, but with only mixed success.

South–South Financing and Investment

A number of developing countries have the ability to provide FTA to other developing countries or foster foreign direct investment in green energy, other sustainable development projects, and activities associated with regime implementation. Such South–South cooperation (SSC) can be defined as an exchange of knowledge and resources in the political, economic, social, cultural, environmental, or technical domain among governments, organizations, and individuals in two or more developing nations. It can take place on a bilateral, regional, subregional, or interregional basis. Through exchanges of experiences and the pooling and sharing of resources, SSC can foster self-reliance among developing countries, open new channels of communication, strengthen economic ties, and lead to more effective and better-coordinated environmental and development policies.[99]

Recent developments in SSC have taken the form of increased volume of South–South trade, South–South flows of foreign direct investment, movements toward regional integration, technology transfers, sharing of solutions and experts, and other forms of exchanges.[100] In fact, South–South trade in renewable energy equipment and services is growing rapidly.[101] Some argue that SSC should be seen as a complement to North–South cooperation; others argue that the two models must always be part of separate discussions due to the principle of CBDR; and still others, usually donor countries, seek to insert references to all types of activity, including SSC, into discussions of FTA, believing that developing countries in a position to do so should have nearly the same responsibility to provide assistance as industrialized countries.

Triangular Cooperation

Triangular cooperation brings together developing countries, providers of development assistance, and international organizations to share knowledge and collectively implement projects that support sustainable development.[102] Triangular cooperation occurs when traditional donor countries and international organizations facilitate SSC through the provision of funding, training, project management, technological systems, and other forms of support. When successful, triangular cooperation enhances aid efficiency, builds synergies between traditional and emerging donors, builds the capacity of donor agencies in developing countries, and improves the quality of SSC.[103] Triangular cooperation carries risks, however. These include lowering quality standards if emerging donors do not have the experience and capacity to provide high-quality development assistance; programs that reflect the experiences and preferences of the donors rather than the beneficiary countries' actual needs, priorities, and strategies; and higher transaction costs because three groups of actors must agree on common goals, standards, and procedures and create the legal, institutional, and budgetary conditions required for successful implementation.[104]

Triangular cooperation is not at the scale of traditional North–South cooperation or even SSC. Yet, it reflects the fact that new sources of finance have emerged (e.g., an increased number of large, private foundations have become active in sustainable development), and some developing countries are losing their status as recipients of traditional development assistance and becoming donors. It also offers traditional donors the opportunity to scale up aid programs by joining forces with new donors and then switch to supporting the new donors as they take on progressively larger roles. Triangular cooperation, if properly implemented, can accelerate this process, and thereby enrich the entire system of international sustainable development cooperation.[105]

Public–Private Partnerships

Public–private partnerships (PPPs) are increasingly promoted as a way to finance environment and development projects, potentially including the SDGs. Although there is no universally agreed-upon definition, PPPs are often described as a medium- or long-term contractual arrangement between the state and a private-sector company; an arrangement in which the private sector participates in the supply of assets and services traditionally provided by government, such as hospitals, schools, prisons, roads, bridges, tunnels, railways, water and sanitation, and energy; and an arrangement involving some form of risk sharing between the public and private sectors.[106] The 2008 financial crisis brought about renewed interest in PPPs. Facing constraints on public resources, while recognizing the importance of investment in infrastructure to help their economies grow, governments increasingly turned to the private sector as an additional source of funding.[107] It will be interesting to see if this pattern repeats itself in the economic aftermath of the COVID-19 pandemic.

As with every initiative, critics point out that not all PPPs are well designed, implemented, transparent, assessed, or effective at helping countries that need it the most.[108] When they work well, however, PPPs give governments and international organizations access to new resources (financial, technical, and infrastructural). Civil society networks gain access to increased public and private funding, as well as in-kind and technical support. And businesses get access to risk and expectations management, market and community development expertise, contracts, and positive publicity.[109] One example is the UNCCD Land

Photo 5.4 The United Nations Convention to Combat Desertification launched the Land Degradation Neutrality Fund at COP13 in Ordos, China.

Courtesy Franz Dejon, IISD/*Earth Negotiations Bulletin*, http://enb.iisd.org

Degradation Neutrality Fund, which is an impact investment fund that blends resources from the public, private, and philanthropic sectors to support achieving land degradation neutrality through sustainable land management and land restoration projects implemented by the private sector.[110] Although not a PPP per se, the Basel Convention has developed initiatives on plastics, mobile phones, computers, and e-waste involving companies, NGOs, international organizations, and governments that contain similar elements (see Chapter 3).

Conclusion

The effectiveness of an environmental regime, that is, the extent to which it produces measurable improvements in the environment, is a function of regime design, particularly the strength of the key control provisions aimed at addressing the environmental threat, as well as the level of implementation (the extent to which countries adopt domestic regulations to enact the agreement) and compliance (the degree to which countries conform to these regulations and other regime rules and procedures). Many factors can inhibit or promote the effectiveness of an environmental regime. Among the most fundamental are eight broad sets of obstacles that can make it difficult to create or strengthen regimes so that they contain strong and effective control measures:

- Structural or systemic obstacles that arise from the structure of the international system, the structure of international law, and the structure of the global economic system;
- Lack of sufficient concern, hospitable contractual environments, or necessary capacity;
- Lowest-common-denominator problems;
- Time-horizon conflicts;
- Obstacles that stem from the characteristics of global environmental issues themselves, including the inherent links among environmental issues and important economic and political issues, unequal adjustment costs, scientific complexity and uncertainty, the presence of different core values and beliefs, and the involvement of large numbers of actors;
- Obstacles that stem from the interconnections among environmental issues;
- Regime design difficulties; and
- Changing realities in the global economic and ecological systems that have created new and sometimes conflicting views regarding how to apply the principle of CBDR.

Once regimes are created, certain factors can negatively influence national compliance with their requirements. These include inadequate translation of regime rules into domestic law; insufficient capacity or commitment to implement, administer, monitor, or enforce policies; misperception of relevant costs and benefits; high costs of compliance; inadequate or poorly targeted FTA; poorly designed regimes; and the sheer number of international environmental agreements and the lack of coordination among them.

Despite these obstacles, options exist to strengthen compliance with environmental agreements. Among the most important are elevating concern, creating market incentives, eliminating counterproductive subsidies, augmenting domestic capacity, increasing and more effectively targeting technical and financial assistance, emphasizing and supporting improved reporting and monitoring, enhancing coordination among regimes and conventions, applying sanctions, and employing positive and negative publicity.

Issues of financial resources, including the politics and provision of financial assistance, are central issues in global environmental politics. Given the political and economic obstacles preventing significant increases in financing for environmental regimes, as well as the potentially large amounts needed to assure their effectiveness, it is necessary for MEAs to seek alternative sources for such resources. Several options exist, including focusing existing bilateral and multilateral assistance on projects directly supportive of environmental regimes and sustainable development, developing revenue from regime mechanisms such as emissions trading, creating new revenue streams from pollution taxes, canceling debts owed by poor countries or exchanging them for tangible sustainable development actions, and greening global trade and investment. PPPs, SSC, and triangular cooperation also have potential to increase the flow of financial and technical assistance.

In spite of daunting obstacles to the creation and effective implementation of international environmental agreements, successful examples do exist. Examining the obstacles to creating strong agreements and options for increasing compliance provides insights into additional tools for creating effective global environmental policy.

Notes

1 United Nations Environment Programme (UNEP), *Auditing the Implementation of Multilateral Environmental Agreements (MEAs): A Primer for Auditors* (Nairobi: UNEP, 2010), 3, http://wedocs.unep.org/handle/20.500.11822/17290.

2 The figures of 1150 and 1500 come from the International Environmental Agreements Database Project (http://iea.uoregon.edu) directed by Ronald Mitchell.

3 Broader and influential discussions of implementation and compliance include Edith Brown Weiss and Harold K. Jacobson, eds., *Engaging Countries: Strengthening Compliance with International Environmental Accords* (Cambridge, MA: MIT Press, 1998); James Caermon, et al., eds., *Improving Compliance with International Environmental Law* (London: Earthscan, 1996); David Victor, Kal Raustiala, and Eugene Skolnikof, eds., *The Implementation and Effectiveness of International Environmental Commitments* (Cambridge, MA: MIT Press, 1998); Oran Young, ed., *The Effectiveness of International Environmental Regimes* (Cambridge, MA: MIT Press, 1999); Edward Miles, et al., *Environmental Regime Effectiveness* (Cambridge, MA: MIT Press, 2001); Ronald Mitchell, "Problem Structure, Institutional Design, and the Relative Effectiveness of International Environmental Agreements," *Global Environmental Politics* vol. 6, no. 3 (August 2006): 72–89; and Oran Young, "Effectiveness of International Environmental Regimes: Existing Knowledge, Cutting-Edge Themes, and Research Strategies," *PNAS* vol. 108, no. 50 (2011): 19853–19860.

4 The discussion of the first five sets of factors draws extensively on publications by one of the coauthors. See particularly David Downie, "Understanding International Environmental Regimes: Lessons of the Ozone Regime" (PhD diss., University of North Carolina, Chapel Hill, 1996); and David Downie, "Global Environmental Policy: Governance Through Regimes," in *Global Environmental Policy: Institutions, Law, and Policy*, 2nd ed., eds. Regina Axelrod, David Downie, and Norman Vig (Washington, DC: Congressional Quarterly Press, 2005).

5 Classic examples include Thucydides, Niccolò Machiavelli, and Thomas Hobbes. Influential modern examples include Reinhold Niebuhr; Hans Morgenthau, *Politics Among Nations: The Struggle for Power and Peace*, 5th ed. (New York: Knopf, 1973); Robert Jervis, "Cooperation Under the Security Dilemma," *World Politics* vol. 30 (1978): 167–186; and Kenneth Waltz, *Theory of International Politics* (Reading, MA: Addison-Wesley, 1979).

6 Waltz, *Theory of International Politics*.

7 Joseph Grieco, "Anarchy and the Limits of Cooperation: A Realist Critique of the Newest Liberal Institutionalism," *International Organization* vol. 42 (Summer 1988): 485–507.

8 Jervis, "Cooperation Under the Security Dilemma"; Kenneth Oye, ed., *Cooperation Under Anarchy* (Princeton, NJ: Princeton University Press, 1986), 1–22.

9 Mancur Olson, *The Logic of Collective Action* (Cambridge, MA: Harvard University Press, 1965).

10 Garrett Hardin, "The Tragedy of the Commons," *Science* vol. 162, no. 3859 (December 13, 1968): 1243–1248; J. Samuel Barkin and George Shambaugh, eds., *Anarchy and the Environment: The International Relations of Common Pool Resources* (Albany: State University of New York Press, 1999).

11 Robert Keohane, *After Hegemony: Cooperation and Discord in the World Political Economy* (Princeton, NJ: Princeton University Press, 1984).

12 Robert Jervis, *Perception and Misperception in International Politics* (Princeton, NJ: Princeton University Press, 1976).

13 M. A. Giordano and A. T. Wolf, "Sharing Waters: Post-Rio International Water Management," *Natural Resources Forum* vol. 27 (2003): 163–164.

14 1972 Stockholm Declaration and Action Plan, UN Document A/CONF.48/14, 118.

15 Peter Sand, *Lessons Learned in Global Environmental Governance* (Washington, DC: World Resources Institute, 1990), 21.

16 See, for example, Naomi Klein, *This Changes Everything: Capitalism vs. the Climate* (New York: Simon & Schuster, 2014).

17 Discussions of trade and environment include Chris Wold, Sanford Gaines, and Greg Block, *Trade and the Environment: Law and Policy*, 2nd ed. (Durham, NC: Carolina Academic, 2011); Erich Vranes, *Trade and the Environment: Fundamental Issues in International and WTO Law* (New York: Oxford University Press, 2009); Kevin Gallagher, *Handbook on Trade and the Environment* (Northampton: Edward Elgar, 2009).

18 For a general discussion, see the Carbon Tax Center's website: www.carbontax.org.

19 Intergovernmental Panel on Climate Change (IPCC), *Climate Change 2014: Synthesis Report—Contribution of Working Groups I, II and III to the Fifth Assessment Report of the Intergovernmental Panel on Climate Change* (Geneva, Switzerland, IPCC, 2014).

20 Peter Haas, Robert Keohane, and Marc Levy, eds., *Institutions for the Earth: Sources of Effective International Environmental Protection* (Cambridge, MA: MIT Press, 1993). This discussion slightly expands their definition of the three conditions.

21 For discussion of aspects of this and the next category, see Lawrence Susskind, *Environmental Diplomacy: Negotiating More Effective Global Agreements* (New York: Oxford University Press, 1994); and Sand, *Lessons Learned in Global Environmental Governance*.

22 Downie, personal observations. The stated reason was Sudan's concern that listing would lead to cost increases, something Sudan was reportedly told by a company that makes fenthion. Ecuador insisted that the 2015 official meeting report reflect that its delegation had been approached by private-sector representatives in "unacceptable" ways seeking to persuade it to oppose listing paraquat. The listing was subsequently blocked by only two countries. For summaries of the debates outlined in this section, see the official 2015, 2017, and 2019 COP reports on the Secretariat website and the daily and summary reports produced by the *Earth Negotiations Bulletin*, https://enb.iisd.org/vol15/.

23 Sand, *Lessons Learned in Global Environmental Governance*.

24 Most spills occur in industrial facilities and laboratories and are relatively contained but can expose particular individuals to high doses. Large spills and area contaminations also occur as a result of industrial accidents; fires; accidents involving trains, ships, or trucks transporting chemicals; and inadequate pollution controls at production facilities. Famous examples include the explosions in 2008 at a large chemical plant in Guangxi Province, China, that released toxic gas into the air and contaminated the Longjiang River, forcing evacuation of nearby towns. In 1991, seven train cars carrying the pesticide metam sodium derailed, spilling chemicals into the Sacramento River and killing downriver plant and aquatic life for forty-three miles. In December 1984, a cloud of poisonous gas escaped from a Union Carbide chemical plant that produced the pesticide sevin in Bhopal, India, killing thousands of people and exposing hundreds of thousands. In 1983, the US government purchased the town of Times Beach, Missouri, and relocated more than 2200 residents because the land was so badly contaminated from nearby industries.

25 WHO and UNEP, *State of the Science of Endocrine Disrupting Chemicals* (Geneva: WHO and UNEP, 2013).

26 IPCC, *Climate Change 2014: Synthesis Report*; IPCC, *Global Warming of 1.5°C* (Geneva, Switzerland: World Meteorological Organization, 2018).

27 Recent examples include deliberations on pentachlorophenol, short-chained chlorinated paraffins, and dicofol. Personal observations by David Downie during these meetings. See also the official reports from the Persistent Organic Pollutants Review Committee meetings, available from the Stockholm Convention Secretariat, and reports by the *Earth Negotiations Bulletin* (https://enb.iisd.org/vol15/).

28 e.g., IISD, "Summary of the Eleventh Meeting of the Rotterdam Convention's Chemical Review Committee: 26–28 October 2015," *Earth Negotiations Bulletin* vol. 15, no. 238 (October 31, 2015).

29 Observations by David Downie during the POPs and mercury negotiations.

30 David Downie, personal observations during the mercury negotiations. See also the official reports of these negotiations (which Downie helped to draft), as well as the *Earth Negotiations Bulletin* (www.iisd.ca/vol28).

31 See Knut Midgaard and Arild Underdal, "Multiparty Conferences," in *Negotiations: Social-Psychological Perspectives*, ed. Daniel Druckman (Beverly Hills, CA: Sage, 1977), 339; and Pamela Chasek, *Earth Negotiations: Analyzing Thirty Years of Environmental Diplomacy* (Tokyo: United Nations University Press, 2001), ch. 3.

32 Barkin and Shambaugh, *Anarchy and the Environment*.

33 Research continues on developing biofuels from plants that can grow on marginal land without fertilizer or from algae that can be grown in greenhouses with recycled water, which could alleviate many of these negative impacts.

34 Ronald Mitchell, "Regime Design Matters: Intentional Oil Pollution and Treaty Compliance," *International Organization* vol. 48, no. 3 (Summer 1994): 425–458. See also Ronald Mitchell, "Problem Structure, Institutional Design, and the Relative Effectiveness of International Environmental Agreements," *Global Environmental Politics* vol. 6, no. 3 (August 2006): 72–89.

35 Harold K. Jacobson and Edith Brown Weiss, "A Framework for Analysis," in *Engaging Countries: Strengthening Compliance with International Environmental Accords*, eds. Edith Brown Weiss and Harold K. Jacobson (Cambridge, MA: MIT Press, 1998), 4.

36 J. Timmons Roberts, Bradley Parks, and Alexis Vásquez, "Who Ratifies Environmental Treaties and Why? Institutionalism, Structuralism and Participation by 192 Nations in 22 Treaties," *Global Environmental Politics* vol. 4, no. 3 (August 2004): 22–64.

37 In addition to those cited earlier or later, examples of this literature include Peter Sand, ed., *The Effectiveness of International Environmental Agreements* (Cambridge, MA: Grotius, 1992); Ronald Mitchell, *Intentional Oil Pollution at Sea* (Cambridge, MA: MIT Press, 1994); Ronald Mitchell, "Compliance Theory: A Synthesis," *Review of European Community and International Environmental Law* vol. 2, no. 4 (1993): 327–334; Patrick Bernhagen, "Business and International Environmental Agreements: Domestic Sources of Participation and Compliance by Advanced Industrialized Democracies," *Global Environmental Politics* vol. 8, no. 1 (2008): 78–110; and David McEvoy and John Stranlund, "Self-Enforcing International Environmental Agreements with Costly Monitoring for Compliance," *Environmental and Resource Economics* vol. 42, no. 4 (2009): 491–508.

38 Sand, *International Environmental Agreements*, 82.

39 Michael Kelly, "Overcoming Obstacles to the Effective Implementation of International Environmental Agreements," *Georgetown International Environmental Law Review* vol. 9, no. 2 (1997): 462–463.

40 For example, in an experiment conducted by WWF, volunteers declared or displayed a cactus to customs officials in several countries, including the United Kingdom, Switzerland, Germany, Sweden, Denmark, and the United States. Although virtually all cacti are protected under CITES, officials asked no questions in any of these countries about the plant species or its origins. See Bill Padgett, "The African Elephant, Africa and CITES: The Next Step," *Indiana Journal of Global Legal Studies* vol. 2 (1995): 529, 538–540, as cited in Kelly, "Overcoming Obstacles," 469–470.

41 Personal observations by David Downie during meetings of the Stockholm, Rotterdam, and Basel Conventions, 2013–2019.

42 Personal observations by David Downie during negotiation of the Minamata Convention.

43 David Vogel and Timothy Kessler, "How Compliance Happens and Doesn't Happen Domestically," in Weiss and Jacobson, *Engaging Countries*, 24.

44 Andrew Heimert, "How the Elephant Lost His Tusks," *Yale Law Journal* vol. 104 (1995): 1473, as cited in Kelly, "Overcoming Obstacles," 465.

45 e.g., Nelleman, UNEP, and INTERPOL, *Green Carbon, Black Trade*; Environmental Investigation Agency and Telepak, *The Final Cut: Illegal Logging in Indonesia's Orangutan Parks* (Washington, DC: Environmental Investigation Agency, 1999); Christian Vasco, et al., "The Socioeconomic Determinants of Legal and Illegal Smallholder Logging: Evidence from the Ecuadorian Amazon," *Forest Policy and Economics* vol. 78 (May 2017): 133–140; Gitika Bhardwaj and Obed Owusu-Addai, "How Poverty Is Contributing to Deforestation Across Africa," Chatham House, Expert Comment, December 7, 2018, www.chathamhouse.org/expert/comment/how-poverty-contributing-deforestation-across-africa.

46 Peter Tsai and Thomas Hatfield, "Global Benefits from the Phaseout of Leaded Fuel," *Journal of Environmental Health* vol. 75, no. 5 (December 2011): 8–14.

47 UNEP and Kenya Forest Service, *The Role and Contribution of Montane Forests and Related Ecosystem Services to the Kenyan Economy* (Nairobi: UNEP, 2012).

48 Matthew Wald, "Fossil Fuels' Hidden Cost Is in Billions, Study Says," *New York Times*, October 19, 2009; Committee on Health, Environmental, and Other External Costs and Benefits of Energy Production and Consumption, National Research Council, *Hidden Costs of Energy: Unpriced Consequences of Energy Production and Use* (Washington, DC: National Academies Press, 2010).

49 UNEP, *UNEP Year Book 2014 Emerging Issues Update* (Nairobi: UNEP, 2014), 43.

50 Robert Costanza, et al., "The Value of the World's Ecosystem Services and Natural Capital," *Nature* vol. 387 (May 15, 1997): 253–260.

51 Robert Costanza, et al., "Changes in the Global Value of Ecosystem Services," *Global Environmental Change* vol. 26 (May 2014): 152–158.

52 For information, see The Economics of Ecosystems and Biodiversity (TEEB) website: www.teebweb.org.

53 See Patrick ten Brink, et al., *The Economics of Ecosystems and Biodiversity for Water and Wetlands: A Briefing Note* (Geneva: UNEP TEEB, 2012); and Daniela Russi, et al., *The Economics of Ecosystems and Biodiversity for Water and Wetlands: Final Consultation Draft*, UN Document UNEP/CBD/COP/11/INF/22, September 26, 2012.

54 UNEP FI and Global Footprint Network, *A New Angle on Sovereign Credit Risk: E-RISC—Environmental Risk Integration in Sovereign Credit Analysis* (Geneva: UNEP, 2012).

55 e.g., Nicholas Stern, *The Economics of Climate Change: The Stern Review* (Cambridge: Cambridge University Press, 2007); McKinsey & Co., *U.S. Greenhouse Gas Emissions: How Much and at What Cost?* (New York: McKinsey, 2007); Frank Ackerman and Elizabeth Stanton, *The Cost of Climate Change: What We'll Pay If Global Warming Continues Unchecked* (Washington, DC: Natural Resources Defense Council, 2008); Ernst von Weizsäcker, et al., *Factor Five: Transforming the Global Economy Through 80% Improvements in Resource Productivity* (London: Earthscan, 2009); Economics of Climate Adaptation (ECA) Working Group, *Shaping Climate Resilient Development: A Framework for Decision-Making* (Washington, DC: ECA, 2009); Council of Economic Advisers to the President of the United States, *The Cost of Delaying Action to Stop Climate Change* (Washington, DC: The White House, 2014); US Environmental Protection Agency (EPA), *Climate Change in the United States: Benefits of Global Action* (Washington, DC: EPA, 2015).

56 ECA Working Group, *Shaping Climate*.

57 "Too Hot to Work: Climate Change Puts South-east Asia Economies at Risk," *Guardian*, October 27, 2015; Jeremy Pal and Elfatih Eltahil, "Future Temperature in Southwest Asia Project to Exceed a Threshold for Human Adaptability," *Nature Climate Change* (2015), doi: 10.1038/nclimate2833.

58 See Tammy Thompson, et al., "A Systems Approach to Evaluating the Air Quality Co-benefits of US Carbon Policies," *Nature Climate Change* vol. 4 (October 2014): 917–923.

59 Coral Davenport, "Economies Can Still Rise as Carbon Emissions Fade," *New York Times*, April 7, 2016.

60 Ibid.

61 Michael Renner, et al., *Green Jobs: Towards Decent Work in a Sustainable, Low-Carbon World* (Nairobi: UNEP, 2008).

62 Andy Gouldson, et al. *Accelerating Low-Carbon Development in the World's Cities* (London and Washington, DC: New Climate Economy, 2015).

63 For specific information, see the relevant reports of the ozone regime's Implementation Committee, available at the Ozone Secretariat's website: http://ozone.unep.org.

64 John Vidal, "Many Treaties to Save the Earth, but Where's the Will to Implement Them?" *Guardian*, www.theguardian.com/environment/blog/2012/jun/07/earth-treaties-environmental-agreements.

65 Personal observations.

66 David Downie and Jessica Templeton, "Pesticides and Persistent Organic Pollutants," in *Routledge Handbook of Global Environmental Politics*, ed. Paul Harris (New York: Routledge, 2013).

67 UNEP, *GEO 5: Global Environmental Outlook—Environment for the Future We Want* (Nairobi: UNEP, 2012).

68 See Stern, *The Economics of Climate Change*, xvii and chs. 14–17; International Monetary Fund (IMF), *Fiscal Monitor: How to Mitigate Climate Change* (Washington, DC: IMF, 2019); Justin Caron, et al., "Exploring the Impacts of a National U.S. CO_2 Tax and Revenue Recycling Options with a Coupled Electricity-Economy Model," *Climate Change Economics* vol. 9, no. 1 (2018): 1–40; Carbon Tax Center's website (www.carbontax.org); and Eric Marx, "More than 2,000 Companies Call for Lowering Emissions Using a Price on CO_2," *Environment and Energy Publishing*, May 22, 2015.

69 For discussion, see UNEP and WTO, *Trade and Climate Change: A Report by the United Nations Environment Programme and the World Trade Organization* (Geneva: WTO Publications, 2009).

70 Thomas Cottier, Olga Nartova, and Anirudh Shingal, "The Potential of Tariff Policy for Climate Change Mitigation: Legal and Economic Analysis," *Journal of World Trade* vol. 48, no. 5 (October 2014):1007–1037. Such provisions were even included as part of climate change legislation that passed the US House of Representatives in 2009 (HR 2454: American Clean Energy and Security Act of 2009) but did not pass in the Senate.

71 David Coady, et al., "How Large Are Fossil Fuel Subsidies," *World Development* vol. 91 (March 2017): 11–27.

72 For specifics on fossil fuel subsidies in the United States, see *Federal Financial Interventions and Subsidies in Energy in Fiscal Year 2016* (Washington, DC: US Energy Information Agency, 2017). The Trump administration has evidently not issued an update to this study.

73 J. Samuel Barkin and Elizabeth DeSombre, *Saving Global Fisheries: Reducing Fishing Capacity to Promote Sustainability* (Cambridge, MA: MIT Press, 2013).

74 See Victor, Raustiala, and Skolnikoff, *The Implementation and Effectiveness of International Environmental Commitments.*

75 Personal communications from party representatives and regime officials.

76 Examples include the Alliance for Responsible Atmospheric Policy, an industry group, which tracked ozone-depleting substance production for many years, and the Environmental Investigation Agency's investigations of CFC smuggling.

77 For information, see www.traffic.org.

78 For information on IFAW's wildlife crime prevention activities, see www.ifaw.org.

79 See Susskind, *Environmental Diplomacy.*

80 Personal communications.

81 See the website of the Environmental Performance Index: www.epi.yale.edu.

82 For discussion, see Mitchell, *Intentional Oil Pollution at Sea,* 47–48.

83 e.g., Edith Brown Weiss, "The Five International Treaties: A Living History," in Weiss and Jacobson, *Engaging Countries,* 115–116.

84 For example, see Pamela Chasek, "Confronting Environmental Treaty Implementation Challenges in the Pacific Islands," *Pacific Islands Policy* vol. 6 (2010).

85 Personal observation by the authors during negotiations on the ozone, chemical, climate, and mercury regimes. For specific examples, see *Earth Negotiations Bulletin* reports from the negotiations at http://enb.iisd.org.

86 See particularly Jeffrey Sachs, *The End of Poverty: Economic Possibilities for Our Time* (New York: Penguin, 2005); and Jeffrey Sachs, *Common Wealth: Economics for a Crowded Planet* (New York: Penguin, 2008).

87 See, for example, Simone Borghesi and Massimiliano Montini, "The Best (and Worst) of GHG Emission Trading Systems: Comparing the EU ETS with Its Followers," *Frontiers in Energy Research* vol. 4 (29 July 2016), https://doi.org/10.3389/fenrg.2016.00027.

88 Stephen Seidel and Daniel Blank, "Closing an Ozone Loophole," *Environmental Forum* vol. 7 (1990): 18–20.

89 For information, see www2.gov.bc.ca/gov/content/environment/climate-change/planning-and-action/carbon-tax.

90 For an early example, see International Institute for Sustainable Development, "Financing Climate Change: Global Environmental Tax?" *Developing Ideas* vol. 15 (September–October 1998).

91 UN Commission on Sustainable Development, *Financial Resources and Mechanisms for Sustainable Development: Overview of Current Issues and Developments, Report of the Secretary-General,* E/CN.17/ISWG.II/1994/2, February 22, 1994, 24.

92 "Levy on International Air Travel Could Fund Climate Change Fight," *Guardian,* June 8, 2009, 13.

93 See, for example, John Vidal, "Oil Nations Asked to Consider Carbon Tax on Exports," *Guardian,* November 21, 2012.

94 The original proposal, by Nobel Prize–winning economist James Tobin, was for a 0.5 percent tax on speculative currency transactions that would raise $1.5 trillion annually and was aimed at deterring such transactions. The United Nations Development Programme (UNDP) proposed a much smaller tax. See UNDP, *Human Development Report 1994* (New York: Oxford University Press, 1994), 69–70; Martin Walker, "Global Taxation: Paying for Peace," *World Policy Journal* vol. 10, no. 2 (summer 1993): 7–12.

95 See section 921 of the United Nations Reform Act of 1999, commonly referred to as "Helms-Biden."

96 Updated information on the HIPC initiative can be found on the World Bank and IMF websites: www. worldbank.org/debt and www.imf.org/external/np/exr/facts/hipc.htm.

97 Jim VandeHei, "G-8 Leaders Agree on $50B in Africa Aid," *Washington Post*, July 9, 2005.

98 See the Jubilee USA Network website: www.jubileeusa.org.

99 International Trade Union Confederation, "Briefing Note: What Are South–South and Triangular Cooperation?" August 3, 2012, www.ituc-csi.org/briefing-note-what-are-south-south?lang=en.

100 See United Nations Office for South–South Cooperation, www.unsouthsouth.org/.

101 UNEP, *South Trade in Renewable Energy: A Trade Flow Analysis of Selected Environmental Goods* (Nairobi: UNEP, 2014).

102 "Triangular Cooperation," OECD, www.oecd.org/dac/dac-global-relations/triangular-cooperation. htm.

103 Guido Ashoff, "Triangular Cooperation: Opportunities, Risks and Conditions for Effectiveness," *Development Outreach*, October 2010, 23, https://openknowledge.worldbank.org/handle/10986/6081.

104 Ibid., 23–24.

105 Ibid., 24.

106 e.g., María José Romero, *What Lies Beneath? A Critical Assessment of PPPs and Their Impact on Sustainable Development* (Brussels: Eurodad, 2015), 4.

107 World Bank Public–Private Partnership in Infrastructure Research Center, "Potential Benefits of Public–Private Partnerships," http://ppp.worldbank.org/public-private-partnership/overview/ppp-objectives.

108 For representative discussion and examples, see: Romero, *What Lies Beneath?* 6; Karin Bäckstrand, "Multi-stakeholder Partnerships for Sustainable Development: Re-thinking Legitimacy, Accountability and Effectiveness," *European Environment* vol. 16 (2006): 290–306; Kacper Szulecki, Philipp Pattberg, and Frank Biermann, "Explaining Variation in the Effectiveness of Transnational Energy Partnerships," *Governance* vol. 24, no. 4 (2011): 713–736; Jonathan Volt, "Opinion: Why Does United Nations Secretary-General Insist on Placing Public–Private Partnerships in the Heart of the Post 2015 Development Agenda?" Earth Systems Governance Project, March 23, 2015.

109 United Nations Foundation, *Understanding Public-Private Partnerships* (Washington, DC: UN Foundation, 2003).

110 For more information on the LDN Fund, see www.unccd.int/actions/impact-investment-fund-land-degradation-neutrality.

Chapter 6

Environmental Politics and Sustainable Development

Abstract

The relationships among environmental protection, economic development, and social development—the three dimensions or pillars of sustainable development—are central to the current landscape of global environmental politics. Thus, it is not surprising that North–South economic issues have been and remain a prominent element of global environmental politics. Numerous developing countries still perceive global economic relations as fundamentally inequitable. This often shapes their policy responses to global environmental issues and their negotiating strategies. Many developing countries argue that the North is responsible for many of the planet's environmental woes and must adopt more sustainable consumption and production patterns and significantly reduce the use of natural resources and fossil fuels before the South follows suit. Yet at the same time, the most significant increases in pollution, population, resource use, and greenhouse gas emissions are occurring in developing countries. This chapter begins by discussing North–South relations in the sustainable development context. It then outlines economic and trade issues that affect environmental politics before concluding with a look at the relationship between the environmental protection and sustainable development agendas, culminating with the United Nations 2030 Agenda for Sustainable Development and its seventeen Sustainable Development Goals.

Keywords: additionality, common but differentiated responsibilities, economics, environmental politics, North, South, polluter pays principle, sustainable development, Sustainable Development Goals, trade

As the case studies in this book demonstrate, environmental issues are inextricably linked with economic and social issues. While other factors are also important (see Chapters 3, 4, and 5), the relationships among environmental protection, economic development, and social development—the three dimensions or pillars of sustainable development—are central to the current landscape of global environmental politics.

Thus, it is not surprising that North–South economic issues have been and remain a prominent element of global environmental politics. Despite the growth of many emerging economies, including Brazil, China, India, and South Africa, to name a few, numerous developing countries still perceive global economic relations as fundamentally inequitable. This often shapes their policy responses to global environmental issues and their negotiating strategies. Many developing countries argue that the North is responsible for many of the planet's environmental woes and must adopt more sustainable consumption and production patterns and significantly reduce the use of natural resources and fossil fuels before the South follows suit. Yet at the same time, the most significant increases in pollution, population, resource use, and greenhouse gas (GHG) emissions are in developing countries.

This chapter looks at several central issues at the intersection of global environmental politics and development. We begin by discussing North–South relations in the sustainable development context. We then outline systemic economic changes and economic and trade issues that affect environmental politics. We conclude with a look at the evolution of the relationship between the environmental protection and sustainable development agendas, culminating with the United Nations 2030 Agenda for Sustainable Development and its seventeen Sustainable Development Goals.

North–South Relations, the Environment, and Sustainable Development

Historically, many developing countries perceived global environmental issues as a North–South issue and, sometimes, even as an effort to sabotage their development aspirations. This perspective emerged back in 1971 at a seminar held in Founex, Switzerland, which laid the groundwork for the 1972 Stockholm Conference on the Human Environment. The Founex Report that emerged from the seminar was the first paper to identify key environment and development objectives and relationships and the policy and conceptual differences separating developed and developing countries.[1] The tone and substance of the report foreshadowed key elements of the South's rhetoric during the subsequent fifty years of global environmental conferences and regime negotiations. The Founex Report provides critical testimony that these interests (1) have remained largely unchanged over time and (2) lie at the heart of today's global politics of sustainable development.[2] As the Founex Report states:

> The developing countries would clearly wish to avoid, as far as feasible, the [environmental] mistakes and distortions that have characterized the patterns of development of the industrialized societies. However, the major environmental problems of the developing countries are essentially of a different kind.
>
> They are predominantly problems that reflect the poverty and very lack of development in their societies ... These are problems, no less than those of industrial pollution, that clamor for attention in the context of the concern with human environment. They are problems which affect the greater mass of mankind ... In [industrialized] countries, it is appropriate to view development as a cause of environmental problems ... In [the southern] context, development becomes essentially a cure for their major environmental problems.[3]

Although many developing-country officials, particularly in environment ministries, recognize the seriousness of environmental degradation and how it negatively affects their economic future, the viewpoints expressed in the Founex Report help explain why many developing countries often regard global environmental regimes as peripheral to their core concerns and sometimes even suspiciously—as a means by which some industrialized countries seek to maintain or even gain new control over resources, intellectual property, and technology located in the South.

The 1972 Stockholm Conference on the Human Environment treated the environment as part of the broader development process in order to allay these concerns. This helped focus discussion on specific problems facing developing countries and implied that additional financial resources would be sought, primarily through existing development assistance channels.[4] Along these lines, the resulting Stockholm Declaration and Action Plan specifically noted (in Recommendations 102–109) that environmental concerns should not be a pretext for discriminatory trade policies or reduced access to markets and that the burdens of environmental policies of industrialized countries should not be transferred to developing countries. Recommendation 109, in particular, called on states to ensure that concerns of developed countries with their own environmental problems should not affect the flow of assistance to developing countries and that this flow should be adequate to meet the additional environmental requirements of such countries.[5]

Emergence of Sustainable Development

In the wake of the Stockholm Conference, the UN raised international environmental awareness through governments, nongovernmental organizations (NGOs), and the world's business and scientific communities. However, environmental and development issues were often addressed separately. Stockholm successfully brought international attention to the need for cooperation on environmental problems but did not resolve any of the inherent tensions in linking environmental protection with social and economic development.[6]

In 1983 the UN General Assembly established an independent commission to formulate a long-term agenda for action on the broad issues of environment and development. Chaired by Norway's environment minister, Gro Harlem Brundtland, the commission conducted fifteen public hearings over three years at locations around the world. Both governments and civil society participated in the hearings. The commission's 1987 report, *Our Common Future*, stressed the need for development strategies in all countries that recognized the limits of natural ecosystems to regenerate themselves and to absorb waste products. Recognizing "an accelerating ecological interdependence among nations,"[7] the commission emphasized the link between economic development and environmental issues and identified poverty eradication as a necessary and fundamental requirement for environmentally sustainable development. In addition, the report noted that the goals of economic and social development must be defined in terms of sustainability in all countries: developed or developing, market-oriented or centrally planned.[8] It also determined that a series of rapid transitions and policy changes were required, including keeping population levels, pollution, and consumption in harmony with the ecosystem, reducing mass poverty, increasing equity within and among nations, increasing efficiency in the use of energy and other resources, reorienting technology, and merging environment and economics in decision making.[9]

The Brundtland Report also called on the UN General Assembly to convene an international conference to review progress and promote follow-up arrangements. This became the 1992 Earth Summit (formally known as the UN Conference on Environment and Development or UNCED), which achieved a pact, underpinned by a set of core principles that had their origins in the Brundtland Report, among countries of the North and countries of the South that linked environmental and developmental concerns.

The Rio Principles

On the twentieth anniversary of the Stockholm Conference, governments gathered in Rio de Janeiro, Brazil, to move the sustainable development agenda forward. The 1992 Earth Summit attracted greater official and unofficial interest than had the Stockholm Conference. The summit and the two years of preparatory work that preceded it showed that there were still significant differences between developed and developing countries on many environmental issues. Each group provided different inputs to the agenda-setting process. Developed countries wanted to focus on ozone depletion, climate change, acid rain, and deforestation. Developing countries preferred exploring the relationship among sluggish economic growth, consumption and production patterns, and the economic policies of the developed countries. They emphasized that an "environmentally healthy planet was impossible in a world that contained significant inequities."[10]

The major output of the Earth Summit was a global plan of action for sustainable development, called Agenda 21. Agenda 21 demonstrated an emerging consensus on the issues affecting the long-term sustainability of human society, including domestic social and economic policies, international economic relations, and cooperation on issues concerning the global commons. The summit also produced the Rio Declaration on Environment and Development, which led to the institutionalization of several principles that have roots in Stockholm but have become features of nearly all post-Rio global environmental treaties and politics. Three that have particular relevance for North–South relations are additionality, common but differentiated responsibilities (CBDR), and the polluter pays principle.

The first of these principles is additionality, which is not explicitly stated in the Rio Declaration but underlies most of Agenda 21 as well as the climate change, ozone, and persistent organic pollutants regimes. The principle of additionality arose out of developing countries' concern that instead of raising new funds for addressing global environmental issues, the industrialized countries and international financial institutions would simply divert resources previously targeted for development. Thus, the principle of additionality sought to ensure that new monies would be made available to deal with global environmental issues.[11]

Despite assurances given to the South, however, this principle suffered a setback soon after the Earth Summit during the negotiation of the desertification convention. Early in these negotiations, it became clear that the industrialized countries were not going to make new funds available. This dismayed developing countries, particularly those in Africa, and became a major source of contention during the negotiations. Ultimately, the Global Mechanism was established under the 1994 UN Convention to Combat Desertification (UNCCD), its role essentially being to use existing resources more efficiently to meet the action needs of the convention (see Chapter 4).[12] Nevertheless, the fact that the UNCCD regime began without new and additional financial resources to combat desertification damaged the principle of additionality.[13]

Both the principle of additionality and demands for "new and additional" funding to assist developing countries' implementation of global environmental agreements were also harmed by sharp reductions in official development assistance (ODA) in the 1990s. In response, developing countries started to use the threat of retreating from previous consensus agreements on environmental issues as leverage. However, commitments made at the March 2002 UN Conference on Financing for Development reversed the ODA declines. In 2005, donors also committed to increase ODA at the Group of Eight summit in Gleneagles, Scotland,[14] and at the UN Millennium +5 Summit.[15] These pledges, combined with other commitments, implied an increase in aid from nearly $80 billion in 2004 to $147.55 billion at its peak in 2016. Yet, it still represented only 0.32 percent of combined gross national income, far below the target of 0.7 percent.[16] (See Box 6.1.)

Ten years after the Rio Earth Summit, bilateral ODA from Organisation for Economic Co-operation and Development (OECD) members (developed countries) to non-OECD members (developing countries) for global environmental objectives (climate change, biodiversity, desertification, and other treaties/agreements), as measured by the OECD's Development Assistance Committee (DAC), had only reached $4.84 billion, or 6 percent of $80.49 billion total ODA. When ODA for projects that have a significant environmental benefit, even though the principal reason for the funding was not the environment (for example, a project for providing clean drinking water, which may be aimed at human health and well-being but has a secondary environmental benefit, or agricultural funding that can also help adapt to climate change), is included, the 2002 total reached $8.78 billion, or 11 percent of total ODA. Fifteen years later, ODA from the DAC member countries for global environmental objectives had increased to 20 percent of total ODA, or $29.03 billion, and when added to other projects that also had environmental benefits, the total increased to $85.67 billion, or 58 percent of total ODA.[17] (See Figure 6.1.) Regardless of this increase, however, ODA from DAC member countries alone is not nearly enough for all developing

❖ BOX 6.1   THE 0.7 PERCENT ODA TARGET[18]

The best-known international target in the aid field is raising official development assistance (ODA) to 0.7 percent of donors' national income. The target grew out of a proposal by the World Council of Churches in 1958 to transfer 1 percent of donor countries' income to developing countries. But it had a major problem: governments had no means of programming or even predicting the private element of capital flows, which in many years make up more than half the total.

This drawback stimulated efforts to define a separate sub-target for official flows. The Dutch economist Jan Tinbergen led this work after he was appointed chair of the United Nations Committee on Development Planning in 1964. Tinbergen estimated the capital inflows that developing economies needed to achieve desirable growth rates, and proposed a target for official flows—both concessional (grants and subsidized loans) and non-concessional—of 0.75 percent of gross national product (GNP), to be achieved by 1972. Some, but not all, developed countries accepted this target, but without the date, at the second meeting of the United Nations Conference on Trade and Development (UNCTAD), held in New Delhi in 1968.

This idea was then taken up by the Pearson Commission, appointed by World Bank President Robert McNamara in 1968. The Commission's 1969 Report proposed that ODA "be raised to 0.70 percent of donor GNP by 1975 and in no case later than 1980."[19]

In the late 1960s, intense negotiations occurred in the United Nations regarding future development programs. Aid volume was a key sticking point between developed and developing countries. For most of the negotiations, developing countries pressed for the UNCTAD target of 0.75 percent of GNP in total official flows. But when negotiations stalled a couple of weeks before the UN General Assembly was due to vote on the resolution, they substituted the Pearson Commission target of 0.7 percent of GNP in official development assistance. This broke the impasse, and although most donor countries expressed reservations, UN General Assembly Resolution 2626 (XXV) included the goal that "Each economically advanced country will progressively increase its official development assistance to the developing countries and will exert its best efforts to reach a minimum net amount of 0.7% of its gross national product" by the mid-1970s.

During the 1970s, the new target gained acceptance, with exceptions. The United States made it clear that, while it supported the general aims of the resolution, it did not subscribe to specific targets or timetables. Switzerland was not a member of the United Nations at the time, and did not adopt the target. All other developed countries have at one time or another accepted it, at least as a long-term objective, and it has been repeatedly re-endorsed at international conferences. However, in 2019 only Sweden, the United Kingdom, Norway, Denmark, and Luxembourg met or exceeded the target.[20] Finland achieved it once, in 1991. The Netherlands dropped below the target in 2013 for the first time since 1975.[21] None of the other thirty members of the Organisation for Economic Co-operation and Development's (OECD) Development Assistance Committee (DAC) has ever met the 0.7 percent target.[22]

countries to meet their global environmental commitments. In addition, the economic impact of the COVID-19 pandemic may affect the ability of many countries to devote more funds to environmental protection (even given the long-term economic advantages of doing so) and of many donor countries to provide funds.

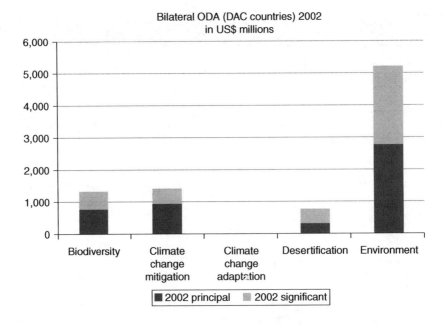

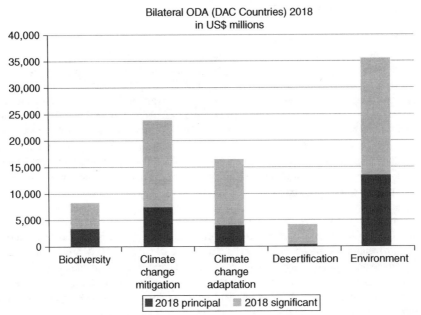

Figure 6.1 Bilateral Aid Activities Targeting Global Environmental Objectives 2002 and 2018

Notes: Funding source is Organisation for Economic Development and Co-Operation Development Assistance Committee (OECD DAC) member countries only.

Funding for climate adaptation activities was not measured separately in 2002.

Data source: OECD, "Aid activities targeting Global Environmental Objectives," Accessed June 28, 2020, https://stats.oecd.org/Index.aspx?DataSetCode=RIOMARKERS#.

Developing countries continue to argue that the North should bear the financial burden of measures to reverse existing ecological damage and meet much of the burden of avoiding even more serious damage in the future. This is a key component of the principle of CBDR. This principle states that global environmental problems are the common concern of all nations, and all nations should work toward their solution (common responsibilities), but action should be differentiated in proportion to the responsibility for creating the problem and the financial and technical resources available for taking effective action (differentiated responsibilities).

The CBDR principle enjoys broad support among developing countries and has been explicitly acknowledged in nearly all global environmental agreements since the mid-1980s. Specific regime rules reflect the principle in a number of ways: the different schedules for industrialized and developing countries to reduce and then eliminate ozone-depleting substances under the Montreal Protocol (as discussed in Chapter 3, developing countries are given additional years before they must phase out particular chemicals); the calls for industrialized countries, and only industrialized countries, to freeze their GHG emissions under the United Nations Framework Convention on Climate Change (UNFCCC); the absence of developing-country commitments to reduce GHG emissions under the Kyoto Protocol; references in many regimes requesting that parties take into account "the special situation" of landlocked developing countries, small island developing states, or least developed countries; and provisions to provide developing countries with financial and technical assistance (FTA) to help them implement the ozone, climate, biodiversity, desertification, hazardous waste, chemicals, and mercury regimes.

At the same time, as discussed in Chapter 5, important differences exist regarding how countries believe the CBDR principle should influence global environmental policy both in general and on specific issues. Developing countries emphasize historical responsibilities for causing global environmental problems, the large disparities in current per capita contributions (e.g., in per capita GHG emissions or resource consumption), and their need to devote resources to lifting millions of people out of extreme poverty and underdevelopment. It would be unfair, counterproductive, and perhaps immoral, they maintain, for developing countries to devote scarce resources to combating global environmental problems at the expense of addressing economic and social development. Thus, many developing countries argue that the CBDR principle demands not only that industrialized countries should take far more significant action and provide greatly increased FTA but also that developing countries should take on commitments only to the extent that they receive sufficient FTA to allow them to implement the requirements under a global regime without having a negative impact on their economic development. This means, for example, that the FTA must meet all of the extra, or incremental, costs for using alternatives to the ozone-depleting chemicals or coal-fired power plants that industrialized countries used during their economic development.

In contrast, although most industrialized countries allow that historical responsibility is relevant to policy discussions, they also emphasize the common responsibility of all countries to contribute to solving global environmental problems, which implies a need for developing countries to avoid duplicating the unsustainable historical development patterns of the industrialized world. They also point out that some developing countries are currently among the most important contributors to particular environmental problems and that it will be simply impossible to address these issues, in particular climate change, mercury pollution, and deforestation, if these developing countries do not act, and act soon. Thus, many industrialized countries maintain that, although it is appropriate for them to act first and to provide FTA, developing countries must also take action; particular levels of FTA are not a precondition for developing countries to take responsible action; and developing countries experiencing rapid levels of economic growth or that have large impacts on particular environmental problems have more responsibility to act on those problems than other developing countries.

These differences have been on full display in the climate negotiations. The United States and some other countries have argued that certain developing nations should agree to take significant action to reduce their GHG emissions from burning fossil fuels (e.g., China and India) and deforestation (e.g., Brazil and Indonesia). Many (but not all) developing countries rejected these arguments, citing their low per capita emissions, their need for energy and economic development, inadequate FTA provisions, and the responsibility of industrialized countries for creating the problem. The Paris Agreement is the first climate agreement without the CBDR principle at its core (see Chapter 3). Nevertheless, developing countries have not jettisoned the principle as part of their negotiating briefs.

The polluter pays principle seeks to ensure that the economic and other costs of environmental action should be borne by those who create the need for that action. As with other Rio Principles, developing countries have argued that the polluter pays principle has been steadily diluted. They point to an increasing pattern of pushing treaty implementation steadily southward, including in the climate, desertification, and biodiversity regimes, by seeking relatively fewer changes in behavior patterns in the North and relatively more in the South, even though northern behavior gave rise to most of the problems in the first place.[23]

Developing counties also regularly criticize the governing structures of international organizations such as the World Bank, which allows a minority of donor countries to outvote the rest of the world. Developing countries have stated that institutions making decisions on how to spend funds on the global environment should have a democratic structure, that is, one in which countries are more equally represented. Thus, developing countries did some of their toughest bargaining in environmental negotiations when they resisted the donor countries' proposed governance structure for the Global Environment Facility (GEF) and successfully negotiated more equal representation on the GEF Council (see Chapter 2).

Developing countries have also called for the transfer of environmental technologies on concessional or preferential terms to be part of environmental treaties. In the Montreal Protocol negotiations, for instance, developing states requested a guarantee from industrialized countries that corporations would provide them with patents and technical knowledge on substitutes for ozone-depleting substances. This has also been a major issue in the climate change and chemicals negotiations. Although significant investments involving the latest technologies have occurred in some developing countries in the climate and ozone sectors, the outright transfer of patents has not.

For these and other reasons, many developing countries remain frustrated with global environmental politics, in part due to their criticism that the global economic system remains unfairly skewed in favor of advanced industrialized countries. On the one hand, some argue that the concept of sustainable development has allowed developing countries to incorporate long-standing concerns about economic and social development into the environmental agendas, and that by doing so, they have influenced the nature of global environmental discourse.[24] On the other hand, some claim that the South has seen few development benefits from its involvement in global environmental politics. Much of North–South environmental relations in the years since the 1992 Earth Summit has focused on what the South sees as the North's failure to deliver what was promised or implied at Rio: new and additional financial resources, technology transfer, and capacity building.

Changing Economic Realities

The relationship between the global economy and the natural environment goes a long way toward explaining the evolution of sustainable development politics. The post-World War II global economy of the 1950s and 1960s included a sharp divide between developed or industrialized countries in the North and developing countries in the South. At that time, developed countries accounted for 90 percent of world manufacturing output and 90 percent of exports.[25] In addition to this imbalance in production and exports, there was an imbalance in living standards and political power.

By 1974, encouraged by a surge in commodity prices and the Organization of Petroleum Exporting Countries' (OPEC) successful manipulation of oil supplies, developing countries attempted to restructure the global economic system. The South called for a bold but largely unrealistic plan, the New International Economic Order, containing a list of demands for the redistribution of wealth, which would include a new system of international commodity agreements, a unilateral reduction of barriers to imports from developing states into industrialized countries, the enhancement of developing countries' capabilities in science and technology, increased northern financing of technology transfer, and changes in patent laws to lower the cost of such transfers.[26]

After the late 1970s, however, the New International Economic Order faded from the global political agenda as economic trends turned against the South. Some officials in the North consequently felt even more strongly that it could disregard southern demands for change. Yet, although some northern observers might have considered the New International Economic Order agenda "discredited,"[27] it remained unfinished business for much of the South and was still considered a goal "very much worth pursuing."[28]

In the 1980s, commodity prices, debt, and trade issues shaped the economic picture in developing countries. Falling commodity prices devastated the economies of countries heavily dependent on commodity exports. Between 1980 and 1991, the price of a weighted index of thirty-three primary commodities exported by developing countries, not including energy, declined by 46 percent.[29] Meanwhile, heavy debt burdens, taken on at a time when commodity prices were high and northern banks were freely lending dollars from Arab oil revenues, siphoned off much of the foreign exchange of many developing countries. By 1995, the total external debt of the least developed countries was $136 billion, a sum that represented 112.7 percent of their GNP that year.[30]

But the global economy was also changing. Spurred by the revolution in information technology, trade liberalization, economic reforms, the demise of the Soviet Union, Chinese economic growth, and the increased movement of capital and technology from developed to developing countries, global GDP more than quadrupled in size from 1988 to 2018, increasing from $19.27 trillion to $85.91 trillion.[31] Although this economic growth reached practically every region of the world, a handful of large developing countries—led by China, India, and Brazil—accounted for a major share of global growth. Other emerging economies, such as Indonesia, Mexico, Russia, Turkey, and Vietnam, also grew at a rapid pace. This enabled developing countries to expand their share of global GDP, fueling speculation that the world's economic balance of power has had shifted away from the United States and Europe.[32]

However, despite this growth, significant income gaps exist between and within the industrialized and developing world. Europe and North America, which represent 15 percent of the world's population, control about 57 percent of total household wealth (see Figure 6.2). The richest 10 percent of the world's population hold 83 percent of the world's wealth. The top percentile alone account for 43.9 percent. The bottom 57 percent of the world's population account for only 1.8 percent.[33]

Yet these numbers are not as stark as they were even a decade ago, reflecting the growing prosperity of emerging economies, especially China, and the expansion of the middle class in parts of the developing world. This group, which has tripled in size since 2000 (from 514 million people to 1.7 billion), now controls 32.6 percent of global wealth.[34]

Much of the economic growth in the emerging economies resulted from an expanded emphasis on international trade and investment in adherence with neoliberal economics—a political-economic movement, increasingly prominent since 1980, that deemphasizes or rejects government intervention, believing that progress and even social justice can be achieved through economic growth, which in turn requires freer markets. For example,

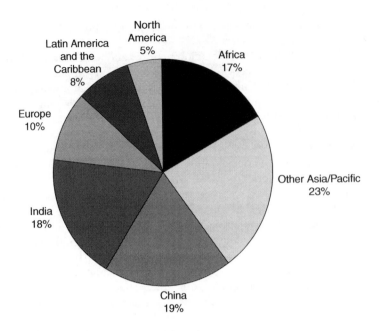

Figure 6.2a Global Population Distribution (2019)

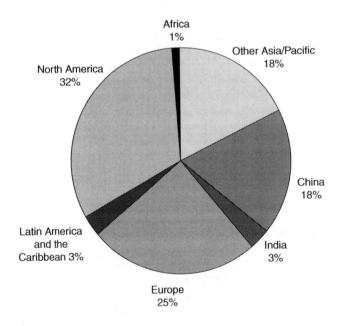

Figure 6.2b Global Wealth Distribution (2019)

Data sources: United Nations, Department of Economic and Social Affairs, Population Division (2019), World Population Prospects 2019, Online Edition, https://population.un.org/wpp/ Download/Standard/Population/ and Credit Suisse Research Institute, *Credit Suisse Global Wealth Report 2019*. (Zurich, Switzerland: Credit Suisse Research Institute, October 2019).

neoliberals argue that the best way to protect the environment is by overcoming poverty through increased privatization, foreign direct investment, and free trade. The belief that poor countries could grow themselves out of poverty by reducing trade barriers and other regulations, encouraging foreign investment, and adopting other elements of "economic liberalization" took on an almost religious zeal in some economic and policy circles within rich countries.[35]

Yet many industrialized countries did not adhere to this philosophy in practice. During the early 1990s, trade barriers erected by industrialized countries against imports of manufactured and processed goods from developing countries increased even as most developing countries (under pressure from international financial institutions) were lowering their barriers to imports.[36] Tariffs on certain sectors of particular interest to developing countries, including agriculture, textiles, clothing, fish, and fish products, tended to be the highest in industrialized countries, limiting market access.[37] Furthermore, new kinds of nontariff barriers to trade (such as antidumping and countervailing duty actions), export-restraint agreements (such as the Multi-Fiber Arrangement), and direct subsidies were used to protect industries in the industrialized countries against less expensive imports due largely to cheaper labor from developing countries.

During this period, the emphasis on trade liberalization raised concern among environmentalists because of its potential impact on both the earth's ecosystems and policy choices. Many environmental NGOs see trade liberalization as helping to increase greater consumption of natural resources and creating pressures to dismantle environmental regulations.[38] They note that the global trade system had evolved for decades without much thought about its impact on the environment, with counterproductive results. When the General Agreement on Tariffs and Trade (GATT), the central pillar of the international trading system, was negotiated just after World War II, there was no mention of the word *environment*. For the next forty years, trade officials and their environmental counterparts pursued their respective agendas on nearly parallel tracks that rarely, if ever, intersected. Little attention was paid to potential connections between trade liberalization and environmental protection.

The GATT and the World Trade Organization (WTO) constitute a regime that seeks to promote a common set of international trade rules, a reduction in tariffs and other trade barriers, and the elimination of discriminatory treatment in international trade relations.[39] The WTO, which governments created in 1995, has the mandate to rule on a broad spectrum of issues, from trade in goods and services to intellectual property rights, including issues affecting human health, the use of natural resources, and the protection of the environment.

The preamble to the treaty that established the WTO recognized that the organization should ensure "the optimal use of the world's resources in accordance with the objective of sustainable development."[40] This was a last-minute victory for environmentalists, although the preamble is nonbinding. With this in mind, and with a desire to coordinate policies in the field of trade and the environment, the WTO also created a Committee on Trade and Environment (CTE) and ensured that the subject would have a place on the WTO agenda. The CTE was tasked with making "appropriate recommendations on whether any modifications of the provisions of the multilateral trading system are required."[41] Yet, after more than twenty-five years, these recommendations have not appeared.

Some trade negotiators had hoped that trade and environment-related decisions would be part of a successful outcome of the Doha Development Round of trade negotiations. The 2001 Doha Ministerial Declaration included more language on both economic development and environmental issues, including fishing subsidies, than any of its predecessors. Liberalizing global agricultural trade was the linchpin of the agenda. Many developing countries depend on exporting basic agricultural products but have trouble accessing markets in many developed nations that support their farmers with subsidies. The OECD estimates that these subsidies total nearly $300 billion annually. Agricultural lobbies in the United States, Europe, and Japan have consistently exercised their considerable political clout to convince lawmakers to maintain such subsidies. The Doha Round of trade negotiations also sought to further reduce barriers to trade in services, such as business and finance, and non-agricultural goods.[42]

However, WTO member states failed to complete these negotiations, and, after years on life support, the Doha Round was officially declared dead in December 2015. Many countries were so frustrated by the stalemate that they began to negotiate bilateral and regional trade deals. For example, the United States concluded the Trans-Pacific Partnership with Japan, Vietnam, and nine other countries in early 2016 after seven years of negotiations. Even though Donald Trump withdrew the United States from the agreement in 2017 after he became president, the remaining eleven countries (Australia, Brunei Darussalam, Canada, Chile, Japan, Malaysia, Mexico, New Zealand, Peru, Singapore, and Vietnam) signed the Comprehensive and Progressive Agreement for Trans-Pacific Partnership, which entered into force on December 30, 2018. The United States and the European Union (EU) began negotiating the Transatlantic Trade and Investment Partnership in 2013, but the Trump administration halted the talks in 2017. China has signed many bilateral and regional agreements and in 2012 launched negotiations on the Regional Comprehensive Economic Partnership, which originally included ten countries from the Association of Southeast Asian Nations (ASEAN) plus Australia, China, Japan, New Zealand, and South Korea. India pulled out of talks in November 2019 but could still rejoin. Countries were expected to sign the agreement in late 2020.[43]

Although regional agreements can be useful, they threaten to segregate the world into overlapping trading blocs with different rules, including for environmental protection. And most of these agreements—in which countries agree to eliminate tariffs for products made within the trading bloc—do not include the world's least developed countries.[44]

At the start of the Doha Round, American and European officials committed to producing a trade agreement that would promote development in poorer countries without asking them to reduce import barriers to the same extent as industrialized nations. But as some large developing countries, particularly China, began exporting far more than they were importing, wealthier countries started demanding that they also lower import barriers and cut subsidies to their farmers. China and India refused,[45] which some blamed for blocking the entire trade agreement, while others put the onus on developed countries, arguing they were "keen to abandon the Doha Development Round … simply because [they] were not willing to give up on the massive agricultural subsidies that distort global trade."[46]

The following sections examine some of the key issues along the trade and environment nexus: specifically, the relationship between environmental treaties and the WTO, how environmental issues have been addressed in the dispute settlement process, ecolabeling, standards and certification, subsidies and the environment, and liberalizing trade in environmental goods and services.

The Relationship Between Multilateral Environmental Agreements and the World Trade Organization

More than twenty multilateral environmental agreements (MEAs) incorporate trade measures to help them achieve their goals.[47] This means that the agreements use restraints on trade in particular substances or products, either among parties to the treaty, between parties and non-parties, or both. Although this represents a relatively small number of MEAs, they include some of the most important, including the Convention on International Trade in Endangered Species of Wild Fauna and Flora (CITES); the Montreal Protocol; the Basel, Rotterdam, Stockholm, and Minamata Conventions; and the Cartagena Protocol on Biosafety. Under all of these treaties, trade in the specified products (e.g., endangered species, ozone-depleting substances, hazardous wastes, toxic chemicals, mercury, or genetically modified organisms) is banned or restricted among parties or between parties and non-parties (see Box 6.2).

❖ BOX 6.2   SELECTED MEA TRADE MEASURES

Convention on International Trade in Endangered Species of Wild Fauna and Flora:

- invokes trade restrictions against parties and non-parties to protect listed species of animals and plants threatened with extinction and endangerment
- uses a permit-and-listing system to prohibit the import or export of listed wildlife and wild-life products unless a scientific finding is made that the trade in question will not threaten the existence of the species

Montreal Protocol on Substances That Deplete the Ozone Layer:

- prohibits trade in ODS with non-parties unless the non-party has demonstrated full compliance with the control measures under the protocol
- uses trade provisions to encourage the phase-out of ODS and to discourage the establishment of "pollution havens" in which parties shift their manufacturing capabilities to non-parties

Basel Convention on the Control of Transboundary Movements of Hazardous Wastes and Their Disposal:

- uses trade measures to limit the market for the transboundary movement and disposal of hazardous waste between OECD and non-OECD countries
- parties must not permit hazardous waste or other wastes to be traded with a non-party unless that party enters into a bilateral, multilateral, or regional agreement

Rotterdam Convention on the Prior Informed Consent Procedure for Certain Hazardous Chemicals and Pesticides in International Trade:

- parties can decide, from the convention's agreed list of chemicals and pesticides, which ones they will not import
- when trade in other listed substances does occur, labeling and information requirements must be followed, including those that allow for the prior informed consent of the importing party
- if a party decides not to consent to imports of a specific chemical, it must also stop domestic production of the chemical for domestic use, as well as imports from non-parties

Cartagena Protocol on Biosafety:

- parties may restrict the import of some living GMOs as part of a carefully specified risk-management procedure
- living GMOs that will be intentionally released into the environment are subject to an advance informed-agreement procedure, and those destined for use as food, feed, or processing must be accompanied by identifying documents

Trade-restricting measures in an environmental agreement may serve one of two broad purposes. First, they may control a type of trade that produces, contributes to, or encourages environmental damage. A good example is CITES, which requires import and export licenses for trade in some endangered species and prohibits them for others. The Basel Convention seeks to restrict or ban the movement and trade of hazardous waste, seeing such movement as a source of environmental harm. Since the import of toxic substances by countries unaware of their potential for harm can lead to environmental damage, the Rotterdam Convention establishes information exchange and labeling requirements for certain toxic chemicals and pesticides, and allows parties to ban imports of listed substances or require their prior informed consent.

Second, environmental agreements may include trade measures as a means to increase regime participation, compliance, and effectiveness. Some regimes use trade measures as an additional incentive to join and adhere to the MEA by barring non-parties from trading in restricted goods with parties. Non-parties to the Basel Convention, for example, cannot ship certain wastes to any party, nor can they import wastes from them. Some, like the Montreal Protocol, have provisions that allow parties to impose trade sanctions on countries found to have significantly violated regime rules. Others use trade restrictions to enhance regime effectiveness, again by restricting trade in certain controlled substances (as a means to reinforce controls on production and use). This prevents leakage, that is, situations where non-parties or parties with exemptions simply increase production of a restricted good and ship it to the parties that have restricted their own production.[48]

A potential problem with MEA trade measures is that they might conflict with WTO rules. An agreement saying that parties can use trade restrictions against some countries (non-parties) but not against others (parties) could violate Articles I, III, and XI of the GATT (provisions addressing most-favored nations and national-treatment principles, as well as provisions on eliminating quantitative restrictions). Free-trade advocates worry that countries might use trade-restricting measures in an MEA to seek economic gain or to reward friends and punish enemies rather than to protect the environment. Environmentalists worry that countries affected by MEA trade restrictions might challenge their legitimacy before the WTO, which could weaken the MEA.

Most analysts argue that the latter should not be a problem when the countries involved are parties to the MEA. In such cases, the countries have voluntarily agreed to be bound by the MEA's rules, including the trade measures, as spelled out in the agreement. However, problems can arise when the agreement only sets out objectives that might be relevant to trade but leaves it to the parties to make domestic laws to achieve them. The Nagoya Protocol to the Convention on Biological Diversity (CBD) leaves it up to national governments to determine whether changes are necessary to national patent laws for applicants to disclose the use of any traditional knowledge or genetic resources used in their invention. Although WTO members have expressed hope that disputes among parties might be settled within the MEAs themselves, a party complaining about the use of such nonspecific trade measures could choose to take its case to the WTO.[49]

The situation is further complicated if a party to an MEA uses trade measures in the agreement against a non-party but both countries are WTO members. Here, the non-party has not voluntarily agreed to be subject to the MEA's trade measures. As with party-to-party measures, the trade-restricting party may be violating the non-party's rights under WTO rules, but here the non-party might take the matter to the WTO even if the measures are specifically spelled out in the MEA.

This raises the crucial question of which regime, the MEA or the WTO, should be accorded primacy when they conflict. However, the CTE has not made much progress on these issues, largely due to the collapse of the Doha Round of trade negotiations.

Environmental Issues and the World Trade Organization Dispute Settlement System

Potential conflicts between WTO provisions and trade restrictions established by individual nations outside of MEAs are much more common. Since environmental policy affects, and is affected by, most economic and trade policies, it is not surprising that conflicts between trade liberalization and environmental protection have increased in both number and diplomatic prominence. Indeed, the first case heard by the WTO Dispute Settlement Body involved the environment.[50]

Environmental trade measures (ETMs)—policies that seek to regulate or restrict trade as a tool to address environmental problems—include import prohibitions, product standards, standards governing production of natural resource exports, and mandatory ecolabeling schemes.[51] Exporters disadvantaged by such environmental measures sometimes charge that the policies are actually intended to protect domestic producers from foreign competition.

The United States has historically taken the lead in defending the right of national governments to use ETMs for domestic and international environmental objectives and, consequently, has been the target of several cases brought before WTO dispute panels. The United States used trade restrictions in conjunction with its lead-state efforts to end commercial whaling, to protect dolphins from being killed by tuna fishers, to protect marine mammals from destructive drift nets, and to support CITES. This includes the sweeping bans on ivory and ivory-containing products the United States enacted in 2016 to augment protection of the increasingly endangered African elephant.[52] Sometimes the United States has used the threat of ETMs for similar purposes. For example, US threats to ban South Korean fish products from the US market and prohibit Korean fishing operations in US waters helped persuade South Korea to give up both whaling and driftnet operations in the Pacific Ocean.[53]

When a country believes that an ETM unfairly restricts market access, it can file a complaint, and a WTO dispute-resolution panel has the authority to determine whether a particular trade measure is or is not compatible with the GATT trade rules. The panels consist of trade specialists from three or five contracting parties with no stake in the issue and who have been agreed to by both parties to the dispute. Dispute panel rulings are normally submitted to the WTO Council (which includes all parties to the agreement) for approval. Decisions carry real weight. If a country fails to bring its law into conformity with the decision, other states are allowed to implement retaliatory trade measures. This is more threatening to small countries than large trading countries such as the United States. Few small countries will risk taking significant retaliatory measures on their own against the United States or the EU, as these could prove counterproductive.[54]

US laws employing ETMs have been challenged before the GATT/WTO disputeresolution panels on several occasions. The panel's first decision, on the US–Mexican tuna–dolphin dispute, helped to shape the politics of trade and environment issues. In 1991 Mexico filed a complaint with the GATT charging that a US embargo against Mexican yellowfin tuna was a protectionist measure put in place to benefit the US tuna industry. The embargo had been imposed under an amendment to the 1972 Marine Mammal Protection Act, which allowed the use of trade sanctions against countries that killed too many dolphins while catching tuna (the Mexican fleet killed dolphins at twice the rate of the US fleet).[55] The panel ruled that the US ban violated the GATT because it concerned only the process of tuna fishing in international waters rather than the product. This was a historic decision that reflected the tendency of most trade specialists to view ETMs as setting dangerous precedents that could harm the world trade system.[56]

Two other environmental complaints brought under WTO dispute settlement rules also set precedents. In the first, Venezuela and Brazil claimed that they were being discriminated against by a US Environmental Protection Agency rule under the Clean Air Act that required all refineries selling gasoline into the US market to use the 1990 US industry standard as a baseline. Because fuel from foreign refineries was not as clean in 1990 as that from US refineries, the importing countries were beginning their clean-up efforts from a different starting point. In 1997, the WTO panel ruled in favor of Venezuela and Brazil, and the Environmental Protection Agency revised its rules.[57]

The second case stemmed from US efforts to implement the Endangered Species Act. In December 1995, the US Court of International Trade, in response to a lawsuit brought by the Earth Island Institute, an NGO, ruled that in order to export shrimp to the United States, countries that trawl for shrimp in waters where marine turtles live must be certified by the US government to have equipped their vessels with turtle-excluder devices (TEDs). In January 1997, India, Malaysia, Pakistan, and Thailand charged that this US ban on imported shrimp violated WTO rules that no nation can use trade restrictions to influence the (fishing) rules of other countries. The United States argued that relatively simple and inexpensive TEDs could be placed on shrimp trawlers to save the turtles. If properly installed and operated, TEDs allow most sea turtles to escape from shrimp trawling nets before they drown, with minimal loss of shrimp compared with non-TED nets. TEDs have been mandatory on all US shrimp trawlers since December 1994.

In April 1998, the WTO dispute settlement panel held that the US import ban on shrimp was "clearly a threat to the multilateral trading system" and consequently "not within the scope of measures permitted under the chapeau of Article XX [General Exceptions]." The United States appealed the decision. In October 1998, the appellate body found that the US ban legitimately related to the "protection of exhaustible natural resources" and thus qualified for provisional justification under Article XX(g) and was allowable. The decision may have set a positive precedent for the use of unilateral trade measures for environmental purposes, but it also found that the US import ban had been applied in an unjustifiably or arbitrarily discriminatory manner and cited seven distinct flaws in the legislation. It found, for example, that the requirement that exporters adopt "essentially the same policy" as that applied by the United States had an unjustifiably "coercive effect" on foreign countries. It also found that the United States had not seriously attempted to reach a multilateral solution with the four complaining countries and that the process for certification of turtle protection programs was not "transparent" or "predictable."[58]

In response to the appellate body decision, the United States adjusted its policy. The revised guidelines still prohibit the import of shrimp harvested with technology adversely affecting the relevant sea turtle species. But instead of requiring the use of TEDs, it allowed the exporting country to present evidence that its program to protect sea turtles in the course of shrimp trawling was comparable in effectiveness to the US program. The guidelines note, however, that the Department of State is not aware of technology as effective as the TED.[59]

Ecolabeling, Standards, and Certification

Ecolabels—labeling products according to environmental criteria established by governments, industry, or NGOs—help consumers exercise preferences for environmentally sound production methods, such as wood harvested from sustainably managed forests rather than clear-cutting, fish caught from sustainable fisheries, or tuna caught with methods that do not kill large numbers of dolphins. Although some ecolabels are conferred by the product firms themselves or by trade associations, the ones with the most credibility are third-party ecolabels awarded by independent entities that use clear and consistent criteria to evaluate the process and production methods by which a product is made, grown, or caught. While governments sponsor ecolabel programs, some of the most important are private, voluntary schemes. Third-party ecolabels have already demonstrated their potential for attracting the attention of producers where international policy making has failed, as shown by the case of the Forest Stewardship Council (FSC) and timber products.

After the 1992 Earth Summit failed to produce an agreement to stop deforestation, a group of businesses, environmentalists, and community leaders joined together to create a voluntary, market-based approach that sought to improve forestry practices worldwide. That meeting marked the birth of the FSC.[60] By 1995, the FSC had begun setting standards for sustainable forest management, criteria for potential certifiers to meet, and releasing labels to signify that a product has been certified by FSC standards—harvesting trees in a way that protects water, soil, indigenous rights, and wildlife, as well as ensuring reforestation and good community and labor relations. FSC hoped to create a larger market for certified forest products and to use that market to leverage more sustainable forest management. Today, FSC's governing body comprises more than 1100 member organizations and individuals equally divided among environmental, social, and economic voting chambers. FSC members include environmental organizations such as WWF, Greenpeace, and Friends of the Earth, as well as companies such as IKEA, Home Depot, the Walt Disney Company, and International Paper. FSC also has the support of a large and growing number of companies that have united themselves in various countries into buyers' groups committed to selling only independently certified timber and timber products.

The unprecedented FCS initiative resulted in arguably greater levels of dialogue and progress than the formal international negotiations on forests and began to change forest-management practices worldwide. By 2020, more than 198 million hectares of forested land were FSC certified in eighty-two countries around the world—the equivalent of more than 10 percent of the world's production forests. FSC works with 150,000 small holders around the world and is increasingly working with indigenous groups who live in and around certified forests.[61]

In 1997, WWF and Unilever, the world's largest buyer of seafood, created the London-based Marine Stewardship Council (MSC). Operating independently since 1999, MSC has developed the leading standard for sustainable and well-managed fisheries and uses an eco-label to recognize and reward environmentally responsible practices. Consumers concerned about overfishing can choose seafood products that have been independently assessed against the MSC standard and labeled to prove it. As of 2020, fisheries responsible for nearly 15 percent of marine catch have been certified to the MSC Fisheries Standard. More than 36,000 products are sold with the blue MSC ecolabel, including fresh, frozen, smoked, and canned fish, fish-oil dietary supplements, and other items. This amounts to more than $5 billion in global annual sales, all of which can be traced back to certified sustainable fisheries.[62] However, it is worth noting that the annual world trade in fish and fishery products is about $152 billion,[63] and MSC proponents understand that global fisheries remain severely threatened and there is a long way to go to ensure sustainable fish production.

While FSC and MSC are among the most prominent, there are more than 460 different types of ecolabels. The large number can certainly confuse consumers regarding which systems are the most valid (see Figure 6.3). However, a 2018 report by the Changing Markets Foundation found that "rather than being an accelerator for positive change, this 'flood' of certification creates confusion for consumers and the industry and is standing in the way of genuinely sustainable consumption."[64] The report investigated an array of ecolabeling programs in seafood, textiles, and palm oil, ranging from product labels, such as the MSC, to industry-wide initiatives aiming to improve the environmental performance of a sector as a whole, such as the Higg Index in textiles. The report concludes that many schemes are so focused on getting a majority of industry players on board, or meeting the growing demand for certified products, that they lower their standards on sustainability. The report recommends that certification schemes be more ambitious, not compromise to satisfy the priorities of different companies, and become more comprehensive by covering the entire life cycle of a product.[65]

Although some ecolabeling initiatives have proven successful, they also have the potential to be used in unfair and discriminatory ways and can be accused of such even when they are not. In May 2012, the WTO's highest court issued its first ever ruling on ecolabeling. The court ruled that the US government dolphin-safe label violated WTO law by discriminating against Mexican tuna. The judgment was immediately lambasted by environmentalists and US consumer advocates who saw the judgment as an attack on US dolphin protection. However, the point of criticism was not necessarily the high standards used vis-à-vis Mexican products but, rather, the low standards used vis-à-vis all other products. The judges specifically criticized the US law for being unable to guarantee that non-Mexican products eligible for the label were, in fact, fished in a dolphin-safe manner. Thus, the label violated the WTO's Technical Barriers to Trade Agreement, which states that regulations must be

Figure 6.3 Examples of Ecolabels

implemented in a non-discriminatory manner, treating all foreign products in a given sector equally and no less favorably than similar domestic products.[66]

Some developing countries remain hostile to particular third-party ecolabeling programs because they threaten to reduce markets for a domestic industry using what others judge an unsustainable practice. Both developed and developing countries have also expressed more justifiable concerns about other ecolabeling programs that appear skewed in favor of domestic producers and against foreign competitors. This type of ecolabeling conveys an advantage to a domestic industry by virtually mandating a particular technology or production process, ignoring that another technology or process may be equally or more environmentally sound and more suitable in the country of origin.

Subsidies and the Environment

Another important issue on the trade and environment agenda is the need to eliminate subsidies that harm the environment. A subsidy may be defined as any government-directed intervention that, whether through budgeted programs or other means, transfers resources to a particular economic group. Subsidies distort markets by reducing prices and sending signals to producers and consumers that fail to reflect the true costs, including environmental harm, of production. Subsidies on goods traded internationally also give unfair price advantages compared to similar goods from countries that provide no subsidies.

Subsidies can have significant negative impacts on the environment, especially in the commodity sectors (e.g., agriculture, forests, fossil fuels, fisheries, and mining). They draw more investment into these sectors and exacerbate the overexploitation of land, forests, water, and fish. They also reduce the cost of particular practices, products, or technologies that harm the environment, such as flood irrigation, mining, fossil fuel extraction and use, or excessive use of pesticides, while making more sustainable products and practices appear less attractive economically.[67]

Fisheries subsidies are one of the factors that have led to massive overfishing. According to the UN Food and Agriculture Organization (FAO), nearly 90 percent of the world's marine fish stocks are now fully exploited, overexploited, or depleted.[68] Billions of dollars of damaging subsidies continue to be poured into fishing every year, despite governments' agreement on long-standing goals to eliminate them. Estimated at $35.4 billion per year worldwide in 2018,[69] subsidies are used to make fuel cheaper, support boat building, or help fleets purchase larger or more effective nets and other supplies. Nearly a quarter of all subsidies provided to fishing fleets are for fossil fuel. These are considered among the most harmful because they make it affordable for more vessels to spend more time at sea and emit more GHGs. Taken together, fishing subsidies increase the size of fishing fleets, augment the ability of individual ships to catch more fish, reduce their cost of operation, and make fishing seem more profitable than it really is—all of which help to drive the global decline in fish populations.

China provides the most fishing-related subsidies, 21 percent of the global total, followed by the EU (11 percent), the United States (10 percent), and South Korea (9 percent).[70] Japan and the EU each provide over $2 billion in capacity-enhancing subsidies to their fleets, much of which engages in distant water fishing that exacerbates overfishing in the waters of other countries, especially developing countries, and in the high seas. Fish remains one of the most traded food commodities worldwide, and 54 percent of this trade comes from developing countries. For these countries, the fish trade generates more income than most other food commodities combined. The sustainability of fisheries, which subsidies help deplete, is therefore essential to the livelihoods of tens of millions of people, especially in developing countries, where 97 percent of fishers live.[71]

Photo 6.1 During the 2017 UN Ocean Conference, most delegates called on World Trade Organization negotiators to address harmful fisheries subsidies.

Courtesy of UN Photo/Kim Haughton.

Since the establishment of the WTO, some members have focused on the elimination of fisheries subsidies as possibly the greatest contribution that the multilateral trading system could make to sustainable development. The lead-state coalition, known as the Friends of Fish (Argentina, Australia, Chile, Colombia, Ecuador, Iceland, New Zealand, Norway, Pakistan, Peru, and United States), have pointed to the win-win-win nature of such action: good for the environment, good for development, and good for trade. But a veto coalition consisting of heavily subsidizing members (the EU, Japan, and South Korea) have argued that the empirical evidence that eliminating subsidies would benefit the environment was still weak. Japan and South Korea insisted that poor fisheries management, rather than subsidies, was the root cause of stock depletion.

The Doha Ministerial Declaration explicitly called for negotiations aimed at clarifying and improving WTO rules on fisheries subsidies. At the 2015 WTO ministerial conference, governments failed again to reach a deal. In response, a group of WTO members released a ministerial statement pledging to reinvigorate WTO work in order to achieve ambitious and effective disciplines on fisheries subsidies, a move welcomed by conservation groups.[72] Two years later, at the 2017 Buenos Aires Ministerial Conference, ministers agreed to conclude these negotiations by aiming to adopt an agreement to curb harmful fisheries subsidies by the 12th WTO Ministerial Conference,[73] which was scheduled for June 2020 but postponed until at least 2021 due to the COVID-19 pandemic.

Liberalizing Trade in Environmental Goods and Services

The environmental goods and services sector includes activities, processes, goods, and services that "measure, prevent, limit, minimize or correct environmental damage to water, air and soil, as well as problems related to waste, noise and ecosystems," including cleaner technologies, renewable energy technologies, products and services that reduce environmental risk, pollution, and resource use.[74] When new domestic environmental regulations are introduced, one way that companies, governments, and consumers respond is by demanding goods and services that can alleviate associated compliance costs. In other words, there is greater demand for products that protect the environment. Opening markets to environmental goods and services allows the spread of new resource-efficient technologies.[75]

The WTO emphasizes that reducing tariff and nontariff barriers on environmental goods and services will facilitate trade and economic development because domestic purchasers will be able to acquire environmental technologies from foreign companies at lower costs. The environment will benefit because of the wider availability of less expensive products and technologies, which in turn will improve the quality of life by providing better access to clean water, sanitation, and clean energy. Finally, the liberalization of trade in environmental goods and services will help developing countries obtain the tools they need to address key environmental priorities as part of their ongoing development strategies.[76]

The negotiations on reducing trade barriers for environmental goods and services could have an impact on several MEAs. Their outcome could affect the price and market availability of products and technologies to replace ozone-depleting substances and persistent organic pollutants under the Montreal Protocol and Stockholm Convention, respectively. They could improve the availability of technologies for the environmentally sound management of hazardous wastes under the Basel Convention or to reduce mercury emissions under the Minamata Convention. They could increase the availability and lower the cost of green energy and energy efficiency technologies to help countries implement their commitments under the Paris Agreement on climate change. Trade liberalization could also contribute toward fulfilling the technology-transfer mandates contained in the UNFCCC and similar provisions in other MEAs. However, despite a statement in the Ministerial Declaration that initiated the Doha trade round instructing WTO members to negotiate the reduction or elimination of such trade barriers, WTO members have been unable to do so. Many states have provided lists of proposed environmental goods for tariff reductions, including air pollution control, renewable energy, waste management, water treatment, environmental technologies, and carbon capture and storage. Further progress came in July 2014 when a group of countries accounting for nearly 90 percent of global trade in environmental goods announced that they would negotiate an Environmental Goods Agreement. Initial discussions were based on an Asia-Pacific Economic Cooperation Forum (APEC) list of fifty-four environmental goods. Talks then expanded the list to include more than 300 products[77] covering a range of environmental categories, including goods related to cleaner and renewable energy (solar panels, wind turbines), energy efficiency, air pollution control (soot removers and catalytic converters), environmental monitoring and analysis (air and water quality monitors), and solid and hazardous waste management (waste incinerators, crushing and sorting machinery, and wastewater treatment filters and disinfection equipment), among others. However, these negotiations, like most of the Doha Round, have been stalled since December 2016.

The Outlook for Trade and Environment

Efforts to manage an increasingly open global trade system face perhaps their greatest set of challenges in seventy years. These include the re-emergence of trade wars, WTO paralysis, rapidly changing economic and trade dynamics among many countries, the impact of four years of the most pro-tariff US administration since World War II, and fall-out from the COVID-19 pandemic. At the same time, the trade and environment agenda has matured, the range of issues under discussion has expanded, and the priorities, strategies, and diversity of actors have advanced in ways that environmental proponents see as positive. While views vary by issue, most developing countries are more open to discussion of the environment–trade nexus than they were three decades ago. Indeed, on issues such as fisheries and fossil fuel subsidies, some developing countries are key players in demanding action at the environment–trade interface.[78]

Yet many of the issues described in this section remain unresolved after many years of negotiations. While they clearly have benefits for certain interests, and produce short-term economic gains, subsidies and environmental trade barriers generate enormous negative externalities. Support for economic policies that include environmental and social considerations remains central to calls for reforming trade and advancing sustainable development.[79] The roles that industrialized countries, the largest developing countries, emerging economies, less developed countries, intergovernmental organizations (IGOs), NGOs, and multinational corporations play on these issues will continue to evolve, as will the relationship between trade and environment within the sustainable development agenda.

Balancing the Environmental and Sustainable Development Agendas

In the decades since the release of the Brundtland Report and the 1992 Earth Summit, the international community has made various attempts to operationalize this concept of sustainable development. Developing countries, with the support of a number of IGOs, including the United Nations Development Programme, have emphasized programs that focus on human development. The human development approach, developed by the economist Mahbub Ul Haq and anchored in the Nobel Laureate Amartya Sen's work on human capabilities, argues that the fundamental aim of development policy should be to expand the opportunities that people have to lead meaningful lives.[80] Economic growth is seen as a means toward this end, not an end in itself. Gross domestic product (GDP) and economic growth should not be used as the leading or principal indicators of national progress in many countries, as neither was ever intended to be used as a measure of well-being. In the 1970s and 1980s the development debate considered using alternative focuses beyond GDP, including employment and whether people had their basic needs met.[81]

For many years, discussions focused on human development existed in a parallel universe to those focused on sustainable development. Although both concepts are often associated with each other, they were largely developed, researched, and measured separately. Distinctions were made between the disciplines of environmental sustainability and human development, which contributed to the apparent disconnect between both the fields and associated research. Thus, large gaps existed in the understanding of how to balance human development and environmental sustainability.[82] This disconnect persisted in the Millennium Development Goals.

The Millennium Development Goals

In 2000, the UN General Assembly held a Millennium Summit of world leaders to address the pressing challenges facing the world's people in the twenty-first century. Set against a backdrop of widespread concern about the social and ecological implications of globalization, the Millennium Assembly placed the relationships among poverty, environmental decline, and economic development firmly in the international spotlight.[83] Following the Summit, the UN General Assembly adopted resolution 55/162 to mandate the Secretary-General to prepare a long-term road map toward implementation of the Millennium Declaration.[84] The drafting process was led by then UNDP Administrator Mark Malloch-Brown, and the resulting September 2001 report set forth the Millennium Development

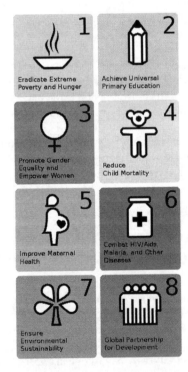

Photo 6.2 The Millennium Development Goals (MDGs) were a specific package of eight goals and eighteen targets to be accomplished by 2015.

Courtesy Kjerish, Wikimedia Commons, https://commons.wikimedia.org/w/index.php?curid=53986556.

Goals (MDGs): a set of eight goals and eighteen targets for the world to pursue and hopefully achieve by 2015.[85]

The MDGs were directed toward eradicating extreme hunger and poverty, improving living standards, and achieving important and laudable development milestones (see Photo 6.2). Only one was focused on sustainability. Although the MDGs did not garner initial support, especially from environmental NGOs and some developing countries, during their fifteen-year lifespan they became the world's central reference point for development cooperation.[86]

Yet, while noble, the MDGs were also limited, with their focus on the human development agenda: poverty, health, and education in developing countries.[87] As such, the MDGs left out many factors known to contribute to global poverty, including war and political instability, discrimination and social inequality, vulnerability to natural disasters, corruption, and inadequate rule of law. Moreover, the lone environmental goal was added almost as an afterthought. As Malloch-Brown commented, "The document had gone to the printing presses as I passed the head of the UN's environmental programme ... and a terrible swearword crossed my mind when I realised we'd forgotten an environmental goal ... we raced back to put in the sustainable development goal."[88] As such, MDG 7, "Ensure Environmental Sustainability," was insufficient to advance integration of the human development and sustainable development agendas.

That said, there is broad agreement that the MDGs provided important targets and policy focal points for governments and IGOs and served as rallying points for NGOs to hold governments and the UN system accountable. Indeed, agreeing on and pursuing the MDGs likely saved the lives of millions and improved conditions for many more.[89] Nevertheless, as with most global programs, progress was uneven across regions and countries, and, more troubling to some observers, many of those left behind were among the poorest and most disadvantaged because of their gender, age, disability, ethnicity, race, or geographic location.

The Sustainable Development Goals

Many agreed that the MDG experience, while imperfect, demonstrated that when concrete objectives exist to guide the international community toward collective goals, it becomes easier for governments, IGOs, NGOs, foundations, and interested corporations to work together to reach them. Thus, by 2010, the UN and governments had already begun discussions on what should follow the MDGs, given that they would expire in 2015.

At the same time, preparations had begun for a major global sustainable development conference, scheduled to mark the twentieth anniversary of the Earth Summit. In June 2012, the international community returned once again to Rio de Janeiro for the UN Conference on Sustainable Development (UNCSD, also referred to as Rio+20). The UNCSD's agenda focused on securing a renewed political commitment for sustainable development; assessing progress made to implement the outcomes of the sustainable development summits in 1992 and 2002; and addressing new and emerging challenges.

During the UNCSD preparatory process, a new proposal emerged that sought to bridge the sustainable development and human development agendas. Colombia, with support from Guatemala, submitted a proposal for consideration:

> The international community urgently needs benchmarks so that it can harness and catalyse multidimensional and multisectoral approaches to addressing critical global challenges. Accordingly, Colombia has proposed, together with Guatemala, that one of the outcomes of the Rio Conference ... should be the adoption of a set of Sustainable Development Goals [SDGs], modelled on the Millennium Development Goals, to help define the post-2015 framework.[90]

After lengthy negotiations, the Rio+20 outcome document, titled *The Future We Want*, agreed that countries would collectively develop

> sustainable development goals [that] should be action oriented, concise and easy to communicate, limited in number, aspirational, global in nature and universally applicable to all countries while taking into account different national realities, capacities and levels of development and respecting national policies and priorities.[91]

The process of developing the SDGs (also known as the Global Goals for Sustainable Development) began in early 2013. Unlike the MDGs, which were crafted by a group of UN experts under the guidance of the UN Secretary-General, the SDGs were negotiated by governments in an Open Working Group that met thirteen times between March 2013 and July 2014. Although governments knew that it would be inherently difficult to negotiate a set of goals as concise as the MDGs, lead states had a larger agenda. The SDGs were intended both to be universal—in other words, an agenda that recognizes shared national and global challenges among all countries (not just developing countries)—and to offer a paradigm shift away from outdated development assumptions of the past.

Photo 6.3 The United Nations projected the seventeen Sustainable Development Goals on its headquarters building during the Sustainable Development Summit in September 2015.

Courtesy Pamela Chasek.

Following the conclusion of discussions in the Open Working Group in July 2014, governments agreed on a process to reach final agreement on both the SDGs and a broader post-2015 development agenda. These negotiations began in January 2015 and concluded in early August 2015 with the provisional adoption of the document "Transforming Our World: The 2030 Agenda for Sustainable Development." The agenda, with the SDGs and targets as the cornerstone, also contains a declaration and sections on means of implementation, follow-up, and review.[92] The 2030 Agenda for Sustainable Development was formally adopted by heads of state and government during a summit at UN Headquarters in New York in September 2015.

The seventeen SDGs (see Box 6.3), which collectively include 169 targets, seek to end poverty and hunger and achieve sustainable development by promoting inclusive economic growth, protecting the environment, and promoting social inclusion. Individual SDGs address human rights, gender equality, women's and girls' empowerment, and peaceful and inclusive societies. And, as often repeated throughout the negotiations, unlike the MDGs, the SDGs are supposed to ensure that no country or person is left behind.

❖ BOX 6.3   THE SUSTAINABLE DEVELOPMENT GOALS

1. End poverty in all its forms everywhere
2. End hunger, achieve food security and improved nutrition, and promote sustainable agriculture
3. Ensure healthy lives and promote well-being for all at all ages
4. Ensure inclusive and equitable quality education and promote lifelong learning opportunities for all
5. Achieve gender equality and empower all women and girls
6. Ensure availability and sustainable management of water and sanitation for all
7. Ensure access to affordable, reliable, sustainable and modern energy for all
8. Promote sustained, inclusive and sustainable economic growth, full and productive employment, and decent work for all
9. Build resilient infrastructure, promote inclusive and sustainable industrialization, and foster innovation
10. Reduce inequality within and among countries
11. Make cities and human settlements inclusive, safe, resilient, and sustainable
12. Ensure sustainable consumption and production patterns
13. Take urgent action to combat climate change and its impacts (taking note of agreements made by the UNFCCC forum)
14. Conserve and sustainably use the oceans, seas, and marine resources for sustainable development
15. Protect, restore and promote sustainable use of terrestrial ecosystems, sustainably manage forests, combat desertification and halt and reverse land degradation, and halt biodiversity loss
16. Promote peaceful and inclusive societies for sustainable development, provide access to justice for all and build effective, accountable, and inclusive institutions at all levels
17. Strengthen the means of implementation and revitalize the global partnership for sustainable development

Source: United Nations, "Transforming Our World: The 2030 Agenda for Sustainable Development" (New York: United Nations, 2015), https://sustainabledevelopment.un.org/post2015/transformingourworld.

As with previous sustainable development action plans and programs, including the MDGs, the SDGs have been subject to criticism. Some governments and NGOs have complained that seventeen goals are too unwieldy to implement or sell to the public as policy priorities. Some critics argue that the 169 targets are a recipe for failure: a lengthy agenda adopted with great fanfare in September 2015 only to be quickly forgotten and destined for a bookshelf, gathering dust.[93] Others have noted that the number of SDGs and targets show what happens when a bureaucratic process runs out of control: "The organisers sought to consult as widely as possible, with the result that each country and aid lobbyist got a target for its particular bugbear ... Something for everyone has produced too much for anyone."[94]

However, many others believe that the number of goals is necessary because they reflect the complexity and interconnectedness of today's challenges. From this perspective, it is better to have seventeen goals and numerous targets that include action on women's empowerment, climate change, the environment, good governance, and peace and security, for example, than fewer goals that do not address these issues. To achieve truly sustainable development, these challenges must be addressed in an integrated way. It does not make any sense to try to reduce extreme poverty while ignoring the role that the environment and good governance play in building prosperity.[95]

As for the wide-ranging consultations, supporters noted that unlike the MDGs, the SDGs were the deliberate product of a grassroots process, which began with input from a broader range of advocacy groups, everyday citizens, and governments than ever before, marking a paradigm shift.[96] The political inclusivity of the negotiating process and the breadth of the goals represent recognition that governments alone cannot achieve sustainable development. It requires the participation of businesses and civil society as well as the political commitment of world leaders. As noted in the 2019 *Global Sustainable Development Report*, "The 2030 Agenda is both a normative orientation and a guide for action. It identifies and pursues development priorities while requiring coherence among all policy areas and sectors, at the local, regional, national and transnational levels."[97]

Since the adoption of the SDGs, there have been signs of success and concerns about shortcomings in implementation. Each year, the UN High-level Political Forum on Sustainable Development (HLPF) reviews implementation of the SDGs, and individual countries present their "Voluntary National Reviews" on their own implementation. These national reviews, as set out in the 2030 Agenda, facilitate the sharing of successes, challenges, and lessons learned with a view to accelerating SDG implementation. Collectively, the reviews show that governments have begun incorporating SDGs into national plans and policies.[98] Many have set up coordinating structures for coherent implementation. In most cases, NGOs and other stakeholders are included in technical working groups and advisory committees set up by governments for SDG implementation, and many countries have highlighted the crucial role that subnational and local authorities play in implementing the SDGs. Between 2016 and 2019, 142 countries submitted at least one voluntary national review, and some have carried out second or third reviews, for a total of 158 reports.[99] In 2020, forty-seven countries presented their voluntary national review, with twenty-six presenting for the first time.[100]

Progress in implementing the SDGs is measured through 232 global indicators adopted by a UN expert group with government input, and national indicators developed by countries themselves.[101] At current rates, several of the SDG targets should be attainable by 2030, including reducing child mortality and full enrollment in primary school, although this could be affected by the impacts of the COVID-19 pandemic on the economies and health-care, social, and educational systems of countries around the world. It is worth noting that these goals and targets are carry-overs from the MDGs. Several other targets may also be reached with additional effort, including access to electricity, eliminating open defecation, literacy, and desirable levels of expenditure on scientific research and development.[102]

However, despite early efforts, the world is not on track for achieving most of the 169 targets. In fact, data show that international community is not even moving in the right direction on some issues, in particular economic inequalities, climate change, biodiversity loss, and waste. The 2019 *Global Sustainable Development Report* continues:

> Critically, recent analysis suggests that some of those negative trends presage a move towards the crossing of negative tipping points, which would lead to dramatic changes in the conditions of the Earth system in ways that are irreversible on time scales meaningful for society. Recent assessments show that, under current trends, the world's social and natural biophysical systems cannot support the aspirations for universal human well-being embedded in the Sustainable Development Goals.[103]

In September 2019, heads of state and government met at the quadrennial HLPF held under the auspices of the United Nations General Assembly. They adopted a statement acknowledging shortcomings in SDG implementation and committed to launching an "ambitious and accelerated response" to make the coming decade one of action and delivery.[104] This call for accelerated action by all stakeholders and all levels has resulted in countries committing to over 232 actions, 80 percent of which address actions that leverage interlinkages between SDGs. Examples include:

- Finland pledged to achieve carbon neutrality by 2035 and become carbon negative soon thereafter.
- The United Kingdom announced a £515 million education package for reaching the most marginalized girls in Africa and investing in a new financing facility for education that combines guarantees and grants of donors to leverage additional finance for girls' education in lower-middle-income countries.
- India set a target of installing 175 GW of renewable energy capacity by the year 2022, which includes 100 GW from solar, 60 GW from wind, 10 GW from bio-power, and 5 GW from small hydropower.
- Kadiwaku Family Foundation, a philanthropic organization in the Democratic Republic of the Congo, has committed to promoting inclusive entrepreneurship and has already trained 650 youth with disabilities.
- The Dzivarasekwa Community Waste Transfer Centre in Zimbabwe was established so that community members can bring certain types of trash and instantly get paid by recycling companies. The program provides an additional source of income and raises environmental protection awareness while reducing the amount of waste produced by the community.
- UNDP's office in Colombia has committed to improving biodiversity conservation by strengthening local institutions and organizations in the Amazon region, including in low-carbon management and peace-building.[105]

The SDGs have contributed to resource mobilization and new and targeted programs, and, more broadly, provided a framework that encourages and supports coordinated and integrated approaches toward sustainable development. As noted, however, the international community is clearly not on track to achieve most of the SDGs and targets, and this was true even before the global health and economic crises that started in 2020. With this in mind, the 2020 meeting of the HLPF changed its agenda to focus on the COVID-19 pandemic and its impact on the SDGs. A background paper prepared for the meeting notes that while the crisis is threatening progress toward the SDGs, it also makes their achievement all the more urgent and necessary. "A transformative recovery from COVID-19 should be pursued, one that addresses the crisis, reduces risks from future potential crises and relaunch[es] the implementation efforts to deliver the 2030 Agenda and SDGs during the Decade of Action."[106] Nevertheless, it remains to be seen whether national and local governments, IGOs, the private sector, NGOs, and other stakeholders can and will dramatically step up the pace of implementation needed to achieve the SDGs and the 2030 Agenda.

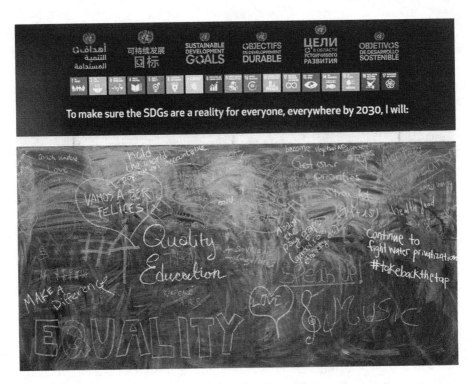

Photo 6.4 A UN art installation asks people to make sure the Sustainable Development Goals are a reality for everyone.

Courtesy Mike Muzurakis, IISD/*Earth Negotiations Bulletin*, http://enb.iisd.org

Conclusion

The evolution of global environmental politics cannot be understood without examining the evolution and intersection of environmental protection, economic development, and social development—the three dimensions of sustainable development. As the linkages between environmental issues and economic and social development are increasingly apparent, the boundaries of global environmental politics have broadened and now must include the politics of economic and social development. The difficulty of sorting through environmental and development priorities carries through to the trade arena and the challenge of achieving a broadly acceptable balance between free trade and environmental protection within the context of the WTO, including on issues as diverse as endangered species protection, fisheries subsidies, and environmental goods and services, to name but a few.

Many developing countries continue to maintain that global economic relations are fundamentally inequitable or that global environmental policy must not impact economic development, and this often shapes their policy responses to global environmental issues and related negotiating strategies. They press industrialized countries to renew their commitments to the Rio Principles, particularly additionality, CBDR, and polluter pays. Many industrialized countries maintain that they are fulfilling their commitments but in new ways that reflect significantly different economic realities than those that existed in 1992, and that the unforgiving pace of environmental degradation requires significant action not only by them but also by many developing countries.

Despite the apparent tension among various economic, social, and environmental goals between, and within, developed and developing countries, many respected observers argue that in the long run, economic health depends on social and ecological health. The SDGs mark a coordinated effort based on this belief. Through the SDGs, all countries have pledged to take action both within their own borders and in support of wider international efforts. For the first time, a UN development plan recognizes the interlinkages among sustainability of ecosystem services, poverty eradication, economic development, and human well-being.

However, given the record of the first five years of the SDG era, it is fair to ask whether these global goals can operationalize sustainable development. Although the goals contain elements of the three dimensions of sustainability, many are still presented and measured using a siloed approach that looks at the goals and targets as separate elements, existing in isolation from each other, rather than as a holistic, integrated agenda. Some goals even conflict, and the overall framework is not always internally consistent and, as a result, may not be sustainable.[107]

Nevertheless, implementation efforts continue, and many countries, IGOs, and NGOs maintain their commitment, at least publicly, to the ideals expressed in the preamble to the 2030 Agenda: "We are resolved to free the human race from the tyranny of poverty and want and to heal and secure our planet." It continues:

> We are determined to take the bold and transformative steps which are urgently needed to shift the world onto a sustainable and resilient path. As we embark on this collective journey, we pledge that no one will be left behind.[108]

Notes

1 *Development and Environment* (Paris: Mouton, 1971), report and working papers of experts convened by the secretary-general of the UN Conference on the Human Environment, Founex, Switzerland, June 4–12, 1971.

2 Adil Najam, "The View from the South: Developing Countries in Global Environmental Politics," in *The Global Environment: Institutions, Law and Policy*, 2nd ed., eds. Regina Axelrod, David Downie, and Norman Vig (Washington, DC: Congressional Quarterly Press, 2005), 224–243.

3 *Development and Environment*, 5–6, as cited in Adil Najam, "Why Environmental Politics Looks Different from the South," in *Handbook of Global Environmental Politics*, ed. Peter Dauvergne (Cheltenham, UK: Edward Elgar, 2005), 111–126.

4 Lars-Göran Engfeldt, *From Stockholm to Johannesburg and Beyond* (Stockholm: Government Offices of Sweden, 2009), 81.

5 Ibid., 67; UN, *Report of the United Nations Conference on the Human Environment*, A/CONF.48/14/Rev 1 (1973), www.un-documents.net/unche.htm.

6 Pamela Chasek, "Sustainable Development," in *Introducing Global Issues*, 6th ed., eds. Michael Snarr and D. Neil Snarr (Boulder, CO: Lynne Rienner, 2016), 294.

7 World Commission on Environment and Development, *Our Common Future* (New York: Oxford University Press, 1987), 5.

8 World Commission on Environment and Development, *Our Common Future*, 43.

9 Engfeldt, *From Stockholm to Johannesburg*, 111.

10 Marian Miller, *The Third World in Global Environmental Politics* (Boulder, CO: Lynne Rienner, 1995), 9.

11 Najam, "The View from the South." See also Andrew Jordan, "Financing the UNCED Agenda: The Controversy over Additionality," *Environment* vol. 36, no. 3 (1994): 16–34.

12 Pamela Chasek, "The Convention to Combat Desertification: Lessons Learned for Sustainable Development," *Journal of Environment and Development* vol. 6, no. 2 (1997): 147–169.

13 Najam, "The View from the South."

14 See the final communiqué from the Gleneagles Summit, 2005, www.g7.utoronto.ca/summit/2005gleneagles/communique.pdf.

15 See the outcome document from the 2005 UN summit, www.un.org/summit2005.

16 OECD, "Trends and Insights on Development Finance," Development Co-operation Profiles (Paris: OECD Publishing, 2019), https://doi.org/10.1787/2dcf1367-en.

17 OECD, "Aid Activities Targeting Global Environmental Objectives," Accessed January 9, 2019, https://stats.oecd.org/Index.aspx?DataSetCode=RIOMARKERS#.

18 This information is excerpted from OECD, "History of the 0.7% ODA Target," original text from *DAC Journal* 2002, vol. 3, no. 4: III-9–III-11, revised March 2016, www.oecd.org/dac/stats/ODA-history-of-the-0-7-target.pdf.

19 "Partners in Development—Report of the Commission on International Development," Lester B. Pearson (Chairman), New York, Washington, and London, 1969, p. 18.

20 "Aid by DAC members increases in 2019 with more aid to the poorest countries," Organisation for Economic Co-operation and Development (OECD), April 16, 2020, www.oecd.org/dac/financing-sustainable-development/development-finance-data/ODA-2019-detailed-summary.pdf.

21 OECD, *Development Cooperation Report: Mobilizing Resources for Sustainable Development* (Paris: OECD Publishing, 2014), 337, doi: http://dx.doi.org/10.1787/dcr-2014-en.

22 However, non-DAC donors Turkey and the United Arab Emirates, whose ODA is not counted in the DAC total, provided 1.10 percent and 0.95 percent, respectively, of their gross national income (GNI) in development aid. See OECD, "Trends and Insights on Development Finance," Development Co-operation Profiles (Paris: OECD Publishing, 2019), https://doi.org/10.1787/2dcf1367-en.

23 Najam, "The View from the South." See also Anil Agarwal and Sunita Narain, *Global Warming in an Unequal World: A Case of Environmental Colonialism* (New Delhi: Center for Science and Environment, 1991); Anil Agarwal, Sunita Narain, and Anju Sharma, eds., *Green Politics: Global Negotiations*, vol. 1 (New Delhi: Center for Science and Environment, 1999).

24 Najam, "The View from the South."

25 Raymond Ahearn, *Rising Economic Powers and the Global Economy: Trends and Issues for Congress*, Congressional Research Service Report 7-5700 (Washington, DC: Congressional Research Service, 2011).

26 See Karl Sauvant and Hajo Hasenpflug, eds., *The New International Economic Order: Confrontation or Cooperation Between North and South?* (Boulder, CO: Westview, 1977).

27 James Sebenius, "Negotiating a Regime to Control Global Warming," in *Greenhouse Warming: Negotiating a Global Regime*, ed. Jessica Tuchman Mathews (Washington, DC: World Resources Institute, 1991), 87.

28 South Commission, *The Challenge to the South: The Report of the South Commission* (Oxford: Oxford University Press, 1990); Mohammed Ayoob, "The New-Old Disorder in the Third World," *Global Governance* vol. 1, no. 1 (1995): 59–77; Adil Najam, "An Environmental Negotiation Strategy for the South," *International Environmental Affairs* vol. 7, no. 3 (1995): 249–287; Najam, "The View from the South," 224–243.

29 This was part of a longer-term decline in the real prices of primary products in the world market, caused by slow growth in demand, the development of cheaper substitutes, and overproduction. See UNDP, *Human Development Report 1992* (New York: UNDP, 1992), 59.

30 UNDP, "Financial Inflows and Outflows," *Human Development Report 1998* (New York: Oxford University Press, 1998). The term *least-developed countries* (LDCs) was originally used at the UN in 1971 to describe the "poorest and most economically weak of the developing countries, with formidable economic, institutional and human resources problems, which are often compounded by geographical handicaps and natural and man-made disasters." There are currently forty-seven LDCs. See https://unctad.org/en/Pages/ALDC/Least%20Developed%20Countries/UN-list-of-Least-Developed-Countries.aspx.

31 Ibid.

32 M. Ayhan Kose and Eswar Prasad, *Emerging Markets: Resilience and Growth amid Global Turmoil* (Washington, DC: Brookings Institution Press, 2010), 1.

33 Credit Suisse Research Institute, *Credit Suisse Global Wealth Report, 2019* (Zurich: Credit Suisse Research Institute, 2019), 9.

34 Ibid.

35 Mark Halle, "Sustainable Development Cools Off: Globalization Demands Summit Take New Approach to Meeting Ecological, Social Goals," *Winnipeg Free Press*, July 29, 2002.

36 World Bank, *Global Economic Prospects and the Developing Countries* (Washington, DC: World Bank, 1992), 13.

37 *Barriers to entry* are any obstacle that impedes a potential new entrant (a company or country) from entering a market to produce or sell goods or services. Barriers to entry shelter incumbent companies against new entrants. They can include government regulations, subsidies, intellectual property rules, restrictive practices, pre-existing supplier or distributor agreements, control of resources, economies of scale, advantages independent of scale, consumer preferences, and other factors.

38 Kevin Gallagher, "The Economics of Globalization and Sustainable Development," in "Trade, Environment and Investment: Cancún and Beyond," special issue, *Policy Matters* vol. 11 (September 2003).

39 General Agreement on Tariffs and Trade (GATT) and World Trade Organization (WTO), preamble to "Agreement Establishing the World Trade Organization," WTO, 1994, www.wto.org/english/docs_ e/legal_e/04-wto.pdf.

40 Ibid.

41 WTO Decision on Trade and Environment, GATT Doc. MTN/TNC/45/MIN (15 December 1993).

42 James McBride and Andrew Chatzky, "What's Next for the WTO?" Council on Foreign Relations Backgrounder, December 10, 2019, www.cfr.org/backgrounder/whats-next-wto.

43 William Reinsch, Jack Caporal, and Lydia Murray, "At Last, an RCEP Deal," Center for Strategic and International Studies, December 3, 2019; Reuters, "RCEP Trade Pact on Track for 2020 Signing: Ministers," *New York Times*, June 23, 2020.

44 New York Times Editorial Board, "Global Trade After the Failure of the Doha Round," *New York Times*, January 1, 2016, A22.

45 Ibid.; and Joseph Stiglitz, "In 2016, Let's Hope for Better Trade Agreements and the Death of TPP," *Guardian*, January 10, 2016.

46 Devinder Sharma, "Time to Admit Honestly That WTO Is Dead!" *ABP Live*, January 9, 2016, www. abplive.in/blog/time-to-admit-honestly-that-wto-is-dead.

47 For a matrix of selected MEAs and their trade provisions, see WTO, "Matrix on Trade Measures Pursuant to Selected Multilateral Environmental Agreements," WT/CTE/W/160/Rev.8, October 9, 2017, www.wto.org/english/tratop_e/envir_e/envir_matrix_e.htm.

48 UNEP and IISD, *Environment and Trade: A Handbook*, 2nd ed. (Winnipeg, Canada: IISD/UNEP, 2005), 66.

49 Ibid., 67.

50 Richard Tarasofsky, *Trade, Environment, and the WTO Dispute Settlement Mechanism*, report commissioned by the European Commission, June 2005, 4, www.ecologic.eu/sites/files/publication/2015/4_1800_cate_wto_dispute_settlement.pdf.

51 The term *environmental trade measures* is used in Steve Charnovitz, "The Environment vs. Trade Rules: Defogging the Debate," *Environmental Law* vol. 23 (1993): 490. Charnovitz lists all of these forms of environmental trade measures except mandatory ecolabeling.

52 Jada F. Smith, "U.S. Bans Commercial Trade of African Elephant Ivory," *The New York Times*, June 2, 2016, www.nytimes.com/2016/06/03/world/africa/elephant-ivory-ban.html.

53 Sang Don Lee, "The Effect of Environmental Regulations on Trade: Cases of Korea's New Environmental Laws," *Georgetown International Environmental Law Review* 5, no. 3 (Summer 1993): 659.

54 One exception was when Ecuador sought WTO approval for retaliatory sanctions against the European Union (EU) for the EU's failure to comply with the WTO ruling on its banana-import regime, which discriminated against some South and Central American banana-exporting countries. However, realizing that, as a small country, imposing punitive tariffs on EU imports would have little impact on the EU but a devastating effect on Ecuador's consumers, Ecuador said it would target intellectual property rights and services in retaliation. See International Centre for Trade and Sustainable Development (ICTSD), "Ecuador, U.S. Reject EU Banana Proposal; Ecuador to Cross-Retaliate," *Bridges Weekly Trade News Digest* 3, no. 45 (November 15, 1999).

55 Daniel Esty, *Greening the GATT: Trade, Environment and the Future* (Washington, DC: Institute for International Economics, 1994), 188. In an ironic twist, research undertaken by the Inter-American Tropical Tuna Commission found that dolphin-safe tuna fishing results in catching tuna at least thirty-five times more immature (because young tuna do not school beneath groups of dolphins as mature tuna do) and thus threatens to deplete tuna fisheries. See Richard Parker, "The Use and Abuse of Trade Leverage to Protect the Global Commons: What We Can Learn from the Tuna-Dolphin Conflict," *Georgetown International Environmental Law Review* vol. 12, no. 1 (1999): 37–38.

56 For environmental critiques of the decision, see Steve Charnovitz, "GATT and the Environment: Examining the Issues," *International Environmental Affairs* vol. 4, no. 3 (Summer 1992): 203–233; Robert Repetto, "Trade and Environment Policies: Achieving Complementarities and Avoiding Conflict," *WRI Issues and Ideas* (July 1993): 6–10. For an alternative view of the decision, see John Jackson, "World Trade Rules and Environmental Policies: Congruence or Conflict?" *Washington and Lee Law Review* vol. 49 (Fall 1992): 1242–1243.

57 Janet Welsh Brown, "Trade and the Environment," in *Encyclopedia of Violence, Peace and Conflict*, vol. 3, ed. Lester Kurtz (San Diego, CA: Academic Press, 1999), T12–14.

58 The appellate body also noted that the United States had not signed the Convention on Migratory Species and the United Nations Convention on the Law of the Sea, ratified the Convention on Biological Diversity, or raised the issue of sea turtles during recent CITES conferences. These inconsistencies on protecting endangered species do not prove, of course, that the US intention in the shrimp/turtle case was not to protect endangered sea turtles.

59 See "Revised Guidelines for the Implementation of Section 609 of Public Law 101–162 Relating to the Protection of Sea Turtles in Shrimp Trawl Fishing Operations," Public Notice 3086, *Federal Register*, July 1999.

60 Forest Stewardship Council. "Looking Back on 25 Years of FSC," https://fsc.org/en/page/25-years-fsc.

61 For additional information about the Forest Stewardship Council, see www.fsc.org.

62 For more information, see the Marine Stewardship Council's website: www.msc.org.

63 Food and Agriculture Organization of the United Nations (FAO), *State of World Fisheries and Aquaculture 2018* (Rome: FAO, 2018), 54.

64 Changing Markets Foundation, *The False Promise of Certification*, May 2018, http://changingmarkets.org/wp-content/uploads/2018/05/False-promise_full-report-ENG.pdf.

65 Ibid.

66 Marie Wilke, "Tuna Labeling and the WTO: How Safe Is 'Dolphin-Safe'?" *BIORES* vol. 6, no. 2 (June–July 2012): 16.

67 See WTO, Committee on Trade and Environment, *Environmental Benefits of Removing Trade Restrictions and Distortions: Note by the Secretariat* (Geneva: WTO, 1997); Gareth Porter, *Fisheries Subsidies, Overfishing and Trade* (Geneva: UNEP, 1998); International Monetary Fund (IMF), *Energy Subsidy Reform: Lessons and Implications* (Washington, DC: IMF, 2013).

68 FAO, *State of World Fisheries and Aquaculture: Meeting the Sustainable Development Goals* (Rome: Food and Agriculture Organization of the UN, 2018), 6.

69 U. Rashid Sumaila, et al., "Updated Estimates and Analysis of Global Fisheries Subsidies," *Marine Policy* vol. 109 (2019): 103695. doi: https://doi.org/10.1016/j.marpol.2019.103695.

70 Ibid.

71 Mukhisa Kituyi and Peter Thomson, "90% of Fish Stocks Are Used Up—Fisheries Subsidies Must Stop Emptying the Ocean," World Economic Forum, July 13, 2018, www.weforum.org/agenda/2018/07/fish-stocks-are-used-up-fisheries-subsidies-must-stop/.

72 See the ministerial declaration at www.wto.org/english/thewto_e/minist_e/mc10_e/fishsubsippmc10_e.pdf.

73 WTO, "WTO Members Prepare to Intensify Fisheries Subsidies Negotiations in 2020," News release, December 6, 2019, www.wto.org/english/news_e/news19_e/fish_06dec19_e.htm; WTO, "Fisheries Subsidies Negotiations Chair Introduces Draft Consolidated Text to WTO Members," News release, June 25, 2020, www.wto.org/english/news_e/news20_e/fish_25jun20_e.htm.

74 OECD, "Opening Markets for Environmental Goods and Services," September 2005, www.ciaonet.org/attachments/11402/uploads.

75 OECD, "Trade and the Environment," Trade Policy Brief, February 2019, https://issuu.com/oecd.publishing/docs/trade_and_the_environment.

76 "Eliminating Trade Barriers on Environmental Goods and Services," WTO, www.wto.org/english/tratop_e/envir_e/envir_neg_serv_e.htm.

77 James Bacchus and Inu Manak, "The Green New Deal is Missing a Critical Element: Trade," *The Hill*, March 28, 2019, https://thehill.com/opinion/finance/436119-the-green-new-deal-is-missing-a-critical-element-trade.

78 Carolyn Deere Birkbeck, "Environment and Trade 2.0," Hoffmann Centre for Sustainable Resource Economy, Chatham House, October 10, 2019, https://hoffmanncentre.chathamhouse.org/events/2019/10/environment-and-trade-20/.

79 Ibid.

80 See, for example, Mahbub ul Haq, *Reflections on Human Development* (New York: Oxford University Press, 1995); Amartya K. Sen, "The Choice of Discount Rates for Social Benefit-Cost Analysis," in R. C. Lind (ed.), *Discounting for Time and Risk in Energy Policy* (Washington, DC: Resources for the Future, 1982), 325–352; and Amartya K. Sen, *Development as Freedom* (New York, NY: Random House, 1999).

81 UNDP, "About Human Development," Accessed January 10, 2020, http://hdr.undp.org/en/humandev.

82 See, for example, Eric Neumayer, "Human Development and Sustainability," Human Development Research Paper 2010/05 (New York: UNDP, 2010).

83 Pamela Chasek and Richard Sherman, *Ten Days in Johannesburg: A Negotiation of Hope* (Cape Town: Struik, 2004); and International Institute for Sustainable Development (IISD), *Millennium Review Meeting Bulletin* vol. 104, no. 2 (March 16, 2005), https://enb.iisd.org/crs/ecosocprep1/sdvol104num2e.html.

84 UN General Assembly, "Follow-up to the Outcome of the Millennium Summit, Resolution 55/162," December 18, 2000.

85 United Nations, "Road Map Towards the Implementation of the United Nations Millennium Declaration: Report of the Secretary-General," UN General Assembly A/56/326 (2001).

86 Macharia Kamau, Pamela Chasek, and David O'Connor, *Transforming Multilateral Diplomacy: The Inside Story of the Sustainable Development Goals* (London: Routledge, 2018), 23–24.

87 Ibid., 28; Liz Ford, "Sustainable Development Goals: All You Need to Know," *Guardian*, July 19, 2015.

88 Mark Tran, "Mark Malloch-Brown: Developing the MDGs Was a Bit Like Nuclear Fusion," *Guardian*, November 16, 2012.

89 For specifics, see United Nations, *The Millennium Development Goals Report 2015* (New York: UN, 2015).

90 Colombian Ministry of Foreign Affairs, "Inputs of the Government of Colombia to Draft Zero of the Outcome Document," November 30, 2011.

91 UN, *Report of the United Nations Conference on Sustainable Development*, A/CONF. 216/16 (New York: UN, 2012), 46–47.

92 See UN, *Transforming Our World: The 2030 Agenda for Sustainable Development*, A.69/L.85, August 15, 2015, https://sustainabledevelopment.un.org/post2015/transformingourworld.

93 Liz Ford, "UN Begins Talks on SDGs, 'Carrying the Hopes of Millions and Millions'," *Guardian*, September 24, 2014, www.theguardian.com/global-development/2014/sep/24/un-begins-talks-sdgs-battle-looms-over-goals.

94 "Unsustainable Goals," *Economist*, March 25, 2015.

95 Howard LaFranchi, "In New UN Goals, an Evolving Vision of How to Change the World," *Christian Science Monitor*, September 1, 2015.

96 Ibid.

97 United Nations, *The Future is Now: Science for Achieving Sustainable Development*, Global Sustainable Development Report 2019 (New York: United Nations, 2019), 8.

98 United Nations, *2019 Voluntary National Reviews Synthesis Report* (New York: UN Department of Economic and Social Affairs, 2019).

99 Ibid., 2.

100 For more information, see https://sustainabledevelopment.un.org/vnrs/.

101 The Inter-Agency and Expert Group on Sustainable Development Goal Indicators developed the global indicator framework that was agreed by the United Nations Statistical Commission at its forty-eighth session in March 2017 and adopted by the General Assembly in July 2017 in the resolution on Work of the Statistical Commission pertaining to the 2030 Agenda for Sustainable Development (A/RES/71/313).

102 United Nations, *The Future Is Now*, 11.

103 United Nations, *The Future Is Now*, XX.

104 UN General Assembly, Political Declaration of the High-level Political Forum on Sustainable Development Convened Under the Auspices of the General Assembly, Resolution 74/4, October 15, 2019, https://undocs.org/A/RES/74/4.

105 UN Department of Economic and Social Affairs, "SDG Acceleration Actions," https://sustainabledevelopment.un.org/sdgactions/.

106 High-level Political Forum on Sustainable Development, "Launching the Decade of Action at a Time of Crisis: Keeping the Focus on the SDGs While Combatting COVID-19," Secretariat Background Note, 2020, https://sustainabledevelopment.un.org/content/documents/26298HLPF_2020_impact_COVID19.pdf.

107 ICSU ISSC, *Review of the Targets for the Sustainable Development Goals: The Science Perspective* (Paris: International Council for Science, 2015).

108 UN, *Transforming Our World.*

Chapter 7

The Future of Global Environmental Politics

Abstract

Since the 1970s, the world has seen an unprecedented level of international activity and cooperation on environmental issues. More governments and nonstate actors are active participants in environmental politics than in any other global issue area. The proliferation of multilateral environmental agreements represents an achievement in international diplomacy. However, international activity does not necessarily produce success, cooperation does not necessarily lead to effective action, and past accomplishments do not necessarily lead to even greater achievements. What the future holds depends in part on how global environmental politics intersects with other complex global realities. This concluding chapter examines the challenges of global environmental governance in a changing international system and how institutional structures have evolved to meet these challenges. We conclude by returning to the concepts of paradigm shift as we look toward the future.

Keywords: COVID-19, environment, development, governance, sustainable development, United Nations, United Nations Environment Programme

As 2019 came to a close, many looked ahead to the new year, which was expected to be a landmark year for the environment and sustainable development. Not only did 2020 mark the seventy-fifth anniversary of the establishment of the United Nations, but it was supposed to be an important year for biodiversity, climate change, chemicals, and oceans governance. But on December 31, 2019, Chinese authorities alerted the World Health Organization (WHO) to an outbreak of a novel strain of coronavirus causing severe illness, which was subsequently named COVID-19. By the end of January 2020, the WHO had declared the outbreak a "Public Health Emergency of International Concern" as COVID-19 started to spread beyond Chinese borders.

In February 2020, the first major environmental negotiations of the year had taken place as scheduled. The thirteenth Meeting of the Conference of the Parties to the Convention on Migratory Species of Wild Animals convened in India, marking what was supposed to be the first in a series of international biodiversity conferences in 2020 leading up to the UN Biodiversity Conference scheduled for October 2020, which was expected to adopt a new global biodiversity framework under the Convention on Biological Diversity. The International Seabed Authority's Council met in Jamaica to continue negotiations on environmental guidelines for deep seabed mining. And the Intergovernmental Panel on Climate Change (IPCC) met in Paris to agree to an outline of the synthesis report for IPCC's Sixth Assessment Report, which is expected to be concluded in 2022.

The working group negotiating the post-2020 global biodiversity framework was supposed to meet in Kunming, China, but, due to concerns about COVID-19, the meeting was moved to the headquarters of the Food and Agriculture Organization (FAO) in Rome, Italy, at the last minute. However, by the time the meeting opened, COVID-19 had already spread to Italy. On each day of the meeting, delegates were screened at the entrance before they could enter FAO headquarters. By the end of the week there were over 800 cases in Italy and rising. Less than two weeks later, on March 11, 2020, when the WHO declared COVID-19 a pandemic, the first caused by a coronavirus, there were over 12,000 cases in Italy and 118,000 cases in 114 countries.[1]

By mid-March 2020, international travel, conferences, and the entire global economy had ground to a halt as the pandemic spread. The UN suspended all in-person meetings and closed its headquarters in New York. The World Trade Organization postponed its twelfth Ministerial Conference. Each day, news came about other environmental conferences and meetings that had been postponed or canceled, essentially emptying the 2020 calendar. Questions quickly arose about how the global environmental agenda, as well as the entire international agenda, would move forward during this unprecedented pandemic. Multilateralism had ground to a halt.

Yet even before the COVID-19 pandemic, there was concern that multilateralism was waning and leadership was lacking. Nearly fifty years after the UN first addressed the human environment at the Stockholm Conference and nearly thirty years after the Rio Earth Summit, the optimism surrounding the promise of a paradigm shift to sustainable development had faded for some, and others were downright pessimistic. The excitement of negotiating new treaties had been replaced by implementation battles over financial and technical assistance (FTA), accountability, additionality, the application of the principle of common but differentiated responsibilities (CBDR), and other issues. Multilateral environmental agreements had failed to reverse, or even slow down, many of the most threatening global environmental trends, including climate change, biodiversity loss, and damage to our oceans.

At the same time, the stakes continue to rise. In addition to the global macrotrends presented in Chapter 1, the economic costs of environmental degradation keep growing. Many global environmental regimes still require significant change, in particular economic and social development strategies and changes in consumption of natural resources and production of goods, to be effective. Combating climate change requires major changes in the way the global economy is structured. The ambitious global environmental agenda is arguably in danger of being overwhelmed by economic and political forces that threaten the health of the planet.

This concluding chapter examines the challenges of global environmental governance in a changing international system and how the institutional structure has evolved to meet these challenges. We conclude by returning to the concepts of paradigm shift as we look toward the future.

Global Environmental Governance in a Changing International System

Since the 1970s, the world has seen an unprecedented level of international activity and cooperation on environmental issues. More governments and nonstate actors are active participants in environmental politics than in any other global issue area. The proliferation of multilateral environmental agreements (MEAs) represents an achievement in international diplomacy. However, international activity does not necessarily produce success, cooperation does not necessarily lead to effective action, and past accomplishments do not necessarily lead to even greater achievements. What the future holds in store depends in part on how global environmental politics intersects with other complex global realities.

The first of these complex realities involves the broad changes in the international system. The East–West Cold War politics that dominated the 1972 Stockholm Conference were replaced by a North–South dynamic at the 1992 Rio Earth Summit after the Cold War came to an end. At the Earth Summit, there was a simple grand bargain: poor countries would become more environmentally sustainable if the rich countries would pay most of the costs.[2] This was codified in many MEAs, including the Montreal Protocol, the UN Framework Convention on Climate Change (UNFCCC), the Convention on Biological Diversity (CBD), and the UN Convention to Combat Desertification (UNCCD). Today, another transition is taking place. The simple, two-sided world of rich countries and poor countries no longer exists. Consequently, it has become a struggle to determine which countries should take which actions, and which ones should provide and receive FTA.

As we discussed in Chapter 6, the past twenty-five to thirty years saw the rapid development of emerging economies, led by Brazil, China, India, and Indonesia (see Table 7.1). China has surpassed Japan and all European countries to become the second largest national economy. China has the second largest defense budget (after the United States), consumes the most natural resources, and emits the most greenhouse gases (GHGs). In 1974, Organisation for Economic Co-operation and Development (OECD) member states made up 78 percent of the world's gross domestic product (GDP). By 2018, this had dropped to 61 percent. As a result, the old model of OECD countries taking action first and paying the incremental costs for developing countries' action may no longer make sense. In fact, many countries considered to be "developing" have larger GDPs than some OECD countries. For example, according to the World Bank, in 2018, Bangladesh's GDP of $274 trillion was larger than OECD member Hungary's GDP of $157.8 trillion, and Ethiopia's GDP of $84.3 trillion was larger than OECD member Luxembourg's GDP of $70.9 trillion. In fact, there are sixty-two developing countries with GDPs bigger than OECD member Estonia's GDP of $30.7 trillion.[3]

Yet great inequalities remain. For example, if you add the top four non-OECD countries (China, India, Brazil, and Russia) to the thirty-six OECD countries, these forty countries represent 84 percent of the world's GDP. The forty-seven least developed countries (LDCs) comprise more than 1 billion people (about 13 percent of the world's population) but only 1 percent of the world's GDP.[4] And the more than 100 countries remaining contribute just 15 percent of the world's GDP.

Large disparities also exist among and within developing countries. The LDCs' annual average per capita income is measured at $1089, with some countries, such as Malawi, as low as $380—less than $1 a day. At the other end of the spectrum is Qatar (technically a developing country), with annual average per capita income (for its citizens) as high as $63,410.[5]

Nevertheless, the per capita income of nearly all developing countries, including the BRICS countries (Brazil, Russia, India, China, and South Africa), is considerably below both the OECD and global averages (see Table 7.2). As a result, these countries argue that the principle of CBDR is still valid because changes in GDP do not negate historical responsibilities for causing global environmental problems, the large disparities in current per capita contributions (e.g., in per capita GHG emissions or resource consumption), and their need to devote resources to lifting millions of people out of extreme poverty.

In contrast, most industrialized countries agree that historical responsibility and current per capita emissions are relevant to policy discussions, but they also emphasize the common responsibility of all countries to contribute to solving global environmental problems, which implies a need for developing countries to avoid duplicating the unsustainable historical development patterns of the industrialized world. They also note that many large developing countries are now among the largest contributors to many global environmental problems.

Table 7.1 Top 20 Countries Ranked by GDP, 1993 and 2018

Rank	Country	1993 GDP ($ trillions)	Rank	Country	2018 GDP ($ trillions)
1	United States	6858.6	1	United States	20,544.3
2	Japan	4454.1	2	China	13,608.2
3	Germany	2071.3	3	Japan	4971.3
4	France	1322.8	4	Germany	3947.6
5	Italy	1064.9	5	United Kingdom	2855.2
6	United Kingdom	1061.4	6	France	2777.5
7	Canada	577.2	7	India	2229.5
8	Spain	525.1	8	Italy	2083.8
9	Mexico	500.7	9	Brazil	1868.6
10	China	444.7	10	Canada	1713.3
11	Brazil	437.8	11	Russia	1657.6
12	Russia	435.1	12	Rep. of Korea	1619.4
13	Rep. Korea	386.3	13	Australia	1433.9
14	Netherlands	353.6	14	Spain	1419.0
15	Australia	311.5	15	Mexico	1220.7
16	India	279.3	16	Indonesia	1042.2
17	Switzerland	264.4	17	Netherlands	913.6
18	Argentina	236.7	18	Saudi Arabia	786.5
19	Belgium	224.7	19	Turkey	771.3
20	Sweden	211.2	20	Switzerland	705.1

GDP at purchaser's prices is the sum of gross value added by all resident producers in the economy plus any product taxes and minus any subsidies not included in the value of the products. It is calculated without making deductions for depreciation of fabricated assets or for depletion and degradation of natural resources. Data are in current US dollars. Dollar figures for GDP are converted from domestic currencies using single-year official exchange rates.

Source: World Bank Databank, accessed March 28, 2020, http://data.worldbank.org/indicator/NY.GDP.MKTP.CD.

For example, China and India are first and third in GHG emissions, and developing countries as a group emit far more mercury than OECD countries and are home to the highest rates of deforestation. In addition, per capita contributions to global environmental problems in a few developing countries are on a par with those of industrialized countries; most notably

Table 7.2 Average Gross National Income Per Capita in Select Countries and Groupings, 2018

Switzerland	$84,410
Norway	$80,610
United States	$63,080
Qatar	$61,150
OECD Average	$40,095
World Average	$11,124
Turkey	$10,420
Russia	$10,230
China	$9,460
Brazil	$9,140
South Africa	$5,750
India	$2,020
LDC Average	$1,080
Burundi	$280

Source: World Bank, GNI (gross national income) per capita, Atlas method (current US$), May 16, 2020, http:// data.worldbank.org/indicator/NY.GNP.PCAP.CD/countries.

China, which now has higher per capita GHG emissions—and far higher cumulative GHG emissions—than many developed countries (see Chapter 3).

While many developing countries are far wealthier than they were at the 1992 Earth Summit, great differences still exist in per capita income between developing and developed countries—and between the LDCs and many other developing countries. Industrialized countries have still contributed more to most environmental problems over time, but the current contributions of some developing countries significantly exceed those of many industrialized countries, while many other developing countries contribute almost nothing. These new realities in the international system, both positive and negative, make the creation and implementation of effective global policy all the more difficult.

A second new reality is the proliferation of stakeholders and potentially influential actors—including countries, evolving coalitions of countries, international organizations, nongovernmental organizations (NGOs), corporations, philanthropies, states and provinces, cities, and others—and the consequential difficulty of creating and imposing top-down, system-wide policies. The 1992 model was based on the concept of a top-down global deal negotiated by governments through a consensus-seeking process in which a relatively small number of large countries or country coalitions (e.g., the Group of 77 (G-77)) had consistent influence across issue areas.[6] The current model is far more bottom up, voluntary, and leader-driven across different stakeholder groups.[7] In today's multipolar world, many countries and shifting coalitions have different sets of cross-cutting interests on different issues and pursue them diligently. This makes it more difficult to achieve the broad consensus required in most environmental regimes to strengthen control measures, particularly if consensus by all parties is required (see Chapter 5). We can see negative impacts of this in the chemicals regimes when one or a few states stall or even prevent agreement to add new substances to the control measures (see Chapter 3).

Moreover, outside of the European Union (EU), the most powerful countries and coalitions—including China, India, Russia, and the United States—are not providing the necessary global environmental leadership. In addition, although many corporations see tremendous economic opportunity in sustainable products and practices, the current system is also one in which some powerful economic interests and corporations wield significant influence opposing new and stronger global environmental agreements—in part because the economic costs of most of the environmental externalities they cause are not included in their business models. For example, in the United States, influential corporations and their allies have prevented ratification of the Kyoto Protocol, the three chemicals conventions (Basel, Stockholm, and Rotterdam), and the CBD, worked to build doubt among the public about the basic science of climate change, and negatively affected American implementation of the Montreal Protocol with regard to eliminating methyl bromide.

On the positive side, the proliferation of actors has opened new avenues of influence for those seeking more effective global environmental policy. International organizations and environmental NGOs play more substantial roles in agenda setting and regime implementation. As noted in Chapter 2, many states, cities, municipalities, and large businesses are reducing GHG emissions even when their national governments refuse or are unable to do so. More nonstate actors have become part of norm-setting and norm-implementing institutions and mechanisms in global governance, which denotes a possible shift from purely intergovernmental regimes to more public–private and private–private global policy making.[8] These include the hazardous waste reduction and management partnerships developed as part of the expanded Basel Convention, as discussed in Chapter 3, and the ecolabeling initiatives developed by networks of NGOs, manufacturers, and retailers, as described in Chapter 6.

The expanded set of active, interested, and influential actors is seen at the informational side events at climate, biodiversity, and other MEA conferences, which are often the most informative and dynamic sessions. The governments, local authorities, NGOs, business and industry innovators, indigenous peoples, scientific and research communities, and other groups that participate in these panel discussions and events share best practices, research breakthroughs, innovations, and success stories, which then spread around the world at the subnational level. However, these types of initiatives are no panacea if global environmental governance is ineffective, nor can they replace the ability of effective governments to enact and implement policy at the national level. Environmental action by private and subnational public actors cannot and should not seek to replace state action but, rather, should work in tandem.[9]

A third reality is the fragmentation of global environmental issues. Far from a holistic, precautionary, and non-incremental approach, which was once deemed a requirement for global environmental governance, environmental policy is instead fragmented into many separate and unequal regimes.[10] This has resulted in intersecting but sometimes conflicting agendas, inconsistencies across regimes dealing with common issues, and competing demands for resources. The biodiversity and desertification regimes are also major stakeholders in how commitments evolve under the climate change regime regarding land-use change and forests. Efforts to conserve endangered species of sharks take place under both the Convention on International Trade in Endangered Species of Wild Fauna and Flora (CITES) and the Convention on Migratory Species (CMS), with mixed results. Whales are covered by CITES, CMS, and the International Whaling Commission. Many chemicals covered in the ozone regime are also GHGs, but this has not always produced positive results. For many years, a large coalition of governments argued that because hydrofluorocarbons (HFCs), powerful GHGs, were invented to replace ozone-depleting chemicals banned under the Montreal Protocol, they should be dealt with under the ozone regime, not the UNFCCC, especially because the ozone regime has binding targets and timetables. Other countries, however, argued that because HFCs are only GHGs, not ozone-depleting chemicals, they should only be dealt

Photo 7.1 Activists dressed as endangered shark species walk the hallways at the Conference of the Parties to the Convention on Migratory Species.

Courtesy Franz Dejon, IISD/*Earth Negotiations Bulletin*, http://enb.iisd.org

with under the climate regime. This jurisdictional debate delayed the agreement to phase out HFCs under the Montreal Protocol for many years, as described in Chapter 3.

Across international organizations, including within the UN system, multiple organizations address similar environmental and development issues, sometimes in pursuit of competing goals and often without effective coordination and collaboration, which yields wasteful competition and duplication. Within nations, different ministries often advocate for different domestic policies and negotiating positions at the global level that reflect their particular interests with respect to agriculture, industrial development, energy, foreign affairs, trade, and other issues rather than a holistic approach to sustainable development. Thus, while debates over global environmental governance and sustainable development reflect the need for more synergistic policy development and implementation, the responsibility for negotiating and implementing solutions to global environmental problems remains fragmented across both MEAs and government ministries.[11]

A fourth reality is the need for universality. Although there are many definitions of universality, in the environmental arena it often refers to recognition of the interconnectedness of national and global environment and development challenges and universal commitments to address them. Many environmental challenges, such as illegal trade in wildlife, are global issues, due to the interconnectedness of the global marketplace. Sustainably managing and protecting global public goods, such as biodiversity and the climate, entail global responsibility and concerted multinational cooperation.[12] Such issues are universal in that they affect everyone, regardless of wealth or income, gender or race, and need to be addressed by all countries, both individually and collectively, or the resulting policies will not be effective. This was explicitly referenced in the 2030 Agenda for Sustainable Development.

Several years before the 1992 Rio Earth Summit, a shift occurred in participation patterns at intergovernmental environmental negotiations. In perhaps the most notable example, African countries took on the role of lead states in the negotiations that created the 1989 Basel Convention. In another critical case, while few developing countries actively participated in the creation of the ozone regime, they played a significant role in the negotiations that produced the first strengthening of the Montreal Protocol and, in particular, the concurrent historic 1990 agreement that created the regime's financial mechanism. The active involvement of many states, and many different types of states, became the norm in the early 1990s during the negotiations of the UNFCCC and CBD.

But universal participation in negotiations, which is positive if it builds a truly global consensus, does not always mean universal ratification and implementation, which are required so that key countries do not remain outside a regime. For example, as noted in Chapter 3, although the negotiation of the Kyoto Protocol was open to all parties to the UNFCCC, the largest per capita GHG emitter, the United States, participated in the negotiations but never ratified the treaty, and major developing countries with growing GHG emissions, such as China and India, did not have commitments. As a result, by the end of the first commitment period in 2012, the Kyoto Protocol covered only about 15 percent of global GHG emissions, thus failing to slow down global warming.[13] Similarly, and as also discussed in Chapter 3, a number of large countries have not ratified, and thus need not implement, the control measures on all of the toxic chemicals added to the Stockholm Convention. As outlined in Chapter 4, multiple countries are key veto states in the negotiations on marine biodiversity in areas beyond national jurisdiction. Addressing global environmental issues requires universal participation in policy creation and implementation by all the major actors, or it will not succeed.

A fifth reality is that despite its flaws, the intergovernmental negotiating process itself is still a necessity. "Getting action in the United Nations," a diplomat once complained, "is like the mating of elephants. It takes place at a very high level, with an enormous amount of huffing and puffing, raises a tremendous amount of dust and nothing happens for at least 23 months."[14] Many who see the need for urgent action on environmental problems are skeptical of entrusting complete responsibility to the slow and often cumbersome "huffing-and-puffing" multilateral negotiating process within the UN. As discussed in Chapter 5, environmental problems do not wait patiently while governments negotiate. When governments did not adopt a successor agreement to the Kyoto Protocol in Copenhagen in 2009, the earth's average temperature continued rising for six years while the 2015 Paris Agreement was under negotiation. Even with the Paris Agreement, unless countries significantly increase their current commitments to reduce emissions, temperatures will continue rising, likely to around 3°C above preindustrial levels, breaching the 2°C threshold that scientists say is the limit of safety, beyond which the effects—droughts, floods, heat waves, storms, and sea-level rise—will be profound and likely catastrophic and irreversible.[15]

Although not every MEA has been negotiated within the UN system, since 1972, the UN or one of its specialized agencies—primarily the United Nations Environment Programme (UNEP)—has been recognized as the main venue for addressing global and regional environmental issues. Although there are frustrations inherent in this process, and governments are not the only important actors, as described in Chapter 2, the international system still centers on states, and governments seldom surrender decision-making authority to a supranational body. As a result, the international community is still forced to employ the slow method of intergovernmental negotiation as the primary tool to address global environmental issues.[16]

Finally, 2020 brought a new reality—COVID-19. At this writing, the long-term human and economic toll of this pandemic is yet to be determined. Yet, as MEAs and governments grapple with the challenges of meeting virtually, less frequently, or not at all, the nature of multilateralism and global environmental politics could change dramatically.

The Continuing Evolution of Global Environmental Governance

Since the United Nations Conference on Sustainable Development (UNCSD or Rio+20) in 2012, many international organizations have sought to evolve and improve their ability to

Photo 7.2 The UN as a whole has evolved to embrace sustainable development as a central theme as a result of the 2030 Agenda for Sustainable Development and the SDGs and is making associated governance changes.

Courtesy Kiara Worth, IISD/*Earth Negotiations Bulletin*, http://enb.iisd.org

address environmental and sustainable development concerns, albeit not always successfully. The MEAs, their secretariats, and the associated Conferences of the Parties (COPs) have taken a variety of actions, some in response to the realities outlined in the previous section. UNEP, the main international organization in global environmental affairs, saw its governance structure changed and its financial situation improved following Rio+20, and it has also pursued internal improvements. The UN as a whole has evolved to embrace sustainable development as a central theme, supporting pursuit of the 2030 Agenda for Sustainable Development and the Sustainable Development Goals (SDGs) and making associated governance changes. This section highlights key aspects of the ongoing evolution of global environmental governance.

Evolution of Multilateral Environmental Agreements

As we have seen, after the momentum created by the 1972 Stockholm Conference, the attention to environmental issues and the commitment to take normative action led governments to adopt numerous agreements to address specific environmental issues. During this first phase, which spanned the 1970s and 1980s, more than 100 global and regional MEAs were adopted. However, the sector-by-sector approach followed by most of the early MEAs ignored the interdependence of environmental issues and the need for an ecosystem approach to the preservation of environmental quality. Moreover, the early MEAs generally failed to adequately integrate environmental standards into economic development policies, ignoring the call to do so expressed in the Stockholm Declaration.[17] Nearly all of the agreements also lacked meaningful mechanisms to hold states accountable for breaching an obligation to respect and protect the environment. In general, the conservation approach adopted in most of the MEAs from this period can be considered more "utilitarian than ecological."[18]

The environmental conventions and agreements adopted during the second phase, starting just before the 1992 Earth Summit and continuing through the Minamata Convention on Mercury in 2013, reflected a greater willingness within the international community to respond to scientific evidence concerning the significant and even irreversible environmental threats to human health and the environment created by ozone-depleting chemicals, GHG emissions, overfishing, deforestation, toxic chemicals, mercury emissions, loss of biodiversity, and other damaging human activities.[19] This led to another spate of negotiations that resulted in the UNFCCC, CBD, UNCCD, Stockholm Convention, Rotterdam Convention, and Minamata Convention and the expansion of the Montreal Protocol and CITES, among other MEA developments. Although the effectiveness of these agreements has varied, their creation and, in many cases, expansion represent important achievements in global environmental governance.

More recently there has been a third phase, which is concerned with implementation and effectiveness. Even with so many MEAs on the books, there are few true success stories. The evolution of global environmental governance shows that, although progress has been made in establishing a network of treaty obligations and soft law, "the main challenge remains how to guarantee at the global level that the regulatory system of human activities is systematically aligned with natural and ecological systems that govern life on the planet."[20] So, it is logical that, moving forward, environmental negotiations are likely to continue to focus on implementation, monitoring, and compliance to ensure that existing MEAs are actually making a difference on the ground.

A critical issue in implementation is compliance, the degree to which countries actually follow the rules they establish to put the international regime into action in their countries. In general, international environmental law suffers from a serious deficit of enforcement mechanisms. Unlike international trade or even human rights law, there is no dispute settlement body or international court of the environment. Implementation of international environmental standards is largely left up to national governments that enact domestic laws and, in some cases, soft international enforcement mechanisms such as noncompliance procedures that permit "some level of moral and political suasion to be applied to states unwilling or unable to respect the standards set in the multilateral treaties to which they are Parties."[21]

A major question is whether new provisions or significant reform of international institutions is required to improve the quality and effectiveness of national implementation of global environmental governance. On the one hand, there is a discernible trend toward broader acceptance of an enhanced role for international institutions in the supervision and implementation of environmental law. On the other hand, significant resistance persists with regard to delegating adjudication or enforcement powers. Many countries even object to delegating significant monitoring responsibilities on domestic implementation, especially if the proposal impacts a state's perception of its sovereign right to manage natural resources and pursue economic and social development strategies of its own choosing.[22] As a result, there is no simple solution to this problem. The trend toward concentrating on implementation is clear, but ready solutions, especially on the issues of compliance and the need for more effective FTA, as discussed in Chapter 5, are difficult to foresee.

In response to worries about fragmentation, some governments and other actors seek greater collaboration among existing MEAs. The Basel, Stockholm, and Rotterdam Conventions, as described in Chapter 3, embarked on a "synergies" process in 2007 that resulted in a decision taken by all three COPs in 2010 to enhance coordination and cooperation.[23] This resulted in a joint secretariat, joint meetings of the COPs of the three conventions, and increased coordination in certain implementation activities and, in some cases, the provision of FTA. This synergies process has helped parties to improve the use of available resources through more coordinated national policy frameworks and institutional mechanisms for regulating chemicals and wastes; reduce administrative costs associated with the conventions; better coordinate technical assistance activities; make more efficient use of financial resources to support developing countries' implementation of the conventions; and develop a more integrated, life-cycle approach for the environmentally sound management of chemicals and wastes.[24] The synergies process was facilitated by the fact that the three conventions address related issues and all three were already at least partially administered by UNEP and had secretariats located in Geneva.[25]

A liaison group of biodiversity-related conventions is also attempting to improve cooperation and coordination.[26] Although the process is not nearly as developed as the initiative underway among the Basel, Stockholm, and Rotterdam Conventions and is also hindered by different secretariat locations and administrative arrangements, the formative efforts are indicative of a trend. So, too, is the decision by parties to the Montreal Protocol to adopt the Kigali Amendment to facilitate reductions in the use of HFCs, which are also addressed in the climate regime. The Global Environment Facility (GEF) attempts to fund projects that have co-benefits in multiple issue areas, such as projects in the chemicals focal area that also address hazardous waste because they improve life-cycle management or projects that seek to protect a forested area as a biodiversity preserve but that also provide climate benefits because a healthy forest acts as a sink for carbon dioxide (CO_2).

Evolution of the United Nations Environment Programme

Since UNEP's establishment in 1972, it has been the lead UN organization on the environment, as described in Chapter 2. At the same time, the UN institutional framework for environmental issues has grown in size and complexity, with an increasing number of UN institutions, agreements, meetings, reports, and actors. Although governments discussed UNEP reform options for years with limited success, the Rio+20 process provided a new impetus.

There were two main camps among those advocating reform. One side included institutional reformists who wanted to improve the current system of treaty regimes and international institutions. The other included those who believed that far deeper changes were necessary, possibly including the creation of a UN Environment Organization, and replacing UNEP with this more powerful organization. Many in the first group focused on strengthening key institutions in specific issue areas and negotiating stronger and more effective global regimes. They also called for increased coherence and coordination among the goals and processes of the major global environmental, financial, trade, and development institutions and systems.[27] Some also supported elevating the precautionary principle to an official guiding principle of global environmental policy.

In the second group, France, Germany, and the EU spearheaded support to create a UN Environment Organization with the status of an official specialized UN agency, a status that UNEP did not have. They argued that this would increase the availability of financial resources and provide a more efficient and effective structure for governance and leadership. Some governments and NGOs also argued that this model could be the first step in an active effort to bring all of the environmental treaties together under a single umbrella organization. Other proposals were even more ambitious, such as creating a new world environment organization that would be modeled on and intended to counterbalance the World Trade Organization (WTO). Some proposed that this organization could operate as a type of global environmental legislature, entrusted with setting international standards on certain issues and given the authority to enforce them against laggard countries, similar to the WTO's ability to judge whether domestic laws and regulations violate global trading rules and order changes.[28]

After intense debate in Rio in 2012, the final agreement fell short of creating a UN Environment Organization or transforming UNEP into a specialized agency—and far short of establishing an organization with legislative or WTO-like authority.[29] Rio+20 did agree to allow all member states to be part of UNEP's Governing Council (instead of only fifty-eight) as well "as other measures to strengthen [UNEP's] governance as well as its responsiveness and accountability to member states" and to have "secure, stable, adequate and increased financial resources from the regular budget of the United Nations and voluntary contributions to fulfill its mandate."[30] Instead of UNEP becoming an umbrella organization for MEAs, the outcome merely encouraged parties to MEAs to consider further measures to enhance coordination and cooperation,[31] which in practice supported efforts such as the synergies initiative.

The first universal Governing Council, renamed the UN Environment Assembly (UNEA) of UNEP, convened in 2014 under the overarching theme "Sustainable Development Goals and the Post-2015 Development Agenda, Including Sustainable Consumption and Production." UNEA-1 called for the full integration of the environmental dimension into the sustainable development agenda, acknowledging that a healthy environment is an essential requirement and key enabler for sustainable development. UNEA also appealed for ambitious universal implementation of the SDGs and inclusive social and economic development in harmony with nature. By trying to position itself at the center of efforts to integrate the economic, environmental, and social dimensions of sustainable development, UNEP wanted to ensure that it was not left behind in the shift from the Millennium Development Goals (MDGs) to the SDGs.

The theme of the second UNEA meeting was "Strengthening the science-policy interface." Assessing the state of the environment and recommending policies to improve it is at the core of UNEP's mandate. This is what is meant by the science-policy interface. But this aspect of UNEP's mandate has long been inadequate. UNEP has no scientific body to feed science into UNEA's decision making. Despite the vast number of global environmental assessments, there has been no explicit linking between the science of environmental problems and the societal and political actions needed to solve them. As discussion at UNEA-2 indicated, UNEA remains institutionally disconnected from science and would benefit from greater incorporation of science into decision making and from systematic linkage with assessment mechanisms.[32] UNEP is not alone in this regard, as evidenced in the UNCCD case study in Chapter 4.

Each subsequent UNEA meeting has explored broad themes linked to the SDGs. The third session of UNEA in 2017 considered the overarching theme of pollution. Discussions focused on combating the spread of marine plastic litter and microplastics, a topic receiving a great deal of attention around the world. UNEA also adopted resolutions on a range of pollution-related issues such as eliminating exposure to lead paint and promoting environmentally sound management of used lead-acid batteries, environment and health, improving air quality globally, water pollution, soil pollution, and pollution prevention and control in areas affected by terrorist operations and armed conflicts.[33] The fourth session in 2019 examined innovative solutions for environmental challenges and sustainable consumption and production. Delegates adopted the first UN-endorsed resolution on circular economy and "industry symbiosis" (bringing companies together in innovative collaborations, finding ways to use the waste from one as the raw materials for another). UNEA-4 also sent a strong signal that most countries believe single-use plastic products should be reduced or phased out, putting the plastics industry on notice. But participants also expressed concern that the agenda was too wide-ranging, and that UNEP and its member states had not done enough substantive work to prepare for the meeting.[34]

To some degree, UNEA has achieved the goal of bringing the attention of more governments to the environmental agenda and generating political momentum and action. The number of states, international organizations, NGOs, and other stakeholders participating in UNEA has increased significantly. However, according to a report to the Nordic Council of Ministers, UNEA's full potential remains untapped, and integrated solutions across themes as well as links with broader realms, including trade and human rights, are still underdeveloped. In particular, UNEA's relationship with the MEAs is still vague, and decision making continues to operate largely in silos without an overall strategy or mechanism for cooperation to facilitate integrated solutions.[35]

As its fiftieth anniversary approaches, UNEP faces the challenge of proving its worth. Not only must it strengthen the science-policy interface and continue to improve its agenda-setting role, UNEP must now also demonstrate that it can provide leadership in implementing the environmental dimension of sustainable development within the UN system and create coherent and accurate monitoring and evaluation frameworks to provide a credible platform for action on the SDGs and beyond.

High-level Political Forum on Sustainable Development

Rio+20 also set in motion a major change in how governments address sustainable development at the UN by calling for the establishment of the High-level Political Forum on Sustainable Development (HLPF) to "provide political leadership, guidance and recommendations for sustainable development."[36] The HLPF operates under both the UN Economic and Social Council (ECOSOC) and the UN General Assembly (UNGA). The highest level of the forum convenes every four years, gathering heads of state and government for two days at the beginning of the annual UNGA session in September. The HLPF also meets annually for eight days—including a three-day ministerial meeting—under the auspices of ECOSOC to ensure regular high-level discussions. To date, the focus of the HLPF has been reviewing progress toward the SDGs and the implementation of the 2030 Agenda for Sustainable Development. As part of its follow-up and review mechanisms, the 2030 Agenda encourages member states to "conduct regular and inclusive reviews of progress at the national and subnational levels, which are country-led and country-driven."[37] These Voluntary National Reviews serve as a basis for the regular reviews by the HLPF, as described in Chapter 6.

From 2016 to 2019, the HLPF reviewed clusters of SDGs, eventually completing an in-depth review of all seventeen SDGs. This review was capped off in September 2019, when heads of state and government met for what was called the "SDG Summit" and took stock of progress during the first four years of SDG implementation. Over 150 side events and special events, hosted by NGOs, governments, the private sector, and intergovernmental organizations, also took place during the Summit, showcasing progress and best practices in implementing one or more SDGs. On the face of it, the first phase of the HLPF had met expectations.

Photo 7.3 "If women stop, the world stops." As discussions at the High-level Political Forum in 2019 focused on SDG 8, decent work, and economic growth, representatives from the Women's Major Group reminded delegates about the important role women play in the global workforce.

Courtesy Kiara Worth, IISD/*Earth Negotiations Bulletin*, http://enb.iisd.org

Despite cautious optimism about the process, the substantive conclusion of HLPF's first review cycle was clear: the world is not on track to achieve most of the SDGs by 2030. As described in Chapter 6, progress has been made in reducing poverty, but tens of millions still live in extreme poverty. Economic inequality is high and rising. Women and children remain marginalized. Systemic threats, including climate change and biodiversity loss, threaten to undermine progress.[38] Participants also highlighted elements of the HLPF process in need of improvement. The annual agenda is overburdened and at times resembles the diplomatic equivalent of speed dating rather than meaningful dialogues. Being more selective about what can or should be discussed at the global level, and what can be dealt with at the regional level, could be one way of lightening the agenda and improving implementation.[39]

When governments created the HLPF after Rio+20 they also established a review process, and in 2016 the General Assembly agreed to conduct this review in 2020.[40] All agreed that this review process presents a timely opportunity to reposition the HLPF toward the implementation of its mandate as the central intergovernmental forum for the international governance of sustainable development. However, due to the COVID-19 pandemic and the shuttering of UN Headquarters for most of the year, the substantial review of the HLPF was postponed until the crisis has passed.[41] When the HLPF did meet in a virtual format in July 2020, the focus was on maintaining momentum on SDG implementation in light of the impact of the COVID-19 pandemic.

Does Evolution Mean Change?

The ongoing evolution of the institutional architecture of global environmental governance does not guarantee that environmental conditions will improve, GHG emissions will decline, trade in endangered species will cease, levels of air and water pollution will drop, the earth's protective ozone layer will be restored, or the world's biodiversity, fisheries, land, and forests will be effectively conserved. Institutional developments are important, but perhaps the biggest obstacle to improving the architecture and impact of global environmental governance is political will.

Many internationally agreed-upon treaties, declarations, and documents require or call for new policies and practices to protect the environment, but actual progress in doing so has been limited. Some of the political, economic, and corporate leaders who oppose increased action in particular issue areas appear to believe that they live in isolation from well-accepted ecological, economic, and technological trends. Some dismiss the idea that climate change, biodiversity loss, persistent organic pollutants (POPs), hazardous wastes, or mercury emissions undermine the future of their country or interests. Some worry that strengthening environmental governance could challenge the fundamental concept of state sovereignty or interfere inappropriately with free markets or corporate flexibility. Some argue that strong environmental policies will hinder national economic growth. There are other political, economic, and corporate leaders, however, who agree that more significant action is necessary, and that aspects of the system need to be changed to prevent significant damage to the environment, human health, the economy, and national security, but so far they have not been able to build the domestic or international coalitions necessary to create and implement more ambitious environmental policies.

The challenge of amassing the necessary political will is illustrated by the debate over a "Global Pact for the Environment." To address a lack of progress in implementing international environmental law and governance, an international network of 100 experts from over forty countries, coordinated by the Club des juristes (a French legal think tank), proposed the Global Pact. Their draft international treaty reflected the precautionary and polluter pays principles and the right to an ecologically sound environment.[42] Senior French politicians, led by French President Emmanuel Macron, drafted a corresponding UN General Assembly resolution, which seventy-one other countries co-sponsored. In May 2018, governments adopted resolution 72/277, "Towards a Global Pact for the Environment," which set up a working group to identify and consider gaps in international environmental law and environment-related instruments, and to articulate ways to address those gaps.

This working group met three times in 2019 and submitted recommendations to the General Assembly. Perhaps not surprisingly, however, once detailed discussions began, some governments strongly resisted the concept of a legally binding global pact, and no agreement could be reached on even general recommendations until proposals for a new binding instrument were taken off the table. Thus, the final recommendations were weak, especially when compared with the ambition of the original French project. According to the *Earth Negotiations Bulletin*, "fear [among governments] played a role and ultimately shaped the outcome: fear of losing sovereignty, fear of complicating existing MEA regimes, fear of opening up established principles and their varied/contested application, and, significantly for developing countries, fear of committing to steps that they lack the capacity to implement."[43] The UNGA adopted the recommendations as resolution 73/333 and called on UNEA to consider the proposal at its fifth session.[44]

The future of the Global Pact is expected to be considered as part of the planning for the fiftieth anniversary of the Stockholm Conference and UNEP. Some believe that ideas embodied in the original draft pact will not go away because they tap into and resonate with a wider set of emerging public concerns about the adequacy of national and international responses to environmental degradation and especially climate change, concerns exemplified by the Sunrise Movement and the Fridays for Future climate movement inspired by Swedish youth activist Greta Thunberg.[45] Others argue that a new global pact is not the appropriate next step for improving global environmental protection. They posit that a more fundamental consideration is needed to understand why the current system is failing to address environmental issues more effectively, what type of potential remedies might be effective, and whether an overarching international agreement on the environment would even make a difference.[46] Clearly, many close observers agree, if governments do pursue a new agreement,

Photo 7.4 Tens of thousands of students, led by Greta Thunberg, took to the streets on Friday, September 20, 2019 in advance of the UN Climate Summit to demand climate action.

Courtesy Kiara Worth.

they must ensure that there is clarity concerning its purpose, its obligations, and its intended legal effect, including in relation to other MEAs.[47]

There is no doubt that global environmental governance is not nearly as ambitious or effective as many would like it to be. Whether the UNEA, HLPF, possible Global Pact, and the MEAs discussed in Chapters 3 and 4 can make global environmental governance more effective in ameliorating the increasingly serious ecological challenges facing humankind remains to be seen. But as the international community evolves and the interrelationship between environment and development deepens, the political will to further strengthen the structures of global environmental governance will become even more important.

Conclusion: The Prospects for Global Environmental Politics

Can the international community develop effective cooperative efforts to address global environmental problems successfully? The case studies presented in this book show that, on some issues, it can. With the ozone layer, states have devised a regime that has been innovative in its rule making and largely effective and cost-efficient in phasing out most of the damaging chemicals. Governments have significantly reduced the use of lead in gasoline, the production and use of certain POPs, and the hunting of endangered whale species.

But the most successful regimes have also had favorable circumstances. The ozone case involved a relatively small number of chemical producers and product manufacturers who discovered cost-effective substitute chemicals and technologies. The whaling ban passed because only a few countries wanted to continue to hunt whales and there was no large worldwide market for whale products. The ivory ban initially succeeded because a few major countries were able to shut down most of the market for elephant ivory. Most of the POPs eliminated to date had already been banned in OECD countries and thus, ready substitutes were available for other countries. However, none of these regimes have been completely successful. The black market for ivory still exists, although many countries, including China, have banned legal ivory sales, and elephant poaching continues unabated; Japan and Norway still hunt whales; the ozone layer has not fully recovered; and exceptions exist for some banned POPs, while many others have not been added to the regime. The adoption of the Paris Agreement was celebrated with great fanfare, but it hasn't stopped the last five years from being the warmest years on record.[48]

We have outlined the importance of continuing efforts to improve regime effectiveness. Parties can strengthen regimes by tightening the requirements or expanding them to new areas, improving compliance with those requirements, developing new, nonbinding programs that support the goal of the regime, and broadening state participation in the regime. Parties have significantly expanded the ozone regime by strengthening controls on the original chemicals it covered, added many more chemicals to its control measures, and created the Multilateral Fund to attract developing-country participation and help fund the use of non-ozone-depleting chemicals. The Basel Convention reacted to difficulties in reducing shipments of hazardous waste by expanding its scope, developing guidelines and partnerships that seek to avoid the creation of such waste, and promoting its environmentally sound management. The Rotterdam and Stockholm Conventions have added numerous chemicals to their control measures. CITES has expanded the list of species it covers and encouraged the development of a network of NGOs and law enforcement agencies to combat illegal trade. The IWC adopted the whaling ban. Nearly all environmental regimes have significantly expanded not only their number of parties but also the number of countries seeking to address the issue.

The tools for expanding a regime are not panaceas, however. The biodiversity regime developed seven well-received thematic work programs that address marine and coastal biodiversity, agricultural biodiversity, forest biodiversity, island biodiversity, inland waters biodiversity, dryland biodiversity, and mountain biodiversity. Yet, because the core causes of biodiversity loss continue, the international community failed to meet both the 2010 target for significantly reducing biodiversity loss and the Aichi Biodiversity Targets, as noted in Chapter 4. The UNCCD has achieved universal ratification, significantly increased international recognition of the problem of land degradation in the drylands, and developed an important new paradigm for focusing action, but broad progress remains difficult because combating land degradation must work hand in hand with efforts to address poverty eradication, water resources management, agriculture, deforestation, biodiversity conservation, climate change, and population growth. The success or failure of this regime is a key indicator for the overall success or failure of sustainable development rather than just an indicator of the success of an environmental regime.

As we have seen, international organizations affect the creation, expansion, and success of global environmental policies and other actions that impact the environment by helping to set the global agenda (e.g., UNEP), bringing states together to negotiate and managing the talks (UNEP, FAO), monitoring global environmental trends (UNEP), conducting comprehensive scientific assessments (Intergovernmental Panel on Climate Change (IPCC), Intergovernmental Science-Policy Platform on Biodiversity and Ecosystem Services (IPBES)), and providing financial support for environmental activities (GEF). But these organizations do not always have the mandate, ability, or backing of a sufficient number of states with the necessary political will to promote strong regimes. Financial resources are also a critical issue. The GEF provides significant resources, but even if these were allocated in the most effective and efficient way possible, they could accomplish only a fraction of what is needed to support effective international cooperation in biodiversity, climate change, chemicals and waste, land degradation, international waters, and sustainable forest management.

The world's global trade and financial institutions—the World Bank, the International Monetary Fund (IMF), and the WTO—also play important roles. The World Bank and the IMF have both aligned themselves with the 2030 Agenda, so they can assist countries in implementing the SDGs.[49] The WTO has not produced a major international trade agreement since governments abandoned the "Doha Round" of negotiations in 2015. While WTO members are negotiating an agreement to cut fishing subsidies to allow the recovery of depleted fish stocks, key differences remain. As noted in Chapter 6, due to COVID-19, negotiations have stalled, and the WTO ministerial meeting originally scheduled for 2020, which was supposed to adopt this agreement, has been postponed to at least 2021.[50]

The leadership of the industrialized countries, especially the United States, is key to effective regimes. When the United States actively engages in trying to achieve consensus on stronger institutions or actions, it has often been able to overcome reluctance on the part of other industrialized countries, as in the negotiations on ozone depletion, African elephants, whaling, mercury, and the Paris Agreement on climate change. When the United States has been a veto state, as in the case of the hazardous waste trade, or has played a much lower-profile role, as in cases of desertification and biodiversity, the resulting regime has been negatively affected. The US executive branch has wavered on some of these issues for years, through multiple administrations, and Congress has often been a force impeding US leadership. Over four years, the Trump administration had the worst environmental record of any modern president, rolling back or reversing more than 100 environmental rules and regulations, including Obama-era limits on carbon dioxide emissions from power plants, cars, and trucks as well as regulations on mercury, clean air, water, and toxic chemicals.[51]

China, India, and the EU have joined the United States as countries whose leadership is important on global environmental issues. The size of their economies, resource consumption, and GHG emissions, as well as their central roles in international trade and financial relations, make their full participation in environmental regimes essential in the twenty-first century.

Although their resources and interests are increasingly diverging, developing countries as a group must also show leadership, move beyond the traditional interpretation of the principle of CBDR, and participate fully in more global environmental regimes. As shown in the provisions of the Minamata Convention on Mercury and the Paris Agreement on climate change, governments understand that if major developing countries do not take action, there is nothing that developed countries alone can do to prevent significant environmental harm. Developing countries need to take the initiative and accept new commitments in return for financial or other incentives, but the commitments and compensation need not be uniform for all developing countries. The Stockholm Convention on POPs, the Minamata Convention, and the Paris Agreement provide important examples of how to craft MEAs that acknowledge the special situation of many developing countries without establishing strict differentiation between developed and developing countries with respect to all regime obligations.

There is increasing awareness among business and industry groups regarding the implications of global environmental threats and global environmental regimes for their interests. As a result, more corporations and trade associations are playing active roles in global environmental politics. Because treaties could impose significant new costs or open new opportunities, the business community recognizes that early involvement in the negotiating process will often bring long-term benefits once a regime is in place.

Sometimes this involvement is negative. Some corporations and industry associations have worked against strong international or national environmental measures. Exxon/Mobil reportedly funneled more than $32 million to researchers and activist groups promoting disinformation about global warming, as well as to members of Congress and corporate lobbying groups that deny climate science and block efforts to fight climate change.[52] The agro-industrial complex in the United States, along with the chemical companies producing methyl bromide, worked to create a large loophole in the phase-out provisions for methyl bromide under the Montreal Protocol.

At other times, corporate interests have assisted the creation of strong environmental regimes. During the Montreal Protocol negotiations, US chemical companies that manufactured chlorofluorocarbons (CFCs) realized that significant regulations were on the way and developed alternatives. Their success enabled US negotiators to take a stronger position and emerge as a lead state in the negotiations. The Munich Climate Insurance Initiative, which brings together insurers, climate experts, economists, and independent organizations, is working on the innovative uses of risk-transfer tools to manage climate risks in conjunction with the UNFCCC. Companies that produce or use renewable energy employ ever greater numbers of people and have become influential in promoting green energy and GHG reduction policies at the local, state, and national levels.

Domestic commitments to support global environmental policy are unlikely to happen without environmental movements and civil society influencing national public opinion and pushing governments into action. At the international level, NGO networks on climate change, chemicals, biodiversity, and land degradation monitor treaty implementation and facilitate public participation in national action programs and strategies. The Trade Records Analysis of Flora and Fauna in Commerce (TRAFFIC) monitors the international trade in endangered species. International NGOs such as Greenpeace and WWF contribute substantial ideas on climate change, marine pollution, marine biodiversity, whales, and fisheries. Youth activism, especially on climate change, has pressured governments from the streets and within the UN system. The most important challenge for NGOs and civil society, however, is to build tangible support in reluctant states for implementing and strengthening global environmental regimes.

Global environmental politics has grown significantly more complex since the first global environmental conference in Stockholm in 1972. Many more issues, treaties, institutions, and policy initiatives exist, and the environment is now integrated into a broad array of international economic, trade, and development issues. In some ways, this growth is a sign of the progress made in the last fifty years by the international community in learning how to address global environmental issues.

Yet, these steps are not enough to meet the significant challenges the world faces.[53] Aspects of the exclusionist paradigm based on neoclassical economics continue to influence important policy discussions. The shift to a sustainable development paradigm and application of the precautionary principle—something that seemed imminent in 1992—has not come to pass. Some hope that the 2030 Agenda for Sustainable Development and the SDGs may facilitate such a shift. Yet, questions about universality, CBDR, accountability, and political will still remain. Proponents of the SDGs hope that individual national commitments will add up to worldwide results that help all people live better lives, especially those living in extreme poverty, while also leading to a healthier environment. For the first time, the UN development agenda recognizes, in an operational sense, the interlinkages among preserving the sustainability of ecosystem services, reducing pollution, economic development, poverty reduction, and human well-being. However, it is easy to agree that the shift to sustainable development is necessary. Almost no one challenges that statement. The difficulty is to reach agreement on what that means, develop appropriate policies, and muster the political will to implement them effectively.

This book has examined the principal paradigms, actors, issues, and challenges in global environmental politics. What the future will bring is unclear. As we saw in 2020, a new virus strain can upend economic systems and suspend multilateral diplomacy in a matter of weeks. Today's environmental challenges are global in nature, unprecedented in scope, and closely linked to economic and social development. The need for innovative and creative global solutions is greater than ever.

Notes

1 World Health Organization, "WHO Director-General's Opening Remarks at the Media Briefing on COVID-19—11 March 2020," March 11, 2020, www.who.int/dg/speeches/detail/who-director-general-s-opening-remarks-at-the-media-briefing-on-covid-19-11-march-2020.

2 Andrew Deutz, "Rio+20: What Does Success Look Like in the Post-Copenhagen Era?" *Guardian*, June 19, 2012.

3 World Bank, "GDP at Market Prices (Current US$), World Development Indicators," https://data.worldbank.org/indicator/NY.GDP.MKTP.CD.

4 UN Office of the High Representative for the Least Developed Countries, Landlocked Developing Countries and Small Island Developing States, "About LDCs," https://unohrlls.org/about-ldcs/; World Bank, "GDP at Market Prices."

5 World Bank, "GNI Per Capita, Atlas Method (current US$)," October 24, 2020, http://data.worldbank.org/indicator/NY.GNP.PCAP.CD/countries.

6 Deutz, "Rio+20."

7 Ibid.

8 Philipp Pattberg and Oscar Widerberg, "Theorising Global Environmental Governance: Key Findings and Future Questions," *Millennium: Journal of International Studies* vol. 43, no. 2 (2015): 687.

9 Robert Falkner, "The Crisis of Environmental Multilateralism: A Liberal Response," in *The Green Book: New Directions for Liberals in Government*, eds. Duncan Brack, Paul Burall, Neil Stockley, and Mike Tuffrey (London: Biteback Publishing, 2013), 347–358.

10 Pamela Chasek, Lynn Wagner, and Peter Doran, "Lessons Learned on the Roads from Rio," in *The Roads from Rio: Lessons Learned from Twenty Years of Multilateral Environmental Negotiations*, eds. Pamela Chasek and Lynn Wagner (New York: Routledge, 2012), 256.

11 Ibid., 259–260.

12 UNEP and Office of the High Commissioner for Human Rights, "Universality in the Post 2015 Sustainable Development Agenda," UNEP Post-2015 Note #9 (Nairobi: UNEP, 2014), https://wedocs.unep.org/handle/20.500.11822/8721.

13 IISD, "Summary of the Doha Climate Change Conference: 26 November–8 December 2012," *Earth Negotiations Bulletin* vol. 12, no. 567 (December 11, 2012): 26.

14 Richard Gardner, "The Role of the UN in Environmental Problems," in *World Eco-Crisis*, eds. David A. Kay and Eugene Skolnikoff (Madison: University of Wisconsin Press, 1972).

15 Fiona Harvey, "Paris Climate Change Agreement: The World's Greatest Diplomatic Success," *Guardian*, December 14, 2015, www.theguardian.com/environment/2015/dec/13/paris-climate-deal-cop-diplomacy-developing-united-nations.

16 Pamela Chasek, *Earth Negotiations: Analyzing Thirty Years of Environmental Diplomacy* (Tokyo: United Nations University Press, 2001), 1–2.

17 Francesco Francioni and Christine Bakker, "The Evolution of the Global Environmental System: Trends and Prospects," Transworld working paper 8, January 2013, 5, http://transworld.iai.it/wp-content/uploads/2013/01/TW_WP_08.pdf.

18 Ulrich Beyerlin and Thilo Marauhn, *International Environmental Law* (Oxford: Hart, 2011), 10–11.

19 Francioni and Bakker, "The Evolution of the Global Environmental System: Trends and Prospects," 5.

20 Ibid., 20.

21 Ibid., 21.

22 Ibid.

23 *Synergies* is the name given to this process within the three treaty regimes.

24 UN Department of Economic and Social Affairs, Basel Convention, Rotterdam Convention, Stockholm Convention, UNEP, and Food and Agriculture Organization of the UN, *Synergies Success Stories: Enhancing Cooperation and Coordination Among the Basel, Rotterdam and Stockholm Conventions* (New York: UN, 2011), 4.

25 The Rotterdam Convention is co-administered by UNEP and the FAO and also has an office in Rome.

26 The Liaison Group of Biodiversity-related Conventions includes the Convention Concerning the Protection of the World Cultural and Natural Heritage, Convention on Biological Diversity, Convention on International Trade in Endangered Species of Wild Fauna and Flora, Convention on the Conservation of Migratory Species of Wild Animals, Convention on Wetlands of International Importance especially as Waterfowl Habitat, International Plant Protection Convention, International Treaty on Plant Genetic Resources for Food and Agriculture, and the International Whaling Commission.

27 Adil Najam, David Runnalls, and Mark Halle, *Environment and Globalization: Five Propositions* (Winnipeg, Canada: IISD, 2007), 32. See also Adil Najam, Mihaela Papa, and Nadaa Taiyab, *Global Environmental Governance: A Reform Agenda* (Winnipeg, Canada: IISD, 2006).

28 James Gustave Speth, "Beyond Reform," *Our Planet* (February 2007): 16. For more on the World Environmental Organization proposal, see Daniel Esty, "The Case for a Global Environmental Organization," in *Managing the World Economy: Fifty Years After Bretton Woods*, ed. P. Kenen (Washington, DC: Institute for International Economics, 2004), 287–307; Frank Biermann, "The Rationale for a World Environment Organization," in *A World Environmental Organization: Solution or Threat for Effective Environmental Governance*, eds. Frank Biermann and Steffen Bauer (Aldershot, UK: Ashgate, 2005): 117–144.

29 A specialized agency is an autonomous organization linked to the UN through a special agreement, such as the Food and Agriculture Organization, the International Atomic Energy Agency, and the International Labor Organization, among others.

30 UN, *Report of the United Nations Conference on Sustainable Development*, A/CONF.216/16 (New York: UN, 2012), 18.

31 Ibid., 17–18.

32 Niko Urho, Maria Ivanova, Anna Dubrova, and Natalia Escobar-Pemberthy, "International Environmental Governance: Accomplishments and Way Forward," Technical Report (Oslo: Nordic Council of Ministers, 2019), 12, 47.

33 IISD, "Summary of the Third Session of the United Nations Environment Assembly: 4–6 December 2017," *Earth Negotiations Bulletin* vol. 16, no. 143 (December 9, 2017).

34 IISD, "Summary of the Fourth Session of the United Nations Environment Assembly: 11–15 March 2019," *Earth Negotiations Bulletin* vol. 16, no. 153 (March 18, 2019).

35 Urho, Ivanova, Dubrova, and Escobar-Pemberthy, "International Environmental Governance: Accomplishments and Way Forward," 87.

36 UN, *Report of the United Nations Conference on Sustainable Development*, 16.
37 UNGA, Transforming Our World: The 2030 Agenda for Sustainable Development, Resolution 70/1, October 21, 2015, www.un.org/ga/search/view_doc.asp?symbol=A/RES/70/1&Lang=E.
38 IISD, "Summary of the 2019 Meeting of the High-level Political Forum on Sustainable Development: 9–19 July 2019," *Earth Negotiations Bulletin* vol. 33, no. 55 (July 22, 2019): 19.
39 Ibid.
40 UN General Assembly, "Follow-Up and Review of the 2030 Agenda for Sustainable Development at the Global Level," Resolution 70/299, August 16, 2016.
41 Faye Leone, "Governments and Experts Exchange Proposals for Improving HLPF," SDG Knowledge Hub, April 16, 2020, http://sdg.iisd.org/commentary/policy-briefs/governments-and-experts-exchange-proposals-for-improving-hlpf/.
42 See "Draft Global Pact for The Environment," https://globalpactenvironment.org/uploads/EN.pdf.
43 IISD, "Summary of the Third Substantive Session of the Ad Hoc Open-Ended Working Group Towards a Global Pact for the Environment: 20–22 May 2019," *Earth Negotiations Bulletin* vol. 35, no. 3 (May 25, 2019): 11.
44 UN General Assembly, "Follow-Up to the Report of the Ad Hoc Open-Ended Working Group Established Pursuant To General Assembly Resolution 72/277," Resolution 73/333, September 5, 2019.
45 IISD, "Summary of the Third Substantive Session of the Ad Hoc Open-Ended Working Group Towards a Global Pact for the Environment," 11.
46 Susan Biniaz, "10 Questions to Ask About the Proposed 'Global Pact for the Environment'," Sabin Center for Climate Change Law, Columbia University, August 2017, http://columbiaclimatelaw.com/files/2017/08/Biniaz-2017-08-Global-Pact-for-the-Environment.pdf.
47 Ibid.
48 Climate Central, "Top 10 Warmest Years on Record," January 15, 2020, www.climatecentral.org/gallery/graphics/top-10-warmest-years-on-record.
49 See, for example, IMF, "Review of Implementation of IMF Commitments in Support of the 2030 Agenda for Sustainable Development," Policy Paper No. 19/013, June 3, 2019, www.imf.org/en/Publications/Policy-Papers/Issues/2019/06/03/Review-of-Implementation-of-IMF-Commitments-in-Support-of-the-2030-Agenda-for-Sustainable-46960; and World Bank, "World Bank Group and The 2030 Agenda," www.worldbank.org/en/programs/sdgs-2030-agenda.
50 Emma Farge and Philip Blenkinsop, "WTO Chief Roberto Azevedo to Depart a Year Early," Reuters, May 14, 2020, www.reuters.com/article/us-trade-wto/wto-chief-roberto-azevedo-to-depart-a-year-early-idUSKBN22Q191.
51 Nadja Popovich, Livia Albeck-Ripka, and Kendra Pierre-Louis, "The Trump Administration Is Reversing 100 Environmental Rules. Here's the Full List," *New York Times*, October 15, 2020, www.nytimes.com/interactive/2020/climate/trump-environment-rollbacks.html.
52 Suzanne Goldenberg, "ExxonMobil Gave Millions to Climate-Denying Lawmakers Despite Pledge," *Guardian*, July 15, 2015. See also John Cook, Geoffrey Supran, Stephan Lewandowsky, Naomi Oreskes, and Ed Maibach, *America Misled: How the Fossil Fuel Industry Deliberately Misled Americans About Climate Change* (Fairfax, VA: George Mason University Center for Climate Change Communication, 2019), www.climatechangecommunication.org/america-misled/.
53 Neil Carter, *The Politics of the Environment: Ideas, Activism, Policy*, 2nd ed. (Cambridge: Cambridge University Press, 2007), 268.

Index